The family life cycle in European societies

Le cycle de la vie familiale dans les sociétés européennes

edited by / sous la direction de

JEAN CUISENIER

with the assistance of / assisté de

MARTINE SEGALEN

Mouton · The Hague · Paris

Cet ouvrage a été publié avec le concours du Centre National de la Recherche Scientifique. Les contributions qu'il rassemble ont été présentées dans une première version et discutées au cours du XIIIe Séminaire International de Recherches sur la Famille, qui s'est tenu à Paris du 24 au 28 septembre 1973. Ce Séminaire a été organisé grâce au concours du Service de Coordination de la Recherche du Ministère de la Justice, de la Caisse Nationale des Allocations Familiales, et du Centre National de la Recherche Scientifique.

ISBN: 90-279-7822-0

Printed in the Netherlands

Foreword

GERRIT A. KOOY

This publication enables the reader to experience something of the atmosphere and the scientific importance of a seminar held in Paris in 1973 under the auspices of the Committee on Family Research. Therefore, the chairman of that organization in the period 1970–1974 could not possibly decline the invitation received from the editor of this book to "compose a prelude to its central themes". (Accepting such invitations is inherent to the role of chairmen and ex-chairmen of sponsoring organizations.) It is to be hoped, then, that what immediately follows will meet the expectations of the inviting party and satisfy the possible curiosity of the reader concerning the historical background of this publication.

In 1949 a group of sociologists from various countries established the International Sociological Association. This new organization did not accept individual membership, but became a kind of federation of existing national sociological associations. As such it was able to serve the interests of sociologists throughout the world. Among its important achievements, quadrennial world congresses with mass participation as well as a number of publications of high scientific standing can be mentioned. Nevertheless, the ISA did not seem to serve the interests of the various sociological subdisciplines to such an extent as it might do, if the organization were to provide an infra-structure for international communication and interaction between the representatives of these subdisciplines. Consequently, the ISA began to encourage the establishment of so-called research committees, small groups of people who accepted the task to further the interests of their subdiscipline within the organization. One of the several committees which were established was the Committee on Family

Research, formed in 1959. According to the rules of the ISA as they held until 1966, membership in the committee was limited to 18 persons. The concept of membership in the committee was rather ambiguous until the ISA revised its statutes in 1970. The creation of new categories of ISA membership in that year opened the possibility that the committee might become an organization of all those individuals paying individual membership and research committee fees to the ISA and having been accepted as members by the committee. Thus, what actually had been a service center being led by a few individuals, was given opportunity to continue its development in a democratic professional association of family sociologists all over the world. At the present moment, the committee has evolved from its original character to that of such a professional association. However, the objectives of the CFR – an organization with some 145 members from 26 different countries in the middle of 1974 – have remained the same.

From the very beginning, the objectives of the CFR have been the following: to stimulate family research in all countries, but with special emphasis on methodologically underdeveloped countries; to stimulate comparative family research; to improve the quality and efficiency of international and intranational family research. In order to fulfill this three-fold task the committee has developed and is still developing five types of activities: namely, sponsorship of international seminars on family research; organizing of world congress programs on family sociology each fourth year; publication of inventories of research; furtherance of cross-national research projects; publication of papers presented during CFR meetings. Thanks to considerable sacrifices in time and energy of a relatively small group of activists these objectives have been realized to a substantial extent. *Hic* and *nunc* it would go too far, if an attempt were made to enumerate all CFR achievements, but it seems appropriate to deal with the ISFR's (International Seminars on Family Research) at some length.

The first ISFR was organized at a moment that the Committee on Family Research had not yet been established. It was Nels Anderson, then director of the Unesco Institute in Cologne, who succeeded in bringing together a group of family researchers from various countries for a seminar in 1954. After this first ISFR, four others followed which also had no relation with the Committee on Family Research. However, the sixth seminar which was held at Opatija, Yugoslavia, in 1961, took place under the auspices and thanks to the active involvement of the CFR. The six seminars that have been held in Washington, D.C. (1962), Oslo (1963), Tokyo (1965), Teheran (1968), London (1970), and Moscow (1972) also owe their realization to CFR's active participation in the prepatory activities. So far each ISFR attempted to encourage close relations between researchers who were either established in or just beginning a career in family sociology. The main purpose of each of the seminars was training and furtherance of good sociological research on the family. As between 150 and 200 different family sociologists from widely diverse countries have participated in these exhausting, but scientifically stimulating meetings, one already can reasonably hypothesize that this main purpose has been fulfilled. However, the series of seminars also resulted in several more or less voluminous publications which reached a large group of readers. Just one example of these publications may be mentioned. The Tokyo seminar of 1965 led to the publication of *Families in East and West*, an excellent source book for those who are interested in socialization practices or the importance of consanguineal groupings in various parts of the world. Hitherto, the Moscow seminar has not yet resulted in a publication of a selection from its papers. However, it seems plausible that the Karchew-Sussman editing team will be able to publish a Russian and an English version of the twelfth ISFR in the near future.

From the point of view of the CFR, the thirteenth seminar in the French capital meant a change in policy. Although the strange phenomenon *family sociologist* can be considered in a *fundamentalist* and in a *heterodox* way, it can be maintained that the non-family sociologist was traditionally excluded from participation in the ISFR's. The seminars were organized for the in-group and, when a representative of another discipline or sub-discipline intruded, it was more or less by accident. Honesty requires one to say that this first interdisciplinary seminar had not been purposefully pursued as an interdisciplinary meeting by the committee's governing board. The board just did its best to seduce another decent and over-busy *VIP* somewhere in this world to render the material and personal services for another seminar. The results were not overwhelming in the beginning. Several solicitations were declined, but then it happened that secretary John Mogey found the *VIP* who seemed to guarantee the continuation of CFR's most cherished tradition: Jean Cuisenier. Thanks to him a thirteenth seminar within a measurable space of time became a realizable possibility. However, what Dr. Cuisenier had clearly in mind was an interdisciplinary seminar. According to him, the seminar in Paris should imply the mutual confrontation of the family sociologist, the anthropologist, the demographer, and the historian. The board members of the CFR, although they saw no reason to oppose this wish of their discussion partner in the French capital, realized that they accepted a considerable risk. Exchanges of thought among family sociologists should always be perfectly clear for the participants in the discussion, for all of them have studied at least a number of the same American textbooks. Nevertheless, these exchanges are often deeply frustrating and confusing, not so much because of the scientific level of most family sociologists, but rather because of the multidimensional character of their field which encompasses various theoretical views, often reconcilable only with difficulty. Due to wise leadership, the discussions of the past had normally been positive learning experiences instead of seriously traumatic events. Although the leadership of this thirteenth seminar might be as excellent or even more excellent, the risk of frustration and confusion was considerably greater this time. In the meanwhile, all those involved hoped that this meeting of birds of such different feathers would prove to non-family sociologists as well as family sociologists that an interdisciplinary seminar can be highly rewarding, too.

The theme chosen for the thirteenth ISFR immediately received the full consent of the governing board of the CFR. The chairman agreed with Dr. Cuisenier and the other board members in selecting "the European family cycle" as the theme of the thirteenth seminar. This agreement represented a reaction to an apparent lack of interest among European family sociologists in a theoretical and research development that has taken place 99% in the United States. Irrespective of one's personal evaluation of the sophisticated developmental approach, this youngest of the various approaches within family sociology finds its defendants among the most outstanding contemporary family sociologists. Therefore, continuing negligence of the developmental approach might hamper the further growth of a practically relevant European family sociology. In the opinion of the chairman a seminar on the European family cycle would enable us to discover through research done in Europe and theoretical discussion with the most renowned American defendants of the developmental approach, whether European family sociology should change its course.

The 1973 ISFR became a great success both as a scientific meeting and as a social event. Jean Cuisenier, the instrumental leader, and Martine Segalen, the expressive leader, assisted by an efficient and friendly staff, provided what the seminar participants from 21 countries had hoped the meeting alongside the Bois de Boulogne would produce. As a matter of course, it is absolutely impossible to make the reader a full participant in the Paris venture of 1973. What might be maximally realized is to provide him or her with an ordered selection of the 37 papers, plus an introduction and conclusion. Jean Cuisenier who had already carried the heavy burden of the seminar as such, was prepared to accept a further exhausting CFR assignment. The Director of the Centre d'Ethnologie Française fulfilled his editing role with the same skill as his role of seminar leader. Therefore, this book on the European family cycle should find many users among both researchers and policy makers.

Contents / Table des matières

List of contributors / Liste des auteurs

Anne Boigeol, Service de coordination de la recherche du Ministère de la Justice, Paris, France

Rada Boreli, Institut de Sociologie, Yougoslavie

Robert Chester, Senior Lecturer in Sociology, Department of Social Administration, University of Hull, England

Jacques Commaille, Service de coordination de la recherche du Ministère de la Justice, Paris, France

Jean Cuisenier, Directeur du Centre d'Ethnologie française, C.N.R.S., France

Wilfried A. Dumon, Sociological Research Institute, University of Louvain, Belgium

John Eriksen, Institute of Applied Social Research, Oslo, Sweden

Ruža First-Dilić, Zagreb University, Yugoslavia

Gérard Frinking, Institut néerlandais d'Etudes démographiques (N.I.D.I.), Pays-Bas

William J. Goode, Department of Sociology, Columbia University, New York, U.S.A.

Jean-François Gossiaux, Chef de travaux, Ecole des Hautes Etudes en Sciences sociales, Paris, France

Elina Haavio-Mannila, Institute of Sociology, University of Helsinki, Finland

Joël M. Halpern, Department of Anthropology, University of Massachusetts, Amherst (Mass.), U.S.A.

Tamara K. Hareven, Department of History, Clark University, Worcester (Mass.), U.S.A.

R. M. D'Hertefelt-Bruynooghe, Sociological Research Institute, University of Louvain, Belgium

Reuben HILL, Regents' Professor of Family Sociology, University of Minnesota, Minneapolis (Minn.), U.S.A.

Nikolina ILIEVA, Associate Professor, Candidate of Economic Sciences, Higher Institute of Dramatic Art, Sofia, Bulgaria

Takeji KAMIKO, University of Osaka, Japan

Jean KELLERHALS, Université de Genève, Suisse

Gerrit A. KOOY, President of the Committee on Family Research, University of Wageningen, the Netherlands

Cvetko KOSTÍĆ, Institut de Sociologie, Yougoslavie

Renate KÜNZEL, Working Group for the Sociology of Law, Federal Republic of Germany

Peter LASLETT, Cambridge Group for the History of Population and Social Structure, Cambridge, England

Françoise LAUTMAN, Chargée de recherche, Centre d'Ethnologie française, C.N.R.S., France

Jacques LAUTMAN, Maître de recherche, Centre d'Ethnologie française, C.N.R.S., France

John MOGEY, Boston University, Boston (Mass.), U.S.A.

Vera OSHAVKOVA, Research Associate, Institute for Trade Union Problems, Sofia, Bulgaria

Rhona RAPOPORT, Institute of Family and Environmental Research, London, England

Robert N. RAPOPORT, Institute of Family and Environmental Research, London, England

Roy H. RODGERS, Professor of Sociology, University of Oregon, Eugene (Oreg.), U.S.A.

Martine SEGALEN, Attachée de recherche, Centre d'Ethnologie française, C.N.R.S., France

Veronica STOLTE-HEISKANEN, University of Helsinki, Finland

Victor THIESSEN, Department of Sociology, Dalhousie University, Canada

Per Olav TILLER, Institute of Applied Social Research, Oslo, Sweden

Jan TROST, Group for Family Research, Uppsala University, Drottinggatan, Sweden

Andrzej TYMOWSKI, Institut du Commerce intérieur, Pologne

Introduction
Le cycle de la vie familiale: origine et champ de l'interrogation

JEAN CUISENIER

Moins de trois ans se sont écoulés depuis que j'ai proposé à notre comité de prendre comme thème de séminaire "le cycle de la vie familiale dans les sociétés européennes". Le sujet, certes, n'était pas absolument neuf – puisque les premières formulations, que l'on doit à Reuben Hill et Evelyn Duval, datent de 1948 –. Mais le moment me paraissait venu pour qu'on tente une évaluation des recherches entreprises dans cette perspective, qu'on examine les acquisitions les plus récentes, qu'on se demande si le corps de concepts élaborés à cette fin était bien appliqué et réellement pertinent pour le traitement des données européennes. Je risquais donc une première esquisse de l'interrogation dans la lettre adressée aux participants, et dont il faut ici rappeler les termes:

> Par cycle de la vie familiale, on entend la succession des moments qui marquent les opérations d'une unité de vie familiale depuis sa formation jusqu'à sa dissolution. Du concept de cycle, il y a un premier usage, purement *descriptif*: il sert également aux ethnographes pour exposer la succession typique des grands événements de la vie familiale, formation du couple, naissance et éducation des enfants, mariage et formation de nouveaux couples, transformation ou non du vieux couple par divorce ou remariage, dissolution de l'unité par divorce ou mort des conjoints. On ne s'interroge pas, en ce cas, sur les facteurs qui déterminent les événements, ou sur les rapports de position qui lient ces évènements. On n'insiste pas sur la spécificité du temps propre dans lequel les acteurs de la vie familiale ordonnent leurs opérations. On ne relève pas les différences qui existent entre ce temps propre et le temps calendaire, qui règle les

activités des êtres humains comme membres d'une société globale, d'une part, et le temps biologique, qui scande leurs rythmes d'êtres vivants selon la loi du grandissement, de la maturation et de la sénescence.

Du concept de cycle, il y a un autre usage, *analytique*, qu'il faut définir. Par cycle de la vie familiale, on vise alors une succession de moments marqués par des coupures spécifiques. Des économistes, comme Chayanov, Titmuss ou Fooke ont montré que la balance producteurs/consommateurs, telle qu'elle change dans l'unité domestique avec les années de mariage, est, si l'on veut rendre compte de certains comportements, une variable d'un pouvoir explicatif plus grand que l'âge du chef de famille. Des psychosociologues comme Evelyn Duvall ou comme Rodgers se sont attachés à discerner dans le cycle des séquences et des unités temporelles partiellement indépendantes des séquences calendaires et des rapports d'âge entre membres de l'unité domestique. En tous ces cas, le cycle est traité comme une suite de *phases* distinctes, et le travail de l'analyse consiste à découper l'unité du cycle en autant de phases qu'il est pertinent pour le traitement d'un problème particulier.

Mais il faut tenter d'aller plus loin, et rechercher si la suite des phases du cycle, telles qu'elles apparaissent à l'analyse, obéit à une logique, et laquelle. Il faut, pour cela, prendre au sérieux le précepte qui veut que l'on traite la famille comme un système social. S'il est vrai que la société familiale fonctionne selon un temps cyclique, alors chaque phase est à considérer comme un état de système, la succession des phases comme un système d'états de système. Les dernières questions à formuler sont donc les suivantes: la succession des phases du cycle, qui sont chacune autant d'états du système familial, peut-elle être traitée comme une série de positions dans un espace de relations? Si oui, la succession des phases du cycle obéit-elle à des lois structurales, et lesquelles? Comment ces lois varient-elles selon les cultures, les sociétés, les classes de la société?

En posant ces questions, on vise moins à bâtir une théorie du cycle de la vie familiale qu'à proposer un cadre d'analyse. Trop souvent, on traite des grands faits de la vie familiale séparément. Mariage, fécondité du couple, éducation des enfants, divorce, distribution des rôles dans la société familiale sont plutôt à considérer dans leurs relations réciproques. Si l'on invite à analyser la vie familiale par le concept du *cycle*, c'est pour marquer l'importance qu'il y a aujourd'hui, à ressaisir, dans une vue unitaire, la variété des transformations qui affectent le système familial.

Mon but, dans ce propos liminaire, n'est évidemment pas de répondre à ces questions: c'est aux contributions soumises à ce séminaire de le faire. Mon but n'est pas, non plus, de construire le sujet lui-même: c'est à Reuben Hill et Roy Rodgers de s'expliquer pleinement eux-mêmes. Je dois plus simplement introduire aux débats, tracer la portée et les limites de notre interrogation.

Introduire veut dire: “mener jusqu'au sujet lui-même”. Il se peut que le but soit unique et indivisible. Les cheminements vers le but sont, en revanche, nombreux et variés, parce que les terrains d'où naissent les questions sont eux-mêmes divers et distincts. Ainsi l'introduction doit-elle expliciter quelles sont les origines de l'interrogation, quel est son champ, quelles sont les perspectives selon lesquelles il convient de la développer.

Où se placer pour s'interroger sur le cycle de la vie familiale dans les sociétés européennes?

Un choix possible est de prendre comme société de référence la nôtre propre à chacun de nous, là où il est situé, et de repérer les problèmes qui viennent à l'expression dans cette société. Et de fait, en France comme en Angleterre, en Yougoslavie comme en Roumanie, les transformations de la vie familiale dans le temps sont si vives et si profondes que la société globale est concernée, et que de multiples problèmes sociaux sont posés. Des agences gouvernementales fonctionnent, un peu partout, pour traiter ces problèmes pratiquement. Mais leurs responsables savent aussi bien que les sociologues, sinon mieux, que pour changer une règlementation, définir une jurisprudence, doser des dépenses, il faut anticiper sur l'évolution en cours, avoir quelques idées, donc, des formes sociales à l'œuvre, et des conflits qui s'engagent. Dans quelle mesure les idées des responsables d'agences gouvernementales sont-elles les idées qui prévalent dans la société globale, dans quelle mesure sont-elles des idées propres à des groupes d'acteurs déterminés? Le discerner est une tâche assez difficile pour justifier à elle seule les efforts les plus soutenus. Ce n'était pas, toutefois, la tâche de ce séminaire. Qu'il suffise, ici, de caractériser le premier choix: partir des *problèmes* sociaux que posent les transformations du cycle familial dans les sociétés européennes, c'est s'engager dans la voie d'une évaluation des *réponses sociales* qu'y apportent les familles, les associations et les agences gouvernementales.

Un deuxième choix consiste à partir d'un type de l'organisation familiale délibérément construit, et tenu pour idéal, puis à définir les variables d'après lesquelles un groupe ainsi organisé évolue dans le temps, enfin à examiner comment les données européennes appelées selon un tel schéma varient en effet. Le type généralement pris comme référence est le type idéal de la famille conjugale, dont on peut se demander quel idéal il figure: celui que visent les familles européennes elles-mêmes, ou celui que leur attribuent les sociologues dans leur projet de référer à un modèle unique, pour mieux en saisir, les formes diverses d'organisation familiale effectivement observables en Europe. Or rien, théoriquement, ne désigne la famille conjugale comme type idéal par rapport auquel saisir la réalité des cycles familiaux. La méthode qui consiste à bâtir un modèle de l'organisation familiale et du cycle, à dresser la liste des variantes possibles, à examiner les variantes effectivement données dans l'observation, est parfaitement détachable de l'usage qui en a été fait, et qui a toujours privilégié la famille conjugale et son cycle comme type de référence. D'autres modèles peuvent être bâtis, comme cela a été fait pour d'autres sociétés que les sociétés européennes.

La troisième voie a pour point de départ l'étude des formes diverses d'organisation familiale et du cycle qui apparaissent réellement dans l'histoire des sociétés européennes. Au lieu d'être fait par construction, comme dans le cas précédent, l'inventaire des formes est dressé par observation et reconstitution sur pièces d'archives. Les catégories à manier sont alors celles de la pratique sociale et des règles administratives, puisque ce sont les catégories que manipulent les documents. Mais pour être comparables et mobilisables dans un projet de connaissance scientifique, ces catégories doivent être subsumées sous des catégories plus larges, que seule une orientation théorique de la description peut fournir.

Telles sont les trois voies qu'on peut distinguer pour en venir au cycle lui-même, les trois voies qu'ont réellement suivi les contributions soumises à discussion. Mais dans quel champ limiter l'investigation?

Il faut bien, par convention, prendre des décisions.

Décidons donc que nous nous limiterons, dans l'espace, au continent européen, et aux sources européennes des types de familles observables dans les pays non-européens de peuplement européen. Cette limitation se justifie moins pour des raisons théoriques, car le concept de cycle est d'ambition universelle, que pour des raisons pratiques liées aux conditions du recueil et de l'exploitation des données. Il n'y aurait pas grand sens, en effet, pour notre propos à comparer des types d'organisation familiale aussi différente que ceux qu'offre un échantillonnage ethnographique des cultures.

Décidons aussi de nous limiter dans le temps. Ce que nous allons considérer, ce sera l'organisation familiale et son cycle dans les sociétés européennes contemporaines. Par contemporanéité, entendons ici la similitude de position historique des sociétés qui sont passées par la révolution démographique. La date de celle-ci varie, on le sait, selon les sociétés: du 18e siècle au début du 20e siècle probablement. Sur ce point comme sur le point précédent, ce sont des raisons pratiques qui prévalent pour le découpage du champ.

Ainsi repéré, le champ est assez vaste pour que l'interrogation s'y déploie à l'aise: c'est la tâche à laquelle les contributions présentées dans cet ouvrage vont maintenant se livrer.

I. *Cycle theories and history of the concept*

Théories du cycle et histoire du concept

1. Social theory and family development

REUBEN HILL

In this introductory chapter I seek to stimulate the reader to reexamine the family life cycle concepts he may have been using and to develop a frame for analysis that is more encompassing than the frameworks currently in vogue for ordering family life cycle data. Eleven years ago Professor John Mogey convened the Seventh International Family Research Seminar in Washington D.C. to discuss research and theory bearing on the theme, "The transition from marital to parental roles in marriage", in which several of the concepts of the family development conceptual framework were explicated and their utility for generating research propositions was assessed.

Has anything new been added over the past decade, either methodologically or theoretically to which we should be paying attention? My impression based on the published literature is that there has been precious little progress in the past decade on the issue of measurement and the sharpening of the classificatory categories we use for distinguishing phases of the family life cycle, whereas the picture with respect to conceptualization seems much brighter. Perhaps, this is as it should be; namely, that progress in conceptualizing should precede improvement in operationalization and measurement of concepts, but I would argue that the two activities should be mutually reenforcing and should move forward together rather than in lead-lag sequence.

CHALLENGES FOR CONCEPTUALIZATION IN FAMILY DEVELOPMENT FROM RELEVANT FORMULATIONS IN CONTIGUOUS SPECIALISMS

There has been in the past decade an increasing stimulation from the intersecting of several disciplines addressing the issues of development and change for which the family is becoming a common object of study. For example, family historians and historical demographers for the first time are challenging the ahistorical views of many family scholars. The incipient field of study on the sociology of time offers many challenging concepts relevant to family development. Social anthropologists and ethnographers are being increasingly read for their observations of the critical transitions in the developmental cycle of domestic groups. The meticulous work of consumption economists and statisticians on family budgets is being belatedly recognized by family historians and family sociologists as a means of assessing trends in values and in life cycle variations, in levels of living and in "life satisfactions" which they term "subjective welfare". Anthropologists, consumption economists and family sociologists are converging in their interests about intergenerational continuities, intergenerational transfers, and intergenerational solidarities. Sociologists seeking a better way of comparing societies have recently developed a program of scholarly conceptualization and work on age stratification paralleling earlier productive work on social stratification. Their formulations intersect at a number of points with the interests of family scholars on life cycle phenomena. Finally, we should note that genetic psychologists and human development researchers have conducted longitudinal research, now being analyzed from a life course perspective.

These several developments, originating in different disciplines, have added enormously to the vocabulary of concepts which scholars in family development will need to rework into their own taxonomy of preferred concepts, and present an abundance of empirical generalizations challenging previous views. The net effect has been to increase the diffuseness of family development as a research domain, to augment the redundancy of terms and concepts, and the richness of descriptive work to be integrated by family scholars. Let me treat some of these issues in more detail in the pages which follow.

Time concepts requiring attention by family development scholars

Of the three basic conditions affecting all social systems, *numbers*, *space*, and *time*, family development and the issues of categorizing such development into phases are primarily concerned with the pervasive issue of *time*. The numerical dimension of societies has been the preoccupation of demography, whereas the concentration and dispersion of human populations in social space has generated the science of human ecology. (In family sociology the study of family situations reflects this interest: see Bossard and Boll, 1943; Chombart de Lauwe, 1956; and Scheflen, 1971.) But the temporal boundaries of life and the sequential ordering of action as a central feature of social order is so minimally developed that no one has even invented a name for the science of the temporal dimensions of life, according to Wilbert Moore whose book, *Man, Time and Society* (1963) would be a challenge to family scholars. Historians may argue that their concern with chronology, the ordering and dating of past events, makes them eligible for this task, but their work has tended to exclude the rhythms and cycles, the speed and direction, the strains in time allocations, and the strategies of planning that mark the phenomena of time in human experience. To be sure, contemporary family historians are focusing on some of the above issues for historical time periods. But their contributions to date have been mainly in reconstructing family structure (size of families, degree of extendedness of families, reflecting *numbers*) and to a limited extent the utilization of space by families, discovering over historical time relatively recent concern by the masses with the value of privacy in family living. To my knowledge, with the possible exception of Lutz Berkner (1972) on Austrian data, family historians have not yet coped with the dimensions of time and career management, or with the way family structure changes over its developmental cycle, or with the changes in normative content of family positions over the life span of families for any historical period of time.

Let me extend our horizons a bit by examining the aspects of time that family development as a conceptual approach renders residual. From Rodgers' chapter in this book, it will be apparent that the focus taken by students of the family life cycle narrowed relatively early to the issues of development of the *conjugal family*. Attention has been given almost exclusively to the temporal boundaries demarcated by the ceremonialization of the formation of the conjugal family unit in marriage and the dissolution of this family unit by the death of the participants, and to the orderly changes in family structure which occur within that social time span. This focus has left residual many of the most interesting issues of family time, namely, the sequential ordering of events, timing of actions, and the synchronization of activities in rhythms by day and night, by days of the week, by seasons of the year, by family rituals occurring annually (anniversaries) and by significant rites of passage such as birth ceremonies, coming of age ceremonies and so on. Beginnings are being made, however, to incorporate some of the ceremonies of passage in the work of the Rapoports (1963) and the social anthropologists (Fortes, 1962) as critical episodes of transition demarcating phases of the developmental cycle.

The *timing* of family actions and their *synchronization* over the family's career have not yet been incorporated in the family literature nor have the several "time utilization" studies in Europe and America undertaken the analysis of the family as a time budgeting association. Hill (1970) and his colleagues have made a beginning at examining this phenomenon descriptively for three different generations of the same family line. He discovered variations in achievement "on time" of family long term goals by generation, with some families seeing themselves as "behind schedule", some "on schedule", and some "ahead of schedule". The concept of "career management" was coined by Hill in this study to account for the relative success and failure of families to synchronize their activities and to husband their resources to achieve their goals *on schedule*.

The reader may wish to ask what problems would be encountered in incorporating into a more encompassing approach to family development the several aspects of timing and career management that have been treated as residual to date.

If we take the focus of the scholars in family development as given, namely, the orderly changes in family structure and functioning over the life span of the family formed by the marriage of two adults, there is the necessity of differentiating this new nuclear unit from the parental families in which the new family heads were reared. The social anthropologist Lloyd Warner has coined the term "family of procreation" for the former and "family of orientation" for the latter. Most Western family scholars take the family of procreation as their point of reference and treat the families of orientation of the new family heads as significant kinsmen (central members of the kinship network) with whom a variety of transactions occur over the family's developmental cycle. In contrast, many Eastern scholars and social anthropologists[1] located in societies where extended families are normatively supported find the most interesting unit to study developmentally to be what the Japanese sociologists term the "lineal family", the vertically linked multi-generation family. In Japan the form such a lineal family takes is the "stem family" pattern of one married son and his wife remaining in his family of orientation while his siblings leave the parental family at marriage to establish conjugal units of their own (Eitaro Suzuki, 1942: 1–50). The developmental cycle of the stem family is divided by Morioka (1967) into four demarcated stages:

Stage I: Two couples of successive generations cohabitate, but headship lies with the father. This is an especially difficult period for the daughter-in-law and not too comfortable for her husband and parents-in-law. The service the daughter-in-law renders to her parents-in-law is more important than the love of the young couple. If she fails to gain the acceptance of her husband's parents, she is very often divorced by them regardless of the love or will of her husband (Koyama, 1961: 35).

Stage II: The headship has been transferred to the son, with the retirement or death of the father. This is a stage of transfer of authority not only for the son but also for his wife who assumes hegemony over thc household – it may be a period of tension between the generations since succession is accompanied by a shift of management of the resources accumulated by the parents.

Stage III: This stage begins with the death of the mother and ushers in the first experience of the couple and their children as a conjugal or nuclear family. It ends with the marriage of their heir and the renewal once again of Stage I, thus completing the cycle.

Morioka has brought together data from Suzuki's work in the 1930's with data from the Japanese census for 1950 and 1960 to compare the average length of time each of these stages lasts for the three time periods (see Table 1). Nuclear family living (Stage III) appears shorter and multi-generation living longer, it would appear, over the time periods compared by Morioka.

I. P. Desai (1964) finds the normative support for the extended family which Indians call the "joint family" so strong in his study, *Some Aspects of the Family in Mahuva* (1964), that he questions the wisdom of regarding the nuclear family form as legitimate in India. It is in effect either "a

Table 1. *Years in four stages of the stem family life cycle in Japan*

Stage	1930 (in years)	1950 (in years)	1960 (in years)
I	5.5	14.4	15.7
II	4.0	5.5	0.3
III	20.0	7.0	6.8
	29.5	26.9	29.0

joint family in becoming" or the remnants of a "joint family that was". Examining the histories of more than 383 families, he ascertains that only two percent have been nuclear in form over their entire history; 24 percent began as nuclear units, experienced joint family living for a period and are now once again nuclear units; another 20 percent began as nuclear, became joint and have persisted as joint families for the balance of their career; an important proportion began their family career in the joint form and ultimately contracted to the nuclear form (36 percent), and the balance of the families reported a continuous condition of joint family living for the entire family span (16 percent). Desai offers this variety of patterns as evidence for the numerical importance of nuclearity as a form experienced by the great majority of Indian families at some point in their careers (just as a period of childlessness is a part of the experience of all Western marriages). He notes, however, that there is a high tendency to turn to joint family living as the desirable form of family life (just as the great majority of Western marriages undertake the status of natural or adoptive parenthood to fulfill the normative requirements for becoming a family in the Western world). The sheer variety of Desai's family careers in moving back and forth from conjugal to joint family forms suggests that to do justice to the developmental cycle would require a more complex arrangement of phases than the three stages demarcated by Morioka for the Japanese stem family. Indeed, when Morioka seeks to make cross-national comparisons of the Japanese and the Chinese lineal families and later the American conjugal family life cycle, he utilizes a more elaborate system of classification.[2]

An intriguing question which has not been pursued by advocates either of the conjugal or of the lineal family, as the preferred focus for family developmental analysis, is the issue of temporal boundaries where lineages are the focus of attention. There is more than mild interest in what types of family lines persist over hundreds of years and what types die out. The Japanese as contrasted with the Chinese and the Koreans have developed a system of adoption of the son-in-law when they face the prospects of no surviving sons, or no sons willing to continue the family traditions and care for the aging parents. If one of the major tasks of a family is to assure its own replacement, this issue begs attention by students of family development and is perhaps even more critical in a period of debate over the desirability of zero population growth.

I do not pretend to have exhausted in the preceeding pages the potentialities as yet little realized of assessing *family time* in its manifold aspects, but perhaps some of the concepts I have presented from the vocabulary of social time will stimulate readers to put them to use: temporal boundary setting by phases of equilibrium and of transition; sequential ordering of events; timing of plans and actions, and the synchronizing of activities of family members internally and externally with extra-familial agencies; career and life cycle management, structuring the future by forward planning, and, finally, managing time, a scarce commodity of increasing value over much of the family's career. These several issues will obviously be approached differently if the "lineal family" is the point of reference rather than the conjugal unit that Western scholars have preferred to date.

The sociology of age stratification and family development

The emerging sociology of age stratification provides a broad approach that can guide and stimulate scholars in family development. Translations can be made directly of a number of age stratification concepts that pertain to the "life course of individuals", such as "birth cohorts" and "generations" to their family equivalents, namely, the "developmental careers of families", "marital cohorts", and "vertically linked generations of nuclear families". To assess this burgeoning field of study I commend for reading especially Volume III, *A Sociology of Age Stratification*, in *Aging and Society* by Matilda Riley, Marilyn Johnson, and Anne Foner (1972). A chapter in that volume by John Clausen on "The life course of individuals" treats the developmental careers of individuals, marriage and the family cycle, occupational career development, cross-age relationships (intercohort and intergeneration), aging and identity changes and an overview of the life course where all of these are interrelated. I can only hint at challenges to our conceptualizations in family development in the paragraphs that follow.

The conceptual approach of the sociology of age structure and stratification emphasizes three universal processes: (1) aging and (2) cohort succession, as these interpenetrate and interact with (3) social change.[3] Certain rudiments of the sociological theory of age can be suggested by Figure 1. This figure represents schematically the life spans of three selected cohorts; each cohort consists of people born at the same time. The people within each cohort *age*. That is, over time they pass through a sequence of roles from birth to death (such as dependent child, student, worker, spouse, retiree), learning to play new roles and relinquish old ones, striving to maintain their identities, accumulating knowledge and attitudes and social experiences, and undergoing biological and psychological

Figure 1. *Processes of cohort flow and aging showing selected cohorts over time*

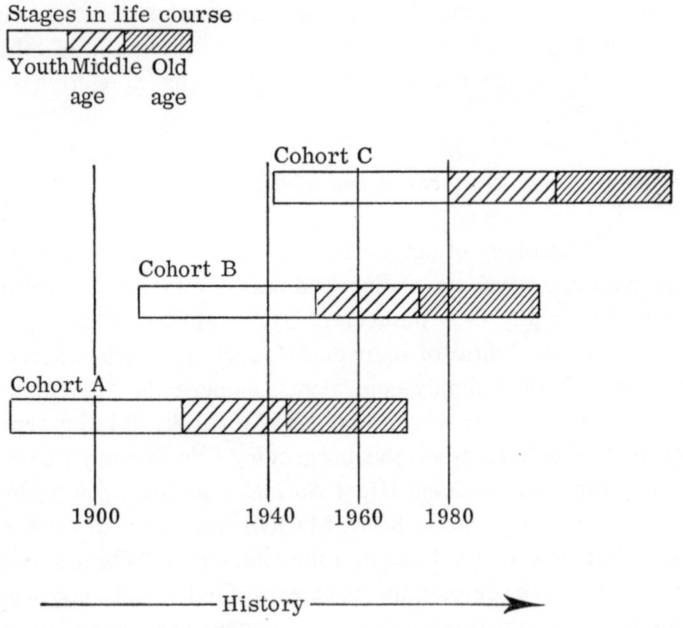

Source: Matilda White Riley, Marilyn Johnson and Anne Foner (1972), *Aging and Society*, Volume III: *A Sociology of Age Stratification*, New York, Russell Sage Foundation: 10.

Figure 2. *Processes of marital cohort flow and development showing selected cohorts over the developmental cycle*

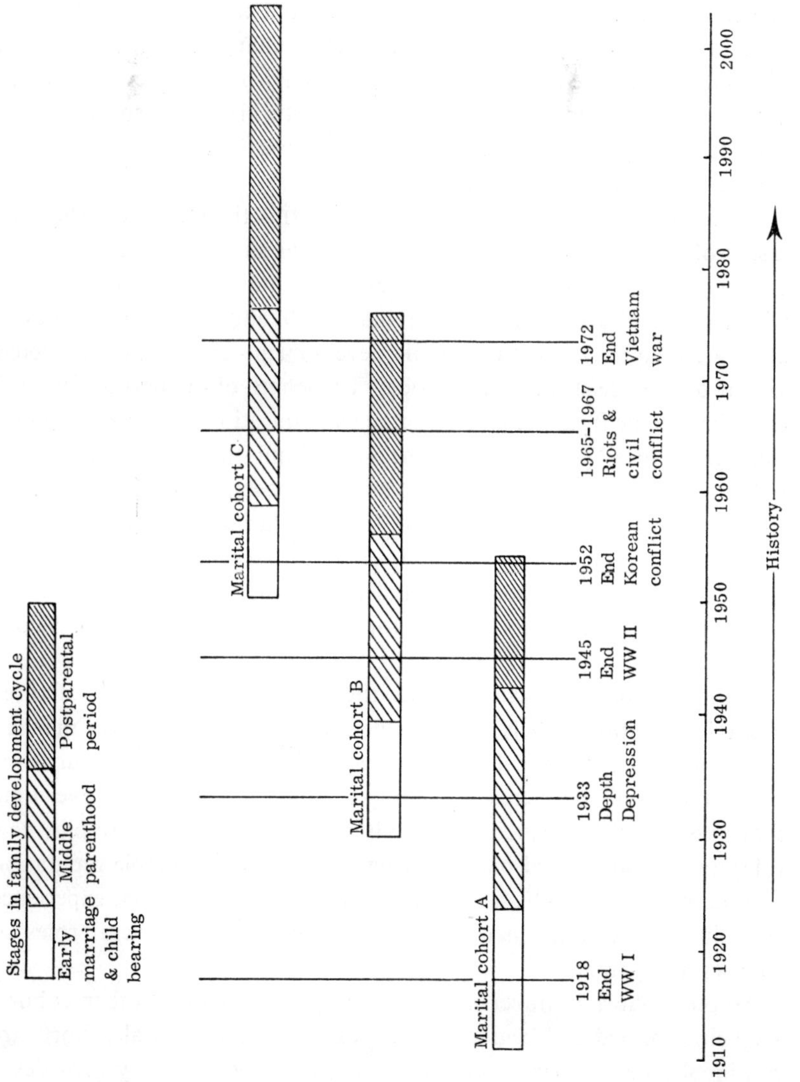

Source: Based on actual data from the first two generations and estimates for the third generation of the same family lines from the study by Reuben Hill (1970), *Family Development in Three Generations*, Cambridge, Schenkman: 84, Chart 4.01.

development and change. Moreover, changes in the social structure – designated as "history" at the bottom of Figure 1 – are constantly occurring (as society undergoes wars, famines, periods of prosperity and depression, changes in the state of science and the arts, revolutions in tastes and life styles, and so on). As society changes, each new cohort encounters a unique sequence of social and environmental events. Hence the life-course patterns of people in one cohort will differ in some respects from the life course patterns of other cohorts. In this sense, different cohorts age in different ways.

Let us now redraw Figure 1 as Figure 2, this time depicting the processes of *marital cohort flow* and *development* showing selected marital cohorts over time. We will use some events as indicators of social change which have had decisive impacts on many U.S. and European families to illustrate the principles at the family development level that are rendered salient by the age stratification model. The length of the bars in Figure 2 take their shape from actual data on marital duration and developmental stage from three generations of the same family lines from the metropolitan areas of Minneapolis-St. Paul, Minnesota (see Hill, 1970: 84, Chart 4.01). I have had to estimate from acutarial tables, however, the duration of the postparental period for the youngest of the three marital generations (Marital cohort C) included in the Minnesota study, because its career has many years to go before reaching the end of its developmental cycle.

Figure 2 represents schematically the developmental careers of three marital generations. Each marital generation consists of couples married at roughly the same time. The couples within each generation mature over time while taking on increasing family responsibilities. That is, over time they pass through a sequence of family role clusters, learning to play new roles and relinquish old ones, striving to build an acceptable reputation and identity as a family, accumulating knowledge and social experience as well as developing increasing competence in their several roles of spouses and parents.

As one cohort is traversing its developmental career, other cohorts are being formed and beginning their careers – new marital cohorts are continually being formed. Our illustration in Figure 2 only provides a picture of three of many possible cohorts, but these three are selected because they represent generations as well as cohorts, separated as they are by the years required for new marital generations to be generated. The length of time that marital cohorts spend in given stages of child bearing, and child rearing before launching their children into marriages of their own, and indeed the discretionary time of the postparental period varies by marital generations as is depicted in Figure 2. Note that the grandparent generation (Cohort A) had a more elongated period of childbearing and childrearing with a much shorter postparental period before widowhood than the subsequent generations. Closer childspacing and an earlier return to the labor force accounts for the shorter period of child bearing for Cohort C, but later entrance into the labor force and later age at marriage of this cohort's children will prolong the child-rearing phase for this generation now in middle parenthood.

Changes in social structure shown at the bottom of Figure 2 as the impact of history are illustrated by the critical events of World War I, the severe economic depression of the 1930's, the prolonged affluence and prosperity associated for some countries following World War II and the Korean war, the race riots and civil disturbances of the sixties, and the debilitating and socially divisive experiences associated with the prolonged Vietnam conflict. As society responds to such changes, each new marital cohort encounters a unique sequence of social and environmental events. Hence, not only the life course patterns of people in one cohort will differ from the life-course patterns of other cohorts in some respects, but the developmental patterns of families of different generations work themselves out in different ways. Let me illustrate by drawing from the career strategies of Cohorts A, B, and C; the three generations in my Minnesota research (Hill, 1970: 310–311):

> The career strategies of the grandparent generation appear to have involved settling for most modest goals, a more cautious development of resources, and a less achievement oriented occupational career, lagging the succeeding generations year by year from early marriage onward.
>
> The grandparent generation entered marriage at a later age, and lacking knowledge and competence in family planning methods, bore more children at closer intervals over a longer period of time than its generational successor. At the mercy of an unplanned economy and limited occupational opportunities, this generation shifted jobs infrequently while remaining in the blue collar class, acquired home and adequate amenities only after children were launched. Unprotected by life insurance over most of its career and prevented from building a nest egg for retirement after launching its children because

of the economic depression, this generation launched its children into marriage later and over a longer period of time with altogether a longer period of childbearing, childrearing and leave taking. Educational aspirations for its children were lowest of the generations, with most of its children over achieving these goals.

The career strategy of the parent generation appears to have been most prudent in its family planning and development of resources. Having high educational aspirations for its children, over half setting college education as the goal, and having high housing aspirations, the middle generation has had a strategy of controlling spacing and number of children, high occupational mobility, delayed home ownership, but early acquisition of protective life insurances and retirement provisions to achieve a high level of life cycle management.

This generation entered marriage during the Great Depression at a prudent age, spaced children farthest apart and closed their families early with the smallest total number of children, augmented the family income by the early reentry of the wife into the labor force to take advantage of war-born opportunities for employment. Deferred from military service because of age and family responsibilities, the breadwinner upgraded his occupational position by shifting jobs frequently. Home ownership was postponed latest of the generations, whereas children were launched nine years earlier, thus enabling this generation to be in a position to be helpful financially to both the grandparent and married child generations.

The married child generation's career strategy shows the most forward planning of any generation, acquiring more rapidly than its predecessors both life insurance and retirement provisions and being most precocious in its timing of home ownership. It leads all the generations in its acquisitions and economic achievements year by year over its shorter life span, although it is also the most extended in its utilization of credit. Its strategy of life cycle management is a combination of risk taking in the volume of its durable goods and automobile acquisitions and of prudential hedging in its heavy investments in protective insurances and retirement plans.

Couples of the married child generation entered marriage youngest at slightly more modest jobs than their parents when they married, but with more than half its wives working and expecting to remain in the labor force. Although they have the highest aspirations for their children, they have spaced them closest together of the generations and have expectations of a larger family size than their parents. The close spacing may cause this generation to be badly off-phase later in the life span compared with their parents, since by now their closer spaced children are in college and will be getting married within a short period bringing a pile-up of expenses which occur in educating and marrying off children. The child generation may gain enough margin to survive this error in life cycle management, however, since it leads the generations year by year in its acquisitions of housing amenities and durable goods, in its occupational advancement, and in its rapidly advancing income level.

Implications for cross-sectional and longitudinal studies. In an earlier paper (Hill, 1964) I discussed in some detail the advantages and limitations of longitudinal research and cross-sectional research for testing hypotheses about family development. Figure 2 further clarifies, it seems to me, the issues to which we should become sensitized. First, cross-sectional studies conducted at a given time and in a given place (indicated by the vertical lines in Figure 2) are indispensable for comparing families of different durations of marriage, as we found it convenient to do at a period of overlap in Figure 2 in the aftermath of the Korean conflict. Each generation of couples was coping with the events of that period in similar and in different ways. The typical cross-sectional study, however, usually samples the entire marital duration spectrum (rather than a tri-modal sample such as is depicted in Figure 2) to study at one point in time the responses of several different marital cohorts on such issues as labor force participation, consumer behavior, leisure time use, family life styles and so on.

Informative as cross-sectional studies are, they are often open to fallacious interpretation (Riley, 1973). The difficulties arise because couples in the several marital duration categories at a given time differ both in developmental stage and in the cohorts to which they belong. The cross-sectional differences reflect a combination of differences in stages of development and generational or cohort differences. Thus, by overlooking the possibility of developmental stage differences, the investigator runs the danger of a "generation fallacy". Conversely, by overlooking the possibility of generational differences, the researcher can – and all too frequently does – run into the alternative danger of a "developmental fallacy". The task is to disentangle the impacts of maturation of the marital couples over their developmental careers (which vary with time) from the impacts of historical events (which vary with time) from the impacts of the differences among the generations (which vary cross-sectionally).

Widely regarded as a remedy for avoiding such fallacies is the longitudinal study, suggested by a single bar in Figure 2. Family histories of the members of a single marital cohort do indeed focus on developmental processes, yielding much valuable information on the intercontingent careers of family members at crucial points of transition. There remains, however, a special hazard in interpreting longitudinal data, since the developmental career of any particular cohort or generation reflects its own unique historical background, the number of children and age composition of the families involved, and the special sociocultural and environmental events to which these families are exposed. Riley (1971) has coined the expression, "cohort centrism", to designate this generation specific bias that tends to color all generalizations derived from such longitudinal data. Our illustrations presented earlier in this discussion of the differences in developmental strategies in career management developed by the three generations appear to be due to the peculiar social and economic impacts of the historical times in which they lived and point up well the formation of cohort centrism in the Minnesota generations studied (see pp. 19–21).

Correctives possible through cohort studies. Cohort centrism may be avoided through comparisons of the developmental career patterns of successive cohorts, suggesting the ranges of variation in developmental patterns by different cohorts and possible clues to historical or environmental correlates. Analysis of the full set of data schematized in Figure 2, for example, has the special property of allowing simultaneous examination of developmental differences and differences among generations, thus helping to map the complicated interrelationships between the two. Clearly size of samples required may make the full analysis prohibitively expensive for most of us at this time.

A most ingenious attempt to establish the linkage of life course patterns with historical events in social change is the longitudinal analysis undertaken by Professor Glen H. Elder (1974) of the University of North Carolina from baseline data gathered on California children and their parents in 1934–1935, followed up in postwar interviews in the 1950's and 1960's. Two cohorts of children, born in 1920–1921 and 1928–1929, respectively, were therefore adolescents and young children respectively when their families experienced the impoverishment of the depression years. The Elder research is a unique work which joins together the contextual data about the depression period with base line data about the personality and family characteristics of participants in that period against which to measure short term and long term adaptations to the changing conditions between the 1930's and the 1950's and the 1960's. He is enabled by his combination of cohort analysis (with two cohorts), longitudinal analysis (with four time measures), and period analysis (with depression and World War II) to address a number of issues that have not been adequately joined in family sociology:

1. Do families grow in the face of economic deprivation in their capacities to cope with stress and critical situations, or do they experience defeat and demoralization?
2. Do families socialize their children in line with the critical situations they encounter in the present or do they prepare them for a more beneficent future?
3. Is there a generation gap in the present time? If yes, is it a consequence of the peculiar upbringing of today's middle aged parents marked by their depression socialization which prepares them poorly to understand their own adolescent young functioning under affluent conditions?

The utility of combining longitudinal with cohort analysis to correct for the misinterpretations of cross-sectional findings is nowhere better illustrated than in the different interpretations of maternal employment data. The cross-sectional data for recent decades (U.S. National Manpower Council, 1957: 125–129) show peak participation of women in the labor force in their early twenties and again at about ages 40–50, with a dip among women during the child rearing years. Rephrased in terms of the developmental careers of families, this information would be read as high employment in early marriage, dropping sharply during the years of childbearing and middle parenthood with a sharp rise in the launching and postparental years. A direct interpretation would be that there are family norms against the wife-mother working during the period of childrearing that depress her participation for that period. A cohort analysis of the underlying processes shows the insufficiency of such a direct interpretation. There appears from the analysis of the experiences of successive cohorts to be a long-term revolution in the occupational involvement of women – from the cohorts marrying at the turn of the century whose participation remained uniformly low until the postparental period just before the retirement of the husband from the labor force, to the participation of more recent cohorts that seems to be rising (with a smaller and smaller dip for childbearing) over most of the family's developmental careers. For example, the three generational cohorts in Figure 2 had quite different longitudinal careers which do not coincide at all with the National Manpower's cross-sectional picture (Hill, 1970):

> Timing the entry, departure, and the reentry of the wife into the labor force differs sharply for each of the generations. Fewer than ten per cent of the wives of the grandparent generation were working gainfully until the postparental period when 20 percent entered the work force. In the parent generation, 20 percent were already employed at marriage (during the Depression), about half dropping out for the childbearing period and by the third decade 50 percent were back in the labor force. Sixty percent of wives in the youngest generation were employed at marriage dropping to 25 percent during the first years of the childbearing period but reentering quickly, to reach 40 percent employed by the tenth year of marriage.

Cohort analysis redirects the search for explanation of a key aspect of family life in the middle years, shifting the focus from cross-sectional factors (such as family norms about when it is decent and respectable for a mother to work) to societal trends (such as rising education and equality of opportunity) in the radical restructuring of masculine and feminine roles in the interface between the family and the occupational structure. Imaginative use of cohort analysis – judiciously interspersed with cross-sectional and longitudinal studies – can generate fresh insights and testable hypotheses about the processes of family development, generational (cohort) succession, and social change that condition the wide range of issues of concern to family development scholars.

Developmental implications of modern systems theory

In a paper prepared for colleagues in Belgium (Hill, 1971) I presented the consequences of a confrontation between the general non-substantive modern systems theory as interpreted by Buckley (1967) and the substance-bound family development framework as it has developed in the United States (Hill and Rodgers, 1964) on three issues of systemness: (1) The issue of interdependence of units, (2) The issue of openness and boundaries, and

(3) The issue of equilibrium seeking versus growth and change of structure in response to internal and external stressors. There can be identified a number of points where the use of the modern systems perspective would liberate the conceptual framework of family development from some of the shortcomings of the organismic and mechanical models from which the framework has drawn so many of its analogies.

Interdependence of units in the family system. In espousing the view of the family as a social system, the developmental approach has emphasized the interrelatedness of parts which exist in the family association. The concept of system has carried with it the idea that change in one part brings about changes in other parts of the system, a state of interdependency which in the family involves interacting positions and reciprocal roles.

The phenomenon of interdependence of parts as stated by the family development framework would appear to modern systems theorists to be much too simple in organization and rigid in the interrelations of its parts. It resembles too closely the workings of mechanical models and does not allow for the complexity and fluidity of a socio-cultural system as viewed by modern systems scholars. They see "sub-units" as at least partially interrelated within the relatively stable patterns of social order. In Gestaltist fashion, they subscribe to the premise of non-summativity of parts; that is, the effects of system membership on individual or system behavior are greater and at times lesser than a simple summation of the behavior tendencies or characteristics of the individuals comprising the system. Indeed, the identifying characteristic of a system is the organizing network of these relatively causal and constraining interrelationships of the components. In these respects the two perspectives are in fundamental agreement. But the modern systems theorists part company with family developmentalists who say that every part of the system is related to all its companion parts so that a change in one part will effect a change in all other parts and subsequently the whole system. Modern systems theory would make room for the frequent empirical observations that the marital sub-system within the family is often quite insulated from the perturbations in the sibling sub-system and the parent-child sub-system. There is room within their conceptualizations for the phenomenon of "role slippage" and "role strain", to which Goode (1960) has referred, and for the development of mechanisms which buffer between contending units to delay and even nullify the impacts of role changes in one position on other positions. Relations between parts can often be expressed better as "step functions" than as linear functions, consonant with threshold theories of change.

To sum up, the family development framework might well be rewritten to present the phenomenon of interdependence of parts as a variable, changing in degree over the family life cycle, low in the beginning of marriage as the phenomenon of organization emerges and varying over time thereafter. Interdependence will also vary from family to family in a cross section of the population, leaving room for a possible judgment of "over-organization" or "under-organization" for some families when viewed from the standpoint of coping with the needs of their growing members and an ever-changing social environment.

Boundary maintenance and the family. Viewing the family as a boundary maintaining system suggests that it is partially closed, semi-autonomous, and when coping with internal issues may seem to exclude the world from its affairs. The network of relationships that links family members together arises from shared normative expectations. These shared expectations unite family members and at the same time they also serve to differentiate the family unit from other associations. Our kinship terminology, too, emphasizes the distinctness of the nuclear family, set apart from the rest of its kindred.

The issues of boundary setting and boundary maintenance appear to be most pressing at the beginning of the family cycle when the young husband and wife feel more at home in the predictable network of expectations of their respective parental families than in the new husband-wife relationship. Again, much later in the cycle, boundary problems recur when the family is launching its young adult members into jobs and marriage because of the uncertainties about the precise obligations of their attenuated membership in the parental family, especially where they may not yet have achieved economic independence.

In the most recent revisions of the family development framework (Rodgers, 1973) greater attention is now being given to linkages between the family and other associations. Viewing the transactional aspects constitutes a real modification of the earlier view of the family as a closed system. The family is now viewed as neither independent of other social systems nor is it wholly dependent; thus it is termed a "semi-closed system", opening up *selectively* to transact business with other associations. I commend Rodgers' discussion of family careers-transactional analysis as the most definitive treatment of this issue (Rodgers, 1973).

The family can be seen to have liaison roles built into its positions including rules for transacting business with teachers, employers and the helping professions. Thus, for example, among the many roles of the wife-mother position is the integrating role of tension management within the family. The liaison role with the helping professions concerned with tension management is often built into the wife-mother position to support this integrative role. The wife-mother position also often contains the role of liaison with the school, the church, and the retail enterprises of the marketplace. The breadwinning role of the husband-father, quite as naturally, links the family to the occupational world and, to a more limited extent, to the political structure. Thus both parental positions have roles linking the family to the wider community.

The differences between the modern systems theorists and the family development scholars on the degree of openness may be largely semantic. Modern systems writers reserve the term "closed system" for mechanical models that have no exchange whatsoever with their environment. Such systems if not fed with renewed energy from the environment tend to run down and lose whatever differentiated structure they have. In contrast to closed systems, open systems are found primarily in the biological and social realm where there is a constant exchange between the system and its environment. Energy continually flows in and out of the system through permeable boundaries. As a result of this exchange, the environment is able to effect change in the system and, conversely, the system can alter its environment. Olson's (1968: 267) definition of a social system assumes openness, but stresses a clearly defined boundary: "A social system is a model of a social organization that possesses a distinctive total unity beyond its component parts, that is distinguished from its environment by *a clearly defined boundary*, and whose sub-units are at least interrelated within a relatively stable pattern of social order".

The family development perspective chooses to speak of the family as a "relatively closed system". Its advocates have been impressed by the problematic nature of establishing and maintaining boundaries. With the accent on the family as *closed* except when *selectively opening*, this framework has taken the view that events occurring within the family are likely to be better explained by antecedent influences originating within the family than from external events.

Operating at the more abstract level of socio-cultural systems, modern systems theorists assert that the establishing of boundaries for social organizations is more problematic than for physical objects since they lack natural and clearly delineated physical limits. They assert that boundaries can be partially defined in terms of the degree of permeability of boundaries. In general, boundaries serve to separate the system from its environment and are one of the qualities of "systemness". In the case of the family, it should be noted that the coincidence of the household with the nuclear family unit does demarcate rather well certain physical boundaries between the family and non-family units, making the family an easier system than many other social organizations to differentiate visually and physically. The phenomenon of neo-local residence also tends to facilitate boundary establishment between nuclear family units of the same family lines.

The confrontation between the two perspectives on this issue has highlighted for me the gain from undertaking a comparative analysis of different social cultural systems with respect to the dimensions of openness, permeability of boundaries, and accessibility of the public to information about decisions which occur within the system. From such a comparative analysis, the family as a social system may turn out to be maintaining its privacy more successfully than most other social systems because of the intimate functions performed behind its closed doors and the legal sanctions that can be brought to bear against violating the sanctity of the home.[4]

The family as an equilibrium-seeking system. In its present formulation, the family developmental framework is at war within itself about the issue of equilibrium seeking and equilibrium maintenance, and we may welcome a resolution of this dilemma from the formulations of the modern systems perspective. In one part of the family developmental framework, the family is seen as a growing, changing structure due to its ever variable size and age composition, making equilibrium an ephemeral phenomenon of questionable heuristic value. A successful family from this vantage point would need to be responsive to the new needs of its members, to changes in the environment in the form of expectations for modification in family performance, and would make a virtue out of providing a wide range of experiences to promote the growth of members which would require still further changes in its structure.

To give conceptual support for this view of the family, the concepts of individual and family developmental tasks were incorporated into the framework. Each position in the family system is open to change in its normative content as a consequence of changes in role definitions in any other positions to which it is related reciprocally. At the level of the family collectivity, a similar responsiveness is implied to the changing expectations of external agencies for family performance over its career. Such a developmental view of the family has not been exactly compatible with assertions in the framework about the family as an equilibrium-seeking system which have been drawn from the conceptual vocabulary of the structure-function theorists.

I think the resolution of the dilemma of the family development framework by modern systems perspectives lies in the discussion of feedback processes which Buckley believes are centrally characteristic of social systems. He believes that social systems are open internally as well as externally, that is, social systems use as a partial basis for their functioning and programming mismatch information from both within and outside the system. Our usual view of feedback in family development has been essentially negative, as input information from outside the system indicating a discrepancy, incongruence, or divergence between the system's behavior and some desirable developmental goal. This information about the effects of the system's behavior or actions has served as input data which the system uses as a basis for altering its operations and reducing its divergence from the internally represented environmental goal. In addition, however, the social system receives feedback information about the status or condition of its members and their relationships, which again signals incongruence or disparity between component states and the system's values. This internal feedback, a form of "systemic self awareness", can be again used as input on the basis of which the system may alter its operations, its organization, or its goals. Thus we have a double system of feedback to reduce errors and bring family behaviors into congruence, drawing on information both from the external environment and from the internal system. Maruyama (1963) has characterized feedback into *negative* (error activated, deviations counteracting) and *positive* (also deviation activated, but deviation amplifying) feedback processes. It is the latter type of feedback process which would be quite new to family development thinking. The primary difference between positive and negative feedback processes is the nature of the systemic changes following the input of internal or external deviation information. The negative feedback process is such that, after receiving mismatch information, deviation counteracting operations are triggered so as to bring the system's behavior back into congruence or convergence with the extant internal standards or the system's governing criterion values. The negative feedback process then, is basically toward maintaining a "sameness", or status quo. It is a change resistant set of operations!

The positive feedback, or deviation amplifying process, also begins with error or mismatch information, resulting from a comparison of data about behavior with internal standards or external criteria. The difference is that the subsequent operations do not act to reduce the discrepancy but rather to increase the divergence between the system's status and the original goal or values. Buckley and others view positive feedback processes as constructive, as system enhancing, and as centrally contributing to the maintenance of system viability, while recognizing that they may also occasionally have potentially destructive outcomes. Indeed, positive feedback processes are the vehicles by which social systems grow, create, and innovate and are referred to as morphogenic processes (literally, form or structure changing processes). Is it possible that the naming and classifying of this second type of feedback process is what the family development framework has required in order to integrate its irreconcilables, equilibrium seeking, and the changes needed in structure to cope with the changing age composition of its members?

Modern systems scholars postulate that social systems must be capable of changing their basic structure, organizations, and values in order to remain viable. Viewing the family system over its career, it is evident that it must be capable of enduring basic changes of structure with each of its several crises of transition: when the childless couple become parents, when the first child enters kindergarten, and when adolescents are launched into jobs and marriage, among others. The impetus for basic changes in structure can come from within the system and its components (as, for example, might occur by spontaneous or induced change in the state of a component) as well as from the environment (as in adaptation to environmental forces and pressures).

Morphogenesis can take the form of change in inter-component relations (greater autonomy and decreased constraint); qualitative changes in the nature of relationships (such as between a sexually maturing son and his mother), change of governing values, purposes, and standards; basic changes in internal and external input operations (as in the increased earning power of the adolescent); and the ascendence of components or sub-systems with new and different properties and attributes in the governing or management of the system (such as may occur in family *governance* when adolescents graduate into young adulthood while still living at home).

Another idea integrally related to positive feedback suggested by

Cadwallader (1959: 154–157) is the necessity of a constant flow of varied information, experience, and input into the system called "variety". A family mapping the environment for variety would be willing to hear and consider a wide range of political or moral views even though some of these ideas conflicted with their own values. Cadwallader has also postulated that creative, viable systems must contain a mechanism for preventing the locking in of old but dysfunctional operations and programs. This would be most relevant for family development where the protective nurturing patterns, functional for the care of helpless and dependent infants, become rapidly dysfunctional for the supervision of mobile children and autonomy seeking adolescents. I have elsewhere termed this process "de-parentalization", giving up the protective, possessive, caretaking roles of early parenthood to enter into a new set of reciprocities with one's adolescent children in what approaches the symmetry and mutual respect of colleague relationships. If the infant-care phase is overvalued by parents, the later pressures from growing children and adolescents for redefinition of their positions in line with their changing capacities will be resisted, and the recognition of autonomy implied in collegial relations among family members who have become young adults may not be achieved.

In my judgment, with these concepts of positive feedback, mapping for variety, and morphogenesis, the modern systems perspective has opened for view a wider scope of operation for the family as a social system by identifying the range of processes at work in the adaptations of social systems to their environments. To be sure, for those goals of family living which are relatively timeless or are likely to change only over a long span, the type of negative feedback and self correcting processes usually referred to as morphostatic may well be appropriate. The family surely incorporates some such goal states. In mapping the changing environment and the responses of its members to bring about a minimizing of incongruity and mismatching, the family may be reinforcing what is a desirable organization on behalf of its members. *However, to promote growth and development* of the family as a system over its life span with respect to the continuously changing needs of its members, coordinated with its increasing responsibilities in the society, the positive feedback processes which make for deviation amplification and changed structure appear important to insure the viability of the family system. I would hope we would soon reconceptualize family development to incorporate these features of morphogenesis into its framework.

To recapitulate, the confrontation which we have undertaken has suggested a number of points where the use of the modern systems perspective would emancipate and liberate the family development framework from the shortcomings of the organismic and mechanical models from which the framework has drawn so many of its analogies. The sociocultural systems of our society, of which the family is surely a prototype, may be assumed to be organized systems, internally and externally open, purposeful, self-regulating, and self-directing, dependent on communication and information as the basis for organization, and governed by the principle of maximizing viability. A maximally viable social system is characterized by complex structural relationships, high levels of communication and interaction between its components and subsystems, by highly flexible organization, a minimum of rigid constraints in intercomponent relationships, and considerable intra-system determinism and causality of system and component behavior. To become maximally viable, a system must possess effective morphogenic or positive feedback processes, and must have available to it a constant flow of varied and novel inputs, plus provision for information, storage and retrieval.

May a hundred flowers bloom!

I have tried in the foregoing pages to translate for family oriented scholars the seminal concepts and propositions from general social theory dealing with social time, age stratification, and modern cybernetics systems that should be taken into account as we revise the conceptual framework of family development from which improved developmental career categories can be constructed:

Social time concepts	*Age stratification concepts*	*Modern systems concepts*
Temporal boundaries	Life course	Systemness
Time allocation	Birth and marital cohorts	Boundary setting
Timing of actions	Cohort succession	Closed *vs.* open systems
Synchronizing of activities	Cohort centrism	Permeability of boundaries
Career management	Cohort effects	Step functions
Career strategies	Period effects	Mismatch information
Life cycle management	Generation fallacy	Feedback, negative and positive
	Developmental fallacy	Morphogenesis
		Morphostasis

There are two parallel tasks which developmentally oriented scholars confront. The first is conceptualizing family development as a dependent variable with sufficient scope and clarity to promote its understanding and suggest its determinants. This requires attention to the multiple dimensions involved, to the systemic properties of the concepts, and at least, descriptively, would argue for a rich and varied bundle of sensitizing concepts to do the phenomenon justice. It is to the task of explicating and elaborating on family development as a dependent variable that the foregoing pages of challenging concepts from contiguous disciplines would be most profitably directed. Such a bundle of interrelated and interdefined concepts would be maximally useful in undertaking family histories where the task was systematic ideographic description. Unfortunately, such a multi-faceted cluster of concepts would be too cumbersome to operationalize for use in survey research with hundreds of families. A drastic process of factorial reduction would be required to achieve a manageable set of dimensions.

The second task is to construct a classificatory device which is simple enough to be readily used as an independent variable where the "family developmental effects" could be specified as a means of limiting the generalizability of propositions. This is, in effect, what the current versions of the family life cycle stages are used for. The device needs to be sufficiently simple and manageable that it can be used widely. Therefore a limited number of dimensions would be incorporated which could be easily assessed in questionnaires along with other demographic type data.

Résumé

Théorie sociale et développement de la famille

Au cours des dix dernières années, un climat d'émulation grandissante est dérivé de la rencontre de plusieurs disciplines autour des problèmes du développement et du changement pour lesquelles la famille est en passe de devenir l'objet commun de leur étude. Ainsi, les spécialistes de l'histoire de la famille et ceux de la démographie historique critiquent les vues an-historiques de nombreux sociologues de la famille. Le tout nouveau champ d'études que nous offre la sociologie du temps ne manque pas de concepts stimulants ayant trait au développement de la famille. Grâce à leurs observations, les anthropologues sociaux et les ethnologues sont devenus de plus en plus lus pour leurs observations relatives aux périodes critiques de transition du cycle développemental des groupes familiaux. Les historiens et sociologues de la famille ont fini par reconnaître que les travaux méticuleux réalisés par les statisticiens et les économistes de la consommation sur les budgets des familles constituaient un moyen d'évaluer certaines tendances dans les valeurs et les variations du cycle de vie, dans le niveau de vie et les satisfactions qu'ils appellent "le bien-être subjectif". Les anthropologues, économistes de la consommation et sociologues de la famille témoignent le même intérêt pour les manifestations de continuité, de transfert et de solidarité d'une génération à l'autre. Cherchant à améliorer les méthodes de comparaison entre sociétés, les sociologues ont récemment établi un programme de conceptualisation scientifique et d'étude sur la stratification des âges parallèle aux travaux antérieurs sur la stratification sociale. Les chercheurs, qui se penchent sur les problèmes de psychologie génétique et de développement humain, ont effectué des études longitudinales qui sont actuellement analysées sous l'angle du cycle de vie.

Tous ces travaux ont beaucoup enrichi le vocabulaire conceptuel dont les chercheurs traitant du développement de la famille auront besoin pour leur propre taxonomie de concepts préférés et pour présenter toute une série de généralisations empiriques remettant en question les conceptions antérieures. Ces travaux ont en outre permis d'accroître la diffusion du développement de la famille en tant que domaine de recherche, d'augmenter le nombre de certains termes et concepts, et d'enrichir les matériaux de nouveaux travaux descriptifs.

Les concepts de temps. Des trois conditions fondamentales affectant tous les systèmes sociaux, *nombres*, *espace* et *temps*, le développement de la famille et les problèmes consistant à établir des phases pour analyser ce développement sont avant toute chose conditionnés par le *temps*. Le *réglage temporel* des diverses actions de la famille et leur *synchronisation* dans le cycle de la famille n'ont pas encore été incorporés dans la littérature traitant des problèmes de la famille; par ailleurs, les nombreuses "études d'utilisation du temps" effectuées aux USA et en Europe n'ont pas encore produit d'analyses de la famille en tant qu'association disposant d'un budget temps. Le concept de "gestion du cycle de vie" (career management) a été créé pour expliquer comment les familles parviennent tant bien que mal à synchroniser leurs activités et gérer leurs ressources pour parvenir *en temps voulu* aux objectifs qu'elles s'étaient fixés.

La structure des âges. Cette nouvelle discipline qu'est la sociologie de la stratification des âges fournit une méthode très souple à ceux qui s'intéressent au développement de la famille. On peut ainsi directement traduire un certain nombre de concepts de stratification des âges appartenant au "cycle de vie des individus" comme les "cohortes de naissances" et les "générations", en leurs équivalents familiaux, par exemple le "cycle développemental des familles", les "cohortes conjugales" et les "générations de familles nucléaires à liens verticaux".

L'approche conceptuelle de la sociologie de la structure et de la stratification des âges souligne trois processus universels: 1) le vieillissement et 2) la succession des cohortes s'imprégnant 3) du changement social et interagissant avec lui. Il conviendrait ici d'expliquer certains des principes de la théorie sociologique de l'âge. Une cohorte désigne un groupe d'individus nés au même moment. Dans chaque cohorte, les individus vieillissent. Autrement dit, avec le temps, ils passent par une série de rôles de la naissance à la mort, (comme par exemple enfant-charge, étudiant, adulte actif, époux, retraité) en apprenant de nouveaux rôles et abandonnant ceux qui deviennent périmés, s'efforçant de maintenir leur identité, accumulant connaissances, attitudes et expériences sociales, subissant les phénomènes d'évolution et de changements biologiques et psychologiques. En outre, des changements appelés "histoire" surviennent constamment dans la structure sociale: la société passe par des périodes de guerre, de famine, de prospérité et de dépression, d'évolution dans les sciences et les arts, par des révolutions dans les goûts, et les styles de vie, etc. A mesure que la société évolue, chaque nouvelle cohorte rencontre une séquence unique d'événements sociaux. Dès lors, le schéma du cycle de vie des individus d'une cohorte diffèrera en certains points de celui d'une autre cohorte.

Dans le cadre du développement de la famille, on peut traduire ce phénomène en transformant les cohortes d'âges en cohortes conjugales ou générations conjugales. Chacune de ces générations consiste en couples qui se sont mariés environ à la même époque. Les couples de chaque génération évoluent dans le temps à mesure que leurs responsabilités familiales s'accroissent. En d'autres termes, ils passent, dans le temps, par une série d'ensembles de rôles familiaux, apprenant à en assumer de nouveaux et à renoncer aux anciens, s'efforçant de se bâtir une solide réputation et une identité en tant que famille, accumulant connaissances et expériences sociales, et acquérant une compétence grandissante dans leurs divers rôles de conjoints et de parents.

En faisant un bon usage de l'analyse des cohortes – judicieusement combinée à des études transversales et longitudinales – on peut aboutir à des perspectives tout à fait inattendues ainsi qu'à des hypothèses vérifiables sur les processus du développement de la famille, la succession des générations et le changement social qui conditionnent tout le vaste champ des problèmes sur lesquels se penchent les spécialistes du développement de la famille.

Les effets de la théorie des systèmes. Pour un certain nombre de problèmes, on pourrait, en employant la théorie des systèmes, débarrasser le cadre conceptuel du développement de la famille de certains défauts dus à des modèles mécaniques et organicistes d'où ce cadre a tiré tant de ses analogies.

Interdépendance des unités dans le système de la famille. En adoptant le point de vue de la famille comme système social, l'approche utilisée par les théoriciens du développement de la famille a mis en lumière l'interdépendance des éléments existant dans l'association familiale; cette interdépendance sous-entend des positions interagissantes et des rôles réciproques.

Cette approche pourrait bien être réécrite de façon à présenter ce phénomène d'interdépendance des divers éléments comme une *variable* qui change de degré tout au long du cycle de la vie de la famille, commençant par être faible au début du mariage – lorsque ce phénomène d'organisation se met en place – puis variant avec le temps. L'interdépendance variera également d'une famille à l'autre si l'on étudie une population à un certain moment, tout en laissant la possibilité de juger si les familles sont "sur-organisées" ou "sous-organisées" en ce qui concerne la manière dont elles font face aux besoins de leurs membres et d'un environnement social en constante évolution.

Le maintien des limites et la famille. Si l'on considère la famille comme un système qui maintient des limites, on constate qu'il est partiellement fermé, semi-autonome et lorsqu'il est aux prises avec des problèmes internes, il semble exclure le reste du monde de ses affaires. En se plaçant sur le plan plus abstrait des systèmes socio-culturels, les théoriciens des systèmes estiment qu'il est plus malaisé d'établir les limites d'organisations sociales que d'objets physiques puisque ceux-là n'ont pas les limites physiques bien clairement définies de ceux-ci. Toujours selon eux, ces frontières peuvent être partiellement définies en termes de leur degré de perméabilité. En général. les frontières servent à séparer le système de son environnement et sont l'une des caractéristiques de "système".

La famille comme système de recherche d'un équilibre. D'un côté la famille est perçue comme une structure qui grandit et qui change selon sa taille et l'âge de ses composants, faisant de l'équilibre un phénomène éphémère ayant une valeur heuristique discutable. Cette conception de la famille n'est pas tout à fait compatible avec celle qui la considère comme un système à la recherche d'un équilibre, selon les arguments tirés du vocabulaire conceptuel des théoriciens de la fonction-structure.

Les théoriciens des systèmes postulent que les systèmes sociaux doivent être capables de modifier leur structure de base, leur organisations et leurs valeurs afin de rester viables. Si l'on juge le système familial d'après son cycle, il est évident qu'il doit être en mesure de supporter des changements de structure à chacune de ses multiples crises de transition.

Pour conclure brièvement, cette discussion s'est efforcée de traduire pour les sociologues de la famille, les concepts et propositions de base de la théorie sociale générale – portant sur le temps social, la stratification des âges, les systèmes de cybernétique – qui devraient être pris en considération à mesure que nous révisons le cadre conceptuel du développement de la famille à partir duquel on pourrait construire des catégories améliorées du développement du cycle de la vie des familles. Certains des concepts-clé de chacun des trois secteurs de la théorie sociale sont énumérés ci-dessous afin de rappeler ce que chacun peut ajouter au vocabulaire des chercheurs qui s'intéressent au développement de la famille.

Concepts de temps social	*Concepts de la stratification des âges*	*Concepts des systèmes*
Frontières temporelles	Cours de vie	Etat de système
Allocation de temps	Cohortes des naissances, cohortes conjugales	Etablissement des limites
Réglage temporel des actions	Succession de cohortes	Systèmes fermés opposés à systèmes ouverts
Synchronisation des activités	Importance des cohortes	Perméabilité des frontières
Gestion du cycle	Effets des cohortes	Fonctions graduelles
Stratégies du cycle	Effets des périodes	Information non cohérente
Gestion du cycle de vie	Erreur de perspective générationelle	Effet rétroactif, négatif, positif
	Erreur de perspective développementale	Morphogénèse
		Morphostase

Notes

1. Cambridge social anthropologists Fortes and Goody (in Goody, ed., 1962: 4–6) find merit in expanding the developmental cycle into phases which will encompass both the family of orientation of participants and their families of procreation in a developmental cycle which they term the "developmental cycle of domestic groups". Three main phases are identified: (1) The phase of expansion that lasts from the marriage of two people until the completion of their family of procreation (during which all the offspring are economically, affectively and jurally dependent upon them); (2) the phase of dispersion or fission which begins with the marriage of the oldest child and continues until all the children are married; and (3) the phase of replacement which begins with the struggle for control of the parental family resources and only ends with the death of the parents and their replacement in the social structure of the family they founded by the families of their children, more specifically by the family of the father's heir among the children.
2. Morioka's ingenuity in comparing the effects of demographic constraints, nuptiality and fertility norms on the length of stages of the Japanese and American families for two decades is well worth noting. He used Glick's demographic stages which

focus primarily on plurality patterns and rites of passage. See Morioka (1967: 596–606). I have devoted as much attention as I have to the work of the Japanese scholars because they are making substantial investments of time in family life cycle analyses. John Mogey's report (1969), *Sociology of Marriage and Family Behavior 1957–1968*, published in *Current Sociology*, XVII, 1/3: 1–364, shows fifty-five different publications by the Japanese (1957–1968) on family development and the family life cycle, or about one half of the total world output (outside the United States) about these topics. This compares with a total of 427 Japanese publications on all research domains covered by the Mogey report. Many of these publications are of high methodological quality and deserve careful study. The chapter by Professor Kamiko in this book copes well with the twin issues of ideology and morphology with respect to extended family forms and warrants the reader's close attention.

3. I have drawn generously in this section from Matilda Riley's concise condensation in the proposal by Orville Brim, Jr. and his associates of the conceptual framework of the sociology of age stratification (Brim *et al.*, 1973: 6–13).
4. On the other hand, we should be prepared from comparative analysis that the emphasis on privacy and the sanctity of the home which Americans take for granted is far from universal. Bert N. Adams notes that these two patterns only became salient in Western Civilization in the late Middle Ages, see Adams (1971), *The American Family: A Sociological Interpretation*, Chicago, Markham: 55–57.

References

Adams, Bert (1971), *The American Family: A Sociological Interpretation*, Chicago, Markham.

Berkner, Lutz K. (1972), "The stem family and the developmental cycle of the peasant household: an Eighteenth-century Austrian example", *American Historical Review*, 77: 398–418.

Bossard, James H.S., and Boll, Eleanor S. (1943), *Family Situations*, Philadelphia, University of Pennsylvania Press.

Brim, Orville G. Jr., *et al.* (1973), "Work and personality in the middle years", unpublished manuscript prepared for the Social Science Research Council, New York, June.

Buckley, Walter (1967), *Sociology and Modern Systems Theory*, Englewood Cliffs, N. J., Prentice-Hall.

Cadwallader, M. (1959), "The cybernetic analysis of change in complex social organization", *American Journal of Sociology*, 65: 154–157.

Chombart de Lauwe, Paul H. (1956), "L'influence de la rue sur l'enfant", *Ecole des Parents*, June: 17–28.

Clausen, John (1972), "The life course of individuals" in M.W. Riley *et al.* (ed.), *Aging and Society*, Vol. III: *A Sociology of Age Stratification*, New York, Russell Sage Foundation: Ch. 11.

Desai, I.P. (1964), *Some Aspects of the Family in Mahuva*, Baroda, India, Sadhana Press.

Elder, Glen H. (1974), *Children of the Great Depression*, Chicago, University of Chicago Press.

Fortes, Meyer (1962), "Introduction" in Jack Goody (ed.), *Developmental Cycle in Domestic Groups*, Cambridge, England, Cambridge University Press.

Goode, William J. (1960), "A theory of role strain", *American Sociological Review*, 25, August: 483–496.

Hill, Reuben (1964), "Methodological problems with the developmental approach to family study", *Family Process*, 31, March: 186–206.
—— (1969), "Sociological frameworks appropriate for family oriented psychiatry", *Voices; The Art and Science of Psychotherapy*, 5, Spring: 65–74.
—— (1970), *Family Development in Three Generations*, Cambridge, Mass., Schenkman Company.
—— (1971), "Modern systems theory and the family: a confrontation", *Social Science Information*, 10: 7–26.
—— and Rodgers, R. H. (1964), "The developmental approach" in Harold T. Christensen (ed.), *Handbook of Marriage and the Family*, Chicago, Rand McNally: 171–211.
Koyama, Takashi (1961), *The Changing Social Position of Women in Japan*, Paris, UNESCO.
Maruyama, M. (1963), "The second cybernetics: deviation amplifying mutual causal processes", *American Scientist*, 51.
Mogey, John (1969), *Sociology of Marriage and Family Behavior, 1957–1968*, *Current Sociology*, XVII/1–3: 1–362.
Moore, Wilbert E. (1963), *Man, Time and Society*, New York, Wiley and Sons.
Morioka, Kyomi (1957), "Life cycle patterns in Japan, China and the United States", *Journal of Marriage and the Family*, 29, August: 595–606.
National Manpower Council (1957), *Womanpower*, New York, Columbia University Press.
Olsen, Marvin E. (1958), *The Process of Social Organization*, New York, Holt, Rinehart and Winston.
Rapoport, Rhona (1963), "Normal crises, family structure and mental health", *Family Process*, II/1, March: 68–80.
Riley, Matilda W. (1973), "Aging and cohort succession: interpretations and misinterpretations", *Public Opinion Quarterly*, 37, Spring: 35–49.
Riley, M. W., Johnson, M., and Foner, A. (1972), *Aging and Society*, Vol. III: *A Sociology of Age Stratification*, New York, Russell Sage Foundation.
Rodgers, Roy H. (1973), *Family Interaction and Transaction*, Englewood Cliffs, New Jersey, Prentice-Hall.
Scheflen, Albert E. (1971), "Living space in an urban ghetto", *Family Process*, 10/4, December: 429–450.
Suzuki, Eitaro (1942), "On cyclical regularity in generational development of the Japanese family" in T. Toda and E. Suzuki (eds.), *Family and Rural Village*, Tokyo, Nikko-shoin: 1–50.

2. The family life cycle concept: past, present, and future

ROY H. RODGERS

Introduction

My assignment, as defined by the Program Committee through President Cuisenier, is to "delineate the history of the concept, its main uses, as well as its future". To carry out fully only the first two aspects of that assignment would represent a major effort (setting aside for the moment my ability to forecast the future). I will proceed, therefore, in the following way. First, I will survey the historical background of the family cycle concept, identifying only the major events in that history. Reuben Hill and I have presented a more complete history elsewhere (1964: 172–185). Second, I will attempt to identify some of the major ways in which the concept is used currently, using the somewhat imprecise definition of "current" that work which has appeared within approximately the past decade. My recent book on the developmental approach (Rodgers, 1973) provides more depth for those who wish it. Finally, I will engage in a small amount of self-indulgence by attempting to indicate a future course for the concept. I am acutely conscious that this volume is part of that future. I confess my inability to predict the direction which the Seminar papers may take developmental analysis! Let me begin, then, with a bit of history.[1]

The family life cycle concept in history

I have found it useful to divide the history of the family life cycle concept into three periods: that work which occurred prior to 1948, that which appeared from 1948 to 1964, and that which came after 1964. The years 1948 and 1964 are not chosen arbitrarily. In both years an event took place which, viewed retrospectively, represents a major turning point in the utilization of the concept in family theory and research. But, rather than beginning in the middle of the story, let us turn to the beginning.

Pre-1948 events. B.S. Rowntree (1903) divided the family life cycle into three parts: one of poverty when children are young, one of relative prosperity when the children grow up and become wage earners, and a second period of poverty in old age. This formulation is the earliest explicit discussion that I know of which analyzes the family in a developmental way. His work, of course, was an attempt to understand the pattern of poverty in late 19th-century and early 20th-century England. This focus on the economic aspect of the family followed an established European approach used by such eminent early family students as Frederic Le Play (1855; 1871) and which is still followed by some European and American scholars. In the earliest American work of significance, the rural sociologists Sorokin, Zimmerman, and Galpin (1931) carried out an economic analysis of the family life cycle which emphasized the changing composition of family membership – another aspect which survives in the contemporary work. Their efforts stimulated a number of similar studies (Lively, 1932; Kirkpatrick, Cowles, and Tough, 1934; Loomis, 1934; Duncan, 1941; Blackwell, 1942). A forerunner of many of the later studies of consumer economics and the family cycle was the work of Howard Bigelow (1948), who moved to a considerably more elaborate set of stages of the cycle. All of these are representative of the first of three themes which can be found in family life cycle work, viz., the treatment of the family life cycle as an independent variable used to explain various types of family phenomena (in the cases cited, economic phenomena).

A second theme appears in the pre-1948 work. This theme treats the family cycle as interaction process. The theme was not clearly developed at this point, but it was a clear factor in the work of Glick (1947) in his comparisons of the 1890 and the 1940 American family based on U.S. Census data. For, while Glick based his analysis on pure demographic data, he drew many interesting speculative conclusions concerning the changes which may occur in the interactive experiences of families as a result of their changing demographic character. His later publications (1955; 1957; 1965) carry these sorts of analyses out in an even more explicit manner.

At about the same time that Glick was working on his first analysis of census data, another kind of analysis was taking place using the setting of family housing as its focus. A committee chaired by Evelyn Duvall participated in a conference on family housing sponsored by the Woman's Foundation. Their work, published in a book edited by Frederic Gutheim (1948), identified the changing needs of families for differing kinds of space over their life cycle which result from the changing interactive patterns.

The third pre-1948 theme of considerable significance to the family life cycle approach is drawn from the human growth and development studies which flourished in the United States from the 1920s. While this work was essentially aimed at describing and explaining the developmental changes of the individual human being, it provided two important elements for family life cycle study. First, its method emphasized longitudinal analysis, rather than cross-sectional studies and demonstrated that such a method was feasible. Second, out of this work came a major idea, that of individual "developmental task", which Duvall (1971) testifies provided a very important impetus to the work which she and Reuben Hill had been doing in family life cycle analysis. And, so, we come to that benchmark point which closes the "primitive period" in the history of the family life cycle approach and propels it into a period of major progress.

From 1948 to 1964. Evelyn Duvall and Reuben Hill had been brought together at the University of Chicago by their common interests in family study. We can see now that the request to Professors Duvall and Hill to co-chair the Committee on the Dynamics of Family Interaction at the 1948 National Conference on Family Life provided the basis for a new level of sophistication in family cycle analysis. Dr. Duvall reports (1971) that the Committee produced "several hundred pages of mimeographed working papers". Those working papers stimulated a number of family students in American universities to expand further this approach.

The 1948 Conference was followed in 1950 by an Interdisciplinary Workshop on Family Research at the University of Chicago. That workshop devised the initial conceptualization of *family* developmental tasks (Hill, 1951 : 21–22) and outlined those tasks for the first stage of the family life cycle (Duvall, 1962: IX). Duvall also reports that it was the outline from this workshop which she used and elaborated for her book *Family Development* which first appeared in 1957 and has seen three revisions since then. This book was the first major publication of the approach.

Meanwhile, Reuben Hill (who also participated in the 1950 workshop) was carrying on a different line of activity. He developed graduate seminars at the University of North Carolina and at the University of Minnesota specifically devoted to the further systematization and specification required if the conceptual framework were ever to become a viable theory. A number of master's theses and doctoral dissertations bear witness to the stimulation which these seminars engendered. In my doctoral dissertation (Rodgers, 1962), I attempted to synthesize the theoretical work of those seminars and to put the conceptual framework to an empirical test. The intent of the empirical test was to demonstrate that the conceptual approach allowed for a number of alternative formulations of the idea of "family life cycle stages" depending upon the type of family behavior for which explanation was being sought. I argued for the abandonment of the use of the terms "stage" and "cycle", replacing them with the concepts "category" and "career". For the most part that plea has fallen on deaf ears, though the career concept is increasingly used interchangeably with the concept of "cycle".

The chapter in Christensen on the developmental approach (Hill and Rodgers, 1964) represents a cumulative report of the work of those seminars, as well as some attempts at new conceptualizations. Because the Christensen volume was widely read, the chapter had a considerable impact on scholars interested in theorizing developmentally. It is for this reason that I see 1964 as the second benchmark period. While it is certainly not true that the *Handbook* presentation resolved all the theoretical problems, it was in such a state of conceptual development and so widely disseminated that it provided a sufficient springboard for further intensive theoretical and empirical work.

Up to this point, the *published* materials on the developmental theory (as compared with mimeographed "working papers" and unpublished theses) were extremely meager. In their landmark article on conceptual frameworks in family study only four years before, Hill and Hansen (1960: 311) were able to cite only Duvall's book and a chapter by Hill (1961) as "definitive and illustrative material" published from an explicit developmental perspective. By 1964 Hill and I were able to add Deutscher's study of postparental family life (actually published in 1959, but with very limited distribution), the empirical study by Blood and Wolfe (1960) of Detroit families which carried out some life cycle analyses, and my dissertation (also published with very limited distribution). None of this work was international in treatment. (It must be confessed that we missed the publications of Brant and Khaing (1951) on Burmese family cycle, Collver (1963) comparing India and United States family life cycles and we were as yet unaware of the published work of Koyama (1959) and Morioka (1953; 1962). Undoubtedly, there are other additions possible to this list of our sins of omission.)

From 1964 to the present. The scarcity of publications in the period prior to 1964 comes quickly to an end. From 1964 on there is a steady production of journal articles and books which involve a developmental orientation to the family. Scanning the bibliography which I prepared for my book (in no sense an exhaustive search of the literature – especially as it fails to account fully for recently produced materials since the completion of the manuscript) produced about fifty published items with a developmental orientation. These items have several interesting characteristics.

First, there are a number of new names appearing in the developmental literature for the first time. Magrabi and Marshall (1965) published a proposed "game-tree model" for research on developmental tasks. (It is unfortunate that, to my knowledge, neither author has followed up on their model with actual research.) Jan Stehouwer (1965) reported on three-generation households in Denmark. Helen Z. Lopata (1966) gave her first report on the life-cycle of the social role of the housewife which was later expanded to a full monograph (1971). Michel (1967) compared data on French families with similar data from Blood and Wolfe's (1960) American families and Safilios-Rothschild (1967) compared her data on urban Greek families with Michel's French families. Newcomer William Silverman joined seasoned developmentalist Reuben Hill (1967) to compare Belgian and American family task allocation patterns. Rossi (1968) reported on the "Transition to parenthood", Burr (1970) and Rollins and Feldman (1970) reported on life cycle characteristics of marital satisfaction, and Lewis (1972; 1973) reported on his developmental framework for premarital dyadic formation.

A second characteristic of the past decade is the increased amount of publication with international and, in some cases, comparative data. In addition to the work cited above, Blood (1967) followed up his work with Wolfe in Detroit by comparing those couples with a group of Tokyo marriages. For the first time in a Western publication Kiyomi Morioka (1967) published some of his work on life cycles with comparisons of Japanese, Chinese, and American forms. The Rapoports, having carried on considerable work on marital careers in the United States (Rapoport, 1964; Rapoport and Rapoport, 1964; 1965), continued their interest with the study of "dual-career" families in England (1969, 1971a, 1971b). Finally, Dorrian Sweetser (1968) continued her reports on intergenerational relations in Scandanavia with a report on Finnish families.

A third, and possibly the most significant, characteristic of the literature of the past decade is the evidence of considerable commitment on the part of several scholars to a program of developmental exploration. This is exhibited in the publication of a series of articles and/or a major monograph with theoretical and empirical contributions of considerable substance. The following social scientists, either individually or in collaboration, are notable in this regard: Aldous, for her work on intergenerational continuity; Blood, for work on husband and wife relationships; Deutscher, for work on the post-parental period; Wells Goodrich and collaborators, on patterns of newlywed marriage and conflict resolution; Hill, for both theoretical and methodological clarification, for empirical work in a number of settings, and especially for three generation family analysis; Lopata, for analysis of the housewife role; Morioka, for analysis of extended family life cycles; Rapoport and Rapoport, for dual career analysis; Rodgers, for attempts at conceptual and methodological clarification and systematization; Rollins and Feldman, for developmental analysis of husband-wife relationships; and Shanas and Streib, for intergenerational analysis.

Finally, there is a general sense of the legitimacy of the developmental approach in the literature of the past decade. Writers, especially in the more recent publications, appear to carry the implicit assumption that readers will be generally familiar with the developmental orientation. They appear to believe that use of the developmental approach does not have to be justified and that (while no means completely systematized either theoretically or methodologically) there is much insight and potential explanation of human family behavior to be gained from taking the developmental perspective. All in all the maturing state of developmental analysis is apparent in the topics studied and the beginnings of cumulative findings. (It is also to be recognized that the papers in this volume are additional evidence of the maturing status of the approach.) While this evidence is rewarding to those of us who have invested our efforts heavily in the approach, we are quite aware that we have not arrived. Where *do* we stand in this fifth decade of concentrated developmental analysis of the family?

The present status of the developmental approach

Undoubtedly, there are as many views of the present state of the developmental approach as there are viewers. Reuben Hill opened this seminar with one such view. His paper, it seems to me, demonstrates again the maturity to which I alluded above. Hill devotes his attention, not to basic conceptual issues but, on the contrary, to some rather sophisticated extensions of the developmental approach related to new developmental conceptualizations of social time, age stratification, and modern systems analysis. This sort of treatment is a considerable distance from the issues I recall being discussed in those early seminars at the Universities of North Carolina and Minnesota!

In my own recent attempt to state the developmental analytical approach as fully as possible (Rodgers, 1973), I found the formulations which I had habitually used to organize the field inadequate for the task. I concluded that the reason for this was that developmental work had moved into such diverse concerns that a new set of categories was required to encompass the current situation. I shall summarize the approach that I developed as the vehicle for indicating how I view the present state of developmental analysis.

Developmental analysis may be viewed as concerned with the *interactional* or *transactional* arena of family behavior. This distinction may be stated as follows (Rodgers, 1973: 64–65):

> In the interactional arena of family dynamics, the emphasis is on analysis of the processes which occur within the family system. Explanations of behavior observed are derived from other behavior or from normative patterns of a particular family. If there is a certain pattern of decision making observed, for example, the explanation for its sources is based on other elements internal to that system, such as normative structure which attributes to some actors authority or expertise in decision making and to others less authority or expertise.
>
> We already have established, however, that the family is only more-or-less a closed system. Many internal processes have their explanations partially, if not wholly, in external elements. In this situation, then, the transactional arena becomes involved. For example, a great deal of discussion and interaction may take place in certain families over how to handle a situation with an aging parent. The norms and expectations governing such an interaction

> are not found totally within that system. Some of them are derived from expectations based in relationships with other relatives, including the aging parent, or with friends and acquaintances. In addition, there are certain societal norms concerning relationships of this sort. In other words, this particular issue does not exist in the vacuum of the nuclear family system but is involved intricately with other relationships external to it.
>
> There is a broader aspect to the transactional arena in family behavior. A number of components of the internal relationships are almost totally dominated by relationships external to the family. A husband's occupational role strongly will influence a great many areas of his family life. Ability to spend time with family members, some of the recreational pursuits followed, participation in certain types of community organizations, and a host of other elements of his occupational life-space govern his ability or his inability to relate to family members.

It is recognized that this analytical distinction between interactional and transactional arenas is arbitrary and that much behavior is relevant to both internal and external normative patterns.

Within each arena I have proposed that developmental analysis be viewed as concentrating on *three facets of family dynamics* – the societal-institutional, the group-interactional, and the individual-psychological. In the first facet falls behavior derived from the general normative structure of the society. The second facet contains family behavior derived from norms developed in the family career experience. The third facet involves family behavior arising as a result of taking into account characteristics of individuals within the family group. Once again, the arbitrary nature of these distinctions is recognized. Any given behavior pattern, of course, is probably a result of a combination of more than one of these facets and may overlap the two arenas.

Except in the most general sense, developmental theorists and researchers have not handled the range of behavior encompassed by these classifications. Therefore, I have found it beneficial to identify the chief "functional areas" of family behavior which appear to be the primary focus of any piece of work. I have used the six functional categories devised by Bennett and Tumin (1948:49): (1) reproduction or recruitment of new group members; (2) maintenance of biological functioning of group members; (3) socialization of new members; (4) production and distribution of goods and services; (5) maintenance of order; and (6) maintenance of meaning and motivation for group activity.

Finally, developmental analysis may be viewed as having been concerned with the modal family patterns of a given society and with a variety of non-modal patterns. My own volume, written with United States readers in mind, places its central emphasis on the modal United States family career patterns which are most nearly approximated by the urban Protestant white middle class group. Non-modal patterns analyzed include studies of atypical role complexes and family careers, patterns resulting from role complex or family stresses, and analysis of cross-cultural and sub-cultural patterns. A number of generalizations concerning the state of our work may be made within each of these categories. Space limitation prohibits detailed discussion.

The first generalization which can be made is that much more work has been done on the developmental analysis of the interactional arena than of the transactional arena of family behavior. There is a considerable amount of attention paid to transactions between the extended family and the nuclear family. However, other potential work on family transactions with the economic system, the governmental/political system, the educational system, or the religious system is essentially non-existent. Both the conceptual development and the empirical data are lacking in most areas.

A second major generalization is that most work deals with the group-interactional facet of family behavior. The societal-institutional facet appears in many cases to be taken for granted as "known" – though it can be shown that we do not have the systematic data available to indicate the kinds of societal norms which prevail for the entire career of any cultural family system. I suspect, however, that it is possible to generate a considerable amount of this information by the secondary analysis of anthropological and other data already in existence. Individual-psychological facet material, however, may be more difficult to gain. Most studies of individual development utilize the family as one of several variables in the explanation of individual behavior. The family development perspective calls for assessing the impact of individuals on the career of families as the primary interest and only secondarily being concerned with the family's impact on the individual's developmental career.

A third set of generalizations may be made about the functional areas which have been covered in developmental analysis. (Keep in mind that it has already been asserted that most work exists in the interactional arena and within the group-interactional facet of that arena.) Probably the least amount of work has occurred in the analysis of the maintenance of biological functioning over the family career. Some developmental analysis of the relationship between housing and family careers has been accomplished, but essentially nothing similar exists concerning nutrition, health and medical care, or sanitation. These latter areas would appear to account for a considerable amount of the life space of most families.

Similarly, while there is a wealth of study on the socialization process from an individual perspective, very little developmental analysis of family socialization process has occurred. This is undoubtedly a further reflection of the low activity in the individual-psychological facet of family developmental study.

Work on recruitment and reproduction from a developmental perspective has been relatively sparse. Notable exceptions exist in the areas of fertility control and some significant starts occur in mate-selection analysis from a developmental view. We do not have a solid body of literature in this functional area, however.

Turning from these three functional areas with relatively minor activity by developmental analysts, it is possible to identify much more work on the division of labor, the maintenance of order, and the maintenance of meaning. We have a good solid body of developmental literature analyzing the changing role complexes with respect to various tasks to be carried out in families over their careers, with respect to the decision-making, power, and authority career patterns, and with respect to marital and family satisfaction over the career. (I have proposed that most work on satisfaction with marriage and family may be reduced to the question of whether the kinds of relationships which exist in the family continue to hold meaning for the participants. Thus, I have placed this material in the maintenance of meaning category (Rodgers, 1973: 130–131; 140–152).) There is still need, however, for more work on the dimension of family disorganization and conflict management in the maintenance of order area and on the dimension of values and philosophy of life in the maintenance of meaning area.

To summarize, then, the developmental study of modal family careers has been most heavily concentrated in the group-interactional facet of the interactional arena on topics of division of labor, maintenance of order, and maintenance of meaning. Transactional arena analysis, societal-institutional and individual-psychological facet analysis, and study of the recruitment-reproduction, maintenance of biological functioning, and socialization functions in the group-interactional facet are still generally lacking.

Finally, in turning to the study of non-modal family patterns, let me simply say at the outset that this is generally an unexplored area for developmental investigators. I will only indicate, then, the kinds of topics that I have identified within some broad categories and identify those few developmental studies that have been attempted. I have divided the non-modal study into three major groups:

(1) studies of atypical role complexes and family careers;
(2) studies of role complex and family career stresses; and
(3) cross-cultural and sub-cultural studies.

Atypicality in the family career may be viewed as resulting from atypical structures, inability to play roles, and unwillingness to play roles. Thus, in the structural area it is possible to analyze excess or deficit in structure (situations in which there are either more or fewer than the modal number of positions occupied) and atypical formations (in which families may be formed in some non-modal manner such as through remarriage, adoption of children, and the like). Inability to play roles may result from various types of physical or mental disability in one or more members, from having one or more family members addicted to drugs or alcohol, or from cultural deprivation of some kind. Finally, the unwillingness to play roles category includes such patterns as separation, desertion, infidelity, running away, and suicide. The only major work accomplished from a developmental point of view is Farber's (1959; 1960a; 1960b; 1963) studies of families with severely mentally retarded children. Indeed, it is Farber's (1961) conceptualization of the family as a set of mutually contingent careers which has been so important to the framework.

To be distinguished from the kinds of variant family careers that may result from these atypicalities are those career patterns arising as a result of some stressful situation. I have categorized the studies which might be carried out on role complex and family career stress according to the sources from which stress might originate. Thus, natural disasters, economic and political events which might produce stress, and technological change may all be viewed as having a societal-institutional source. I can cite no explicitly developmental work here, though there are a number of studies of family response to economic problems and war related difficulties. Group-interactional sources of stress may be seen arising from critical transition points in the family career or particularly vulnerable periods in the family career. Rossi (1968) and the Rapoports (1963; 1964; 1965) provide excellent examples of the study of critical transitions. Aldous and Hill (1969) have gathered together data from a number of studies which give indications of some of the vulnerable periods in the family career. Finally, individual-psychological sources might also be categorized according to whether they arise from critical transition points in the positional career or from certain vulnerable periods of the positional career. No examples of developmental analysis in this latter area come to mind. In general, then, the developmental study of stress throughout the family career remains a relatively untapped domain.

I turn now to the final area of non-modal study. I have earlier indicated that there is a significant growth in developmental study which includes data on non-United States families or, even more significantly, compares two or more cultural patterns. This volume has added significantly to that bibliography. There is the other matter of sub-cultural developmental analysis. In the United States we might think of ethnic and racial variations, socioeconomic subcultures, and religious groupings. It may be equally possible to identify significant sub-cultural family patterns in other societies. I cannot cite any significant studies from a developmental point of view of United States sub-cultural family patterns.

Earlier I asserted that I sensed a growing state of maturity in the developmental approach to family study. It should be readily apparent, however, why I was quick to point out that we have not yet arrived. The overall assessment of our present state must include both the recognition of some solid progress in our understanding of the human family career and some large areas of near or total ignorance. I have said many times that this is what makes this area so intellectually intriguing to me personally. We have done a great deal – but there is much to be accomplished in the future.

Where do we go from here?

Whenever I think about what lies ahead for developmental study of the family, I am put in a state of ambivalence. I am both excited by the challenge that exists and overwhelmed by it. There is no need for any family student to fear the loss of something to do if he takes the developmental approach! Yet the developmental analyst works from a strong beginning.

In my view the future of developmental work lies now in the hard work of theory building. I believe that we have enough development of the conceptual framework and, in some areas, enough empirical data that we may begin to develop propositions for testing. By this process we can continue to expand into those yet unexplored areas, but at the same time move the general approach forward theoretically. Wesley Burr's (1973) recent book on theory construction in family sociology provides developmentalists with a challenge. He states (Burr, 1973: 218): "At the present time the theoretical ideas that have been generated in the developmental approach have been minimal, and only a small number of the concepts in this framework have been used in these theoretical ideas." He goes on to identify a few propositions derived from developmental work. I believe that there are others which can also be formulated. I do not share Burr's apparent doubts about the explanatory usefulness of the developmental approach, though I am quite ready to admit that it is time that we began to put our work to more rigorous and sophisticated test. In my view this involves a conscious shift from the kind of *exploratory* work in which we have been engaged to the more demanding attempts at *explanatory* analysis. We will encounter, of course, instances in which we will need to develop new conceptual devices. And we will encounter serious methodological barriers. However, I am convinced that the focus which systematic propositional development and testing requires will be the most productive approach for the growth of developmental analysis.

Résumé

Le concept du cycle de la vie familiale – présent, passé et futur

Historique. Le but que je me fixe est de "cerner l'histoire de ce concept, son utilité principale ainsi que l'avenir qui lui est réservé". Dans ce résumé succinct, je ne puis entrer dans les détails comme je l'ai fait dans la version anglaise du texte (pour un historique plus complet se reporter à Hill et Rodgers, 1964: 172–185). Avant 1948, les données permettant une étude sur le développement du cycle de la famille étaient essentiellement de nature descriptive et contenaient trois points importants: le cycle de la vie familiale comme variable indépendante, comme processus interactionnel et/ou comme aboutissement de l'évolution humaine et d'études sur le développement. La période 1948–1964 fut marquée par des efforts en vue d'approfondir les bases conceptuelles et empiriques de l'approche développementale; deux importantes publications sont à signaler à ce propos (Duvall, 1957; Hill et Rodgers, 1964) ainsi que plusieurs thèses et documents de travail non publiés. Depuis 1964, on a pu constater un constant accroissement du nombre des articles de revues et ouvrages ayant pris une orientation vers le développement du cycle de la famille; les chercheurs ont été plus nombreux et plus variés, le contenu de leurs publications de plus en plus international et s'engageant parfois résolument vers un programme d'études sur le développement, justifiant ainsi cette approche. Dans l'ensemble on peut se féliciter de la maturation de l'analyse développementale dans les sujets étudiés et des résultats qui commencent à s'accumuler.

Etat actuel des recherches. Dans ma récente tentative en vue de définir l'approche développementale (Rodgers, 1973), j'ai mis au point un ensemble de catégories permettant de lui donner une structure. Je me servirai de celles-ci pour exposer mon point de vue sur l'état actuel des recherches dans ce domaine. On pourrait les résumer ainsi: l'analyse développementale 1) traite du domaine interactionnel ou transactionnel du comportement familial (Rodgers, 1973: 64–65); 2) dans l'un ou l'autre domaine, elle peut aussi bien se concentrer sur l'aspect société-institution, groupe-interaction et/ou individuel-psychologique de la dynamique de la famille; 3) peut s'occuper spécifiquement d'une ou de plusieurs "régions fonctionnelles" du comportement (Bennett et Tumin, 1948: 49) des catégories ci-dessus; et 4) peut se pencher sur des schémas familiaux modaux d'une société donnée ou sur différents schémas non modaux.

A mon sens, les généralisations suivantes sont valables dans l'état actuel de l'analyse développementale.

1. On s'est plutôt intéressé au domaine interactionnel que transactionnel, aussi bien sur le plan conceptuel qu'empirique.
2. La plupart des travaux traitent de l'aspect groupe-interaction. Nous avons besoin d'un plus grand nombre de données sur les types de normes sociétales qui dominent tout au long du cycle familial dans une culture quelconque, afin de combler les lacunes de l'aspect société-institution. Nous avons également besoin de nouvelles données relatives à l'influence des individus sur le cycle familial pour compléter nos connaissances concernant l'influence de la famille sur l'individu, et ce pour mieux comprendre l'aspect individuel-psychologique.
3. Dans les divers domaines fonctionnels étudiés, la plupart des travaux ont porté sur la division du travail, le maintien de l'ordre et de la signification. Peu a été fait sur le maintien du fonctionnement biologique, les processus de socialisation de la famille (par rapport à la socialisation de l'individu), ou sur les fonctions de recrutement et de reproduction.
4. Relativement rares sont les études sur les schémas familiaux non modaux, conçus sur le plan développemental quel que soit le domaine.

Pour conclure, il convient aussi de reconnaître les progrès indéniables réalisés dans notre compréhension du cycle de la famille ainsi que dans d'autres domaines que nous ignorions totalement ou presque.

Futur. C'est avec enthousiasme et quelque appréhension que je m'attaque aux problèmes encore à résoudre. L'avenir de l'analyse développementale dépend désormais des efforts fournis en vue de construire une théorie. Nous disposons d'une structure conceptuelle adéquate et, dans certains cas, de suffisamment de données empiriques pour pouvoir mettre au point des propositions à tester. Wesley Burr (1973: 218–233) a récemment donné un modeste coup d'envoi dans cette direction. Je pense qu'il reste encore d'autres propositions à formuler à partir du matériel déjà disponible. Je ne partage pas les doutes de Burr au sujet de l'utilité d'expliquer cette approche (1973: 218), mais il est clair que du genre d'efforts exploratoires fournis par le passé, il faut absolument passer maintenant à une analyse beaucoup plus approfondie. Naturellement, nous aurons besoin de mettre au point de nouveaux dispositifs conceptuels et méthodologiques. Cependant, je suis convaincu que c'est dans un développement systématique des propositions et de leur mise à l'épreuve que nous trouverons l'approche la plus fructueuse de l'analyse développementale et de son perfectionnement.

Note

1. I must issue a disclaimer similar to Reuben Hill's in his presentation. This treatment will deal most heavily with American scholarship. I am hopeful that one of the major outcomes of the Seminar will be wider dissemination of the work that scholars have accomplished internationally in this field.

References and selected bibliography

Adams, Bert N. (1968), *Kinship in an Urban Setting*, Chicago, Markham Publishing Co.

—— (1970), "Isolation, function and beyond; American kinship in the 1960's", *Journal of Marriage and the Family*, 32, November: 575–597.

Aldous, Joan (1965), "The consequences of intergenerational continuity", *Journal of Marriage and the Family*, 27, November: 462–468.

—— and Hill, Reuben (1965), "Social cohesion, lineage type, and intergenerational transmission", *Social Forces*, 43, May: 471–482.

—— (1969), "Breaking the poverty cycle: strategic points for intervention", *Social Work*, 14, July: 3–12.

Bennett, John W., and Tumin, Melvin W. (1948), *Social Life*, New York, Alfred A. Knopf, Inc.

Berardo, Felix M. (1968), "Widowhood status in the United States: perspective on a neglected aspect of the family life-cycle", *The Family Coordinator*, 17, July: 191–203.

Blackwell, G. W. (1942), "Correlates of the state of family development among farm families on relief", *Rural Sociology*, 17: 161–174.

Bigelow, H.F. (1948), "Financing the marriage" in H. Becker and R. Hill (eds.) *Family, Marriage, and Parenthood*, Boston, D.C. Heath: 393–421.

Blood, Robert O. (1967), *Love-Match and Arranged Marriage: A Tokyo-Detroit Comparison*, New York, The Free Press.

—— and Wolfe, Donald M. (1960), *Husbands and Wives*, Glencoe, Ill., The Free Press.

Bott, Elizabeth (1957), *Family and Social Network*, London, Tavistock Publications Ltd.

Bowerman, Charles E., and Elder, Glen H. (1964), "Variations in adolescent perception of family power structure." *American Sociological Review*, 29, August: 551–567.

Brant, C.S., and Khaing, M.M. (1951), "Burmese kinship and the life cycle", *Southwestern Journal of Anthropology*, 7, Winter: 437–454.

Brim, Orville G. (1966), "Socialization through the life cycle" in Orville Brim and Stanton Wheeler (eds.), *Socialization After Childhood: Two Essays*, New York, John Wiley and Sons, Inc.; 1–49.

—— (1968), "Adult socialization" in John A. Clausen (ed.), *Socialization and Society*, Boston, Little, Brown, and Company: 182–226.

Buric, Olivera, and Zecevic, Andjelka (1967), "Family authority, marital satisfaction and the social network in Yugoslavia", *Journal of Marriage and the Family*, 29, May: 325–326.

Burr, Wesley (1970), "Satisfaction with various aspects of marriage over the life cycle: a random middle class sample", *Journal of Marriage and the Family*, 32, February: 29–37.

—— (1973), *Theory Construction and the Sociology of the Family*, New York, John Wiley and Sons, Inc.

Clausen, John A. (1966), "Family structure, socialization, and personality" in L.W. Hoffman and M.L. Hoffman (eds.), *Review of Child Development Research*, Vol. 2., New York, Russell Sage Foundation: 1–53.

—— (1968), "Perspectives on childhood socialization" in John A. Clausen (ed.) *Socialization and Society*, Boston, Little, Brown and Co.: 130–181.

Clark, Lincoln H. (1955), *Consumer Behavior*, Vol. 2., *The Life Cycle and Consumer Behavior*, New York, New York University Press.

Collver, Andrew (1963), "The family cycle in India and the United States", *American Sociological Review*, 28, February: 86–96.

Cutler, Beverly K., and Dyer, William G. (1965), "Initial adjustment process in young married couples", *Social Forces*, 44, December: 195–201.

Deutscher, Irwin (1959), *Married Life in the Middle Years: A Study of the Middle Class Urban Postparental Couple*, Kansas City, Mo., Community Studies, Inc.

—— (1962), "Socialization for postparental life" in Arnold M. Rose (ed.), *Human Behavior and Social Processes*, Boston, Houghton Mifflin Company: 506–525.

—— (1964), "The quality of postparental life: definitions of the situation", *Journal of Marriage and the Family*, 26, February: 52–59.

Duncan, O.D. (1941), *Analysis of Farm Family Organization in Oklahoma*, unpublished Doctoral Dissertation, Baton Rouge, Louisiana, Louisiana State University.

Duvall, Evelyn M. (1971), *Family Development*, 4th edition, Philadelphia, J.B. Lippincott Co.

Eckhardt, Kenneth W., and Shriner, Eldon C. (1969), "Familial conflict, adolescent rebellion, and political expression", *Journal of Marriage and the Family*, 31, August: 494–499.

Evans, Richard H., and Smith, Norman R. (1969), "A selected paradigm of family behavior", *Journal of Marriage and the Family*, 31, August: 512–517.

Farber, Bernard (1959), "Effects of a severely mentally retarded child on family integration", *Monographs of the Society for Research in Child Development*, 24.

—— (1960a), "Family organization and crisis: maintenance of integration in families with a severely mentally retarded child", *Monographs of the Society for Research in Child Development*, 25.

—— *et al.* (1960b), "Family crisis and the decision to institutionalize the retarded child", *Council of Exceptional Children Research Monograph Series*, Washington D.C., National Education Association, Ser. A, 1.

—— (1961), "The family as a set of mutually contingent careers" in Nelson Foote (ed.), *Consumer Behavior: Models of Household Decision-Making*, New York, New York University Press: 276–297.

—— and Jenne, W.C. (1963), "Family organization and parent child communication: parents and siblings of a retarded child", *Monographs of the Society for Research in Child Development*, 28: 3–78.

Feldman, Harold (1964), *The Development of the Husband–Wife Relationship*, Ithaca, N.Y., Department of Child Development and Family Relations, Cornell University.

Foote, Nelson (1961), *Household Decision-Making*, New York, New York University Press.

Geismar, Ludwig (1973), *555 Families: A Social-Psychological Study of Young Families in Transition*, New Brunswick, N.J., Transaction Books, Inc.

Glick, Paul C. (1947), "The family cycle", *American Sociological Review*, 12, April: 164–174.

—— (1955), "The life cycle of the family", *Marriage and Family Living*, 18, February: 3–9.

—— (1957), *American Families*, New York, John Wiley and Sons, Inc.

—— and Parke, Robert Jr. (1965), "New approaches in studying the life cycle of the family", *Demography*, 2: 187–202.

Goodrich, D. Wells, *et al.* (1968), "Patterns of newlywed marriage", *Journal of Marriage and the Family*, 30, August: 383–391.

Hansen, Donald A. (1965), "Personal and positional influence of normal groups: propositions for research on family vulnerability to stress", *Social Forces*, 44, December: 202–210.

Herbst, P.G. (1952), "The measurement of family relationships", *Human Relations*, 5, February: 3–35.

—— (1954), "Family relationships questionnaire" in O.A. Oeser and S.B. Hammond (eds.), *Social Structure and Personality in a City*, London, Routledge and Kegan Paul, Ltd.: 315–321.

Hess, Robert D., and Toney, Judith V. (1967), *The Development of Political Attitudes in Children*, Chicago, Aldine Publishing Co.

Hill, Reuben (1951), "Interdisciplinary workshop on marriage and family research", *Marriage and Family Living*, 13, February: 21–22.

—— (1961), "Patterns of decision-making and the accumulation of family assets: a longitudinal and intergenerational study", in Nelson Foote (ed.), *Consumer Behavior: Models of Household Decision-Making:* 57–80.

—— (1964), "Methodological issues in family development research", *Family Process*, 3, March: 186–206.

—— (1965), "Decision making and the family cycle" in Ethel Shanas and Gordon F. Streib (eds.), *Social Structure and the Family: Generational Relations*, Englewood Cliffs, N.J., Prentice-Hall, Inc.: 112–139.

—— (1970a), "The three generation research design: method for studying family and social change" in Reuben Hill and René König (eds.), *Families in East and West*, Paris-The Hague, Mouton: 536–551.

—— (1970b), *Family Development in Three Generations*, Cambridge, Mass., Schenkman Publishing Company, Inc.

—— (1971), "Modern systems theory and the family: a confrontation", *Social Science Information*, 10, October: 7–26.

—— and Aldous, Joan (1969), "Socialization for marriage and parenthood" in David A. Goslin (ed.), *Handbook of Socialization Theory and Research*, Chicago, Rand McNally and Company: 885–950.

—— and Hansen, Donald A. (1960), "The identification of conceptual frameworks utilized in family study", *Marriage and Family Living*, 22, November: 299–311.

—— and Rodgers, Roy H. (1964), "The developmental approach" in Harold Christensen (ed.), *Handbook of Marriage and the Family*, Chicago, Rand McNally and Company: 171–211.

——, Stycos, J.M., and Back, Kurt (1959), *The Family and Population Control*, Chapel Hill, N.C., University of North Carolina Press.

Kirkpatrick, Clifford (1967), "Familial development, selective needs, and predictive theory", *Journal of Marriage and the Family*, 29, May: 229–236.

Kirkpatrick, E.L., Cowles, Mary, and Tough, Roselyn (1934), "The life cycle of the farm family", *Research Bulletin*, 121, Madison, Wisconsin: University of Wisconsin, Agricultural Experiment Station.

Kohlberg, Lawrence (1969), "Stage sequence: the cognitive-developmental approach to socialization" in David Goslin (ed.), *Handbook of Socialization Theory and Research*, Chicago, Rand McNally and Company: 347–480.

Komarovsky, Mirra (1962), *Blue Collar Marriage*, New York, Random House, Inc.

Koyama, Takashi (1959), "Cyclical changes in the family composition" in Y. Okada and S. Kitano (eds.), *Ie: Its Structural Analyses*, Tokyo, Sobunsha: 67–83.

Lansing, John B., and Kish, Leslie (1957), "Family life cycle as an independent variable", *American Sociological Review*, 22 October: 512–519.

Le Play, Frédéric (1855), *Les Ouvriers européens*, Paris, Imprimerie Royale.

—— (1871), *L'Organisation de la famille selon le vrai modèle signalé par l'histoire de toutes les races et de tous les temps*, Paris, Tequi.

Lewis, Robert A. (1972), "A developmental framework for the analysis of premarital dyadic formation", *Family Process*, 11: 17–48.

—— (1973), "A longitudinal test of a developmental framework for premarital dyadic formation", *Journal of Marriage and the Family*, 35, February: 16–25.

Lively, C.E. (1932), "The growth cycle of the farm family", *Bulletin*, 51, Wooster, Ohio, Ohio Agricultural Experiment Station.

Loomis, C.P. (1934), *The Growth of the Farm Family in Relation to Its Activities*, Raleigh, North Carolina, North Carolina State College, Agricultural Experiment Station.

Lopata, Helena Znaniecki (1966), "The life cycle of the social role of the housewife", *Sociology and Social Research*, 51, October: 5–22.

—— (1971), *Occupation Housewife*, London, Oxford University Press.

Magrabi, Francis M., and Marshall, William H. (1965), "Family developmental tasks: a research model", *Journal of Marriage and the Family*, 27, (November: 454–461.

Michel, Andrée (1967), "Comparative data concerning the interaction in French and American families", *Journal of Marriage and the Family*, 29, May: 337–344.

Morioka, Kiyomi (1953), "A new approach to the family study: theory and method of family life cycle", *Monthly Bulletin of Family Courts*, 5, February: 66–73.

—— (1962), "A study of the family life cycle", *Shakaikagaku Hydron*, 4: 1–41.

—— (1967), "Life cycle patterns in Japan, China, and the United States" *Journal of Marriage and the Family*, 29, August: 595–606.

—— (1973), *Family Life Cycle*, Tokyo, Baifu-kan.

Neugarten, Bernice L., and Weinstein, K.K. (1964), "The changing American grandparent", *Journal of Marriage and the Family*, 20, May: 199–204.

Rainwater, Lee (1965), *Family Design: Marital Sexuality, Family Size, and Contraception*, Chicago, Aldine Press.

Rapoport, Rhona (1964), "The transition from engagement to marriage", *Acta Sociologica*, 8: 36–55.

—— and Rapoport, Robert (1964), "New light on the honeymoon" *Human Relations*, 17: 33–56.

—— (1969), "The dual-career family", *Human Relations*, 22, February: 3–30.

—— (1971a), "Early and late experiences as determinants of adult behavior", *British Journal of Sociology*, 22, March: 16–30.

—— (1971b), *Dual-Career Families*, Harmondsworth, Middlesex, England, Penguin Books Ltd.

Rapoport, Robert, and Rapoport, Rhona (1965), "Work and family in contemporary society", *American Sociological Review*, 30, June: 381–394.

Rheingold, Harriet L. (1969), "The social and socializing infant" in David Goslin (ed.), *Handbook of Socialization Theory and Research*, Chicago Rand McNally and Company: 779–790.

Rodgers, Roy H. (1964), "Toward a theory of family development", *Journal of Marriage and the Family*", 26, August: 262–270.

—— (1966), "The occupational role of the child: a research frontier in the developmental conceptual framework", *Social Forces*, 45, December: 217–224.

—— (1973), *Family Interaction and Transaction: The Developmental Approach*, Englewood Cliffs, New Jersey, Prentice-Hall, Inc.

Rodman, Hyman (1967), "Marital power in France, Greece, Yugoslavia, and the

United States", *Journal of Marriage and the Family*, 29, May: 320–324.
Rollins, Boyd C., and Feldman, Harold (1970), "Marital satisfaction over the family life cycle", *Journal of Marriage and the Family*, 32, February: 20–28.
Rossi, Alice S. (1968), "Transition to parenthood", *Journal of Marriage and the Family*, 30, February: 26–39.
Rowntree, B.S. (1903), *Poverty: A Study of Town Life*, London, MacMillan.
Safilios-Rothschild, Constantina (1967), "A comparison of power structure and marital satisfaction in urban Greek and French families", *Journal of Marriage and the Family*, 29, May: 345–352.
Shanas, Ethel, and Streib, Gordon F. (1965), *Social Structure and the Family: Generational Relations*, Englewood Cliffs, N.J., Prentice-Hall, Inc.
Smith, Thomas E. (1970), "Foundations of parental influence upon adolescents: an application of social power theory", *American Sociological Review*, 35, October: 860–873.
Silverman, William, and Hill, Reuben (1967), "Task allocation in marriage in the United States and Belgium", *Journal of Marriage and the Family*, 29, May: 353–359.
Smith, Ruth H., *et al.* (1969), "Privacy and interaction within the family as related to dwelling space", *Journal of Marriage and the Family*, 31, August: 559–566.
Sorokin, P.A., Zimmerman, C.C., and Galpin, C.V. (1931), *A Systematic Sourcebook in Rural Sociology*, Vol. II, Minneapolis, University of Minnesota Press.
Sprey, Jetse (1969), "The family as a system in conflict", *Journal of Marriage and the Family*, 31, November: 699–706.
Stehouwer, Jan (1965), "Relations between generations and the three-generation household in Denmark" in Ethel Shanas and Gordon F. Streib (eds.), *Social Structure and the Family: Generational Relations*, Englewood Cliffs, N.J., Prentice-Hall, Inc.: 142–162.
Straus, Murray A. (1963a), "The family interaction schedule", Minneapolis, Minnesota Family Study Center, University of Minnesota.
—— (1963b), "The family patterns profile", Minneapolis, Minnesota Family Study Center, University of Minnesota.
Streib, Gordon F. (1965), "Intergenerational relations: perspectives of the two generations on the older parent", *Journal of Marriage and the Family*, 27, November: 469–476.
Sweetser, Dorrian (1968), "Intergenerational ties in Finnish urban families", *American Sociological Review*, 33, April: 236–246.
Troll, Lillian E. (1971), "The family of later life: a decade review" *Journal of Marriage and the Family*, 33, May: 263–290.
Udry, J. Richard, and Hall, Mary (1965), "Marital role segregation and social networks in middle-class middle-aged couples", *Journal of Marriage and the Family*, 27, August: 392–395.
Winch, Robert F., *et al.* (1967), "Ethnicity and extended familism in an upper-middle-class suburb", *American Sociological Review*, 32, April: 265–272.
Zigler, Edward, and Child, Irwin L. (1969), "Socialization" in Gardner Lindzey and Elliott Aronson (eds.), *The Handbook of Social Psychology*, 2nd ed., Vol. 3., Reading, Mass., Addison-Wesley Publishing Company, Inc.: 450–589.

3. Family cycle and theory construction*

WILLIAM J. GOODE

The rapporteur can choose one of several tasks in commenting on such a wide range of papers. One of these is simply to make a summary. However, I believe it is not feasible to summarize so rich a set of papers, with so vast a quantity of empirical materials. Moreover, a quick summary would inevitably distort the variegated facets of these subtle perspectives.

A second mode of analysis would be to take up each paper, and suggest how it does or does not contribute to the development of the field. Such a procedure suggests that the analyst knows precisely where each new brick will be placed in the cathedral that is under construction. However I am convinced we cannot as yet know where each of these will be placed, or whether it is usable at all. In any event, that procedure puts one in the role of the school teacher who gives a high or low grade to those who have written their papers. Finally, that mode of analysis contains within it a further problem, that the audience is not likely to have remembered all of the specific points made in each paper. If one remedies that defect by restating the point, then one is once more attempting to summarize, with its inevitable distortions.

Instead, I wish to adopt a third procedure, which is to consider some of the explicit and implicit themes, suggestions and ideas that are found in these papers, and to note how they might lead to a more fruitful orientation. That is to say, I would like to consider them primarily as a way of

* Editor's note: William Goode acted as rapporteur for the session devoted to "The changes of family cycle in European societies since the 18th century". We publish his introduction to the session, in which he refers to various papers presented by the participants. Most of them are published here: those by Ilieva, Kostić and Boreli, First-Dilić, Rodgers, Hill, Trost, the Rapoports and Thiessen, Halpern, Laslett, Haavio-Mannila. The papers by Pecheva, Turner and Weitzman are not published.

raising our theoretical sights, or altering our theoretical view so that we may uncover some new ways of thinking about these topics.

In different language, I wish to bring out some of the theoretical themes implicit in these papers, even when they are focused on specific, detailed, and even concrete findings. When I say "theoretical", I mean something rather specific. The term does not have to do with a higher level of pretentiousness, or a cosmic perspective, but rather: *structures of empirical propositions.*[1] In using the term, I do not mean any reference of the thought modes to be found in, say, physics. Some sociologists do cherish the illusion that all sciences should follow that mode of thought, and that sociology will become a science only to the extent that it can present a set of neat definitions, mathematical deductions, and experimental tests. In fact, no other science has followed physics in these respects. Each one has developed its own style of thought, most of them not mathematical at all. For example, neither chemistry nor biology has been mathematico-deductive throughout most of their history. Our own field may actually turn out to be closer to biology in structure, at least for the next century. What we may find in sociological analysis is nodes, or small units of empirical propositions linked together, without any powerful overarching architectonic theory, or perhaps many subsets of neatly deductive mathematical forms.

Of course, we have already been involved in many theoretical issues. For though the earlier discussions dealt with technical and methodological problems, it was clear that those problems grow from unresolved theoretical and conceptual issues. Indeed, as the historian of science well knows, the progress of a field is marked by the progress of methodological techniques, while theoretical development lags; and the sudden jumps of theory, without adequate corresponding technical, methodological or even empirical developments.

With reference to the family cycle itself, we have encountered a curious surprise or paradox in our conference. On the one hand, we observe a set of scholars who throughout a rather long intellectual history have been devoted to developing many typologies of the family cycle. Before us we have papers by Ilieva, Pecheva, First-Dilić, Kostić and Boreli, all of whom have offered or assumed one or more versions of a family cycle typology. Elsewhere you have read papers by Rodgers and, of course, the long series of papers by Hill and his associates over some decades. All of these are occupied with creating a typology, i.e., a more or less detailed way of classifying a particular species, an animal, an organism, a system.

On the other hand, we observe a succession of scholars, equally dedicated, who say in effect "there is nothing there to classify. The object does not exist at all". We have read many such criticisms, and many have been offered here as well. Jan Trost especially has offered a strong criticism of this notion. Yesterday, Weitzman offered a detailed comment on the varied quality and complexity of people's lives, that render such classifications almost worthless. The Rapoports are also focusing on a project which will describe some of the wide variety of human experience in family life, and thus implicitly reject the family cycle as a clearly identifiable structure.

Thus we face this interesting paradox: two sets of scientific observers and analysts, one of which wishes to classify in minute detail a particular organism or system; on the other side, a group of equally able people who assert there is nothing there to classify. It is all an illusion. It is not only that the emperor does not have any clothes; there is no emperor at all.

Such a disagreement almost always suggests, in the history of the field, that the wrong theoretical question has been posed. When equally dedicated and percipient analysts deny each other's "obvious" observations, then surely we have asked the wrong question. On the other hand, to suspect that we have asked the wrong question does not automatically create or generate the right question.

The query that has been posed grows, of course, from a special intellectual orientation, which has been fruitful from time to time in the social sciences, i.e., the biological analogy. In the life of the organism, it is possible to observe some kind of life cycle. We should keep in mind, however, that in biology that cycle is most evident in embryology, and much less so in other aspects of biological science. More fundamentally, in biological thought, except for broad philosophical speculations about the meaning of life, the life cycle is actually a *narrative device*. It is much less often a theoretically fruitful framework for analysis. Indeed, we too may, after we have developed an adequate typological device called the family cycle, be able eventually to discard it, except as a narrative skeleton for locating family events.

Elusive variables

Before going on to suggest how we might use the family cycle or life cycle more fruitfully, let me first point to a conceptual problem that we cannot explore here. I believe that both the life cycle and the family cyle belong to an entire class of variables which we might label "slippery" or even "greasy". They are tantalizing variables. We perceive that they are important, but we cannot easily specify any significant propositions in which they are shown to have precise causal power. Or, we see that they are causal, but we cannot show why. They remain relatively obscure. Many of them deal, in one way or another, with the problem of time.

By way of elucidation and illustration, let me note a few of those. Several of them, as I have just noted, deal with time, especially time in *history*. Contrary to the humanist assertions one frequently runs across, time is not a variable in itself. Things happen *in* time, but time itself does not *cause* things to happen. Yet we do use time in that framework.

Another such time variable is *sibling order*, the order in which siblings are born and socialized. However, after we have shown that first-born sons are different in important ways – for example, a very high percentage of the people listed in any *Who's Who* in any country are first-born sons – it turns out that the analysis of sibling order is immensely complex. As soon as we begin to consider girls as well as boys in a series of siblings, and consider the complexities of different orders of male-female and first-middle-later born, then most of our generalizations either break down, become very weak or highly contingent, or they are obscure in meaning. They also seem to vary greatly among different samples.

Another such variable is the "consumption of time" in social life. If we consider time as an economic good, we are immediately aware that we do utilize our social relations partly in time, consumption, and savings terms. We do decide to do this or that, depending on the cost in time as well as money. However, once again we do not know how to make neat propositions about time and social relations. It is worth remarking, on the other hand, that several of our colleagues in economics have begun to do this and at least claim to be developing some powerful propositions over the past decade.[2]

The place of biological variables in social life may fall into the same category: e.g., human energy, health, or for that matter physical beauty. We all know they are "important", but again it is difficult to state precise propositions in which those variables are the prime movers.

Family life stages viewed as variables

It is clear that when we look closely at the family cycle or life cycle notion, we see that we have not developed a body of good theory, i.e., sets of empirically linked propositions. This is so in part because that "variable" seems very elusive, and in part because we have formulated the variables so *concretely* that we can't fit our phenomena easily into that set of classes. Fruitful variables are rarely concrete. Consequently, the critic can say (as does Trost, for example) that depending on how precisely one defines the stages of the family cycle only some 35 percent to 60 percent of all families fit the cycle at all after five years of marriage, to say nothing of those people who do not enter a formal marriage at all. Surely, a classification, or a typology of variables, must be viewed as unfruitful if it is defined so concretely that a large part of the population cannot be fitted into it at all.

From a larger perspective, however, you can argue that this brute fact either destroys the idea completely, or we should instead view it as a challenge.

One way of viewing it as a challenge theoretically is to think of each *stage* in the family cycle as a variable in itself, and ask ourselves what are the behavioral, familial, attitudinal, or value patterns that correlate negatively or positively with different stages? That is to say, we can view the succession of phases in family life as stochastic, or perhaps even as a set of Markov chains, each link of which increases or decreases the probability of some succeeding event.

In that case, it is much less important whether all families fit the stages, the links, or the types. For they become fruitful if each variable or stage does link up with other important variables or consequences. You may then develop powerful correlations just the same.

One can see immediately that there are some consequences that would flow from such a slight shift in perspective. For example, if one marries and divorces, one does not then return sociologically to the beginning point. The chances have increased that the next courtship will be somewhat different. One is not then defined sociologically as a single person. We know already that the second courtship is different, the forms of marriage are different, whom one marries is different, and so on.

I believe, then, that if we view each phase as a variable, or each phase as a variable that increases the probability of one set of succeeding events rather than another, we can utilize the family cycle notion much more fruitfully.

Haavio-Mannila does not attempt a sweeping critique of this kind, but nevertheless formulates some interesting propositions that would fit my suggestion. For example, she notes that if a couple does not go through the stage of parenthood – in some criticisms, the fact that some do not become parents is viewed as a destructive comment on the family cycle notion – it is more likely that wives then need a wide circle of friends in order to be happy. She also suggests that in the *late* stages of marriage a man with a low level of sexual activity will be less happy.

A third such finding is that feelings of anxiety are more common among employed mothers of preschool children than among the nonemployed. Once again, we are referring to a *phase* in the family cycle, i.e., the presence of preschool children, and the relationship between it and other variables, such as anxiety or mothers' employment.

Now one must concede that many such findings will not be powerful propositions. Many of Mannila's findings are time- and space-specific. They are what I call "historically accidental". One would not expect to find precisely those relationships in other times and places. For example, the development of sexual satisfaction among wives in the later stages of marriage is almost certainly a product of the sexual inhibitions peculiar to our special historical epoch, one that is now passing. It is not transcultural; it is not transhistorical.

Family cycle and time links

As social scientists, we are properly suspicious of mere correlations. As our elementary texts point out so often, correlations may be spurious in many different ways. That proper caution should not, however, cause us to forget that if there is a causal link at all, it *will* show up in a correlation of some kind. Consequently, some correlations will eventually become the building blocks of theory.

Such correlations, when they grow from the attempt to link the phases of a family cycle with other variables, also require us to consider several other fruitful outcomes of the family cycle perspective. These have in part been noted in the papers before us, but I wish to state them more explicitly. One or more of them can be found in the papers by Halpern, First-Dilić, Ilieva, Pecheva, and Turner, as well as (especially on the empirical side) Laslett. These broader perspectives are three major types of time links. They are: (1) the links between the family life cycle and historical processes; (2) between the life cycle and cohorts or generations; and (3) between the family life cycle and family systems themselves. These should be viewed as three separate perspectives or ways of organizing data. We cannot consider all of them, but they should at least be noted for future analysis.

First, the family cycle requires us to collect *longitudinal* data. We cannot be certain we have found any cycle at all unless we use such diachronic data. Again, elementary textbooks in the methods of social research have many times pointed out that cross-tabulations from a single synchronic sample cannot always substitute for diachronic data. Even averages that are drawn from a sample of people of different chronological ages will not give us longitudinal data. This is a point which Hareven has brought out, but it also appears in many other papers. To emphasize this methodological and theoretical assertion does not, of course, mean that we should cast out synchronic data; we shall always need them too. What is important is to recognize that once we seriously look at families in their phases, we are also required to collect longitudinal data.

Secondly, if we use such data, and wish to obtain family cycles, we are also then forced into some *historical* consideration of the family itself – that is, how a given family system, or a system of family cycles, changes over time. When we do so, our time dimensions become much larger. We must then think in a framework of *several* generations in depth, or we cannot define a real family *cycle*.

Moreover, third, since long time periods are forced upon us by this perspective, we are then pushed into other historical analyses. We must also introduce some consideration of the different effects through *history* of war and depression, national growth, changes in national boundaries, and alterations in sexual behavior, family values, and so on, throughout the *family* cycle. The analysis must then become complex, contingent, and even obscure, because that is the nature of historical analysis over longer periods of time.

Fourth, what we thought were important historical changes, like the supposed changes in the composition of the conjugal family unit, may not be very great at all, when we view them over a longer time perspective. This relates to a fifth point, that perhaps in many systems what we had come to think of as the idealized type of family system, the one that is valued most highly by the society, may actually turn out to be only one stage in the development of particular families over their family cycle. Thus, for example, I made the suggestion over a decade ago that both the

Arab and Indian family systems (among others) are likely to be joint or extended in their household patterns only at one phase in the cycle of the family, and most especially when a given family becomes economically or politically successful. That is, if we look at longer time perspectives, and consider generations or cohorts separately, we may find that what was viewed as the ideal family "system" is merely one phase of a family cycle of several generations in depth.

The notion of the "idealized family system", which I have emphasized in my writings in the past, leads us once more to the suggestion made earlier in this discussion, that we might fruitfully utilize some part of the family cycle concept by treating each phase as an independent variable, as heightening or lowering the probability of one or another successive stage. Haavio-Mannila did this in a tentative way, and Halpern did so implicitly as well. For example, in his paper on Yugoslavia, he has noted that even with the declining size of the family over a century's time, in a rural familistic society we might nevertheless encounter more family units embedded among and in active interaction with a live extended kin network than a century ago. How could this happen? How could it happen, that a family *system* is changing over historical time, by declining greatly in numbers, but also enlarging the number of *relationships* with live members?

The answer is of course very simple, although it does not (as Halpern argues) deny any of the current theses as to the impact of industrialization on the family system. Indeed, *longevity* is the variable that correlates with the completion of a family cycle over time. Far more people live out a normal life span in rural Yugoslavia, and thus make it possible to complete a family cycle that perhaps only infrequently was completed in the past.

That in itself is an obvious proposition, but it does suggest a broader theoretical question. Under which conditions are families more or less likely to complete what seems to be the modal or even ideal family cycle of their culture? – Affluence or poverty? Political power or impotence? High managerial skills on the part of older women? And so on. Doubtless, members of our conference can suggest other variables that might maximize or minimize the chances of going through one or more stages of any family cycle that might be conceptualized.

This challenge is still more daringly accepted by Laslett, whose data turn our family cycle question around somewhat by placing it in a much longer time dimension, generational analysis, and family system analysis. Thereby he forces us to consider these new dimensions of the family cycle and demonstrates the fruitfulness of the approach even when we cannot accept it as empirically or typologically adequate.

One part of his data is not well known to most social scientists, but most participants in this conference are now familiar with the facts. We now know that only a low percentage of all families in most times and places live in multigenerational, extended households. That finding has been brought out in many analyses of the past twenty years – some of my own, some by Marion J. Levy and Ansley Coale, and of course notably in the work of Professor Laslett. As we now know, under most conditions of birth rates, death rates, and age at marriage, we cannot have a high percentage of extended households. Indeed, that problem is raised once more in the present conference papers on Yugoslavia today, with reference to the *zadruga*.

However that fundamental fact is related to several others, and here we must think of the relationship between family cycle and generations, as well as family cycle and life cycle, for we now can see clearly that the longer time perspective of history does not suggest that the recent impact of industrialization has altered the family cycle or the family system as much as has been supposed – again, of course, this is a challenge that I offered over a decade ago, in my *World Revolution in Family Patterns*.

Next, consider the fact that Western marriages have mostly occurred between men and women of the same age, with about 30 percent of wives, more or less, being older than their husbands. Most husbands and wives married in their mid- or late twenties. Would that not, then, make a difference in the spousal relations throughout the family cycle? Would it not be likely that their marriages would be more companionate and less authoritarian? Indeed, would this not affect whom they chose to marry, or whom they tried to marry? Would it not affect the extent to which elders tried to lay a heavy hand upon them in the mate choice process? That is to say, when marriage as a phase in the family cycle occurs late in the life cycle, and both man and woman are about the same age, it then becomes more difficult for the elder generation to maintain control.

These differences are strong, when the comparison is made between Western family cycles over the past 500 years, as contrasted with those in India.

Or let us consider a next example, socialization, with respect to the relative age of parents and children. If the stages of the individual life cycle have any influence, is it not likely that the greater age discrepancy between parents and children in Western countries would make a difference in the socialization process? Does this not create a different type of interaction between the generation or cohort, and the family cycle itself? Does this mean, for example, that Western parents needed less ideological support to achieve their parental authority than, say, Japanese or Indian parents, where the age discrepancy was less?

As a third aspect of cycling, relating to cohorts or generations and socialization, we note that a substantial percentage of young people in Laslett's sample went into some form of domestic service. The upper classes once followed this pattern as well. It is possible that only about 40 percent of the young escaped some form of service in other people's families. Thus we have an interesting pattern of outsiders coming in to take part in some phase of the family cycle. Of course a very high percentage of households included servants, and this pattern continued in England through much of the nineteenth century. We might suppose, guess, or speculate that the later stages of marriage correlated with having outsiders in service within the household.

That circumstance might well make for differences in the socialization of the young. We can look at the situation from two perspectives, (a) those who are in service themselves, and (b) the households where these outsiders dwell. The former are being socialized by *surrogate* parents. Does this make a difference in their socialization experience? Does it make a difference in the family cycle itself? The Puritans certainly thought that surrogate parents possessed a great advantage. They believed, for example, that one's own parents would be too loving and would not keep a firm enough hand on the child.

But does it also make a difference in the socialization of the very young if they are surrounded by an additional group of "outside" people who are in service? Those servants are also socializers, are also part of the family cycle. They were likely to be only slightly older than the younger children. Were they then like older siblings in their correction? For we know that they were not working assiduously all day long; they were often engaged in more or less familial types of activities, and they were not always of a markedly lower class origin.

The paper by Turner notes this relationship in other connections, and also notes the extent to which families exchanged children with one another. Did this exchange affect socialization in that kind of society? Hareven does not raise this question explicitly, but her data on boarding house life in the United States suggests similar questions. A very high percentage of people spent part of their lives in boarding houses and surrogate types of large family systems. That is, such an experience was part of a widespread family cycle pattern in the United States.

These matters also raise further perspectives and questions; one of the most important is one that Hajnal raised two decades ago, and that Professor Laslett and I have independently raised here and there in prior publications. It is also raised in the papers from our Eastern European colleagues, the question of East and West in Europe itself: if those differences are as profound as they sometimes seem to be, why did they exist, and what were their consequences? For they suggest that both the family cycle and the family system were different.

A further aspect of this great difference, though it is one that differentiates all of the Western European from most of the rest of the world, is the *investment* pattern in the two types of socio-economic structures. In turn, we may view the difference in the investment pattern as linked tightly with the family cycle itself.

In the Eastern type of familistic system there has been a greater investment in the *family system itself*, or if you will, in the completion of the family cycle. By contrast, in Western Europe, and most especially in the industrializing countries, there has been a far greater withholding of energies from the familial sector: not permitting a given person to enter the marriage phase of the family cycle until he or she is adult, has spent some years in adulthood, and has acquired some economic competence, so as to be able to establish an independent family. Thus the actual marriage and parenthood phase comes much later in the age of the cohort.

That is a very striking difference, with many consequences, and we can reread some of the data before us today with this perspective in mind. One important consequence was that in the Western European, industrializing, system, there were many adults who had not yet established families, and who were therefore available for the new type of production system when it finally emerged historically on the scene of modern Europe.

The phasing of life cycles within the family cycle

All of the foregoing are at least in part questions about the family cycle, and what I have tried to do is no more than offer a few perspectives that I think might be fruitful in reconsidering the family cycle orientation.

They are partly questions that arise from transforming the family cycle notion into phasing variables.

Let us, however, consider phasing variables in a slightly different way: the phasings of the *life cycle* of husband and wife, of parents and children, of kinfolk and couples. I want to comment on these matters independently, since just as the family cycle leads us into the past, so does it lead us into the present and even itno the future. How have these phasings differed in the past? How will they differ in the future?

Certainly we see that if there were different phasings in the past between husband and wife, parents and children, couples and kinfolk, the actual family cycle must have been different; for the *family* cycle itself is made up of those different phasings of the individual *life* cycle.

Now when we look at the phasings themselves one of the interesting things that we note is that, by and large, societies do not name and distinguish many specific phases in the life of the individual, as they do not indeed for the life cycle of the family itself. Even India, which has a traditional four-age system (the last of which, the *Ashram*, is retirement from the world) uses only those four. Of course when they are named and distinguished socially, they are likely to express ideals rather than reality.

That is, by and large, societies recognize only very crude passages of time in the phasings of life cycles, and do not attempt to worry overmuch about how husbands and wives are psychologically or chronologically phased together, or whether these are even relevant for discussing the life cycle.

This is not so surprising, because social structures in general invest very little in the matching, the adjustment, and the happiness of spouses. The larger social structure is relatively unconcerned with the happiness of people, and I believe even with the *functioning* of families, *except* as they contribute to the larger system.

On the other hand, people in the modern world, especially since World War II, have moved more and more firmly towards the notion that individual happiness does matter greatly, and it has therefore become socially important. As a consequence, the matching of psychological or chronological phases as part of the family cycle has become individually and socially more important.

In the past, of course, infants married in some instances, old men were sometimes married to young girls, and so on. Where extended kin and elders maintained considerable control over who married whom, they could also maintain some control over marital interaction if that was important, whatever the matching or mismatching of the phases in the life cycle of husband and wife.

But though societies have not invested much energy in the relationship of phases in the life cycle as they form part of the family cycle, there are bits of folk wisdom that have been passed on from generation to generation about these phasings. I would not call most of these *norms*. That is, I do not believe that by and large they were expressed as *moral prescriptions*. They are rather cognitive descriptions or predictions of what might happen, i.e., how the family cycle might be played out over time, if certain harmonies or disharmonies existed in the life cycles of the marrying man and woman. Let me note some of these ideas about complementary phasing of life cycles, just to remind you that they exist. Perhaps some of you, with a broader knowledge of folk beliefs, can state many similar notions. Needless to say, not all societies are in agreement with these.

One of them is that old men should not marry very young women, because as the man's sexual powers wane, the woman's will grow. Therefore he will not be able to control her. Note that it is defined as socially important that she *be* controlled, an important goal of men in all family systems.

Secondly, the man should be some years older than the woman, but the woman should not be older than the man, because his authority can be threatened. Now, these observations should not stimulate you to assert that some people have violated these rules (e.g., the Chinese in the last period of the Ch'ing Dynasty). If people had never violated such rules, no such folk wisdom would ever have been stated.

Third, "old man" is a phase which can be matched in marriage with some phases of a woman's life, but "old woman" should not be matched in a new marriage with any phase of a man's life.[3]

In a very high percentage of societies, it has been viewed as incongruous or shameful for the older woman to entertain the notion of marriage. She has "finished" her marital cycle. In especially Catholic countries in the Western and Eastern European zones, as in India and China, the widow was likely to be defined as having completed the marital cycle, and social pressures were mounted against any such new union on her part.

As sociologists and anthropologists, we know why that was so. A marriage is an investment, especially an investment in future phases of the family cycle. Consequently, an investment in an old woman would not be viewed as worthwhile.

Other connections are equally obvious, e.g., the relationship with patriliny, i.e., making the woman part of the husband's line. Her remarriage with a new man, after years of life in her former husband's lineage, might pollute his name, his honor, and his lineage.

There is, however, an important qualification of this notion in folk knowledge about the complementary phases of the life cycles of spouses. It is observable that wherever a woman owns property in her own right, but is old or is a widow, she can more easily be defined as *not* having yet completed the marital cycle. If she marries again, a man would then get control over that property. The laws of property have always been conceived, passed, and enforced by men. Even in Western European societies where the remarriage of older women was viewed as somewhat incongruous, that view was always relaxed for older women with wealth.

One may phrase this folk wisdom still more generally: the more patriarchal the society is, the less a man will be criticized for marrying a woman much younger than he is. A corollary is: the higher the man's rank, the less criticized he is for marrying a much younger woman.

I believe that many of you could develop similar notions from your own folk knowledge. My basic assertion is, however, that societies have not concerned themselves greatly with these aspects of matching the life cycle of husbands and wives, parents and children, or couples and kinfolk.

In the immediately contemporary world, we are concerned far more with the matching of these phases in the family cycle. For to the extent that individuals choose their own mates and family elders do not, the class factors, ethnic background, and religion will play a lesser role in the choice of spouses. Where people do not stay in the social networks of their parents or their natal neighborhood as part of those family cycles, that social and geographic mobility increases the likelihood that people with the same ascribed traits will *not have the same life cycle experiences*. They will not be at the same phase in the life cycle when they marry, even if they are at roughly the same ages, or come from the same class background.

That is especially so nowadays with respect to the discrepancy between spouses and children because they do not have the same experiences even at the *same phase* of their individual life cycle. By contrast, in less rapidly moving historical epochs, children and parents might well have gone through similar life experiences when each reached the same chronological age.

A further aspect of the complementary phasing should be noted: because women enjoy more freedom now, and in the future will enjoy still more freedom than in the past, they do not have to adjust so completely to the phasing patterns of their husbands as in the past. In fact they may develop new phases of their own; or, phrased differently, husbands must increasingly adjust to a new set of problems in their personal life and family cycles, i.e., the new and independently conceived life phases of their own wives. We may also predict that the chances will be lower in the future that husbands and wives will be in phasal harmony, or perhaps we should instead predict that people who become husbands and wives will look more carefully to ascertain whether they are in phasal harmony.

Final comment

Now all of these variables create a complex set of options for the individual. They do undermine to some extent any simple concrete classification of family cycle. But this line of criticism, implicit in so many of the papers today, also suggests that though we cannot force all people and all families into a Procrustean bed, lopping off the appendages that do not fit the type, and thus losing reality, we need not do so anyway.

For, in fact, if we treat each phase as a variable in itself, we can see that each one does affect some later behaviors, attitudes, and family patterns; and each is affected in turn by them. Each phase may be viewed as a set of time-links, acting as a screening or linkage process, increasing or decreasing the probabilities of certain successive alternatives in a life or family cycle.

Thereupon, a host of interesting theoretical propositions and even broader perspectives begins to emerge, as I have tried to sketch them here. In part I have derived them directly from explicit comments by some of the authors; and others I have developed by bringing out, I think, implicit perspectives in some of these papers. All of them, I believe, reach most deeply into important elements of the social structure, and they raise significant questions about diachronic data, longitudinal data, generational depth, and historical perspectives. These perspectives and questions suggest that family variables are not only dependent, not only affected by political and economic variables; they are also independent in their own right. Thus we can see how, even when we look at the phasal aspects or cycle variables, we can relate all of them to larger social structures. We can see how they might interact with one another, and we are once more able to understand how potentially fruitful a family cycle approach might be, even if we cannot neatly put all families into a finite, precise, concrete typology or taxonomy of family cycles.

Résumé

Cycle de la vie familiale et construction théorique

Deux conceptions du *Cycle de la vie familiale* semblent s'opposer dans les exposés entendus au cours de ce séminaire. Certains sociologues de la famille développent et raffinent une typologie du cycle de la vie familiale; d'autres réfutent cette typologie estimant qu'elle ne s'applique pas à son objet. Ne peut-on réconcilier ces deux orientations de recherche en considérant que le cadre classificatoire offert par le concept du *CVF* constitue un ensemble de variables dont la formulation doit rester suffisamment générale pour se prêter à la classification du plus grand nombre possible de situations se rapportant à la famille? Il s'agirait de considérer chaque stade du cycle comme une variable, et d'analyser les attitudes et les modèles de valeurs qui s'y rattachent.

De plus le concept de *CVF* invite à tenir compte de la dimension temporelle, et suppose que l'on ajoute à nos analyses synchroniques l'étude des données longitudinales, afin d'examiner les changements historiques de la famille. Ceci conduit à une plus vaste question théorique: quelles sont les conditions nécessaires pour que les familles puissent suivre ce qui semble être le cycle familial modal de leur culture?

L'emploi du *CVF* se révèlera fécond si l'étude porte sur l'organisation et la succession des séquences temporelles. Quelle était la succession typique des phases du cycle dans la société d'autrefois, quels rôles y étaient attachés dans les relations entre mari et femme, parents et enfants, couples et ascendants? et comment cette succession et ces rôles ont-ils été modifiés? Quels facteurs peuvent affecter leur succession dans le futur?

Si nous traitons chaque phase du cycle comme une variable, il nous faut voir l'interaction réciproque entre celles-ci et les comportements et les attitudes qui lui sont propres. Chaque phase sera donc traitée à la fois comme une variable dépendante et aussi indépendante.

Notes

1. For a more detailed exposition of this definition, see William J. Goode (1973), *Explorations in Social Theory*, New York, Oxford University Press.
2. See, for example, Gary S. Becker (1965), "A theory of the allocation of time", *Economic Journal*, September; and Staffan B. Linder (1970), *The Harried Leisure Class*, New York, Columbia University Press.
3. Of course, as the comparative social analysts will remember, in a system where a man may inherit his brother's wives, an older woman might well be remarried even towards the end of her life. It should not be necessary to point out, however, that it was a *duty* of the surviving brother to take over the responsibility for the older wife of the dead brother; it was not a privilege, and the marriage was not viewed as a "new marriage".

II. *Uses of the concept for sociological analysis*

Application du concept à l'analyse sociologique

4. The life cycle of the Yugoslav peasant farm family

RUŽA FIRST-DILIĆ

In spite of increasing interest throughout the world in the developmental approach to family study, three critical points relevant for this paper can be made. *First*, although it is frequently stressed that the main concept of the developmental approach – that of stages of the family life cycle – is borrowed from rural sociology, it is difficult to find recent studies of the rural family using this approach. With the exception of McCann's study (1960), studies of this type were carried out mostly between the two World Wars. *Second*, in the past, theory development and research were concentrated in the Western countries, while family scholars from predominantly peasant societies of Middle and Eastern Europe seemed not to be enthusiastic about it. For example, the developmental approach has not yet been employed in any study of marriage and the family in Yugoslavia. *Third*, there is a paucity of empirical evidence concerning the changing role structure of the family. Students of the family find it increasingly necessary, however, to have more precise information concerning the interplay between the changing familial role structure and family life.

The present investigation is an attempt to cope with these deficiencies in Yugoslav family, as well as rural sociology. We have sought to obtain initial information concerning the relationship between the life cycle of the peasant farm family in Yugoslavia and its changing marital role structure.

The objectives of this paper are twofold: (1) to identify the life-cycle stages of the peasant farm family as determined in 16 selected villages in Croatia, and (2) to ascertain the role-performance patterns of husband and wife in the peasant farm family, as the family shifts from one stage to another. The stages of family development were then utilized as independent variables in order to explain changing marital behavior in terms of both work and authority-role relationship.

Location of study: the Yugoslav peasant farm family

The Yugoslav farmer is of the peasant type, with the following distinctive common characteristics: he is (1) a small-scale agricultural producer (2) who, together with other family members, provides labor for operating the farm, (3) who farms for immediate family consumption rather than for the market, and (4) whose value in agricultural production for family consumption exceeds that in sales. Peasant farmers own 86 percent of the total arable land of 10,200,000 hectares (39,372 square miles), while the average area of land held by the peasant is about 3.0 hectares (9.39 acres). According to the Agricultural Enumeration in 1969, there were 2,634,000 small farm holdings, with 12,084,000 people living on them.[1] The average size of the household is 3.9 persons, while an average farm holding has 4.7 members. The accommodation facilities per farm holding cover 10.1 square meters *per capita* (12.08 square yards); 76.6 percent of the total number of farm holdings have electricity; only 12.0 percent of the peasant farmers own any agricultural machinery.

The contemporary peasant farm family is in a phase of transition from a subsistence type of productive association to a market-oriented, consumer unit. Although this transition is rather slow, its presence is evident and determines the changing intra-familial structure. When the peasant farm family was primarily a productive association, the head of the household (the oldest male) was the exclusive organizer of production, the proprietor of the farm, the main decision-maker, and the representative of the family in its relations with the outside world. In such a constellation, both the females and the younger generation were deprived of any but the working dimension of family life. Even in such delicate questions as mate selection and family planning, the persons directly involved were not allowed decision-making power.

Today two family types exist in Yugoslavian villages. The first one – still prevailing – is the three-generational *stem family* in which nuclear families are related patrilineally rather than bilineally. Since there is not enough arable land for all children and their families to make a living, daughters provided with a dowry and all sons but the oldest are exported from their family of origin, thus creating the second contemporary type – a *neolocal family*.

As a consequence of the process of individualization of the farm family and the occupational differentiation of its members, a process of redistribution of the patriarchal authority is taking place. In the developed villages authority is redistributed along the parentalistic line: decisions are reached by both husband and wife, while the younger generation is excluded. In the underdeveloped rural areas this process occurs along the paternalistic line, involving males only, regardless of their generation but taking into consideration their age.

To get married and to establish a home and family is still the predominant value among the Yugoslav rural population. This is of special importance for the farm population because of its basic orientation toward the continuation of family farming. As a consequence, there is a strong (economic) interest in preserving a marriage "at any price", making it highly probable that the primary group will complete the full life cycle of marriage and family. Both familial and societal norms prescribe the appropriate role behavior for each member of the family and determine how these roles are expected to change as each member ages. During the course of a marriage, the age and member composition of the family change and so does the pattern of intra-familial interaction.

Framework for analysis

The unit of analysis is the peasant farm family, perceived as the family task-performance and decision-making unit. In the light of the above brief discussion, the peasant farm family is defined as a unit consisting of the interacting head of the family and his wife, who operate a small holding, provide labor for farm, barnyard,[2] household, and family maintenance activities, and reach the respective decisions. Two types of marital interaction are assumed here to be the most crucial in affecting the marital dyad and indicating variations in their role relationship: marital division of labor and marital power structure.

At the behavioral level, the dependent variable is the *structure of the peasant farm family*, defined in terms of conjugal role relationship. The structure of such a family revolves around a changing pattern of relationship between the head of the family and his wife; this pattern is established between them as the processes of division of labor and division of power take place within the family framework over a period of years.

In the relationship of conjugal roles, four basic constellations are possible: (1) the husband is work performer and/or decision-maker; (2) the wife is work performer and/or decision-maker; (3) work and/or authority is shared between husband and wife; and (4) neither husband nor wife performs any task and/or reaches any decision. These relationships can vary from family to family, with regard to (a) the scope of relative role performance (i.e., of individual task performance and/or decision-making of one spouse) and (b) the scope of shared role performance (i.e., of joint – simultaneous or successive – task-performance and/or decision-making of both spouses) (Wolfe, 1959).

The ratio between the relative and shared role performance provides a basis for the construction of patterns of marital division of labor and power structure. Three qualitative types relevant to this study may be delineated: (1) autocratic, (2) transitional, and (3) democratic.

The autocratic marital interaction pattern conforms to Blood and Wolfe's (1967) concept of role stereotypy: work and/or authority roles are segregated on the basis of traditional male *vs.* female prescriptions. The democratic pattern is understood as role differentiation on the basis of complementary role specialization, while the possible transitional types are located between these two end patterns. Within the autocratic pattern, two subtypes are distinguished: a purely autocratic type (all the tasks or all the decisions are carried out by only one spouse) and a dominant type (the relative participation of one spouse is greater than the relative role performance of the other). There are also two possible subtypes within the democratic type: syncracy or sharing (all tasks and decisions are reached jointly) and autonomy or specialization (there is balanced division of labor and/or a balanced division of power between the spouses) (First-Dilić, 1971).

Only one variable has been selected to account for the comparison of peasant farm families in terms of their labor and power structure: *the family life cycle.* The basic time units of the family life span – stages of development – are demarcated by (1) *age composition of the family* and (2) *change in family size.*[3] The individual life cycle of the oldest child for the period during which he lives with his family of orientation is partially used to identify the emergence of a new stage in family life (Duvall, 1962). In the peasant farm family, it is necessary to consider not the "first" child, but the "oldest" present in the family, because, regardless of the age order, peasant offspring at 15 may be launched into (child and early) marriage, non-farm jobs, or city school, thus creating an overlap between certain stages. Furthermore, the often-used criterion of retirement from active employment (Hill and Rodgers, 1964) cannot be applied to our peasant farm population because there is not yet compulsory old-age pension for this category of Yugoslavian citizens. The criterion of school placement is acceptable only for the preschool and elementary school period; those offspring who continue their schooling are no longer members of the village and the agricultural community.

The four-stage family life cycle discussed by Sorokin and others (1931) is not well-suited for a discussion of today's peasant who is faced with a situation of compulsory education. Moreover, they suggest that a very typical stage for the peasant farm family is that of couples with one or more adult, self-supporting children. The *questio facti* is, however, to define this adulthood. A fifteen-year-old peasant farm offspring who works on the family farm is self-supporting but is neither socially nor legally adult. *Whether one is self-supporting* has been used as the third criterion for dividing up the life span of the peasant farm family in Yugoslavia.

A combination of these three criteria permits inferring seven stages, as follows:

I Pre-child family (newly married couple, childless for the first 5 years of marriage);

II Pre-school family (oldest child below school age);

III School-age family (oldest child 7 to 14; possibly younger siblings);

IV Family with adolescent(s) (oldest child 15 to 18; possibly younger sibling);

V Family with self-supporting young adult(s) (oldest child 19 or over; until the first child leaves home);

VI Child-launching family (from the time when the first child leaves home until the last leaves);

VII Post-child family (after all children have left home, until death of either spouse).

So conceived, stages I, II and III are on the temporal continuum. Stages IV, V and VI, although they suggest continuity (even in families with only one child), in fact overlap one another.

Blood and Wolfe's study (1960) suggests that the ability of the husband to influence family decision-making decreases as the family moves through its life cycle. Bott's study (1971) indicates that the first stage of the family life cycle is characterized by more joint activity than any of the later stages, while McCann's study (1960) found no relationship between family authority patterns and the family life cycle. Hill's (1965) data show that the work-role specialization becomes more sharply defined with the years. Thus, the marital work-role structure has been shown to evolve from sharing to individual performance, while the evidence is inconclusive in the area of marital power structure.

The general hypothesis being tested in the present study is that *the peasant farm family structure changes as the family progresses through the set of stages of development.*

Method

The secondary analysis presented in this paper is based on the data collected as a part of a larger study with a very general aim: to describe the position of women in the peasant farm family in Croatia (one of six federal republics constituting the S.F.R. of Yugoslavia). Data collection was started in 1968 and completed in 1970.

Peasant farm families from 16 purposely selected villages in Croatia represent the universe of the original study.[4] A multi-stage quota sampling procedure was used to draw the parental sample of 320 families,[5] from which the subsample of 158 complete nuclear families was selected for the present analysis. Another 27 married couples were included as subjects of the study. These are aging couples who have already been through the stages of child-bearing, -rearing, and -launching, and were designated in the post-child stage of the family life cycle. Because no newly married couples could be found for the parental sample, the data for the first stage (i.e., the pre-child family) are missing.

The data were collected by interviewing both husbands and wives. The present analysis, however, considers only the information reported by peasant farm wives. Coding scales for each of the variables were devised from appropriate questions on the verbatim interview protocols.

Following Lewin's (1966) concept of a behavioral field, the peasant farm family was understood as a field of marital behavior, constituted by different interrelated areas of family functioning. The behavioral field of the family was differentiated into the following areas for their various activities: (1) farm area, (2) barnyard area, and (3) household area.[6]

The marital division of labor is operationalized in terms of task performance, while the decision-making process is perceived as the operational measure of the conjugal power structure. Thus the unit of measure is a particular task (15) and/or a decision (12), respectively.

The following tasks were selected and grouped into family functioning areas:

1. Farm area tasks: ploughing, digging, manuring, sowing, pruning, mowing.

2. Barnyard area tasks: feeding livestock, milking, caring for poultry, gardening.

3. Household area tasks: buying groceries, household necessities, and major household equipment and furniture; painting and papering.

Since particular tasks did not overlap with particular decisions – which is a disadvantage – the selection involved the following decisions:

1. Farm area decisions: buying, selling, or renting a farm, buying major farm equipment, buying fertilizer, trying new crop varieties.

2. Barnyard area decisions: buying or selling livestock, selling agricultural products, construction of farm buildings.

3. Household area decisions: borrowing money, building a new house, household repairs, buying major household equipment and furniture, buying a vehicle.

These units of measure (tasks, decisions) were combined into a composite measure in order to arrive at the pattern of marital role relationship at the level of each area as well as of the family as a whole.

Since the original study was undertaken as an investigation of the broad area of rural family organization, the interviews covered a wide range of questions concerning age at marriage of both spouses, family size, schooling, duration of marriage, marital interaction, etc. Thus, it was possible to delineate a combination of several factors used in *ex post* determination of stages of the peasant farm family life cycle: (1) age of husband at the time of the original study, (2) age of wife at the time of the original study, (3) size of the family, (4) duration of marriage, and (5) length of time in the current stage. Calculations are based on median values for years reported at the time of the original study as well as for the number of persons living in the household at the time of reporting.

The data are cross-sectional rather than longitudinal; they come from six separate groups of peasant farm families in different stages of development, and the data obtained on a given dimension are treated as if they were longitudinal.

Findings

The research was descriptive, and thus the conclusions are tentative, of the nature of hypotheses requiring further validation. Furthermore, the results obtained will be presented only in percentage cross-tabulations, with no testing of differences, because requirements needed for such a statistical test were not available.

The following discussion will be structured according to the objectives of the study.

Out of the total number of peasant farm families used in this analysis, none was in pre-child stage; 9.2 percent were in pre-school stage; 22.2 percent in the school age stage; 12.4 percent were families with adolescent; 13.5 percent, families with self-supporting young adult; 28.1 percent, child-launching families; 14.6 percent were post-child families. The controlled characteristics through the family life cycle are presented in Table 1.

Table 1. *Median profile of the life cycle of the peasant farm families*

	Stages					
Properties	II	III	IV	V	VI	VII
Age of husband	32.5	36.1	44.1	45.8	54.7	58.2
Age of wife	28.5	37.2	39.5	43.9	46.3	54.5
Size of the family	4.0	4.0	5.0	4.5	3.0	2.0
Length of marriage	7.0	16.0	18.7	24.3	23.8	35.0
Years in the stage	5.0	5.3	2.0	4.0	3.5	4.5

Comparing couples of different durations of marriage but charting the results as if they were drawn from a cohort of married couples that had been followed through time, a median profile of the peasant farm family development has been obtained. These findings are of descriptive value, serving as a framework for marital role-structure analysis.

According to the developmental approach to the family study, marital role allocation changes as the structure of the family ranges over the family cycle. Blood and Wolfe (1967) found that work-role differentiation of the couple increases over time, with the honeymoon period involving more sharing than any later stage. Silverman and Hill (1967) supported this elaboration. Our findings confirm the above statement.

A trend has been found toward work-role specialization: each spouse tends to have an area of family functioning which he or she dominates

Table 2. *Task performance, by areas and stages in family life cycle (in percentages)*

Stages	Areas of family functioning	Marital interaction patterns				
		Husband dominant	Wife dominant	Syncratic	Transitional	Total
II	a	53.8	30.8	7.7	7.7	100.0
	b	—	85.8	—	14.2	100.0
	c	7.2	57.1	14.3	21.4	100.0
III	a	74.4	12.8	5.1	7.7	100.0
	b	2.5	90.2	—	7.3	100.0
	c	17.1	68.3	7.3	7.3	100.0
IV	a	50.0	25.0	5.0	20.0	100.0
	b	—	85.7	4.8	9.5	100.0
	c	14.3	61.9	19.0	4.8	100.0
V	a	52.6	10.5	15.8	21.1	100.0
	b	—	100.0	—	—	100.0
	c	31.6	42.1	5.3	21.0	100.0
VI	a	82.0	12.0	2.0	4.0	100.0
	b	—	92.0	2.0	6.0	100.0
	c	28.0	48.0	2.0	22.0	100.0
VII	a	74.1	—	22.0	3.7	100.0
	b	—	92.6	—	7.4	100.0
	c	55.6	25.9	7.4	11.1	100.0

a = farm area; b = barnyard area; c = household area.

(depending on the prevailing number of chores he is directly responsible for). The farm *wife has working autonomy* in the barnyard area over the entire family life cycle; at the beginning of this cycle (stages of pre-school, school age and adolescent family) she is dominant in the household area, but later on her work engagement diminishes while that of her husband increases; in the farm area she participates predominantly during the pre-school stage, with decreasing trends as the cycle goes on. On the other hand, the farm *husband has autonomy* in the farm area, which is greater in the later than in the earlier stages of the cycle; he has almost no participation in the barnyard area; in the household area, his work participation increases over the cycle, thus becoming greater than his wife's in the post-child stage. This is due to earlier aging of farm wives and their physical incapacity to continue carrying the burden of work responsibilities in both household and farm area; however, they continue to perform chores in the barnyard area. *Sharing* is little practiced in task performance; it is of some importance only in the last stage when farm tasks are considered. As the transitional pattern covers mostly cases in which a third person is involved in task performance, it is of a higher rate in the stages with adolescents and self-supporting young adults.

There is not much data concerning the relationship between stages in the family life cycle and marital authority-role relationship. The major contributions are those of Blood and Wolfe (1967), Hill (1965, 1970), and Hill and Rodgers (1964). As long as children are in the family of origin, the authority belongs to the husband; after his retirement, his authority declines. It seems that middle-age is the peak of wife dominance. Geiken (1964) reported that couples married for under one year are ready to share their decisions to a greater extent than those married for over one year.

Table 3. *Decision making, by areas and stages in family life cycle (in percentages)*

Stages	Areas of family functioning	Marital interaction patterns				
		Husband dominant	Wife dominant	Syncratic	Transitional	Total
II	a	53.8	—	38.5	7.7	100.0
	b	35.3	—	64.7	—	100.0
	c	29.4	—	70.6	—	100.0
III	a	51.3	5.2	43.5	2.6	100.0
	b	48.8	2.4	48.8	—	100.0
	c	36.4	2.4	61.2	—	100.0
IV	a	55.0	—	40.0	5.0	100.0
	b	52.2	—	47.8	—	100.0
	c	43.5	4.3	52.2	4.3	100.0
V	a	68.2	—	31.8	—	100.0
	b	60.0	4.0	36.0	—	100.0
	c	48.0	—	52.0	—	100.0
VI	a	71.4	2.0	26.6	—	100.0
	b	69.3	1.9	28.8	—	100.0
	c	59.6	3.8	36.6	—	100.0
VII	a	59.3	—	37.0	3.7	100.0
	b	59.3	—	40.7	—	100.0
	c	51.9	—	48.1	—	100.0

a = farm area; b = barnyard area; c = household area.

The empirical evidence collected in our study suggests that authority-role relationship within the peasant farm families is differentiated into husband dominant and syncratic patterns. The peasant farm husband is dominant (even autonomous) in decision-making pertaining to the farm area over the whole family life span, with a tendency to gain power as the family moves from stage III (school age) to stage VI (launching), while in stage

VII (post-child) he loses his power to a certain degree. The same tendency of weakening has also been noticed in the other two areas, although in general the husband's power was not so high there. On the other hand, as the family group grows older, the peasant farmer gains in power in both economic yard and household areas, while the sharing – dominant at the beginning of the cycle – weakens. The peasant wife's autonomy as well as dominance are minimal. Although highly engaged in the activities of the peasant farm family, peasant women do not make major farm decisions autonomously.

Figure 1. *Percent of family role structure, by types of marital interaction, marital interaction patterns and stages of family life cycle*

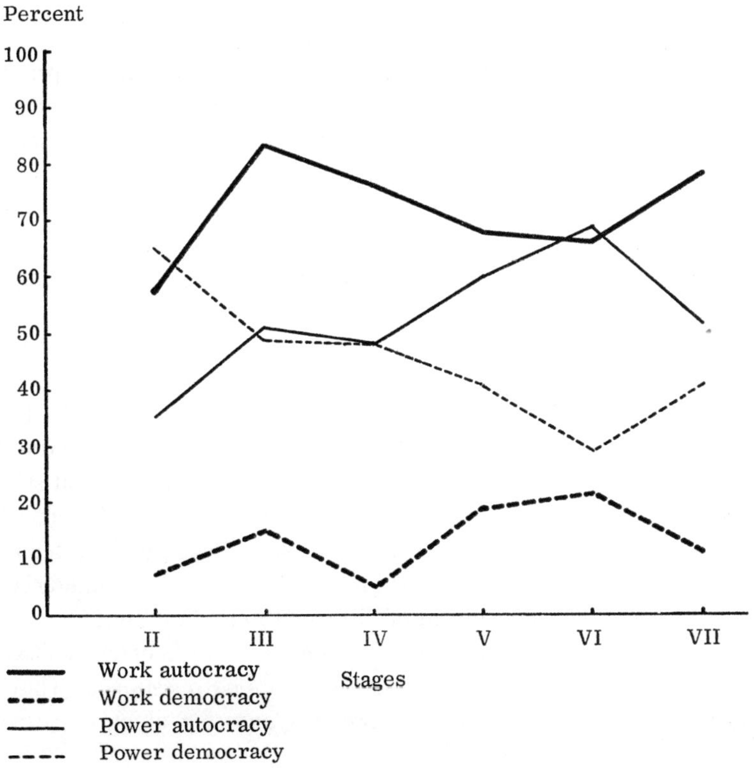

The distribution of marital authority patterns obtained on the level of the family shows that the older the family, the more autocratic task role performance there is and the less democratic decision-making (Figure 1).

Those tendencies are not linear, however; namely, certain oscillations are noticed in the school-age and adolescent stages of the family life cycles which may be explained by critical changes in family life when the first child starts school. The overlapping of the adolescent stage with the following two stages can exert a certain influence as well. Furthermore, the results of power structure on the level of the family are consistent with those on the area level as far as the last stage is concerned: there is a sharp decrease in the autocratic pattern rate and an increase in the democratic pattern rate, probably as a consequence of the reduced power of the peasant farmer.

Conclusions

We have attempted to identify the life-cycle stages of selected peasant farm families in one Yugoslavian Republic. The main problem raised here is connected with the overlapping of stages IV (family with adolescent), V (family with self-supporting young adult), and VI (child-launching family), as a consequence of the child marriages which still exist in some rural areas of the country. It seems that there are no strict criteria for delineating the stages in life development of the peasant farm family in Yugoslavia.

Furthermore, the number of stages is also questionable. In future research it would be appropriate to add an eighth stage designated as aged-family and involving post-parental farm couples where the husband is 60 or over and the wife 55 or over, and the couple has no one to run the farm. This category has been purposely omitted from the present study, although it represents a specific segment of the farm population, with distinctive social, economic, and health problems; it can be expected that their marital interaction pattern will reflect these distinctive differences.

Whatever the accomplishment of this paper in itself, it must be seen as a first attempt of its type, based on the secondary analysis of data collected for a larger study; their appropriateness can be questioned. Though incomplete, the present analysis represents one step along a path on which further research is needed.

RÉSUMÉ

Le cycle de la vie de la famille de l'exploitant agricole yougoslave

Les objectifs de la présente analyse sont doubles:
1. identification des étapes du cycle de la vie d'une famille d'exploitants agricoles yougoslaves, d'après une étude effectuée sur 16 villages croates sélectionnés et,
2. évaluation des normes des rôles du mari et de la femme dans la famille d'exploitants agricoles yougoslaves, à mesure que celle-ci passe d'une étape à l'autre.

L'unité d'analyse est la famille de l'exploitant yougoslave perçue comme une unité de tâches prescrites et de pouvoir de décision. Elle a été définie comme l'unité d'interaction composée du chef de famille et de sa femme qui gèrent une petite exploitation, fournissent du travail à la ferme et à la basse-cour, ce qui permet de subvenir aux besoins de la famille et du ménage, et prennent les décisions respectives qui s'imposent.

Trois types qualitatifs de division du travail conjugal et de structure du pouvoir conjugal ont été définis – autocratique, transitionnel et démocratique – fonction du partage plus ou moins accentué des rôles.

La variable du cycle de la vie de la famille a été choisie pour expliquer la comparaison effectuée entre familles d'exploitants d'après leur travail et la structure du pouvoir. Une combinaison de trois critères – composition de l'âge de la famille, changement des dimensions de la famille, famille ayant un enfant adulte – a permis de déduire sept stades du cycle de la vie de la famille qui sont les suivants:

1. famille au stade pré-parental,
2. famille au stade pré-scolaire,
3. famille au stade scolaire,
4. famille avec adolescents,
5. famille avec jeune adulte indépendant,
6. famille au stade du départ des grands enfants,
7. famille au stade post-parental.

L'hypothèse générale testée dans la présente étude est que la structure de la famille d'exploitants agricoles se modifie à mesure que cette famille passe d'un stade de développement à un autre. Cette hypothèse a été vérifiée à l'aide des données recueillies en 1968, 1969 et 1970 dans 158 familles paysannes nucléaires au complet et 27 couples d'exploitants agricoles mariés. Un processus d'échantillonnage à stades multiples a été utilisé pour extraire l'échantillon de 16 villages sélectionnés en République de Croatie. Les unités de mesure – tâches et décisions particulières – ont été combinées afin de déduire le modèle de relation des rôles conjugaux au niveau de chaque domaine d'activité – la ferme, la basse-cour, la maison – ainsi qu'au niveau de la famille dans son ensemble.

Les résultats ont révélé que 9,2% des familles en étaient au stade pré-scolaire, 22,2% au stade scolaire, 12,4% étaient des familles avec adolescents, 13,3% des familles avec jeunes adultes indépendants, tandis que 28,1% en étaient au stade du départ de leurs enfants, et 14,6% des familles post-parentales.

Les données empiriques indiquent que chaque conjoint tend à avoir un domaine de fonctions familiales qu'il ou elle domine. La femme est autonome dans son travail dans le domaine de la basse-cour pendant tout le cycle de la vie familiale. En outre, elle domine dans le domaine de la maison au début du cycle, tandis que plus tard, c'est le mari qui domine dans l'ensemble des tâches. Le domaine de la ferme est sous l'autorité du mari, alors qu'il ne participe pas aux travaux effectués dans le domaine de la basse-cour.

Le rapport du rôle d'autorité est nettement différencié en un modèle syncratique et un modèle où le mari domine. Le mari paysan est dominant dans les décisions touchant au domaine de la ferme pendant tout le cycle familial avec une tendance à gagner en autorité jusqu'à la période du départ des enfants puis, au contraire, à diminuer jusqu'au stade post-parental. Au contraire, à mesure que le groupe familial prend de l'âge, le mari gagne en autorité à la fois dans le domaine de la basse-cour et de la maison au détriment de la femme.

Notes

1. According to this Enumeration of 1969, 36.4 percent of the total Yugoslavian population are peasant farmers, while 60 percent still live in villages.
2. In Yugoslavia, barnyard refers to the production unit that comprises barn, garden, poultry, and livestock. It has some importance for the family income because most often it is the surplus of the barnyard production that is marketed.
3. Empirical evidence shows that demographic data about the changes in the family are predominantly utilized to account for differentiating stages of family development. These data cover information such as number of family members, ages of children, years married, birth of first and last child, entering of first and last child into jobs and marriage, etc. The theoretically more sophisticated schemes for delineating stages of family development are, in fact, based on such demographic data (Hill, 1964: 190–191).
4. The villages are Vera, Šarengrad, Garčin, Glogovica, Bačkovica, Nova Rača, Leštakovec, Vidovec, Tržić Tounjski, Zagorje Donje, Bunić, Krbavica, Pakoštane, Vrana, Vrsar, and Kaštelir. They were distributed in 8 counties; two villages per county were chosen, one developed and the other underdeveloped.

   The universe of the population was defined as: (1) families living in the selected villages (2) with income chiefly derived from farming (3) where the wife of the household head was not employed outside the home.
5. Three criteria were relevant for arriving at quota categories: (1) type of farming (full-time, part-time), (2) family composition (nuclear, extended), and (3) standard of living (upper, middle, lower). From the pool of nuclear families in which the wife was born between 1910 and 1950, and extended families with at least one complete nuclear family of a younger generation where the wife was born between 1910 and 1950, selection of 20 families in each village was made.
6. The area of kitchen activities and decisions was not considered as typical only of the peasant farm family functioning and thus was purposely omitted from the analysis. The child-rearing area was not included because it was not measurable in the post-child stage of the family cycle.

References

Blood, Robert O., Jr., and Wolfe, Donald M. (1967), *Husbands and Wives. The Dynamics of Married Living*, New York, The Free Press.

Bott, Elisabeth (1971), *Family and Social Network*, London, Tavistock Publications.

Duvall, Evelyn Millis (1962), *Family Development*, Philadelphia, J. B. Lippincott Company.

First-Dilić, Ruža (1971), "Structure of the Yugoslav nuclear farm family: work and authority role differentiation", unpublished thesis. Ames Library. Iowa State University of Science and Technology.

Geiken, Karen F. (1964), "Expectations concerning husband-wife responsibilities in the home", *Journal of Marriage and the Family*, 26: 349–352.

Hill, Reuben (1964), "Methodological issues in family development research", *Family Process*, 3: 186–206.

—— (1965), "Decision making and the family life cycle" in Ethel Shanas and Gordon F. Streib (eds.), *Social Structure and the Family: Generational Relations*, Englewood Cliffs, Prentice-Hall.

—— (1970), *Family Development in Three Generations*. Cambridge and London, Schenkman Publishing Co., Inc.

—— and Rodgers, Roy H. (1964), "The developmental approach" in Harold T. Christensen (ed.), *Handbook of Marriage and the Family*, Chicago, Rand McNally & Company.

Lewin, Kurt (1966), *Principles of Topological Psychology*. New York, McGraw Hill Book Company, Inc.

McCann, Glenn C. (1960), "Consumer decisions in the rural family in the South", paper prepared for the Annual Meeting of the American Sociological Association, New York, August.

Silverman, William, and Hill, Reuben (1967), "Task allocation in marriage in the United States and Belgium" *Journal of Marriage and the Family*, 29: 353–359.

Sorokin, P., Zimmerman, C.C., and Galpin, C.V. (1931), *A Systematic Source Book in Rural Sociology*, Minneapolis, University of Minnesota Press.

Wolfe, Donald M. (1959), "Power and authority in the family" in Dorwin Cartwright (ed.), *Studies in Social Power*, Ann Arbor, The University of Michigan: 99–117.

5. Social change and the child-rearing phase. Resources and network of the modern urban family in Norway

JOHN ERIKSEN and PER OLAV TILLER

1. *Introduction*

The analysis to be presented here aims at summarizing Norwegian data from three representative surveys of households pertinent to the question of kinship and neighbor networks, economic resources and helping patterns in the modern urban family in the child-rearing phase. The data are preliminary to a planned project on the adequacy of officially administered social and family service schemes as a compensation for resources represented by kinship and neighborhood contacts lost through mobility.

Although none of these studies aimed at investigating the phenomenon of household or family cycle, some of the findings lend themselves relatively easily to an analysis in these terms.

Naturally, households assumed to represent – at a certain time – different cyclical stages also belong to different age cohorts, a problem that cannot be solved except in longitudinal or retrospective studies. One such study is under way at our institute, the "occupational life history project".[1] To illustrate some of the possibilities with the retrospective method, the following unpublished observation from that study can be mentioned:

A year-by-year counting of the composition of the household to which the respondent has belonged, shows that men born in 1921 have experienced an average of 13 changes in the household composition. These changes may be increases or decreases in the number of household members or any change in the respondent's set of family relations in the household, e.g., through establishing a household of his own, household members moving out, children being born, etc. In a sense, then, the average 50 years old has lived in 14 different households. For men born in 1931 and 1941 respectively, the corresponding figures are 12 and 10. Of the oldest cohort, 34% have had 15 or more household "situations" in the course of their 50 years of life. Of the next cohort, those born in 1931, 28% have experienced 15 or more situations during their 40 years, and of the youngest group, 16% have seen 15 or more households in 30 years.

It seems that relatively little change in the surrounding household takes place between 40 and 50 years of age or between 30 and 40 compared with the period before 30, which covers both one's own childhood and part of the child-rearing age. However, the average 50 years old has experienced a change in the household situation every four years, the 40 years old even more changes, namely three new situations in every ten years, while the youngest men have seen a new situation every third year.

Thus, while the number of different role incumbents may show great stability in a system within society over time, the individual family goes through continuous changes in composition and functioning over relatively short periods.

2. *Social change: mobility and occupation*

Social change in Norway – or the changes that Norwegian society is undergoing – encompasses several dimensions. One common factor at the basis of much of this development is rural-urban mobility, which at present has high speed, having started later in Norway than in most other industrial countries. This mobility again is a multi-dimensional phenomenon. Changes in the residence of the household entail changes in several other aspects of the situation. A few characteristics of different population groups – varying in residence – may serve the purpose of illustrating some of these dimensions.

As mobility to urban areas started relatively late in Norway, the primary sector of the economy (agriculture, fishing, forestry, etc.) is still important, and even today a fairly large proportion of the population lives in rural areas.[2] The proportion of the population earning its living from the primary sector has been reduced from nearly one third in 1946 to less than one fifth in 1960, which is still a rather high figure compared to Sweden's 13.8% and U.S.A.'s 6.5%.[3] During the same period the secondary sector (manufacturing, construction, etc.) shows a slight increase, while the tertiary sector (commerce, transport, communication, services) has increased from 27.5% in 1946 to 33.6% in 1960. The increase in population dependent upon income from pensions, capital, etc. (10.7% in 1947 to 12.4% in 1960) is partly explained by the changing age structure of the population, with relatively more old people constituting own households and being dependent on public pensions and welfare schemes for their living. As for residence, this development has continued, and since there is a correspondence between residence and occupation, there is reason to conclude that there has also been an increase in the size of the tertiary sector. The 1970 census figures show the urban population to have increased with another 11% from 1960.

This brief sketch of a very complex social situation in change may be summed up as follows: (1) shift from the primary to the tertiary sector in the economy, manufacturing, construction, etc. playing a stable role, and (2) mobility from rural to urban areas, which is a prerequisite for the change within the economy, but can also be viewed as a consequence of this change.

In the surveys the urban-rural dimension was operationally defined by type of residence with four values on an ordinal scale:

1. *Large town*, densely populated area (20,000 inhabitants or more)
2. *Small town* or small densely populated area (2,000 to 19,999 inhabitants)
3. *Village* (200–1,999 inhabitants)
4. *Sparsely populated* area.

The importance of various industries was measured by number of main household providers earning their main living from the different industries. 55% of the Norwegian households lived in large and small towns (as defined here) in 1970, and nearly one third in sparsely populated areas. The tertiary sector was the most important one, occupying more than 40% of the main household providers. This sector is especially dominant under urban conditions. But even more clearly, the primary sector is connected with rural life. Manufacturing, construction and handicraft showed much less variation on the urban-rural dimension. Thus constructed these data in many ways reflect the same development as mentioned above with historical time as one variable, a development from rural life where agriculture, forestry, fishing, etc. are the dominant industries, to urban life more and more based on living from industries like commerce, transport, communication, catering and other services, public as well as private.

It was also found that the number of households headed by a person outside labor force is largest under the most urbanized conditions (17% in large towns) and least in villages (10%). This variation is partly explained by the mobility – especially of young people – from the countryside to town-like areas. But young people also move out of large towns. Thus, there is a disproportionately large number of old people in the most rural as well as in the most urban areas.

This trend is consistent with the frequently claimed development toward increasing strain on people in their jobs, in their families and generally as members of a more and more complex society, reflected in a development of more and more comprehensive welfare schemes and pensions. People living under urban conditions will according to this view be more exposed to this strain than people in rural areas. On the other hand, mobility and lack of job opportunities in the rural districts, increase the need for public welfare schemes. In Norway, disability pensions have in fact been used as a kind of permanent unemployment benefit in such areas.

As type of economy also determines the kinds of jobs available, it is not unexpected to find that white collar jobs now constitute the largest single group of occupations (28%), and as expected it varies markedly along the urban-rural dimension. The various kinds of services and administration are closely connected with modern production (in a wide sense) under urban conditions.

In general these figures reflect the fact that the consequences of technological and economic development have been different for different kinds of jobs. In rural areas there is a large number of self-employed people, most of them self-employed farmers without hired help due to mechanization and structural changes within this sector. On the other hand, these changes together with the reduced importance of agriculture, has created a need for new job opportunities: these "freed" workers often have poor qualifications for modern urban-type jobs. One fourth of the main providers in sparsely populated areas are unskilled workers.

This relative disadvantage of the rural worker in competition for urban jobs is also evident in their level of education. Theoretical and vocational education is a factor of major importance in adjustment to occupational life. The vast majority of the heads of rural households – 80–90% – has only primary education or primary education plus some vocational training, as against 45% for the most urban households. And correspondingly, very few (3%) of the households in sparsely populated areas are headed by a person with at least "gymnasium".[4] The figure for large-town households is 20%.

Housing and residence are also interrelated. The typical dwelling in Norway is a separate single family house. Of all households 43% live in such houses. In rural areas this percentage is 60, and even in rather urbanized areas (small towns) this is the type of dwelling for half of the households. Larger towns are dominated by apartment houses with five or more dwellings (56%). Thus, rural areas are dominated by small houses (one or two households) at a good distance from each other. The more urban the area, the larger and the more concentrated are the houses. For people grown up with typical rural housing conditions, adjustment to modern suburban life – with large apartment houses, among other things – is likely to represent a special factor of strain.

Tenure status is another aspect of change in housing connected with rural-urban mobility. 75–80% of the rural households own their own house, while almost two thirds of the most urban households are tenants. Owning one's own home represents a large degree of security and control with one's situation. In one sense, therefore, rural-urban mobility means relative deprivation with regard to housing.

The main topic of this paper is the situation of the household in the child-rearing phase. The figures – though not controlled for the age of children – indicate that such households constitute a much smaller proportion of all households in large towns than in other districts (Table 1).

Households with children might be expected to comprise more members than those without. As Table 1 shows, rural households are generally larger than urban ones. This confirms the impression that household size varies inversely with degree of urbanization. Table 1 also shows that childless households are a typical urban phenomenon, while "extended" households are most frequent in the least urbanized areas.[5]

Concerning the proportion of single-person households, we find a particularly high figure for large towns. These households will comprise many providers not in labor force and dependent on pensions, welfare schemes and social security. However, the number of single-person households in the most rural areas is not particularly low. This is because rural-urban mobility is selective with regard to age, and single-person households represent both early and late stages in the household cycle.

Table 1. *Household's place of residence and household types and household size (%)*

	Large town	Small town	Village	Sparsely pop. areas	All households %	All households N
Type of household I						
Married couples with children	58	70	70	71	67	527
Married couples without children	20	10	19	13	15	120
Single parents	3	3	3	3	3	23
Single persons	19	17	8	13	15	122
Sum	100	100	100	100	100	792
Type of household II						
Single persons and couples without children	35	24	24	24	28	218
Nuclear families (single parents included)	59	70	69	66	65	517
"Extended" households	6	6	7	10	7	57
Sum	100	100	100	100	100	792
Household size						
Average number of members	3.09	3.33	3.61	3.86	3.46	
Percent with 1 or 2 members	48	27	30	26	31 (N = 245)	
Percent with 6 or more members	3	7	9	18	8 (N = 70)	

3. *Household type and phase*

In our effort to single out and locate households in the typical child-rearing phase, a first step may be to introduce at the age of the provider. Table 2 indicates that providers between 30 and 40 years of age are most often found in small towns and those between 40 and 50 in the more rural areas. The age groups assumed to represent the earliest and latest stages of the household cycle are found in large towns.

Table 2 relates provider's age to household type. From these figures it seems reasonable to speak of the age levels from 25 to 50 years as the typical child-rearing age of the providers. Single-person households are – as explained above – likely to consist of young (below 25) or old (above 60) providers.

Table 2. *Main provider's age and place of residence and household type (%)*

	Less than 25 years	25–29 years	30–39 years	40–49 years	50–59 years	60–69 years	70 years or more	Sum
Place of residence								
Large town	7	11	20	23	13	15	11	100
Small town	7	10	28	18	20	10	7	100
Village	5	7	18	28	18	17	6	100
Sparsely pop. areas	4	8	18	26	19	13	9	100
Sum (%)	6	9	21	23	19	13	9	100
Sum (N)	46	71	163	182	146	98	68	774
Household type								
Married couples with children	5	11	29	29	19	6	11	100
Married couples without children	5	9	6	13	15	31	21	100
Single parents	5	5	22	31	27	5	5	100
Single persons	13	3	3	9	17	26	29	100
Sum (%)	6	9	21	24	19	13	8	100
Sum (N)	46	71	163	182	144	97	66	769

Households in the child-rearing stage should typically consist of provider, spouse and one or more children.[6] From the previous tables we should expect this household type to be more frequent in the rural than in the urban population. This is because other households – childless couples and single providers representing the early and late stages in the household cycle – are "over-represented" in urban areas (Table 3).

Table 3. *Place of residence and type of household, dichotomized (absolute figures and %)*

	Urban N	%	Rural N	%	All households N	%
Provider-spouse-children (PSC) households	229	54	204	60	433	56
Other households	198	46	138	40	336	44
Sum	427	100	342	100	769	100
%	—	56	—	44	—	100

4. *Economic resources*

As one objective of this paper is to explore economic resources and social networks and their interrelationships in the urban household in its child-rearing phase, we shall first describe the economic resources of four types of households (Table 4). If we look at total income – all kinds of cash-flow into the household, not only income from work – urban households are better off than rural ones. Most clearly, this is the case with families in their child-rearing phase. But, generally, PSC-households have a markedly larger average total income than other households.

Table 4. *Household type/place of residence and average total cash income in Norwegian kroner (Round figures)**

	PSC-households		Other households		All house-holds
	Urban	Rural	Urban	Rural	
Average income per household	42,700	35,300	30,000	26,700	34,700
Average income per "consumer unit"	12,500	9,200	14,700	12,000	11,800
Average income per "consumer unit" after direct taxes (approximately)	9,400	7,000	9,600	7,800	—
Number of households	222	191	186	129	728

* Income figures in Table 4 refer to 1969.

However, since households vary in size and composition, average income per household is not a good measure of economic resources or capacity. This has been taken into consideration in calculating income per "consumer unit" for the different types of households. Parent(s) have been counted as full unit(s) and children as two thirds, and as it is relatively cheaper to run large than small households, also additional adult members have been counted as two thirds of a unit. When economic resources are calculated in this way, urban households are still better off than rural households, but the differences are strongly reduced, especially for families in their child-rearing phase. The situation for PSC-households *vs.* other households has been reversed, the latter having the largest average income per consumer unit.

However, PSC-households pay less direct taxes than do other households. The effect of this on total economic resources at disposal is difficult to calculate with some accuracy, in particular per consumer unit. In general, the above differences will be reduced, resulting in slightly lower average income for PSC-households than for other households. Large needs during the child-rearing period, to establish a home and provide for children, are not matched with large resources compared to other stages in the family cycle. The main factor in income differences is not type of household, but place of residence.

Our data – not to be reported in detail here – also show that households in their child-rearing stage are almost exclusively dependent on income from work. For rural PSCs, income from own business (mainly farms) plays an important role. Other households have a more varied income pattern, and other sources than work are also more important. One example is income from public welfare schemes and pensions. Most PSC-households will report such income (mainly child allowance), but even for the generally larger rural PSCs, this source is of minor importance compared to other households, often solely dependent on old age pension, disability pension, etc. It should be noted that there is rather little difference between urban and rural PSC-households with regard to income structure (except income from own business). But cash income only is an insufficient measure and does not take care of more informal economic adjustments and exchange outside the market and money economy.

Cost of living – especially housing and transport – is higher in urban than in rural areas, in particular for PSC-households. However, the average income "per unit" is about the same for the four categories of households.

If the typical PSC-household finds itself in a particularly strained economic situation, it should be of interest to see whether such households avail themselves of other ways to meet economic demands.

As would be expected, we found consumption of own products to be more common in rural than in urban households. However, among urban households, such consumption was most frequent in the PSCs. As regards especially cheap purchases, the rural-urban difference was less marked. But again, PSC-ones reported highest frequency.

This suggested importance of additional sources of income is not recognized by urban PSCs, who almost never report them to be very important, and particularly often state that they are of minor importance.

This lack of recognition may have normative sources. One of the most important norms concerning the family in the child-bearing and child-rearing stages is the relative economic independence and autonomy of the family unit. We have seen that this unit less often represents an extended household among urban than among rural residents. Therefore these norms might be expected to be particularly strong in the urban setting. This is consistent with the modern urban image of the family as typically dependent on *one* source of survival only, namely the bread-winner.

5. *Network*

Additional income – as well as economic support – may be dependent on the social relations of the household, more particularly, the social network of the family. Available kin networks have been considered as an insurance against break-down through crisis, whether due to illness, unemployment or sudden accidents. Households with children witness particular demands for stability in order to provide for offspring and in general fulfill the norms pertaining to this phase of life.

First, mobility entails a loosening of ties with the family of orientation: the younger generation leaves the place of birth, where the parents still live, and goes to towns. Our survey data showed that half of the households have providers who have always lived in their present place of residence. However, of the urban household providers less than 40% live in the community where they were born.

This means that urban providers less often may be expected to live close to their parents – and partly also to siblings (i.e., their family of origin) – than heads of rural households (Table 5). Except for distance to parents, PSC-households live close to relatives less often than others.

Residential proximity or distance must be assumed to influence the frequency and type of communication. But also, a family's needs for assistance and support from kin may promote contact between relatives.

First, if proximity is a decisive factor, face-to-face contact should be most frequent with nearby relatives. Since PSC-households have parents at a closer distance than have other households, face-to-face contact should also be more frequent for these (Table 6).

Table 5. *Proximity: travel time of households to relatives less than one hour (%)*

	To parents			To parents-in-law		
	PSCs	Others	All	PSCs	Others	All
Urban	46.5	34.0	43.6	42.6	42.5	43.5
Rural	64.2	66.7	64.5	57.0	66.7	58.1
All	56.8	47.9	55.5	51.4	59.5	52.3
	To children, grand-children, children-in-law			To siblings, siblings-in-law		
	PSCs	Others	All	PSCs	Others	All
Urban	55.0	63.1	60.0	50.3	53.0	51.3
Rural	42.4	58.5	47.6	56.3	58.9	56.9
All	46.4	62.3	53.7	53.8	55.5	54.3
	To further removed kin					
	PSCs	Others	All			
Urban	29.0	25.3	27.6			
Rural	31.6	43.6	33.9			
All	30.5	31.7	30.9			

Table 6. *Face-to-face contact between households and relatives once a month or more (%)*

	With parents			With parents-in-law		
	PSCs	Others	All	PSCs	Others	All
Urban	68.6	58.8	66.2	63.4	57.6	62.4
Rural	79.3	52.0	76.7	71.0	71.0	71.0
All	76.9	56.6	71.9	68.1	62.5	67.4
	With children, grand-children, children-in-law			With siblings, siblings-in-law		
	PSCs	Others	All	PSCs	Others	All
Urban	76.8	84.4	81.2	61.7	71.6	65.4
Rural	74.5	75.0	74.7	65.6	56.3	63.6
All	75.3	80.5	77.6	64.0	66.3	64.7
	With further removed kin					
	PSCs	Others	All			
Urban	18.6	21.8	19.7			
Rural	27.0	28.9	27.4			
All	23.8	24.6	24.0			

As expected, PSC-households more often show this type of contact than the others. Also, among the PSC-households, the rurals most often had parents in the vicinity, and these have more often face-to-face contact with parents than urbans. The same holds for parents-in-law.

PSC-households, as compared with others, have relatively more face-to-face contact with parents than with parents-in-law, i.e. more with the husband's than with the wife's parents. Face-to-face contact with descendant kin is more frequent in urban than in rural households. In the latter, children will more often have left the place and gone to towns or other places.

With siblings, there is *less* frequent face-to-face contact in the urban than in the rural PSC-households, which fits their general pattern of infrequent contact. Again, other forms of contact with siblings may be more common in urban than in rural households.

With further removed kin face-to-face contact is particularly infrequent in the urban PSC-households, so that these households in general must be said to be characterized with low face-to-face contacts with relatives, with the exceptions of own children, grandchildren and children-in-law.

Telephone communication with relatives was found to be more frequent for urban households than for rural ones, with the exception of such communication with children and with further removed kin. Since urban households had more face-to-face contact with children, the need to use telephone may be less. With further kin, however, distance and lack of face-to-face contact is not compensated in this way. One should keep in mind that urban households probably more often have telephone than rural ones. This therefore pertains only to those with telephone. Since both parties require telephone, such communication will be more frequent between urbans than between urbans and between urbans and rurals.

In urban PSC-households the data indicated that telephone communication seems to compensate for lack of face-to-face contact with siblings, parents and parents-in-law, and in rural ones with children.

Communication by mail gave the same picture. An exception was a particularly frequent exchange of letters between rural households without children at home and their children, grand-children and children-in-law. This indicates particularly strong ties between rural parents and their children. Another striking figure which fits the pattern was a remarkably low figure for urban PSCs' communication by mail with children. The relatively high frequency of face-to-face contact here does not fully explain this trait: rural PSC-households had almost as much face-to-face contact with children, but much more frequent communication by mail. However, rural households generally have more children, some living close, permitting face-to-face contact, some having moved out, requiring contact through mail.

The degree of attachement with different types of relatives was measured by a question of perceived solidarity. Again we found an indication of particularly strong ties between rural parents and their children. With all relatives, except siblings, rural PSC-informants reported stronger feelings of solidarity than urban ones. With siblings, strong feelings of solidarity were particularly often reported by urban PSC-households, while rural childless households least often reported this.

In general, attachment – contact and solidarity – seemed more restricted in urban PSC-households, relatively seen, to the family of orientation, while rural PSCs showed a wider range of attachment to relatives.

6. *Contact and support*

To what extent is this network – or parts thereof – in operation as a source of support and assistance to the members? We have been – in particular – concerned with the needs of the households in the child-rearing phase and with the alleged situation of these urban households as finding themselves in an "economic strait-jacket".

With these figures we are not studying a cyclical phase proper, but, instead, comparing a population group where the members have children still living at home, with other households. (We shall later try to "isolate" the phase in which we are particularly interested.) Do these people, then, avail themselves of relatives as a source of support? Or do they themselves represent a source of support for their relatives? Two questions were asked concerning relatives, neighbors and friends, one about the respondent's and his household's expectation of help from these sources, the other about the respondent's and his household's willingness to give help, in critical situations (Table 7).

In general, rural respondents report more willingness to help as well as expectation of being helped, excepting help from relatives, where urbans at least as often show expectation as rurals. In general, PSC-households more often than others report both willingness to help and expectations of being helped. The highest frequencies for expectation is found in rural PSC-households for all three sources, and the lowest in childless house-

Table 7. *Households' expectation of help from relatives and willingness to help relatives* (%)

	Expect help from relatives			Willing to help relatives		
	PSCs	Others	All	PSCs	Others	All
Urban	91.7	90.2	91.7	93.1	89.5	91.7
Rural	93.5	84.6	91.5	95.4	90.1	94.2
All	93.0	87.4	91.3	94.7	89.7	93.1
	Expect help from friends			Willing to help friends		
	PSCs	Others	All	PSCs	Others	All
Urban	84.3	84.6	84.4	87.3	83.5	85.8
Rural	88.2	75.6	85.5	91.0	87.9	90.3
All	86.7	80.9	84.9	90.0	85.3	88.3
	Expect help from neighbours			Willing to help neighbors		
	PSCs	Others	All	PSCs	Others	All
Urban	74.0	59.7	68.5	75.5	65.4	71.5
Rural	79.9	67.8	77.2	85.1	80.2	84.1
All	77.6	63.8	73.6	81.4	71.4	78.4

holds from neighbors. The highest frequencies for willingness to help is also found in PSC-households for all three recipients, and the lowest again for childless urban households toward neighbors.

In urban households, the presence or absence of children seems of decisive importance for neighbor relations and in rural ones for relations with relatives and friends. Looking at the frequencies for all six questions we find the same ranking for all four groups, excepting the childless urban households who express less willingness than expectation concerning relatives and the same concerning friends.

These figures do not indicate that neighbor relations compensate for lack of kinship contacts. One might expect them to be of great importance for the urban family, particularly in the child-rearing-phase. Respondents were asked about the quality of their relations with neighbors. Of urban households, PSC-families reported less often than others good neighbor relations, although the difference was small. In the rural group, PSC-households more often than others reported good relations. There was no difference between PSC- and other households generally.

Generally, more attachment to friends than to neighbors was indicated for all groups. In some cases, however, these friends may be found among neighbors. Respondents were therefore asked if they had neighbors whom they regarded as friends.

Of the urban households, PSC-families reported more often than others that they considered their neighbors as friends. In the rural group, PSCs less often considered their neighbors as friends. The most striking difference is that the rural households seen together, more often than the urban considered their neighbors as friends (69% *vs.* 33.5%). Seen together, these data do not indicate that poor or weakened kin relations in the urban households are compensated through relations with friends and neighbors.

7. *Three phases of urban households*

In the final section, we shall make an attempt at elucidating some characteristics of the child-rearing phase in the urban household. The figures are based on the Sweetser study's findings in her representative urban sample.[7]

By dividing the sample of households on the basis of the existence of children in the household and their age, we arrive at a grouping corresponding to three phases:

I. Households without children. These will mostly be households in an early phase of the family cycle, since they have not (yet) produced children.

II. Households with children under 20 years of age only. This group will represent the child-rearing phase.

III. Households with children 20 years or older. This group will represent the oldest phase, the stage following the child-rearing phase proper.

We have assumed relative proximity to be one of the most important prerequisites for contact and communication. We have also been interested in the question of to what extent young urban households represent a stage in rural-urban mobility. This could be investigated in other ways by means of the urban household study, as Sweetser has shown.[8] At this point it should only be indicated that we expect group III to encompass many families with parents in relative proximity. This is exactly because we expect higher mobility – and therefore greater distance to parents – in younger respondents. Therefore, this is not a phase characteristic, but an indicator of social change.

As expected, group III contained particularly many providers with fathers in the vicinity. This group also had a high number whose fathers lived farther away from the respondent than four hours. (The latter number represents few cases and is thus uncertain.) Group II was in an intermediate position. Group I had few in either extreme category; 41% of their fathers lived at a distance between 1 and 4 hours.

To the extent that parents are widowed (or divorced), and thus do not live together, the relative distance to mothers and fathers for the group as a whole may not correspond completely. In contrast with the figures for fathers, group I had the highest percentage with mothers living at great distance. This might mean that widowed fathers tend to move closer to their children or their children closer to them in group III. Group II had the highest percentage of mothers nearby. There will be more mothers than fathers alive, particularly for the older groups. It therefore seems reasonable to conclude that mothers who are widows live close to children in phase II.

Proximity or distance does not necessarily mean contact or lack of contact. However, some types of contact may be especially dependent on proximity, for example, visits without invitation. A correspondence between proximity and visiting without invitation seemed to hold for group II, but visits to or from fathers were also most frequent in this group. Group I might be expected still to be relatively dependent on the parents, and parents of respondents in group III might be more dependent on their adult children. Therefore, the high frequencies for group II may be a phase phenomenon, e.g., reflecting a common interest in the youngest generation, children and grandchildren.

Where personal contact is concerned, the respondents also answered a question about face-to-face contact with parents within the last month.

The results correspond well with those from the household composition study (Table 6). In that study 77% of all PSC-households reported face-to-face contact with parents once a month. Of the corresponding group here (group II) 76% reported such contact with fathers and 78% with mothers.

These figures deviate somewhat from those for visiting. Face-to-face contact was most common in group III both as regards fathers and mothers. This fits in with the fact that group III most often had fathers living nearby, and quite often also mothers. The difference between visiting and face-to-face contact may be explained by relatively frequent visiting between providers and parents in group II, but with relatively lower frequencies of meeting outside visits. In group III the face-to-face contacts with mothers may take place during visits only.

Lack of opportunity for visiting and face-to-face contacts might be compensated through communication by mail or telephone. If this is the case, we should expect a higher frequency of telephone contact in group I than in the other groups. These respondents both more often had parents in great distance and low frequency of face-to-face contact with mothers as well as visits to or from mothers. Here, the number with telephone contact once a month seemed much higher than in the other study, where 40% reported such contact, as against the 45–52% here. However, in the first study, the question was: "How often – ?", while here the respondents were asked: "How often during the last month –?" It is not unlikely that this latter formulation introduced a bias.

A compensation for lack of other contact as expected for group I was not evident. Instead, group II, who most frequently visited parents or were visited by them, had the highest frequency of telephone contact with parents.

Again, this points to common interest between parents and children in the child-rearing phase. The same holds for communication through mail.

The high frequency of exchange in phase II holds for fathers, but not for mothers. The low number for mothers is an exception from the general picture of this phase. However, communication by mail would be the first communication type seen as unnecessary in view of the high frequency of telephone contact as well as visits without invitation.

From these data one may venture the conclusion that providers who at present find themselves in phase II have a relatively high degree of contact with their parents: they more often than the other groups exchanged visits with parents and letters with fathers, and they more often had telephone contact with mothers and fathers.

The child-rearing phase may represent a limitation in the flexible use of economic resources. One might further assume that kinship ties are maintained for some purpose or other. Our next step is to see whether the high degree of contact with parents corresponds to an access to economic or other support for providers in phase II. Respondents were asked whether they had received economic aid or help in the home from parents and whether they had given such aid to parents within the last year. We find exchange of economic support to be most frequent in group I. This is reasonable to the extent that this group represents the phase of home establishing. Also natural is the predominance of the father as donor in this respect. More surprising it may be that this group also often contributes economically to parents, particularly to mothers. However, *some* of the younger will have relatively light economic burdens and parents who are not too well off.

Table 8. *Economic support and home help to and from parents* (%)

Households	To fathers	From fathers	To mothers	From mothers
Economic support				
I. without children	9	25	16	21
II. with children under 20 years only	3	12	5	7
III. with children 20 or older	7	15	7	4
Home help				
I. without children	52	28	73	44
II. with children under 20 years only	33	23	37	29
III. with children 20 or older	30	12	41	8

For all three groups economic aid is more often received than given, except for group III concerning mothers (Table 8).

The most striking fact is that group II, while having a relatively high degree of contact and communication with parents, shows the lowest frequencies in 3 of the four cells, i.e., they particularly seldom receive or give economic support in relation to parents. Thus, in the phase where visiting, telephone-communication and exchange of letters with parents were most frequent, economic exchange with parents seems to be at a minimum. In the group assumed to represent the child-rearing phase, we see *no connection between contact and economic support given or received.*

Home help (shopping, helping around the house) might be an alternative to economic support. Therefore, phase II might be the predominant recipient here. It is this phase that sees the most heavy household tasks and where home help from parents might mean considerable alleviation.

Here, group II is no longer lowest, but group III. An exception is the lowest frequency in group II for home help given to mothers. This is reasonable in view of the suggested size of household tasks in group II. As with economic support, the highest frequencies are seen in group I. A dominance of given as compared to received home help is seen in all three groups, but particularly for mothers in group III. These mothers will relatively often be widows.

While respondents more often give than receive home help, the opposite is the case for economic support. This might suggest an exchange of home help against economic support. We shall later try to see if this may be the case.

As with economic support home help seemed unconnected with degree of contact or communication. This is the more striking, since home help should be expected at least to entail contact between the parties. Nor seems distance to be of importance: group I had the highest frequency of mothers living at great distance, and still this group sees most of home help, both given and received. Group II had most often mothers in the vicinity, and still least often gives home help to mothers and does not particularly often receive help from them.

We examined closely the relationship between distance to parents and help given or received. First, how is economic support related to distance?

The figures for economic support to and from mothers were low and the percentage uncertain. Concerning fathers, proximity was related both to giving and receiving economic support. However, respondents in group III particularly often had fathers in the vicinity, and this group did not particularly often receive economic support from fathers. Group II showed no specific trend as to distance, had a medium frequency of help to fathers, but the lowest frequency of help *from* fathers, etc. The low degree of exchange of economic support in group II therefore seems to be a phase phenomenon and cannot be explained by distance or proximity.

Still more likely should be an interdependence of proximity and home help, and home help varied more consequently with proximity than did economic support. Mothers nearby most often both give and receive home help. But again, group II *least* often both gave and received home help to and from mothers nearby. The low exchange of home help with mothers therefore takes place in spite of proximity. Also, group I, though having most often "distant" mothers, most often received home help from mothers. We are beginning to see indications of an impact of norms pertaining to the household in phase II concerned with independence, autonomy and self-sufficiency.

Finally, the economic situation might be decisive for the degree of support or help both given and received. We therefore categorized the income of the provider in four groups. Income data in this study refer to total household income, number of household members not taken into account (*cf.* Table 5). Therefore, the income level of typical child families is lower than indicated by the figures in Table 9. The fact that household group II relatively seldom receives economic support from parents, cannot be explained by their seemingly high income. And this may explain the low amount of support given *to* parents. Group I naturally comprises particularly many with low incomes, and this may explain the frequent economic support from parents in this group.

The table also shows the relationship between income and help given and received.

Table 9. *Annual income and household phase, economic support and home help* (%)

	Annual income (in Norw. kroner)			
	0–24,000	25,000–30,000	31,000–45,000	More than 45,000
Households				
I. without children	40	19	21	20
II. with children under 20 years only	10	33	36	21
III. with children 20 or older	33	25	21	21
Economic support				
given to:				
Mother	8	10	6	11
Father	3	4	7	7
received from:				
Mother	19	2	7	17
Father	19	10	10	27
Home help				
given to				
Mother	47	44	44	53
Father	43	32	36	44
received from:				
Mother	36	27	30	35
Father	30	18	23	26

We find that households in the highest *and* lowest income groups are those that most often receive economic support from parents. These two groups also most often give home help to parents. In both these groups an exchange of home help against economic support may take place. However, it will be seen that the differences in frequency of help are greater between "phases" than between income groups as regards economic support received and home help given. It seems that exchange of help may be explained as a necessity where resources are small and as a surplus phenomenon when they are large.

An indication of the more strained economic situation of phase II may be given through the relationship between given and received economic support for the three groups. We would expect a particularly higher relative receiving from parents than giving to parents in phase II (Table 10).

Table 10. *Household phase and received and given economic support*

		Household phase		
		I	II	III
% receiving economic support from fathers / % giving economic support to fathers	=	2,8	4,0	2,1

8. *Conclusion*

The analysis presented above has revealed trends that give a rationale for a study of the adequacy of officially administered social and family service schemes to compensate for such resources that may be represented by kinship and neighborhood networks lost through mobility. In general the data indicate that the urban family in the child-rearing phase finds itself in a particularly strained situation. We have seen that the assumed higher economic demands for the family in this phase are not balanced by a correspondingly favorable economic situation. We have also seen indications of a lower degree of kinship ties in the urban than in the rural households with young children, and a lack of compensation through neighbor relations. In accordance with norms of autonomy and independence the urban family in the child-rearing phase seems estranged from such contacts that might represent resources of financial support and home help. In such families we would predict a high degree of vulnerability in times of crisis and a heightened need for social and family services, the adequacy of which will be limited to the degree that they do not instigate or further social processes that might counteract the relative isolation of the nuclear family.

Résumé

Le changement social et la phase d'éducation de l'enfant
Ressources et réseau de la famille urbaine moderne en Norvège

Les données analysées dans le présent article constituent les préliminaires d'un projet relatif à l'étude des ressources des familles, du réseau social et des services sociaux, avec insistance sur la phase de l'éducation des enfants; ces données sont fondées sur trois études représentatives des familles norvégiennes.

La mobilité rurale-urbaine a entraîné des changements dans les modèles de résidence des familles ainsi que des changements dans le type d'économie, de composition et de dimension de la famille. La famille typique des nouvelles zones résidentielles est une petite unité familiale ou un foyer d'une seule personne, généralement un individu dans les premières ou les dernières phases de sa vie d'adulte. La phase d'éducation des enfants est sur-représentée dans ces zones comme on peut le voir, à la fois d'après l'âge parental (25–29 ans) et le type de famille (parents et jeunes enfants seulement).

On avait émis l'hypothèse que l'urbanisation entraînait une rupture des anciens réseaux sociaux fondés sur la parenté et/ou le voisinage, ce qui était supposé rendre la famille urbaine moderne particulièrement vulnérable en temps de crise, et partant, plus dépendante des modèles officiels d'aide sociale. (En outre, le revenu en nature – consommation des propres produits – est très rare dans ces familles.) Si les familles, lors de la phase d'éducation des enfants, sont souvent en contact avec des parents et grands-parents, il apparaît que dans les familles urbaines, la fréquence de ces contacts ainsi que de ceux avec des parents plus éloignés, était bien moins élevée que dans les autres familles (bien que les rapports par lettre et par téléphone soient plus fréquents dans ces dernières familles). De même, les sentiments de solidarité réciproque avec parents et parenté étaient moins marqués dans les familles urbaines pendant la phase d'éducation des enfants. Etayant notre hypothèse, ces dernières familles déclarèrent moins s'attendre à l'aide de la part de la parenté, des amis et voisins que les familles rurales de même type. Ceci est également vrai en ce qui concerne leur désir d'aider des personnes appartenant aux mêmes catégories.

Parmi les familles urbaines, seules celles ayant des enfants de moins de vingt ans, vivent particulièrement près des mères, rendent souvent visite à leurs parents et ont de fréquents contacts avec leurs mères. Et pourtant, l'aide économique donnée par les parents (et également envoyée aux parents) est très rare dans ces familles. Il en va de même pour l'aide à la maison, si l'on excepte la basse fréquence d'aide domestique qu'apportent les parents aux familles n'ayant que des enfants adultes. Néanmoins, l'aide à la maison exige une certaine proximité des foyers et comme les familles urbaines habitent à plus grande distance des parents que les ruraux, elles doivent en général ne compter que sur leurs propres ressources. Quant à la situation économique, on constate que l'aide économique des parents est la plus fréquente au sommet et à la base de l'échelle des revenus. Ceci est également plus valable – jusqu'à un certain point – pour l'aide accordée aux mères et non aux pères, puisque – bien naturellement – les familles ayant un revenu particulièrement bas ne peuvent venir en aide à leur père. L'aide apportée et reçue dans la maison suit le même modèle général. Il semble que cette réciprocité de l'échange s'explique comme une nécessité là où les ressources sont modestes et comme un phénomène d'excédent lorsqu'elles sont abondantes. En général, la famille urbaine dans la phase d'éducation des enfants, semble se trouver dans une situation économique particulièrement dure. L'absence de réseau social de ressources n'est pas mieux compensée par un revenu relativement supérieur par unité de consommation dans ces familles que dans d'autres. D'autres familles ont un modèle de revenu plus varié (revenu en nature, pensions, etc.). Il semble que cette dépendance presque totale du revenu salarial constitue une vulnérabilité particulièrement grande chez la famille urbaine dans la phase d'éducation des enfants.

Notes

1. Natalie Rogoff Ramsøy (1973), *The Norwegian Life History Study: Design, Purpose, and a Few Preliminary Results*, Oslo, INAS; and Kari Skrede (1973), *Sosial bakgrunn*

og oppvekstforhold. En sammenligning av de tre årskullene i yrkeshistorieundersøkelsen (*Social Background and Conditions of Child Development. A Comparison of the Three Age Cohorts in the Occupational Life History Project*), Oslo, INAS.

2. For comparison between some Western countries with regard to the relative importance of the various industries see for example Ståle Seierstad (1972), "Norsk økonomi" (Norway's economy), Ch. III in Natalie Rogoff Ramsøy (ed.), *Det norske samfunn* (Norwegian Society), Oslo, Gyldendal: 93.
   Data for the proportion of the population living in urban and rural areas in different countries are given in *Demographic Yearbook, 1970*, New York United Nations, 1971: 147–152, Table 5.
3. Seierstad, *ibid.*
4. "Gymnasium": (junior) college, preparatory for university entrance, students about 16–19 years old.
5. "Extended" households as used here are other households than single persons, married couples without child(ren) and/or other households member(s) and nuclear families (single parents included).
6. Households consisting of Provider and Spouse and Child(ren) and no other members are designated as PSC-households from here on.
7. Dorrian A. Sweetser (1973), *Urban Norwegians: Kinship Networks, and Sibling Mobility*, Oslo. INAS report 73(2).
8. *Ibid.*

6. Family developmental tasks and happiness

ELINA HAAVIO-MANNILA

Family developmental tasks belong to the most important concepts in family development research (Duvall, 1962: 27–52; Hill and Rodgers, 1964: 187–190; Hill, 1964: 189). As a social group, a family must come to terms with certain basic conditions, functional prerequisites, essential for its survival, continuity and growth (Duvall, 1962: 27). Reproduction, physical maintenance, protection, education and socialization, recreation, status-conferring, and affection-giving have been listed as core tasks which all families can be expected to undertake. "When these basic tasks for families are particularized by the sequences in which they must be performed and the hierarchy of importance which they have at different points in time, they become family *developmental* tasks. Thus, the family development task concept permits the analyst to highlight for each stage of development the tasks that have primacy, those which are secondary, and those which are still to be activated" (Hill and Rodgers, 1964: 187). According to the family development theory, successful accomplishment of the developmental tasks results in happiness and satisfaction: "*A developmental task is a task which arises at or about a certain period in the life of an individual, successful achievement of which leads to happiness and to success with later tasks, while failure leads to unhappiness in the individual, disapproval by the society, and difficulty with later tasks*" (Havighurst, 1953: 2; Duvall, 1962: 31–32).

The concept of family developmental tasks can be tied to the discussion concerning basic human needs. The family is a social group in which the satisfaction of many basic needs is in all societies legitimate and appropriate. Of the having-loving-being needs (Allardt and Uusitalo, 1972: 12) especially the loving needs are generally supposed to be satisfied in the family. The whole institution of marriage is ideally based on the primacy of love in the relationship between the spouses. Parental love and companionship are also considered very important in family life. Material needs (having) are also often satisfied through family: children and stay-at-home wives or husbands get their living from the income earned by the family provider. Needs for self-actualization (being) are perhaps less often than loving and having needs satisfied in the family. However, insubstitutability, an operational definition of being value, can be tied to a person's family role. A person may feel him- or herself easily substitutable at work, but not in the family. In this way his family role may rescue him from alienation.

The family developmental tasks vary in different stages of the family life cycle. Also the role of the family in satisfying basic human needs varies according to the family life cycle. Other institutions like work, friendships, politics, school, etc. may always or at certain stages provide opportunities to satisfy human needs to a greater degree than does the family.

This paper is composed of two parts. In the first part we *describe* married couples in Helsinki at different stages of the family cycle: (1) families without children in which both spouses are less than 30 years old, (2) families with preschool-age children, (3) families with preschool and school-age children, (4) families with only school-age children, (5) families with children above school-age (15 years), and (6) families without children in which one or both of the spouses is at least 30 years old. In all families both the husband and the wife were interviewed, and we shall compare their replies. As dependent variables we use factual information about *division of labor* as regards the provider and child care roles, *material resources and consumer patterns* in the family, *human relations inside the family*, especially the *sexual life* of the spouses as well as their *extrafamilial relationships* with friends and co-workers. We also have more attitudinal information about *happiness*, *satisfaction*, and *anxiety* connected with family and work life.

These variables are related mainly to the physical maintenance, recreation, and affection-giving functions of the family. Of the previously mentioned core tasks of the family those of reproduction, protection, education, and status-conferring will not be discussed. If we tie our variables to the value or need tricotomy of having-loving-being we may state that the material resources of the family, like income and also health, represent the having dimension, and human relations inside and outside the family the loving dimension. The being dimension is not studied here.

The last part of the paper tries to *test the hypothesis presented in the family developmental task theory*. According to this, different tasks have primary importance at different stages of family development. The achievement of just these tasks is crucial to satisfaction at that stage. If those developmental tasks are not achieved, the result will be unhappiness and dissatisfaction. On the basis of family research we present the following tentative hypotheses:

1. Good material resources are most important for families with children.
2. Wife's employment is most difficult when children are under school-age.
3. Sexual relations are more important in the earlier stages of marriage than in the later ones.
4. Friends and co-workers are more important to childless families than to families with children.

We shall examine how happiness, satisfaction, lack of anxiety and pain are related to the achievement of the family tasks which are important at each stage of the family life cycle. We are, however, very much conscious of the diversity of family life, and of the possibilities of many alternative solutions to the same problems. "Deviant" families, which do not follow such common assumptions about "proper" family developmental tasks as we present in our hypotheses, may have found ways to run their families contrary to popular expectations. Nowadays, for example, women's possibilities to shape their own lives have at least somewhat increased. It is not impossible or even frustrating to work outside the home while children are small if daycare facilities are appropriate. And sexual relations may be as important later in life than at the beginning of the marriage, even though their frequency has declined. We could continue to make opposite hypotheses to those presented above. We want to underline the tentative, mainly operational character of our hypotheses.

Research material

The interview material for the study was collected in 1970–1971 in Helsinki. The main sample was the same as that used for the crossnational study on family modernization directed by Marvin B. Sussman and sponsored by the Family Committee of the International Sociological Association. It was chosen among married couples with school-age (7–15 years) children in ten randomly selected city areas of Helsinki, distant suburbs excluded. The sample was stratified according to social class of the husband and to migrant status. Half of the families selected for the sample were supposed to represent middle class, half working class. The highest social strata (1–3 according to a 9-point classification scale by Urho Rauhala, 1965) including, for example, persons with academic education were left outside the sample. The other stratifier was the migrant status; half of the families had moved to Helsinki during the year preceding the interview, half had been born in Helsinki. In addition to the sample drawn for the international study I myself collected data from younger couples with and without children and from older couples without children. This sample was stratified according to social class in the same way as the original sample.

The response rate remained very low in the original study (about 50%). This was partly caused by the length of the questionnaire which was told to the respondents beforehand. The interview lasted two or three evenings, about 6–10 hours for each spouse. The husband and the wife were interviewed simultaneously in different rooms by two sociology students. The questionnaire about sexual life was filled by the respondents themselves in writing and was put in a sealed envelope so that the interviewer could not read it.

Altogether 157 families or 314 persons were interviewed. 76 of the families belonged to the international sample. It was difficult to reach the migrant families in the sample. Their proportion remained at 30% instead of the intended 50% in the original sample. Because of the stratification of the sample the families do not statistically represent all families in Helsinki. There are too few upper class families in the whole sample and too many recently migrated families in the sample of parents with school-age children. The stratification according to social class was the same in all stages of the family life cycle, and as a result of this, there are 40–50% middle class families in all family life cycle groups studied, except among the youngest families without children (67%).

Table 1 shows the average ages of the husbands in the six family life cycle groups under study. The age interval between the stages is 6–7 years with the exception of the first two stages – A = young families without children and B = families with preschool-age (0–6 years) children – between which it is only one year. Older families without children (stage F) are of the same age as those having school children only (stage D): husbands are on average 39 years of age. In the figures, stage F will be presented at the same point of the continuum as stage D. In the tables, however, it has the position of the last group.

Table 1. *Average age of husband, number of children, wife's employment, and home help, according to stage in the family life cycle*

	Stage in the family life cycle*						
	A	B	C	D	E	F	All
Average age of husband, years	25	26	32	39	46	39	34
Average number of children	0	1.2	2.4	1.8	3.0	0	1.5
Wife is employed, %	95	81	69	81	69	92	81
Family has some kind of help in household, %	—	5	16	12	12	8	9
Number of families interviewed (N)	(21)	(38)	(26)	(43)	(16)	(13)	(157)

*A = young families without children (both spouses under 30 years)
B = families with preschool children (0–6 years)
C = families with preschool and school children
D = families with school children only (7–14 years)
E = families with children at and post school-age
F = older families without children (at least one of the spouses is 30 years or older)

Division of tasks in the family: the provider and the child care roles

The number of children in the child families ranges from 1.2 in the earliest (B) to 3.0 in the latest (E) stage of family life cycle. On average the child families have 1.9 children. According to a nationwide household survey in Finland in 1966 the number of children in households in which the oldest child was 0–7 years was 1.77, in households with an 8–12 year old as the oldest child, 2.11, and in households with the oldest child between 13 and 20 years, 1.75 children (Pesola, 1971: 38). The number of children in our Helsinki sample is not very deviant from that in the whole country. Our preschool child families are smaller and postschool child families larger than is the case in Finland on the average.

In four of five families the wives participate in taking care of the economical provider functions (Table 1). There are fewest – about 70% – employed mothers in families with many children, that is in families with school *and* either preschool or postschool children (stages C and E). On the other hand, over 90% of the childless wives are working outside the home. The existence of a large family to take care of seems to be closely related to wives' employment which, however, in Helsinki is very common in all families.

Even though the wives are often employed, there is very little outside help in the household: only every tenth family has some kind of household or cleaning help. Outside help is most common in families with school children. The care arranged for preschool children varies a lot. Half of the preschool age children of employed mothers are cared for at home by household helpers, relatives, or family members. Sometimes the spouses shift turns so that one can look after the child while the other is working. The other half spends their daytime in public day care centers or in private homes which take care professionally of other people's children. With the development of family life, the proportion of children taken care of by family members increases. In general, the public day care is not well developed in Helsinki. Only a quarter of preschool children of employed mothers in our sample have had access to a creche or kindergarten. In the whole city of Helsinki 24% of children under school age of employed mothers are taken care of by public daycare institutions (Eskola, 1973: 337).

Social and material resources of the families

The educational background of husbands and wives is very similar. The young families without children (stage A) have a much higher educational level than the other families. There is a big difference between stages A and B even though the families are not very different in age. This may reflect the tendency of young educated people to postpone childbirth more than is the case in marriages of persons with less educational resources. Among the middle aged families those with children are, however, better educated than the childless couples. We shall return to this result later.

From the point of equality of the sexes it is frustrating to see how small the effect of education is in the occupational realm. Equal education of the sexes does not result in equal rewards in *prestige* and *income*. This result is not explained by the difference in the amount of occupational training between the sexes: 46% of the husbands but also 40% of the wives have some kind of vocational education. The wife's special role in the family is one explanation of this, although studies including unmarried women show that it does not explain everything (for example, Eskola and Haavio-Mannila, 1972). In our material (see Figure 1) the difference between the spouses is especially marked in stage C, in families with preschool *and* school children, in which the wives fairly often stay at home. If we look at the income of employed persons only, the picture becomes a bit "lighter": employed wives earn about 650 Finnish marks per month, taxes deducted, their husbands about 1,100 Fmks. Only 14% of the employed wives earn as much or more than their husbands; 33% earn less than half the income of their husbands.

Figure 1. *Income according to stage in the family life cycle*

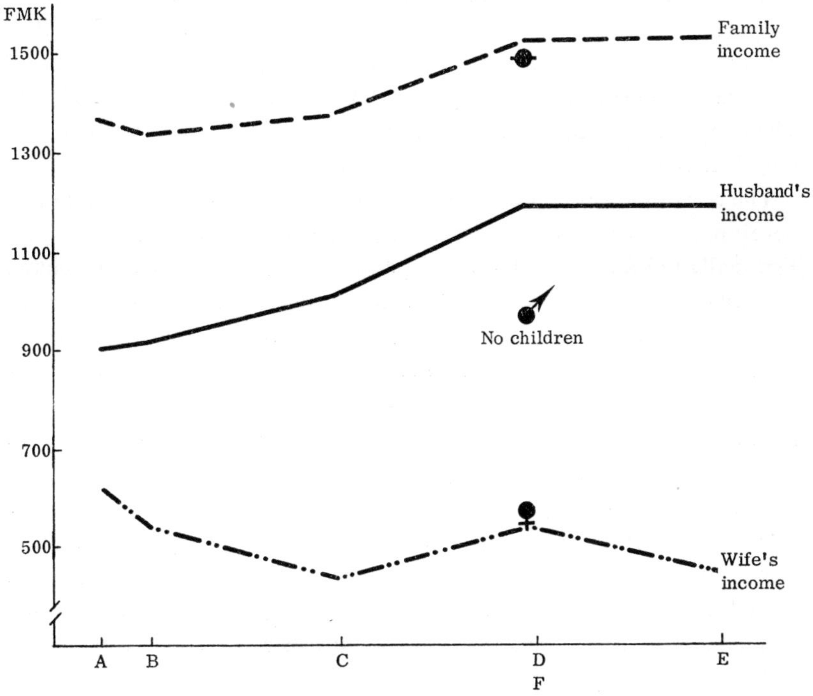

Middle aged families without children have, apart from low education, also lower social prestige and income than families with children of the same age. One may here refer either to the "status symbol" value of children, or to the importance of good economical resources for raising children. Poor families no longer have as many children as before the time of effective birth control methods.

The total family income increases until the latest stage in the family life cycle. This increase is mainly due to increase in husband's income. Wife's income declines from stage A to stage C when the family still has children under school-age but increases in stage D when all the children are at school-age. In the older families it again drops. Total family income of the latest stage E is fairly high even though both husband's and wife's incomes are already rather low. This is probably caused by the high amount of social benefits, tax reductions and children's incomes in these large families.

In Finland, according to the nationwide household survey in 1966 (Pesola, 1971: 89–91), the compulsory expenses for food, dwelling, clothing etc. are highest in families with adolescent children. Even though the total sum of money consumed is fairly large in these families, they can dispose of less money for alternative expenses such as education, durable equipment, and entertainment than families with younger children. The proportion of alternative, "luxury" expenses is, however, smallest in the older families which have already launched their children.

The rise in the amount of some of the compulsory expenses with family development is apparent on the basis of our Helsinki material, too. Especially the food and clothing expenses increase from phase to phase. Housing expenditure is almost the same throughout the family life cycle. This is related to the extremely difficult situation of young families in finding a dwelling. Neither do the entertainment expenses show any marked variation according to family life cycle. Middle aged childless families have lower expenses on all items studied than families with children in the same age category.

Even though the economic position of the family improves as the family passes through its life cycle, the economic demands of the later stages are greater than those of the earlier stages. Reaching a good economic standard is an important family developmental task for families with children. We shall later investigate how its achievement is related to happiness and lack of anxiety.

Sexual relations

One of the basic functions of marriage is to give an outlet to the sexual drive in stable and secure conditions. Sexual life is one expression of the loving value. A happy sex life satisfies a great part of the loving needs of an individual.

A special "sex questionnaire", originally prepared for a national study on sexual life in Finland by Kimmo Leppo, Osmo Koskelainen and Kai Sievers, was presented to our respondents as a pilot study for that large survey, the results of which will be published in 1974. It includes questions about sexual norms, attitudes and behavior. Only part of the results can be presented in Figure 2 and Table 2.

Figure 2. *Proportion of those who have had sexual intercourse at least five times during last month according to stage in the family life cycle*

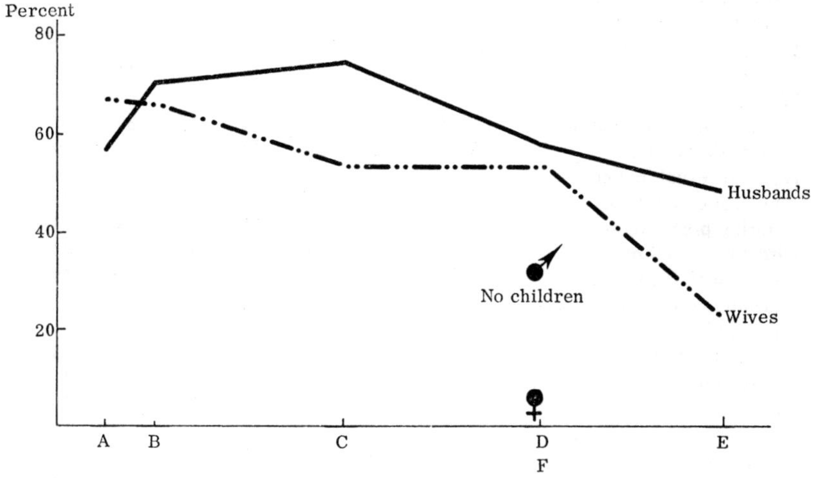

The *appreciation of sexual enjoyment* as one of the most positive things in life does not vary very clearly according to stage in family life cycle and sex. In the middle stages, C and D, the wives appreciate sexual enjoyment most whereas husbands consider it as positive through the family life cycle.

According to several other indicators of strength and frequency of sexual life, husbands are more openly sexual than the wives: they consider their sexual drive stronger, they prefer to have and report having sexual intercourse more frequently, and have had more extramarital sexual relations. But some defects or disturbances in the sexual life are as common among husbands and wives: *impotency* in case of husbands, and *frequent lack of orgasm* in case of wives. These difficulties are most common in the beginning of the marriage (stage A) and in the middle of family life cycle (stage D). The oldest couples are no longer suffering from them. In general the sexual drive and activity declines with family development. The slowing down of sexual life with increasing age has been documented in earlier studies, for example by Kinsey (1953: 77) and Zetterberg (1969).

Table 2. *Characteristics of sexual life according to the stage in the family life cycle (H = husbands, W = wives) (%)*

		Stage in the family life cycle						
		A	B	C	D	E	F	All
Definitely considers sexual life one of the most positive things in life	H	57	69	62	74	62	85	68
	W	67	49	79	81	46	62	66
Considers own sexual drive at least fairly strong	H	38	75	45	41	38	23	49
	W	29	22	25	28	8	15	23
Would prefer to have sexual intercourse at least three times a week	H	70	81	62	64	75	39	67
	W	71	51	29	42	—	—	39
Has had sexual intercourse at least eleven times during preceding month	H	34	31	29	22	8	—	23
	W	39	11	8	11	—	8	15
Discusses sexual matters often with the spouse	H	62	47	42	51	23	8	44
	W	62	53	60	47	31	15	48
Has suffered from impotency during last year/Does not get orgasm always or almost always in sexual intercourse	H	57	31	36	43	17	50	40
	W	52	43	34	46	33	30	41
Has had extramarital sexual relations during lifetime	H	14	34	40	36	70	46	36
	W	14	11	19	11	8	8	12
Considers own sexual life to be very happy	H	14	19	21	23	15	8	18
	W	24	19	33	32	8	—	23

Relations with friends and co-workers

Family is not the sole source of human relationships which are important to the satisfaction of the loving needs. The term *friendship* refers to close relations between persons who can freely discuss with each other, be open and honest in their interpersonal relations, and first of all, *trust each other*, as our respondents define the concept. Trustworthiness, reliability seems to be the key word in friendship: a friend does not deceive you or let you down.

The number of close personal friends of the same sex seems to decline with the advancement of family life cycle for both spouses (Figure 3). The same thing happens in the number of close male friends of the wives, too: young wives have more male friends than the older ones. But the husbands seem to get more "girl friends" in the most advanced stage of the family life cycle (E). Also the number of married couples met regularly declines according to the responses of the wives but increases in the

Figure 3. *Number of married couples as friends (—), friends of own sex (--), and friends of the other sex (. . .) according to stage in the family life cycle*

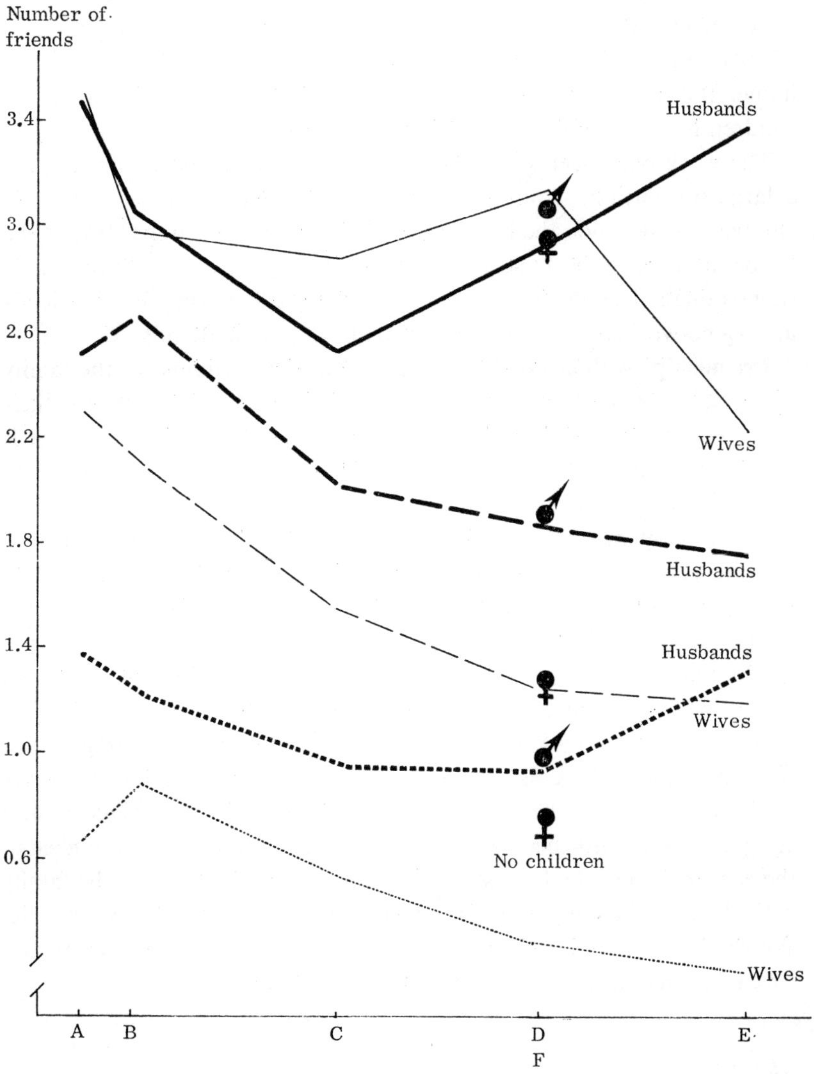

opinion of the husbands. The sex roles seem to favor older husbands' friendships with women but not older women's friendships with men.

Wives become more and more isolated from all kinds of friendships with increasing age. Only the childless middle aged wives fairly often have male friends. Maybe a family with children offers enough company and friendship to wives at the stages of family life when children are still at home. But what happens to the wives without good friends after the children have left home and the husband dies?

The work place seems to offer friendship and companionship to quite a large proportion of our respondents. *Friendships between co-workers* emerge mostly inside the boundaries of the same sex group: 80% of the husbands have some male friends at work but only 47% have female friends there. The percentages for wives as regards having female friends among co-workers is 65 and as regards having male friends, 37.

Friendships with co-workers are scarce in the beginning of the family life cycle when the spouses are new at their jobs. Among husbands their frequency declines with each stage in the family life cycle after stage B but for wives the lowest frequency is in the middle stages when the family demands most of her and when many wives even stay at home. Later the wives develop more ties with co-workers even though these may not become very close. Middle aged wives without children have especially many ties with co-workers of both sexes. They may in this way get some compensation for lacking parental relations.

The tendency for men to have close ingroup relations at work can clearly be seen. Men enter into alliance with each other and very often exclude female co-workers from their circles. This is disadvantageous to women's careers. It is also related to the formal segregation of the sexes in the work places. The possibilities and the need to feel solidarity and companionship with people outside the immediate family are higher in the earlier than in the later stages of family life cycle. Perhaps the family with children is enough to satisfy the loving needs of middle aged people. We shall later examine the importance of friends to the satisfaction and lack of anxiety in different stages of family life cycle.

Dissatisfaction and anxiety

To study the importance of the family developmental tasks we need some measure of happiness. We shall use two indicators of wellbeing and satisfaction:

(1) a *happiness and satisfaction* scale composed of feelings of happiness in marriage and sexual life, work satisfaction and satisfaction with overall life, and
(2) a scale measuring *feelings of anxiety and pain* related to success at work, economical position of the family, getting old, losing the interest of the other sex, love for the spouse or other persons, and future of children.

In earlier studies it has been found that "marital happiness declines over the life-span from the honeymoon through the childbearing and child-rearing period to reach its lowest point when the children are adolescents and leave the home, at which point the scores improve and remain higher than before, on into old age" (Hill, 1964: 197). The same tendency can be seen from Figure 4. Unhappiness and anxiety are highest in the middle stages of family life. The sharp decline in stage D and increase in E for wives may be due to the small sample.

Figure 4. *Index of dissatisfaction and unhappiness according to stage in the family life cycle*

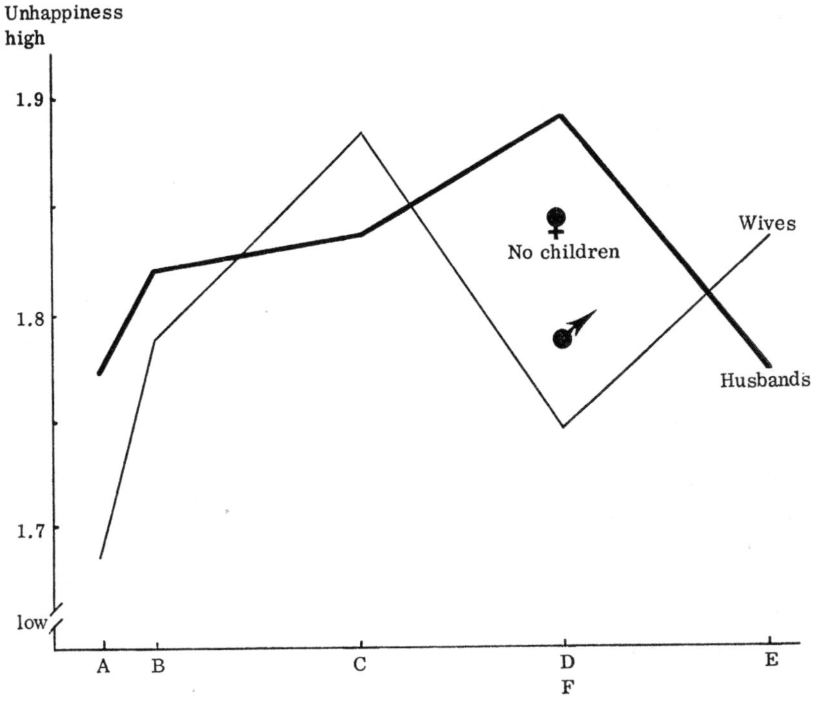

Anxieties and pains do not follow quite the same pattern as dissatisfaction (Figure 5). The number of anxieties and pains is lowest in stages A and C, that is when the young couple does not yet have children (A), and when the oldest children are at school and there are also small children in the family (C). The rise in anxiety in families with preschool children only (stage B) may be related to changes caused by the arrival of children. When the children mature, anxiety decreases for a while but it comes back at the later stages. Childless couples have a low number of anxieties. This is due to the lack of anxiety about the future of children which is very common in the child families.

Figure 5. *Number of feelings of anxiety and pain according to stage in the family life cycle*

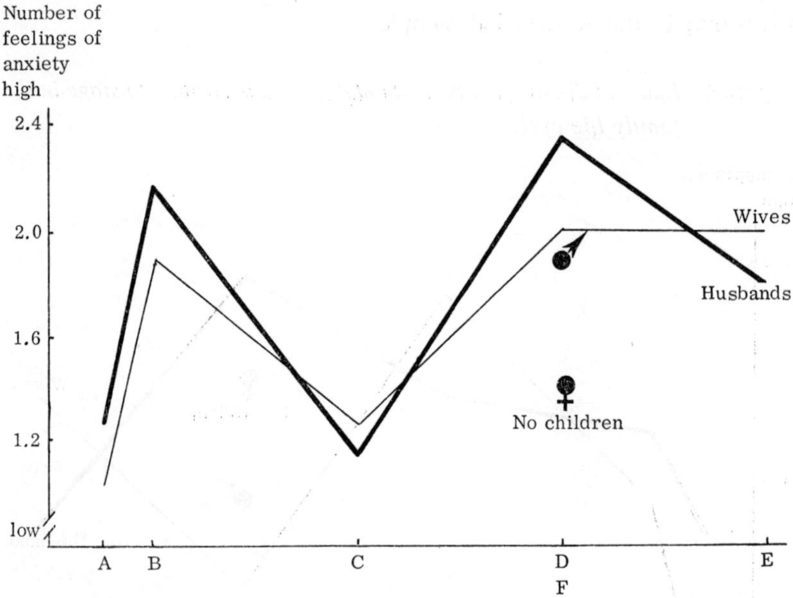

Even though the different indicators of unhappiness and anxiety seem to appear at different stages of the family life cycle, as such they correlate positively with each other. There is a positive correlation between the answers of husbands and wives, too. Especially the number of anxieties, and the marital and sexual happiness of the husband is correlated with that of the wife.

The family life cycle has at its different stages different characteristics.

The material resources increase but also the compulsory expenses are rising so that the actual standard of living does not rise at quite the same tempo. Sexual activities, but also their disturbances, slow down with increasing age. The number of close friends declines as families mature. Only the husbands at the last stage investigated here have more female friends than earlier. They also prefer more frequent sexual activity than husbands in the earlier stages. This may be some kind of "wildness of the fifties". This is not an unhappy period in their life. The oldest wives on the contrary do not experience any increasing activity in their human relations as do their husbands. This may be related to the climacterium period which seems to be an unhappy period for a woman.

The best time in marital life is the beginning, before the children have arrived and the couple is still young. The differences between the sexes are at that point minimal. Later they increase in a very traditional way.

Achievement of family developmental tasks and happiness

After having presented the variation of certain family tasks, resources, relationships, and feelings through the family life cycle from marriage to the stage when the family has adolescent children we now turn to the testing of our hypotheses about the proper achievement of developmental tasks and happiness. Our main task is to show that achievement of certain things at the "right" phase of family living leads to happiness and satisfaction.

The first family developmental task examined here is related to the economic function of the family. The material needs rise when children arrive and grow older. Thus it is especially important to have a good family income at the later stages of marriage, rather than at the earlier ones. Our hypothesis "Good *material resources* are most important for families with children" receives support from Table 3. Both dissatisfaction and anxiety are, in the later stages of family life when all children have reached school-age (stages D + E), connected with the low economic standard of the family. In the earlier stages husbands (not wives) in the higher income families are more dissatisfied than husbands in the lower income families. The other indicator of unhappiness, feelings of anxiety and pain, shows that differences between high and low income families are larger in the earlier and middle stages than in the later stages of the family life cycle. In all phases of family life poor families are, however, clearly more anxious than the rich ones.

Table 3. *Dissatisfaction and anxiety according to stage in the family life cycle and family income (scale means)*

Stage in the family life cycle	Family income per month, taxes reduced	Dissatisfaction		Anxiety		(N)
		Husbands	Wives	Husbands	Wives	
No children (A+F)	small (less than 1,700 Fmks)	1.73	1.76	1.62	1.29	(21)
	large	2.00	1.77	1.29	1.00	(14)
	difference	−.27	−.01	.33	.29	
Children under school age (B+C)	small	1.76	1.87	2.07	1.76	(42)
	large	1.96	1.73	1.10	1.45	(20)
	difference	−.20	.14	.97	.31	
Children at school age (D+E)	small	1.92	1.82	2.28	2.07	(29)
	large	1.79	1.71	2.10	1.93	(30)
	difference	.13	.11	.18	.14	

The second hypothesis "*Wives' employment* is most difficult when children are under school-age" is based on common sense knowledge and research findings. The practical arrangement of daycare for children is not easy in Helsinki, and ways of organizing vary considerably. The easiest way for a mother would be to stay at home, but this solution is seldom available because of the economical necessity of wife's employment in most of the working and lower middle class families. The hypothesis receives support (Table 4) when we look at the anxiety variable among the wives: feelings of anxiety are more common among employed than non-employed mothers of preschool children. Such is the case among mothers of school children, too, but to a more limited degree. The fathers of school-age children whose mothers are employed, are especially anxious, much more so than the fathers of younger children. Older men seem to find it particularly difficult to adjust themselves to the employment of their wives.

The dissatisfaction variable reveals almost no difference between the employed and nonemployed wives or their husbands. Most dissatisfaction is found among the nonemployed mothers of preschool children. They are especially unsatisfied with their work when we look at the individual items of satisfaction. Due to changing role expectations of women the young stay-at-home mothers feel frustrated because they are not able to find "self-actualization" in the work life. The household tasks do not

Table 4. *Dissatisfaction and anxiety according to stage in the family life cycle and wife's employment (scale means)*

Stage in the family life cycle	Wife's employment	Dissatisfaction		Anxiety		(N)
		Husbands	Wives	Husbands	Wives	
No children	employed[a]	1.83	1.75	1.48	1.09	(32)
Children under school age	employed	1.82	1.79	1.74	1.80	(48)
	not employed	1.83	1.92	1.81	1.25	(15)
	difference	−.01	−.13	−.07	.55	
Children at school age	employed	1.88	1.77	2.29	2.04	(45)
	not employed	1.86	1.78	1.71	1.83	(12)
	difference	.02	−.01	.58	.21	

a. There were only two nonemployed wives among the childless families. They have been left out.

satisfy these often quite well-educated women. But even though these homemothers of small children are unsatisfied with their work, they are not anxious as their employed sisters are. The employment of mothers has its costs, even though the work life, and overall life of the working mothers is according to their statements very satisfactory.

Sexual activities were found to decrease with the development of the family life cycle. We thought that it was a natural development and stated our hypothesis as follows: "*Sexual relations* are more important in the earlier stages of marriage than in the later ones". This hypothesis is not at all supported by our data (Table 5). For husbands the frequency of coitus has almost no effect on dissatisfaction and anxiety. Only in the older marriages those with low sexual activity feel somewhat more anxiety than those with a high frequency. This is contrary to the hypothesis, and shows that the importance of sexual activity does not decrease with age.

For the wives we get strong support in the opposite direction of relationship than that suggested by the original hypothesis. In the earliest stage of marriage those wives who have had frequent sexual intercourse are the most unhappy and anxious. In the later stages there is no difference in the dissatisfaction scores but anxiousness is more common in the sexually passive group. High frequency of sexual intercourse seems to be especially important for the lack of anxiety in the later stages of marriage.

As a compensation for lack of companionship of children, it is suggested that good friends are especially important for the childless families. Our fourth hypothesis stated: "*Friends and co-workers* are more important to

Table 5. *Dissatisfaction and anxiety according to stage in the family life cycle and frequency of sexual intercourse (scale means)*

Stage in the family life cycle	Frequency of sexual intercourse	Dissatisfaction Husbands	Dissatisfaction Wives	Anxiety Husbands	Anxiety Wives	(N)
Young without children (A)	low (less than five times during preceding month)	1.78	1.56	1.33	.67	(9)
	high	1.77	1.77	1.23	1.31	(13)
	difference	.01	−.21	.10	−.64	
Children under school age (B+C)	low	1.89	1.86	1.80	1.95	(20)
	high	1.80	1.81	1.74	1.52	(43)
	difference	.09	.05	.06	.43	
Children at school age and older without children (D+E+F)	low	1.86	1.77	2.20	2.03	(35)
	high	1.89	1.81	2.05	1.75	(36)
	difference	−.03	−.04	.15	.28	

childless families than to families with children". This hypothesis receives quite a lot of support from Table 6, especially in the case of wives. Childless wives without a wide friendship circle are the most unhappy and anxious ones. On the other hand, wives and husbands with children at school-age and a wide friendship circle are very often expressing feelings of anxiety. Maybe they have too many things to take care of whereas the childless and isolated persons are really lacking human contacts and community. According to Allardt's results, all the four Scandinavian countries had a kind of Happiness-factor which invariably had high loadings in the variables measuring perceived happiness and felt security and support. This factor also tended to have high loadings in the Loving-variable and on the scale measuring Doing (employment) (Allardt, 1973: 44). Unhappiness and anxiety of childless wives without friends is an example of the close relationship between community (loving) and life satisfaction and mental health (we have not called our anxiety scale a mental health variable even though our unpublished data from another study show that the anxieties measured here correlate strongly with neurotic symptoms).

We may summarize the results related to the testing of our hypotheses about achievement of developmental tasks and happiness in the following way:

Table 6. *Dissatisfaction and anxiety according to stage in the family life cycle and manysidedness of friendship circle (scale means)*

Stage in the family life cycle	Friendship circle	Dissatisfaction Husbands	Dissatisfaction Wives	Anxiety Husbands	Anxiety Wives	(N)
No children (A+F)	limited[a]	1.94	2.00	1.50	2.20	(14)
	manysided	1.76	1.67	1.48	.76	(21)
	difference	.18	.33	.02	1.44	
Children under school age (B+C)	limited	1.80	1.91	2.11	1.46	(19)
	manysided	1.83	1.77	1.60	1.79	(43)
	difference	−.03	.14	.51	−.33	
Children at school age (D+E)	limited	1.84	1.69	1.90	1.81	(21)
	manysided	1.86	1.86	2.34	2.23	(38)
	difference	−.02	−.17	−.44	−.42	

a. The sum scale consists of the following items: has really close friends of own and other sex, has other good friends of own and other sex, has married couples as friends, majority of co-workers of own and other sex are friends. The maximum score is 7. The cutting point is between 3 and 4 types of friends.

In the earlier stages of marriage too frequent sexual activity may be problematical to the wife. Adjustment to frequent intercourse seems not to be easy in the beginning of marital life. If the marriage remains childless, a limited friendship circle causes unhappiness. *In the families with preschool children* low income is problematical, wife's employment bothers her, and the husbands are suffering if they have only a limited friendship circle. Now infrequent instead of frequent sexual intercourse is problematical to the wife. *In the last family life stages studied*, low family income, wives' employment, low sexual activity, and a wide (but maybe loose?) friendship circle are connected with anxiety. In the later stage of family life the social (loving) situation of the family seems to make more difference than earlier when the general satisfaction level is higher and anxiety less frequent.

The sample of this study is so small that many results are not statistically significant. We have, however, found some regularities which are supported by earlier studies, and may thus at least to a certain degree be considered to be reliable. The family developmental task hypotheses found quite good support from our data. We might continue to test more hypotheses of that sort.

At the end some social policy implications of the empirical results may be suggested:

1. Low income is particularly stressful for families with children. Increased family allowances may solve some problems here as well as measures connected with the equalization of incomes.

2. While children are small, wife's employment causes anxiety but at the same stage of family life cycle her staying at home makes her dissatisfied with (home)work and overall life. The anxiety of employed mothers might be lessened by better children's daycare arrangements and increased help in household chores by public services and husband's participation in them. The dissatisfaction of the stay-at-home wives is more problematic. It is related to the status of homework in general. Women's liberation movement has stressed the importance of employment for the society and for the self-actualization of women themselves. It may have made the full-time housewives feel themselves inferior to the employed ones, and in this way caused dissatisfaction. Practical measures to make the life of home-mothers more satisfactory are not easily invented in present day conditions of housing and family structure.

3. The importance of active sexual life in the later stages of marriage particularly for wives' lack of anxiety implicates that there is not enough information about the sexual needs of women at more advanced ages.

4. The unhappiness of childless couples without friends shows the importance of human relationships, companionship, and "community" outside the immediate family to probably all groups in the population except the "self-sufficient" nuclear families with children.

Résumé

Les tâches développementales de la famille et son bonheur

En tant que groupe social, la famille doit composer avec certaines conditions de base, certaines nécessités fonctionnelles qui sont essentielles à sa survie, sa continuité et sa croissance. L'équilibre physique, les fonctions de reproduction, de protection, d'éducation et de socialisation, de divertissement, l'acquisition d'un statut et l'échange d'affection, ont été cités comme les premiers devoirs requis de toute famille. Selon Hill et Rodgers, "lorsque ces devoirs familiaux de base sont précisés par les phases au cours desquelles ils doivent être accomplis et par la hiérarchie d'importance qu'on leur confère à diverses périodes, ils deviennent des tâches développementales de la famille. Ainsi ce concept permet au chercheur de mettre en relief, pour chaque phase du développement, les tâches prioritaires, les tâches secondaires et celles qui doivent encore être réalisées". Cette théorie sous-entend que la réalisation de ces tâches développementales ont le bonheur et la satisfaction pour aboutissement.

On peut lier ce concept à la discussion relative aux besoins fondamentaux de l'homme. La famille est un groupe social dans lequel la satisfaction de nombreux besoins fondamentaux est légitime et appropriée, quelle que soit la société. Des besoins tels "avoir", "aimer" et "être" (Allardt et Uusitalo, 1972: 12), ce sont surtout ceux d'"aimer" que l'on suppose en général devoir être satisfaits au sein de la famille.

Les tâches développementales familiales varient avec les diverses périodes du cycle de la vie de la famille. Et le rôle qu'elle joue en satisfaisant les besoins fondamentaux de l'homme varie avec le cycle de la vie familiale. D'autres institutions comme le travail, l'amitié, la politique, l'école, etc., peuvent toujours, à certains moments de l'existence, apporter de plus grandes satisfactions que la famille.

Dans la première partie de cet article, 157 couples mariés d'Helsinki ont été décrits à différents stades du cycle de la vie familiale: 1) couples sans enfant dans lesquels les conjoints ont tous deux moins de 30 ans; 2) familles avec enfants d'âge pré-scolaire; 3) familles avec enfants d'âge pré-scolaire et scolaire; 4) familles avec enfants d'âge scolaire seulement; 5) familles avec enfants ayant passé l'âge scolaire; 6) familles sans enfant, dans lesquelles un ou les deux conjoints a 30 ans au moins. Dans toutes ces familles, le mari et la femme ont été interviewés. Des renseignements précis ont été demandés pour servir de variables dépendantes au sujet de la diversité du travail – tant pour le conjoint pourvoyant aux besoins matériels du foyer que pour celui qui prend soin des enfants – des ressources matérielles et modèles de consommation, relations humaines au sein de la famille, surtout sur la vie sexuelle et les relations extra-familiales avec amis et collègues, et au sujet de la santé. Des données concernant le bonheur, la satisfaction et l'anxiété ont également été analysées en tenant compte de la phase du cycle familial.

Dans la seconde partie, l'on s'efforce de tester l'hypothèse présentée dans la théorie de l'évolution des tâches de la famille. Selon celle-ci, plusieurs tâches sont d'importance primordiale à différentes périodes du développement familial. L'accomplissement de ces tâches est capitale à ce niveau; senon, il en résulterait l'insatisfaction et l'anxiété.

Les résultats liés au test de plusieurs hypothèses relatives à l'accomplissement des tâches développementales de la famille et de son bonheur, peuvent être résumées comme suit:

Aux premiers stades du mariage, l'activité sexuelle fréquente semble engendrer anxiété et mécontentement parmi les épouses mais non leur mari. S'habituer à une vie sexuelle active n'est pas chose aussi facile pour une femme que pour un homme. Si le mariage reste sans enfant, l'épouse en souffre quand son cercle d'amis est limité. Dans les familles avec enfants en âge pré-scolaire, le *stress* est lié à un revenu bas dans le cas des deux conjoints. L'épouse qui a un emploi à l'extérieur devient inquiète mais si elle reste chez elle, elle est insatisfaite. L'époux souffre si son cercle d'amis est limité. A ce stade, les rapports sexuels peu fréquents engendrent des problèmes pour l'épouse. Aux derniers stades de la vie de la famille étudiés ici (les couples les plus âgés avaient la cinquantaine) les revenus familiaux peu élevés, l'emploi à l'extérieur de la femme, l'activité sexuelle réduite et un cercle d'amis très étendu mais très lâche, sont à l'origine de l'anxiété.

Dans les derniers stades de la vie de la famille, la situation matérielle de l'"avoir", et sociale de l'"aimer", semble présenter une influence particulière. Dans les premiers stades, le niveau général de satisfaction est plus élevé et l'anxiété moins fréquente. Ceci pourrait constituer une des raisons pour lesquelles les variables "avoir" et "aimer" ne sont pas autant liées au mécontentement et à l'anxiété dans les familles jeunes que dans les familles plus âgées.

Enfin, ces résultats empiriques pourraient être l'occasion d'émettre quelques

suggestions en matière de politique sociale:
1. Un revenu modéré constitue un réel *stress* dans les familles ayant des enfants. Des allocations familiales et autres mesures aplanissant les différences de revenu entre familles avec ou sans enfants sont nécessaires.
2. Tandis que les enfants sont jeunes, l'emploi de la femme à l'extérieur provoque l'anxiété mais au même stade, si elle reste au foyer, elle devient insatisfaite par les travaux ménagers et la vie en général. L'anxiété de la femme travailleuse pourrait être amoindrie par de meilleures crèches et une aide accrue dans les travaux ménagers fournie par des services publics et la participation effective de l'époux aux charges de sa femme. L'insatisfaction des épouses au foyer est plus difficile à résoudre. Elle est liée au statut du travail ménager en général. Les mouvements féministes ont souligné l'importance de l'emploi à l'extérieur pour la femme et de la réalisation de soi. Ceci a pu donner aux ménagères à plein temps un complexe d'infériorité par rapport à celles qui ont une profession et engendrer leur insatisfaction. Il n'est pas facile d'inventer des mesures pratiques pour rendre agréable la vie des mères au foyer, dans les conditions d'habitat et de structure familiale actuelles.
3. L'importance d'une vie sexuelle active dans les stades ultérieurs du mariage pour que l'épouse n'éprouve pas d'anxiété sous-entend que l'on n'est pas assez informé sur les besoins sexuels de la femme d'âge mûr.
4. Le mécontentement des femmes sans enfant qui n'ont pas d'amis démontre l'importance des relations humaines, de l'amitié et de la "communauté" extérieure à la famille immédiate comprenant probablement tous les autres groupes de la population sauf les familles nucléaires avec enfants qui se suffisent à elles-mêmes.

REFERENCES

Allardt, Erik (1973), "About dimensions of welfare, an exploratory analysis of a comparative Scandinavian survey", *Research Group for Comparative Sociology*, University of Helsinki, 1.

—— and Uusitalo, Hannu (1972), "Dimensions of welfare in a comparative study of Scandinavian societies", *Scandinavian Political Studies*, Vol. 7: 9–27.

Duvall, Evelyn M. (1962), *Family Development*, Philadelphia and New York, J.B. Lippincott Company, second edition.

Eskola, Irja (1973), "Children's day care in Finland" in Pamela Roby (ed.), *Child Care – Who Cares?*, New York, Basic Books.

—— and Haavio-Mannila, Elina (1972, 1975), "The careers of professional women and men in Finland", *Research Reports*, Institute of Sociology, University of Helsinki, 185, and *Acta Sociologica*, Vol. 18, N° 2–3: 174–201.

Havighurst, Robert J. (1953), *Human Development and Education*, New York, Longman's, Green & Company.

Hill, Reuben (1964), "Methodological Issues in Family Research", *Family Process*, Vol. III/1, March: 14–33.

—— and Rodgers, Roy H. (1964), "The developmental approach" in Harold T. Christensen (ed.), *Handbook of Marriage and the Family*, Chicago, Rand McNally Company: 171–211.

Kinsey, Alfred C., Pomeroy, Wardell B., Martin, Clyde E., and Gebhard, Paul H. (1953), *Sex Behavior in the Human Female*, Philadelphia, W.B. Saunders Company.

Pesola, Ritva (1971), "Perheen käyttäytymisestä kuluttajana perheen eri elinvaiheissa vuoden 1966 kotitaloustiedustelun kulutusmenojen valossa", Master's thesis in Sociology, University of Helsinki.

Rauhala, Urho (1965), *Suomalaisen yhteiskunnan sosiaalinen kerrostuneisuus*, Porvoo, Werner Söderstöm Oy.

Zetterberg, Hans (1969), "Om sexuallivet i Sverige", *Statens Offentiga Utredningar*, 2, Stockholm.

7. Social indicators for the analysis of family needs related to the life cycle

VERONICA STOLTE-HEISKANEN

To say that the family is a functional part of society, and as such the relationship between society and the family is a fundamental concern of family sociology is to state an often-heard truism that hardly needs repeating. Yet, up till the recent years there has been regrettably little empirical evidence to show this "fundamental concern" to be more than a generally endorsed principle.

Partly because of empiricism in research orientations and partly as a consequence of the dominance of structural functionalism in Western sociology, much of family sociological research has focused on micro-level analyses of the nuclear family and its internal mechanisms, in isolation from society and its other institutions (Stolte-Heiskanen, 1972). There have been, however, some important developments that point to re-orientations in family sociology toward a broader and more comprehensive direction. First of all, a number of important analyses have appeared that challenge the previously held notion of the nuclear family both as a universally functional and structural phenomenon unique to modern industrial societies (e.g., Aires, 1962; König, 1970; Gordon, 1972). Secondly, doubts are being increasingly cast upon the concomitant assumption of the functional necessity of the isolation and insulation of the family from the larger society (Litwak, 1970; Sennett, 1970). Both of these basic conceptual reorientations have contributed to the growing awareness of what has been termed as "bridging type concepts" between the family and other units (Hill, 1966: 14).

The resurgence of more macro-sociological interests in sociology in general too has had its repercussions in family sociology. Specifically, developments in general systems theory have provided an important stimulus for viewing the family in a larger context. The emergence of the so-called developmental approach also re-focused family research toward the morphological aspects of family structures and made us aware of the importance of social space and time (Hill, 1972).

Changes and reorientations in family sociology, or the social sciences in general, do not occur in a vacuum. At least to some extent these trends also reflect a more general reorientation in the social sciences towards a growing awareness of the need for "socially relevant" research. The frequently noted disintegration of what has been defined as "the traditional forms of hierarchical structural embeddedness of the functional division of labor", is manifested in the increasing vulnerability of contemporary industrial organizations, in the growing contradictions between the importance of the worker as a consumer and his structural alienation, in the problems created by the growing amount of socially superfluous time (leisure), and the erosion of traditional, historically formed and locally varying partial structures of social and political control (Meszaros, 1971). This has brought increasing challenges to the premises of traditional political economy and the individualistic tradition of utilitarianism (Bosnjak, 1972).

Social scientists and policy makers alike are becoming increasingly aware of the fact that the emphasis on economic growth in highly industrialized societies has not brought all the beneficial results to the populations that have sometimes been claimed or assumed. As a consequence, both policy makers and social scientists are beginning to respond to the growing collective pressure for "humanistic social action" on an organized societal scale. In the realm of policy makers this is reflected in re-evaluations and formulations of social welfare and policy. In the social sciences this has been simultaneously accompanied by the emergence of the policy sciences and its concretization in the so-called social indicators movement that focuses on the gap between social needs and social action.

The present paper is an attempt to outline a potential conceptual framework for the analysis of the relationship between the family and the larger social system, utilizing the concepts of social policy, or social indicators as potential "linkage mechanisms" between the family and the social system. To this end some concepts of both the general systems theoretical approach and the developmental approach in family sociology are utilized, along with some broader structural orientations.

Social indicators

The so-called social indicators "movement" emerged in the 1960's in Western industrialized societies as a consequence of the growing dissatisfaction with the available tools for measuring and modifying the growing problems with which societies are being confronted. The "movement" may be described as part of the generally emerging "politics of relevance" that aim toward the rationalization of policy-making in general (Zapf, 1972: 234). The basic underlying principle is to describe how the population in a society lives and what measures can be, or are being, taken to improve the level of living or the "quality of life". Or, as Gross has so succinctly put it, "how to best describe the state of the nation" (Gross, 1966: 154). Thus, social indicators are primarily tools for describing the state of societal welfare and the factors affecting it, with the ultimate purpose of these descriptions serving as a basis for social policy effecting the observed changes.

While the idea of social indicators has received widespread interest and enthusiastic support both by social scientists and policy makers, the reception has not been totally uncritical. Many of the problems and controversies center around the methodological issues of measurement. In this respect the question of quantifying the qualitative is most problematic. As Afanasjev pointed out, the most important questions concerning societal information involve those qualitative aspects that most often cannot be presented in formal terms: factors related to social groups and classes, to the position of the individuals, their needs and benefits, the motives for their actions, the nature of their actions themselves, their emotions, psychological states, social experiences, etc. (Afanasjev, 1971: 183). Yet these are the very factors that are most difficult to summarize in quantitative terms.

Another problem is raised by the fact that social indicators, as any social bookkeeping system, are products of the very societal institutions that they aim to describe. As such these measures are influenced by exactly the same limitations that concern all complex institutions in society, including those that at the same time influence the phenomena that they aim to describe (Biderman, 1966: 69).

On a different level, the frequently random and isolated development of indicators in the absence of any theoretical framework, or even overtly antitheoretical orientation (e.g., Schonfield and Shaw, 1972), makes the indicators often of little analytical value (Land, 1971; Zienkowski, 1971).

As a tool of social policy, it is obvious that the very concept of social indicators is a normative one, and rests on more or less explicitly formulated values that define the goals. While this is often explicitly recognized, far less attention is being paid to the more serious question of the assumption of the existence of a *consensus* concerning these goals and their implementations. Undoubtedly the question of "whose social indicators" is a most significant one that deserves far more discussion.

Social indicators as an analytic concept

In general there are two different approaches to indicators of the social state of affairs. On the one hand, the so-called "matter-oriented" approach follows essentially the tradition of national statistics and aims at distilling meaningful information from great quantities of statistical data. On the other hand, the "idea-oriented" approach considers indicators as more abstract concepts describing the welfare, quality of life, possibilities of systems, etc. (Niitamo, 1972). In a sense these two different approaches reflect the dual nature of the concept of social indicators: they make it possible to modify societal reality and to make social policy more rational (matter-oriented), and they are tools of scientific knowledge of reality and its development (idea-oriented) (Girardeau, 1972: 200).

The present paper primarily concerns the latter aspect of social indicators, namely its potentials as a concrete tool of analysis of *linkage mechanisms* between the family and society. Social indicators can be conceived also as empirical measures of societal inputs into its subsystems (i.e., family) that either may reflect feedback responses to the changing needs of the family, or/and may aim at modifying the structure, function, goals, ideology, etc., of the subsystem. As such the focus here is on the elaboration of the family as a societal subsystem from the perspective of macro- and micro-changes and the changing needs that these changes imply.

A systems approach to the family

The assumption that the family is a functional part of a larger totality (society) implies that it is an open system that is interdependent with inputs from society and itself produces outputs that in turn have input feedbacks to society. From a structural perspective on the most general level we can assume that the two fundamental functional input-output linkages between the family and society are those concerning (1) *the reproduction of labor power*, and (2) *the "ideological apparatus" of society* (Althusser, 1971). From the point of view of the family this is correspondingly reflected in the universal functions of the *biological, economic, social, and spiritual* reproduction of man.

This is schematically summarized in Figure 1.

Figure 1. *Functional relationship between family and society*

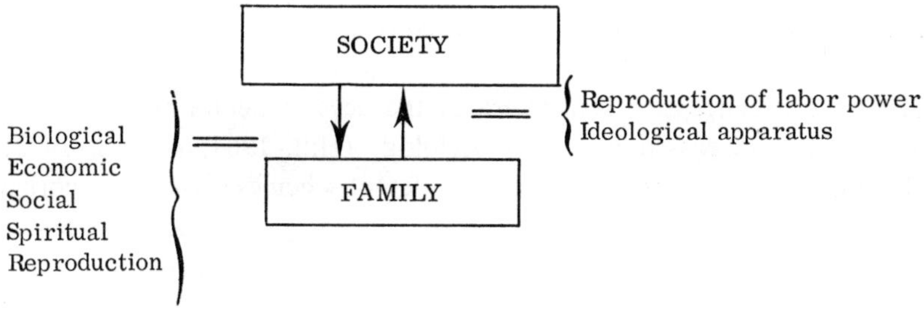

Defining the functional relationship between the family and society on this level of abstraction gives a historical perspective, both in terms of the changes that have occurred in these functions concomitant with broader historical-cultural developments and within the development of the family's individual life-span. There are temporal variations in the intensity and form with which the basic functions are carried out – be it a question of historical time on a societal scale or on the level of the microcosm of the family life-cycle. From this perspective the dynamic aspects of the interaction between the family and society come to the fore. At the same time, it points to the close convergence between the general systems-theoretical framework and the developmental approach in family sociology.

The relevance of general systems theory for family sociology has been systematically outlined by Hill (1971). For the present purposes it needs only to be repeated that the family may be viewed as a "relatively closed (or open) system": a purposive, goal-oriented, task-performing system that maintains a morphogenic equilibrium with its environment. This implies that in the process of interaction and survival, the family as a system responds to change by changing its structure. The concept of change makes the interrelationship between systems-theoretical and developmental conceptual frameworks evident. Thus, one can consider on the one hand consequences of macro-changes in society, and on the other micro-changes in the internal structure and organization of the family as "families form and pursue their careers over their life-span". These changes and morphogenic responses create in turn new needs in the family. The analysis of the linkage mechanisms that reflect societal inputs in response to these needs is one potential way in which the micro- and macro-level analyses of system interactions can be combined.

The developmental approach and the life-cycle

The general conceptual framework of the developmental approach has been widely discussed in family sociology (Hill, 1964; Aldous, 1972; Duvall, 1971; Rodgers, 1973). While different schemes exist to categorize the different phases of the life-span of the family, they seem to center around three basic criteria: the number of positions in the family, the age composition of the family, and the age-role content of the husband-father position (Hill, 1964: 191–192). In order to make the consequent family typology more universal, the third criterium may be modified to that of head of the household, and a fourth criterium of marital status may also be added. In the analysis of contemporary families, particularly with regard to change and family needs, there is no point in limiting our concept to an ideal type of nuclear family (see, for example, Trost, 1973).

From the point of view of the assumed basic input-output relationships between the family and society, the classification scheme of the stages of the family life cycle presented by Hill can be reduced to the following categories:

I.	Establishment	– newly married family without children
II.	New parents	– couples or one parent with one or more children under school age
III.	School-age family	– couples or one parent with school-age children
IV.	Post-parental family	– couples or one parent after children have left home and/or entered the productive sector. Also "middle aged" couples without children
V.	Aging family	– couples or parent after retirement.

The life-cycle approach focuses on the micro-changes that occur in the internal structure, organization and interaction of the family. This approach, however, can be combined to take into consideration also the family as a social system as it stands in relation to the larger totality of society. In a previous paper, a scheme for levels of analysis of the family within a larger social system context was outlined (Stolte-Heiskanen, 1974). These different levels of analysis may be viewed as roughly corresponding in structural terms to the context of the four basic societal functions of the family outlined above, and they can now be reformulated by taking into account the different stages of the life-cycle. From a systems frame of reference, these can also be considered as different subsystems of the family. At the same time the concepts of changing needs as a result of social structural and temporal developments can also be incorporated.

Family subsystems and family needs

In a very general sense, the *biological* functions of reproduction, survival and physical protection of family members may be defined as the *ecological* system level. This focuses on the demographic and morphological structure of the family as it stands in relationship with its environment. In this sense one can speak of the age and sex composition of the family, or from a societal aggregate point of view of the demographic structure of the population and the basic rates of natality, mortality, morbidity, and population movements. These rates, of course, correspond to the basic biological functions and processes occurring on the micro-level of the family. The term "ecological" rather than "demographic" is used to emphasize that also the spatial and temporal aspects of adaptation and interaction both within the family and in relation to its environment fall into this category.

From a strictly biological point of view the family functions related to the survival and physical protection of its members in general have lost much of their importance. New societal institutions, such as public health services and legal institutions have emerged to replace these functions. One important exception, however, remains in the case of very young children whose physical care and protection is still expected to be carried out within the family. Thus, from a developmental point of view many of these basic biological functions of reproduction and physical protection of family members are now concentrated in the first two stages of the life cycle. On the other hand, as a result of urbanization and industrialization the increased employment of mothers outside the home and the growing number of one-parent families have created new needs for arrangements for the physical welfare and protection of the young. These same needs become again important in the Aging family stage of the life cycle.

The post-urban era has also brought about major changes in the spatial and temporal aspects of family systems. As a result new needs have emerged concerning housing and the physical environment. Not only the functional aspects of housing and utilization of dwelling space, but also collective services, health conditions of the environment, transportation, etc., have created new needs that cannot be met entirely within the family. While obviously the need for housing is constant throughout the life span of the family, those aspects of physical planning that are related to the physical accessibility of place of work and other institutions and the working environment are most significant in the economically most active phases of the life-cycle.

The *economic* functions of the family can be located in the *structural* system. In this context the family is located in the societal stratification system that defines its role within the socio-economic organization of society and it stands in functional interrelationship as a unit of production and consumption. Within this subsystem are to be included the internal organization of the family, which includes the division of labor and defines the various roles and statuses and the variety of functions associated with them. From the life-cycle point of view, of course, most of the dynamics of family development concern the rearrangements within these internal structural configurations.

It is obviously in this subsystem that the most far-reaching changes have occurred as a consequence of broader social processes. In modern industrialized societies the family has changed from a primarily production unit to one of consumption. This, however, is not to under-estimate the remaining – and in class societies, perhaps the growing – importance of the family as a decisive agent in the reproduction and formation of future producers.

The fact that the family is increasingly becoming a unit of consumption makes the basic economic needs of the family now even more important. The necessity of maintaining and raising the material well-being as well as the purchasing power of families implies the most fundamental need for provisions for sufficient income from work. Closely connected with this fundamental need is the need for adequate and sufficiently secure working opportunities. These needs are of primary importance in the first four stages of the life cycle, while in the Aging family stage the needs connected with social security become most acute. The dominance of small, two-generational family systems no longer makes it possible for problems of old age, invalidity, sickness, and unemployment to be handled by the family alone, and creates needs for other institutions. As a consequence of the increased participation of women in the labor force new needs have also arisen for assistance to families where mothers are working outside the home.

As a result of the rapidly changing technological and economic basis of production, the possibilities of entering the productive sector are increasingly becoming dependent on occupational education. As such, the family's function of reproduction and formation of new producers has brought forth the need for instrumental skills required for productive participation in society. This need for provisions for education and re-education of family members in this technical-instrumental sense has become an economic necessity, particularly in the School-age family stage, and from the point of view of re-education, in the Post-parental family stage of the life cycle. The extent to which this need can be met may have far-reaching consequences for the location of the family in the stratification system and the general degree of inequality in society.

The *social* reproduction functions of the family can be located in the *cultural* subsystem that defines the superstructural elements of the family as well as society. In this context we can speak of the ideals, norms, and goals of the family and the sanctions and prescriptions associated with different roles and statuses. In terms of its interaction with society, via socialization, socio-cultural values, acceptable goals, norms concerning the allocation and distribution of resources and rewards, and rules regulating patterns of interaction, are transmitted via the family to the future generation. It is in this sense that the family, along with other socializing institutions of society, can be considered as an "ideological apparatus" of the state or society.

While the family has lost its function as an exclusive socializing agent, it still lays the basis for the acquisition of culture and values from other institutions of society. This has created new needs for the family to obtain information, knowledge and capacities to transmit these values. The cultural, educational, and recreational institutions and the mass media are some of the most important institutions that must be effectively linked to the family.

While obviously the socio-cultural needs of the family are present all through the life cycle, they are of greatest importance in the socializing phases of the life cycle, especially in the early stages before it is possible for the new generation to participate in competing institutions of socialization. However, also to be considered are the new needs connected with the active and constructive utilization of leisure time by the family as a whole and by its individual members, insofar as these activities are increasingly oriented outside the home. Cultural and recreational facilities, the channels for active participation in various voluntary organizations and communal life, fulfill some of these functions. These functions may again gain greater importance in the Aging family stage, when there is a greater amount of free time available while the ability to utilize the existing institutions has diminished.

The *socio-psychological* context of the family may be defined as corresponding to the *spiritual* functions of the family, and defines the affective-expressive components of family relations. This would include mechanisms that contribute to the emotional development, well-being, security and identification of the family members. In this context we can also speak of family cohesion or family solidarity.

It has often been observed that the emotional functions of the family have been gaining in importance as other instrumental functions have diminished. It is generally assumed that in face of the growing overall alienating effects of our industrial-technological civilization the family provides a haven of emotional security, identification, and a sense of purpose that shields and compensates the individual members from the impersonal institutions of the "outside world". One may, of course, raise the question whether the positive aspects of this function of the family may not have been unduly overemphasized at the expense of disregarding their over-individuating and isolating consequences. It does, however, point to the growing need of the family for space and time to be together, as well as for knowledge and information that promotes harmony within the family. Obviously these spiritual functions of the family are of equal importance throughout all phases of the life cycle, although they vary in content and consequent needs for different institutions that help to meet them.

Linkage mechanisms between family needs and societal institutions: social policy and social indicators

The above outline of different subsystems associated with basic family functions, their morphology throughout the life span and the concept of emergent family needs is more illustrative than systematic. Obviously, family needs will substantially vary with different types of socio-cultural structures, levels of societal development, within different social classes, and among different family forms and stages of the life cycle. The determination of these concrete variations is a matter of future empirical research for which this outline may be a starting point. The systematic empirical analysis and quantitative description of these needs and their development on an aggregate level is what would constitute one type of social indicators.

For the present purposes this analytic scheme serves to draw attention to the study of the kinds of societal inputs whose goals are to respond in some way to these needs that may or may not exist in society.

The detailed description of the structure and nature of the various societal institutions in different social systems would demand an elaborate model of society. This is hardly within the scope of this paper. One can, however, assume that in general terms social systems comprise economic, political and ideological institutions that concern the material and non-material resources and services of society and the distribution of these resources and services to different social groups. The existing mechanisms on an organized societal scale, the specific, concrete function of which is the allocation and administration of these resources and services and which determine the nature of their redistribution, may be defined as *social policy*. Thus, social policy in this context may be defined as the linkage mechanism which via societal inputs interrelates the family to society and its various institutions that function to fulfill the various family needs. As a linkage mechanism social policy can then be empirically studied in terms of its effectiveness for transmitting the existing institutional resources and in creating new resources and services in response to new needs. The quantitative empirical analysis and description of these inputs on an aggregate level constitutes another form of social indicators. Thus, social indicators as an empirical "bridging type concept" for the interaction between the family and society can be summarily illustrated by the scheme represented in Figure 2. Again, it must be emphasized that this scheme is illustrative, and it is not intended to be substantively comprehensive. Obviously temporal variations in the course of family development must be also systematically taken into account. Here they are only illustrated by indicating the primacy of these needs in different phases of the life cycle (in parenthesis).

Figure 2. *The position of social indicators between family and society*

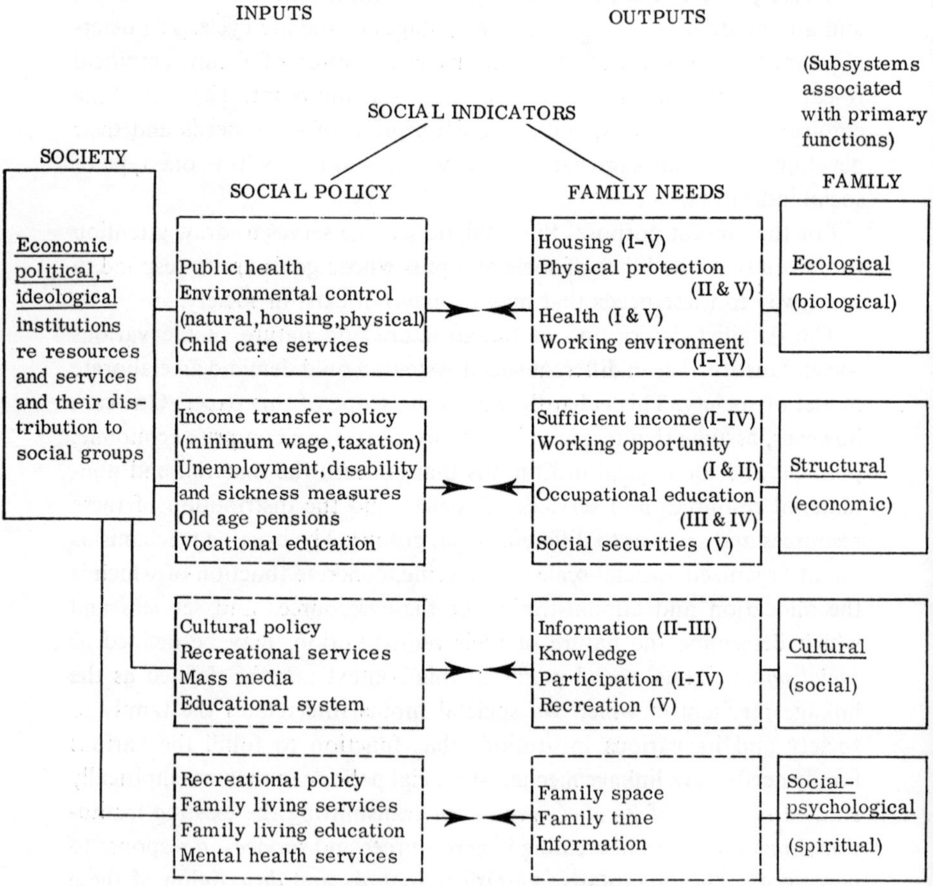

The conceptual scheme presented here is one potential approach to the systematic analysis of the interaction between the family and the larger societal totality. In concrete empirical research it can give a systematic description of the family and its interrelation with various societal institutions. The construction and analysis of the interrelationship between social indicators of social policy and social indicators of family needs can give a picture of the degrees of congruency between societal inputs and family needs. This could make the causal analysis of the sources of the gaps possible. Are the existing gaps between inputs and needs due to the absence of adequate societal institutions and/or the absence of effective linkage mechanisms? Or is the "inefficiency" of the linkage mechanisms due to the value system and the absence of adequate goals?

From the point of view of the family, this would also shed some light on the dynamics of contemporary family living. In the past the interaction between the family and societal institutions has been far too often studied only from the point of view of "problem families" and family pathology. The recognition of the fact that in modern societies the family is not an isolated social group can also shed light on the consequences for the functioning of "normal families" when some needs are or are not systematically met by society.

The present analysis has focused on only one aspect of the interrelationship between the family and the larger societal totality, namely on the societal inputs. Obviously, one must also go a step further and ask what are the consequences of the relationships between family needs and societal inputs on the basic functions of the family from the point of view of society. This, in turn, would demand a systematic analysis of family outputs in terms of its societal role in the reproduction of labor and as an ideological apparatus. This would not only give us a better understanding of the family but could also serve as a theoretical basis for the creation of a more realistic social policy.

RÉSUMÉ

Des indicateurs sociaux pour l'analyse des besoins familiaux reliés au cycle de la vie

L'intérêt généralement croissant pour les analyses macro-sociologiques se reflète aussi dans la sociologie de la famille par le souci croissant de l'établissement de concepts liant les phénomènes de niveau micro- et macroscopique.

Le présent article tente de déterminer un cadre conceptuel potentiel pour l'analyse des relations entre la famille et le système social. Les concepts de politique sociale ou indicateurs sociaux sont élaborés comme un "mécanisme de liaison" potentiel entre la famille et le système social. Les indicateurs sociaux sont conçus comme des mesures empiriques de l'impact de la société sur le sous-système familial qui reflètent soit des réponses rétroactives aux besoins changeants de la famille, soit visent à modifier la structure, la fonction, les buts, l'idéologie, etc. de la famille.

Les deux liaisons fonctionnelles fondamentales entre la famille et la société sont supposées être celles concernant 1) la reproduction du pouvoir du travail et 2) l'appareil idéologique de la société. Celles-ci peuvent être réduites, au niveau de la famille, aux fonctions universelles de reproduction biologique, économique, sociale et spirituelle. Ce cadre doit fournir une perspective historique permettant l'analyse des changements qui ont eu lieu dans ces fonctions en même temps que les développements historico-culturels plus larges, et à l'intérieur du cycle de la vie familiale.

Ces quatre fonctions fondamentales de la famille à tour de rôle peuvent être conceptualisées comme des sous-systèmes différents de la famille. En même temps, ceux-ci peuvent être analysés en relation avec les nouveaux besoins de la famille, en conséquence des changements sociaux, structuraux et temporels.

Les fonctions biologiques de la famille peuvent être définies comme la base écologique du système; les fonctions économiques comme le niveau structurel; les fonctions sociales comme le niveau culturel du système et la fonction spirituelle comme le niveau social et psychologique. Au sein de ce schéma conceptuel, les conséquences des changements sociaux plus importants pour les changements dans les besoins de la famille sont analysés à différentes étapes du cycle de la vie. Les étapes du cycle de vie peuvent être classées en utilisant le schéma modifié de Hill avec les étapes de formation du couple: jeunes parents, famille avec enfants d'âge scolaire, famille post-parentale et famille vieillissante.

Pour finir, les indicateurs sociaux et la nature de la politique sociale sont examinés dans leurs mécanismes de liaison entre famille et institutions sociales. La politique sociale est définie comme les mécanismes sociaux dont les fonctions concrètes spécifiques sont l'allocation, l'administration et la redistribution de ressources et services sociaux. Son efficacité à transmettre les ressources institutionnelles existantes et à créer de nouvelles ressources en réponse à de nouveaux besoins peut être étudiée empiriquement.

References

Aldous, J. (1972), "The developmental approach to family analysis", mimeo., Minneapolis.

Afanasjev, V. (1972), *The Scientific Management of Society*, Moscow, Progress Publishers.

Althusser, L. (1971), "Ideology and ideological state apparatuses", in *Lenin and Philosophy and Other Essays*, London, NLB: 123–173.

Aries, P. (1962), *Centuries of Childhood: A Social History of Family Life*, New York, Knopf.

Binderman, A. (1966), "Anticipatory studies and stand-by research capabilities" in R. Bauer (ed.), *Social Indicators*, Cambridge, Mass., M.I.T. Press.

Bosnjak, V. (1972), "Social policy, social development and the needs of the child and family", mimeo., paper presented at the IIIrd ICOFA Congress, Dubrovnik.

Duvall, E.M. (1971), *Family Development*, Philadelphia, J.B. Lippincott Co.

Girardeau, C. (1972), "Towards a system of social statistics", *Social Science Information*, XI, June: 189–202.

Gordon, M. (ed.) (1972), *The Nuclear Family in Crisis: The Search for an Alternative*, New York, Harper Row.

Gross, B.M. (1966), "The state of the nation: social system accounting" in R. Bauer (ed.), *Social Indicators*, Cambridge, Mass., M.I.T. Press: 154–271.

Hill R. (1964), "Methodological issues in family development research", *Family Process*, III, March: 186–205.

—— (1966), "Contemporary developments in family theory", *Journal of Marriage and the Family*, XXVIII/4.

—— (1971), "Modern systems theory and the family: a confrontation", *Social Science Information*, X, October: 7–26.

Land, K. (1971), "Les indicateurs sociaux aux Etats-Unis et en France", *Revue Française de Sociologie*, XII/4.

Litwak, E., and Figueira, J. (1970), "Technological innovation and ideal forms of family structure in an industrial democratic society" in R. Hill and R. König (eds.), *Families in East and West*, Paris-The Hague, Mouton: 348–396.

König, R. (1970), "Old problems and new queries in family sociology" in R. Hill and R. König (eds.), *Families in East and West*, Paris-The Hague, Mouton: 602–622.

Meszaros, I. (1971), *The Necessity of Social Control*, London, The Merlin Press.

Niitamo, O.E. (1972), "Sosiaali-indikaattoreista SEV-maissa", *Social Indicators in Socialist Countries.*, Kansantaloudellinen Aikakauskirja, 4: 353–363

Rodgers, R.H. (1973), *Family Interaction and Transaction. The Developmental Approach*, Englewood Cliffs, Prentice Hall.

Schonfield, A. and Shaw, S. (1972), *Social Indicators and Social Policy*, London, Heinemann.

Sennett, R. (1970), *Families against the City*, Cambridge, Mass., Harvard University Press.

Stolte-Heiskanen, V. (1972), "Contextual analysis and theory construction in cross-cultural family research", *Journal of Comparative Family Studies*, III, Spring: 33–49.

—— (1974), "Holistic *vs.* particularistic approaches to family policy", *Transactions of the ICOFA Seminar 3* (in print).

Trost, J. (1973), "The family life cycle. An impossible concept?", paper presented at the 13th International Seminar of the ISA Committee on Family Research, Paris.

Zapf, W. (1972), "Social indicators: prospects for social accounting system", *Social Science Information*, XI, June: 243–278.

Zienkovski, L. (1971), "Content and measurement of socio-economic development", *The Review of Income and Wealth*, 4.

8. The internal structure of the three-generation household

TAKEJI KAMIKO

The purpose of this paper is to analyze the internal structure of the Japanese stem-family household in one of its life-cycle stages. Indeed, the proportion of stem families in Japan has considerably decreased after World War II, but even as of 1970 roughly one-fourth of Japanese households are stem-family households (Yuzawa, 1973: 7). The average size of the stem family being larger than that of the nuclear family, the proportion of the population living in the stem family is expected to be considerably bigger than the above mentioned one-fourth.

The numerical importance of the stem family in Japan as compared with Western industrial countries and even with Eastern European countries is well attested to by the following proportions in several countries of old people aged 65 and over, living with their married children: more than 6 out of 10 married and approximately 7 out of 10 unmarried in Japan (Yuzawa, 1973: 151); 0.5 or less out of 10 married and less than 2 out of 10 unmarried in Western industrial countries (Denmark, U.S.A., and Britain); about 2 or 3 out of 10 married and about 4 out of 10 unmarried in Eastern European countries (Poland and Yugoslavia) (Shanas, 1973: 507).

Among occupations, by far the highest percentage of the stem family is found among farmers and the next highest among the self-employed, which is also the case with the European countries. (Baumert, 1954: 507; Rosenmeyer, 1968: 674; Rosenmeyer and Köckeis, 1963: 417–423).

The following pages cover the research we (T. Himeoka, K. Masuda, H. Mitsukawa, H. Tsuchida, A. Hasegawa, T. Mitsuyoshi, H. Oikawa, T. Nomura, H. Tokuoka, T. Kamiko) conducted on the inner structure of the intact three-generation household of contemporary Japan. By the term *intact three-generation household* is meant the household where parents, one of their married children, his (or her, but, as you will see, mostly his) spouse and child(ren) live in the same house. In some cases parents' unmarried child(ren) live with them.

The intact three-generation household, thus defined, is the stem family in the most characteristic stage of its life cycle. The life cycle of the stem family can be divided into three stages – the stage of the intact stem family which includes parents, their eldest married son, and his wife (the intact three-generation household occurs in this stage), the stage of the broken stem family which includes mother, her eldest married son, and his wife, and the stage of the ideologically stem, but morphologically nuclear, family, the period when the mother is dead and her eldest son's eldest son not yet married.

Method of the research

Four hundred twenty-five households in Osaka City and 99 households in three farm villages near Osaka City were studied. As to the urban sample, one-fifth of all the intact three-generation households inhabiting six wards of Osaka City were randomly selected. The six wards were so selected as to represent the whole city according to five criteria including population density, occupation of the inhabitants, number and size of business. The number of households thus selected amounted to 1,047. Concerning the rural sample, we tried to study all the intact three-generation farm households in the three villages, numbering 159.

The reduced number of households finally studied is due to several causes. The samples were selected from the civil register, and 18% of the urban and 13% of the rural sample turned out not to be the actual intact three-generation households, although they were indicated as such on the civil register. In many cases, actually, older and younger generations were living apart.

Seventeen percent of the urban and 8% of the rural sample refused to be interviewed; 24% of the urban and 17% of the rural sample could not be contacted because of absence, changed address, illness, etc.

The mother and her daughter-in-law (in a few cases her daughter) were interviewed separately. Some fifty questions were asked of the former and some sixty of the latter. The 425 urban and 99 rural households, mentioned previously, are the households whose mother and daughter-in-law (or daughter) we could interview successfully. The interview of the urban sample was carried out in June and August 1970 and that of the rural sample in March 1971.

Sample characteristics

The smallest number of members of the intact three-generation household is 5, and 73% of the urban and 85% of the rural sample comprise 6 or 7 members; 85% of city and 84% of village fathers are 65 years old or older; 85% of city and 89% of village mothers are 60 years old or older; 89% of city and 90% of village husbands, 90% of city and 88% of village wives are 26 to 45 years old.

The vast majority of the older generation (67% of city fathers, 89% of village fathers, 70% of city mothers, 81% of village mothers) have 9 years of school education or less, whereas the majority of the younger generation (83% of city husbands, 56% of village husbands, 74% of city wives, 64% of village wives) have 10 or more years of school education.

Ninety-five percent of fathers and mothers of both city and village are healthy on the whole. Only 1.4% of city fathers and 0.5% of city mothers are bedridden.

The married child living with parents is, in most cases (in 84% of urban and 76% of rural cases) the eldest son or his surrogate (later-born son who is the oldest of the living sons).

Table 1. *Sex and birth order of the married child living with parents* (%)

	First-born son	Later-born son	First-born daughter	Later-born son where first-born is dead	Other	Total	N
Urban	64.2	9.4	2.4	19.5	4.5	100	425
Rural	73.8	11.1	9.1	2.0	4.0	100	99

In most cases (89% of urban and 76% of rural cases) the two couples have been living together without interruption since the marriage of the younger couple.

Research findings

The data accumulated by our research have been and are still being analyzed in various ways by my colleagues and me. Here, only a part of the findings obtained until now, which will give a general, bird's-eye view of the life lived by the three-generation household of contemporary Japan, will be described. The findings will be expounded under two major headings: (1) inner structure of the three-generation household, (2) life-cycle stages of the two-couple household.

1. Inner structure of the three-generation household

a) Housing arrangements

The most remarkable thing we know from Table 2 is the degree to which, both in the city and in the village, main living facilities are shared by the two generation couples. Almost none of older rural couples have their own kitchen, bath, toilet, and entrance, and only 6% of them have their own living room. The picture is not very different for older urban couples, although 21% of them have their own living room, and 10% and 12% of them their own kitchen and toilet, respectively. This fact suggests that the communality of living of older and younger generation couples is of a very high degree.

Table 2. *Living facilities for the exclusive use of older people* (%)

	Kitchen		Living room		Bath		Toilet		Entrance		T.V.	
	U	R	U	R	U	R	U	R	U	R	U	R
Absent	89.7	98.0	78.8	92.9	97.2	99.0	87.5	96.0	91.8	99.0	58.9	82.8
Present	10.2	0.0	21.0	6.1	2.4	0.0	12.0	3.0	8.0	0.0	40.9	16.2
Unknown	0.2	2.0	0.2	1.0	0.5	1.0	0.5	1.0	0.2	1.0	0.2	1.0
Total	100	100	100	100	100	100	100	100	100	100	100	100
N	425	99	425	99	425	99	425	99	425	99	425	99

U = urban; R = rural

b) Communality of daily living

The high degree of communality of living suggested by the housing arrangements is abundantly confirmed by the answers of the respondents to the questions concerning their daily living.

In nearly all the sample households (89% of the urban and 100% of the rural sample) cooking is almost always done for the entire household, and in almost as many households (84% of the urban and 99% of the rural sample) the entire household eats together (Table 3). This is in strong contrast to the finding by Blume (1962: 55) that in Cologne 42% of married couples aged 65 and over living with their children cooked only for themselves.

Table 3. *Communality of dining and cooking* (%)

	Yes			No					
	Always	Almost always	Sometimes	Seldom	Never	Other	Unknown	Total	N
Eat together									
Urban	78.4	5.2	2.6	1.4	11.5	0.7	0.2	100	425
Rural	98.0	1.0	0.0	0.0	0.0	1.0	0.0	100	99
Cooking done for the entire household									
Urban	85.9	3.1	0.5	0.9	8.7	0.7	0.2	100	425
Rural	97.0	3.0	0.0	0.0	0.0	0.0	0.0	100	99

In a very small proportion of urban, and almost no rural, households, the two generation couples execute their main household tasks separately, as can be seen in Table 4.

Table 4. *Percentage of households where older and younger couples do household tasks separately*

	Shopping	Dishwashing	Sweeping	Laundering	N
Urban	13.4	13.4	28.9	27.3	425
Rural	1.0	1.0	8.1	4.0	99

A measure of the communality of living was devised. Scores 1, 2, 3, 4, and 5, respectively, were given to the answers Yes, always; Yes, almost always; Yes, sometimes; No, seldom; No, never, to the following five questions: Is the cooking done for the entire household? Do the older and younger couple eat together? Do older and younger couples treat each other's guests undiscriminatingly? Do older and younger couples know each other's friends and the destinations of the outings of each other? Do older and younger couples take care of the entire house in each other's absence?

Table 5 shows the percentages of urban and rural sample households which got the average score of 1 through 5. The average score was calculated by adding up the scores given to the answers to the five questions and dividing the sum by the number of questions. Table 5 clearly shows that communality of living of older and younger couples is exceedingly high. Eighty-six percent of the urban and 98% of the rural samples share, to a very high degree, the five important aspects of daily living. Incidentally, the above-mentioned five questions were asked the mothers.

Table 5. *Degree of communality of living* (%)

Average score	1	2	3	4	5	Unknown	Total	N
Urban	47.1	38.4	7.3	6.1	0.5	0.7	100	425
Rural	60.6	37.4	2.0	0.0	0.0	0.0	100	99

The high degree of communality of living of the two generation couples was again confirmed by the responses to the question asked the mothers: Do you feel you and the younger couple share a single home? As Table 6 shows, 85% of urban and 95% of rural mothers feel that the two generation couples perfectly or almost perfectly share a single home, and no more than 7% of urban and 1% of rural mothers feel that the two generation couples are completely or almost completely living as two different families.

Table 6. *The feeling of sharing a single home* (%)

	The two couples share a single home		↔	Live as two different families				
	1	2	3	4	5	Unknown	Total	N
Urban	70.4	14.8	7.3	3.5	3.5	0.5	100	425
Rural	80.8	14.1	3.0	1.0	0.0	1.0	100	99

c) Livelihood

In four out of five urban households and in almost all (97 out of 99) rural households, the earnings of household members are pooled, and the whole sum is treated as the household income, being managed and expended on a completely communal basis (Table 7). Indeed, in the case of farm households and that of the self-employed, the whole or the predominant part of the income comes from the household enterprise and is not attributable to individual household members. This fact also highlights the degree of communality obtaining in the three-generation family household.

Table 7. *Communality of the management of livelihood* (%)

	Communal	Partly separate	Completely separate	Unknown	Total	N
Urban	80.0	9.4	10.4	0.2	100	425
Rural	98.0	2.0	0.0	0.0	100	99

Table 8 shows the percentages of the separate responses to the question asked the young wife of the household: What is the proportion to which each generation couple contributes to the household purse? The question is admittedly unsuitable to the farm household or to the household of the self-employed because, as was pointed out above, their income is not an aggregate of individual member's earnings but comes from the household business in one piece. But a sizable number of respondents of the farm households and those of the self-employed seem to have answered the question by interpreting it to mean: What is the relative contribution of each generation couple to the household enterprise? Still, remarkably enough, 37% of farm respondents answered that the individual contribution to the household purse of each generation couple is unknowable.

Table 8. *Contribution to the household purse* (%)

	Older couple all or most	Each couple fifty-fifty	Younger couple all or most	The whole house-hold	Other	Unknown	Total	N
Urban	20.5	16.9	45.9	—	11.5	5.2	100	425
Rural	12.1	6.1	40.4	37.4	3.0	1.0	100	99

d) Power structure

Of the several questions we asked the younger wife to probe the power structure of the household, the following four might be of cross-cultural applicability: Which of the two couples takes care of money matters for the entire household? Who represents the household on formal occasions, for example, when formally associating with kinsmen? Who finally makes major household decisions when there is difference of opinion among household members? What is the ratio of power between older and younger couples in daily household decision-making? Tables 9–12 show the percentages of several responses to the above questions.

These tables show that the locus of power presiding over the household is not identical for all the sample households. Older as well as younger couples, or fathers as well as husbands, occupy the position of the actual household head in a sizable proportion of the households. Evidently the seniority or the relative age is not the only determinant of the power

Table 9. *Which couple controls household money matters?* (%)

	Older couple	Younger couple	Indeterminate	Half/half	Separately	Other/unknown	Total	N
Urban	37.2	38.8	5.7	2.6	8.0	7.8	100	425
Rural	41.4	48.5	5.1	1.0	0.0	4.0	100	99

Table 10. *Who represents the household?* (%)

	Father	Husband	Separately	Other/unknown	Total	N
Urban	62.6	19.5	8.0	9.9	100	425
Rural	44.4	37.4	8.1	10.1	100	99

Table 11. *Who makes final decisions?* (%)

	Father	Mother	Husband	Wife	Separately	Other/unknown	Total	N
Urban	50.4	8.5	33.7	1.9	4.9	12.2	100	425
Rural	38.4	2.0	44.4	4.0	4.0	7.1	100	99

Table 12. *Power ratio of the two couples* (%)

Older : Younger	Urban	Rural
0 : 10	5.4	7.1
1–2 : 9–8	5.4	6.0
3–4 : 7–6	13.0	23.3
5 : 5	42.1	28.3
6–7 : 4–3	24.5	23.2
8–10 : 2–0	5.5	8.1
Other/unknown	4.2	4.0
Total	100	100
N	425	99

structure within the household. The problem of the correlates of the household power structure will be dealt with later in the second section of the research findings when we deal with the problem of the life-cycle stages of the three-generation household.

e) Affective relationship between generations

Two clusters of questions were utilized to measure the affective relationship between older and younger couples. One cluster, asked of mothers, is composed of the following six questions: Do you think that the younger couple takes good care of you and your spouse in everything? Do you think you, your spouse, and the younger couple converse on anything without reserve? Do you think you, your spouse, and the younger couple discuss with each other freely, when deciding important household affairs? Do you feel you and your spouse often differ in opinion from the younger couple? Are you and your spouse happy to have been able to live under the same roof with the younger couple? Do you feel that you, your spouse, and the younger couple live without restraint among you?

The other cluster of questions, asked of the young wife, try to probe the conflict between the two couples. They concern the frequency of conflict, who disagrees with whom, who gives way, etc.

Table 13 summarizes the responses of the older wives to the first cluster of questions. The average score was calculated by adding up the scores given to several answers to the six questions and dividing the sum by the number of questions. Scores 1 through 5 were given, respectively, to answers: Yes, always; Yes, almost always; Average, or Don't know; No, seldom; No, never. As for the fourth question, the scores were given in the reverse order. The percentages in Table 13 are those of the older wives who got the several average scores.

Table 13, which tells us that most (82% of urban and 86% of rural) older wives are completely or almost completely satisfied with the affective relationship and with the degree of mutual communication they have with younger couples, suggests that the two generation couples are living literally as a single family in the affective or expressive sphere of life as well.

Table 13. *Affective relationship between the two generation couples* (%)

Average score	1	2	3	4	5	Unknown	Total	N
Urban	14.8	66.8	16.7	1.4	0.2	0.0	100	425
Rural	50.5	35.5	12.1	1.0	0.0	1.0	100	99

Of course this fact does not preclude the existence of conflicts within the household between older and younger couples. As we see in Table 14, approximately one-third of both urban and rural younger wives admitted that conflicts occurred frequently or sometimes between older and younger couples. But the remaining two-thirds answered that there were few or no conflicts between the two couples. Conflicts occurred most frequently between older and younger wives and next most frequently between older and younger husbands among the urban sample, and most frequently between older and younger husbands and next most frequently between older and younger wives among the rural sample.

Table 14. *Are there conflicts between older and younger couples?* (%)

	Yes		No				
	Frequently	Sometimes	Seldom	Never	Unknown	Total	N
Urban	5.8	29.9	45.9	18.4	0.7	100	425
Rural	3.0	30.3	48.5	17.1	1.0	100	99

The findings, thus far reported, sufficiently prove that the two generation couples of the sample households are leading an essentially communal life, are living essentially as a single family. They cook and eat together, share household tasks, pool the incomes and consume them together as a unit, and have the feeling that they are living as a single family.

f) Rural-urban differences

The general conclusion of the preceding section that older and younger couples in the three-generation household live essentially as a single family is, on the whole, valid for the urban as well as the rural sample. Still, there are some differences not to be overlooked between the two samples.

The difference most abundantly evidenced by our research is concerned with the communality of living between the two generation couples within the household. Far more urban older couples than their rural counterparts have their own kitchens, living rooms, toilets, and T.V. sets (Table 2). While there are absolutely no farm households where the two couples do not pool their incomes and each of them manages its own money matters, slightly more than one-tenth of the urban sample are such households. Moreover, there are nearly one-tenth urban households where each of the two couples partly controls its own purse, while there are only two such households out of 99 farm households (Table 7).

In significantly more urban households than rural ones, the two couples do not share household tasks. In nearly one-tenth of urban households, each of the two couples always or almost always cooks its own meals, and in 13% of urban households each of the two couples eats alone, while there are no such households among rural sample (Table 3). Each of the two couples does its own shopping and dish-washing in 13% of the urban sample but only in 1% of the rural sample. Each couple does its own sweeping in 29% of the urban, but only in 8% of the rural sample and does its own laundering in 27% of the urban, but in no more than 4% of rural, sample (Table 14).

Concerning the measure of communal living described previously, far more urban households (14%) as compared with the rural sample (2%) got the score indicating lower degree of communal living (Table 5).

Reflecting the above mentioned rural-urban differences in the degree of communal living, and as we have already seen, a significantly larger proportion (7%) of older urban wives as compared with older rural wives (1%) feels that the two couples are living completely or almost completely as two different families (Table 6).

A second clear-cut rural-urban difference concerns the actual history of, and the attitudes towards the co-residence of two generation couples. First, as to the history of co-residence, a good deal more younger urban couples (11%) than younger rural couples (2%) have had the experience of living in their own houses apart from their parents.

Concerning the attitudes towards co-residence, considerably more younger rural wives (60%) than urban ones (40%) wish to live under the same roof with one of their children even after the child gets married.

Asked whether they preferred a son or a daughter to live with – a purely hypothetical question, because the question was asked irrespective of the sex of the child(ren) of the respondents – one out of four of younger urban wives, but only one out of ten rural ones, answered that the co-residence is undesirable and to be avoided. Far more younger rural wives (51%) than urban ones (24%) preferred a son and more younger urban wives (15%) than rural ones (9%) preferred a daughter.

The two groups of rural-urban differences, which were described above, one group concerning the communality of living and the other the co-residence of the two generation couples, allow us to infer: (1) that some 10% of our urban sample are really a composite of two independent nuclear families, each accounting for its own cost of living and performing its own expressive as well as instrumental family activities, and another

10% are a composite of two semi-independent nuclear families, while almost every household of our rural sample is actually living as one single family; (2) that the two kinds of urban households just mentioned, a composite of two independent nuclear families and a composite of two semi-independent nuclear families, are just the two stepping-stones in the process of nuclearization of the Japanese family, namely, the transformation from the stem family to the nuclear family. The two couples in those urban households, especially the younger couple, seem to live in the two-couple household chiefly because they cannot afford to live in two separate houses. According to the data we collected, those couples are mostly the poorest ones among our sample.

A third and final rural-urban difference concerns the power structure within the household. Consistently more younger rural couples or husbands than urban ones control the household purse (Table 9), represent the entire household on formal occasions (Table 10), and make final decisions over major household affairs (Table 11). A good deal more younger rural couples (36%) than urban ones (24%) have dominant power within the household (Table 12).

These findings contradict the widespread notion that the rural family is more traditional than the urban family. The traditional Japanese family is conceived as the stem family where parents, their eldest son, his wife and children lead a completely communal life and where the father presides over the entire household as a patriarch.

The findings, previously expounded, concerning the rural-urban differences in the communality of living and in the actual history of, and the attitude toward, the co-residence of the two generation couples, confirm the view that the rural family is more traditional than the urban family. But the findings concerning the rural-urban difference in power structure flatly contradict that popular notion.

One might be tempted to compare the age composition of the rural and the urban sample in search of an explanation for the unexpected finding that more younger rural couples than urban ones have dominant power in the household. But there is no significant difference between the age composition of the rural and the urban sample.

One plausible hypothesis would be that the above mentioned rural-urban difference in the household power structure is the effect of the rural-urban difference in the nature of employment. In farming, which is, first of all, manual labor, the older couple's contribution to production or income earning declines more rapidly than in the case of urban occupations. This fact might well explain the lesser power within the household of the older rural couple as compared with that of the older urban couple.

2. Life-cycle stages of the two-couple household

As we have seen, the period of two couples living together under the same roof constitutes one stage, the most characteristic stage in the life cycle of the stem family. Our findings about the power structure in the sample households suggest that this stage can be divided into two sub-stages, the stage in which the older couple maintains leadership and the stage in which the younger couple has replaced the older as leaders.

Judging from Tables 9, 11, and 12, approximately as many older couples as younger ones occupy the position of leaders in the household. This does not mean that, in approximately half of our sample households, the older couple continues to maintain leadership until their deaths and in nearly as many households the younger couple occupies the position of power from the beginning to the end of the co-residence. Table 15 through Table 19 make it quite clear that, as the older couple advances in age, its power is gradually yielded to the younger couple.

Table 15. *Which couple controls household money matters?* (%)

	Age of husband					Age of father				
	–30	–35	–40	–45	46–	–60	–65	–70	–75	76–
Urban sample										
Older couple	62	51	33	18	20	66	43	35	30	25
Younger couple	26	25	49	55	68	14	41	42	45	63
Other responses	12	24	18	27	12	20	16	23	25	12
Total	100	100	100	100	100	100	100	100	100	100
N	66	112	123	60	40	58	109	109	69	56
Rural sample										
Older couple	72	60	32	18	11	100	88	81	46	14
Younger couple	11	32	64	76	78	0	13	19	54	86
Other responses	17	8	4	6	11	0	0	0	0	0
Total	100	100	100	100	100	100	100	100	100	100
N	18	25	28	17	9	16	24	32	13	14

Table 16. *Who makes final decisions?* (%)

	Age of husband					Age of father				
	–30	–35	–40	–45	46–	–60	–65	–70	–75	76–
Urban sample										
Father	71	48	43	31	21	66	46	47	41	22
Husband	13	22	35	43	51	12	26	30	38	52
Other responses	16	30	22	26	28	22	28	23	21	26
Total	100	100	100	100	100	100	100	100	100	100
N	75	139	148	68	43	68	131	135	76	60
Rural sample										
Father	67	52	29	17	20	81	42	38	23	0
Husband	17	32	39	78	80	13	29	41	69	93
Other responses	17	16	32	6	0	6	29	22	8	7
Total	100	100	100	100	100	100	100	100	100	100
N	18	25	28	18	10	16	24	32	13	14

Table 17. *Power ratio of the two couples* (%)

	Age of husband					Age of father				
Older : Younger	–30	–35	–40	–45	46–	–60	–65	–70	–75	76–
Urban sample										
0–2 : 10–8	8	6	9	16	25	5	12	7	14	18
3–4 : 7–6	7	5	19	22	15	5	11	14	14	23
5 : 5	41	55	38	32	35	42	42	49	38	34
6–7 : 4–3	34	22	23	25	20	39	26	18	25	18
8–10 : 2–0	6	8	6	3	0	5	7	8	1	4
Other responses	4	4	6	2	5	5	3	4	7	4
Total	100	100	100	100	100	100	100	100	100	100
N	73	120	127	63	40	64	117	115	71	56
Rural sample										
0–2 : 10–8	0	17	18	6	30	15	0	13	8	43
3–4 : 7–6	6	13	32	41	30	8	17	19	46	43
5 : 5	33	29	21	41	20	23	52	28	15	14
6–7 : 4–3	39	29	21	12	10	38	26	28	23	0
8–10 : 2–0	17	13	4	0	10	15	0	9	8	0
Other responses	6	0	4	0	0	0	4	3	0	0
Total	100	100	100	100	100	100	100	100	100	100
N	18	24	28	17	10	13	23	32	13	14

Table 18. *Who represents the household?* (%)

	Age of husband					Age of father				
	–30	–35	–40	–45	46–	–60	–65	–70	–75	76–
Urban sample										
Father	86	71	65	43	24	86	71	64	56	25
Husband	4	9	21	38	44	5	10	17	30	50
Other responses	10	20	14	19	32	9	19	19	14	25
Total	100	100	100	100	100	100	100	100	100	100
N	72	119	127	63	41	64	116	115	71	56
Rural sample										
Father	78	67	43	6	10	81	54	48	23	0
Husband	6	21	39	67	80	6	29	26	69	86
Other responses	17	13	18	28	10	13	17	26	8	14
Total	100	100	100	100	100	100	100	100	100	100
N	18	24	28	18	10	16	24	31	13	14

Table 19. *Who is the formal household head?* (%)

	Age of husband					Age of father				
	–30	–35	–40	–45	46–	–60	–65	–70	–75	76–
Urban sample										
Father	86	83	67	62	39	86	78	70	65	52
Husband	6	12	30	35	59	5	17	27	31	46
Other responses	8	6	3	3	2	9	5	3	4	2
Total	100	100	100	100	100	100	100	100	100	100
N	72	120	127	63	41	64	117	115	71	56
Rural sample										
Father	100	80	75	50	30	100	88	81	46	14
Husband	0	20	25	50	70	0	13	19	54	86
Other responses	0	0	0	0	0	0	0	0	0	0
Total	100	100	100	100	100	100	100	100	100	100
N	18	25	28	18	10	16	24	32	13	14

The demarcation of the two substages is not very easy. First, there is no definite norm regulating at what age or on what occasion older couples transfer the leadership to the younger. At one extreme an older couple may transfer the leadership to the younger at the time of the latter's marriage, at the beginning of the co-residence, and, at the other extreme, the transfer may not take place until the father's death, namely, until the end of the co-residence. In most households, however, the transfer takes place some time in between, but the time and occasion vary among households.

Secondly, the transfer does not take place once and for all. Leadership in the household has various aspects, as is indicated by the headings of Tables 15 through 19, and, as those tables show, leadership in some aspects is transferred later than leadership in other aspects. The tables tell us that the transfer of the management of household money matters from the older to the younger couple takes place earliest, the transfer of the power of making final decisions next, and the transfer of the roles of formally representing the household and of being the formal household head takes place still later.

It is in order here to make clear what is meant by formal household head. Every city or town in Japan has its register of inhabitants. In the register, inhabitants are grouped in households. The name, sex, date and place of birth, kinship relationship with other household members, etc., of the individual household member are registered. The person who heads the list of household members and who is the base of reckoning their kinship relationship is what is meant here by formal household head. The formal household head coincides mostly, but not always, with the actual household leader. A considerable number of sons continue to acknowledge their father as formal household head long after they have replaced him as the actual household leader.

The demarcation of the substages is difficult, but it is not impossible. Of the four aspects of household leadership, namely, management of household money matters, making final decisions, representing the household, and being the formal household head, the former two can be regarded as exercises of actual leadership and the latter two as aspects of honorary leadership. Granting this, we may set the time of the transfer of household leadership at the time when the older couple has retired, sometimes with reluctance, from the roles of managing household money matters and of making final household decisions and has yielded them to the younger. We can estimate, from Tables 15 through 17, the approximate ages of father and son at the time of the transfer of household leadership.

The transfer of the above-mentioned two roles as well as the leadership as a whole is indeed a gradual and prolonged process. But, in the majority of urban cases, the transfer, as defined above, seems to be completed by the time the father is a few years older than seventy and the son a few years younger than forty, and in the majority of rural cases a few years earlier.

Correlates of the relative power of older and younger couples were searched for. In addition to age, which we have seen to be highly correlated with the relative power, economic resources, physical health, occupation, school achievement, kinship relations between older and younger couples, etc., were found to be significantly correlated with the relative power of the two couples.

Some of these correlates, e.g., school achievement and kinship relationship, cannot be utilized to account for the transfer of household leadership, for they do not change with time, while the transfer of leadership implies change of relative power.

Economic resources and physical health do change with the passage of time. Earning power, and consequently contribution to the household purse, and physical health of the older couple decline with the passage of time. The degree to which the relative power of the two couples changes in accordance with the change of the relative contribution of the two couples to the household purse and with the decline of health of the older couple is well borne out by our data. I presume, therefore, that the most potent factors determining the transfer of household leadership are the decrease of earning power and the decline of health of the older couple, specifically of the older husband.

Résumé

La structure interne du ménage comprenant 3 générations

Cet article est fondé sur l'étude faite sur la structure interne des ménages à 3 générations, dans le Japon contemporain.

On a interviewé successivement 425 ménages comprenant 3 générations intactes à Osaka, une ville de 3 millions d'habitants et 99 ménages paysans à 3 générations intactes, près d'Osaka. L'expression "ménages à 3 générations intactes" s'applique aux ménages dans lesquels les parents, un de leurs enfants marié, son épouse et ses enfants vivent sous un seul et même toit.

On a interviewé des mères et leurs belles-filles.

Furent examinés d'abord l'aménagement du logement, le partage des tâches ménagères, les moyens d'existence, la structure du pouvoir à l'intérieur de la famille, enfin les relations affectives au sein de la famille avec une attention particulière pour la relation entre les 2 couples.

Les résultats ont montré que dans la grande majorité des cas urbains et dans presque tous les cas ruraux, les 2 couples constituaient un ménage entier. Incidemment, ce fait semble avoir un lien avec le problème de l'universalité ou de la non-universalité de la famille conjugale.

La seconde partie des résultats relatés dans cet article traite des différences entre ville et campagne. Trois différences majeures apparaissent. D'abord, quoique la vie communautaire entre les 2 couples à l'intérieur de la famille soit, dans pratiquement tout l'échantillon rural, presque parfait, objectivement et subjectivement, dans quelque 10% des familles urbaines la communauté de vie entre les couples des 2 générations est très réduite.

La seconde différence entre la ville et la campagne réside dans le fait qu'une grande partie de couples urbains plus jeunes (11%) comparés aux couples ruraux (2%) ont fait l'expérience d'une vie sous leur propre toit, séparés de leurs parents. De la même façon, davantage de jeunes couples ruraux (60%) comparés aux couples urbains (40%) souhaitent vivre sous le même toit qu'un de leurs enfants même après le mariage de celui-ci.

La troisième et dernière différence ville-campagne concerne la structure du pouvoir, à l'intérieur de la famille. Dans les familles rurales plus que dans les familles urbaines, les couples plus jeunes, ou les maris, avaient le pouvoir de décision sur les affaires de la famille.

La dernière partie de l'article est consacrée à délimiter les sous-cycles à l'intérieur de l'étape de cohabitation des 2 couples. Cette étape peut être divisée en 2: (1) période au cours de laquelle le père est le chef du ménage, (2) celle au cours de laquelle le fils en est le chef. Selon les données recueillies au cours de notre recherche, le transfert de direction du ménage est achevé dans la majorité des cas urbains, lorsque le père a dépassé 70 ans et que le fils a un peu moins de 40 ans; dans la majorité des cas ruraux, quelques années plus tôt.

References

Baumert, G. (1954), *Deutsche Familien nach dem Kriege*, Darmstadt, Eduard Roether.

Blume, O. (1962), *Alte Menschen in einer Grossstadt*, Göttingen, Schwartz.

Rosenmeyer, L. (1968), "Family relations of the elderly", *Journal of Marriage and the Family*, XXX/4.

Rosenmeyer, L., and Köckeis, E. (1963), "Propositions for a sociological theory of aging and the family", *International Social Science Journal*, XV/3.

Shanas, E. (1973), "Family-kin networks and aging in cross-cultural perspective", *Journal of Marriage and the Family*, XXXV/3.

Yuzawa, Y. (1973), *Zusetsu: Kazokumondai*, Tokyo, Nippon-Hosokyokai.

9. Construction of the life cycle of the family. Some remarks on the availability of information

W. A. DUMON and R. M. D'HERTEFELT-BRUYNOOGHE

Hill (1964: 189) makes a clear distinction between family development studies at the descriptive and at the analytical level. The descriptive studies "place their emphasis less on *what* the behavior is than on *when* it occurs, more on the timing and sequences of family behavior, than on the content of behavior alone". Studies on the composition of family life cycles certainly can be classified under these descriptive studies. The clear-cut differentiation between descriptive and analytical studies may serve as an appropriate tool for categorization and classification purposes and even for developing and stimulating different methods and techniques of investigation.

The results obtained by both methods do not merely supplement each other, but studies on one level may have direct bearing on studies on the other level. Hill, for instance (1964: 189–190), suggests that empirical studies will lead to refinement of the definition of stages of development, which may have a bearing on the predictability of family behavior. To this might be added that, in case changes do occur, even merely in the length of one or more stages of the life cycle, it could be hypothesized that these changes themselves might affect the behavior within this life cycle (in terms of role theory, anticipatory behavior might increase or decrease according to the expectation of the time lapse before which the role will be performed). Put differently, changes in the composition of the life cycle (which might be revealed by studies on a descriptive level) may have quite some bearing on the behavior within the different stages (which might be revealed by studies on an analytical level).

The composition of the life cycle of the family, therefore, is not only a matter of concern for students of population but also for students of the family.

Table 1. *Selected studies on family life-cycle composition*

Year and nature of source		Author	Information area covered	Years concerned	Source of information	Ref.
(a)	(b)	(c)	(d)	(e)	(f)	(g)
(1946)S	1947 S	P.C. Glick	U.S.A.	SY (1890 + 1940)	Census + VS	(1)
(1954)D	1955 S	*Id.*	*Id.*	SY (*id.* + 1950 + 1952)	*Id.*	(2)
(1959)—	1962 S	*Id.* & others	*Id.*	SY (*id.* + 1959 + 1980)	*Id.*	(3)
—	1963 S	A. Collver	India (Banares)	SY (1956)	Survey	(4)
—	1963 D	P.R. Uhlenberg	U.S.A. (Massachusetts)	Co (1830/1920)	Census	(5)
—	1965 D	P.C. Glick & R. Park	U.S.A.	Co (1880/1890–1930/1939)	Census + VS	(6)
(1966)S	1967 S	K. Morioka	Japan	SY (1950 + 1960)	Census + VS	(7)
(1973)D	—	C. Young	Australia	Co (1910/24)	Survey	(8)

Notes: (a) The year between brackets indicates the year in which the study originally was presented. As to the nature of the source, *S* stands for Sociology, *D* for Demography.
(b) The years without brackets indicate the date of publication.
(e) *SY* stands for Selected Years, *Co* for Cohort.
(f) *VS* stands for Vital Statistics.
(g) See References for full information on material in this table, p. 186.

Table 1 gives some evidence which might suggest that the editing policy of scholarly journals goes along the same lines. Indeed, contributions with similar or comparable content, even by the same author, are published in journals on population as well as on sociology of the family. So, this paper will be limited to some remarks of a technical nature on the composition of the life cycle of the family.

Availability of information

Table 1 reveals that the studies have changed in the course of time with respect to the method employed. Before Glick's paper on new approaches (1965), information referred more to given points in time than to composed birth cohorts. This is rather important because information on given points in time coincides with the construction of a synchronic life-cycle composition, whereas the ability to work with birth cohorts coincides with the construction of a longitudinal type of life cycle. Survey data and census data allow cohort analysis because they give information on relevant characteristics of a circumscribed population at a given moment. Vital statistics, as published, on the contrary give information on events that did occur over a given span of time (usually one year). Therefore information obtained from vital statistics only allows the presentation of data of different nature relating to different cohorts but occurring at the same moment or at the same time span. The composition of family life cycles based on information from vital statistics, i.e., cross-sectional data, results in a synthetic pattern or a family life cycle of synchronic type.

Table 1 reveals that information obtained from census data and vital statistics relate to a whole nation, whereas survey data, not only due to the very nature of the survey but also due to other factors, only apply to particular regions or particular groups within a society. Moreover, information obtained from census and vital statistics enables us to go back in history (retrospective studies) and to look forward (prospective studies), whereas with survey research the number of cohorts studied is more restricted, yielding information on more current situations.

Making a distinction between the period of reference and the period in which the information became available results in the conclusion that the census is or can be a better source of information than survey research (as far as construction of life cycles is concerned). The information available on the U.S.A., both as to length of period of reference as well as to the levels of available information, excels available information on any other nation. The information is based mainly on census data and partly on vital statistics. Survey data on other nations, therefore, give the impression of substituting for census data.

Availability of material for constructing the life cycle (Belgium as an example)

The information necessary for the construction of a family life cycle depends on two of its characteristics: (a) the starting point of the life cycle; (b) the different stages to be distinguished within the life cycle. Since marriage is considered as the beginning of a new family (family of procreation), marriage generally is taken as the reference point for the start of the family cycle. From Glick (1947) to Young (1973), moment of marriage has been taken as the starting point of the family life cycle. The Belgian family life cycle as constructed here (Figure 1) respects this rule. Yet, certain objections can be formulated against taking the wedding ceremony as a starting point of the family life cycle. Using a developmental frame of reference implies that the family is referred to as an immanent developing system. It cannot be excluded *a priori* that the family development started before the formal wedding ceremony. In societies in which one or more processes such as pre-marital pregnancy, trial marriage, consensual union (or even separate living arrangements for late adolescents or older children) frequently occur, the wedding day is a poor point of reference to be used as the beginning of the family cycle.

As far as the number of stages is concerned and the criteria along which these stages are built up, ever since Duvall (1957) the developmental stages through which the first or oldest child went were taken as reference points for the different stages of the life cycle of the family. Rodgers (1962), however, took into account the developmental phases of the youngest child as well. Hill (1964) recognizes three sets of data for differentiating stages of the family life span: (a) numbers of positions in the family; (b) age composition of the family; (c) employment status of the husband/father. Hill adds to this that the scheme that has been constructed on these three sets of criteria has advantages and disadvantages. He states "Employing these three sets of readily available data" (1964: 94), "the scheme above has the advantage of simplicity in that it draws from data easily available" (1964: 192). The emphasis put

Table 2. *Information necessary to construct a family life cycle*

Husband/wife (parents)				Children	
Age at		Duration of marriage at			
(1) First marriage	(AFM)				
(2) Birth first child	(ABF)	(3) Birth first child	(DBF)		
				(4) Number of children	(TNC)
(5) Birth last child	(ABL)	(6) Birth last child	(DBL)	(7) Time interval between first and last child	(INT)
(8) Marriage first child	(AMF)	(9) (First) marriage first child	(DMF)	(10) Age at marriage (first child)	(FCM)
(11) Marriage last child	(AML)	(12) (First) marriage last child	(DML)	(13) Age at marriage (last child)	(LCM)
(14) Death a) Husband	(ADH)				
b) Wife	(ADW)				

on the easiness to obtain these data undoubtedly refers to survey research. In census operations these data can easily be obtained, but this information is not always collected and, if collected, not always computed, and, if computed, not always published.

In order to construct a family life cycle for a given population the data reported in Table 2, at the minimum, have to be available. Taking the Belgian situation as an example, Table 3 indicates the information that is available, or can easily be computed from published materials (differentiated as to souce of information), and information which is to be estimated, i.e., which is not available.

Table 3. *Availability of information required to construct a family life cycle (Belgium/1973)*

Information	Available	To be computed	Estimates to be constructed (not available)
AFMw	VS		
AFMh	VS		
ABFw	VS	AFMw + DBF	
ABFh		AFMh + DBF	
ABLw	(E)VS	AFMw + DBL	
ABLh		AFMh + DBL	
AMFw			ABFw + AFMh (?) or AFMw(?)
AMFh			ABFh + AFMh (?) or AFMw(?)
AMLw			ABLw + AFMw(?) or AFMh (?)
AMLh			ABLh + AFMw(?) or AFMh (?)
ADW	VS		
ADH	VS		
DBF	VS		
DBL	(E)VS		
DMF			DBF + AFMh (?) or AFMw(?)
DML			DBL + AFMw(?) or AFMh (?)
TNC	census		
INT		DBL − DBF	
FCM			AFMh (?) or AFMw(?)
LCM			AFMw(?) or AFMh (?)

Note: The small characters *w* and *h*, respectively, stand for wife and husband. (*E*) stands for estimate, i.e., computed information from vital statistics. For the other abbreviations refer to Table 2.

Most of the information required is not readily available. The available information originates almost exclusively from one source: the vital statistics. This implies that the life cycle constructed is of a synchronic type. Hill (1964–1965), treating problems of data collecting, characterizes the synchronic method as "a poor substitute for the more costly longitudinal study". This remark here applies implicitly to survey research. Basically, the same objection can be made to the construction of a family life cycle based on on document analysis. However, if good, reliable data were available (i.e., ready-made or to be computed), such a synchronic

Figure 1. *Synchronic life cycle of the family in Belgium (for selected years*)*

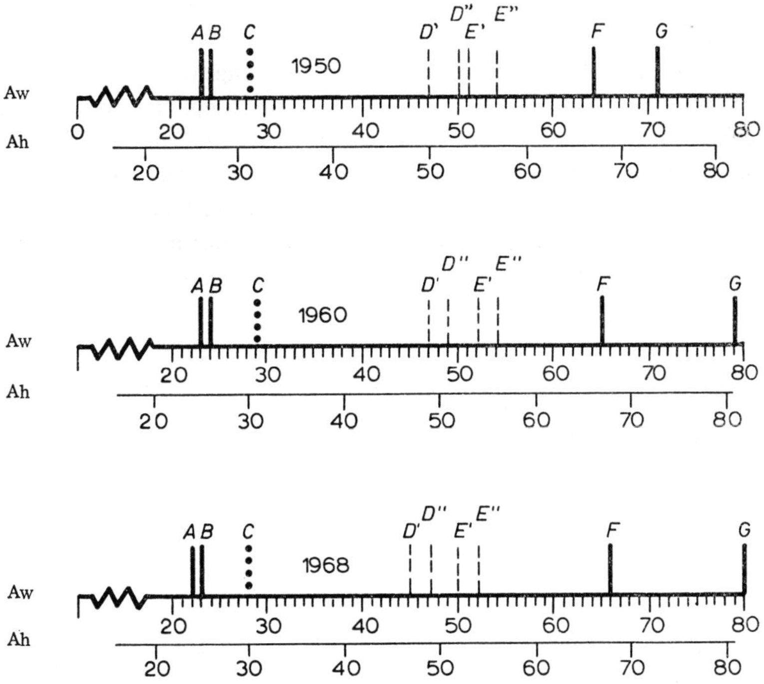

Code	Stage		
A	Marriage	Aw	Median age wife (years)
B	Birth first child	Ah	Median age husband (years)
C	Birth last child	———	Reliable data
D	Marriage of first child	••••••	Computed data (fairly reliable)
E	Marriage of last child	— — —	Mere estimates (reliability poor)
F	Death of husband - if first		
G	Death of wife - if last		

(' if female / " if male)

* The years 1950, 1968 are, respectively, the first and the last ones on which published information is available (by July 1, 1973). For References see p. 186.

type of construction could have some uses. It could serve as a tool for comparative research, the advantage being that it can be constructed in a short period of time, in a great number of countries simultaneously, and at given time intervals (e.g., each year). To this might be added that some other measures (such as, for instance, the divorce rate) also are computed in an essentially synchronic way.

Measures computed from published vital statistics do not allow the use of means (arithmetic or geometric) as measures of central tendencies. The modus is suited for nominal data. This leaves the median as the measure to be applied. The median has the advantage of being applicable for computing published materials of which the beginning and the end categories are almost always open (so the arithmetic mean cannot be applied). It should be noticed, however, that the statistical measure used could produce some differences in the results. For instance, age at marriage (male/1968 Belgium) arithmetic mean: 27y. 7m.; median 23y. –m.; modus 22y. In almost all studies (Table 1) the measure of central tendency applied is the median.

A construction of a life cycle of the Belgian population based on the data available as indicated above is given in Figure 1. This construction reveals that using vital statistics only allows obtainment of a result comparable to the presentation of the life cycle as presented by Glick in 1947. Therefore, in the next section attention will be paid to information available, at least potentially, from material collected for census purposes.

Information available in the census (Belgium 1970)

As indicated earlier in this report, the census can be a rich source of information in order to construct the family life cycle for a given (census) population. The three criteria set by Hill (1964) can be compared with the actual information collected in census operations. Table 4 maps the information required compared with the information collected for a given country (Belgium), at a given time (1970).

The information available is most complete concerning the wife; some information concerning husband and children only is available related to the wife/mother, being filled out on the wife's file. As a result the life history of the wife seems to be the most appropriate axis along which a family life cycle can be constructed. Lack of information about the date of marriage of the children implies that the data collection of the census

Table 4. *Information required versus information collected (Census 1970/ Belgium)*

	Husband	Wife	Each child
C1 C2 Concerning members who do not belong to the household at the time of data collection			
(1) Date of birth	H	H	Iw + H
(2) Date of current marriage	H	Iw	—
Date of previous events:			
(3) Marriage(s)	NC	Iw	—
(4) Divorce	NC	Iw	—
(5) Separation	NC	Iw	—
Concerning members who no longer belong to the household at the time of data collection			
(6) Date of birth	—	—	Iw
(7) Date of marriage	—	—	NC
(8) Date of decease	Iw	NC	NC
C3			
(9) Occupation	Ih	Iw	—

Note: C1, C2, C3, respectively, refer to the three criteria set by Hill (1964). *H* and *I* refer to the two types of documents on which the census data are filled out: *H* stands for the file containing the information on the household as a unit; *I* stands for the file on each individual the household is composed of. The suffix *w* refers to the file on the wife. *NC* stands for not collected. The dash (—) indicates that the information is not required.

only allows differentiation, within the family cycle, of the first stages of the cycle. This also implies that the cycle as a whole can be constructed, however, without differentiating the later stages. Projections of time of decease, however, should be estimated from vital statistics, since census data do not reveal any information on the decease of the wives or about the decease of widowers (the information being collected on the wife's file).

As a result, as far as the Belgian census 1970 is concerned, out of the data collected a series of ten tables will provide some information on the family life cycle, centering on the first stages of the family life cycle. All of these ten tables to be published contain similar information. Data will be computed on women in first marriage, having given birth to 1 child (respectively to 2 to 10 children) by age at marriage, marriage duration and year of birth of the only child (respectively 2 to 10 children).

Conclusion

Survey and census are rich sources of information for constructing the life cycle of the family. Both allow cohort analysis. It should be noted, however, that this cohort analysis is of a retrospective nature, i.e., based on a residual population. In fact the birth cohorts distinguished are in some respects "surviving" cohorts, i.e., women of the same birth cohort, surviving at a given time (the time of investigation). As far as the women (married ones) of the same birth cohort deceased previous to the time of investigation would give a different life cycle picture, the survey and census results would be biased. Neither the amount nor the direction of this potential bias, however, have been estimated.

Survey data apply mostly in the practice of social research to a population of a restricted area and refer to a restricted time period. Census data, not having these disadvantages, must be completed with information from vital statistics, the time of decease having to be estimated from this source.

Vital statistics, as published, only allow synchronic life-cycle construction. The registers or files of vital statistics, however, contain information about marriages, births and deaths, although it is not always possible to relate these events to specified birth cohorts. Therefore, in order to construct a family life cycle based on the life history of the wife/mother, it is necessary that the vital statistics (files or registers) contain information on their husbands and their children or should refer to their files. Only if births and marriages of the children are related to the date of birth (or marriage duration) of their mothers, and with indication of their rank order in their families of procreation, will it be possible to compute family life cycles for any birth cohort of women. Unlike survey or census, this technique would allow following given birth cohorts through their family history, i.e., not retrospective but longitudinal.

RÉSUMÉ

Construction du cycle familial
(quelques remarques concernant la disponibilité des données)

La construction du cycle familial est une forme de recherche de nature descriptive qui peut toutefois avoir des implications au niveau analytique. Des modifications dans la durée de certaines étapes du cycle familial peuvent en effet avoir une influence sur le comportement au cours de ces étapes, notamment par le biais des attentes de rôle.

Il y a une évolution dans les méthodes utilisées pour la construction du cycle familial. Avant 1965, l'information se rapportait à certains événements advenant à un moment donné, plutôt qu'à des cohortes de naissances. Une construction sur la base d'événements advenant à un moment donné fournit un cycle familial synchronique, tandis que les données concernant des cohortes de naissances permettent la construction d'un cycle familial longitudinal. Les enquêtes démographiques et les recensements permettent une analyse par cohortes, parce qu'ils procurent des informations concernant des caractéristiques essentielles d'une population donnée à un moment donné. Les statistiques démographiques procurent des informations concernant des événements advenus dans une unité de temps donnée, généralement un an. La construction d'un cycle familial à partir de statistiques démographiques ne peut se faire que sur la base d'événements se rapportant à des cohortes différentes mais advenus dans la même unité de temps. Ces données "cross-sectionnelles" produisent un modèle synthétique ou un cycle familial synchronique. Bien que la construction d'un cycle familial se fasse à partir de données relativement simples, ces données s'avèrent être peu disponibles, du moins en ce qui concerne la Belgique.

L'information est principalement fournie par une seule source: l'état civil. Il résulte de cet état de fait que le cycle familial élaboré pour la population belge est de nature synchronique. Bien que la méthode longitudinale soit généralement estimée supérieure, une construction synchronique peut néanmoins être utile à condition que l'on dispose de données précises. Pareil cycle familial synchronique peut servir d'instrument à des recherches comparatives. Il présente les avantages suivants: la méthode est économique et peut être appliquée simultanément dans différents pays à des intervalles réguliers (par exemple chaque année).

En ce qui concerne les données des recensements de la population, les informations sur le cours de la vie des femmes sont les plus détaillées. L'information concernant l'époux et les enfants n'est accessible que par le biais de la femme, de sorte que le cours de la vie de la femme semble être le point de départ le meilleur pour construire un cycle familial. Par contre, les données des recensements ne fournissent aucune information concernant la date de mariage des enfants. Elles ne peuvent donc servir qu'à délimiter les premières étapes du cycle familial. La projection de la fin du cycle familial, c'est-à-dire le moment du décès, ne peut être estimée qu'à partir des statistiques démographiques, étant donné que les données des recensements ne fournissent aucune indication sur le moment du décès de la femme, ni sur celui des veufs (du fait que ces informations ne figurent que dans les questionnaires des femmes). En outre, l'analyse des cohortes de naissances sur la base de données des recensements est de nature rétrospective, puisque basée sur une population résiduelle (cohortes de survivants). Il en résulte une marge d'erreur non estimée, correspondant à la différence entre le cycle familial des femmes survivantes et des femmes mariées décédées des mêmes cohortes de naissances. Les mêmes remarques valent d'ailleurs pour les enquêtes démographiques.

Jusqu'à présent, les statistiques démographiques ne permettent pas d'analyser les événements enregistrés selon des cohortes de naissances. Afin de construire un cycle familial sur la base du cycle de vie de la femme, l'information relative à chaque événement devrait pouvoir être mise en rapport avec l'information disponible pour l'épouse/mère. Il ne sera possible de construire un cycle familial pour n'importe quelle cohorte de naissances de femmes, que si la naissance et le mariage des enfants peuvent être mis en relation avec la date de naissance ou la durée du mariage de leur mère, compte tenu de leur rang dans la famille d'origine.

Contrairement à l'enquête démographique et au recensement, cette technique permettrait de suivre certaines cohortes de naissances à travers leur histoire familiale, non pas rétrospectivement, mais longitudinalement.

REFERENCES

Concerning Table 1

(4) Collver, A. (1963), "The family life cycle in India, and the United States", *American Sociological Review*, 28, Jan.: 86–96.
(1) Glick, P.C. (1947), "The family cycle", *American Sociological Review*, 12, Jan.: 164–174.
(2) —— (1955), "The life cycle of the family", *Marriage and Family Living*, 17, Feb.: 3–9.
(3) —— Heer, D.M., and Beresford, J.C. (1962), "Family formation and family composition: trends and prospects" in M.B. Sussman (ed.), *Sourcebook in Marriage and the Family*, Boston, Houghton Mifflin Company: 30–40.
(6) —— and Park, R. (1965), "New approaches in studying the life cycle of the family", *Demography*, 2, 187–202. Also in: R.F. Winch and H.R. Barringer (eds.), *Selected Studies in Marriage and the Family*, 3rd ed.: 166–177.
(7) Morioka, K. (1967), "Life cycle patterns in Japan, China and the United States", *Journal of Marriage and the Family*, 29, Aug.: 595–606.
(5) Uhlenberg, P.R. (1963), "A study of cohort life cycles: cohorts of native born Massachusetts women, 1830–1920", *Population Studies*, 23: 407–420.
(8) Young, C. (1973), "The life cycle of the family in Australia", contributed paper presented to the International Population Conference, Liège, Sept., 8 pp.

Concerning Figure 1

(Belgium) Nationaal Instituut voor de Statistiek (N.I.S.)
—— 1947, *Volkstelling 1947*, *Deel VII*, *Telling van de families*, Tables 10, 15.
—— 1961, *Volkstelling 1961*, *Deel VII*, *Telling van de families*, Tables 13, 28.
—— 1951, *Statistisch Bulletin*, Vol. 47, (Dec.), Table 25, 2233 and Table 27, 2243.
—— 1961, *Statistisch Tijdschrift*, Vol. 47, (Dec.), Table 22, 1978–1979 and Table 23, 1980.
—— 1962, *Statistisch Tijdschrift*, Vol. 48, (March), Table 13, 476–478.
—— 1970, *Bevolkingsstatistieken*, Vol. 2, Tables 7, 61; 23, 41–42; and 24, 43–61.
—— 1971, *Bevolkingsstatistieken*, Vol. 3, Table 5, 21–24.

Other references

Duvall, E.M. (1957), (1971), *Family Development*, 4th ed., Philadelphia, J.B. Lippincot: 576.
Glick, P.C. (1957), *American Families*, New York, J. Wiley: 240.
Hill, R. (1964), "Methodological issues in family development research", *Family Process*, 3, March: 186–205.
—— and Rodgers, R.H. (1964), "The developmental approach" in H.T. Christensen, *Handbook of Marriage and the Family*, Chicago, Rand McNally: 171–211.

III. *Familial events and their relation to the concept*

Faits familiaux dans leurs rapports avec le concept

10. Cycle de la vie domestique et incidences de l'hétérogamie religieuse: le cas des mariages mixtes entre juifs et catholiques en France

FRANÇOISE LAUTMAN

On peut reprocher au principe de la division du cours de la vie domestique par catégories selon la durée du mariage et la présence ou l'âge des enfants, de conduire à mesurer en fait le réel à un type idéal de famille. Sous la trompeuse apparence du réalisme et de la souplesse, de la prise en considération du vécu et des variations possibles de l'appartenance à tel ou tel type d'organisation familiale selon le temps de leur évolution propre où se situent les familles étudiées, la théorie cache la notion contraignante de famille normale.

La rareté de ses applications à l'étude de situations familiales dites deviantes (mères célibataires, seconds mariages, familles à problèmes...) au profit des études comparatives internationales et entre classes sociales, appuie ces critiques. Elle était déjà constatée et déplorée par Hill et Rodgers eux-mêmes en 1964, sans que la situation se soit notablement modifiée depuis (Hill et Rodgers, 1964).[1] Ainsi, Rodgers dans un ouvrage récent donne-t-il plus une liste des structures familiales atypiques à étudier qu'un bilan d'études accomplies (Rodgers, 1973).[2]

Il apparaît cependant que l'étalonnage des familles "normales" ainsi constitué doit pouvoir contribuer à la mesure de l'importance réelle de la déviance supposée: à savoir, les familles "atypiques" évoluent-elles de la même façon que les autres, ou des problemes spécifiques perturbent-ils le cours ou telle ou telle phase de leur vie?

Dans le cas de mariages mixtes, l'approche développementale permet en outre un nouvel examen de données qui leur sont spécifiques; le devenir des liens avec et entre les familles et les groupes d'origine, par exemple, prenant au moment de la formation du couple un accent particulier dans le cas de mariages qui transgressent une loi communément jugée si nécessaire à la survie des groupes, et avec l'espérance souvent avouée de leur fusion ou de leur disparition ou de l'assimilation à l'un des groupes. L'attrait éprouvé pour le groupe du conjoint et les caractères qu'il en porte, joue par ailleurs un rôle dont psychologues et sociologues s'accordent à signaler l'importance au moment de la formation des couples hétérogames; loin d'épouser l'autre malgré sa nationalité, sa race, ou sa religion, l'attrait du bizarre ou de la transgression de l'interdit est souvent un élement déterminant (Abraham 1914, Loewenstein 1952).[3] Enfin la théorie de l'échange compensatoire réciproque (Merton, 1941) rend compte de nombre de mariages hétérogames dans lesquels, plus ou moins consciemment, les époux s'apportent mutuellement les avantages sociaux de leurs catégories respectives: l'exemple le plus cité étant le mariage américain du riche noir et de la pauvre blanche, où l'une sacrifie en statut ethnique ce qu'elle gagne en statut économique, tandis que l'époux acquiert en prestige social ce qu'il manque à gagner sur le plan financier.

Idéalisme humanitaire, malédictions sectaires, exogamie névrotique et échange compensatoire réciproque ramènent également à ce que le fait même des mariages mixtes semble nier: l'importance primordiale des liens familiaux aux groupes sociaux.

Il nous a semblé interessant de mesurer leur évolution au cours de la vie conjugale dans le cas de mariages mixtes entre juifs et catholiques. Qu'advient-il de la nature et de l'intensité des relations avec les familles de chacun des époux? Quels sont leurs comportements et leurs représentations à l'égard de leurs groupes religieux et sociaux propres? et à l'égard de celui du conjoint? Qu'advient-il des rapports de leurs enfants avec ces mêmes familles et groupes d'origine? Cette évolution retentit-elle sur les motivations profondes qui ont déterminé le choix du conjoint? Est-elle ressentie comme un échec du couple?

Ne disposant que d'un nombre de cas restreint, nous avons préféré isoler pour la comparaison les effectifs de deux temps du cycle de vie domestique, dont l'un est généralement perçu, outre qu'il en est le point de départ, comme la période euphorique de la vie conjugale: moins de cinq ans d'union; et l'autre comme l'époque des difficultés et des insatisfactions majeures: la période de présence au foyer d'enfants adolescents ou jeunes adultes, 15 à 25 ans d'union. La comparaison avec des couples homogames juifs ou catholiques interviewés dans les mêmes conditions, est assurée par la présence de deux groupes de contrôle. Dans tous les cas, les deux membres du couple ont été séparément interrogés (tableau 1).

Tableau 1. *Sous-groupes mixtes et groupes de contrôle*

	Femme juive/ Homme catholique	Femme catholique/ Homme juif	Femme convertie au judaïsme	Couples juifs	Couples catholiques
–5 ans	15	19	11	20	20
15–25 ans	13	28			

Nous n'avions pas éliminé, lors de la collecte des entretiens, la possibilité d'un sous-groupe de couples mixtes dont l'un des époux soit converti. Dans les faits nous avons rencontré presqu'uniquement des conversions de jeunes femmes catholiques au judaïsme; leurs maris sont le plus souvent des sépharades originaires d'Afrique du Nord et le profil de ces couples est si accentué que nous les présentons ici comme contrepoint: tous les traits propres aux mariages mixtes s'y trouvent paradoxalement amplifiés.

Les catégories socio-professionnelles sont, pour autant qu'elle soit connue, représentatives de la population juive de France, et réparties de façon équilibrée:

- 19 petits et gros commerçants
- 20 cadres moyens
- 29 cadres supérieurs et professions libérales
- 13 artistes et étudiants

Le déséquilibre des deux derniers groupes n'est qu'apparent; les étudiants se destinent d'une façon générale aux professions libérales et aux emplois supérieurs et cette dernière catégorie comporte un certain nombre d'enseignants ou d'architectes, par exemple.

1. *Cycle familial et attachement au groupe d'origine*

Dans les trois quarts des cas, les mariages se font, quelque soient les groupes, à niveau de pratique religieuse égal, restaurant ainsi sur le plan des comportements une certaine homogamie. Dans les autres cas, le membre juif du couple est un peu plus souvent pratiquant que l'autre. Les pratiquants sont également plus nombreux dans le groupe de contrôle juif que chez les catholiques. Mais juifs ou catholiques, les époux de nos couples mixtes pratiquent rarement; 80% d'entre eux se déclarent non pratiquants ou athées. L'examen de leur passé religieux ne les montre cependant pas issus de milieux plus détachés; leurs parents ont été pratiquants aussi souvent que ceux des groupes de contrôle, et eux-mêmes ont le plus souvent reçu une éducation religieuse. L'abandon de la foi et de la pratique s'est produit à l'adolescence, ou jeune adulte; ils arrivent au mariage avec un profil religieux ou plutôt areligieux déjà fixé et qui ne se modifie pas au cours des 20 ans de mariage que nous examinons. Ce n'est donc pas à des transformations du sentiment religieux que l'on pourra attribuer leur évolution. Il est donné dès le départ et laisse aux deux groupes d'origine leur seul aspect d'inscription sociale.

La représentation de cette inscription a été mieux mesurée pour les juifs; l'attachement ou le rejet du judaïsme, en tant que minorité présentant des traits plus aigus et plus conscients. Aussi y insisterons nous davantage.

On peut y voir trois catégories:

- ceux qui se déclarent totalement détachés.
- ceux qui se sentent liés au judaïsme, d'une façon négative, par le "regard des autres" ou par la solidarité devant l'antisémitisme; l'un d'eux dit: "Je suis un juif de Sartre".[4]
- ceux qui témoignent d'attachement positif sentimental (les souvenirs d'enfance ou d'éducation sont souvent invoqués), spirituel (attachement philosophique ou aux traditions), ou total: "Je suis juif par toutes mes fibres".

70% des juifs du groupe de contrôle se trouvent dans le troisième groupe, 10% seulement se déclarent détachés. Les détachés sont plus nombreux parmi les mariages mixtes, principalement parmi les femmes juives, et l'attachement "de circonstance" du second groupe est plus fréquent. Mais il n'en reste pas moins qu'au contraire de ce qu'on voit pour la pratique, la majorité témoigne d'attachement, sous une forme ou sous une autre, au judaïsme (tableau 2).

Tableau 2. *Attachement au judaïsme*

	Détachés (%)	Attachement de "circonstance" (%)	Attachement positif (%)	N
Femme juive	46	21	32	28
Homme juif	19	32	49	47
Homme juif/ Femme convertie	0	25	75	11
Couples juifs	10	20	70	40

$\chi_2 = 3{,}47$ significatif à .10; $\surd = 1$.

L'attachement n'apparaît pas lié de façon univoque à la pratique, par exemple, de ceux qui demandent la conversion de leur femme, et dont aucun ne se déclare détaché bien qu'un seul soit pratiquant. Il n'y a pas non plus de différence notable entre les jeunes mariés et les couples anciens, si ce n'est l'évocation plus fréquente chez ceux-ci des persécutions, liée au souvenir de la guerre. Là aussi le profil est tôt fixé et semble précéder le mariage.

Il en va différement de l'inscription et de la pratique religieuse des enfants. Négligeant les prescriptions de l'église catholique qui veut que tous les enfants des mariages mixtes lui appartiennent, aussi bien que celle du judaïsme qui ne reconnaît que les enfants des femmes juives, plus de la moitié des jeunes mariés inscrivent leurs enfants dans l'une ou l'autre religion, plus souvent celle du père (tableau 3).

Tableau 3. *Religion des enfants des couples mixtes*

	Catholiques (%)	Juifs (%)	Sans religion (%)	N
Femme juive	38	24	38	28
Homme juif	20	40	40	47

$\chi_2 = 4{,}60$ significatif à .10.

Tableau 4. *Indifférence religieuse des enfants des couples mixtes*

	Non pratiquants (%)	Sans religion (%)
-5 ans	x	33
15-25 ans	25	45

x La pratique des jeunes enfants est difficile à évaluer.

Tout apparaît comme si, le premier effort d'inscription fait, les parents et les enfants reculaient devant l'antagonisme des groupes et les conflits familiaux possibles à l'occasion de leur éducation et de leur pratique religieuse, et se réfugiaient dans l'abstention. La rencontre des groupes est là manquée et le terrain reste souvent vide: 67% des enfants sont baptisés ou circoncis, mais 20 ans après, 70% des enfants ne pratiquent aucune religion. Alors que respectivement 50% des enfants du groupe juif de contrôle et 45% des enfants du groupe catholique se trouvent dans le même cas. On rencontre ici, jalonnées dans le temps familial, les mêmes données que Goldberg et Bok (1970) sur les enfants des couples mixtes juifs-chrétiens en Belgique, selon lesquelles ils possèdent moins bien l'une et l'autre culture que chaque membre des deux communautés. Affrontés à deux cultures ils risquent de n'en adopter aucune et la double exposition est souvent un appauvrisement.

Nous avons vu que dans la majorité des cas, les époux sont et restent attachés à des groupes dont ils continuent de se sentir membres. Si bien attachés à leur groupe que si l'on demande à chaque époux comment il se situe à l'égard de la religion de l'autre, on voit apparaître plus d'indifférence, voire d'hostilité que de sympathie ou d'union. 45% des jeunes mariées converties au judaïsme elles-mêmes se déclarent indifférentes, ou simplement curieuses ou tolérantes à l'égard de leur nouvelle religion.

D'une façon générale, les hommes manifestent plus souvent de l'hostilité, plus rarement de la sympathie envers la religion de leurs épouses; celles-ci sont plus souvent simplement indifférentes. On est loin de la fusion des groupes. Si l'on mesure les différences entre les jeunes mariés et les époux ayant 20 ans d'union, on voit l'indifférence rester pratiquement stable chez les partenaires juifs: elle est le fait de 61% des femmes juives mariées depuis longtemps contre 67% des jeunes mariées, et de 50% des hommes juifs dans le même cas, contre 52% des jeunes mariés. Parmi les catholiques, l'indifférence est nettement plus forte avec le temps, passant de 54 à 70% chez les hommes et de 31 à 62% chez les femmes.

Dans tous les groupes, enfin, l'hostilité semble croître avec le temps; si les hommes juifs font exception, c'est à cause du nombre exceptionnellement élevé de jeunes maris hostiles à la religion de leurs épouses (tableau 5).

Tableau 5. *Sentiments à l'égard de la religion du conjoint*

	Hostilité (%)	Indifférence (%)	Intérêt (%)	Sympathie (%)	N
A. Conjoints catholiques					
H –5 ans	6	54	34	6	15
F –5 ans	0	31	38	31	19
H 15–25 ans	7	70	23	0	13
F 15–25 ans	3	62	7	28	28
B. Conjoints juifs					
H –5 ans	26	52	22	0	19
F –5 ans	6	67	27	0	15
H 15–25 ans	15	50	32	3	28
F 15–25 ans	16	61	16	7	13

A. $\chi_2 = 4{,}44$ significatif à .05; $\surd = 1$.
B. χ_2 non significatif.

Comment cet attachement à son propre groupe et l'indifférence envers celui du partenaire se traduisent-ils dans les comportements, et y-a-t-il là-dessus évolution selon la durée de l'union? Nous retiendrons pour indicateurs, le choix des amis et la participation éventuelle à des manifestations culturelles propres à chaque groupe.

Dans près de la moitié des cas, quelque soit le sous-groupe, on déclare ne pas s'intéresser à la religion de ses amis voire l'ignorer; il en est de même dans les groupes de contrôle juif et chrétien, mais pour le reste on y fréquente uniquement respectivement juifs et catholiques. Alors que les couples mixtes présentent une grande diversité de solutions et privilégient selon les cas, juifs ou catholiques, athées ou autres couples mixtes. La balance penche en faveur des catholiques, mais le rapport de nombre des communautés peut être suffisant à l'expliquer: il y a plus de probabilité, pour qui n'a pas de propos délibéré, à se lier en France avec des catholiques qu'avec des juifs. Mais lorsque c'est l'homme qui est juif, les amis sont plus souvent juifs; il en est comme de la religion des enfants, et les liens avec la société juive sont plus forts dans ce sous-groupe.

Ces liens sont plus faibles lorsque la femme est juive et de plus semblent s'effacer avec le temps. Les juives mariées à des catholiques depuis 20 ans voient moins de juifs et de catholiques, plus d'athées ou d'autres couples mixtes que les jeunes.

Parmi les femmes converties au judaïsme, aucune ne reconnaît fréquenter principalement des juifs (là aussi 50% refusent de s'intéresser à la religion des amis) alors que si l'on interroge leurs maris, 30% d'entre eux situent les relations du couple en milieu juif. La même différence d'appréciation entre maris et femmes est le fait de 50% des jeunes hommes juifs et encore de 20% de ceux qui sont mariés depuis longtemps. On peut voir dans la diversité des solutions, et dans la progression du détachement chez les couples où la femme est juive un signe du brassage attendu; mais l'importance du nombre de cas où l'appréciation diffère va dans le sens de la mauvaise perception par chacun de ce qui concerne le groupe de l'autre, à cette différence que, là, le phénomène semble diminuer au cours de la vie conjugale.

Quant aux activités culturelles et sociales propres à chaque groupe, elles ne sont pas abandonnées et la participation, bien que minoritaire, est à peine inférieure à celle des groupes de contrôle; mais chacun y participe dans son groupe et s'y rend seul: un seul cas d'activité partagée, un couple fréquente les réunions des Amitiés Judéo-Chrétiennes où ils se sont d'ailleurs connus. Cette participation est plus forte dans tous les groupes chez les couples les plus anciens; elle est le fait de 20 à 25 % des couples anciens contre 35 % dans le groupe de contrôle juif et 25 % dans le groupe catholique.

Après vingt ans de vie conjugale, l'attachement de chaque époux à son groupe d'origine est intact, amis et activités culturelles restent propres à chacun; les représentations des relations du couple divergent souvent; faute d'un compromis culturel satisfaisant, les enfants s'excluent des deux groupes à la fois, et les sentiments d'antagonisme ou d'indifférence envers la religion du partenaire se sont accrus.

2. *Variations dans le temps familial des interrelations au sein du couple et avec la famille large*

Qu'en est-il des relations proprement familiales qui sont censées contrôler l'inscription sociale des individus? Nombre de juifs évoquent l'attachement au groupe à travers l'attachement à la famille: "C'est la religion de ma famille ..." "solidarité à cause de mes parents" ... "contre l'antisémitisme qui atteint mes parents" ... "souvenirs d'enfance" ... Est-ce la permanence des liens familiaux qui cause, ou permet, celle de l'attachement? Les nouveaux liens établis avec les belles-familles donnent-ils les conditions d'apparition du sentiment d'être solidaire, ou du moins concerné par leurs origines? Les rapports avec familles et belles-familles ont-ils des caractères spécifiques dus à la mixité?

Au moment du mariage, les désaccords exprimés ont très rarement été jusqu'à la rupture et le nombre des approbations l'emporte de beaucoup sur les désaccords. Cependant A. Girard (1964) constate une approbation presque universelle des parents au moment du mariage (79 %) et comparé à cette unanimité, le taux de désaccord rencontré par les couples mixtes est considérable (tableau 6).
Dans les deux sous-groupes, les parents de la femme sont moins défavorables que ceux de l'homme et une analyse plus fine montre que dans les deux cas également, c'est la mère de l'homme qui est le plus opposée au mariage. On retrouve la même configuration dans les groupes de contrôle mais les désaccords sont moins nombreux, et surtout les motifs différents. Ils y sont à peu près toujours d'ordre économique ou social: le

Tableau 6. *Accord ou désaccord des familles au moment du mariage*

	Accord (%)	Désaccord famille femme (%)	Désaccord famille homme (%)	Désaccord des 2 familles (%)	N
Femme juive/ Homme catholique	60	11	25	4	28
Homme juif/ Femme catholique	58	11	24	7	46
Homme juif/ Femme convertie	45	9	27	18	11
% de A. Girard	favorable ou très favorable 79	l'une des deux familles défavorable 17		les 2 familles défavorables ou très défavorables 4	

conjoint ne satisfait pas aux exigences de sa future belle-famille quant à sa profession ou au train de vie qu'il peut offrir. Ces motifs n'apparaissent à peu près jamais pour les couples mixtes; on invoque au contraire l'origine religieuse ou ethnique. On peut alors faire l'hypothèse du rôle catalyseur de la mixité; elle cristallise et amplifie des sentiments latents contre le mariage des enfants, sentiments qui trouvent là le support de justifications socialement reçues.

Il faut remarquer là aussi le paradoxe de la situation des converties, auxquelles non seulement leur appartenance originelle est plus souvent reprochée, mais qui ont plus souvent aussi à faire face au sectarisme des deux groupes. Affronter le cumul des sectarismes apparaît donc comme premier prix de la conversion au lieu des assimilations et des approbations recherchées. L'une d'elles résume sa situation: "J'étais prête à l'assimilation, maintenant je sais que cela ne se fera pas; je le regrette d'ailleurs..."

Si l'on interroge les couples sur la qualité de leurs relations actuelles avec leurs familles et belles-familles, l'optimisme est pourtant de rigueur. Les relations avec les familles sont sauf exception excellentes ou bonnes, mais si on examine les variations de cette euphorie, elles sont plus souvent excellentes que bonnes avec les familles des femmes et plus souvent bonnes qu'excellentes avec les familles des hommes. C'est avec ces dernières seulement qu'elles sont éventuellement nulles.

Elles sont plus souvent bonnes qu'excellentes chez les couples anciens, de façon nette quand la femme est juive, moins clairement pour les couples dont l'homme est juif, mais elles y sont moins souvent déclarées excellentes au début. Quelle que soit la part de la façade ou l'illusion dans l'appréciation des relations avec les familles et belles-familles, les représentations sont donc moins euphoriques après vingt ans de mariage.

Les enfants ne facilitent pas les relations, leur présence est générale chez les couples anciens où elles sont ressenties commes moins bonnes, et chez les jeunes mariés les relations sont plus souvent simplement bonnes qu'excellentes, même avec la famille de la femme, pour les femmes qui ont des enfants. C'est d'autant plus net que le mariage est plus récent comme si le fait de rester sans enfants au début du mariage facilitait l'établissement de bonnes relations avec les familles d'origine. Celles qui ont des enfants à la fin des cinq ans de mariage ont des attitudes plus proches des nouvelles mariées sans enfants que des nouvelles mariées rapidement chargées de famille.

La crainte des conflits au sujet de l'éducation des enfants suffit-elle à distendre les liens familiaux, comme elle a tendance à rejeter dans la neutralité religieuse? Il faut rappeler la thèse souvent évoquée de la faible fécondité des couples mixtes, et de son attribution aux difficultés d'éducation des enfants (Bresler, 1961; Goldstein et Goldscheider, 1966). Il est vrai que les couples ayant vingt ans d'union, c'est-à-dire tous leurs enfants, n'ont ici en moyenne que 2,1 enfants ce qui est peu pour leurs catégories sociales et leur génération, et de toute façon inférieure à la moyenne nationale (2, 4).

La fréquence et le contenu des relations dont la qualité ressentie vient d'être évoquée, suivent, en l'accentuant, la même évolution.

Chez les jeunes couples mixtes, comme dans le groupe de contrôle catholique, les rencontres avec les parents et les frères et sœurs de la femme sont fréquentes. On voit un peu moins parents et frères de l'homme, les rencontres étant plus souvent mensuelles ou exceptionnelles et moins souvent hebdomadaires que dans le premier cas.

Les relations avec les deux familles sont beaucoup plus fréquentes dans le groupe juif et la différence au détriment des belles-familles est insensible; ces liens se détendent moins avec la durée du mariage, et s'ils deviennent un peu plus souvent mensuels, ils ne s'espacent pas davantage, même avec les frères et sœurs, sans invoquer l'éloignement et la dispersion des familles. Alors qu'aucune excuse n'est cherchée à la faiblesse éventuelle des liens dans les autres groupes; ceux qui sont unis depuis vingt ans voient moins que les jeunes couples, parents de l'homme et collatéraux des deux lignées.

D'une façon générale, par l'effet conjugué du "familisme" juif et du caractère privilégié des relations avec la famille de la femme dans notre société, c'est chez les couples mixtes jeunes et dont la femme est juive que les liens avec la famille d'origine sont le plus étroits, et ceci bien que le détachement social et religieux y soit le plus marqué.

Quant au contenu de ces relations, nous avons retenu le fait de demander conseil ou aide matérielle (ici financière, l'aide aux soins des jeunes enfants, par exemple, portant ici sur un trop petit nombre de cas possibles pour y être significative). Les époux mixtes demandent plus rarement conseil à leurs parents ou collatéraux que ceux des deux groupes de contrôle, suggérant à nouveau le malaise au sujet du compromis culturel établi, mais ils demandent aussi souvent une aide matérielle, et la configuration générale reproduit celle des relations; privilège de la lignée féminine et diminution avec la durée du mariage.

Le sens et le rythme de l'evolution de ces familles suivent donc, tout en se situant sur un registre de relations plus difficiles, celui de l'ensemble de notre société. Les couples mixtes n'ont pas plus de rapports avec leurs familles d'origine que la moyenne, ce qui représente pour les juifs une diminution; leur contenu est marqué d'un malaise (désaccord au mariage ... conseils ... enfants ...) qui les appauvrit et elles suivent avec le temps le mouvement général d'éloignement. On ne peut donc pas rendre compte par le poids d'habitudes et de fréquentations familiales de la stabilité, avec laquelle elles font contraste, de l'attachement et de la persistance de l'identité de chacun dans son propre groupe. Elles n'offrent pas non plus de facilités d'assimilation au conjoint.

Dans toute union conjugale, les époux doivent s'adapter l'un à l'autre au prix de certaines concessions. Un compromis s'établit. Dans les mariages mixtes, au lieu d'accommoder simplement deux cultures quotidiennes familiales différentes, ce sont des ensembles plus vastes et structurés qui s'affrontent. C. Carisse (1969) a démontré sur l'exemple des mariages franco-anglais au Canada que le choix ne se fait pas à mi-chemin, mais "au profit d'une culture et au détriment de l'autre", encore que différemment selon les secteurs du comportement. Dans le cas cité par exemple, la culture anglaise domine les secteurs axés vers le pouvoir, alors que la culture française l'emporte pour ce qui concerne l'attachement communautaire. En ce qui concerne les comportements et les représentations analysés précédemment, nous avons vu que l'équilibre se fait en fonction du sexe et se renverse donc selon les sous-groupes: l'homme l'emporte plus souvent sur le plan de l'inscription sociale (amis, religion des enfants, manifestations d'attachement au groupe d'origine ...) la femme sans adhérer à ses positions, observe plus souvent une certaine neutralité sur ces plans, mais l'emporte sur celui des relations familiales avec son propre groupe. L'équilibre ainsi réalisé ne peut que contribuer au malaise puisqu'il conduira plus souvent ceux qui s'inscrivent comme juifs à vivre avec des catholiques et inversement.

Qu'en est-il de la vie quotidienne et des rapports à l'intérieur du petit groupe domestique? L'entretien a porté avec chaque membre du couple, sur ce qu'il retrouvait, pensait avoir reproduit chez lui de la vie familiale quotidienne de sa famille d'origine, et de celle de son conjoint.

Chaque époux est plus souvent conscient des traits issus de sa propre famille que de celle de son conjoint; nous retrouvons là, la mauvaise perception, déjà évoquée, de ce qui concerne l'autre et sa famille, dont on dit souvent n'avoir rien repris ou trop mal la connaître pour l'apprécier. Quant à sa propre lignée, un tiers environ des enquêtes répond de façon évasive "tout et rien" ... "Je ne sais pas" ... et un quart, il s'agit plus souvent de l'époux juif, pense avoir repris la façon de vivre de sa famille en général. L'évocation de traits plus précis est plus souvent le fait aussi d'époux juifs et porte sur des traits que l'on peut considérer comme relevant plutôt de la culture familiale juive (sens de la famille, habitudes de cuisine et de table ...). Les traits évoquant l'organisation domestique (horaires ... façon d'entretenir la maison ...) sont plutôt retenus par les époux chrétiens.

Si on prend en considération la durée, il y a plus de réponses négatives chez les époux anciens que chez les jeunes, la référence à la façon de vivre dans son ensemble diminue, mais la citation de traits précis augmente un peu et ce sont encore une fois les traits de la culture familiale juive. Dans les cas où il s'établit (ou est conscient et avoué) le compromis sur la culture quotidienne s'établit donc à l'avantage du groupe juif mais a tendance à disparaître avec le temps; ce qui est également le cas de plusieurs autres élements du compromis: liens avec les familles, inscription religieuse des enfants ...

Qu'en est-il alors des rapports du couple? Nous avons retenu comme indices, la qualité de la communication entre les époux et la satisfaction ou insatisfaction de la femme. La baisse de la communication et de la satisfaction au cours du mariage, et particulièrement dans la période ou les enfants sont adolescents, est un phénomène général et qui se vérifie également auprès des groupes de contrôle.

Dans l'ensemble, la communication, dont les indicateurs portaient sur les rapports de vie quotidienne (faire parler l'autre s'il a des ennuis, discuter les problèmes de santé et de budget ...) est meilleure que dans les groupes de contrôle; ce qui n'est pas incompatible, et peut être même compensatoire de la mauvaise communication sur les problèmes concernant famille large et groupes sociaux. Elle a toutefois comme partout tendance à baisser avec la durée de l'union.

L'évolution de la satisfaction est encore plus à l'avantage de ces couples; elle suit la règle de la diminution au cours du mariage, mais même à son niveau le plus bas, elle reste supérieure à celle qui se rencontre dans les groupes de contrôle (tableau 7).

Tableau 7. *Satisfaction de la femme*

	Satisfaite (%)	Pas très satisfaite (%)	Insatisfaite (%)	N
Femme juive –5 ans	93	7	0	15
Femme catholique –5 ans	74	26	0	19
Femme juive 15–25 ans	69	8	23	13
Femme catholique 15–25 ans	68	21	11	28
Femme – couples catholiques	60	15	25	20
Femme – couples juifs	55	20	25	20

χ_2 non significatif.

Conclusion

Il semble donc bien que malgré (ou à cause de) tout ce qui les sépare, et que ni le fait, ni la durée du mariage n'abolissent, la réussite de ces couples soit plutôt supérieure à la moyenne, et le type de leur évolution révélateurs d'un fonctionnement parfaitement normal de l'institution conjugale, à travers, et indépendamment de l'institution familiale large, perturbée par leur existence, et de leurs problèmes spécifiques d'inscription sociale. Ce qui rencontre à la fois les théories sur l'exogamie névrotique ou sur l'échange compensatoire réciproque: dans les deux cas le maintien des appartenances et identités respectives des époux est dans la logique de la formation du couple, et permet d'en conserver les avantages psychologiques et sociaux escomptés.

Mais l'approche développementale apporte ici une contribution au réexamen des hypothèses et des connaissances concernant la formation et la signification sociale des mariages mixtes qui rencontre et éclaire également les questions ouvertes par l'accroissement actuel de leur nombre.

Le taux des mariages mixtes a longtemps pu être révélateur de l'importance numérique d'un groupe donné (Price, 1964; Schoenfeld, 1969; Henry, 1966). Les immigrants d'un groupe pionnier, les juifs isolés dans les petites villes, les femmes dont les maris possibles sont morts à la guerre, les membres d'un groupe ethnique ou religieux peu représenté au sein d'une classe sociale, font un nombre élevé de mariages mixtes; ces mariages ne peuvent être imputés à des marginaux ou déviants, et perdent leur caractère de transgression d'interdit. Le nombre des mariages mixtes est révélateur de la nature obligatoire ou simplement préférentielle de l'endogamie au sein d'un groupe, et devant l'augmentation du nombre de ces mariages au cours des dernières années, tout porte à penser que nous devons rejeter l'hypothèse de l'exogamie névrotique dans le cas des mariages mixtes entre juifs et catholiques français que nous avons étudiés ici. A l'image de ce qui se passe dans les petits groupes, le taux élevé de mariages mixtes s'accompagne de la désuétude de l'interdit au profit d'une endogamie plus ou moins préférentielle. L'acte n'a plus le même sens, il n'exprime plus fatalement la fuite hostile de son propre groupe; il est souvent vécu comme échange compensatoire réciproque, c'est-à-dire tentative de jouer de son propre groupe pour acquérir les avantages d'un autre.

Dans la mesure où le mariage mixte met en jeu les rapports de prestige et de statut entre les groupes, il tombe sous le coup des règles d'alliance et rentre dans la norme du mariage. Les mariages mixtes s'expliquent mieux comme lieu d'une combinaison différente des règles sociales que comme leur exception. Ils sont au même titre que les mariages endogames, sous l'effet de la contrainte sociale, mais cette contrainte engage la recherche d'un équilibre nouveau entre les groupes, et non la volonté aveugle de leur survie.

L'image des mariages mixtes cesse alors d'être négative; ils ne doivent plus être considérés comme échappant aux normes sociales; ils se trouvent sous l'influence prioritaire d'autres normes sociales qui règlent la taille et le statut respectif des groupes dans une société, voire le sens de ces groupes comme lieu d'inscription sociale.

Summary

Family life cycle and incidences of religious heterogamy: the case of mixed marriages between Jews and Christians

The analysis of family development according to the duration of the marriage and the presence or the age of children implies that there does exist in fact an ideal type of family. It is interesting to compare the evolution of this type of "normal" family with that of a "variant" type, in the present case that of marriages between Jews and Catholics.

The level of religious observance of mixed couples in our sample is low: 80% declare themselves to be non-practicing or atheists. On the other hand, attachment to the group of origin as a social identification is very strong, particularly as measured in the Jewish husband, and this does not change with time. This social identification does not fail to cause a certain amount of conflict, for whereas 67% of the children are either baptized or circumcised, 70% of these same children do not practice any religion twenty years after: in the confrontation of two cultures, the children are not likely to adopt either. For the latter, the double exposure is often an impoverishment. On the other hand, the partners remain very attached to their group of origin and are more often indifferent, and even hostile, than sympathetic toward the religion of the other. With the passing of time this indifference is almost stable among the Jewish partners; among the Catholics, it grows more pronounced; in all groups, hostile feelings grow with time. These attitudes can be translated into behavior: the choice of friends, for example, and separate participation in cultural and social activities of the own group, participation which does in fact increase in all groups during the marriage. The relations of couples with their family and in-laws reveal a somewhat specific characteristic of the mixed marriage: the two families approve of the marriage only in approximately half of the cases; the mix seems to amplify latent feelings against the marriage of the children, which here find some socially acceptable justifications. Nevertheless, the relations with family and in-laws are viewed with optimism, especially those with the wife's family but they are represented less euphorically after twenty years of marriage. And the presence of children does not render the relations with the larger family any easier. As to the frequency of contacts with the family of origin, and their content (requests for advice and material help), the general configuration shows privilege in the female line, which lessers during the marriage; this is in accordance with what has been observed for the whole of our society but is in contrast with the stability of attachment and the persistence of each one within his own group.

If a compromise is reached on day-to-day culture, this is to the advantage of the Jewish group. But it has a tendency to disappear with time. Communications between the couple and satisfaction of the wife are superior to those encountered in the control groups (homogamous marriages), but these also tend to lessen gradually. It seems, therefore, that despite (or because of) all that separates them, the success of these couples is better than average and that their evolution reveals a perfectly normal functioning to the conjugal institution. Mixed marriage does not, in the cases studied, as it might have done in other circumstances, reflect a hostile flight from one's own group; it is often experienced as a reciprocally compensatory exchange, in other words, as an attempt to use one's own group in order to obtain the advantages of the other. Thus, maintenance of the respective ties and identities of each partner is part of the logic of the formation of the couple and allows them to keep the psychological and social advantages which they value.

Notes

1. "Le problème des familles 'déviantes' n'est pas encore apparu dans ce chapitre. L'examen de la littérature développementale rend manifeste qu'on a peu accordé d'attention aux familles qui ne suivent pas l'ordre normal des étapes, de l'établissement à la dissolution par la mort des partenaires. Le cadre conceptuel présenté ici permet pourtant d'étudier des familles où surviennent mort prématurée des parents ou des enfants, incapacités physiques ou mentales, divorce, séparation et autres. La fréquence de telles situations en fait plutôt des variantes que des anomalies de la vie familiale. Savoir comment elles affectent le modèle de rôles de la famille serait un apport considérable" (Hill et Rodgers, 1964).
2. Rodgers définit les variantes de la formation de la famille (remariage, mariage entre des conjoints ayant une grande différence d'âge, etc. ...) comme l'un des cas de structure familiale atypique. D'autre part il insiste sur les échanges du système familial (family transaction) avec les autres systèmes dont la religion. Il ouvre ainsi la voie à l'approche développementale de familles dont l'insertion sociale est atypique telles que les mariages mixtes (Rodgers, 1973).
3. Les cas retenus pour cette analyse ont été recueillis pour une étude sur 150 couples mixtes juifs-chrétiens (Bensimon et Lautman, 1974, "Aspects religieux et culturels des mariages entre juifs et chrétiens en France", Ethnies, n° spécial).
4. J. P. Sartre (1954) met l'accent sur de tels éléments qui appuient une vision existentielle de la judaïcité.

Références

Abraham, K. (1914), "A propos de l'exogamie névrotique. Contribution à l'étude comparée de la vie psychique des névrosés et des primitifs", *Imago*, 6, 3ème année, réédité in *Oeuvres Complètes*, T II, Paris, Payot: 59–61

Abramson, H. J. (1971), "Inter-ethnic marriage among Catholic Americans and changes in religious behavior", *Sociological Analysis*, 32, Septembre: 31–44.

Atkeson, P. (1970), "Building communication in intercultural marriage", *Psychiatry*, 33/3: 396–408.

Bensimon, D., et Lautman, F. (1974), "Aspects religieux et culturels des mariages entre Juifs et Chrétiens en France", *Ethnies*, 4: 90–117.

Berman, L. A. (1968), *Jews and Intermarriage. A Study in Personality and Culture*, New York-South Brunswick-London, Thomas Yoseloff.

Besanceney, P. H. (1971), *Interfaith Marriages: Who and Why*, Ohio, John Carroll University Heights.

Bresler, J. B. (1961), "The relation of population levels to ethnic groups backgrounds", *Enquiries Quarterly*, 8, mars: 12–22.

Burchinal, L. G., et Chancellor, L. E. (1963), "Survival rates among religiously homogamous and interreligious marriages", *Social Forces*, mai.

Carisse, C. (1966), "Accomodation conjugale et réseau social des mariages bi-ethniques au Canada", *Revue française de Sociologie*, 4: 472–484.

—— (1969), "Orientations culturelles dans les mariages entre Canadiens français et Canadiens anglais," *Sociologie et Sociétés*, 1, mai: 39–52.

Chancellor, L. E., et Monahan, J. P. (1955), "Religious preferences and interreligious mixtures in marriages and divorces in Iowa", *American Journal of Sociology*, 61: 223–239.

Cohen, E. (1969), "Mixed marriage in an Israeli town", *Jewish Journal of Sociology*, 11, juin: 41–50.
Girard, A. (1964), *Le choix du conjoint. Une enquête psycho-sociologique en France*, Paris, Presses Universitaires de France.
Goldberg, B., et Bok, W. (1970), "Dualité culturelle et appartenance", Bruxelles, Centre National des Hautes Etudes juives (ronéo)
Goldstein, S., et Goldscheider, C. (1966), "Social and demographic aspects of Jewish intermarriage", *Social Problems*, 13/3: 386–399.
Heer, D.M. (1962), "The trends of intermarriages in Canada: 1922–1957", *American Sociological Review*, 27: 245–250.
Heiss, J.S. (1960), "Premarital characteristics of the religiously intermarried in an urban area", *American Sociological Review*, 25, février: 47–53.
—— (1961), "Interfaith marriage and marital outcome", *Marriage and Family Living*, 23: 228–233.
Henry, L. (1966), "Perturbations de la nuptialité résultant de la guerre 1914–1918", *Population*, 21, mars-avril: 273–332.
Herberg, W. (1955), "The triple melting pot. The third generation from ethnic to religious diversity", *Commentary*, 20: 101–108.
Hill R. et Rodgers, R.H. (1964), "The developmental approach" in H.T. Christensen (ed.), *Handbook of Marriage and the Family*, Chicago, Rand McNally: 170–209.
Hunt, C.L., et Coller, B.W. (1956), "Intermarriage and cultural change: a study of Philippine-American marriages", *Social Forces*, 35 2: 223–230.
Lazerwits, B. (1971), "Intermarriage and conversion: a guide for future research", *Jewish Journal of Sociology*, 13, juin: 41–64.
Levinson, M.H., et Levinson, D.V. (1959), "Jews who intermarry: sociopsychological bases of ethnic identity and change", *Yivo Annual of Jewish Social Science*, 12: 103–130.
Loewenstein, R. (1952), *Psychanalyse de l'antisémitisme*, Paris, Presses Universitaires de France.
Merton, R.K. (1941), "Intermarriage and the social structure: fact and theory", *Psychiatry*, 4: 361–374.
Mol, H. (1970), "Mixed marriages in Australia", *Journal of Marriage and the Family*, mai: 293–300.
Monahan, T.P. (1970), "Are interracial marriages really less stable?", *Social Forces*, 48/4: 461–473.
—— (1971), "Interracial marriage in the United States: some data on upstate New York", *International Journal of Sociology of the Family*, 1, mars: 94–105.
Price, C.A. (1964), *Jewish Settlers in Australian Canberra*, The Australian National University.
Rodgers, R. (1973), *Family Interaction and Transaction. The Developmental Approach*, Englewood Cliffs, N.J. Prentice Hall.
Sartre, J.P. (1954), *Réflexions sur la question juive*, Gallimard, Paris.
Schoenfeld, E. (1969), "Intermarriage and the small town, the Jewish Case", *Journal of Marriage and the Family*, 31, février: 61–64.
Schwartz, A. (1971), "Intermarriage in the United States", *American Jewish Year Book*, 71: 101–121.

11. Divorce and the family life cycle in Great Britain

ROBERT CHESTER

Introduction

In England the sociological understanding of divorce is not yet far advanced. The literature of the 1950s and 1960s was slight, and was dominated by unsophisticated exegeses of the official statistics which paid scant heed either to theory or to work done abroad (see, e.g., MacGregor, 1957; Fletcher, 1962; but note Rowntree and Carrier, 1958). Field-studies were non-existent, and conventional wisdom attended more to legal and administrative factors than to the dynamics of marital interaction in the context of emergent marriage patterns and the family life cycle. Post-war divorce fluctuations, for instance, were influentially held to reflect the changing real value of legal aid in an inflationary period, even though this simple financial determinism does not survive serious examination (Chester, 1972a). The relative lack of social scientific attention means that in discussing the relationship between marital instability and the family life cycle there are problems in the spheres of theory, conceptualisation, methodology and data, and that what can confidently be reported is somewhat meagre. These difficulties, however, exist in all societies in different ways, and it may be that an exploration of the English case will helpfully illustrate the weaknesses in our apparatus of understanding.

As in other countries, divorcing in England continues throughout all marriage durations, and therefore throughout the family life cycle. The incidence of divorce, however, is not evenly distributed over the cycle, and this is not surprising. It is known that marital satisfactions vary in source and quantity at different developmental stages, and also that there is temporal variation in the opportunities, constraints, costs, and benefits relating to termination of marriage. In principle, the pattern of differential distribution by time might afford important clues to the developmental aspects of marital relations, and good epidemiological data might provide a base for theoretical understanding of marital instability. In practice, satisfactory data do not exist, and for both practical and theoretical reasons would be difficult to gather.

The family life cycle is understood here as a conceptual framework designed to promote the generation of theory rather than as constituting a theory in itself. Whereas most concepts emerge as adjuncts to theoretical ideas, therefore, the developmental theorists have inverted the usual strategy and created the conceptual apparatus first. The cycle is conceived as a progression of changes which may routinely be expected to occur over time in the size, age-composition and role-structure of an elementary family. The approach to divorce within this framework might focus on two main spheres of analysis. One line of investigation would examine the effect of marital disruption on the family life cycle, and this matter will be considered somewhat briefly later in the paper. Initial attention here, however, will be given to the other possibility, the effect of the life cycle on marital stability. Such an approach is basically epidemiological, the hope being that examination of the relationship between instability and different stages of the cycle might (a) identify what has to be explained; (b) suggest hypotheses, preferably of a causal nature; and (c) afford tests of propositions otherwise derived. Among the difficulties besetting an enterprise of this kind are the following:

1. The absence of a standardised depiction of the stages of the family life cycle;
2. The fact that life events which may be importantly related to marital conflict and instability are omitted in typical versions of the cycle (or, more properly perhaps, are subsumed in an undifferentiated fashion);
3. The uncertain serviceability of divorce as an index of the broader, and sociologically more relevant phenomena of marriage breakdown or marital instability;
4. The ambiguity of the temporal distribution of divorce as an indicator of points of marital strain or vulnerability;
5. The fact that official statistics are not presented in relation to stages of the family life cycle, which have to be inferred from other variables.

Some examination of these points will serve to indicate the developments which are needed before a rigorous analysis can be made of the relationship between the family life cycle and the dissolution of marriage.

The family life cycle as a variable

While the life cycle framework undoubtedly facilitates the marshalling of family data and the identification of significant events in family development, it must be confessed that, so far at any rate, the theoretical yield has not proved generous. It would, perhaps, be premature to follow some critics and dismiss the family life cycle as a variable, but it may be as well to be prepared for ultimate disappointment so far as theoretical power is concerned. To be sure, some investigators have used the developmental cycle as a variable in studying such matters as marital satisfaction, and family economic behaviour, and have been enthusiastic about its utility, but different writers have divided the cycle into different numbers of stages. Doubtless different investigatory purposes are suited by different conceptualisations, and in matters such as the estimation of trend direction it may not be crucial how many stages are defined. However, in considering marital instability and its possible origins in developmental progress, it clearly matters whether we simply dichotomise the expanding versus the contracting phases of the cycle or use, say, the fine calibration described by Rodgers (1962) who proposes 24 stages. In fact, most researchers in this school seek a compromise between uninformative brevity and unmanageable complexity, and the most usual conceptualisation is perhaps the 8-stage system proposed by Duvall (1967). However, this scheme is not universally endorsed or adopted, and the lack of standardisation is potentially inimical to comparative or cumulative work. It may be that different areas of substantive interest require different standardisations, and in any case so far as divorce is concerned the issue is slightly academic while typical official statistics permit only imprecise inference of developmental stage from criteria such as age or marriage duration. If, however, it were ever hoped to persuade official quarters to use the family life cycle as an analytical variable, it would be necessary to agree upon a standard scheme (and for purposes of international comparison it would be necessary to allow for different national patterns of schooling).

A further point is that typically most stages of the family life cycle are defined in relation to the age or developmental status of children, and thus accord primacy to the factor of fertility. Again, some stages are very brief while others may span two decades or more. Such definitions therefore ignore some events which may well be relevant to marital instability, or compound them into stages otherwise defined. For example, the only occupational change explicitly described in Duvall's formulation is the retirement of the husband, but there are others which may influence marital harmony or stability. Employment of the mother has been plausibly related to inter-spousal conflict in some investigations (e.g., Nye and Hoffman, 1963), and it may be that the occupational mobility of the husband can create marital instability (Chester, 1974). The point here is that even an apparently clear relationship between a developmental stage and a dependent variable may be the product in fact of a particular aspect of that stage which is not specified as a defining characteristic. The more compendious the developmental stage the greater is the uncertainty in this, and the postparental stage illustrates the point well. During this lengthy phase there exists the "empty nest", a high probability of the re-employment of the wife, the female menopause and any psychological climacteric in men (plus other phenomena of ageing), long and increasing marital duration, plus other matters which may be related to marital satisfactions and conflict. Similarly, it might be asked if those who remain permanently childless are to be regarded as perpetually remaining in Stage 1 of Duvall's scheme. If (unrealistically) they are, then any division of the population by family cycle stages will produce a class of "beginning families" of immensely diverse marriage durations and conditions. If they are not, then it must be decided at what point attention should be restricted to fertile couples only. Or again, of the order of one fifth of English brides are pregnant, and thus experience a truncated Stage 1. Any relationship found between this brevity and marital instability, however, would be contaminated by the fact that premarital pregnancy is itself divorce-disposing (Christensen and Meissner, 1956).

In summary, then, as a variable the family life cycle lacks clear specification. There is no standard scheme, the developmental sequence is associated with simple and ever-increasing marriage duration, and each individual stage is a compound of diverse experiences. Some writers (e.g., Lansing and Kish, 1957) have found stages of the family life cycle more effective than time-based single variables such as age or duration in predicting items of economic behaviour, but generalisation of this superiority to other behavioural spheres cannot be axiomatic. It may eventually be found that many variables of interest to family sociologists are better explained by longitudinally separate components of the family life cycle (such as marriage duration or occupational developments) than by omni-dimensional horizontal stages. The utility of the family life cycle variable has to be demonstrated in each area of family behaviour, and in the case of divorce this has not yet been done even though there is ample evidence that the relationship between time married and propensity to divorce is curvilinear. Some of the relevant data will be discussed later, but meanwhile attention must turn to a different issue.

Marriage breakdown, marriage break-up, and divorce

The epidemiological approach has certain methodological requirements which in the case of marital instability are currently not easy to meet. There must be good definitions, since we cannot count what we cannot classify, and there must be good case-finding and recording, because the faulty construction of rates can lead only to faulty theoretical explanation. Divorce is a discrete and measurable event, and case-finding presents no problems because the legal termination of marriage cannot be clandestine. Total incidence is therefore readily known, although distributional data are also required if the family life cycle is to be used as a variable. In this section, however, it is necessary to examine the adequacy of divorce figures as an index of marital instability.

Because of its legal properties and its finality divorce is an important marital outcome, and merits study in its own right. It is not, however, the only possible manifestation of marital instability, and it would be incautious to infer too readily from divorce cases to unsuccessful marriages more generally. "Why do some marriages fail?", and "Why do some marriages end in divorce?" are by no means identical questions, and a task for research is to discover why only some disrupted marriages terminate in divorce. To clarify this point, and to evaluate the heuristic value of divorce statistics it will be helpful to distinguish some different marriage situations.

The term "marriage breakdown" (which, incidentally, is taken over from ordinary speech) might perhaps be reserved to cover the broadest notion of marital failure, and defined as *the disruption of a marital relationship through significant failure of one or both partners to give an acceptable performance of marital role-obligations*. Such an abstract formulation obviously requires supplementary definitions of key words like "significant", "acceptable", and "obligations", and a decision on whether these matters are to be objectively or subjectively determined. It has the merit, however, of indicating that divorce is a potential outcome of a situation rather than the situation itself, and borrowing from Goode (1966) we might dichotomise marriage breakdown as follows:

I. "*Empty shell marriage*", where cohabitation persists, but with little meaning for the partners and where there is minimal or negative mutual affective support. Marriages, that is, which are socially and legally existent, but which are distinguished by high levels of disharmony or indifference.

II. *Willed termination*, via divorce, annulment, separation or desertion. Marriages, that is, which have broken up as well as broken down, whether or not the legal nexus has been severed.

Even if we regard them as relevant to our purpose, the former type of marriage presents problems of definition and case-finding which are currently unsolved. Some couples undoubtedly do remain together only in protracted disharmony or indifference, and the origins of empty shell marriage may well relate to the family life cycle, but it is doubtful whether we have either a consensual definition of empty shell marriage or adequate instruments of detection and enumeration. For England, anyway, there is virtually no useable information about marriage breakdown which does not eventuate in some form of break-up, and no more will be said of empty shell marriages except that they should not be ignored, and that their nature, numbers and distribution would be fit subjects for research. Attention will turn instead to the various components of willed termination of marriage, all of which must be noted because to a certain extent at least they are functionally-equivalent alternative outcomes of marital disruption. Even this more definable category, however, is resistant to accurate measurement because some of its components are labile and not all are manifested in public records.

Figure 1 attempts to chart the differentiation of marriages into those which experience breakdown and those which do not. Marriage breakdown as defined above appears at 2B, and divides into empty shell marriages at 3A and willed terminations at 3B. The latter represents the minimum figure for instability of marriage, and it is evident that the divorce figure at 5B portrays only part of the total. The relative proportions involved are clearly relevant to our theme, and so we must look at divorce, annulment, and the various types of separation, versions of which exist in most modern societies. In England these forms of termination appear as follows:

Figure 1.

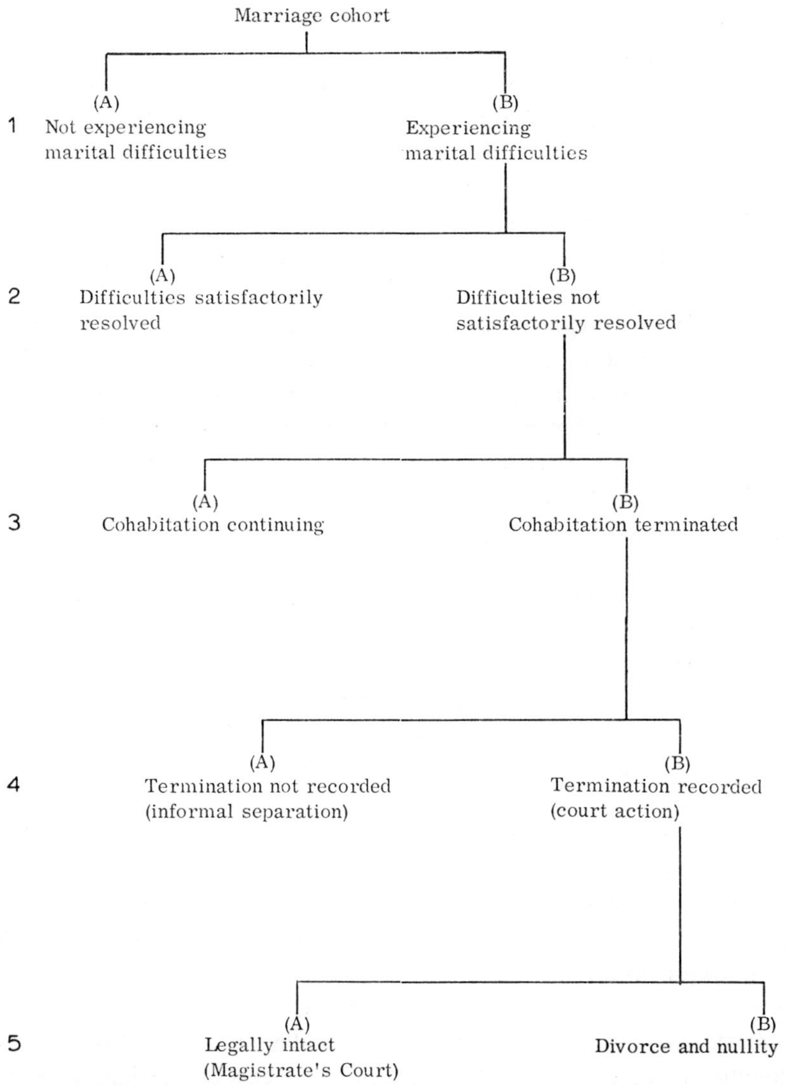

I. *Divorce*, meaning the total dissolution of a marriage.

II. *Annulment*, which technically declares a marriage to be invalid rather than terminated. Like divorce it is granted in the higher courts, and frees the partners to remarry.

III. *Separation*, used as a conceptual compendium to describe situations where the marriage is socially defunct although legally intact, so that the partners cannot remarry. These situations may be classified as:

(a) *Judicial separation.* Also granted in the higher courts, and corresponding to the ecclesiastical divorce *a mensa et thoro*, this is statistically insignificant and may safely be ignored;

(b) *Magistrates' orders.* Various kinds of these are granted in the local courts, normally in connection with maintenance. They are important because applications currently exceed 30,000 per annum, and together with the previous categories these cases are represented at 4B in the diagram;

(c) *Informal separation*, referring to terminations which occur without recourse to law. These cases appear at 4A, and are primarily (but not entirely) responsible for uncertainty about the total of willed terminations. Some couples may arrange private legal settlements, but probably most do not, and anyway such agreements are not publicly recorded.

Divorce is the only category of willed termination that we can measure with certainty. Informal separations cannot even be estimated, and the records of magistrates' proceedings are too uninformative to afford confident measures. Many of these actions are repetitions of earlier proceedings in respect of the same marriage rather than newly-notified cases of marital instability, and an unknown number of orders are effectively dead soon after issue (no court action being required to cancel them in the event of reconciliation). Furthermore, much higher proportions of applications are withdrawn or unsuccessful than in the case of divorce, and little is known about applicants who do not gain an order.

A further noteworthy point is that except for divorce and nullity the categories of willed termination are not necessarily *ultimate* conditions. Informal separation often precedes court action, and many people with magistrates' orders (perhaps about half) go on to divorce after an interval. Knowledge of numbers currently in given situations, therefore, would not indicate ultimate outcomes, and simple totalling would lead to double-counting (Chester, 1971a). Because the components of marriage termination are not permanently discrete we do not have a satisfactory measure of total incidence, and we would only obtain one from either a very long-term longitudinal survey or from studying the marital history of a sample of people in, say, late middle age. Even so, this would give us the experience only of a particular historical cohort, and in England contemporary trends suggest that this would be very misleading about the experience of more recently marrying groups (Chester, 1971a).

Divorce figures alone, then, are an uncertain index of marital instability in relation to the family life cycle even within the contemporary conditions of a given jurisdiction. Equally importantly, this factor makes problems for comparative study, whether the comparison is between different national jurisdictions or between different historical periods in the same society. Valid comparison would require knowledge of *total* marital termination, since the relative proportions of its components would vary not only by real differences in marital stability but also by differences in what Day (1964) conceptualises as the *existential* and *normative* availability of particular options. By the former is meant the legal and financial terms upon which divorce and its alternatives are obtainable, while the latter refers to the acceptability of divorce or its perceived alternatives to spouses and their social circles, and to social opinion generally. There are temporal and geographical variations in the provision of divorce and alternative legal strategies, in grounds recognised and the parties to whom they are available, in financial assistance to litigants, etc. Similarly, there is variation in normative climate, and in assumptions about the appropriateness of different courses of action in particular marital contingencies. Nationally and internationally it seems in general true to say that the divorce option has latterly become more widely available, and more extensively used as an alternative to legal or informal separation. Nevertheless, to make a straightforward comparison of divorce statistics in relation to developmental stages of the family in, say, England, Sweden, Italy and Ireland would more likely mislead us than enhance our understanding.

Summarising this section, then, it may be said that investigation of divorce is a valid and justifiable enterprise, but that this may be as much a study of legal as of marital behaviour. The distribution of divorce may reasonably be studied for what it can tell us about the marital relationship at different stages of the family life cycle, but our real need is for data on termination of marriage more broadly conceived. If, as seems possible in England at least, discordant couples turn increasingly to divorce rather than its alternatives, then the divorce figures will increase in heuristic value. Meanwhile we must be cautious in our inferences, in case the functional alternatives to divorce have a different temporal distribution.

Developmental stages and vulnerability of marriage

The problems of relating marital instability to the family life cycle are not exhausted by the previous discussion, and we must now consider the significance of legal duration of marriage. Statistics indicate that in England as in other countries there is a curvilinear relationship between divorce and time married, with considerable "front-loading" in that peak divorcing occurs in the earlier rather than the later years of marriage. Within the developmental approach the length of time married would be taken as a rough indicator of stage of the family life cycle achieved, with attribution of stage based on standardised demographic data. Even if we make the double assumption, however, that divorce is a serviceable index of instability *and* that developmental stage has more predictive power than simply time married, there are still difficulties in transposing marital duration into developmental stage achieved if the available data are based on legal duration of marriage. This point may be illustrated by the findings from a study of English divorce court records (Chester, 1971b).

Official statistics typically employ the concept of *de jure* duration in the analysis of temporal distribution, and this is measured from the wedding day to the date of the final divorce decree. However, although a marriage has legal reality until the final decree, its socially and sexually effective reality ends when the partners cease to cohabit (even though there may continue to be economic, parental and other transactions between them thereafter). For many investigatory purposes, therefore, the more relevant datum is *de facto* duration, defined as the elapse of time from wedding day to the date of break-up. Even this may overlook a prior period of time in which the marriage has been realistically defunct although not yet terminated by physical parting, but at least *de facto* duration is a better statement of effective endurance of marriage than is *de jure* duration. And, confirming a pattern found in the U.S.A. by Kephart (1954) and Monahan (1962), the English study revealed that *de jure* data overstate effective duration by a margin sufficiently large to embarrass attempts to deduce developmental stage from time married. For the sample studied ($N = 805$) the mean *de jure* duration was 13.7 years, against 9.1 years for *de facto* duration, and the difference between the medians was of similar magnitude. The distribution of intervals between separation and divorce showed that the time-lag ranged up to 30 years, with a median figure of 2.9 years and with one third of the cases extending beyond 4 years. From these figures it seems that, in England anyway, divorce is commonly a *formal* ratification of a long-accomplished event – the *effective* termination of a marriage. In assessing the differential vulnerability of developmental stages, therefore, it is clear that *de jure* duration is an unreliable tool for transposing time into life-cycle categories. An indication of the potential measurement error is shown in Table 1.

Table 1. *Percentage distribution of marriage durations in grouped years (nearest* 1 %)

	0–4	5–9	10–19	over 20
De jure durations	16	29	33	22
De facto durations	38	24	28	10

Duvall's proposed initial stages of the cycle are: I – marriage to birth of first child; II – first child under 2½ years; III – first child 2½ but under 6; IV – first child 6 but under 12. With primary marriages (even if there were premarital pregnancy) we would assume that a couple breaking up within 5 years *must* fall somewhere into the first three stages, with perhaps an emphasis towards stages I and II. The first row of the table shows that on *de jure* duration only 16% of the divorcing couples had durations under 5 years (and thus firm location in Stages I, II or III), whereas the second row indicates that in fact 38% of the couples had effective durations under 5 years. *De facto* duration thus places divorcing couples much more strikingly in these early stages of the cycle, and indeed, detailed inspection shows the peak of breaking-up to be in the third year of marriage, with the most hazardous years running from the first to the fourth wedding anniversaries. Furthermore, it is possible that the briefer the *de facto* duration, the greater is the exaggeration provided by legal duration. Separate analysis of marriages which broke up within 2 years (Chester, 1971c) showed a difference in the means of the two kinds of duration of 6.4 years (against the 4.6 years for all divorces), and a median interval from parting to divorce of 3.8 years (against 2.9 for all cases).

There is another way of indicating the effect induced by differences of duration during the earliest years of marriage. English Census data suggest that by the end of four years approximately 70% of couples in primary marriages have made the transition from Stage I to Stage II (i.e., have produced a child), whereas by the end of two years only 45% have done so. This crucial transition, therefore, is very sensitive to time, and if *de jure* duration overstates the real endurance of marriage by any significant margin then considerable error will be introduced into the attribution of developmental stages. Legal duration gives only the grossest kind of estimate of stage achieved, at least for earlier years of marriage, and once again caution is required in making inferences from officially provided data.

Official statistics

The primary source of information on English divorce is the annual *Registrar General's Statistical Review of England and Wales*, published by the Office of Population Censuses and Surveys (formerly the General Register Office). Some of the regular tables in this publication are cumulative, and every five years or so there is a commentary on the divorce figures in relation to some special topic. Brief details of some aspects of divorce are also available in the *Annual Abstract of Statistics* published by the Central Statistical Office, and this also has cumulative tables. Further and different information can be obtained from *Civil Judicial Statistics*, published by the Lord Chancellor's office, and from the Law Society's *Annual Report on Legal Aid and Advice*. Finally, the reports of the Census of Population have some tables which discriminate those currently of divorced status, although this material has not yet shown itself to be very helpful for research purposes.

From the sociological viewpoint the information provided by these official publications is deficient both in volume and range, although to a great extent the defects are those which are commonly found among collections of routinely-gathered registration data. The tabulation is not necessarily based on sociologically-relevant categories or concepts, desirable items of information are omitted from the tables or not gathered, and cross-tabulations of a complex kind are not undertaken. In justice it should be said, however, that the presentation and detail of the statistics have steadily improved over the past twenty years, and that the official compilers have shown themselves responsive to requests for additions and modifications. The English statistics are, in fact, probably superior to those of many other countries, even though they fall far short of the ideal. They have the virtue of full national coverage which is lacked by the American statistics, and are much fuller than those of, say, Canada and Australia. They certainly do not have the comprehensiveness and convenience of the French documentation newly instituted by the Ministry of Justice however.

The official statistics contain three kinds of information bearing on the family life cycle, and these relate to age at divorce, legal duration of mariage, and fertility (used here in the English demographic meaning of *reproductive performance* rather than *reproductive potential*). Unfortunately, for reasons already discussed, and also because of the way the data are marshalled, these variables can give only the broadest indication of developmental stage. Since all three are mutually related it is not surprising that they concur in the indication they give, which is that in England divorce is most strongly associated with the earlier rather than the later phases of the family life cycle. A brief examination of the statistics is sufficient to demonstrate this, although it must be remembered that such a demonstration does not necessarily indicate a *causal* link between stage of the life cycle and divorce. Unless otherwise stated below, all the statistics presented are taken from the *Statistical Review* for the relevant year.

Age at divorce is a somewhat inconclusive variable, because the table of divorce rates by age does not partition the data by age at marriage, and this creates a margin of uncertainty about the temporal opportunity which divorcees have had to make progress through the stages of the family life cycle. In 1970, however, 40% of the women who divorced were aged under 30 (compared with 27% of the men), 60% were under 35 (men 49%), and 73% were under 40 (men 65%). The sex differences, of course, reflect the higher marrying ages of men, but for both sexes the highest rates of divorce were found in the age group 25–29, at 11.3 per 1,000 married population for women, and 10.7 for men. The next two highest age groups for women were 30–34 (8.9), and 20–24 (7.4), whereas for men the sequence was 30–34 (9.9), and 35–39 (7.6), again reflecting different patterns of age at marriage. These age-specific rates compare with a rate for all ages of 4.7 divorces per 1,000 married population, and bearing in mind both that most people marry at ages of 20 or over and that marriages effectively end some time before divorce, it is safe to conclude that the majority of break-ups leading to divorce are located within Duvall's stages I–IV.

The way in which *de jure* duration misreports the effective duration of marriage has already been discussed, but it is interesting nevertheless to see when divorce occurs in terms of completed years of marriage. In 1966 the mean duration of marriage before dissolution was 13.05 years. This itself suggests early divorcing, and the point is amplified by a consideration of dissolution rates per 1,000 married women. The peak rate is found in the fourth year of marriage, closely followed by the rates for the fifth and sixth years, after which there is a steady decline disturbed only by a noticeable but minor secondary peak at durations around 19 and 20 years. The latter may be related in some way to the launching or postparental stages of the life cycle (Duvall's VI and VII), but as will be noted the relationship between parenthood and divorce is ambiguous.

Statutorily, divorce petitions can be presented during the first three years of marriage only in very rare circumstances, and the very low rates of divorce for the first triennium are thus explicable on purely procedural grounds. It will be recalled that information on *de facto* duration places maximum vulnerability to break-up much earlier than is indicated by *de jure* duration, but even so the legal duration figures do confirm the emphasis on the early developmental stages, since the peak divorce rates are found among couples who can scarcely have moved beyond Stage III. The figures also indicate, incidentally, that where either spouse is under 20 the tendency for divorce to be early is particularly marked.

This information on divorce-propensity by time married (whether the latter is taken directly as a variable or assumed to represent developmental stage) matches oddly with the results of studies of marital satisfaction over time. There are in fact no studies of this kind for English marriage, but assuming that the American findings are applicable it would appear that the relationship between satisfaction and instability is positive rather than inverse as might be expected. American studies broadly concur that marital satisfaction is at a peak in the earliest years of marriage (when divorce is also high) and then declines to a nadir or a plateau in the late stages of the family cycle (the studies are at some odds over the shape of the curve after the downward trend through the childbearing and child-rearing years). The curves of satisfaction and instability thus tend to follow rather than oppose each other, and to common sense this appears paradoxical. Since the divorce figures are unequivocal, a first response might be to assume that the marital satisfaction studies are badly amiss, but it may not be necessary to be so iconoclastic.

To begin with, the relationship between satisfaction and instability may not be the common-sensical one. Cuber and Harroff (1963; 1965), for instance, seem to indicate that marriages may be unhappy and yet stable, perhaps because contentment with the instrumental aspects of marriage can compensate for deficits in marital satisfaction. Again, early break-up of marriage perhaps suggests gross and quickly-discoverable mismatching, and it may be that while *most* couples experience peak satisfaction in the early years there are significant minority numbers of marriages which are of dubious viability from the beginning, and which are rapidly aborted by divorce. This would inflate the figures for early divorce, and possibly account for the initial paradox of peak satisfaction concurrent with peak divorce, but would leave the subsequent parallel decline in both variables to be accounted for. It is perhaps likely that there is systematic variation over the family life cycle in the factors determining marital stability, and that any disruptive push created by declining marital satisfaction is countered or more than countered by such things as increasing interhabituation, lack of optimism about alternative futures, increasing entrapment in mundane obligations, occupational or other non-marital sources of contentment, pleasure from other aspects of marital status, parental factors and so on. The process of becoming un-matched is a gradual one, and perhaps leads to different marital strategies from those adopted in the case of initial mismatching. Nevertheless, it is somewhat disturbing that satisfactions studies accord rather ill with instability patterns, and clearly there is something here to be explained.

Like age and marriage duration data, the fertility patterns of divorcing couples locate instability primarily in the earlier stages of the family cycle. To begin with, some quarter of English divorcing couples are childless, and are therefore notionally in Stage I. More than 70% of these marriages have endured over 5 years however, and one third have lasted more than 10 years. Indeed, childless couples continue to divorce beyond the end of the second decade, and as previously suggested it seems unrealistic to suppose that the conditions implied by the concept of "beginning families" are infinitely extended. It is more reasonable to suppose that permanently childless couples have a cycle of development which has its own logic, and depiction of this seems scarcely to have begun.

It is often held, sometimes axiomatically, that children are a stabilising force in marriage (or that childlessness is destabilising). Monahan (1955) and Chester (1972c) have argued, however, that the alleged fertility deficit of the divorce population may be an artifact of reporting procedures, and that the usually assumed relationship between fertility and stability may be non-existent. However that may be, the English fertility data confirm that the early stages of the family cycle are most implicated in divorce. The presentation of the data does not permit precise inference of developmental stage, but some things can be said. For instance, in 1970 there were 43,000 divorces involving children, and 27,600 of these had durations of less than fifteen years. Thus two thirds of these divorcing couples can scarcely have progressed beyond Stage IV at divorce, and this would be true of an even larger proportion at break-up. Approaching from another angle, there were 93,700 children affected by divorce in 1970, of whom 19% were under 5, 55% under 11, and 73% under 16 at the time of the divorce. Bearing in mind again that marriages effectively break up some time before the divorce, it is obvious that from the child's point of view his family is most likely to break up while it is in one of Stages II–IV. Well under one fifth of the "children" affected by divorce in 1972 were in fact over 20.

Age, duration and fertility thus converge in indicating that if the family life cycle is an analytically strategic variable, then in England it is to Stages I–IV (in Duvall's classification) that we should attend most closely. Remembering the *caveat* that divorce is but one category of willed termination, albeit perhaps the most important, we can add that the meagre available information on magistrates' orders suggests that this form of break-up is also principally related to the earlier developmental stages. A study of the orders made in 1966 (McGregor *et al.*, 1970) showed that 63% were made before the marriage had endured 12 years, and 73% before 15 years duration. These percentages were higher when children were involved in the proceedings, and three-quarters of the wives in fact had children under 16 at the time of the order. As might be expected the wives concerned were relatively youthful when they went to the court, 74% being aged under 40. Thus, although *informal* separations are still a completely unknown quantity, we can say that two of the categories of willed termination in England seem to be similarly related to the family life cycle. Actuarially speaking, it is families in the early developmental stages who are most at risk of break-up, although we cannot yet assert that stage of the cycle is the critical variable.

Conclusion

This paper has not presented time-based data on English divorce in detailed tabular form because this would not have greatly illuminated the foregoing summary commentary. Available information permits only broad inferences about the distribution of marital instability over the family life cycle, and does not allow any sure demonstration that the concept of developmental stage is superior in explanatory or predictive power to other time-related variables. Break-up of marriage clearly occurs most prominently in the earlier stages of the cycle, but causal relationships remain for the present at the level of possibility or plausibility. In lieu of detailed statistical reporting an attempt has been made to explore some of the difficulties which lie in the path of any study of the relationship between the cycle of family development and termination of marriage, and the net result of this is to emphasise the need for caution, and for conceptual and statistical refinement.

Concentration here on the *incidence* of divorce is not intended to suggest that no other relevant issues exist in considering the effect of developmental stages on divorce behaviour. Certain other particularities of divorce vary over the cycle in ways which might afford insight into the developmental aspects of the marital relationship, and two upon which some suggestive information is available are the sex-distribution of petitions and the distribution of grounds. Currently wives obtain nearly two thirds of English divorces, but the female share varies by duration of marriage (Chester, 1970), and detailed information might say something of the marital experience which is afforded to each spouse at different points of the cycle. The grounds cited in the petitions also show a differential distribution by sex, and a variation by duration of marriage as well, and although the relationships between grounds of divorce, complaints about the marriage, and causes of divorce-initiation are not well understood, these variations could say something about maritally offensive behaviour and responses to it in relation to different developmental stages. These aspects of divorce are not sufficiently well-documented for worth-while consideration here, but enough is known to suggest that they represent potentially fruitful fields of enquiry.

The further (and major) matter which has not been pursued in the main body of the text is the effect of marriage break-up in truncating or redirecting the family life cycle, and in creating anomalous patterns of development. The basic paradigm in the developmental approach traces the "normal" family life cycle from marriage to post-retirement and dissolution by death. Divorce and other forms of willed termination deflect this cycle into deviant paths for some, and, through remarriage or unmarried cohabitation, create new families which also may not follow the normal course.

Childless marriages beyond a certain duration already constitute a deviation from the model assumed in the developmental approach, and the need to study the developmental patterns of such unions has been mentioned. When one spouse wilfully departs from a childless marriage, at whatever stage, the family cycle simply terminates, since neither partner can meaningfully be regarded as a residual family. If there are dependent children, however, one spouse is normally left with the responsibility for them, and this does create a residual family which will develop with time. Such development may be as a one-parent family or as a reconstituted family (or both in sequence), and either way the normal developmental path is not followed.

In one-parent families the role-obligations of the missing partner are either redistributed or unfulfilled, and whichever is the case the family's experience in successive developmental stages will differ from that of complete families. Where the absentee is replaced by marriage (or by informal means), the role-structure may be relatively normal but the sequence of stages will not. It is therefore of some consequence to have information about both the extent to which broken families are reconstituted, and of characteristic behaviour patterns in remarriages and residual families.

In England currently some 18% of all marriages involve remarriage for at least one partner, and marriage rates for divorcees are very high, so that undoubtedly reconstitution is a common consequence of marriage break-up. Sometimes the consequence is stable cohabitation with a new partner rather than formal remarriage, but we have no knowledge of the number of irregular unions or of how they differ developmentally from legal marriages. Indeed, there is no study of English remarriage which would tell us, for instance, whether new spouses characteristically take on the full obligations of their predecessors (e.g., parental as well as marital roles). Some information is available about behaviour in one-parent families (e.g., Marsden, 1969; George and Wilding, 1972), but there is no clear estimate of numbers because this condition is frequently a transitory stage between break-up and remarriage, and is therefore experienced by a greater total number than the number of permanently depleted families.

Enough has been said to indicate the desirability of conceptualising, measuring and studying the results of marriage termination in modifying the normal cycle of development. With current rates of willed termination a significant minority of the population will not follow the normal path, and the consequences of marital instability for the family cycle are as noteworthy as the consequences of the life cycle for marital instability. Many (and probably growing numbers) will experience not *the* cycle of development but rather a number of part-cycles or irregular cycles. Fuller knowledge of this, as of the developmental distribution of marriage termination, must wait upon an increased attention from English social scientists, and at the time of writing even an adequate sociography is not yet in sight.

Résumé

Le divorce et le cycle de la vie familiale en Grande-Bretagne

Utilisant des données anglaises, cet article illustre les difficultés à rendre compte de l'instabilité du mariage par rapport au cycle de la vie familiale, et indique la nécessité d'un raffinement conceptuel et statistique. Une analyse, utilisant comme variable indépendante le cycle de la vie familiale et comme variable dépendante l'instabilité maritale, pourrait en principe donner des informations sur les aspects développementalistes de la relation maritale ainsi que quelques bases pour une compréhension théorique. Malheureusement cela comporte de grandes difficultés et notamment:

1. Plusieurs auteurs proposent différents nombres d'étapes pour le cycle de la vie familiale, et l'absence d'une définition standard diminue l'utilité du concept. L'accroissement des phases qui est conceptualisé améliore la sensibilité du concept à l'égard des processus développementaux dans le mariage mais ajoute aussi à la complexité analytique et rencontre des inadéquations dans l'information statistique disponible. Une absence de standardisation crée aussi des problèmes dans le cadre d'une étude cumulative ou comparative.
2. Dans la plupart des versions du cycle familial, les étapes sont définies en relation avec l'âge ou l'état des enfants. Ces deux caractères excluent de l'analyse les couples sans enfants et rend obscure l'influence possible de changements professionnels ou autres événements qui surviennent durant les étapes définies uniquement par la maturation des enfants. En plus, le poids et les événements marquant la transition entre les étapes est variable, ainsi que la durée des étapes.
3. Les statistiques sur le divorce ne sont pas nécessairement de bons indices de l'instabilité maritale parce que les mariages se terminent aussi par une séparation formelle et informelle. Par ailleurs, ceux qui se séparent, divorcent souvent plus tard, ceci présentant des problèmes de compte double. Le divorce est une stratégie légale qui est inégalement disponible pour des groupes différents à différents moments et à différents endroits; et nous avons besoin d'une mesure de l'instabilité maritale plus complexe que celle fournie par les seules statistiques. Les conclusions de ce fait sont sujettes à erreur et doivent être révisées.
4. Le concept de durée du mariage utilisé dans les statistiques officielles se réfère à la durée *de jure* du mariage, du jour du mariage à la date du divorce. Cependant les couples se séparent généralement avant de divorcer, et pour mesurer la vulnérabilité du mariage un concept plus pertinent est celui de la durée *de facto*, qui va du jour du mariage à la date de séparation.

   C'est pourquoi les statistiques officielles tendent à localiser la fin du mariage plus tard dans le cycle de la vie de famille qu'elle ne l'est en réalité.
5. Les statistiques officielles du divorce n'utilisent pas le cycle de la vie de famille comme variable et c'est pourquoi les étapes du développement doivent être déduites

d'autres variables diachroniques tel que l'âge auquel on divorce, la durée du mariage et la fertilité. Celles-ci ne peuvent offrir que des indications imprécises sur l'étape du cycle familial en relation avec la propension différentielle au divorce. Dans le cas anglais les statistiques ne font qu'indiquer que les premières étapes du cycle de la vie familiale sont plus vulnérables au divorce que ne le sont les étapes ultérieures.

Il est donc clair qu'en relation avec l'analyse de l'instabilité maritale le concept du cycle de vie familiale a souvent une utilité quelque peu limitée. En plus, l'article démontre que l'instabilité du mariage influence le cycle de la vie familiale aussi bien que l'inverse. La fin du mariage brise l'étape du développement conceptualisé comme cycle et conduit soit à un remariage et à un cycle nouveau mais différent, soit à des formations familiales (telles que des familles avec un seul père ou mère) qui n'observent pas le chemin normal du développement. Avec des taux élevés et croissants pour les différentes formes de fin de mariage, il est clair qu'une grande partie de la population ne fera pas l'expérience de la suite prévue d'étapes telles qu'elles sont conceptualisées par cycle de la vie familiale, mais verra plutôt un ensemble de cycles partiels ou de cycles irréguliers. Le nombre et la nature de ces derniers nécessiterait d'en faire l'objet d'une recherche, ce qui ne paraît pas être le cas en Angleterre.

NOTE

Great Britain does not constitute a single jurisdiction, Scotland in particular having a separate legal system. All the commentary in this paper relates to the divorce statistics for England and Wales, and also to the situation under the divorce law as it was until 1st January 1971. The effects of the new law from that date are not yet properly visible.

REFERENCES

Chester, R. (1970), "Sex differences in divorce behaviour", *Journal of Biosocial Science*, Suppl. 2: 121.

—— (1971a), "Contemporary trends in the stability of English marriage", *Journal of Biosocial Science*, 3: 389.

—— (1971b), "The duration of marriage to divorce", *British Journal of Sociology*, 22: 172.

—— (1971c), "Some characteristics of marriages of brief duration", *Medical Gynaecology and Sociology*, 6: 9.

—— (1972a), "Divorce and legal aid; a false hypothesis", *Sociology*, 6: 205.

—— (1972b), "Current incidence and trends in marital breakdown", *Postgraduate Medical Journal*, 48: 529.

—— (1972c), "Is there a relationship between childlessness and marriage breakdown", *Journal of Biosocial Science*, 4: 443.

—— (1974), "Social mobility and marital stability: a critical note", forthcoming, *Journal of Marriage and the Family*, May.

Christensen, H.T., and Meissner, H.H. (1953), "Studies in child-rearing: III – premarital pregnancy as a factor in divorce", *American Sociological Review*, 18: 641.

Cuber, J.F., and Harroff, P. (1963), "The more total view: relationships among men and women of the upper middle class", *Marriage and Family Living*, 25: 140.

—— (1963), *The Significant Americans*, New York, Appleton-Century-Crofts.

Day, L.H. (1964), "Patterns of divorce in Australia and the United States", *American Sociological Review*, 29: 509.

Duvall, E. M. (1967), *Family Development*, Philadelphia, Lippincott.
Fletcher, R. (1962), *The Family and Marriage in Britain*, Harmondsworth, Penguin Books.
George, V., and Wilding, R. (1972), *Motherless Families*, London, Routledge and Kegan Paul.
Goode, W. J. (1966), "Family disorganisation" in R. K. Merton and R. A. Nisbet (eds.), *Contemporary Social Problems*, New York, Harcourt, Brace and World.
Kephart, W. M. (1954), "The duration of marriage", *American Sociological Review*, 19: 287.
Lansing, J. B., and Kish, L. (1957), "Family life cycle as an independent variable", *American Sociological Review*, 22: 512.
Marsden, D. (1969), *Mothers Alone*. London, Allen Lane.
McGregor, O. R. (1957), *Divorce in England*, London, Heinemann.
Monahan, T. P. (1955), "Is childlessness related to marital stability", *American Sociological Review*, 20: 446.
—— (1962), "When married couples part: statistical trends and relationships in divorce", *American Sociological Review*, 27: 625.
Rodgers, R. H. (1962), *Improvements in the Construction and Analysis of Family Life Cycle Categories*, Kalamazoo, Western Michigan University.
Rowntree, G., and Carrier, N. H. (1958), "The resort to divorce in England and Wales 1858–1957", *Population Studies*, 11: 188.

12. The connection between the family cycle and divorce rates. An analysis based on European data*

RENATE KÜNZEL

The increase in divorce rates in most countries has led to divorce becoming one of the most frequently discussed problems in "family disorganisation" (König, 1969: 271). This interest in the problem of divorce has up till now, however, hardly led to any ideologically unbiassed analysis of existing circumstances and their causes. On the contrary, divorce is continually considered as an isolated problem and the old prejudice repeated about the institutions of marriage and the family being endangered by the growth of divorce.

In order to contrast this widespread notion with a neutral analysis, the phenomenon of divorce will therefore be considered against the background of total societal changes. We start here from the hypothesis that the socio-economic structure of a society has an effect on the various phases of the family cycle in their course of development and contents and, through these changes, influences the divorce rates. We shall attempt to test this hypothesis in two steps.

* This essay is part of a three-stage research project on the situation of divorced women in the Federal Republic of Germany.

The first stage of the project is an international comparative investigation of cultural and socio-economic relationships in terms of codified norms relating to divorce regulations, and also of the influence of socio-economic structural data on family phases and thus on divorce behaviour. In the second stage of the project an investigation is at present being made, based on attitudes in the West-German public to marriage and divorce, of the extent to which the codified regulations on behaviour in the Law on Marriage and the Family are internalised and harmonise with informal mechanisms of regulation. The third stage will then investigate the problem of divorce on the level of concrete behaviour, i.e., with regard to the details of the day-to-day life of women, particular interest being focussed on the situation of divorced women in the various phases of the divorce process.

The essay presents extracts from the results of the first stage of the project, being, however, restricted regionally to Europe.

1. *Influence of socio-economic structural changes on the course of development and the contents of family cycles*

We shall firstly attempt to demonstrate the connection between the socio-economic structure of a country and the phases of the family cycle. In order to be able to demonstrate the changes in the phases of the family cycle that are associated with social change, we have classified all European countries into two groups according to their level of development. The first group (13 countries) is composed of the *highly industrialised* countries, in which only a small proportion of male employed persons works in the farming sector, but a large proportion in industry and mining, and where academic and technical occupations are relatively numerous. Energy consumption per head is high (basis for calculation is over 5,000 kg. of coal), as is the gross national product per person (over 1,500 dollars a year). The distribution of income is broad – half the income is distributed among 40% to 47% of the population. A large proportion of the population lives in towns of over 100,000 inhabitants (over 30%), and the level of education, measured by the expenditure on education (70 dollars a head and more per annum) and the proportion of students in the total population (60 students and above per 10,000 people), is high.

The second group (15 countries) is *not highly industrialised*, but has attained a *medium* degree of industrialisation, only a few countries being *agrarian*. The proportion of those employed in the farming sector is higher than in the first group, the proportion of academic and technical occupations is lower. Similarly, energy consumption and the share per head in the gross national product lie below the values of the first group. The distribution of income is not so balanced, urbanisation is not so far advanced and the educational level does not attain the standard of the highly industrialised countries.

This classification has been made on the basis of statistical material from different volumes of the *Demographic Yearbook* edited by the United Nations, New York, and the *World Handbook of Political and Social Indicators* (Taylor and Hudson, 1972). All the data used below come from these publications.

We shall compare data from the two groups of countries that are appropriate for characterising the phases of the family cycle. The age of marriage and the expectation of life, which give the lower and upper limits of the possible length of marriage, are indicators for the framework enclosing the various phases of the family cycle. The number of children and the sequence of births, and also the alternation of the wife's intra-family and occupational activities determine the distribution and content of the phases of the family cycle and the constellation of roles within the family. Unfortunately, we only have these rough indicators available to say anything about the phases of the family cycle in the various countries.

The interpretation of socio-economic data with regard to phases of the family cycle is, however, problematic in many respects. It is our aim to demonstrate typical changes in the phases of the family cycle that result from industrialisation, urbanisation and a rise in the level of education in a country. This assumes that there are variables ("universals") independent of time and culture that are associated with these socio-economic processes. If this were not the case, then we could not consider these data independently of their historical and cultural context.

Besides this there is another decisive methodological problem. In investigating the influence of socio-economic structures on the changes in the family phases of individuals we contrast aggregate data, i.e., collective properties, with one another, and cannot infer the behaviour of individuals directly from these. In deducing from the collective to the individual level there is a danger of coming to false conclusions (ecological fallacy), since the aggregate data reproduce the marginal distribution without expressing anything about the internal distributions, which may be concealed or cancelled out in the marginal distribution (Hummell, 1972: 55f).

In order to be able to carry out this analysis at all we start, despite these considerations, from the assumption that the results of the aggregate data lead to hypotheses that can be carried over onto the individual level – i.e., that from the change in the socio-economic structures of different societies and the observable changes in the phases of the family cycle it is possible to deduce interpretable relationships for the behaviour of individuals.

As the analysis of the data material in Table 1 shows, the *marriage age* of men in many highly industrialised countries is 26 years or less, but in most countries with a lower degree of industrialisation it is 27 and above. For women a corresponding tendency cannot be observed on the level of the aggregate data. In the developing industrial countries women marry young, i.e., mostly at the age of 23 or below, whereas in most highly industrialised countries the marriage age of women is 24 and above.

As regards the individual level, we can assume that in developing industrial countries a greater dependence on the family tends to prevent

Table 1. *Level of development of the European countries* and data on the course of development of the family cycle***

Data on the course of development of the family cycle	Developing industrial countries (15)	Highly industrialised countries (13)
Man's medium age of marriage		
26 and younger	20%	31%
27 years	40%	31%
28 years and above	40%	38%
Woman's medium age of marriage		
23 and younger	47%	16%
24 years	20%	46%
25 and above	33%	38%
Man's average expectation of life in his 20th year		
up to 50 years of age	16%	46%
51–52	46%	31%
53 and above	38%	23%
Woman's average expectation of life in her 20th year		
up to 55 years of age	46%	8%
56 years of age	38%	59%
57 and above	16%	33%

* For the definition of the types of countries, *cf.* the first paragraphs of Section 1 of this article.

** Sources: *Medium age of marriage of the man and of the woman:* United Nations, 1969: 498 f.; *Average expectation of life of the man and of the woman in the 20th year of life:* United Nations, 1970: 640 f.

men from marrying earlier. The chance of building up one's own existence independently of the family of procreation rises with advancing industrialisation and the creation of new occupations, which arise in a process of differentiating out of the family sphere (Ogburn and Nimkoff, 1955: 125 f.). This makes it possible for men to marry earlier. As long as men are economically responsible for the family, their age of marriage must be more strongly determined by external factors than that of women, which is determined more by ideological factors (Goode, 1963: 44). Thus, the marriage age of women can be low when it is not usual for them to be in employment and when they live in financial dependence either on the family of procreation or on the family of orientation.

From contrasting the marriage ages of men and women in the various countries it can be deduced, for the individual level, that the age differences between the partners are higher in the developing industrial countries than in the highly industrialised ones, which should not be without significance for the relationship between the marriage partners.

As our data show, the *expectations of life* are also different in the two groups of countries considered, those of men being basically poorer than those of women. Regardless of the level of development of a country, men nearly always have a lower expectation of life than women. In most developing industrial countries the life expectation of a 20-year old woman is at the most 55, that of a 20-year old man 51 to 52; in highly industrialised countries it is 56 and above for women and only 50 for men. Even in the less industrialised countries of Europe a more propitious economic situation and, associated with this, better nutrition and medical care have already led to a rise in the life expectations of the population. The pattern frequently encountered in earlier times of men marrying several times during their lives because of the high mortality of women in child-birth – in 1850 half of the female population died before the age of 45, whereas nearly 90% survive that age today (Myrdal and Klein, 1968: 13) – hardly occurs now. On the other hand, it can be deduced from the results for the various countries that, in the harsh competitive struggle and the intensified drive for productivity at work in the highly industrialised countries, the life expectation of men does not rise to the same extent as that of women.

A significant result that we can deduce from the tendencies appearing in Table 1 is that, with increasing industrialisation, the relationship between age and the phases of the family cycle alters, which means that a restructuring of the family cycles must be associated simultaneously with this (König, 1969: 20). If there is a tendency for the age of marriage to fall with increasing industrialisation and for the expectation of life to rise generally, then the average length of marriages will increase. It can easily be worked out that, when the age of marriage – particularly of men – is high and is associated with a low expectation of life, then the length of marriages must be relatively short, whereas with a low age of marriage and a high expectation of life a considerably greater length of marriages is to be expected.

Now it can be assumed that in the groups of countries under consideration not only the beginning and end, and thus the possible *length* of the phases of the family cycle change, but at the same time their *contents* change too. In the course of industrialisation functions are increasingly transferred out of the family (König, 1967: 78) into other areas of society. Where the family had previously produced for itself many of the things it needed (Ogburn and Nimkoff, 1955: 125 f.), it now turns more and more from being a place of production into a place of consumption ("Séminaire International sur la Famille", 1969: 571), and in doing so changes the role constellation of its members. Where the man's place of work in the sphere of agriculture and handicrafts was at least near to the family, with the professionalisation of many tasks a separation of the private and the occupational spheres comes about. Through more and more tasks being taken away from the family and being professionalised, the area of women's tasks within the family has become considerably restricted (Treinen and Brothun, 1973: 256). It thus becomes possible that

Table 2. *Level of development of the European countries* and data on the content of the family cycle***

Data on the content of the family cycle	Developing industrial countries	Highly developed industrial countries
Population growth	(15)	(13)
up to 1.1%	60%	70%
1.2% and above	40%	30%
Percentage of women in the total of all employed persons	(14)	(13)
under 30%	36%	8%
30–39%	36%	69%
40% and above	28%	23%
Family status of women in employment		
single:	(6)	(11)
under 50%	33%	73%
50% and above	67%	27%
married:	(7)	(12)
under 50%	71%	42%
50% and above	29%	58%

* See Table 1, Note *.

** Sources: *Population growth* (growth rates from 1960 to 1965): Taylor and Hudson, 1972: 295 f.; *Percentage of women in the total of all employed persons*: calculated from United Nations, 1965: 190 f. A certain amount of caution is recommended in comparing the data on the female working population in the various countries: the same occupations – despite the definition recommended by the United Nations – may be differently classified in different countries. The extent to which women's occupations are counted as employment in any particular country may also be an indication of the status of women there; *Family status of women in employment*: calculated from United Nations, 1969: 287 f.

the woman, deprived of her formerly abundant tasks, leaves the intra-family sphere and goes out to work. With this begins a trend to see the function of housewife in a marriage as no longer being the only solution. These changes should manifest themselves, in a comparison between countries, in an increasing *proportion of women in employment*. As Table 2 shows, the proportion of women who are working in relation to all employed persons is in fact lower in the developing industrial countries than in the highly industrialised ones, where, with the exception of one country, 30% or more of all employed persons are women. The developing industrial countries in which the proportion of women in the total of employed persons is 40% or more, are Communist countries, where women are already integrated into the work process to a higher extent, or where activities carried out by women, e.g., in collectivised agriculture, are more frequently classified as employment than in Western countries. Apart from socio-economic data, it becomes clear from this how important political factors can be.

Data on the family situation of women in employment are available for some countries. Although the data are only available for a few countries, we can deduce from them the tendency for employed women in the developing industrial countries to be recruited predominantly from the reservoir of unmarried women, whereas in highly industrialised countries more than half of the employed women are married (Titmuss, 1962: Foreword). In the developing industrial countries the woman's pre-marital employment is presumably not so much a result of changed role expectations – on the contrary it is accepted as a transitional phase before marriage that also offers the chance of acquiring a dowry. With increasing industrialisation it gradually becomes more usual for the dowry to be replaced by occupational training for the woman (Dunckelmann, 1961: 103) and more and more frequent for her to remain in employment after marriage. Nevertheless, life-long employment for women – except in Communist countries, where employment frequently occurs, despite maternity (Treinen and Brothun, 1973: 251) – has not yet become the prevailing pattern. In Western countries, keeping an employment appears to be sanctioned for women predominantly in the first years of marriage (Dunckelmann 1961: 156), when higher expenditures for purchases cannot be met out of the man's income (Dunckelmann, 1961: 144). As long as occupation and career belong to the external sphere in Western societies, while women are identified with internal relationships, i.e., with the family sphere, they see themselves confronted with diverging role expectations. When they take on an occupation they are not relieved of their functions within the family and are thus faced with the dilemma of having to decide either for their occupation or for the family (*cf.* on this, Treinen and Brothun, 1973: 255).

A further decisive difference that changes the family cycles both in their course of development and in their content is in the *number of children* that are on the average brought up in a family. In agrarian and pre-industrial societies, where the standard of living is relatively low and does not rise for generations, there are many children to a marriage and their births extend over a long period of time. With industrialisation, urbanisation and a longer period for education, the investments required to bring up a child rise. All the same, the continual reduction in birth rates with increasing industrialisation can hardly be explained by the higher expenditure. It is rather to be supposed that there are class-specific norms with regard to what is aimed for and regarded as being the ideal number of children, and that these norms are above all determined by cultural traditions (*cf.* Nimkoff, 1965: 351, who refers to the influence of Catholicism). It should then depend on economic factors to what extent these norms are fulfilled. Whereas in 1870 there were 5.8 children to one married woman, of three married women today only one still has more than two children (Myrdal and Klein, 1968: 20), which in addition are planned in shorter and shorter successions of births in the first years of marriage. Whereas 50 years ago a woman spent on the average 15 years of a considerably shorter life in actual child-bearing and nursing of babies, the corresponding average is three and a half years today (Myrdal and Klein, 1968: 20, *cf.* also König, 1969: 20). At the time when children in highly industrialised countries leave home, the parents are 40, and at the most 50 years old (Myrdal and Klein, 1968: 37 f.). A long span of life still lies ahead of them. At this time in the middle classes the husband is frequently just at the peak of his career and thus more strongly oriented to his work than to his marriage (König, 1969: 21). And the wife can no longer concern herself with her tasks in the family: "... her main justification, the work for which she 'gave up everything', is gone ..." (Mead, 1949: 332 f.). Women who gave up their jobs because of the family only find their way back into a job with difficulty, after a long break which they have spent in the family with children (*cf.* the report of the Institut für Arbeitsmarkt und Berufsforschung, 1970: only 17% of the women who were looking for work in Germany in 1968 through the employment exchanges were aged 40 and above). Exceptions to this rule, to a certain extent, are the German Democratic Republic and the Soviet Union, where a return to work occurs more frequently, as also in the U.S.A. (Treinen and Brothun, 1973: 252). Hardly any woman, however, after a break of 15 years or more, can resume a career once it has been interrupted.

The trend to reduce the number of children should, in our comparison, be reflected on the country level: as shown by Table 2, with its data on population growth – an indicator for the size of families – countries with a low or medium degree of industrialisation have higher growth rates than highly industrialised countries. From this a lower number of children per family in the highly industrialised countries can be inferred. We only have data on the average number of children per mother for seven of the highly industrialised countries: in all seven the number of children is under three. We do not possess further data for the countries investigated, e.g., on the length of active maternity.

The more the woman, in the course of industrialisation, is needed outside the family and the smaller the number of children she has to bring up, the more she acquires the chance of building up her own independent existence beside the man and on equal terms with him. The pressure of the changed circumstances will then gradually compel the notion of the woman's "correct place" to be revised (Goode, 1963: 56). Every change, though, that affects the woman's role also affects that of the man, and every change brings consequences for the organisation of the family. A falling age of marriage, rising expectation of life, a smaller number of children and the separation of the private and the occupational spheres in association with the growing integration of the woman into the occupational sphere lead to a change in the family situation and thus in the phases of the family cycle in the highly industrialised countries. An important change should be that the period of time in which the family cycles lie becomes longer and that phases develop that are more and more clearly distinct from one another. And roles and role constellations involving the partners that are relevant to each particular phase of the family cycle can then be worked out, the components of the roles resulting in each case from the concrete tasks and functions that determine this life situation. In the course of life the role constellations of the members of the family and thus the elements of their roles change many times: in the first phase of marriage the two partners live mostly without children. If the wife continues to go out to work in this first phase, although her role configuration has been changed by marrying, she has not at the same time, however, given up other, earlier elements of her role. If a withdrawal from working life is associated with the birth of the first child, then her role configuration undergoes a decisive change; elements of the mother role must be adopted and at the same time the wife's role in relation to her husband is redefined. Yet other role configurations and constellations result when there are children of school age in the family, and others again when one day they leave home. As the children grow up, the woman's intra-family tasks become fewer. The more, in the course of the children phase of marriage, the woman has maintained contact with working life by temporary or permanent employment, the greater is her chance, after the children have left home, of re-integrating herself into an occupation.

The various phases of the family cycle in the highly industrialised countries make plain how, with the passing of time, the role constellations of the marriage partners change several times and thus produce phases of differing stability, the phases without children and the times when the woman can engage in employment having a lower stability. In agrarian countries and developing industrial countries on the one hand the length of marriage tends to be shorter, but what should be more decisive, though, is that the whole of the marriage has more or less the same content and tasks and that there is hardly any formation of phases that are clearly distinguishable from one another, with the consequences that this entails.

We started from the hypothesis that the socio-economic structure of a country determines the family cycle in its course of development and contents. Even though we did not want to exclude cultural influences, our socio-economic analysis has made references to differences in the family cycles in the countries investigated.

2. *Influence of changes in family cycles on divorce rates*

In this second step of our analysis it will now be shown that these changes in the family cycles affect divorce rates. With the aid of the indicators for describing family cycles that we have for each country, we shall now attempt in what follows to establish trends in the frequency of divorce. Our starting point is that changes in the family phases also always lead to changes in the divorce rates. Since not every breakdown of a marriage ends in divorce – "divorce is but one course of action open to those whose marriages fail" – divorce rates are always only an imperfect index of marital disruption (Chester, 1972: 529). Disruptions can have the most diverging consequences, which – as long as they do not lead to divorce – cannot be statistically measured at all. These differing reactions to the disruption of a marriage can be considered as latent crises. If our hypotheses about the connection between the altered family cycle and divorce are valid, then we can also assume that the "latent" crises caused by disruption will show a similar variation.

In the following analysis of divorce trends we assume again that developments observable in each country permit statements to be made about the divorce tendency of individuals. We assume that the rise in divorce rates associated with advancing industrialisation can be explained by changes in the family cycles and that these changes themselves are associated with a change in the role constellations within the families. To what extent the indicators that correlate with the frequency of divorce in the countries investigated are really capable of affecting the divorce tendency of individuals can only be established through empirical investigations on the individual level. Only in this way is it possible to test whether trends that we observed in contrasting aggregate data show up variables that affect the divorce tendency of individuals.

In Tables 3 and 4 the divorce rates in the various countries are shown as dependents of the indicators that describe the course of development and the content of the phases of the family cycle.

With reference to the *age of marriage* of men and women in the various countries it proves to be the case that – as expected – the divorce rates rise with a descending age of marriage: in countries where the men's medium age of marriage is 26 and below and the women's 23 and below, the divorce rates are high; on the other hand, in countries where the man's age of marriage is 27 and above and the woman's 24 and above, the divorce rates are low. The age of marriage should be an important indicator, since the age at which a family is started goes towards determining the course of development and content of family cycles. Thus, various investigations indicate that the age at which a marriage starts is significant for its subsequent stability. Ogburn and Nimkoff (1955: 252; *cf.* also Winch, 1971: 599) found out that it is especially marriages between young people that are insecure. Glick also points out that early marriages are less stable than those contracted at a rather more mature age: thus the medium age of the first marriage of women who were no longer in their first marriage was two years lower than of those who were still in their first marriage (1957: 56). Marriages between young people

Table 3. *Data on the course of development of the family cycle* and on the frequency of divorce***

Data on the course of development of the family cycle	Frequency of divorce high	low	
Man's medium age of marriage			
26 and younger	57%	43%	(7)
27 years	30%	70%	(10)
28 and above	50%	50%	(8)
Woman's medium age of marriage			
23 and younger	56%	44%	(9)
24 years	38%	62%	(8)
25 and above	38%	62%	(8)
Man's average expectation of life in his 20th year			
up to 51 years of age	42%	58%	(12)
52 and above	50%	50%	(10)
Woman's average expectation of life in her 20th year			
up to 56 years of age	50%	50%	(16)
57 and above	34%	66%	(6)

* See Table 1, Note **.

** Source: *Frequency of divorce*: United Nations, 1969: 686 f. The divorce rates given in the table are the mean annual number of final divorce decrees issued in a three-year period centred on the census year, per 1,000 married couples at the time of the census. The number of married couples was estimated to be the mean of the number of married and separated males and married and separated females. If a three-year average of divorce centred on the census year was not available, the average of two years' experience was substituted; if only one year's experience was substituted; if only one year's experience was available, this was used. The data for most countries are from the early 1960s. *Low* here means less than 3.9 divorces per annum in 1,000 existing marriages, and *high*, 4.0 and above.

should be especially insecure when longer periods of education are usual in a given society, financial independence is expected of young people when they get married, and contraceptives are not used effectively (Winch, 1971: 602). Other investigations again indicate that not only a low age of marriage, but also marriages contracted at an advanced age – which then more frequently also remain childless – increase the susceptibility to divorce (Jaulerry, 1971: 148). The age of marriage thus has quite definite consequences for the role constellation of the partners at the start of the marriage.

As we have seen, apart from the age of marriage, *life expectations* affect the length of marriages. On condition that developments on the individual level are reflected in the aggregate data, the countries where the average expectation of life of men and women is low should show lower rates of divorce than those where it is high. (*cf.* the figures in Table 3: in countries with a high expectation of life for women the divorce rates are high. This relationship does not appear in the case of men, however). We assume, though, that, for the course of development of the particular phases, the age of entering into marriage is more decisive than the length of life, since the latter does not produce a different arrangement of the family cycle, but merely lengthens the phase of growing old and thus the childless phase of the marriage and does not cause any additional crises that were not already present on entering this last phase. In countries with a low expectation of life the phase of growing old is shorter and it can be assumed that marriage there is more frequently ended by the death of one of the partners.

The aspects discussed here mark out the framework and divide the family cycle into stages. The result of this variable division is then, in combination with the changing contents of the family cycles, succeeding

Table 4. *Data on the content of the family cycle* and the frequency of divorce***

Data on the content of the family cycle	Frequency of divorce		
	high	low	
Population growth			
up to 1.1%	53%	47%	(10)
1.2% and above	30%	70%	(15)
Percentage of women in the total of all employed persons			
under 35%	—	100%	(7)
35% and above	59%	41%	(17)
Family status of women in employment			
single:			
under 50%	44%	56%	(9)
50% and above	33%	67%	(6)
married:			
under 50%	38%	62%	(8)
50% and above	44%	56%	(9)

* See Table 2, Note **.
** See Table 3, Note **.

phases of greater and lesser stability. The contents of the particular phases should be more decisive than their external distribution. As can be judged from Table 4, countries with a high population growth have lower divorce rates, whereas low population growth correlates with high divorce rates.

A low population growth means that the *number of children* per family is low, and a low number of children per family makes a divorce more probable. Which does not say anything about whether there is a high tendency to divorce because there are few children, or whether there are few children because a strong tendency to divorce already exists.

The decline in the number of children, who in addition are born in a more rapid succession, affects in a decisive way the woman's life pattern, which again affects the susceptibility to divorce. The woman, who in highly industrialised countries is nearly always in employment before marriage and frequently during it too, has to re-define her role when the first child is born; when the children have grown up she again has to find a role identification. Early marriages, with few children born shortly after one another, combined with a high expectation of life are factors that have an effect on the stability of marriages during the various phases of life.

The opportunity for women to become economically independent is perhaps the most decisive factor here. Thus, countries with a smaller *proportion of women in the total of employed persons* have lower divorce rates than those where a higher percentage of women go out to work. Countries where over 50% of working women are married have higher divorce rates than those where the greater number of working women are still single (Table 4). The data from the comparison between countries suggest that there is a close connection between the participation of women in employment and the level of divorce rates. The significance of employment for the susceptibility to divorce has received various interpretations in different investigations. A French investigation shows that women who have an occupation apply more frequently for a divorce than those without (Jaulerry, 1971: 169). Another investigation comes to the opposite conclusion – that women whose marriages foundered within a five-year break in the inquiry had more often worked neither before nor during the marriage than women whose marriages did not fail (Coombs and Zumata, 1970: 99). In order to examine the significance of employment in more detail, empirical investigations are needed that also take into account the nature of the employment and the effect it has on tasks in the family.

Although research results are still divergent and the discussion about the conditions leading to an increase in divorce is not yet completely clarified, we feel we may assume that when there are crises the probability of a divorce rises when a woman is in employment, has no children and shares the housework with her husband. The tendency to divorce should be low when the woman has young children and does not work and the division of labour between husband and wife is complementary, i.e., the former is responsible for all external matters, while the latter is restricted to the intra-family sphere. Stability would be in danger again when the children are grown up and leave home.

The susceptibility to divorce caused by the change in the phases of the family cycle is reflected then, too, in the length of the marriage up to the divorce. When divorce rates depend on the varying stability in the different phases of the family cycle, which themselves are determined by the role constellations, typical points of time develop at which marriages are particularly liable to end in divorce. These points of time are, firstly, very early on in the marriage before the birth of the first child, and secondly, they culminate when the children leave home, the opportunity of taking employment representing an additional factor here. This trend is also confirmed by an investigation in France, where an increase in divorces among young men aged between 20 and 29 and among men over 40 was demonstrated (Roussel, 1970: 282). Streib, too, demonstrated in an investigation an increase in the number of divorces in middle age (1970: 25 f.).

We can state as a result of our analysis that, in the highly industrialised countries, according to the point of time and the content, varying phases of stability and instability succeed one another and these affect the divorce rates. At the same time the particular point in the family cycle at which divorces find themselves should be a contributory factor to their chances of adapting themselves to the new situation.

It is likely that, with the growing independence acquired by women in the course of industrialisation, divorce rates will continue to rise. Although this will make the family, as an individual organisation, more insecure, this does not by any means imply, however, that as an institution marriage is endangered. As long as divorce rates are associated with high rates of remarriage the institution of marriage can still be regarded as being accepted. Within the bounds of this institution normative ideas about the legitimacy of heterogeneous relationships of limited duration can develop that permit a separation after a short period of time. The question then arises, of course, whether the monogamous, life-long marriage, formerly based on religion, can remain as the model of a generally binding claim and whether it needs to remain a claim at all. When with advancing industrialisation the division of labour loads to organic solidarity and thus to a considerable division of labour in an instrumental framework – through bureaucratic organisation –, then the integration of a society no longer needs to take place through a uniform value basis, as is the pre-condition for mechanical solidarity (Durkheim, 1893). It will then be possible to realise a multitude of values. In relation to the family this would mean that the most varying models of marriages could exist side by side in a purely instrumental context, since there would no longer be any compulsion to subordinate them to a general ideology. All the problems so far considered to be moral ones in this field would then become purely administrative matters and would no longer be subordinate to any absolute moral principles.

Résumé

Relations entre le cycle de la vie familiale et les taux de divorce
Analyse de données européennes

Faisant l'hypothèse que la structure socio-économique d'une société affecte les diverses phases de la vie familiale, et donc les taux de divortialité, on considère le phénomène du divorce en relation avec les changements sociaux globaux. Pour tester cette hypothèse, on s'interroge d'abord sur l'influence des changements socio-économiques sur le développement et le contenu des cycles, puis sur l'influence des changements observés dans les cycles sur les taux de divortialité. Les pays européens sont classés en deux groupes selon le niveau de leur développement économique et pour chacun d'entr'eux l'âge moyen au mariage et les espérances de vie sont examinés. Les écarts d'âge entre époux sont plus accentués dans les pays de moindre industrialisation; par contre, l'espérance de vie est plus grande pour les femmes que pour les hommes dans les deux groupes, bien qu'elle soit plus grande dans les pays les plus industrialisés. La combinaison des deux phénomènes (abaissement de l'âge au mariage, et augmentation de l'espérance de vie) concourt à rallonger la durée du mariage dans les pays les plus industrialisés. D'autre part, on observe un certain nombre de changements dans les fonctions familiales (la famille devenant plus un lieu de consommation que de pro-production; les femmes participant plus à la force de travail dans les pays industrialisés; le nombre des enfants et des intervalles inter-génésiques se réduisant; les enfants quittant le foyer des parents à un âge où ceux-ci ont encore de longues années devant eux) qui affectent l'équilibre et la répartition traditionnelles des rôles familiaux.

Ces changements dans les structures et les rôles familiaux ont un effet sur le divorce. Si le taux de divortialité est mis en relation avec l'âge au mariage, on constate que les chances qu'une union s'achève sur un divorce sont d'autant plus grandes que les époux sont plus jeunes.

Si les effets de l'allongement de l'espérance de vie sont complexes à établir, on note qu'il existe une relation étroite entre le divorce et la proportion des femmes actives. Certains moments du cycle sont considérés comme critiques, créant des situations à haut risque de divorce: avant la naissance du premier enfant, après le départ des enfants. Ainsi dans les pays hautement industrialisés, des phases de stabilité et d'instabilité se succèdent au cours du cycle.

Si l'on peut prévoir un accroissement des taux de divortialité dans l'avenir, il n'est pas pour autant certain que l'institution du mariage soit rejetée tant que le divorce est associé à un taux élevé de remariages.

References

Chester, Robert (1972), "Current incidence and trends in marital breakdown", *Postgraduate Medical Journal*, 48, September: 529–541.

Coombs, Lolagene C., and Zumata, Zena (1970), "Prospective fertility study, a research note", *Social Problems*, 18/1: 92–102.

Dunckelmann, Henning (1961), *Die erwerbstätige Ehefrau im Spannungsfeld von Beruf und Konsum* (*The working woman in the field of tension of occupation and consumption*), Tübingen, J.C.B. Mohr (Paul Siebeck).

Durkheim, Emile (1960), *De la division du travail social* (*The division of social labour*), Paris, 1893; 7th edition, Paris, Presses Universitaires de France.

Glick, Paul C. (1957), *American Families*, New York, Wiley.

Goode, William (1963), *World Revolution and Family Patterns*, Glencoe, Ill. Free Press.

Hummell, H.J. (1972), *Probleme der Mehrebenenanalyse* (*Problems of multiple level analysis*), Stuttgart, B.C. Teubner.

Institut für Arbeitsmarkt und Berufsforschung der Bundesanstalts für Arbeit (1970), "Die Rückkehr von Frauen in das Erwerbsleben" (The return of women to working life), Report No 13, Erlangen.

Jaulerry, Elaine (1971), "Les dissolutions d'union en France, étudiées à partir des minutes de jugement" (Dissolutions of marriages in France), *Population*, special number, June: 143–172.

König, René (1967), *Fischer Lexikon: Soziologie*, revised, extended and republished, Frankfurt, Fischer Bücherei KG.

—— (1969), "Die Stellung der Frau in der modernen Gesellschaft" (Woman's status in modern society) in O. Käser, V. Friedberg, K.G. Ober, K. Thomsen, J. Zander (eds.), *Gynäkologie und Geburtshilfe*, Stuttgart, Georg Thieme Verlag: 1–50.

Mead, Margaret (1949), *Male and Female, A Study of the Sexes in a Changing World*, London, Gollancz.

Myrdal, Alva, and Klein, Viola (1968), *Women's Two Roles, Home and Work*, Second edition, revised and reset, London, Routledge and Kegan Paul Ltd.

Nimkoff, M.F. (1965), *Comparative Family Sytems*, Boston, Houghton Mifflin.

Ogburn, W.F., and Nimkoff, M.F. (1955), *Technology and the Changing Family*, Boston-New York Houghton Mifflin.

Parsons, Talcott (1965), "Kinship system of contemporary United States", in Talcott Parsons (ed.), *Essays in Sociological Theory*, Revised edition, Glencoe, Ill., Free Press: 177–196.

Roussel, Louis (1970), "Les divorces et les séparations de corps en France (1936–1967)" (Divorce and separation in France, 1936–1067), *Population*, 25/2: 275–279.

"Séminaire International sur la Famille" (1969), *Population* 24/3: 571.

Streib, Gordon F. (1970), "Old age and the family: facts and forecasts", *American Behavioral Scientist*, 14 1: 25–40.

Taylor, Charles Lewis, and Hudson, Michael C. (1972), *World Handbook of Political and Social Indicators*, Second edition, New Haven and London, Yale University Press.

Titmuss, Richard M. (1962), *Foreword to Pearl Jephcott, Married Women Working*, London, Allen and Unwin.

Treinen, Heiner, and Brothun, Machthild (1973), "Die Stellung der Frau in Industriegesellschaften" (Woman's status in industrial societies), in Karl H. Bonner (ed.), *Die Geschlechterrolle*, Munich, Nymphenburger Verlagshandlung GmbH: 249–280.

United Nations (ed.) (1965), *Demographic Yearbook 1964*, New York.

—— (1969), *Demographic Yearbook 1968*, New York.

——(1970), *Demographic Yearbook 1969*, New York.

Winch, Robert W. (1971), *The Modern Family*, 3rd edition, New York, Holt, Rinehart and Winston.

13. L'avortement dans la perspective du cycle familial

JEAN KELLERHALS

Introduction

La place qu'occupe l'avortement dans le déroulement des cycles familiaux, les représentations et conflits associés à cette démarche en fonction de la situation familiale, sont extrêmement mal connus.

Certes, le réflexion sur l'avortement et son impact sur les nations et les familles ne date pas d'aujourd'hui. Mais elle a été jusqu'à ces dernières années plus marquée par les prises de position éthiques ou politiques que par l'observation méthodique.

Dans les pays francophones tout au moins, il est possible de diviser la littérature parue sur ce thème en deux grandes phases: l'entre-deux guerres (1918–1939) et l'après-guerre (1945 à nos jours). La fin de la première guerre mondiale voit surgir un nombre considérable d'ouvrages, souvent des thèses, s'attachant à montrer les dangers que représente l'avortement pour l'équilibre économique et militaire de la nation. Des auteurs divers (par exemple: Blet, 1921; Raiter, 1925; Tarakdji, 1937; Tallet, 1938; Roy, 1943) s'accordent dans l'ensemble à reconnaître que l'avortement est une sorte de "fléau", une déviance dont l'origine se situe surtout dans la dégradation des mœurs et quelque peu dans les insuffisances de la prévoyance sociale. Les dangers de cette pratique – à laquelle est d'ailleurs associée celle de l'"anti-conception" – sont jugés si grands qu'il convient d'y remédier de manière urgente. Les remèdes proposés sont divers, mais tous partent de l'idée que l'avortement est une sorte de pathologie, indicatrice de l'égoïsme et de l'amoralisme des populations. On proposera donc le rétablissement des tours où étaient déposés les enfants non désirés, le relèvement (par quels moyens?) de la moralité publique, l'interdiction des propagandes sur l'"anticonception", et quelques améliorations sociales relatives aux salaires ou aux filles-mères.

L'après-guerre marque, en ce domaine comme en d'autres, un changement considérable des orientations et des méthodes des chercheurs intéressés par l'avortement. Les études sociographiques commencent, et les ouvrages d'opinion adoptent l'optique sociologique en ce sens qu'ils s'interrogent sur l'avortement comme conséquence des structures sociales. Bien des études statistiques (Hell, 1947; Monsaigeon, 1947; Darasson, 1952) résultent d'observations de clinique médicale. D'autres, moins nombreuses, se livrent à des analyses de sociologie descriptive et introduisent l'idée d'avortement conjoncturel que nous rencontrerons plus loin (Sutter, 1950). Les ouvrages d'opinion insistent à la fois sur les facteurs sociaux de l'avortement et sur la condition misérable des femmes qui doivent y recourir (Lagroua Weill Hallé, 1959 et 1961; Ladret, 1961; Auclair, 1962; Dourlen-Rollier, 1965).

L'évolution des mentalités est plus lente en Suisse romande. De grandes polémiques s'engagent entre les tenants de l'optique traditionnelle (Doornkaat, 1952; Rémy 1953) et les réformistes, encore bien timides (Flournoy, 1953; Hirzel, 1957), avec des tentatives d'arbitrage par des juristes (Graven).

Mais, même après-guerre, les auteurs ont nettement tendance à considérer que l'avortement est le fruit de situations d'urgence sociale, de marginalité économique ou familiale. L'avortement est en somme le résultat de la misère d'une part, de la sur-natalité d'autre part.

Or cela n'est que partiellement vrai. D'autre part, tous les auteurs souffrent (et le disent) du manque d'études empiriques.

Les quelques résultats présentés ci-dessous apparaissent donc comme une des premières recherches systématiques sur le phénomène de l'avortement dans les pays européens. Si une partie de leur intérêt provient de leur nouveauté, c'est également cette nouveauté qui veut que l'étude se cantonne – dans les pages qui suivent tout au moins – à une description analytique plutôt qu'à une explication qui se voudrait exhaustive. C'est également en grande partie à l'innovation que doivent être attribuées certaines limites méthodologiques qui marquent ce travail.

L'étude menée à Genève se caractérise notamment par le fait qu'elle met fin, pour les contextes que nous observons, à bon nombre de stéréotypes. L'avortement y apparaît comme une stratégie "normale", fortement reliée au cycle de vie familiale. La manière dont il est vécu, les motifs qui y conduisent ne s'accordent pas aux hypothèses couramment avancées en matière de marginalité sociale.

De plus, cette étude permet d'évaluer, dans le domaine de comportement considéré, les avantages et les limites de divers indicateurs des cycles familiaux. L'exposé des résultats fournira un matériel permettant, en conclusion, l'énoncé de quelques problèmes suscités par l'utilisation de la méthode dite "du développement" dans les recherches sur la famille.

I. La fréquence de l'avortement légal

Pour mieux situer l'impact de l'avortement comme stratégie d'équilibration familiale, il peut être utile de décrire son importance quantitative dans la société dont nous nous occupons (la Suisse, et plus particulièrement le canton de Genève).

Deux taux conviennent particulièrement:

- la proportion des demandes d'interruption de grossesse par rapport aux naissances vivantes sur une année;
- la proportion (plus grossière dans son estimation) d'interruptions pour cent grossesses.

La proportion des demandes d'avortement par rapport aux naissances vivantes s'établit à 438 pour mille environ. Pour mieux fixer les idées, disons *une demande d'avortement pour deux naissances vivantes.*[1]

Quelques comparaisons avec d'autres pays industrialisés d'Europe montrent que ce taux est très fort pour l'Europe de l'Ouest, mais moyen par rapport à l'Europe de l'Est (Tableau 1).

Tableau 1. *Proportion des interruptions de grossesse pour 1 000 naissances vivantes en 1970*

Danemark	127,1
Grande Bretagne	93,3
Hongrie	1 267,6
Suède	146,2
Tchécoslovaquie	435,8

Source: "Selected abortion statistics", Transnational Family Rese arch Institute, American Institutes for Research, Silver Spring, 1973.

Le deuxième taux, celui de la proportion d'avortements pour mille grossesses, est plus approximatif. Par un calcul assez simple[2] on arrive au rapport – qu'il faut considérer seulement comme un *ordre de grandeur* – de 281 pour mille. Dans un contexte comme Genève, le nombre des interruptions illégales est trop faible pour modifier sérieusement l'estimation qui précède. On peut donc dire, en termes généraux, qu'il y a environ une interruption légale pour quatre grossesses.

Il est bien clair que ces taux sont considérables, et qu'ils situent d'emblée l'avortement comme un mode fondamental de régulation des équilibres familiaux. Si le statut de l'avortement du point de vue normatif reste encore, dans les mentalités, marqué par la notion de déviance, son importance statistique l'apparente aux comportements normaux (Kellerhals, 1973). Cette sorte de contradiction n'est d'ailleurs pas sans effet sur le vécu des femmes face à l'avortement.

Ces grands cadres posés, il faut en venir maintenant à l'analyse de la place de l'avortement dans le cycle familial. Pour cela, quelques indications méthodologiques sont nécessaires.

II. Quelques aspects méthodologiques

1. *L'approche du cycle familial*

L'approche dite "du développement" en matière de sociologie de la famille n'est pas encore à ce point développée qu'elle autorise une seule démarche méthodologique, scientifiquement indiscutable. L'analyse de l'avortement en fonction du cycle familial a donc été menée selon divers angles, devenus aujourd'hui classiques (Duvall, 1962), qui se complètent plutôt qu'ils ne s'excluent.

Les critères suivants, servant à définir des "phases" dans la vie de famille, ont été retenus:

a) *Le critère de la structure des rôles:* Il oppose les familles où seuls les rôles d'épouse et de mari se rencontrent aux groupes où les rôles de parents complètent les rapports conjugaux. L'apparition du premier enfant forme évidemment la ligne de clivage. La naissance du second enfant ajoute à cette structure les rôles de pairs, découlant de la relation entre enfants. Trois phases qualitativement différentes sont ainsi définies, la naissance éventuelle d'enfants supplémentaires ne modifiant que quantitativement la trame des rôles sociaux.

b) *Le critère du contenu des rôles:* Bien que parent du précédent, il met néanmoins en relief le genre d'activités lié au rôle plutôt que le rôle lui-même. Mais comme la définition précise de ces contenus formerait à elle seule l'objet de nombreuses études, on se contentera ici d'indicateurs indirects. Selon des propositions autorisées (Hill, 1964), et du point de vue qui nous intéresse ici, on retiendra deux facteurs de différenciation:

I. *L'âge du dernier enfant* définit, dans les très grandes lignes, le contenu du rôle parental (maternel surtout). Il convient ici de distinguer la petite enfance (0 à 2 ans), où prévaut la liaison constante et toute-puissante entre la mère et l'enfant; la période de préscolarisation (3 à 5 ans) marquée à la fois par une certaine indépendance du rejeton et par l'accaparement de fait de la mère; la période de première scolarisation (6 à 11 ans) qui libère déjà passablement les parents; et enfin la période pubertaire (12 à *n* ans) durant laquelle se développent les rôles égalitaristes entre les divers membres de la famille.

II. *Le travail féminin:* la différenciation entre les familles où le principal rôle instrumental est joué par un des parents seulement et celles où les deux époux ont une profession s'avère de plus en plus fondamentale. Le rôle professionnel de la mère (par opposition à son seul rôle ménager) crée dans la famille une dynamique particulière dont il est essentiel de voir les effets sur la politique de natalité du groupe.

c) *Le critère de la longévité du couple:* Par opposition aux deux critères précédents, il offre à première vue une allure linéaire, définissant moins des "phases" qualitativement différentes qu'un procès durant lequel se développent ou s'estompent tels traits particuliers de la famille. Toutefois, cette première perspective n'est que partiellement justifiée. En effet, en tant qu'indicateur, la longévité du couple définit indirectement les phases suivantes: la première période (0 à 1 ou 2 ans) correspond souvent à la phase conjugale de la famille, marquée par une dominante, dans les tâches fondamentales du groupe, de l'objectif d'*adaptation mutuelle* des rôles et aspirations des époux; la seconde période (2 à 10 ans) correspond à la phase d'expansion de la famille, marquée par la dominante de la *procréation et de la première socialisation*; la troisième période (plus de 10 ans) correspond à la phase de *stabilisation* et de premier retour (avant le retour définitif lié au départ du dernier enfant), à une centration sur l'adaptation mutuelle des époux. Il est par ailleurs très important de voir que ces phases – définies dans les lignes qui précèdent en termes de corrélation statistique – apparaissent également comme des modèles sociaux, c'est-à-dire comme des injonctions de comportement pour un couple occupant une situation donnée. C'est cet aspect de modèle social qui exercera, nous en faisons l'hypothèse, une contrainte particulièrement nette dans le domaine qui nous préoccupe (la natalité et l'avortement).

C'est donc par rapport à ces critères – forcément incomplets – que l'analyse des données sera menée.

2. *Les enquêtes*

Les chiffres et considérations qui suivent sont basés sur deux études par interview qui furent menées à Genève.

La première – appelée ici enquête *Fécondité* –[3] porte sur l'interview de 3 000 résidentes genevoises, définissant une cohorte de femmes enceintes sur 18 mois et fréquentant pour cette raison (accouchement, interruption de grossesse, conservation de grossesse) les services de santé.

La seconde – dénommée ici enquête *Avortement* – porte sur l'interview de 906 femmes, résidentes de Genève, requérant une interruption légale de la grossesse. Cet échantillon, dont la fraction sondée représente environ la moitié, est représentatif des demandes d'avortement. Les interviews ont été effectuées entre le moment où la femme a eu connaissance de sa grossesse et celui où elle s'est présentée devant un expert mandaté pour autoriser l'interruption.

Les deux populations représentées comprennent des personnes de nationalité suisse et étrangère, la condition étant cependant d'être domicilié à Genève. *Les célibataires et les personnes mariées sont également représentées, mais la présente analyse ne portera que sur les personnes mariées.*[4]

Les interviews de la première étude ont été faites d'octobre 1966 à mars 1968. Ceux de la deuxième recherche ont couru de juillet 1970 à juin 1971.

En règle générale, les entretiens ont été conduits dans la langue préférée de l'interrogée.

III. La place de l'avortement dans le cycle familial

1. *Rang de la conception, nombre d'enfants et fréquence de l'avortement*

Au fur et à mesure que s'accroît le rang d'une conception dans un couple, les naissances vivantes issues de cette grossesse diminuent considérablement (tableau 2).

Tableau 2. *Genève – Enquête fécondité.*
Résultat de la conception selon le rang de conception, en %

	Rang de conception					
	1ère	2e	3e	4e	5e	6e
Naissance vivante	86,2	79,7	70,7	60,9	57,1	61,9
Avortements spontanés ou provoqués*	13,8	20,3	29,3	39,1	42,9	38,1
(N)	(2 230)	(1 238)	(519)	(202)	(91)	(42)

* L'Enquête Fécondité ne nous permettait pas de savoir avec rigueur si l'on était en présence d'une fausse-couche spontanée ou d'un avortement provoqué.

Dans cette progression frappante, il est possible de distinguer trois "moments" assez nets:

I. La première conception, correspondant donc au couple sans enfants, n'est pour ainsi dire pas marquée par l'avortement provoqué: il faut en effet – très approximativement – compter avec 10% d'avortements spontanés (fausses-couches); il y a donc environ 3% d'avortements provoqués.

II. Les deuxièmes et troisième conceptions (correspondant environ à la présence d'un à deux enfants) laissent apparaître au contraire une intrusion assez massive de l'avortement comme stratégie d'équilibration: en effet, à la troisième conception, 20% environ des grossesses se terminent par une interruption.

III. Enfin, un nouveau coup de frein est donné lors de la quatrième conception; mais à partir de ce moment, il se produit – contrairement aux idées reçues – une stabilisation des taux d'avortement.

L'examen de l'étude "Avortement" permet d'observer une évolution du même type. Les sujets qui n'ont pas d'enfants n'ont pour ainsi dire pas eu – auparavant – d'interruption de grossesse. Par contre, dès qu'un enfant est présent, l'avortement intervient comme stratégie d'équilibration. Une augmentation du recours à l'interruption se produit encore à partir de la présence de trois enfants (tableau 3).

Tableau 3. *Genève – Enquête Avortement.*
Avortements antérieurs selon le nombre d'enfants du couple, en %

	Nombre d'enfants dans le couple			
	0	1	2	3 et +
A eu un avortement provoqué	2,9	21,1	18,2	26,0
N'a pas eu d'avortement provoqué	97,1	78,9	81,8	74,0
(N)	(34)	(104)	(148)	(50)

Descriptivement, en considérant les demandes d'interruption, on s'aperçoit que l'avortement est loin de se présenter comme une stratégie réservée aux seuls couples surchargés d'enfants. 10% des demandes émanent de couples qui n'ont pas encore d'enfants, 31% de couples qui n'en ont qu'un, 44% de ceux qui en ont deux, et seulement 15% de couples qui en ont trois ou plus. Il ne s'agit donc pas d'un comportement émanant, de ce point de vue, de marginaux de la société.

La question qui se pose alors est de savoir quelle est la signification de l'acte, c'est-à-dire le but qu'il se propose d'atteindre. On est amené à distinguer en ce sens deux genres d'avortements: *l'avortement conjoncturel* et *l'avortement structurel.* Le premier correspond à une volonté de remettre à plus tard l'arrivée d'un enfant qui, dans l'abstrait, est souhaité. Le second correspond à la volonté d'en finir définitivement avec la phase de procréation, le nombre souhaité d'enfants ayant déjà été atteint. Le tableau 4 fait la distinction entre ces deux formes d'avortement.

Tableau 4. *Genève – Enquête Avortement.*
Désir d'enfants ultérieurs selon le nombre d'enfants actuel du couple, en %

	Nombre d'enfants			
	0	1	2	3 et +
Désire encore des enfants	79,4	58,6	33,8	8,0
Ne désire plus d'enfants	20,6	41,4	66,2	92,0
(N)	(34)	(104)	(148)	(50)

Si l'avortement conjoncturel est défini comme le fait d'interrompre la grossesse tout en désirant ultérieurement des enfants, on s'aperçoit qu'environ 40% des demandes tombent dans cette catégorie. L'avortement conjoncturel diminue évidemment de beaucoup avec le nombre d'enfants dans le couple, ainsi que le montre le tableau 4. Il reste majoritaire tant que le nombre de deux enfants n'est pas atteint, il devient presque inexistant à partir de trois enfants. On verra plus bas les incidences de cette distinction sur le vécu de l'avortement lui-même.

2. *L'impact du facteur économique*

Bien que l'avortement comme mode d'équilibration touche l'ensemble des milieux sociaux et ne se prête nullement à une analyse en termes de marginalité, il n'est cependant pas insensible à l'influence des divers facteurs sociaux.

Deux d'entre eux ont souvent fait l'objet d'hypothèses passionnées: la situation économique du couple d'une part, la concurrence du travail féminin d'autre part.

La situation économique et sociale du couple est susceptible de modifier l'impact de l'avortement dans le cycle familial pour deux raisons principales: un moindre niveau socio-économique est fréquemment associé à des pratiques inadéquates de contrôle de la fécondité d'une part (ce qui augmente la probabilité d'une grossesse "non désirée"), et d'autre part ce moindre niveau diminue le nombre d'enfants que le couple peut accueillir, même si par ailleurs il souhaiterait, dans l'abstrait, voir sa famille s'agrandir.

L'analyse des résultats de la conception selon le rang de celle-ci et selon le revenu familial tend à la fois à confirmer cette hypothèse et à limiter son impact quantitatif.

La tendance générale s'observe aisément: au fur et à mesure que le revenu familial s'accroît, l'intervention de l'avortement diminue. De plus, le tableau 5 définit trois grands genres de population. Une sorte de "sous-prolétariat" d'abord, où la quatrième conception se solde dans la moitié des cas par un avortement. Dans une autre sous-population, plus ou moins favorisée (plus de 2 000 francs par mois), les proportions de naissances vivantes varient très peu selon le rang de la conception. Enfin, dans toute une population intermédiaire, comprenant les deux tiers de l'ensemble, les différences relevées sont très proches les unes des autres. C'est pourquoi nous pouvons parler à la fois d'une justification de l'hypothèse mentionnée et de son caractère limité.

Une analyse plus fouillée, de conception à conception, nous montre

Tableau 5. *Genève – Enquête Fécondité.*
Différences dans la proportion des naissances vivantes issues des premières conceptions et des conceptions dont le rang est égal ou supérieur à quatre, selon le revenu familial (en Frs. suisses), en %

Revenu familial mensuel	1ère conception	(N)	4ᵉ conception et suiv.	(N)	Différence dans la proportion de naissances vivantes
moins de 1 000, –	89,5	(153)	50,0	(18)	−39,5
1 000–1 250, –	88,1	(594)	57,4	(54)	−30,7
1 251–1 500, –	88,0	(408)	60,0	(44)	−28,0
1 501–2 000, –	86,8	(608)	63,0	(54)	−23,8
plus de 2 000, –	78,4	(324)	84,2	(19)	+ 5,8

qu'il y a en fait trois stratégies d'avortement selon le milieu économique. Pour les catégories "pauvres" (moins de 1 000 francs par mois), l'avortement est un régulateur tardif: il intervient entre la troisième et la quatrième conception. Pour les catégories "aisées" (plus de 2 000 francs par mois), l'impact – relativement faible – de l'avortement est beaucoup plus précoce: ces familles y recourent surtout lors de la première et deuxième conceptions, avec une stabilisation, voire une diminution par la suite. Pour les catégories de familles intermédiaires (1 000 à 2 000 francs par mois), l'utilisation du frein de l'avortement s'intensifie progressivement, sans marquer de palier net. Il convient donc, pour tirer la leçon de cette constatation, de voir que la dynamique de chaque phase familiale varie selon le type d'insertion des familles dans les structures sociales.

3. *L'impact du travail féminin*

L'importance du travail féminin pour le phénomène observé ici est encore plus nette. L'hypothèse courante est que le rôle professionnel de la femme, qu'elle désire travailler ou y soit contrainte par les circonstances, entre en conflit avec son rôle de procréation. Mais il s'agit de bien faire attention au niveau du social qui est observé. D'autres analyses (Bassand et Kellerhals, 1972) nous ont convaincu qu'en ce qui concerne le plan des représentations et aspirations, le travail féminin professionnel n'était pas en corrélation avec une moindre propension à la procréation. Il est beaucoup plus fréquent de voir les deux aspirations, professionnelle et de procréation, coexister solidement l'une à côté de l'autre. Par contre, s'agissant du plan des réalisations, c'est-à-dire finalement du résultat des grossesses, on peut voir que la corrélation est très forte. Cette sorte de contradiction ne manque pas de créer, chez la femme, une ambivalence psychologique importante.

Qu'en est-il, tout d'abord, du résultat de la conception selon la situation professionnelle de la femme? En un premier temps, on opposera simplement les ménagères, qui n'ont pas d'activité en dehors du foyer, à celles qui ont une profession à l'extérieur (tableau 6).

Tableau 6. *Genève – Enquête Fécondité.*
Résultat de la conception selon le rang de celle-ci et le travail féminin (proportion de naissances vivantes en %)

	Rang de la conception				
Situation de travail	1ère	2e	3e	4e	5e et +
Ménagère	88,9	81,9	76,7	68,0	67,1
(N)	(1 095)	(700)	(313)	(125)	(85)
Avec profession	83,6	77,0	61,7	49,4	43,7
(N)	(1 135)	(538)	(206)	(77)	(48)
Différence dans la proportion des naissances vivantes	5,3	4,9	15,0	18,6	23,4
Proportion de femmes ayant une profession	50,9	43,4	39,7	38,1	36,1

Bien que la proportion de naissances vivantes résultant d'une conception soit toujours plus faible chez les femmes qui travaillent à l'extérieur par rapport aux ménagères, la différence entre ces deux groupes s'accentue très considérablement à partir de la troisième conception. A la cinquième, deux tiers de celles-ci se terminent par une naissance vivante chez les "ménagères" contre la moitié seulement chez les femmes avec profession. Il est alors justifié de parler d'une sorte de concurrence de fait entre le rôle de procréation et le rôle professionnel. Mais il convient de remarquer que cette concurrence se fait surtout à partir du moment où la norme habituelle de fécondité (très généralement 2 enfants, à Genève) a été atteinte.

Cette idée de concurrence *de fait* – puisque nous avons vu l'absence de corrélation au plan des représentations – est très nettement confirmée par l'enquête "Avortement". D'après les données de cet échantillon, la demande d'interruption se produit comparativement beaucoup plus tôt chez les couples où la femme travaille à l'extérieur que chez ceux où elle n'exerce qu'un travail ménager (tableau 7).

Tableau 7. *Genève – Enquête Avortement.*
Place de l'avortement selon le milieu social et le travail féminin, en %

Descendance actuelle du couple	Milieux subalternes*		Milieux de cadres*	
	Ménage	Profession	Ménage	Profession
0–1 enfant	21,0	48,2	44,0	55,8
2 enfants	57,9	38,1	41,3	37,2
3 enfants et +	21,1	13,7	14,7	7,0
(N)	(76)	(139)	(75)	(43)

* Les milieux subalternes comprennent les manoeuvres, ouvriers qualifiés et employés subalternes; les milieux de cadres incluent les indépendants de l'industrie, du commerce, les cadres moyens et supérieurs de l'industrie et de l'administration, les enseignants des divers degrés; le critère employé est celui de la profession du mari.

La pratique d'un travail professionnel pousse, on le voit, à recourir très tôt, dans l'histoire du couple, à l'avortement. Toutefois, cette constatation générale doit être affinée. En effet, c'est surtout dans les milieux subalternes, où le travail féminin est plus qu'ailleurs indispensable à l'équilibre financier du couple, que les différences entre les ménagères et les femmes avec profession sont accentuées. Dans les milieux de cadres, la différence s'estompe beaucoup. La constatation faite au paragraphe précédent se justifie donc également ici: la dynamique des phases familiales est différente selon le mode d'insertion de la famille dans les structures sociales. On observera par ailleurs que la proportion de femmes au travail est nettement supérieure dans les milieux subalternes (64,6 %) que dans les milieux de cadres (36,4 %). Enfin, on remarquera que, malgré tout, l'avortement intervient plus tôt dans les couches aisées de la population que dans les couches défavorisées, ce que nous observions plus haut.

IV. Les représentations de l'avortement selon le cycle familial

1. *Cycle familial et motivation de l'avortement*

Comme toute conduite, l'avortement est "orienté": il manifeste la volonté du couple de se rapprocher de certaines valeurs, d'actualiser certains idéaux.

Il est donc important de voir pourquoi les couples recourent à l'avortement. En d'autres termes, quelles valeurs, quelles aspirations justifient-elles, aux yeux des sujets, le recours à cette forme particulière de rétro-conduite. Cette première question se double de celle de savoir si les phases du cycle familial conduisent à actualiser des valeurs ou aspirations qui diffèrent de phase à phase.

La tâche n'est à vrai dire pas aisée. Des motifs divers entrent souvent dans le processus de décision, et mettre à jour le plus important d'entre eux peut prêter quelquefois à discussion: cette opération est impossible dans un certain nombre de cas.

D'autre part, les motifs conscients ne sont pas toujours l'expression adéquate des dynamismes affectifs plus profonds. Aussi faudra-t-il peut-être plutôt parler ici d'interprétation que de motivation, sans que le rapport entre les deux termes soit très clairement défini.

Enfin, il est bien clair que l'interprétation que les sujets donnent de leur conduite n'est pas non plus l'expression adéquate, parce que clairement consciente, des forces sociales qui pèsent sur eux et entraînent la décision.

Cela dit, il n'en reste pas moins que les valeurs poursuivies par les sujets, la manière dont ils réalisent leur intégration culturelle au système dans lequel ils sont plongés, sont des indicateurs très précieux des dynamismes familiaux et sociétaux.

La diversité très grande des raisons invoquées pour recourir à un avortement oblige le chercheur à regrouper celles-ci en quelques catégories. En fait, quelques valeurs ou aspirations fondamentales sous-tendent, malgré la pluralité des vocabulaires, les conduites en cette matière. Les catégories principales d'interprétation subjective de la conduite sont en l'occurence les suivantes:

- Motif *somatique*
  (la femme juge que la grossesse et l'enfant à venir compromettent une santé physique déjà fortement atteinte) 23,9 %
- Motif *psychologique*
  (semblable au precédent, mais portant sur la santé mentale; le

terme psychologique est pris ici au sens très restreint d'atteinte psychiatrique) 6,2%

- Motif *économique*
  (comprenant les problèmes de logement, de revenu, de travail féminin indispensable au revenu, de plans économiques, de tierces personnes économiquement à charge, d'instabilité de l'emploi, de mobilité économique du couple) 26,4%
- Motif d'*adaptation mutuelle*
  (comprend les problèmes de conflit conjugal, de stabilité affective du couple, de rapports extra-conjugaux) 14,5%
- Motif de *socialisation*
  (comprend les difficultés avec les enfants existants, la volonté de mieux s'occuper d'eux) 13,0%
- Motif de *contrainte*
  (le sujet est contraint de prendre sa décision à cause de la volonté d'un tiers) 2,1%
- Motif d'*eugénisme*
  (comprend les diverses raisons de crainte pour l'état physique ou mental de l'enfant à venir) 3,8%
- *Inclassables*
  (parce que plusieurs motifs également importants forment toute une structure où il serait vain de rechercher une dominante) 10,3%

Face à ces grandes catégories d'interprétation, le problème est alors de savoir si leur fréquence relative en fonction du cycle familial permet de définir des phases de ce dernier, des moments dans la vie du couple où prédominerait, même de manière relative, tel ou tel genre de problème, telle *tâche principale.*

a) *Le critère du nombre d'enfants.*

Voyons tout d'abord les chiffres (tableau 8):

Ce tableau permet-il de dessiner des systèmes d'interprétation différents selon la structure des rôles? Cette démarche paraît en partie justifiée.

La phase des *rôles conjugaux* est marquée très nettement par la prévalence du problème de l'*adaptation mutuelle*, qui forme ici le 40% des motifs. Vient ensuite la grande importance donnée à la question de l'*accession économique*, et cela bien que le couple n'ait encore, comparativement aux autres, que peu de charges. Il s'agit donc d'un système d'interprétation relativement simple, dominé par la volonté du couple d'assurer son "achievement" affectif et économique.

Tableau 8. *Genève – Enquête Avortement.*
Distribution des motifs principaux du recours à l'avortement selon le nombre d'enfants du couple, en %

	Nombre d'enfants			
	0	1	2	3 et +
Motif somatique et psychologique	20,0	31,5	32,8	26,0
Motif économique	25,8	25,8	30,3	16,0
Motif d'adaptation mutuelle	40,0	18,2	7,4	10,0
Motif de socialisation	0,0	8,6	17,5	18,0
Motif d'inadéquation*	0,0	6,7	5,4	12,0
Autres ou inclassables	14,2	9,2	6,3	18,0
(N)	(35)	(105)	(149)	(50)

* Il s'agit d'une sorte de "structure" où les idées dominantes sont que la femme s'estime trop vieille pour procréer à nouveau, et où elle pense qu'il lui serait trop difficile de recommencer le cycle des activités relatives aux soins à donner aux enfants en bas-âge.

La phase d'apparition des *rôles parentaux*, qui correspond bien sûr à une complexité plus grande du système familial, trahit une plus grande diversification des motifs. Malgré les charges nouvelles, *l'importance des motifs économiques ne croît pas*. Les problèmes d'adaptation mutuelle sont en partie résolus. Le couple est confronté ici à diverses tâches, toutes imbriquées, qui font que le système d'interprétation ne se laisse pas définir en un ou deux grands traits.

Il faut souligner ici que seules de légères différences quantitatives se font jour entre la phase dite des "rôles conjugaux et parentaux" (un seul enfant) et celle des rôles "conjugaux, parentaux et de pairs" (deux enfants).

La phase correspondant à la présence de trois enfants ou plus présente deux différences par rapport à la précédente. Cette phase – tout au moins en contexte genevois – marque déjà un dépassement des normes idéales de fécondité. Or, on observe, paradoxalement et contrairement aux stéréotypes les plus courants, une *diminution nette des motivations économiques*. Il y a par ailleurs une *croissance du motif d'inadéquation*: en somme, la grande famille semble plus gêner les acteurs en ceci qu'elle constitue une déviance culturelle qu'en ceci qu'elle entraîne des contraintes économiques très fortes.

En résumé, et pour se contenter des grands traits, le critère du nombre d'enfants différencie surtout deux grands systèmes d'interprétation: celui correspondant à la famille sans enfant et celui où ces derniers sont présents. A l'intérieur du deuxième système, seules des différences partielles interviennent.

Le recours au critère, très voisin du précédent, de la nature conjoncturelle de l'avortement, amène sensiblement aux mêmes conclusions: prédominance des questions d'adaptation économique et d'adaptation mutuelle dans l'avortement conjoncturel, légère prévalence de l'adaptation à la socialisation dans l'avortement structurel.

b) *Le critère de la longévité du couple.*

Le critère de longévité du couple s'impose, à l'observation, comme un indice de clivages très important. De ce point de vue, trois phases essentielles dans la vie de la famille peuvent être distinguées:

1. les deux premières années, durant lesquelles l'objectif central du couple est d'*assurer l'équilibration des rôles et les modes d'échange affectif;*[5]
2. la période de deux à dix ans de mariage qui correspond, au niveau des modèles sociaux, à celle de la *procréation*, la fin *culturelle* de celle-ci correspondant, grosso modo, à la limite de dix ans de mariage (le couple se jugeant, après cette date, trop "vieux" pour avoir de nouveaux enfants, même si les fonctions biologiques le permettent, et les enfants déjà nés étant par ailleurs suffisamment âgés pour qu'une nouvelle naissance représente en fait le recommencement de tout un cycle d'activités);
3. la période de re-centration sur le couple et d'égalitarisme avec les enfants déjà nés, où l'objectif central du couple est d'une part d'assurer sur une nouvelle base ses échanges intellectuels et affectifs, et, d'autre part, de préparer activement l'insertion sociale des enfants déjà nés.

Tableau 9. *Genève – Enquête Avortement.*
Distribution des motifs principaux de recours à l'avortement selon la longévité du couple, en %

	Moins de 2 ans	2 à 10 ans	Plus de 10 ans
Motif somatique ou psychologique	20,0	25,5	35,3
Motif économique	42,9	31,4	12,9
Motif d'adaptation mutuelle	28,6	14,9	9,5
Motif de socialisation	0,0	16,5	12,2
Motif d'inadéquation	0,0	2,7	13,4
Autres et inclassables	8,5	9,0	16,7
(N)	(35)	(188)	(116)

Cette typologie, certes criticable dans les détails, conduit en fait à une bonne différenciation des interprétations de la conduite chez les couples. Le tableau 9 le montre à l'évidence.

Les motifs d'adaptation économique dominent nettement dans la première phase et s'estompent beaucoup (ceci est à nouveau paradoxal) au fur et à mesure que la longévité du couple s'accroît. Il en va de même pour l'interprétation de la conduite en termes d'adaptation mutuelle. La troisième phase est marquée par une recrudescence de l'attention portée à l'équilibre personnel du sujet (somatique et psychologique notamment).

En somme, plus qu'en termes de contraintes objectivement démontrables (une analyse plus longue permettrait de montrer que la situation somatique, économique, relationnelle du couple ne varie pas dans des proportions importantes durant la période globale considérée), le couple interprète sa situation en termes culturels: il est trop tôt ou trop tard, par rapport à des standards sociaux (normatifs ou statistiques), pour procréer. En ce sens, les catégories employées ici sont autant l'expression de modèles sociaux plus ou moins conscients chez les acteurs que celles de concepts ayant une fonction heuristique.

c) *Le critère de l'âge du dernier enfant* (tableau 10).

Il s'agit en fait, dans le cas présent, d'un assez mauvais différenciateur. Il est cependant utile sur deux points. Il souligne d'une part l'importance du motif d'inadéquation. Il confirme d'autre part la diminution nette du problème de l'adaptation économique avec l'évolution du couple (il faut bien sûr considérer que nous nous situons *uniquement*, dans l'ensemble, à l'intérieur d'une tranche d'âge de 20 à 45 ans).

Tableau 10. *Genève – Enquête Avortement.*
Motifs de recours à l'avortement selon l'âge du dernier enfant, en %

	0–2 ans	3–6 ans	7–11 ans	12 et + ans
Motif somatique et psychologique	33,0	24,5	35,2	33,3
Motif économique	35,8	26,6	18,2	12,1
Motif d'adaptation mutuelle	9,0	15,5	11,3	9,1
Motif de socialisation	14,3	15,6	15,5	9,1
Motif d'inadéquation	0,9	2,2	14,1	24,2
Autres et inclassables	7,0	15,6	5,7	13,2
(N)	(33)	(71)	(90)	(112)

2. *Cycle familial et image du fœtus*

L'ambiguïté de la définition culturelle de l'avortement dans notre société autorise une analyse passionnante – et souvent passionnée – de la manière dont cette intervention est vécue par les sujets qui y recourent.

Nous n'examinerons ici que deux aspects de ces représentations:

a) *l'image du fœtus*, c'est-à-dire la nature que l'on attribue à ce dernier. Il peut être vu comme un être possédant, dès la conception, toutes les caractéristiques de l'humain, potentiellement tout au moins. A un autre extrême, il peut être envisagé comme une simple excroissance, sans autonomie propre ni vie réelle;
b) *le jugement moral:* à cause de l'ambiguïté des normes sociales en matière d'avortement, celui-ci peut être vu soit comme relevant de la sphère du choix éthique, soit comme un acte à propos duquel aucune considération éthique ne devrait être faite (comme, par exemple, le fait de subir l'ablation de l'appendice). S'il fait l'objet d'une évaluation éthique, celle-ci peut être fortement négative, plus ou moins négative ou encore positive (ce qui ne se trouvera pas dans notre enquête).

Il est clair qu'en principe la nature des représentations que le sujet se fait de l'avortement conditionnera en partie le conflit ou l'absence de conflit qui marquera sa décision. Ce point sera envisagé dans la section suivante. Pour le moment, il nous intéresse surtout de savoir dans quelle mesure les représentations de l'avortement sont liées au cycle de vie familiale.

Trois grandes catégories d'images permettent de classer les diverses représentations associées au fœtus dans la civilisation occidentale contemporaine.

Le *fondamentalisme* voit le fœtus comme doué de toutes les caractéristiques de l'être humain dès sa conception. Dès la fusion de l'ovule et du spermatozoïde, il y a vie humaine, et par conséquent, un sujet de droit. Le tabou du meurtre s'y applique pleinement. On reconnaîtra ici la position traditionnelle de l'Eglise catholique.

Le *relationnalisme* définit surtout la vie humaine, la personne devrait-on dire, par la relation. Un être humain est un être en relation. Il n'existe somme toute que dans et par les liens qu'il tisse avec d'autres, et par ceux que d'autres créent avec lui. Dès lors, le fœtus acquiert sa nature humaine au moment où d'autres (la mère, le monde social) prennent conscience de lui et forment à son égard des projets précis. Dans la perspective des sujets, il peut s'agir d'un relationnalisme psychologique (le fœtus devient humain au moment où il bouge, c'est-à-dire au moment où la mère prend conscience de lui comme entité partiellement autonome) ou d'un relationnalisme social (le fœtus devient un être humain à la naissance, au moment où il devient une unité démographique autonome et où il accède à la conscience de la différenciation entre soi et autrui – ce qui d'ailleurs se produit bien ultérieurement à la naissance).

Le *positivisme* tente de s'appuyer sur des considérations biologiques pour définir la présence ou l'absence d'un être humain. Ici, le fœtus accède à l'humanité à partir d'un certain stade de son développement biologique, indépendamment de la conscience qu'autrui en a. Les sujets diront ainsi que le fœtus est un être humain "dès qu'il est formé", ... "dès qu'il a des yeux", ... "dès que son cerveau est complet", les estimations des sujets quant aux dates de l'accession à tel stade de développement relevant par ailleurs de la plus haute fantaisie et s'étalant entre deux et neuf mois.

Dans l'échantillon genevois, la perspective fondamentaliste est partagée par une personne sur cinq (19,1 %). L'orientation relationnelle rallie quatre personnes sur dix (41,1 %) et l'orientation positiviste trois personnes sur dix (31,5 %). Il a été impossible de définir clairement l'image du fœtus dans 8,2 % des cas.

Peut-on expliquer en termes sociologiques la prévalence de telle ou telle image? Cette opération paraît, au vu des résultats obtenus, assez difficile. En règle générale, les variables introduites pour tenter d'expliquer la genèse des images sont assez inopérantes.

Un premier ensemble de variables, définissant dans les grandes lignes la position du couple ou de la femme dans les structures sociales, ne permet de confirmer aucune des hypothèses énoncées primitivement à propos de la genèse de la représentation du fœtus. Ni la nationalité (méditerranéenne ou nordique) ni le statut socio-professionnel, ni le travail féminin, ni le désir d'enfants ultérieurs ne sont corrélés avec la perception du fœtus, cette absence de liaison demeurant lorsque les divers facteurs sont "contrôlés".

Un deuxième ensemble, propre au cycle familial, amène à la même conclusion. L'image du fœtus ne varie pas en fonction de la longévité du couple, ni du nombre d'enfants déjà eus, ni de l'âge du dernier enfant.

Si donc les conduites et leurs motivations sont clairement reliées aux différentes phases du cycle, il n'en va pas de même à propos des "images de l'enfant à naître". On verra dans la conclusion ce qu'il est possible de tirer de cette sorte de contradiction.

3. *Cycle familial et jugement moral sur l'avortement*

On pourrait s'attendre à ce que le jugement moral porté sur l'avortement dépende étroitement – et presque exclusivement – de l'identité accordée au fœtus. Si tel était le cas, la stabilité des images du fœtus en fonction des grandes variables sociologiques devrait être associée à une stabilité des jugements moraux en fonction de ces mêmes variables. Or ce n'est pas le cas.

La question à laquelle les interviewées avaient à répondre était celle de savoir si elles jugeaient l'interruption de grossesse comme:
- moralement très répréhensible,
- comme une faute, mais sans gravité,
- comme un acte qui n'a rien à voir avec la morale.

Elles pouvaient en plus donner une réponse "autre".

L'analyse des résultats montre que les évaluations morales négatives dominent nettement. 13,9% des interrogées jugent l'avortement comme très répréhensible, 54,2% le perçoivent comme une faute morale sans grande gravité, et seul un tiers de l'échantillon (31,9%) estime que la conduite examinée sort de la sphère du jugement moral, disant qu'un tel comportement n'a rien à voir avec la morale. C'est bien sûr l'opposition entre l'avortement "objet de jugement moral" et l'avortement "a-moral" qui nous retiendra surtout.

Voyons ce qu'il en est du rapport entre le cycle familial et le jugement porté sur l'avortement.

Une première hypothèse voudrait que le jugement porté sur l'acte soit d'autant moins négatif que l'avortement apparaît comme plus urgent, c'est-à-dire, dans le cas de couples mariés (le raisonnement serait différent dans le cas des célibataires), que l'idéal de grandeur de la famille est atteint, voire dépassé. En ce cas, les avortements conjoncturels devraient refléter un jugement plus sévère que les avortements structurels. De même, et de manière voisine, le jugement devrait aller en se libéralisant en fonction du nombre d'enfants déjà nés.

Les chiffres démentent cette hypothèse (tableau 11).

Contrairement à l'hypothèse, un nombre relativement élevé d'enfants est associé à une très faible représentation de la position "amoraliste" au profit d'une prévalence nette des jugements négatifs. Or il convient de rappeler que dans l'échantillon:
- le nombre d'enfants n'est pas associé à la pratique religieuse,
- l'incidence de l'avortement croît avec le nombre d'enfants.

Tableau 11. *Genève – Enquête Avortement.*
Jugement sur l'avortement en fonction du nombre d'enfants du couple, en %

	Nombre d'enfants			
	0	1	2	3 et +
Acte très répréhensible	7,1	17,6	11,0	17,9
Faute sans grande gravité	50,0	41,2	58,9	67,9
Rien à voir avec la morale	42,9	41,2	30,1	14,3
(N)*	(14)	(51)	(73)	(28)

* La question examinée ici n'a été posée qu'à une femme sur deux dans l'échantillon.

Il faut donc corriger l'hypothèse et la reformuler ainsi: l'accession du couple au nombre désiré d'enfants, voire son dépassement, encourage, dans le même mouvement, le recours de fait à l'avortement comme mode d'équilibration (*cf.* section I) et une perception négative de cet acte. La raison de ce dernier point est peut-être à chercher dans la socialisation normative que la présence d'enfants opère chez les parents. Le fait que l'urgence de la décision n'entre finalement guère en ligne de compte pour définir le jugement porté sur l'acte est renforcé par le fait que l'on n'observe pas, de ce point de vue, de différence nette entre les couples pratiquant un avortement conjoncturel et ceux qui y recourent dans une optique structurelle (tableau 12).

Tableau 12. *Genève – Enquête Avortement.*
Jugement sur l'avortement selon le caractère conjoncturel ou structurel de celui-ci, en %

	Conjoncturel	Structurel
Acte très répréhensible	13,6	14,0
Faute sans grande gravité	59,3	50,9
Rien à voir avec la morale	27,1	35,7
(N)	(59)	(106)

On observe enfin, toujours à titre de vérification de cette dernière hypothèse, une indépendance relative entre le jugement moral et l'âge du dernier enfant (tableau 13).

Tableau 13. *Genève – Enquête Avortement.*
Jugement sur l'avortement selon l'âge du dernier enfant, en %

	0–2 ans	3–6 ans	7–11 ans	12 et + ans
Acte très répréhensible	12,7	14,3	20,6	6,7
Faute sans grande gravité	61,8	55,1	41,2	60,0
Rien à voir avec la morale	25,5	30,6	38,2	33,3
(N)	(15)	(34)	(49)	(55)

V. Le conflit

Dans notre société, l'avortement ne va pas de soi. Tout d'abord, son obtention reste soumise à des procédures assez rigides. Mais surtout, les normes sociales stigmatisent encore fortement cet acte. On ne s'étonnera pas, dès lors, que certaines femmes, placées devant la question de leur grossesse, vivent un conflit souvent assez profond. Ce conflit peut être de deux genres principaux.

a) Il y a tout d'abord la tension entre le désir d'un enfant et l'impossibilité concrète de l'accueillir en ce moment: c'est la question des avortements conjoncturels.
b) Il y a ensuite le conflit entre la nécessité subjective d'interrompre et les images qui sont associées à cet avortement.

Il est bien clair que, dans certains cas, un cumul de ces deux genres de conflit se produit.

Le problème est alors de savoir de quels facteurs dépend le conflit. Nous avons tenté de cerner celui-ci, bien imparfaitement, en posant à la femme la question de savoir si sa décision avait été prise aisément, ou si, au contraire, elle avait eu de sérieuses difficultés à la prendre, soit parce que cette décision allait à l'encontre de ses aspirations profondes, soit parce qu'elle contredisait ses idées relatives à l'enfant, à la vie humaine, ou, plus banalement, que cette décision la plaçait en porte-à-faux avec les tendances idéologiques de son milieu.

Trois grands ordres de facteurs sont susceptibles de régir le niveau de conflit qui marque la décision. Il s'agit tout d'abord de la situation objective du couple dans les structures sociales au sens large: sa nationalité, sa dépendance ou son pouvoir du point de vue socio-économique. Il s'agit ensuite des dynamismes propres au couple et à la famille en tant qu'entité partiellement auto-déterminante: interviennent ici des facteurs tels que la durée du mariage, le nombre d'enfants, l'atteinte de la fécondité souhaitée, le type de travail féminin. Enfin, il s'agit de variables idéologiques: les idées des sujets quant à la nature du fœtus, la pratique religieuse, etc.

Les lignes qui suivent montreront dans l'ensemble que le niveau de conflit est considérablement plus lié au dynamisme interne de la famille qu'à la situation objective du couple dans les structures sociales.

1. *Situation sociale et niveau du conflit*

Deux hypothèses, reliant la position des sujets dans les structures sociales et le degré de conflit susceptible de marquer la décision d'avorter, peuvent être avancées ici:

a) la décision sera d'autant plus aisée que le couple occupe une position socio-économique défavorisée;
b) la décision sera d'autant plus aisée que la femme provient d'une culture qui autorise plus libéralement le recours à l'interruption de grossesse.

Il a été constaté plus haut que cet ordre de facteurs sociaux avait une importance considérable quant à la fréquence et au rythme des avortements. Il est donc d'autant plus frappant de constater, d'après nos données, que la fréquence du recours objectif à l'avortement n'est nullement associée, au plan subjectif, à une facilité plus grande de la décision, ou, en d'autres termes, à un niveau de conflit moins fort. Les deux hypothèses précédentes sont en effet infirmées de manière peu discutable par les données recueillies.

Tableau 14. *Genève – Enquête Avortement.*
Niveau de conflit selon le milieu social et le travail féminin, en %

	Milieux subalternes		Milieux de cadres	
	Profession	Ménage	Profession	Ménage
Décision aisée	66,7	66,7	58,1	57,1
Décision difficile	33,3	33,3	41,9	42,9
(N)	(135)	(75)	(43)	(63)

Il est aisé de constater:

– que le niveau de conflit ne diffère aucunement en fonction du travail féminin, alors même que les femmes exerçant une profession recourent

plus volontiers et de manière plus prompte à l'avortement;
- que les milieux sociaux défavorisés ne vivent pas l'avortement d'une manière plus facile ou plus difficile que les milieux aisés, alors même que les pressions qui s'exercent sur eux paraissent à première vue plus fortes; la différence de 10% qui sépare, dans le tableau 14 les deux milieux n'est guère significative.

Mais on peut objecter à ces chiffres et aux conclusions qui en sont tirées que tout cela est le résultat d'une interaction avec l'origine nationale, dont on sait qu'elle est fortement reliée avec le statut social et le travail féminin. Un contrôle approprié (qui n'est possible que pour les milieux subalternes, les Méditerranéens étant fort peu représentés parmi les cadres) montre qu'il n'en est rien (tableau 15).

Tableau 15. *Genève – Enquête Avortement.*
Niveau de conflit selon la nationalité et le travail féminin dans les milieux subalternes, en %

	Ressortissantes italiennes et espagnoles		Ressortissantes suisses, du reste de l'Europe et de l'Amérique du Nord	
	Profession	Ménage	Profession	Ménage
Décision aisée	63,7	58,6	70,9	71,7
Décision difficile	36,3	41,4	29,1	28,3
(N)	(80)	(29)	(55)	(46)

On reconnaît aisément que le niveau de conflit n'est que très légèrement supérieur chez les ressortissantes italiennes et espagnoles par rapport aux autres nationalités et que le facteur travail féminin ne joue aucun rôle visible.

En résumé, ni l'origine nationale, ni le travail féminin, ni le milieu social ne différencient réellement les niveaux du conflit.

2. *Cycle familial et conflit*

Deux critères du cycle de vie familial jouent ici un rôle assez considérable.

Il s'agit d'abord de la nature conjoncturelle ou structurelle de l'avortement. On se rappelle que cette distinction correspond en fait aux couples qui estiment n'avoir pas encore atteint leur fécondité souhaitée d'une part, à ceux qui, au contraire, l'ont atteinte ou dépassée, d'autre part.

La nature conjoncturelle de l'avortement est associée à un niveau de conflit nettement plus fort que celui observé dans le cas de l'avortement structurel (tableau 16).

Tableau 16. *Genève – Enquête Avortement.*
Niveau de conflit selon la nature conjoncturelle ou structurelle de l'avortement, en %

	Désir d'enfants pour l'avenir		
	Oui	Eventuellement	Non
Décision aisée	49,5	60,8	68,4
Décision difficile	50,5	39,3	31,6
(N)	(91)	(51)	(193)

Le second facteur propre aux dynamismes du couple tient à sa longévité. On a vu plus haut l'importance des modèles sociaux définissant des phases de la vie du couple au cours desquelles il est soit autorisé soit peu recommandé de procréer. En ce sens, il est alors compréhensible que la décision soit d'autant plus aisée que le couple se situe dans un moment social où procréer apparaît comme une conduite étrange, voire déviante (tableau 17).

Tableau 17. *Genève – Enquête Avortement.*
Niveau du conflit selon la longévité du couple, en %

	Durée du mariage		
	moins de 2 ans	2 à 10 ans	plus de 10 ans
Décision aisée	51,4	61,4	65,5
Décision difficile	48,6	38,6	32,6
(N)	(35)	(189)	(116)

Par rapport à ces deux genres de variables relatives au dynamisme de la famille, l'un nettement de l'ordre des représentations, lié aux aspirations du couple, l'autre mettant plus en lumière la situation de la famille en tant qu'entité autonome, il est frappant de constater que les contraintes objectives, matérielles, pourrait-on dire, liées à la présence d'un plus ou moins grand nombre d'enfants, ne paraissent jouer strictement aucun rôle (tableau 18). Cela est d'autant plus étonnant que la majorité des réflexions courantes à propos de l'avortement mettent en rapport la fécondité actuelle du couple et la plus ou moins grande difficulté subjective qu'il a à recourir à l'avortement. Or, nous constatons bel et bien que les contraintes matérielles ne jouent qu'un rôle mineur dans le vécu de la décision, alors que les aspirations et les modèles sociaux la modèlent pour une large part. La chasse aux stéréotypes n'est donc pas terminée.

Tableau 18. *Genève – Enquête Avortement.*
Niveau du conflit selon le nombre d'enfants, en %

	Nombre d'enfants		
	0–1	2	3 et +
Décision aisée	62,4	61,7	60,0
Décision difficile	37,6	38,3	40,0
(N)	(141)	(149)	(50)

Il en va exactement de même pour ce qui est du critère de l'âge du dernier enfant. On se serait attendu à ce qu'un âge élevé corresponde à une plus grande facilité à prendre la décision. Or, ce n'est pas le cas (tableau 19).

Tableau 19. *Genève – Enquête Avortement.*
Niveau de conflit selon l'âge du dernier enfant, en %

	0–2 ans	3–6 ans	7–11 ans	12 et + ans
Décision aisée	60,2	63,3	66,2	66,7
Décision difficile	39,8	36,7	33,8	33,3
(N)	(113)	(90)	(71)	(33)

VI. Conclusion

L'impact du cycle familial sur l'avortement n'est pas univoque. Il doit être apprécié au moins à trois niveaux: celui des actions, celui des représentations et celui du processus de décision.

Au plan des actions, les différents critères utilisés pour définir les phases du cycle familial différencient considérablement les conduites en matiere d'avortement. Tant la structure des rôles que le contenu de ceux-ci conduisent à des stratégies différentes en matière d'avortement.

La position socio-économique des couples joue également un rôle assez marqué.

Au plan des représentations, la majorité des indicateurs du cycle familial permettent de définir des *systèmes d'interprétation de la conduite* (structure des motifs de recours à l'avortement) selon la phase dans laquelle le couple est situé, montrant ainsi les valeurs ou objectifs dominants poursuivis à chacun des stades. *Par contre*, ces critères ne permettent pas de déceler des variations des représentations concernant le fœtus. De même, un seul d'entre eux (le nombre d'enfants) est associé à la nature du jugement moral porté sur l'avortement.

Au plan du processus de décision, nous observons que le niveau de conflit est surtout réglé par la nature conjoncturelle ou structurelle de l'avortement, ainsi que par la longévité du couple, les autres variables ne jouant pour ainsi dire aucun rôle.

De telles différences dans la valeur discriminante des critères du cycle familial conduisent le chercheur à soulever certains problèmes théoriques.

D'abord, une phase donnée du cycle familial n'est pas close sur elle-même, mais inscrite dans l'histoire globale du groupe. Cela signifie que le mode d'équilibre structurel d'un "moment" dépend en partie des phases précédentes, et même de facteurs construits avant que le groupe ne se forme. Ces facteurs (tels que des attitudes par exemple) imprègnent le groupe familial tout au long de sa vie, ne variant pas nécessairement avec le passage d'une phase à l'autre. De même, les conduites actuelles sont ouvertes sur un futur qu'elles anticipent. Elles ne peuvent en conséquence pas toujours être comprises par la seule référence à l'état actuel du système.

Dès lors, si l'idée de sous-systèmes familiaux s'avère précieuse, le problème reste entier de savoir quelles sont les caractéristiques du groupe propres à définir ces sous-systèmes, quelles sont les frontières de chaque phase, et surtout quel est le lien d'une phase à l'autre, l'influence déterminante d'un état antérieur sur un stade ultérieur.

Ensuite, il apparaît clairement que l'importance quantitative et la signification qualitative des phases du cycle dépendent du genre d'insertion du groupe familial dans les structures sociales globales. Les divers évènements constituant le cycle familial apparaissent à des moments différents et prennent des couleurs variables selon que les familles appartiennent à telle classe sociale, sont intégrées de telle manière à la société locale, etc.

La typologie des cycles, et peut-être même leur principe directeur, doit en conséquence être élaborée de manière différentielle. Cette démarche contribue d'ailleurs à éclaircir le lien entre famille et société globale.

Ces remarques ne diminuent en rien l'importance heuristique du concept de cycle familial. Elles tendent seulement à promouvoir d'une part une meilleure spécification des domaines dans lesquels les phases du cycle sont susceptibles d'avoir une importance déterminante et à mettre l'accent d'autre part sur la nécessité d'une analyse différentielle des phases (quantitativement et qualitativement) en fonction du mode d'insertion de la famille dans la société. Il y a fort à parier que le concept de cycle ressorte enrichi d'une telle mise en perspective.

SUMMARY

Abortion in family life cycle perspective

A study of recourse to abortion as a function of various characteristics of the family cycle leads to the following conclusions: (1) The different stages of the family cycle give a clear outline of the quantitative importance of the recourse to abortion. Two factors seem particularly important from this point of view: the passage from the stage of conjugal to that of parental role on the one hand and the presence or absence of a professional activity of the woman on the other. (2) The observed behavior, nevertheless, suggests the hypothesis that the dynamics of each stage in the cycle depend largely on the socio-economic level of the couples under consideration. In this sense, analysis of the cycles should not exclude a study of the effects of social stratification. (3) The actor's interpretation of their behavior can be differentiated only partially according to family cycle criteria. Certainly the behavioral motivations are largely dependent on the position in the cycle of the families. The stage of conjugal roles is clearly marked by motifs of mutual adaptation, while in subsequent stages motifs of socialization and inadequacy increase strongly. This fact tends, therefore, to confirm the idea that each stage has its specific problems of adaptation. On the other hand, the images associated with abortion – i.e., the image that people have of the foetus and the moral judgment made on the interruption of pregnancy – seem to depend much more on socio-cultural factors in a large sense than on the stages of the cycle themselves. (4) The presence or absence of conflict associated with the decision to interrupt a pregnancy depends on two criteria of the cycle. On the one hand, the conjunctural character of abortion is tied to a conflict which is more marked than that which one observes when the behavior is called structural. On the other hand, the longevity of the couple – indirectly defining qualitatively distinct stages – is associated with a lesser degree of conflict. (5) Because of these different points, it seems that notwithstanding the undoubted heuristic utility of analysis of behavior in relation to criteria of the family life cycle, such an analysis should nevertheless take into account the following facts:

- the content of each stage may vary according to the family's placement in the social structure, in a broad sense;
- the impact of the stage on behavior varies according to whether one analyzes the actions themselves or the explanations given by the actors.

These two elements result from the fact that the stages of the cycle constitute semi-open systems, not closed totalities.

Notes

1. Durant l'année 1970, les résidentes du Canton de Genève ont donné naissance à 4 564 nouveaux-nés, alors que, pour la période allant de juin 1970 à fin mai 1971, on a enregistré approximativement 2 000 demandes d'interruption légales de la grossesse.
2. On met au numérateur le nombre de demandes d'interruption et au dénominateur le total formé par les naissances vivantes pour l'année de référence (4 564), plus les morts-nés (32), plus une estimation grossière des interruptions spontanées de la grossesse (711), plus 90% des demandes d'interruption (représentant la proportion de demandes acceptées (1 800)).
3. Cette étude a été financée en grande partie par la Fondation Ford. Ses aspects sociologiques ont été développés par M. Bassand, J. Kellerhals et L. Raymond. La partie plus spécialement psychologique a été prise en charge par W. Pasini. Le lecteur trouvera un exposé plus détaillé de ses objectifs dans une des publications des investigateurs principaux (Bassand, Kellerhals et Raymond, 1968). L'ensemble de l'étude s'est fait sous le patronage de la Faculté de Médecine et plus particulièrement de M. le doyen W. Gesiendorf.
4. L'étude en question a été dirigée par J. Kellerhals et W. Pasini. Elle a été encouragée par le Professeur W. Geisendorf, doyen de la Faculté de Médecine, et par le Professeur J. Bernheim, directeur de l'Institut de Médecine Légale. Elle a en outre bénéficié de la collaboration des médecins-experts. On trouvera certains résultats généraux dans une publication de l'auteur (Kellerhals et Wirth, 1973). Mme G. Wirth s'est chargée des indispensables aspects de coordination du travail sur le terrain et de phases préparatoires à l'analyse.
5. Il est possible d'hésiter sur l'intérêt qu'il y a à choisir la fin de la première année ou celle de la deuxième comme ligne de clivage. Malgré une légère préférence pour la première solution, nous avons choisi la seconde pour des raisons de nombres: couper à la fin de la première année ne nous aurait pas laissé assez de cas dans la première catégorie.

Références

Auclair, M. (1962), *Le Dossier noir de l'avortement*, Paris.

Bassand, M., Kellerhals, J., et Raymond, L. (1967), "Aspects sociologiques de la fécondite et de la contraception", *Médecine et Hygiène*, 781, Genève.

Bassand, M., et Kellerhals, J. (1975), *Famille urbaine et fécondité*, Genève, Georg.

Blet, G. (1921), "Un péril national: l'avortement. Sa répression", Thèse de droit, Mâcon.

Darasson, Dr. (1952), "Etude statistique des avortements criminels traités à la Clinique obstétricale et gynécologique de Marseille (1947–1950)", Thèse de médecine, Marseille.

David, H.P. (1973), "Selected Abortion Statistics", Transnational Family Research Institute, American Institute for Research, Silver Spring.

Dourlen-Rollier, A.-M. (1963), *La Vérité sur l'avortement*, Paris.

—— (1955), *L'Avortement autorisé ou défendu*, Paris.

Duvall, E.M. (1962), *Family Development*, éd. rév., Chicago, Lippincott.

Flournoy, Dr. (1955), *Nouvelles données et réflexions psychologiques sur les avortements médicaux*, Genève.

Hel, Dr. (s.d.), "Les cas d'avortements enregistrés au contrôle médical de la Caisse primaire de la Sécurité sociale de la région parisienne de 1937 à 1946", Thèse de médecine, Paris.

Hill, R. (1964), "Methodological issues in family development research". *Family Process*, 3, mars.

Hirtzel, R. (1957), *Interruption de grossesse?*, Genève.

Kellerhals, J. (1973), "Déviance, systèmes normatifs et dynamique sociale de l'avortement", *Bull. de Méd. Lég.*, Paris, Masson.

Kellerhals, J, et Wirth, G. (1972), "Social dynamics of abortion request", *International Mental Health Newsletter*, 14/3, New York.

Ladret, A. Dr. (1961), *Libre maternité*, Lyon.

Landecker, W.S. (1965), "Les types d'intégration et leur mesure", in R. Boudon et P. Lazarsfeld (eds.), *Le Vocabulaire des sciences sociales*, Paris-La Haye, Mouton.

Lagroua Weill Hallé, Dr. (1959), *Le Planning familial*, Paris.

—— (1960), *La Grand'peur d'aimer*, Paris.

Monsaigeon, A. Dr. (1947), "L'avortement en pratique hospitalière", Statistique pour 1945–1946 à la Clinique chirurgicale de l'Hôpital St. Antoine, *Semaine des Hôpitaux*, 7 janv. 1947.

Raiter, M. (1925), "Avortement criminel et dépopulation. Etude de sociologie criminelle", Thèse de droit, Paris.

Rémy, Dr. (1953), "A propos de l'avortement thérapeutique, *Médecine et Hygiène*, 1, septembre.

Roy, J.E. (1943), "L'avortement, fléau national: causes, conséquences, remèdes", Thèse de droit, Poitiers.

Sutter, J. (1950), "Résultats d'une enquête sur l'avortement dans la région parisienne", *Population*, janv.-mars.

Tallet, X. (1938), *Les Délits contre la natalité, l'avortement et la propagande anticonceptionnelle*, Avignon.

Tarakdji, A. (1937), "L'avortement criminel, étude médico-légale, juridique et psychosociale", Thèse, Paris.

Ten Doornkaat, J. (1952), *Le Problème de l'avortement*, Genève.

14. L'incidence de la surmortalité masculine sur le cycle de la vie familiale

GÉRARD FRINKING

Introduction

Certains changements se produisant dans le déroulement du cycle de vie familiale sont le résultat des facteurs démographiques. Différents auteurs ont montré les conséquences de la baisse de l'âge au mariage, de la fécondité et de la mortalité sur la succession des grands événements de la vie familiale, depuis sa formation jusqu'à sa dissolution.[1] Le fait le plus significatif a été sans doute l'apparition d'une nouvelle phase située entre le départ du dernier enfant et la dissolution du mariage (post-parental stage).

Depuis quelques années un nouveau phénomène démographique se fait jour. L'augmentation de l'espérance de vie à la naissance dans les pays industrialisés semble avoir atteint un plafond, au moins pour les hommes. Il en résulte dans certains pays, où le niveau de mortalité féminine est très faible, un écart considérable entre la vie moyenne des deux sexes (tableau 1).

Tableau 1. *Espérance de vie à la naissance*

Pays	Période	Hommes	Femmes	Ecart
Suède	1969	71,7	76,5	4,8
Danemark	1968–1969	70,7	75,6	4,9
Norvège	1961–1965	71,0	76,0	5,0
Pays-Bas	1966–1970	71,0	76,4	5,4
Islande	1961–1965	70,8	76,2	5,4
Canada	1965–1967	68,8	75,2	6,4
Etats-Unis	1969	67,8	75,1	7,3
France	1969	67,6	75,3	7,7

Source: *Population Index*, 38/4: 514–522.

Bien que la surmortalité masculine ne soit pas un phénomène nouveau, son ampleur est de date récente. Quelques aspects de cette mortalité différentielle sont abordés dans cette communication.

Méthodologie

En étudiant l'influence de la surmortalité masculine sur le cycle de vie familiale, on peut distinguer une approche longitudinale et transversale. La première consiste à suivre dans le temps l'ensemble des personnes nées dans la même année (ou période), c'est-à-dire une génération. Par contre, la deuxième approche est basée sur l'étude de la surmortalité dans une année donnée (ou période).

Pour étudier la mortalité d'une génération il faut disposer d'une longue série de données sur le nombre de décédés par âge et l'effectif de la population correspondante. Ces données font souvent défaut. D'autre part, les changements de la mortalité sont moins sujets aux évenements survenus dans le passé d'une génération, comme c'est par exemple le cas de la nuptialité, mais dépendent beaucoup plus de l'effet des facteurs se manifestant au fil des années, comme les découvertes médicales. Ainsi, l'analyse transversale a-t-elle pris une place dominante dans les études de la mortalité.

L'étude des interrelations des grands faits de la vie familiale pose cependant des problèmes dans un tel type d'analyse. La succession des événements démographiques, comme l'âge au mariage, la fécondité du couple, la dissolution du mariage ne se laisse pas facilement traiter comme un ensemble, sauf dans le cas de l'invariabilité de ces événements. Cette condition est rarement remplie.

L'analyse longitudinale de la surmortalité masculine semble donc l'approche la plus appropriée pour saisir sa signification véritable pour le cycle de vie familiale; surtout, lorsqu'on essaie de relier les transformations affectant le système familial en rapport avec le changement social.[2]

Données

Nous nous sommes limités aux données néerlandaises, où le niveau de surmortalité concorde sensiblement avec la moyenne dans des pays à faible niveau de mortalité ($E_0 > 75$ ans).

Les générations de 1871–1875, les plus anciennes pour lesquelles une table de mortalité pour les deux sexes a été construite, ont une grande mortalité aux jeunes âges. La baisse de la mortalité depuis 1900 a fait augmenter l'espérance de vie à partir de 25 ans jusqu'à un niveau voisin de celui observé en ce moment.

La surmortalité masculine, qui a augmenté considérablement pendant les dix dernières années, est encore négligeable dans ces générations, comme en témoigne le tableau 2.

Tableau 2. *Ecart entre l'espérance de vie aux divers âges*

	Générations 1871–1875			Période 1966–1970		
Age	H	F	Ecart	H	F	Ecart
0	44,5	46,9	2,4	71,0	76,4	5,4
10	56,1	56,5	0,4	62,5	67,6	5,1
20	48,1	48,7	0,6	52,9	57,8	4,9
30	40,7	41,0	0,3	43,4	47,9	4,5
40	32,5	33,0	0,5	33,9	38,5	4,6
50	24,4	25,1	0,7	24,9	29,2	4,3
60	16,7	17,4	0,7	17,1	20,5	3,4
70	10,4	11,0	0,6	10,8	12,7	1,9
80	5,9	6,2	0,3	6,2	6,8	0,6
90	3,1	3,4	0,3	3,2	3,4	0,2

Source: Bureau Central de Statistique, Pays-Bas (1972), Generatie sterftetafels, gehele bevolking Nederland. Feuillets stéreotypés. Sterftetafels voor Nederland, afgeleid uit waarnemingen over de periode 1966–1970, Vol. I, La Haye.

Ceci n'est pas le cas pour la mortalité de la période la plus récente, les années 1966–1970. Ici, l'écart entre la mortalité masculine et féminine est très net. L'effet total de la surmortalité aux divers âges dans les générations, constituant la population pendant la période en question, fournit une indication d'ampleur pour les générations futures.

C'est ainsi, supposant l'invariabilité de la mortalité récente, que nous sommes en mesure de décrire et de prévoir les changements dans le cycle de vie familiale.

Résultats

En combinant les probabilités de survie pour hommes et femmes à partir de leur âge moyen au (premier) mariage, on peut tracer une courbe de survie selon la durée du mariage. Pour cela, nous avons eu recours à deux hypothèses. La première pose l'absence d'une mortalité différentielle selon l'état civil. Cette condition n'est pas tout à fait remplie. D'après des données récentes, montrant une légère supériorité des mariés par rapport à la population totale, son influence sur les résultats obtenus est faible. La deuxième hypothèse suppose l'indépendance du risque de mortalité des hommes de celui des femmes. Sa vérification n'est non plus assurée. Prenons le cas des accidents de la route qui touchent les familles. Cependant les accidents frappent essentiellement les jeunes et ne modifient pas sensiblement l'hypothèse. Un autre exemple de l'interdépendance entre la mortalité des conjoints se situe aux âges élevés. Souvent, après une longue durée du mariage, la disparition d'un des deux conjoints entraîne la mort de l'autre. Une estimation de cet effet sur la probabilité de survie du couple est néanmoins difficile à donner.[3]

La distribution du nombre de mariages qui survivent aux diverses durées de mariage peut se résumer par la moyenne, indiquant la durée moyenne au moment de sa formation. Cette notion est tout à fait comparable à celle de l'espérance de vie à la naissance. On trouve dans le tableau 3 certaines valeurs de l'espérance de vie du couple, calculées à diverses durées de mariage, pour les générations de 1871–1875 et la période de 1966–1970.

Tableau 3. *L'espérance de vie du couple aux diverses durées de mariage*

Durée de mariage	Générations 1871–1875	Période 1966–1970 (a)	(b)
0	34,5	44,2	41,4
5	31,1	39,5	36,7
10	27,6	34,8	32,0
15	24,1	30,2	27,5
20	20,7	25,8	23,2
25	17,2	21,6	19,2
30	13,9	17,7	15,5
35	10,9	14,1	12,2
40	8,3	11,1	9,4
45	6,4	8,4	7,1
50	4,8	6,2	5,2
55	3,6	4,6	3,9

(a) L'âge moyen au mariage de la période 1966–1970.
(b) L'âge moyen au mariage des générations de 1871–1875.

Il apparaît une augmentation de la vie maritale d'environ 30% pour les générations nouvelles par rapport à celle de la période 1871–1875; ceci à n'importe quelle durée du mariage. Cette uniformité est à première vue assez surprenante. On devrait s'attendre à une diminution de cet écart proportionnellement à la durée du mariage. En effet, les données du tableau 2 montrent que l'espérance de vie au-dessus de 40 ans dans les générations anciennes ne diffère qu'à peine de celle de la période récente, au moins pour les hommes. Or, un tel effet se produit lorsqu'on tient compte de la diminution de l'âge au mariage. Dans ce cas, on observe entre les anciennes et nouvelles générations un allongement de la vie maritale de presque 7 ans, soit 20%, mesurée au moment de la conclusion du mariage. L'écart diminue rapidement selon la durée de mariage.

En isolant l'effet de la surmortalité masculine de celui de la baisse de la mortalité en général, on constate un effet négatif du premier facteur sur la durée maritale. La baisse de la mortalité générale a été contrecarrée par la hausse de la surmortalité masculine. Sans ce dernier facteur, l'augmentation de la durée de mariage aurait été de plus de 10 ans, en absence d'un changement de l'âge au mariage. En réalité, on n'observe qu'une augmentation de presque 7 ans.

Plus lourds de conséquences sont les changements se produisant à la mort d'un des deux conjoints. Le tableau 4 donne les détails les plus importants.

Tableau 4. *Quelques caractéristiques du cycle de la vie familiale après la dissolution du mariage*

	Générations 1871–1875		Période 1966–1970	
Caractéristique	H	F	H	F
Pourcentage des survivant(s)	46	54	34	66
Début du veuvage	61,5	61,2	70,3	66,6
Durée du veuvage	15,7	16,6	10,8	15,6
Fin du veuvage	77,2	77,8	81,1	82,2

Dans les générations de 1871–1875 la mort est à peu près égalitaire. Dans 54% des cas le mariage est dissolu par la mort de l'homme. La durée qui sépare le veuf de la fin de sa vie diffère peu de la période du veuvage de la femme. L'inégalité devant la mort prendra une intensité accrue dans les générations nouvelles. Dans deux mariages sur trois la femme survivra à son conjoint. Sa période de veuvage sera à peine modifiée.

Les conséquences futures de la surmortalité masculine se résument de la manière suivante: le nombre relatif des mariages où l'homme meurt en premier, augmentera considérablement. A un âge où le couple aura à peine commencé la phase de la retraite, la femme devra seule affronter l'existence pendant une durée de plus de 15 ans en moyenne. Ces perspectives nécessitent une attention toute particulière. Elles peuvent nous conduire à remettre en question certaines traditions telle que la différence d'âge des candidats au mariage, le travail de la femme, son rôle dans la famille, etc.

Cette image, construite avec des indices moyens de la population, demande à être nuancée. La réalité est infiniment plus complexe. L'inégalité devant la mort ne se limite pas uniquement au sexe, mais s'étend également aux diverses classes de la société.

Les problèmes méthodologiques, propres à la mesure de la mortalité différentielle selon le milieu social, ont freiné sérieusement les recherches dans ce domaine. Actuellement nous ne disposons que de peu d'études dans lesquelles les contours du phénomène ne sont qu'explorés. Une étude américaine de 1960 fait état d'une différence de 3 ans de l'espérance de vie à 25 ans pour les hommes selon le niveau d'instruction. Cet écart est presque de 10 ans pour les femmes.[4] Des recherches françaises ont aussi révélé l'existence d'une mortalité différentielle.[5] Ici, le nombre de survivants à 70 ans pour 1 000 à 35 ans, mesuré pour différentes catégories socio-professionelles, varie entre 498 pour les manœuvres et 732 pour les instituteurs de l'enseignement public. Lorsque ces données seront combinées avec les caractéristiques des conjoints au moment de leur mariage, on obtiendra une image plus complète de l'incidence de la surmortalité sur le cycle de la vie familiale.

Remarques finales

En brossant un tableau des conséquences de la surmortalité, nous avons laissé de côté le remariage des veufs et des veuves. La plus grande fréquence du remariage des premiers à chaque durée du veuvage, accentuant la différence entre hommes et femmes, devrait conduire à porter un intérêt plus grand aux conséquences multiples de la mortalité différentielle dans les sociétés modernes.

Un premier pas consiste à approfondir les aspects démographiques de la surmortalité masculine pour ensuite les jumeler aux autres données touchant le cycle de vie familiale. Seul un tel type de recherches permettra de prévoir les problèmes auxquels nous devrons faire face prochainement.

Summary

The influence of higher male mortality on the family life cycle

For several years now a new demographic phenomenon has become apparent in the industrialized countries. The increase of life expectancy, at least for the male, appears to have reached a perceivable limit. The result is that in certain countries, where the female mortality rate is very low, a considerable difference in average life duration between the two sexes can be observed. The influence of a higher male mortality rate can be illustrated by comparing a few characteristics of the family life cycle during two different periods of time. The periods taken in consideration are the generations born during 1871–1875, and those having reached the average mortality level by 1966–1970. From this comparison, we find the following: the generations born in 1871–1875 average a more or less equal age at death; in 54% of the cases, dissolution of the marriage is caused by the death of the male spouse, while the span of life left to the widower differs little from the span of life left to the widow. We project an increasingly unequal mortality rate for the coming generations: in two out of three marriages the wife will survive her husband, while the period of widowhood in itself is not expected to change considerably in the future. At the approximate time when the couple will have reached the age of retirement, the majority of the wives will have to face a period alone which will average more than 15 years.

Notes

1. Les travaux de Glick se distinguent par l'approche la plus complète des aspects démographiques.
2. Ryder, N. (1965), "The cohort as a concept in the study of social change", *American Sociological Review*, 30/6: 843–861.
3. Une étude anglaise a montré une légère différence entre la mortalité des veufs et des hommes mariés pendant les premiers six mois du veuvage; voir: Young, M. (1963), "The mortality of widowers", *The Lancet*, 7305: 454–456.
4. Kitagawa, E. (1971), "Social and economic differentials in mortality in the United States, 1960", Congrès International de la Population, 1969, II: 980–995, Liège.
5. Calot, G., et Febvay, M. (1965), "La mortalité différentielle selon le milieu social", *Etudes et Conjoncture*, II: 75–159.

15. Age du chef de famille et niveau de vie du ménage

ANDRZEJ TYMOWSKI

Le fait que les mêmes activités rendent certains individus très pauvres et d'autres très riches étonnait déjà Xénophon: un pareil fait, selon lui, était digne d'analyse.

Encore aujourd'hui, la définition et la connaissance des facteurs qui déterminent les revenus et les dépenses d'une famille sont des questions d'intérêt primordial tant pour les personnes responsables de l'économie et de la société que pour les scientifiques, économistes et sociologues. Les recherches en la matière effectuées en Pologne sont assez développées et soulignent généralement[1] l'importance de la taille de la famille, le nombre de personnes actives, le niveau d'instruction, le caractère du travail effectué par les personnes employées (manuel ou non manuel), le lieu de résidence (ville ou campagne, région) et les caractéristiques du passé familial.[2] Le but de cette étude est l'analyse d'un autre facteur, le rapport entre l'âge du chef de famille et sa situation matérielle, définie par le niveau des revenus alimentant l'économie domestique, par l'importance et la structure des dépenses ainsi que par le degré d'équipement.

L'idée d'analyser ce problème n'est pas neuve. Il a déjà été traité par Rowntree,[3] dans ses études sur la population d'York à la charnière des XIXe et XXe siècles. Pendant l'entre-deux-guerres, Halbwachs[4] suggérait le même genre d'analyse et, il y a relativement peu de temps, Lydall[5] et Schmucker[6] en ont réalisé une, chacun indépendamment. Soulignons par ailleurs qu'en Tchécoslovaquie et en Hongrie, l'un des critères déterminants sélectionnés dans les recherches sur les budgets familiaux est l'âge du chef de famille. Cela confirme jusqu'à un certain point l'importance de cette variable.

Les données statistiques exposées dans cette étude ont été recueillies par l'Office central de Statistiques de Pologne lors d'enquêtes sur les budgets familiaux effectuées en 1971. On a également eu recours à des données de 1967 et 1963[7] afin d'établir certaines comparaisons rétrospectives. Il importe aussi de faire connaissance avec certaines définitions de base en usage pour les enquêtes de l'Office.

L'unité analysée est le ménage – composé de deux ou plusieurs personnes – avec une personne au moins travaillant dans le secteur économique socialisé. Un "ménage" comprend deux personnes au moins domiciliées dans le même logement et mettant en commun une partie ou l'ensemble de leurs revenus afin de subvenir à ses besoins (sans recevoir en contre-partie de services déterminés). Il se peut aussi qu'il bénéficie des moyens dont dispose la communauté domestique pour satisfaire à une partie ou à l'ensemble des besoins personnels (sans prêter de services convenus à l'économie domestique). Comme l'indique cette définition, sont écartés du champ d'observation l'économie paysanne privée, soit la majorité de la population rurale en Pologne, ainsi que les inactifs, c'est-à-dire les personnes âgées habitant isolément et vivant de leurs retraites. Ainsi, les enquêtes de l'Office central de Statistiques ont porté sur plus de la moitié de la population (52% environ).

La définition de "chef de famille" n'est pas simple. Dans les communautés domestiques avec une seule personne rémunérée, le chef de famille est tout désigné. Dans les communautés comprenant deux ou plusieurs salariés dont: a) un seulement parmi les autres membres ayant un époux ou des enfants, cette personne est désignée comme le chef (et plutôt le mari que la femme); b) dans le cas où vivent ensemble plusieurs salariés ayant époux ou enfants, c'est le plus âgé qui est chef de famille (également si personne n'a d'époux ou d'enfants).

En définitive, une fois éliminés les ménages de personnes seules, peu représentatifs pour la problématique envisagée,[8] les enquêtes ont porté sur 2 290 ménages de deux ou de plusieurs personnes. Dans plus de 75% des cas, le chef de famille était un homme. Dans les familles de travailleurs manuels cette proportion était supérieure à la proportion correspondante chez les non manuels (respectivement 79 et 69%). Dans l'échantillon analysé, la proportion de ménages de travailleurs manuels s'élève à 60%, et celle des travailleurs non manuels à 40%.

Les classes d'âge du chef de famille se succèdent par tranches de 10 ans; pour les moins de 30 ans, on a constitué deux classes d'âge: "moins de 24 ans" (pratiquement, on devient chef de famille émancipé à l'âge de 19 ans au moins), et "de 25 à 29 ans". Ce principe a été adopté à cause de la nécessité d'analyser de plus près les budgets au moment des grands changements que suscitent l'émancipation et la fondation d'une famille.

L'âge du chef de famille et la structure démographique de la famille

En général, on accorde une attention insuffisante aux problèmes démographiques dans les analyses de la situation matérielle de la famille. Cela ne semble pas juste. Le nombre des membres d'une famille, sa structure d'âge ou de sexe, le nombre de membres à l'âge actif et de salariés qu'elle comprend sont autant de facteurs importants qui, souvent, décident du niveau et de la structure des revenus et des dépenses, du degré auquel la famille a recours à des services collectifs (cantines, restaurants) et du degré d'équipement de la maison. Le tableau démographique des ménages étudiés a également son importance pour la définition d'une politique des impôts, d'une politique sociale et d'une politique de l'emploi.

Le tableau 1 comprend des données qui caractérisent le rapport entre certains des éléments de la structure démographique des ménages considérés et l'âge du chef de famille.
Ces informations portent surtout sur le nombre de membres des familles et le degré de leur activité professionnelle.

L'évolution du nombre moyen des membres de la famille suivant l'âge du chef de famille est nette: elle rappelle une pyramide aplatie. Les moins nombreuses sont les familles dont le chef est jeune ou âgé; les plus nombreuses sont les familles dont le chef est d'un âge moyen. Cette répartition doit être mise en rapport avec le cycle de la vie domestique: fondation de la famille, arrivée des enfants, départ des enfants adultes.

Près des $\frac{4}{5}$ des familles jeunes dont le chef a moins de 24 ans, sont des familles de 2 et 3 personnes, très souvent des ménages sans enfants qui cohabitent avec l'un des parents. Quand le chef de famille a plus de 24 ans, la proportion de ménages avec 1 ou 2 enfants progresse. Ainsi la dominante, pour les chefs de famille de 24 à 29 ans, c'est la famille de 3 personnes tandis que pour les chefs de famille de 30 à 49 ans, c'est la famille de 4 personnes. Quand le chef de famille est âgé, on constate une diminution du nombre des membres; pour les âges compris entre 50 et 59 ans, les deux tiers des familles ne comprennent que 2 ou 3 personnes; lorsque le chef de famille a 60 ans ou plus, les $\frac{3}{5}$ des familles ne dépassent pas 2 membres. Il est à relever que les familles des travailleurs manuels sont généralement plus nombreuses, fondées plus tôt, avec des enfants venant

Tableau 1. *Données démographiques sur les ménages des salariés enquêtés*

Catégories de données	Total	Age du chef de famille (nombre d'années)					
		moins de 24	25–29	30–39	40–49	50–59	60 et plus
A Nombre de budgets considérés	2990	151	400	1072	939	344	84
B Ménages et nombre de leurs membres (en % de l'echantillon considéré)							
2	20	42	25	13	15	30	61
3	33	39	47	35	26	33	17
4	31	13	23	37	36	18	13
5	13	3	4	13	18	5	7
6 personnes et +	3	3	1	2	5	4	2
	100	100	100	100	100	100	100
C Nombre moyen de membres dans un ménage	3,48	2,86	3,11	3,56	3,76	3,31	2,74
dont: salariés	1,67	1,73	1,69	1,63	1,69	1,70	1,63
D Indice d'activité professionnelle	48,0	60,5	54,3	45,8	44,9	51,4	59,5
Nombre de personnes à la charge d'un salarié	2,08	1,65	1,84	2,18	2,22	1,95	1,68

au monde plus tôt également que dans les familles de travailleurs non manuels. Chez les non manuels, un dixième à peine des familles compte 5 personnes ou plus; chez les travailleurs manuels, le $\frac{1}{5}$ des familles atteint cette dimension,[9] une famille moyenne de travailleurs manuels compte 3,55 membres tandis que la famille moyenne de travailleurs non manuels n'en compte que 3,37.

Les changements dans les dimensions de la famille s'accompagnent de changements dans la structure de l'activité professionnelle. Dans les familles jeunes, le niveau d'activité professionnelle est très élevé; sur 10 personnes appartenant à ces familles, 6 sont professionnellement actives. A mesure que le chef de famille vieillit et que le nombre d'enfants croît dans sa famille, le niveau d'activité professionnelle de la famille baisse; 4,5 personnes seulement sur 10 sont professionnellement actives dans les familles où le chef a plus de 40 ans et cette proportion croît quand le chef de famille est plus âgé (au-dessus de 50 ans). Elle rejoint dans la catégorie d'âge la plus élevée, le niveau observé dans les familles les plus jeunes. D'une manière générale, ce niveau élevé d'activité professionnelle participe de la mise au travail de la femme en Pologne qui, depuis des années, se développe de façon continue.

Le niveau d'activité professionnelle dans la famille dépend directement, en fin de compte, du nombre moyen de personnes à charge par personne active, ce qui a une influence décisive sur la situation matérielle. Le degré d'aisance d'une famille dépend, dans une grande mesure, et du niveau d'équipement existant auparavant, et du rapport entre les personnes actives et non actives dans la famille. On peut évidemment observer "qu'une personne n'en vaut pas une autre" car les uns gagnent plus et les autres moins et d'autre part les frais d'entretien d'un enfant, d'une personne adulte et d'un vieillard ne sont pas les mêmes. Néanmoins, le rapport entre les actifs et les inactifs dans une famille est un facteur important.

Ces remarques sur les relations entre la taille de la famille, son niveau d'activité professionnelle et l'âge du chef de famille ont été faites à titre introductif. La suite démontre à quel point elles sont fondamentales.

L'âge du chef de famille et les revenus de la maison

L'importance des revenus peut être calculée par foyer, ou par membre de la famille.

Une analyse des revenus par famille permet de déterminer l'importance et la structure des revenus dans les foyers ainsi que le rapport entre leur niveau de vie, le nombre de personnes actives dans la famille et l'âge du chef de famille. Les études sur les revenus par personne déforment jusqu'à un certain point certaines de ces quantités (par exemple le montant des revenus de la famille) étant donné qu'ils sont avant tout fonction du nombre de ses membres – qui est variable – et, dans une mesure moindre, de l'importance des revenus en chiffres absolus. Pour déterminer et étudier le degré d'aisance d'une famille il est absolument nécessaire de considérer les données sur les revenus par personne dans un foyer (éventuellement par unité de consommation). Voilà pourquoi il est indispensable d'effectuer une analyse des revenus sous les deux aspects si l'on veut donner une idée des variables dépendantes de l'âge du chef de famille (tableau 2).

Tableau 2. *Revenus mensuels des familles et âge du chef de famille*

	Revenus en zlotys							Indice des revenus (total = 100)						
		Age du chef de famille							Age du chef de famille					
Spécification	Total	moins de 24	25–29	30–39	40–49	50–59	60 et plus	Total	moins de 24	25–29	30–39	40–49	50–59	60 et plus
A. Par foyer														
Total des revenus	5077	4410	4653	5130	5302	5097	4757	100	87	92	101	104	100	94
Part en % des revenus représentés par:														
– Le salaire	87	82	87	88	87	87	85							
– Les prestations sociales	9	14	10	9	9	9	11							
B. Par membre de la famille														
Total des revenus	1459	1542	1496	1441	1410	1540	1736	100	106	103	99	97	106	119

L'importance des revenus par foyer oscille entre 4 400 et 5 300 zl. par mois. La courbe qui illustre les revenus des familles en fonction de l'âge du chef de famille décrit une parabole: les revenus des familles les plus jeunes sont relativement bas; ils augmentent avec les années pour atteindre un niveau – dans les familles d'âge moyen (30–49 ans) – de 20% supérieur à celui des foyers jeunes, dans les familles de personnes âgées, le niveau des revenus du foyer se met lentement à baisser, tout en demeurant plus élevé que dans les jeunes ménages des deux subdivisions. L'importance des revenus du ménage suivant les classes d'âge des chefs de famille est en corrélation de plus en plus marquée avec l'évolution démographique de la famille: plus la famille est nombreuse, plus ses revenus sont importants.

Les remarques que nous venons de faire se rapportent au niveau des revenus des foyers. Lorsqu'on examine les revenus calculés par personne membre de la famille, on constate qu'ils évoluent dans le sens inverse de celui qui caractérisait les revenus – précédemment analysés – par foyer: a) dans les classes d'âge du chef de famille où la famille est peu nombreuse, ils sont relativement importants; b) dans les foyers où le chef de famille est jeune ou âgé, les revenus dépassent quelque peu la moyenne, et quand le chef de famille est d'âge moyen, ils sont inférieurs. Autrement dit: à mesure que la famille croît, ses revenus par personne diminuent, ce qui est surtout très accentué dans les familles où le chef est d'âge moyen, c'est -à-dire dans la période où naissent et où sont élevés les enfants. Puis, quand les enfants arrivent à l'âge adulte et quittent la maison, c'est-à-dire quand le père atteint la cinquantaine, les revenus par membre augmentent de nouveau. Si l'on rapproche les données sur l'importance des revenus du nombre des membres de la famille, on s'aperçoit que "plus la famille est nombreuse, plus les revenus sont importants, mais calculés par membre de la famille, ils sont plus faibles".[10]

Les résultats d'analyses détaillées de l'évolution de la structure des revenus de la famille suivant l'âge du chef de famille sont particulièrement intéressants.

Le nombre de personnes que compte la famille, plus précisément le nombre d'enfants, influe avant tout – ce qui est d'ailleurs tout naturel – sur l'importance des allocations familiales. Les allocations familiales commencent à avoir de l'importance dans les familles où le chef a de 25 à 29 ans. Elles comptent plus encore dans les budgets des familles où le chef a de 30 à 39 ans. Leur part diminue quelque peu dans la catégorie suivante pour baisser très nettement dans les budgets des ménages âgés.

Le foyer est donc alimenté en allocations familiales à une période où le niveau de ses revenus par personne est le plus bas. La part des allocations dans les revenus de la famille moyenne, d'après l'échantillon examiné, est infime; elle s'élève à 3% à peine.

Les revenus provenant de pensions et retraites suivent un mouvement inverse. La cohabitation avec des personnes âgées, généralement le père ou la mère de l'un des conjoints, se produit surtout dans les premières années qui suivent le mariage, et de là, la plus grande part des retraites dans les revenus du ménage. Plus tard, la part des retraites diminue et elle reprend à nouveau de l'importance dans les ménages où l'âge du chef dépasse 50 ans (à cette période là, du reste, les pensions d'invalides ont un rôle plus important dans le budget familial que les retraites proprement dites).

La liaison entre l'âge du chef de famille et les revenus provenant de son travail est significative. On observe d'autre part une différenciation nette dans les données se rapportant aux travailleurs manuels ou non manuels, comme le montre le tableau 3.

Tableau 3. *Catégorie d'emploi et âge du chef de famille*

	Rémunération d'un chef de famille de moins de 24 ans = 100				
	25–29	30–39	40–49	50–59	60 et plus
Travailleur manuel	121	139	137	132	123
Travailleur non manuel	123	152	157	152	158

Le travailleur manuel gagne en moyenne 13% de moins que le travailleur non manuel; ses gains les plus élevés se situent entre 30 et 39 ans; au catégories d'âge qui suivent, les gains diminuent, d'abord très lentement, puis de façon plus nette. Les rémunérations des non manuels obéissent à d'autres lois: en principe, à partir de la 30e année, elles ne subissent pas de changements notables et se maintiennent à peu près au même niveau jusqu'à la fin du temps d'activité du travailleur. Dans les deux groupes, la période d'entrée dans la vie professionnelle correspond aux rémunérations les plus faibles.

Indiquons que les gains de la seconde personne active de la famille – généralement de la femme – sont nettement moins élevés que ceux des maris, et cela dans tous les groupes d'âge du chef de famille. Une seule exception à cette règle, les ménages du groupe le plus jeune où l'écart entre les salaires des maris et des femmes – d'une façon générale les moins élevés – se réduit à presque rien.

Pour résumer, les qualifications professionnelles supérieures des personnes d'âge moyen entraînent à vrai dire un accroissement de leurs gains, mais celui-ci demeure trop faible pour compenser l'extension de la famille avec la venue au monde des enfants. Le rôle des allocations familiales en tant qu'instrument permettant, ne serait-ce qu'une compensation partielle, est insuffisante, étant donné le système polonais de traitements et prestations sociales. Leur montant peu élevé et les frais d'entretien d'un enfant sont disproportionnés. Cet état de choses exerce nécessairement aussi une influence sur le modèle de consommation des familles des personnes d'âge moyen, si elles sont pourvues d'enfants.

Age du chef de famille et dépenses du ménage

Le facteur qui introduit le plus de différenciation dans la situation matérielle de la famille, compte tenu d'un degré d'égalité assez prononcé entre les revenus des foyers en Pologne est sa structure démographique, c'est-à-dire le nombre et l'âge des membres de la famille. Afin d'obtenir des données permettant d'établir des comparaisons sur la situation matérielle de familles de taille différente, on divise les revenus – ou les dépenses – de la famille par le nombre de ses membres, c'est-à-dire que l'on examine les relations en fonction d'une personne. Il est vrai que plus la famille est grande, plus les frais d'entretien baissent (ceux qu'occasionne le logement, les frais de nourriture, les dépenses pour certains articles de consommation durable, etc.), mais il est vrai aussi qu'"une personne n'en vaut pas une autre" et que la composition de la famille – adultes, enfants ou personnes à l'âge de la retraite – n'est pas sans importance.[11] La méthode appliquée en Pologne par l'Office central de Statistiques ainsi que le principe adopté pour la répartition de certaines prestations sociales rendent toutefois les comparaisons possibles entre le degré d'aisance des familles suivant les revenus et leur taille.

Nous avons essayé de déterminer la corrélation entre l'âge du chef de famille et les dépenses du ménage: les données qui en résultent sont présentées au tableau 4.

Tableau 4. *Dépenses mensuelles des ménages et âge du chef de famille*

Spécification	Total	Groupe d'âge du chef de famille 20–24	25–29	30–39	40–49	50–59	60 et plus	Indice des dépenses (total** = 100) âge du chef de famille (nombre d'années) 20–24	25–29	30–39	40–49	50–59	60 et plus
Dépenses mansuelles* par personne en zlotys	1359	1486	1408	1341	1312	1424	1578	115	103	99	96	104	116
pourcentage	100	100	100	100	100	100	100	—	—	—	—	—	—
dont:													
– Nourriture	46	43	43	45	46	48	48	108	97	99	99	109	124
* Alcool et tabac	4	4	4	4	3	3	4	133	115	102	89	96	112
* Vêtements et chaussures	16	18	16	16	16	16	14	132	102	97	97	105	105
* Logement	10	12	12	11	9	9	10	143	127	106	81	92	108
– Gaz, énergie électrique, charbon	4	3	4	4	4	4	5	92	92	101	98	109	119
– Hygiène personnelle, protection de la santé, etc.	3	3	4	3	4	4	4	106	111	98	93	104	131
– Culture, éducation etc.	9	9	9	10	9	8	8	116	97	103	98	93	110
– Transports, communications	5	3	5	4	5	5	4	77	118	89	107	105	92
– Autres	3	5	3	3	3	3	3	118	99	95	99	109	128

* Le montant annuel des dépenses des familles n'égale pas obligatoirement celui de leurs revenus et les décalages qui se produisent sont dûs soit à l'apparition d'économies/supplément de revenus, soit à un mode de vie passager au-dessus des moyens de la fammille/supplément de dépenses.

** Moyenne dans les groupes de population considérés.

L'analyse de ces données permet de relever une série très nette de régularités dans la répartition des dépenses.

1. La part des dépenses pour la nourriture dans l'ensemble des dépenses croît avec l'âge de chef de famille. En effet, les personnes âgées sont moins enclines à investir. Dans les familles des personnes les plus âgées, les dépenses pour la viande, la charcuterie, les légumes, le lait et le sucre atteignent leur maximum. Dans les dépenses alimentaires des jeunes ménages, les frais de consommation collective (restaurants, cantines) sont beaucoup plus importants.
2. C'est l'inverse qui se produit dans la répartition des dépenses pour les vêtements et les chaussures: plus le chef de famille est âgé, plus la part de ce groupe de dépenses dans le budget familial diminue.
3. Les frais de logement et d'équipement ont un rapport très étroit avec le stade de développement de la famille. Dans les familles jeunes, ils sont relativement plus élevés: les jeunes sont plus favorables à l'investissement en biens d'équipement du logement: ils achètent volontiers des articles de consommation durable pour leur ménage. Cette régularité serait encore plus accentuée n'étaient les difficultés encore présentes en Pologne de logement, qui allongent nécessairement l'étape de la "mise sur pied du ménage".

Signalons encore les différences entre les budgets familiaux des manuels et ceux des non manuels. Quel que soit l'âge du chef de famille, les non manuels, de tous les groupes d'âge, dépensent relativement moins que les manuels en nourriture, alcool et tabac tandis qu'ils dépensent plus pour leur hygiène, la santé, la culture, l'éducation et le transport.

Les tendances qui se dessinent dans le modèle de consommation des familles en fonction de l'âge du chef de famille ont une relation avec le degré d'équipement en biens de consommation durable (*cf.* tableau 5).

Tableau 5. *Degré d'équipement des ménages en biens de consommation durable* (*sur 100 ménages*)

Spécification	Total	Age du chef de famille					
		moins de 24	25–29	30–39	40–49	50–59	60 et plus
Téléviseur	85	60	76	88	89	84	83
Poste de radio	96	79	82	93	104	106	106
Machine à laver	90	62	76	92	95	94	95
Aspirateur	57	33	46	61	62	56	62
Réfrigérateur	52	23	42	58	55	48	50
Machine à coudre	42	25	26	38	53	51	45

Les ménages les mieux équipés en biens de consommation durable sont ceux où le chef de famille a dépassé la quarantaine. Il est intéressant de relever que certains biens de consommation durable figurent moins souvent dans l'équipement des ménages de personnes âgées, ce qui prouve que ces achats n'étaient pas prioritaires il y a une quinzaine d'années. Aujourd'hui l'acquisition prioritaire est le poste de radio suivi de la machine à laver et du téléviseur. Déjà les $\frac{3}{4}$ des ménages dont le chef de famille est âgé de 25 à 29 ans sont nantis de ces objets. Les ménages plus âgés n'en possèdent que pour les autres biens considérés – aspirateur, réfrigérateur et machine à coudre – arrivent en seconde position et le nombre de ménages qui les possèdent est nettement inférieur. Soulignons aussi que l'achat de la machine à coudre dans les ménages jeunes est beaucoup moins fréquent que dans les ménages aînés au même stade et, que de ce fait, le pourcentage des familles qui en ont est en légère baisse.

Conclusion

L'étude ci-dessus a servi à illustrer certains rapports entre l'âge du chef de famille et la situation matérielle du ménage. La connaissance de ces correlations est importante car elle permet

a) de programmer convenablement la politique de répartition des traitements et prestations sociales afin de les harmoniser avec les changements dans la situation matérielle de la famille durant son cycle;
b) de prévoir les changements à long terme du modèle de consommation en fonction de l'évolution de la structure des âges au sein de la société;
c) de connaître la situation matérielle des familles en fonction des changements qu'elle subit lors du développement de son cycle.

Summary

Age of the family head vs. *household standard of living*

This analysis of the relationships between the age of the family head and the financial situation of a household is based on statistical data from a survey of family budgets for 1971 conducted by the Chief Census Bureau of Poland. Particular attention is given here to relationships between the age of the family head and the demographic structure of a given household, with special regard to the professional activities of its members. The author includes an analysis of family incomes in relation to the age of the family head, and data are presented per household and per family member, taking into account the changes in amount and structure of incomes. Further, expenditures of basic groups of households, as well as extents of stocks of selected durables, in relation to the variable under analysis, are presented, and attention is called to the important differences between the established patterns of white-collar and blue-collar households. In the final remarks, the author stresses the importance of this type of analysis, as much for social policy and proper distribution of social funds, as for forecasting purposes.

NOTES

1. Les méthodes de recherche sur les budgets familiaux et l'emploi des résultats de ce genre de recherche en Pologne ont été présentés dans une contribution spéciale. Cf. Tymowski, A. (1969), "Les enquêtes sur les conditions de vie dans la planification polonaise", *Economie-Statistique*, 11: 49–53.
2. Etant donné les processus actuels d'urbanisation rapide de la population en Pologne, des enquêtes spéciales ont été effectuées sur l'influence qu'exerce le passé sur le modèle de vie matérielle de la famille urbaine, suivant que les parents étaient des citadins ou des villageois. Tymowski, A. (1970), "L'origine et les conditions de vie de la famille" (Pochodzenie a warunki bytu rodziny), *Studia Socjologiczne*, 2: 147–166.
3. Rowntree, (1902), *Poverty, A Study of Town Life*, London.
4. Halbwachs M. (1933), *L'Evolution des besoins dans la classe ouvrière*, Paris: 61–63.
5. Lydall, H. (1955), "The life cycle in income, savings, and asset ownership", *Econometrica.*
6. Schmucker H. (1956), "Der Lebenszyklus in Erwebstatigkeit, Einkommensbildung und Einkommensverwendung", *Allgemeines Statistiches Archiv*, 40.
7. Ces comparaisons ne sont pas faciles étant donné les changements techniques introduits dans la méthode de sélection pour la représentation et la mise en ordre des matériaux.
8. Les études sur les ménages de personnes seules – dans 3/4 des cas, il s'agit de femmes seules – sont présentées séparément dans un livre intitulé *La Femme moderne* (Kobieta Współczesna), au chapitre sur les revenus et les dépenses des femmes seules (Editions Ksiażka i Wiedza, Warszawa, 1966: 237–258).
9. Indiquons toutefois que le nombre moyen des membres de la famille en Pologne ne cesse récemment de décroître. En quatre ans, suivant des enquêtes semblables effectuées en 1967, presque 30% des familles de travailleurs comptaient 5 personnes ou plus; par ailleurs, les écarts entre le modèle de ménage des manuels et celui des non manuels étaient plus marqués qu'aujourd'hui.
10. Elkin, F. (1964), *La Famille au Canada*, Ottawa: 84.
11. Le sujet est traité plus amplement par Presvelou, C. (1968), *Sociologie de la consommation familiale*, Bruxelles: 123–138.

16. Enjoyment careers and the family life cycle*

VICTOR THIESSEN, RHONA RAPOPORT, and
ROBERT N. RAPOPORT

The problem

The focus of this paper is on the inter-relationships between family life cycle stages and the enjoyment of everyday activities. In this we do not presume that enjoyment is localized in family life but rather that it can be experienced in all spheres of life such as family, work and community. Before discussing the data and findings, some comment on our use of the term "family life cycle" is appropriate.

We think that family life cycle can be useful as a conceptual framework in at least three ways:

1. For sheer description. Families live differently according to their life cycle phase; it is important to recognize this ethnographically so that we can avoid perpetuating monolithic descriptions of "The Family" as though a single state of affairs should apply to all families at all phases of the life cycle. The idea of a cycle provides, in this way, a useful framework for ethnography.
2. For process analysis, showing functional relationships between phenomena at one point in time and those at another point.
3. For causal analysis, whereby phenomena at a later stage in the cycle are explainable not by alternative kinds of analysis (e.g., functional relationships with other synchronic variables) but by earlier "critical" events in the life cycle.

* Our thanks are due to the Leverhulme Trust for their support of the study on women's and men's careers, for which the data were originally gathered; and also for their support of the study of leisure and the family life cycle, for which the analysis presented here was made. (See Rapoport R. et al (1975).) Thanks are also due to M.E. Roughley and the staff of the S.S.R.C. data bank at the University of Essex.

To use the concept in any of these ways it is important to clarify certain issues. First, the unit of analysis must be specified. As the concept of family life cycle can appropriately be applied to the extended family, the nuclear family, marital partners or cohabitation partners, it is important to specify which unit one is dealing with in a specific case. In this study, the focus is on marital partners treated empirically as individuals. Secondly, the unit of time must be specified. It is our belief that real time (as measured by the age of the individual or by calendar dates for example) is not fruitful for the type of analysis we wish to perform – which is a process analysis. For this purpose, time should be measured by what we call "normal critical events". These normal critical events are usually status transitions. Engagement, marriage, parenthood and divorce are examples of normal critical events. We use the adjective "normal" to designate that such events are culturally so recognized. They are "critical" because they have far-reaching consequences on subsequent events. Considering the sequence of such events in developmental terms, it seems useful to apply the concept of *career*. This concept, originally confined to occupational sequences, has been applied in other aspects of the life cycle. Goffman talks about the "moral career" of a mental patient. Rodgers refers to the family life cycle as a career. Emery and Trist speak of life careers as the context for occupational roles and sequences. Rollins and Feldman study longitudinal patterns of marital satisfaction in terms that approximate a career model. In this paper we focus on the enjoyment of everyday activities as having career properties: "enjoyment careers". The identification of changes in enjoyment of activities and their relationship to critical events in the family life cycle is offered as a fruitful approach.

In this paper, enjoyment careers are studied through exploring responses to questions asked in one culture (England) for one category of subjects (university graduates) such as:

1) What are the activities that these people enjoy?
2) How does the enjoyment of these activities change over time?
3) In what ways do events from other life sectors affect which activities are enjoyed?

Three aspects of how other life sectors are relevant to the development of enjoyment careers and enjoyment career structures are examined:

1) Normal critical events in the family. (These are usually role transitions of one form or another. In this study, two such critical events are examined empirically – marriage and the birth of children.)
2) Value orientation to work. (i.e., to what extent does the respondent

obtain satisfaction from his work or career.)

3) Value orientation to home and family (analogous to work or career orientation, this is the extent to which a respondent receives satisfaction from his home or family life).

The data and measurement

The data reported here were obtained from two national samples of students who graduated from British universities in 1960 and 1967. Lengthy questionnaires concerning mainly family and career orientations were given to these samples toward the end of 1967. The number of respondents is somewhat over 1,000 in each of these surveys, making the total number of cases 2,122. The questionnaire items employed in this report were identical or very nearly so in the two surveys.

The primary difficulty with the enjoyment approach concerns which activities to include. One would ideally wish to include all those activities which various sub-groups of respondents are theoretically likely genuinely to enjoy at various times in their lives. Such a list could rapidly become unwieldy, particularly if the activities were quite specific. However, from the pragmatic viewpoint of actually obtaining useful information, the list should be short and not too specific. The list of activities actually used in this study (which was not concerned with leisure as such, but rather emphasized career variables) included the following:

(1) active sports, alone
(2) active team sports
(3) being with female friends
(4) being with male friends
(5) walking alone
(6) walking with others
(7) daydreaming, solo hobbies
(8) planning and organizing things on your own
(9) planning and organizing things with others
(10) visiting relatives
(11) music and art alone
(12) music and art with others
(13) being with small children alone
(14) being with small children in groups with other adults
(15) serious reading, study

For each of these activities the respondents were asked, "For each of the periods of your life indicated below, please indicate the activities which you enjoy(ed) *very much* (circle as many as apply)". The time periods listed for the 1967 graduates were "last years in Primary School", "at Secondary School" and "University years". For the 1960 graduates, who had been out of university for some seven years, the time periods were "at school", "University years", and "now". The choice of these seventeen activities proved to be quite good in that at least a quarter of the respondents in one or more of the sub-groups analyzed (the sub-groups will be described later) listed each of the activities as ones they personally either currently enjoyed or enjoyed in the past.

Experience of the critical events of marriage and having children were ascertained by simply asking the respondent his or her marital status and whether or not they had children. The analysis that follows groups all married people together for statistical purposes, but information on the effects of having children deriving from the larger study is used in developing the interpretations of the data. For the 1967 sample, only 7% were married, since this sample was just graduating from university. An additional 28% had definite marriage plans, but analysis of their patterns indicated that anticipatory socialization notwithstanding, they resembled the single respondents more closely than the married ones. Hence, they are reported with the former group in this analysis. In the 1960 sample, which had graduated from university seven years earlier, 83% were married. The very small proportion of respondents who were divorced, widowed or separated (under 2%) were excluded from the analysis because of their small numbers.

Career and family value orientations were measured by the question "Which of the following gives ('do you expect to give you' for the 1967 sample) the most satisfaction in life?". From the various alternatives provided two are of interest here, namely "your career or occupation" and "family relationships". Almost a quarter of the respondents chose career and these are classified as career-oriented. A further 60% chose family and are classified as family-oriented. Respondents who chose neither of these two alternatives (12%) were deleted from analysis.

A number of points must be raised with regard to the interpretation of these measures. First, the ideal study would have been a longitudinal panel study, where the same questions would have been asked of the same respondents at different stages in their life cycle. Neither the time nor the financial resources made this possible. Hence reports for the earlier time periods are based on memory, and are therefore susceptible to selective memory and its biasing consequences. Two factors in the survey design permit a partial evaluation of the extent of this problem. First is the fact that the two surveys are actually taken at two different stages in the life cycle of respondents. As mentioned previously the 1967 sample was just terminating its formal college education and was composed primarily of single respondents. The 1960 sample consisted of college educated young adults who had been in the job market for seven years, most of them having married and established a family of their own. The second factor is that the time periods for the two samples overlap. Thus the time period "University years" is dependent on memory for the 1960 survey, but not for the 1967 sample. Hence any significant discrepancy in this time period between the two surveys reflects one of three possibilities: systematic sampling errors, selective memory on the part of the 1960 graduates, or genuine cultural change between 1960 and 1967. Whenever such significant differences are found, they will be pointed out.

Secondly, although no strong test for the reliability or the validity of this data is available, some partial checks are gratifying. One check on the reliability would be to correlate the solo activities with the corresponding activities enjoyed with others, e.g., "walking alone" with "walking with others". Because of the common content, one would expect moderately high correlations. These were computed utilizing Kendall's Q (Blalock, 1960), resulting in an average Q of .48, which indicated the data to be quite reliable. A second independent test of the reliability was computed for the activities "music and art alone" and "music and art with others". Elsewhere in the questionnaire the respondents were asked to circle from a list the kinds of things they "want very much". Included in that list was "to attend concerts, plays and other artistic/cultural events". One would expect that those who currently enjoy music and art would also want to attend artistic/cultural events. The average Q between these variables was .43, which again indicates that the data is reliable.

No direct tests of the validity of the data are available. However, some of the patterns of sex and marital differences that will be reported are so consistent with previous findings and theoretical expectations, that one is inclined to judge the data as reasonably valid.

A third consideration is the generaliseability of the findings. Here it is best to consider the specific findings themselves as non-generaliseable. They are likely to be culture-bound, time-bound and situation-bound. It must be kept in mind that the sample is British, university-educated and young. How many persons will enjoy which specific activities is undoubtedly strongly affected by all three of these factors. However, the conceptual approach and some of the general findings such as the impact of marriage should be relevant and fruitful in other populations.

Analysis

The notion of a career in the sense used here implies a life cycle from birth to death of an individual. The time span actually involved here is from primary school through to seven years after graduation from university. Within this time span, a number of normal critical events occur, some of which are shared by many, some of which are relatively unique. In this study, the critical events which are examined are: 1) attending primary school, secondary school and university; 2) marriage; 3) parenthood. Of these critical events, the formal educational ones are constant for both samples. The others characterize only segments of the respondents.

The analysis showed that these non-constant critical events, together with sex and value-orientation, strongly affected the individual enjoyment careers.

Enjoyment careers

In this section, the enjoyment careers of some of the activities will be discussed in detail, showing the impact of critical events.

The enjoyment career of walking alone starts off quite low, with less than 20% of each group enjoying this activity in primary school. It rises sharply, so that by secondary school it is in the vicinity of 35% for married males, which is the peak for those who get married. For the singles it continues to rise slowly to about 45% with no difference between males and females. For the married females whose family is their sole satisfaction (second choice family too) there is a sharp decline after marriage so that their enjoyment of this activity resembles what it was during primary school.

The development of music and art as a source of enjoyment is quite similar for all respondents from primary school through university (if marriage plans or marriage itself does not occur). In all cases, the enjoy-

Figure 1. *Enjoyment career structure of married females with family orientation*

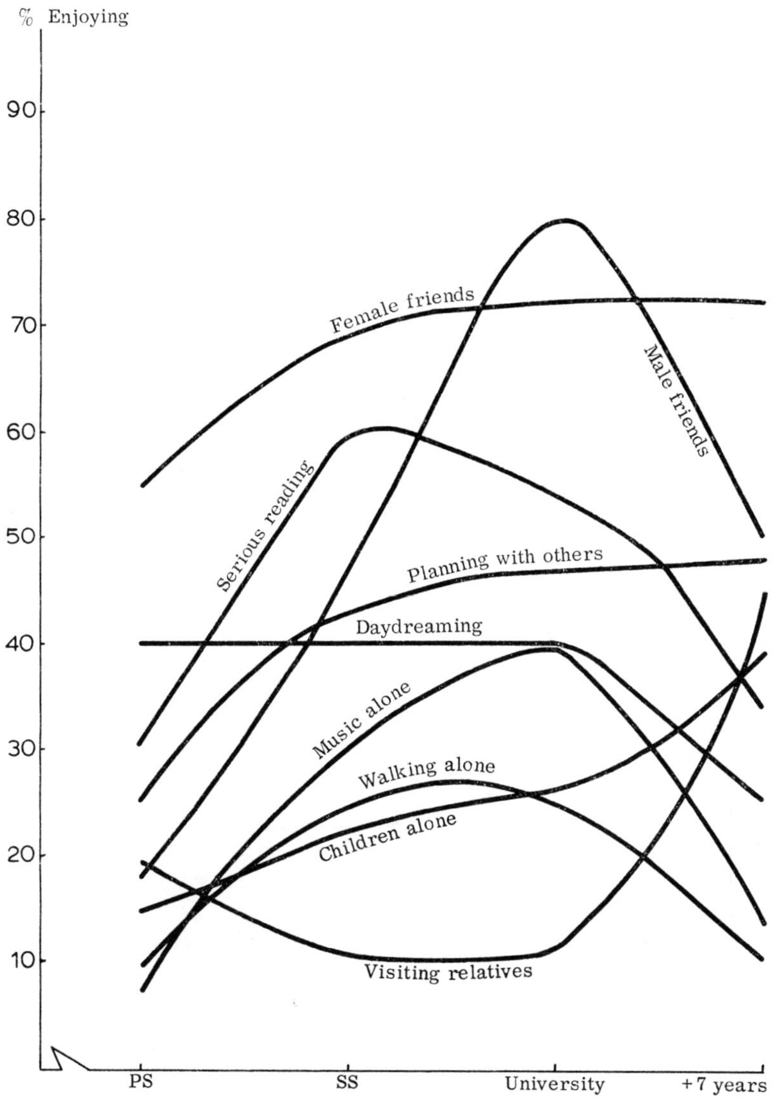

Figure 2. *Enjoyment career structure of single females*

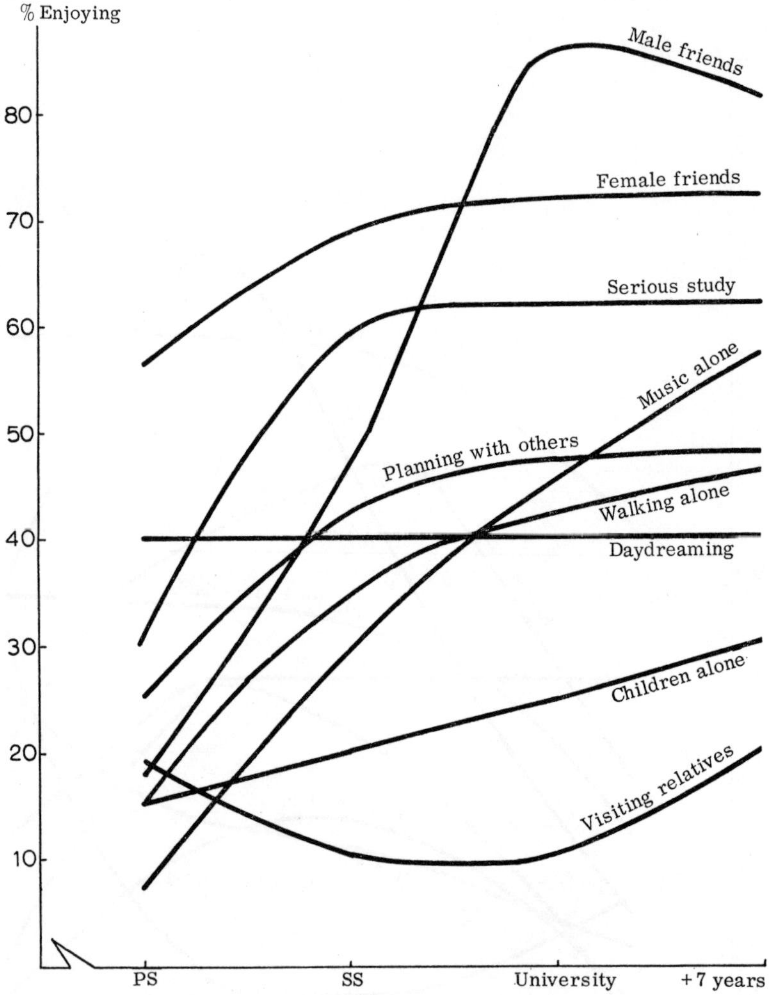

ment of music and art is quite low in primary school (in the vicinity of 10% enjoying this activity), rises rapidly in secondary school and continues to rise, but more slowly, through university. It is at this point that the enjoyment career curves of music and art differentiate. For the single females, the curve continues to rise, reaching its peak at about 50%. For single males, the asymptote occurs at university and remains at about 40%. For married males the curve drops, its end value being about 30%.

Finally, for those married females who are totally family-centered, the enjoyment career curve of music and art alone drops way down to about 15% at the terminal end.

In contrast to a popular view that males are more scholastic than females, the enjoyment career of serious reading and study shows that this activity is enjoyed more by females at all stages. Between secondary school and university it is quite popular with all groups, being enjoyed by 50% or more. This enjoyment continues for all groups except the married female who is family oriented. For her, the enjoyment of this activity begins to decrease around the time she enters university and continues to drop steadily through the time period in this study. Note that it is not marriage itself which is related to this decline, since those females who get married but who combine career with family continue to enjoy serious reading and study.

Being with female friends and with male friends show some remarkably similar patterns dealing with same sex and opposite sex differences. The main points can be summarized as follows:

1) The enjoyment of being with the same sex starts off quite high (about 55% for all groups) and continues to rise to the vicinity of 70% in university. For two groups there is an appreciable decline: married males and career-oriented married females. This latter finding is of particular interest. It suggests the difficulties that married females had in their culture if they went against the norm that the woman's place is in the home. Whether she is ostracized by other females to some extent, or whether she just finds their company less enjoyable cannot be ascertained here.

2) Being with others of the same sex is consistently among the most enjoyed activities for all groups.

3) The enjoyment of opposite sex companionship has the steepest slope of all activities. In primary school it is enjoyed by few. At university it reaches its peak being enjoyed by about 85% of the respondents in all subgroups – more than for any other activity. From this high point there is a decline which is more marked for some groups than for others. The decline is sharpest for those who are married, and particularly those who are family oriented, and least for the singles.

Visiting relatives is not an activity which is enjoyed very much by and large. However, there are some consistent and theoretically interesting and informative variations and patterns. First of all, the typical enjoyment career of visiting relatives is U-shaped. For female respondents the curve is higher at *all* points in the life cycle, in the order of about double the percentage. That is, if 10% of a given category of males (such as single, in primary school) enjoy visiting relatives, then the corresponding figure for females would be roughly 20%. Secondly, if an individual remains single, the enjoyment curve does not rise much after university, particularly if he, the respondent, is a male. Thirdly, if the individual does get married, but is not family-oriented (does not expect to get his major satisfaction from family and home) then the effects of marriage are muted so that the rise in the curve is again minimal. The sex and marriage differences are consistent with the literature on frequency of visiting relatives.

Being with small children, (either alone or in groups with other adults) as a source of enjoyment develops rather slowly for both men and women. For many groups it never does become a major source of enjoyment. It is less likely to be mentioned as a source than is music and art for example, and is more similar (in terms of frequency) with visiting relatives. The enjoyment career curve is not a steep one for most groups.

The curves for single males and females are identical in form; they are smooth and gradually rising, so that between primary school and seven years after university a doubling of the proportion who enjoy being with small children alone has occurred. However, the single female curve is consistently about twice as high as that for single males. For the married male, the enjoyment curve increases its slope starting with definite plans for marriage and continuing so to its terminal point. For the married female, the picture is more complicated. It appears that there is a critical period right after marriage that determines her curve. If at that time the married female seeks her *primary* source of satisfaction outside of the family, then the enjoyment career curve of being with small children drops down way below that of even single females. On the other hand, if the primary source of satisfaction lies within the family, then the enjoyment career curve continues to rise, ending substantially higher than that for any other groups.

There are also some interesting differences in the enjoyment career curves between being with children alone, and being with children in groups with other adults. These differences apply only to the females. Basically, what they show is that the enjoyment curve starts even lower for being with small children in groups and ends lower for single females, but ends high for the totally family oriented married woman. It strongly suggests that it is not the children themselves that are the source of enjoyment, but the surrounding activities that are involved. Thus, single females do not particularly enjoy the activities that surround being with small children in groups with other adults. This interpretation is supported by another set of findings. The analysis showed that among married women, the more family life was at the *centre* of their activities, the *more* they enjoyed being with small children in groups with other adults, but the *less* they enjoyed being with small children alone.

Summary and conclusion

Enjoyment of everyday activities have "careers" or cycles of their own. Most activities in this study are not enjoyed early in life. Rather, one learns to enjoy these activities. Then various events in other life sectors, such as work and family, act to accelerate or dampen such enjoyment. This ebb and flow in enjoyment we call the enjoyment careers.

Each activity has its own enjoyment career. Some, such as daydreaming and solo hobbies, are fairly constant; the enjoyment of such activities neither increases nor decreases to any appreciable extent, and are relatively uninfluenced by other life sectors. Others, such as being with the opposite sex, are not enjoyed until quite late (Secondary School) at which time there is a rapid acceleration so that by the time of university it is the most enjoyed of the activities studied here. This is followed by a rapid decline for those who get married, particularly among females who are family-oriented.

Social activities are more enjoyed than solo activities. In addition, the former show a less rapid decline in enjoyment than the latter. Whether one is talking about sports, or taking a walk, or listening to music, these activities show a more rapid decline if done by oneself than when done with others.

Normal critical life events have a dramatic effect on the enjoyment of many activities. Marriage is one of these events and its impact on the enjoyment of many everyday activities is pervasive. Many things enjoyed before marriage, such as being with the opposite sex, or music and art appreciation are less often enjoyed after marriage, and vice versa.

Normal critical life events, although important in and of themselves, do not directly determine the enjoyment career. These events derive their significance, and therefore their impact, in the context of the value orientations of both the individual and the culture. Marriage does affect the enjoyment of everyday activities. But in our society it affects women more than men, and the nature of the impact is radically different for career-oriented women than it is for family-oriented women. For the family-oriented, activities such as being with children and visiting relatives become more enjoyable while serious reading and study almost vanish. For the career-oriented woman, the reverse is true.

Our findings derive from a special sub-sample of highly educated people from a single national culture, so one would have to exercise extreme caution in generalizing from them or comparing them, for example, with other studies of national culture. What our study does show, is the importance of making explicit how the family life cycle figures into the design, analysis and reporting of any such study. We have shown how a variable like enjoying being with children is subject to change *within* a segment of the population within a culture, according to family life cycle phase. Knowing this alerts one to the need for careful controls on such factors if one is going to compare this variable across national cultures.

Another important point emerging from our analysis has to do with the quality of being *maternal.* Our data show that this type of enjoyment is not directly endowed biologically. Some women *and* some men enjoy being with children more than do others; and those who do not initially, may have to cultivate this capacity. As we have seen, even for women it is a trait that develops slowly and under specific conditions.

This characteristic – of change and development under the impact of conditions specific to different family life cycle stages – applies to other interests as well. It would, accordingly, also be mistaken to think of other characteristics conventionally sex-typed as masculine or feminine, as intrinsic to the two sexes. Our data show that certain interests which may have been enjoyed by both sexes prior to marriage – e.g., sports, sociability – are systemmatically suppressed by women following marriage, but much less so by men.

Our data suggest that there is a peak point for the enjoyment of many activities – such as sociability and sport – and that this peak seems to be somewhere between primary and secondary schools. If suppressed at this point, or shortly after it, the trend seems progressively downwards. Other data suggest that if an interest is extinguished at a critical point early in the cycle, there may be very great difficulty in reinstating it later. For example, it is found in retirement studies that it is difficult to cultivate new interests in people whose capacity to enjoy learning and discovery was not stimulated earlier. The pattern, once established, continues with a relentless momentum that is difficult to dislodge. The theoretical, as distinct from the applied implication of this finding, is that specific early events are likely to be *critical* for subsequent patterns – for enjoyment of children, for enjoyment of marital interaction (including sexual), for aspirations and so on. To explain developmental processes in the family life cycle causally, one requires diachronic as well as synchronic dimensions.

Finally, we should mention ways in which our own analysis presented here is incomplete, and how we feel it may be improved by future work.

a) We need, obviously, to extend the analysis of enjoyment structures through the life cycle.
b) We need to analyze enjoyment careers and structures by family structural types. We have provided an interim analysis of the pattern of different types of individuals for whom family phase or family involvement is an element of classification (e.g., married individuals *vs.* single individuals; family-oriented women *vs.* career oriented women). But we think that family structure as a whole will be important in the kind of analysis already done. It was found that women who are family oriented enjoy being with children in groups of other people. We would hypothesize that this relationship would be clarified by distinguishing between family-oriented women in a conventional family structure (i.e., they do not work at all) and family oriented women in a dual-worker family (i.e. both husband and wife work continuously). The latter, we have the impression, would enjoy being with children but *alone* more than with others. The enjoyment of being with groups of children and others is not, therefore, a product of being family oriented, but of being family oriented in a conventional family structure. Because there are more conventional families than dual-worker families in the sample, the statistical relationship exists, but may tell a misleading story.

The FLC is an important conceptual frame in the ways suggested and demonstrated in this paper. It should be emphasized, however, that we consider that there is not *one* family life cycle which is the model, or template against which all other cycles can be measured as "normal" or aborted or deficient. Any society will contain different kinds of families, and different types of family life cycles may be characteristic of them. The cycles will be linked to biological, psychological and cultural frameworks in different ways, and should be understood in terms of variations. The study of these variations needs to be approached both empirically and conceptually. While computers and factor analyses are useful tools for handling and analysing empirical data, their success as tools of analysis depend on the data as well as on concepts. The data, in turn, also reflect the concepts used to gather them as well as "reality".

Résumé

Le cycle des loisirs

Le loisir est un aspect de la vie familiale qui avec d'autres peut être considéré comme suivant un cycle. Le concept de loisir a été difficile à étudier en raison de la variété des significations qui y sont attachées – loisirs, certaines activités de récréation, certains états émotionnels tels que le plaisir, la détente ou la stimulation. Chacun d'eux peut avoir son propre trajet caractéristique, et chacun peut avoir des rapports différents avec d'autres phénomènes du cycle familial non seulement dans les carrières professionnelles (souvent tenues pour l'inverse du loisir), mais dans les événements du cycle domestique. Cette dernière relation a été beaucoup moins explorée: cet article tente de donner un aperçu sur cette direction de recherche à travers une analyse empirique.

Lorsqu'on a interrogé deux échantillons nationaux de diplômés britanniques (totalisant plus de 3 000 réponses) à propos des activités de détente qu'ils préféraient, l'enquête a montré qu'il existait des cycles de loisirs caractéristiques à ce groupe: des événements critiques (notamment le mariage et le fait d'avoir des enfants) ont un impact sur les cycles de loisirs; et l'impact est différent pour les hommes et les femmes.

On a noté 16 activités quotidiennes, souvent considérées comme des loisirs (par exemple: sports, être avec des amis, la marche, des hobbies, la musique, l'art, etc.) sur des graphiques indiquant que les auteurs des réponses jouissaient de ces activités à l'école, à l'université, et huit ans plus tard (quand la plus grande partie de l'échantillon était mariée et avait des enfants).

Le mariage et les enfants avaient un impact significatif sur les cycles de loisirs. L'impact variait avec le sexe et à l'intérieur même des groupes selon le sexe, selon des orientations de valeur personnelle. Par exemple, les sports (seul et en équipe) sont appréciés de façon croissante par les hommes et les femmes lorsqu'ils passent de l'école à la faculté mais les niveaux d'appréciation baissent pendant les huit années suivant l'université. La baisse est le plus clairement provoquée par le mariage pour les femmes, et par l'arrivée des enfants pour les hommes (qui, plus que les femmes continuent à aimer les sports après le mariage). Ce modèle est valable pour de nombreuses activités – de la marche à pied, l'art et la musique jusqu'à la lecture. Lorsque les femmes ont une carrière professionnelle, elles continuent d'éprouver un fort niveau de plaisir pour la lecture, tandis que les femmes davantage tournées vers les activités domestiques continuent probablement à apprécier à un haut niveau de rêvasserie.

Les rapports d'amitié ou certains types d'association sont également affectés par le mariage et la venue des enfants et de façon différente pour les deux sexes. Le plaisir d'être en compagnie de membres du sexe opposé – plaisir qui croît rapidement pour les hommes et les femmes durant leurs années d'éducation décline rapidement avec le mariage et plus rapidement encore pour les femmes très tournées vers la famille. Celles-ci témoignent d'un grand intérêt pour les visites à rendre aux parents.

Alors que la plupart des cycles de loisirs décrivent une courbe ascendante, puis descendante ou qui se stabilise pour le secteur du cycle étudié, le plaisir des femmes à rendre visite à des connaissances suit un modèle à la forme d'un U, débutant à un niveau élevé dans l'enfance, décroissant puis remontant rapidement après le mariage et les enfants.

Le plaisir d'être avec de petits enfants est affecté par une orientation de valeur aussi bien que par le sexe. Pour les femmes, il semble qu'il existe un point critique après le mariage selon lequel la femme active tire ses sources de loisir de l'extérieur et conséquemment fait preuve d'un plaisir moins élevé d'être avec des enfants. Les femmes orientées vers la famille concentrent dans cette phase leur plaisir à être avec des enfants.

Pour les gens qui restent célibataires, les cycles de loisirs des hommes et des femmes sont très semblables.

Nous pouvons parler de structures de cycles des sous-groupes de la population, selon leur sexe et leur expérience des changements critiques dans leur statut familial. Les 4 structures décrites ici de façon préliminaire concernent les célibataires hommes, les célibataires femmes, hommes mariés et femmes mariées.

Parmi celles-là, l'analyse structurale du cycle montre que des femmes mariées (particulièrement celles qui ont des enfants et celles qui sont tournées vers la famille) font l'expérience du plus grand changement des modèles de cycles de loisir, en substituant le fait d'être avec leurs enfants, de rendre visite à leurs parents à la pratique d'activités sportives artistiques ou sociales. Le mariage et l'éducation des enfants affecte la structure du cycle des loisirs masculins beaucoup moins radicalement du moins dans les groupes décrits, dans la phase en question.

References

Blalock, Hubert (1960), *Social Statistics*, New York, McGraw-Hill Book Co.: 231.

Emery F., and Trist, E. (1973), *Towards a Social Ecology*, London, Plenum.

Fogarty, Michael, Rapoport, Rhona, and Rapoport, Robert (1971), *Sex, Career and Family*, London and Beverley Hills, Sage.

Goffman, Erving (1961), *Asylums*, New York, Doubleday and Co. (Anchor).

Hill, Reuben (1970), *Family Development in Three Generations*, Cambridge, Mass., Schenkman Co.

Rapoport, R., and Rapoport, R.N., with Strelitz, Z. (1975), *Leisure and the Family Life Cycle*, London, Routledge.

Rapoport, Rhona, and Rapoport, Robert (1976), *Dual Career Families Re-examined*, London, Martin Robertson, and New York, Harper and Row.

Rodgers, Roy H. (1973), *Family Interaction and Transaction*, Englewood Cliffs, N.J., Prentice-Hall.

Rollins, B.C., and Feldman, H. (1970), "Marital satisfaction over the family life cycle", *Journal of Marriage and the Family*, 32, February: 20–28.

IV. *Historical and anthropological extensions of the field of investigation*

Elargissement historique et anthropologique du champ d'observation

17. Le cycle familial et le processus de socialisation: caractéristiques du schéma occidental considéré dans le temps

PETER LASLETT

Notre étude a été faite d'un point de vue historique et sociologique et repose sur l'affirmation selon laquelle les institutions et les ensembles culturels doivent posséder une certaine persistence dans le temps, une certaine durabilité, pour être significatifs et représentatifs. Le schéma des structures familiales occidentales, de même que celui du mariage occidental si brillament décrit et analysé il y a une dizaine d'années par John Hajnal,[1] s'est certainement manifesté tout au long de nombreuses générations avant de pouvoir être considéré comme un trait caractéristique de l'occidentalité.

Ce qui est paradoxal, c'est que l'Occident, ou, pour être plus précis, l'Europe de l'Ouest et du Nord-Ouest, ainsi que le reste du monde Anglo-Saxon, ne présente plus avec la même netteté toutes les caractéristiques familiales d'autrefois: en effet, une d'entr'elles a même complètement disparu. D'autre part, dans les régions autres qu'occidentales, le schéma familial des sociétés industrialisées commence à se conformer à celui, modifié, de l'Occident, car nous assistons à notre époque à une convergence des cultures et des institutions. Les données en notre possession à Cambridge suggèrent qu'il a pu y avoir un ensemble particulier de paramètres présents dans le contexte de la famille occidentale à toutes les périodes sur lesquelles nous possédons des informations et qui précèdent le début de l'ère de l'industrialisation. Ces paramètres semblent avoir été présents, sous quelque forme que ce soit, jusqu'à la période que l'on a coutume d'appeler celle de la pleine industrialisation. Maintenant que la sociologie de l'histoire a pris une place parmi les autres sciences sociales, nous devons considérer les cultures et les institutions non seulement comme elles apparaissent à l'heure présente, mais comme elles auraient été si des transformations n'étaient pas intervenues.

Ceci est particulièrement valable dans les études sur la socialisation et la formation de la personnalité et du caractère. C'est en effet de cette seule façon que l'occidentalité elle-même, ou tout autre attribut culturel, peut être mis à jour, puisque pour exister, il doit réapparaître dans le temps, à chaque nouvelle génération. Voici la raison pour laquelle l'aspect de la socialisation primaire, que représente le groupe familial entourant l'enfant en bas âge, est un facteur essentiellement intéressant. La période de la vie des individus qui nous intéresse ici est celle pendant laquelle les parents et leurs enfants entièrement dépendants vivent ensemble, quand les interactions entre les personnes atteignent leur plus haut degré d'intensité et que le groupe humain est le plus compact.

La thèse générale sera de démontrer que le trait déterminant de la famille dans la tradition occidentale, autant que puisse le discerner l'historien social, a été la présence simultanée, pendant la période de socialisation primaire, des quatre paramètres suivants qui, quoique distincts, sont interdépendants.

1. La structure et la composition du groupe familial. En Occident, celui-ci s'est généralement limité aux parents et enfants, à ce qui est appelé le noyau familial, ou simplement le foyer.
2. L'âge de la mère pendant la période de procréation. En Occident, les femmes devenaient mères assez tard, tard dans la vie de la mère et dans sa période de fécondabilité.
3. La différence d'âge entre époux. Elle a toujours été relativement peu importante, avec une faible proportion, mais une proportion d'une signification très nette, de femmes plus âgées que leurs maris, et parfois certains cas de mariages occidentaux tournant vers ce que nous nommons en anglais "companionate marriage".
   En fait, il semblerait que la caractéristique essentielle des familles appartenant à la civilisation occidentale soit qu'environ un cinquième des épouses sont plus âgées que leur mari.
4. L'importante proportion dans les foyers, en tant que membres intégrés, de personnes n'appartenant pas à la famille immédiate, ou même à la famille tout court. C'était le cas des domestiques, c'est-à-dire, des compagnons, des apprentis, des serviteurs et des servantes, et leur présence prédominante dans la société occidentale dénote une particularité dans le cycle de vie individuel de ceux qui travaillaient, ainsi qu'une caractéristique du groupe familial.

Nous serons forcés dans l'étude présente d'étudier l'importance que peuvent représenter chacun de ces traits de la structure familiale occidentale sur la formation de la personnalité d'une façon quelque peu simplifiée et sans beaucoup de preuves pour étayer nos affirmations. Avant de commencer, cependant, il est nécessaire de souligner trois points sur les paramètres auxquels nous venons de faire allusion, et leurs interactions réciproques.

Tout d'abord, c'est le schéma, la combinaison elle-même de ces éléments qui sont proposés comme une description particulière de la société occidentale. Nous ne prétendons pas que les structures familiales simples existaient en Europe occidentale uniquement à l'époque préindustrielle, ni que d'autres sociétés n'aient pas connu dans l'histoire un système de mariage tardif, "companionate marriage", ou la présence de domestiques.

Dans le livre collectif récemment publié par le Cambridge Group for the History of Population and Social Structure, sous le titre *Household and Family in Past Time*,[2] il est bien souligné que les foyers du type le plus simple étaient largement répandus dans toutes les régions étudiées.

Il y a eu sans aucun doute des communautés non occidentales et non-Européennes dans lesquelles le mariage était tardif et les serviteurs peu nombreux, ou bien dont les nombreux foyers étaient d'une structure complexe, bien que la différence d'âge entre les époux ait été faible. Si nous en avions eu la place ici, nous aurions commenté ces différents cas en examinant nos quatre paramètres dans le détail, et les indications qui montrent que dans l'histoire de l'Occident lui-même le mariage entre jeunes époux pouvait être très courant pendant de longues périodes, ou bien les familles simples prédominantes et la domesticité rare, voire même inexistante. Notre hypothèse est sans doute plus inclusive et faible qu'exclusive et forte, quand elle prétend que les quatre paramètres caractérisant l'occidentalité du groupe familial pendant la période de socialisation primaire étaient interdépendants jusqu'à un certain degré, mais jamais totalement.

Le deuxième point que je tiens à préciser se rapporte aux *frontières* du monde occidental que j'essaie de définir d'après ses caractéristiques familiales.

Bien sûr, il est, je pense, superflu de préciser que je ne veux pas faire de division "littérale" des différentes parties du monde, ou même de l'Europe, lorsque je me risque à nommer ces caractéristiques du mariage tardif etc. "occidentales", et à accepter l'implication selon laquelle toute région ne possédant pas ces traits déterminants pourrait logiquement être appelée "orientale". En fait, lorsque nous avons commencé à étudier les structures familiales et à réfléchir sur la famille et le cycle familial, dans le contexte de notre propre pays, la Grande-Bretagne, nous nous sommes aperçus alors que le cycle familial au temps de la socialisation primaire des enfants possédait généralement ces caractéristiques. Toutes les indications obtenues ont révélé la persistance de ces faits (par rapport à trois des quatre paramètres composant le schéma), avec très peu de différence dans l'évolution du temps et des régions de notre pays jusqu'au début et même en pleine période de l'industrialisation. Lorsqu'ensuite nous sommes allés en France, au moins en France du Nord, et dans d'autres pays d'Europe Occidentale, nous avons retrouvé la présence de ces mêmes faits quoiqu'avec moins d'homogénéité et une plus grande variété.

Il serait faux de prétendre que nos connaissances en la matière sont absolument incontestables et puissent être qualifiées d'"historiques", car la situation des autres pays européens occidentaux et celle des pays européens orientaux ne nous est pas aussi familière que celle de l'Angleterre. Nos données sur l'histoire familiale des autres pays du monde sont infimes. Nous connaissons bien toutefois les Etats-Unis et le Japon, et même la Serbie, et pensons que les connaissances acquises à Cambridge sur l'Angleterre pourraient être appliquées et, dans la plupart des cas, largement étendues, à tous les autres pays occidentaux. Mais ce qui nous a frappés dans les communautés autres qu'occidentales, c'est qu'il n'y apparaissait pas un schéma rassemblant tous les paramètres, bien que certaines communautés aient possédé individuellement l'une ou l'autre des caractéristiques en question. D'où la possibilité de l'existence d'un processus de socialisation occidental unique.

Mais l'Occident ainsi défini est, par nombre de ses aspects, différent de l'Occident habituellement décrit dans un certain contexte politique. Par exemple, on peut considérer que, d'après cette définition, une grande partie de l'Italie n'appartient guère au monde occidental, de même que certaines régions de la France méridionale. Comme Hajnal, qui refusait de classer l'Europe méridionale dans l'Europe quand il cherchait à identifier le schéma du mariage européen, je serais enclin à dire qu'au 15e siècle, la Toscane, comprenant Florence à la Renaissance, possédait certains traits qui n'étaient pas "occidentaux"; au 18e siècle, on peut penser que le type de vie à la campagne toscane était même nettement méridional. On peut bien sûr s'étonner de cette définition d'un Occident excluant de telles régions et de cette culture française dont l'"homogénéité nationale" cache une telle diversité de formes et de structures familiales d'une région à l'autre, du Nord au Sud. Ces questions restent à débattre mais montrent bien, à mon point de vue, l'urgence des problèmes soulevés par la sociologie de l'histoire sur la structure de la société, les consensus et l'idéologie politiques, sur la famille dans le contexte social, culturel et idéologique. Dans ce sens, je serais tenté d'affirmer que la sociologie historique constitue *la vraie sociologie critique.*

Il semble en outre qu'il ait existé dans le passé, aux frontières méridionales de l'Occident, une grande variété de structures familiales. Il y avait, dans l'Europe centrale, par exemple, des villages dont les schémas familiaux étaient typiquement occidentaux, et qui étaient proches d'autres villages dans lesquels ces schémas étaient beaucoup moins prononcés, et où des éléments d'autres systèmes cachaient, même occasionnellement, le schéma inverse dans sa forme pure.

Le troisième point que je désire souligner sur les quatre caractéristiques familiales mentionnées définissant la civilisation occidentale est qu'elles sont loin de représenter le processus de socialisation dans sa totalité. Il est évident que d'autres influences étaient, et sont encore en jeu.

Il n'est généralement pas difficile de trouver des listes établies dans le passé qui permettent de connaître avec précision le nombre de personnes qui ont cohabité avec un enfant pendant les cinq premières années de sa vie et donnent des précisions sur les âges pour chaque groupe familial. Mais les membres du ménage ne sont pas les seules personnes ou agents qui peuvent nuancer la personnalité de l'enfant. L'effet des croyances, des coutumes et des normes sur l'éducation des enfants et le modèle de conduite proposé aux jeunes ont certainement une influence pendant le processus de la socialisation. Et on ne peut retirer aucune certitude sur la parenté autre que la famille très proche ou sur la fréquence des rapports qu'elle pouvait avoir avec la famille en question; on commence tout juste à pouvoir évaluer ce que nous pourrions appeler les densités du réseau de parenté dans les communautés du passé: les résultats ne sont pas encore disponibles.

Quant aux effets de l'idéologie sur le développement de l'enfant, nous sommes, je l'avoue, dans la plus grande incertitude; il n'est pas facile, voire même possible, pour l'historien social, de découvrir les méthodes d'éducation des enfants utilisées dans le passé et il est pratiquement certain que l'on ne pourra jamais les mesurer ou les comparer numériquement. Même les rares fois où une attitude bien particulière peut être identifiée dans le contexte de l'époque et du lieu, ou dans le règlement légal ou quasi-légal en application à cette période, il demeure néanmoins des

Tableau 1. *Proportion de ménages étendus et multiples, et taille moyenne des ménages (TMM)*

Pays	Communauté	Comté/Région	Date	Nombre de ménages	TMM	Etendus (%)	Multiples (%)	Total (%)
Echantillon international:								
Amérique coloniale	Bristol	Rhode Island	1689	72	5.85	3	0	3
Angleterre	Ealing	Middlesex	1599	85	4.75	6	2	8
France	Longuenesse	Pas-de-Calais	1778	66	5.05	14	3	17
Allemagne	Löffingen[1]	Württemberg	1687	121	5.77	(5)	(5)	(10)
Italie	Colorno	Parma	1782	*66*	*4.16*	*9*	*11*	*20*
Japan	Nishinomiya[2]		1713	132	4.95	27	21	48
				(87)		(25)	(14)	(39)
Japan	Yokouchi	Suwa County	1676	27	7.0	0	52	52
Japan	Yokouchi	Suwa County	1746	76	5.5	21	28	49
Japan	Yokouchi	Suwa County	1823	98	5.1	28	28	56
Japon	Yokouchi	Suwa County	1846	107	4.4	14	24	39
Pologne	Lesnica	Silesia	1720	311	5.4	5	0	5
Ecosse	Aross-in-Mull	Western Isles	1779	211	5.25	11	3	14
Serbie	Belgrade		1733–1734	273	4.95	15	14	29
Echantillon anglais:								
	Ardleigh	Essex	1796	210	5.48	10	2	12
	Ardleigh	Essex	1851	366	4.48	14	0	14
	Bilston	Staffordshire	1695	192	5.19	11	1	12
	Bilston	Staffordshire	1851	*329*	*5.14*	*15*	*5*	*20*
	Bilston	Staffordshire	1861	*264*	*4.30*	*12*	*1*	*13*
	Chivers Coton	Warwickshire	1686	177	4.41	8	1	9
	Chivers Coton	Warwickshire	1851	*570*	*4.95*	*13*	*3*	*16*
	Clayworth	Notts.	1676	98	4.09	9	0	9
	Clayworth	Notts.	1688	91	4.49	7	1	8
	Clayworth	Notts.	1851	128	4.21	17	4	21
	Colyton	Devon	1851	*342*	*4.94*	*16*	*2*	*18*
	Colyton	Devon	1861	*449*	*4.48*	*14*	*3*	*17*
	Corfe Castle	Dorset	1790	272	4.84	8	1	9
	Corfe Castle	Dorset	1851	513	4.72	14	1	15
	Corfe Castle	Dorset	1861	*297*	*4.31*	*14*	*1*	*15*
	Ealing	Middlesex	1599	85	4.75	6	2	8
	Ealing	Middlesex	1851	*248*	*4.86*	*12*	*1*	*13*
	Ealing	Middlesex	1861	*209*	*4.50*	*19*	*2*	*21*
	Puddletown[3]	Dorset	1724–1725	154	3.97	8	1	9
	Puddletown	Dorset	1851	264	4.91	11	1	12
	Puddletown	Dorset	1861	257	4.77	14	1	15
	Puddletown	Dorset	1871	271	4.89	18	2	20
	Puddletown	Dorset	1881	248	4.46	16	1	17

1. Chiffres approximatifs.
2. Les chiffres entre parenthèses excluent les adoptions.
3. Pas tout à fait complet.

Les chiffres en italiques ont été selectionnés à partir d'échantillons.

		Hommes										Femmes											
		15–19	20–24	25–29	30–34	35–39	40–44	45–49	50–59	60–69	70 +	15–19	20–24	25–29	30–34	35–39	40–44	45–49	50–59	60–69	70 +	Ecart d'âge entre époux	
Angleterre																							
Ealing, 1599	Célibataire	100	100	77	38	62	29	50	12	20	0	100	84	57	36	14	0	12	0	12	0	Moyenne	3.50
Pop. 427	Marié	0	0	23	62	37	71	50	80	66	0	0	15	43	64	64	62	38	86	75	50	Médiane	3.25
																						Proportion de femmes plus âgées	
	Veuf	0	0	0	0	0	0	0	8	14	0	0	0	0	0	21	38	50	14	13	50	que leurs	21 %
	Total	100	100	100	100	99	100	100	100	100	100	100	99	100	100	99	100	100	100	100	100	époux	n = 62
France																							
Longuenesse	Célibataire	100	100	90	89	31	25	26	22	0	33	100	100	73	64	36	10	0	20	0	0	Moyenne	2.35
1778	Marié	0	0	10	11	69	75	73	56	75	33	0	0	18	29	64	85	100	60	75	12	Médiane	1| 0
Pop. 333																						Proportion de femmes plus agées	
	Veuf	0	0	0	0	0	0	0	22	25	33	0	0	9	7	0	5	0	20	25	88	que leurs	27 %
	Total	100	100	100	100	100	100	99	100	100	99	100	100	100	100	100	100	100	100	100	100	époux	n = 48
Serbie																							
Belgrade,	Célibataire	100	67	32	15	17	3	7	7	5	10	23	3	2	4	0	5	0	0	0	14	Moyenne	10.82
1733–1734	Marié	0	33	68	85	83	93	93	90	83	70	77	92	95	87	73	81	60	25	8	14	Médiane	10.18
Pop. 1,357																						Proportion de femmes plus âgées	
	Veuf	0	0	0	0	0	3	0	3	11	20	0	5	3	9	27	14	40	75	92	71	que leurs	0.5 %
	Total	100	100	100	100	100	99	100	100	99	100	100	100	100	100	100	100	100	100	100	99	époux	n = 192
Japon																							
Nishinomiya	Célibataire	100	100	86	71	21	0	0	0	0	0	100	72	17	13	0	0	0	0	0	0	Moyenne	10.36
Hama-Issai-chö,	Marié	0	0	14	18	74	95	91	97	85	46	0	28	83	87	92	76	83	50	31	0	Médiane	9.10
1713																						Médiane	
Pop. 653																						Proportion de femmes plus âgées	
	Veuf	0	0	0	12	5	5	9	3	15	54	0	0	0	0	8	24	17	50	69	100	que leurs	1.9 %
	Total	100	100	100	101	100	100	100	100	100	100	100	100	100	100	100	100	100	100	100	100	époux	n = 105

doutes sur la portée et la fréquence de cette règle.

Du point de vue de ces trois aspects, nous devons pourtant avouer que notre théorie est quelque peu incertaine et incomplète, n'étant pas suffisamment étayée de faits précis pour que la justesse de ces affirmations puisse être prouvée ou valablement contestée. Mais ceci, j'en suis persuadé, est un trait commun à toutes les thèses générales concernant les structures sociales. Pour revenir à nos quatre paramètres, il faut maintenant les examiner en détail pour essayer de déterminer quelles preuves nous possédons véritablement. Ces preuves, ce sont en premier lieu les tableaux publiés en 1972 dans le chapitre 1 du livre *Household and Family in Past Time* qui nous les apportent.

Le tableau 1 montre clairement la complication des structures familiales dans le passé d'après des études faites il y a 2 ans non seulement sur les cinq régions étudiées dans le symposium mais également sur d'autres pays. La nation la plus représentative sur le tableau est l'Angleterre. Vous pouvez remarquer en marge de notre discussion que ces chiffres relatifs à l'Angleterre amènent à la conclusion que la structure des foyers est devenue plus complexe entre le 16ᵉ et 18ᵉ siècles d'une part, et au 19ᵉ siècle, d'autre part, période généralement considérée comme étant celle de la Grande Révolution Industrielle.

Le deuxième tableau représente chacune des 5 communautés qui ont été étudiées dans l'analyse faite au départ sur l'âge des hommes et femmes au moment du mariage et la différence d'âge entre époux, et sur la proportion de femmes plus âgées que leurs maris. Les différences que nous avons évoquées précédemment apparaissent ici clairement entre les 2 premières communautés représentant l'Occident (Ealing en Angleterre et Longuenesse en France du Nord) et les deux dernières représentant des systèmes familiaux contraires (Belgrade et Nishinomiya). Aucune des Françaises n'étaient mariées avant l'âge de 24 ans, seulement 15% des Anglaises (nombre relativement important pour l'Angleterre) l'étaient, contre 28% pour les Japonaises et pas moins de 92% pour les Serbes! La différence d'âge entre les épouses occidentales (2,5, 3,5) n'atteignait pas la moitié de celle des autres (10, 11) et la proportion des femmes plus âgées que leurs époux était d'un ordre plus élevé (25% contre 1,2%). Les mêmes 5 communautés réapparaissent dans le troisième tableau, avec les chiffres pris dans une centaine de villes en Angleterre et dans une communauté coloniale américaine. Ils montrent clairement que les membres de la famille étaient beaucoup moins nombreux dans les foyers occidentaux que dans les autres.

Tableau 3. *Parents résidents en plus des époux et des enfants: nombres, types et proportions*

Type de parent	Angleterre standard: 100 communautés 1574–1821	Angleterre Ealing, Middlesex 1599 Pop. 427	France Longuenesse, Pas-de-Calais 1778 Pop. 333	Serbie Belgrade 1733–1734 Pop. 1,357	Japon Nishinomiya, Hama-issai-chö 1713 Pop. 653	Amérique coloniale Bristol, Rhode Island 1689 Pop. 421
Parent du chef de ménage et/ou de sa femme						
Père	—	1	0	2	5	0
Mère	—	1	3	35	31	0
Sœur	—	4	6	21	18	0
Frère	—	0	3	34	24	0
Neveu	—	3	1	13	5	0
Nièce	—	1	0	12	6	0
Gendre	—	0	2	7	5	0
Bru	—	1	2	9	4	0
Petits-enfants	—	0	2	5	36	4
Autres	—	0	3	28	19	0
Total	—	11	22	166	153	4
% de la population	3.4%	2.6%	6.6%	12.3%	23.4%	1.0%
% de ménages avec des parents	10.1%	13.0%	19.7%	27.0%	53.0%	3.0%

Tableau 4. *Domestiques: nombre, proportion et répartition par âge et sexe*

Age	Angleterre Ealing, Middlesex 1599 Pop. 427 85 ménages Homme	Femme	France Longuenesse, Pas-de-Calais 1778 Pop. 333 66 ménages Homme	Femme	Serbie Belgrade 1733–1734 Pop. 1,357 178 menages Homme	Femme	Japon Nishinomiya, Hama-issai-chö 1713 Pop. 653 132 ménages Homme	Femme	Amérique coloniale Bristol, Rhode Island 1689 Pop. 421 72 ménages Deux sexes	
0–9	0	2	0	0	0	11	0	0	—	—
10–19	41	22	23	24	31	63	43	80	—	—
20–39	31	59	36	47	26	5	52	20	—	—
30+	28	17	41	29	16	21	5	0	—	—
Inconnu	0	0	0	0	28	0	0	0	—	—
Total	100	100	100	100	101	100	100	100	—	—
N	68	41	25	17	121	19	21	5	—	—
Sex ratio (modèle anglais 107 paroisses)	166		145		637		420		56	
Proportion de la population (modèle anglais 13,4%)	25.5%		12.6%		10.3%		4.0%		13.3%	
Proportion de ménages avec domestiques (modèle anglais 28,5%)	34.2%		19.7%		29.6%		13.6%		30.1%	

Tableau 5. *Structure des ménages et domesticité*

		Angleterre Ealing Domestiques			France Longuenesse Domestiques			Serbie Belgrade Domestiques			Japon Nishinomiya Hama-issai-chö Domestiques			Amérique coloniale Bristol Domestiques		
		Avec	Sans	%	Avec	Sans	%	Avec	Sans	%	Avec	Sans	%	Avec	Sans	%
1. Solitaires	a veufs	1	3	12	0	0	1	0	2	2	0	1	7	0	0	7
	b célibataires ou indéterminés	1	3		1	0		2	2		0	8	(10)	1	4	
2. Ménages	a co-résidents apparents	0	0		1	2		0	0		0	3	2	0	0	
sans	b co-résidents autrement rattachés	0	0	2	0	0	6	0	0	2	0	0	(2)	0	0	0
structure	c individus sans lien apparent	1	1		1	0		0	5		0	0		0	0	
3. Ménages	a couples mariés	6	4		1	7		7	37		0	3		1	4	
simples	b couples mariés avec enfants	14	31	78	4	28	76	25	92	67	6	33	43	19	40	90
	c veufs avec enfants	1	1		1	1		0	3		0	5	(48)	0	0	
	d veuves avec enfants	0	9		2	6		1	18		1	9		0	1	
4. Ménages	a ascendante	1	0		1	4		3	15		1	19		0	0	
étendus	b descendante	1	1	16	0	0	14	1	5	15	0	5	27	2	0	3
	c collatérale	2	0		1	2		4	12		1	7	(25)	0	0	
	d ascendante et collatérale	0	1		0	1		0	0		0	2		0	0	
5. Ménages	a noyau second., ascendant	0	0		0	2		2	7		3	3		0	0	
multiples	b noyau second., descendant	1	0		0	0		5	8		4	13		0	0	
	c noyaux collatéraux	0	0	2	0	0	3	0	5	14	0	1	21	0	0	0
	d frérèches	0	0		0	0		2	7		0	3	(14)	0	0	
	e autres	0	0		0	0		0	3		0	1		0	0	
Totaux		85		100	66		100	273		100	132		100 (99)	72		100

Le quatrième tableau indique le nombre correspondant de domestiques, particulièrement élevé pour Belgrade, peut-être en raison de sa nature de capitale provinciale. Il est évident que les chiffres sont plus élevés par rapport à l'Amérique coloniale et surtout à l'Angleterre.
La différence dans la composition des ménages est illustrée au tableau 5, dans lequel est décrite la véritable structure des groupes familiaux des 5 villages étudiés. On peut y étudier les contrastes entre les ménages qui se présentent très fréquemment soit sous forme nucléaire, soit sans structure, en Occident, et les comparer avec les ménages des autres régions du monde où la famille était plus souvent étendue.

Maintenant que nous avons, ou du moins nous l'espérons, donné quelques preuves pour renforcer l'hypothèse exposée, nous allons examiner les quatre paramètres tour à tour et en discuter, en gardant présente à l'esprit l'optique de la socialisation du cycle de vie de l'individu et celui de la famille, en donnant à l'appui quelques données numériques, plus particulièrement axées sur le sujet qui nous intéresse. Nous commençons donc avec le premier paramètre, c'est-à-dire les structures de la famille en Occident et leur caractère restreint prédominant depuis des temps très lointains.

Ce qui nous a paru le plus important est la situation des familles dont les membres pouvaient influencer les enfants pendant les premières années du cycle de leur vie, en Occident et ailleurs. On peut s'en rendre compte dans le tableau 6, dans lequel les années depuis la naissance jusqu'à l'âge de 5 ans sont considérées comme étant celles de la socialisation primaire. Ce tableau révèle des contrastes flagrants, spécialement entre la ville anglaise de Lichfield en 1696, qui, bien que située près de Birmingham, n'était pas un centre industriel, et le petit village rural de Yokouchi au Japon en 1671. A Lichfield, presque tous les enfants appartenaient à des familles de type restreint tandis qu'à Yokouchi, presque $\frac{2}{3}$ d'entre eux vivaient dans des groupes familiaux complexes, chacun d'entre eux contenant au moins 2 unités conjugales. Mais même à Yokouchi, un enfant sur trois vivait dans une famille à type restreint et cette catégorie s'est révélee partout assez importante.

En ce qui concerne le second et le troisième de nos paramètres, les données historiques sont claires et impressionantes. Dans le contexte présent, il suffit de se rapporter au travail déjà accompli par les démographes historiens qui ont opéré des reconstitutions familiales à partir des registres écclésiastiques existant en France, Italie, Angleterre, Japon, et même aux Etats Unis (à l'époque coloniale) pour conclure que dans

Tableau 6. *Socialisation de la première enfance (0 à 5 ans) dans diverses communautés d'autrefois en Angleterre, en France, en Serbie et au Japon, selon la structure des ménages*

		Angleterre Ealing 1599	Angleterre Lichfield 1696	Angleterre Stoke-on-Trent 1701	France Longuenesse 1778	Serbie Belgrade 1733-1734	Japon Yokouchi 1676	Japon Nishinomiya 1713
Ménages	N	33	312	189	27	101	88	13
simples	%	61	94	90	79	66	33	28
Ménages	N	4	11	14	7	16	0	12
étendus	%	8	3,4	6,6	21	14		26
Ménages	N	2	5	4	0	27	15	21
multiples	%	4	1,6	1,9		15	63	46
Autres	N	10	4	3	0	8	1	0
	%	20	1,2	1,4	0	5	4	0
Domestiques résidant dans	N	10	102	33	5	28	0	5
le ménage	%	20	32	16	15	18		11

Note: Ces chiffres sont approximatifs, spécialement ceux de Belgrade. On trouvera une explication des difficultés relatives aux données de cette communauté, et relatives à trois des autres dans Laslett et Wall (1972): 50–51. Les documents relatifs à Stoke (en partie) et à Lichfield sont de très bonne qualité, pour l'Angleterre. En ce qui concerne les chiffres relatifs au Japon, on doit se rappeler que les enfants de 1 et 2 ans sont exclus, et que l'adoption étant pratiquée sur une grande échelle, 42% de tous les enfants des ménages complexes sont touchés par cette pratique; mais du fait que les très jeunes étaient rarement adoptés, la relation prise en compte dans ces chiffres est toujours celle du lien aux parents biologiques.

l'Occident les femmes se mariaient généralement tard, conclusion qui a déjà été établie par Hajnal en 1965. Il est communément accepté qu'il n'y a jamais eu dans les pays occidentaux un âge moyen de mariage inférieur à 20 ans, du moins pas dans une période de temps continu. Ceci a pu être démontré pour le cas de l'Angleterre à partir du Moyen Age, car nos registres commencent en 1538. On sait même que dans un village anglais, sur un laps de temps assez long, il arrivait que les femmes soient plus âgées que leurs maris et que l'âge moyen auquel elles se mariaient approchait parfois les 30 ans. On a noté les mêmes résultats en Norvège pendant le 19e siècle.[3]

Malheureusement, il est peu probable que ce procédé puisse permettre de prouver que les pays dans les autres régions du monde et déjà mentionnés ont eu un régime historique familial différent de celui de l'Occident, au moins pendant la période qui précède le 19e siècle.

D'ailleurs, ce ne sont pas essentiellement les résultats de la démographie historique qui nous interessent car ce qui importe réellement ce n'est pas de savoir si une femme a eu son enfant jeune ou vieille; ce sont les enfants qui présentent de l'intêret, et la façon dont ils vivent au sein de leur famille, sous la protection du père et de la mère. Et les seuls renseignements valables en notre possession viennent comme d'habitude de l'analyse des listes de recensement des habitants, comme dans le tableau 7 qui donne l'exemple de deux communautés, une anglaise et l'autre japonaise.

Le tableau 7 est certes complexe mais sa signification est tout à fait claire. Dans le monde occidental, représenté ici par la ville de Stoke-on-Trent en 1701, pères et mères sont pratiquement du même âge et beaucoup plus âgés que leurs enfants. Dans d'autres parties du monde, comme à Nishinomiya au Japon en 1713, les pères sont sensiblement du même âge que ceux des pays occidentaux, mais sont par contre beaucoup plus âgés que leurs femmes. Les mères sont beaucoup plus proches de leurs enfants par leur âge.

Le schéma suggéré par l'exemple de Stoke-on-Trent et Nishinomiya peut être complété par des exemples tirés d'autres régions d'Occident et d'ailleurs. Dans le recensement islandais de 1729, par exemple, qui constitue peut-être le dénombrement le plus ancien et le plus exact jamais réalisé d'un pays européen pré-industriel, l'âge moyen des mères islandaises était d'environ 32 ans; à Kölked, cependant, un village en Hongrie du type "oriental", en 1819, les mères avaient environ 7 années de moins. Dans ce même village, une mère sur dix seulement était aussi âgée que

Tableau 7. *Ages comparés des mères, pères et de leurs enfants, à Stoke-on-Trent et Nishinomiya*

		Stoke-on-Trent, Staffs., Angleterre 1701	Nishinomiya Japon 1713
Mères et pères		n = 248	n = 114
– Nombre d'années dont l'âge des pères excède l'âge des mères	Moyenne	2,5	9,5
	Médiane	1,6	10,5
	Ecart	−16 à +20	−4 à +28
– Proportion de mères plus vieilles que les pères		29%	2,6%
Mères et leurs enfants		n = 740	n = 261
– Ages des mères à la naissance de leurs enfants	Moyenne	30,4	27,0
	Médiane	30,7	26,7
	Quartile	27,6 à 38,9	23,9 à 34,1
– Proportion d'enfants	– plus jeunes de 25 ans ou moins que leur mère	21%	39%
	– plus jeunes de 30 ans ou plus que leur mère	50%	34%
Pères et leurs enfants		n = 635	n = 239
– Ages des pères à la nais sance de leurs enfants	Moyenne	35.4	36.3
	Médiane	35.4	37.0
– Proportion d'enfants	– plus jeunes de 25 ans ou moins que leur père	15%	3,4%
	– plus jeunes de 30 ans ou plus que leur père	59%	83%

Note: Les chiffres sont obtenus en faisant la différence des âges donnés sur les deux recensements; les veufs et les veuves sont compris s'ils sont accompagnés d'enfants. Les enfants de moins de deux ans sont absents du recensement de Nishinomiya. On n'a pu corriger, ni cette omission, ni les distorsions dues aux remariages, ni les effets consécutifs au départ des enfants.

son mari, tandis qu'en Islande, 22% des mères l'étaient autant ou plus. Il me semble que cette proportion de femmes plus âgées, variant de $\frac{1}{5}$ à $\frac{1}{4}$ constitue l'indicateur le plus significatif du caractère "occidental" des structures familiales apparu dans tous les différents cas étudiés. La conclusion de ces faits, qui a déjà été exprimée auparavant, et suivant laquelle les unions occidentales auraient toujours tendu vers le "companionate marriage", est une hypothèse tout à fait gratuite. Seules les preuves idéologiques ou intellectuelles que nous pourrions découvrir pourraient justifier cette prétention. Néanmoins quelque chose doit pouvoir en être retirée pour l'étude de la socialisation des enfants dans les vieilles institutions familiales européennes.[4]

En Occident donc, les nouveaux-nés semblent toujours avoir eu des mères d'environ 20 à 30 ans au moins. Ailleurs elles étaient de 3 à 4 ans plus jeunes, et pouvaient avoir entre 15 et 20 ans. Un dixième des enfants habitant à Kölked en 1819 et à Yokouchi en 1671 avaient des adolescentes pour mères, mais cela n'a jamais été le cas pour aucun des 100 enfants d'Ealing en 1599 ou de Stoke-on-Trent en 1701. Il appartiendra aux experts en psychologie de l'éducation des enfants de découvrir quelles conséquences respectives créent chez les enfants les différences de maturité de leurs mères, et aussi de découvrir dans quelle mesure un enfant est influencé par le fait que sa mère est plus proche du père de famille par l'âge, souvent même plus âgée et plus expérimentée que lui. Dans d'autres régions, la jeune mère a sans doute dû ressentir son infériorité d'âge, et si l'autoritarisme patriarcal repose dans un complexe social sur la supériorité des années, il n'est pas difficile de deviner où nous devons aller chercher des circonstances prédisposantes. S'il arrivait que les effets que nous étudions soient en réalité plus importants que ceux indiqués par nos chiffres, ce qui est probable, on pourrait dire alors qu'en Occident, mari et femme ont vraiment le même âge ou appartiennent à la même génération, quelque soient les différentiations sociales entre eux. Mais dans d'autres pays, les pères peuvent appartenir à une génération plus vieille, tandis que les mères appartiennent à celle de leurs enfants.

Après nous être penchés sur les 3 premiers de nos paramètres, nous pouvons maintenant exposer le quatrième qui, comme il a été dit plus haut, est plus complexe. Il implique premièrement la présence d'étrangers à l'intérieur du groupe familial, c'est-à-dire celle de la domesticité, et en second lieu il influe sur la socialisation secondaire des domestiques eux-mêmes. En effet, si un garçon ou une fille devenaient domestique entre 12 et 15 ans, ce qui semble avoir été la règle en Europe, cette expérience se déroulait pendant le stade de socialisation secondaire et il s'ensuivait sans doute certaines conséquences sur les enfants des maîtres. On voit sur le tableau 8 le nombre de jeunes gens qui se sont trouvés dans cette situation et quelle période de leur vie on peut étudier.

Nous avons utilisé des données anglaises sur des dates et lieux pour pouvoir mettre en évidence les plus hauts degrés de variation entre les proportions des domestiques à différents groupes d'âge. De toutes façons, l'absence de foyer pour le serviteur qui vivait dans une maison étrangère semble avoir été un fait courant quand ils avaient entre 15 et 25 ans. Ils se mariaient généralement dès qu'ils avaient quitté le service.

Les chiffres apparaissant dans les tableaux 4, 6 et 8 nous amènent à

Tableau 8. *Proportion de domestiques d'individus mariés ou veufs selon les groupes d'âges, en Angleterre, en Serbie et au Japon (en %)*

	Angleterre								Serbie		Japon	
	Ealing 1599		Lichfield 1696		Stoke-on-Trent 1701		Ardleigh 1796		Belgrade 1733–1734		Nishinomiya 1713	
Ages	a	b	a	b	a	b	a	b	a	b	a	b
Hommes												
0–9	0	0	1	0	0	0	0	0	0	0	0	0
10–14	15	0	4	0	3	0	3	0	22	33	0	0
15–19	72	0	47	0	10	0	48	0	47	68	24	0
20–24	78	0	24	18	16	11	38	16	24	85	19	2
25–29	47	29	5	25	20	52	11	52	17	83	8	14
30–34	28	47	1	73	5	73	5	73	13	96	6	26
35–39	43	43	1	76	2	93	4	83	8	93	0	79
40–44	29	71	0	89	0	94	0	79	3	93	0	100
45+	9	89	0	82	1	85	7	80	7	80	0	100
Femmes												
0–9	3	0	0	0	0	0	0	0	1	0	0	0
10–14	7	0	1	0	3	0	5	0	9	0	4	0
15–19	47	0	18	1	30	0	27	0	6	77	8	0
20–24	58	15	42	8	28	17	20	33	0	92	3	28
25–29	36	50	23	38	10	63	9	56	1	97	0	83
30–34	27	63	12	59	7	72	0	89	0	98	0	87
35–39	14	86	4	74	7	73	0	94	1	96	0	100
40–44	0	100	0	78	2	85	3	91	0	100	0	100
45+	5	92	0	76	2	78	6	75	2	95	0	100

a. Domestiques; b. Mariés ou veufs

tirer les conclusions suivantes. En Occident, un cinquième environ des enfants vivaient pendant les premières années de leur vie dans des groupes familiaux comprenant des domestiques. Dans les quatre cinquièmes restants, environ la moitié des enfants, quoique la proportion ait été variable, devenaient des domestiques eux-mêmes entre l'adolescence et leur vingtième année. De cette façon, environ deux cinquièmes des jeunes gens échappaient à ce sort, ou d'être socialisés en la présence de domestiques, ou de devenir domestiques. Une fois encore, on peut souligner qu'il appartient aux spécialistes de l'enfance et de la famille de juger des effets que de telles circonstances ont pu avoir sur la formation de la personnalité. Il me semble qu'il a été très important qu'une si grande proportion de jeunes enfants ait subi l'influence de ces étrangers apparus dans la famille et issus d'une classe sociale différente, inférieure à celle des parents de l'enfant de la famille.[5]

Ces personnes engagées pour leur jeunesse et leur vigueur étaient en nombre 2 à 3 fois supérieur aux réprésentants de la parenté inclus dans le ménage. Bien que la théorie générale sur le processus de socialisation implique que les conséquences découlant du départ des jeunes gens pour aller travailler pendant la période de socialisation secondaire n'aient pas eu une grande portée, il me semble pourtant que ce fait a dû avoir son importance. Dans le vieux monde, en Occident de toutes façons, la forme de subordination aussi bien politique et économique que personnelle était manifestement de type familial.

Les arguments que nous avons avancés ici montrent clairement que la présence de domestiques n'était pas un trait particulier à la civilisation occidentale, et était même assez variable selon les cas. Les anthropologues semblent supposer que la pratique d'échanger de jeunes gens comme domestiques entre maisons peut être notée dans toutes les régions culturelles du monde. Mais la présence de la domesticité dans le contexte de la vie occidentale est absolument indéniable et les exemples choisis dans cette étude me paraissent assez représentatifs. Certains faits semblent indiquer que plus on avance dans le passé social de l'Angleterre, plus grande est l'importance de la place occupée par la domesticité. On ne peut que répéter qu'en Occident, la domesticité existait en tant qu'institution majeure et comme complément des autres particularités familiales que nous avons dépeintes. Et ceci ne se manifestait pas ailleurs. Mais la domesticité a maintenant pratiquement disparu du cadre de la société occidentale. En Angleterre par exemple, elle a cessé de jouer dans l'existence de la famille le rôle que nous avons décrit à une date indéfinie au début du 19e siècle, bien que les domestiques (des femmes en majorité) aient constitué encore un groupe assez important numériquement jusqu'en 1930 environ.

Si une étude était réalisée à l'heure actuelle sur les villes japonaises qui ont été mentionnées ici, on découvrirait certainement que l'âge des individus à leur mariage, la différence d'âge entre époux etc. sont à peu de choses près les mêmes qu'en Angleterre, France ou Amérique. Il en serait probablement de même pour la composition structurale des foyers. Belgrade, maintenant capitale de la Yougoslavie, pourrait être rangée dans la même catégorie "occidentale", l'âge du mariage étant moins tardif (mais le "companionate marriage" plus courant) et la présence de la domesticité assez rare.

Mais la disparition de la combinaison, en tant que combinaison, des caractères qui avaient défini la famille occidentale n'affecte guère l'importance de cette combinaison pour la nature de l'Occidentalité.

Tout ce que j'ai tenté de faire ici, c'est une hypothèse courte, et hardie, une introduction insuffisante à un sujet assez vaste. Mais ce n'est qu'un début. La sociologie historique a beaucoup plus à nous apprendre sur la sociologie de la famille et sur de nombreux autres sujets qui relèvent nettement des sciences sociales.[6]

SUMMARY

Family life cycle and socialisation process: characteristics of the West in historical perspective

This essay attempts to provide a general description of the familial characteristics of the West *over time*, that is historically. As an essay in historical sociology, it is intended to be in deliberate contrast to most discussions of familial sociology in comparative terms, where the comparison is with the situation as it is now, in developed or undeveloped countries. The "family" is defined here exclusively in terms of characteristics of marriage partners, and of the co-resident domestic group. No account is taken of kin relationships between such co-resident groups. This is not because the kinship system of the West is held to be unimportant in defining the family in that area, but because historical evidence is at present available in a fairly easily comparable form for the co-resident domestic group, and we so far have almost nothing on kinship networks, for example, in West European communities. Nearly all of the evidence used comes from a book published in 1972 by the Cambridge Group for the History of Population and Social Structure, and issued by the Cambridge University Press with the title *Household and Family in Past Time*, edited by Peter Laslett with the assistance of Richard Wall. The definition of the domestic group, and discussion of what is meant by "characteristic", will be found in the Introduction to that volume.

Since only the co-resident group is at issue, and since the subject of historical sociology to which this preliminary essay belongs is in such an early stage of its development, it will be obvious that the thesis of this piece is incomplete and tentative, a series of suggestions only. Familial characteristics of the historic West as boldly set out here are five-fold:

1. A relatively late age at first marriage for women
2. A relatively brief age gap between spouses
3. A relatively high proportion of wives older than husbands
4. A relatively large proportion of persons in domestic service
5. A relatively considerable predominance of simple family households or nuclear families.

There may be a sixth characteristic, closely allied to the first, which has been impossible so far to substantiate with historical records going back to any considerable depth in time. This is a relatively high proportion of persons never marrying.

The following observations on the characteristics listed above are of very great importance to the thesis, and should be carefully noted.

1. It is the combination of all or most of them which is suggested as characteristic of the West, *not* the presence of any one of them, or even of two or three. It is now known, for example, from *Household and Family in Past Time*, that the simple family

household was to be found in considerable strength in many areas not thought of as Western in past time, even in Japan. Servants, not always servants of the "Western" type, have been common in many parts of the world for a very long time.

2. Nevertheless it is held that these characteristics are systematically interrelated into a recognisable pattern of familial experience, and especially into a characteristic pattern of primary socialisation which distinguishes the "West". The only justification of the inclusion of this essay in a volume devoted to the familial cycle is its particular concern with one particular phase of that cycle, the phase when man, wife and children are in the stage of primary socialisation, are all together (and very closely together) in the co-resident domestic group.

3. No geographical delineation of the "West" is offered in this essay. The characteristic familial pattern described has been found in England, in northern France, in the colonial and subsequent United States, Iceland, the Low Countries and to a lesser extent in the remainder of the British Isles and in Scandinavia, in each case at times going back to the 18th century or earlier. The crucial temporal stage at issue is that of industrialisation, and great emphasis is laid on the fact that in England, about which most is known and for which our time span of knowledge is greatest, this pattern is found centuries before industrialisation, and may go back a long way in history. What is known so far about the geographical distribution of this pattern of characteristics has been added to some extent, since the essay was originally conceived. Though the new knowledge does little to strengthen the general hypothesis, it certainly does not make against it.

Outside the Europe of the far West (including the United States since colonial times) and of the North-west, there appears to be an intermediate region of ill-defined extent where mixed patterns were found, often in communities situated quite close to each other. Quite extreme instances of "non-Western" characteristics, for example a predominance of complex family forms over simple family forms, have been found in the area surrounding Florence in central Italy, and as far west geographically as Brittany, in the 18th century. It seems clear that the Baltic States of north-west Europe did not conform to the pattern, and that mixed and intermediate communities as to familial forms were to be found in parts of Germany, Austria and particularly Hungary, with some villages with well-defined "Western" patterns situated not far from others which were very different indeed. The general hypothesis, if it survives the discovery of new evidence about new areas and different (hopefully earlier) periods, may well turn out to take the form of an insistence on the *uniformity* of familial characteristics, present well before industrialisation, where industrialisation occurred early, as compared with a lack of uniformity elsewhere. England itself has been called a boringly non-varying society in respect of familial characteristics.

The rest of this brief and tentative essay is given up to suggestions as to how the familial pattern described could have affected socialisation and the formation of character. The first three listed characteristics point to a greater degree of companionship in marriage than we would presumably obtain in areas where wives were married very young indeed, began to have children in their late teens and were educating mothers throughout the twenties, living along with husbands very much older than themselves. Children born to "Western" couples, in contrast, were brought up by mature women, women not so likely to be widowed as elsewhere, and were brought up almost exclusively with their physiological fathers and mothers as rôle models, with a virtual absence within the household itself of any member of the kin of the parents. They did have in their households, however, other primary figures in the form of servants, at least in perhaps a quarter or a third of all households. Where children were born into households not themselves employing servants, they might well belong, perhaps in a half of these remaining cases, to households which exported them as rather older children to be servants elsewhere. This pattern of primary and secondary socialisation is of course not exclusively Western, but its prevalence and importance is reinforced by the fact that in the largest obtainable sample of English households between the 16th and 19th century no less than an eighth of the whole population were persons in service. In individual communities, rural and urban, as high a proportion as 30%, 40% or even 60% of all young English people between the ages of 15 and 24 could be in service. It must be noticed that this parameter, a high level of what the French call "domesticité", has now disappeared altogether from the industrial West. Historical sociology has had to be brought into being to discover its one-time importance.

The life cycle of Westerners under this régime was dominated in its earlier years by the individualistic character of marriage, where each set of spouses was under the imperative necessity of setting up its own establishment before co-residence could begin, and where both wife and husband themselves collaborated to produce the funds necessary to begin that separate establishment. Here the position of young Western people as employees, whether of their own parents, or of their masters if they were servants, is of crucial importance, as well as the habits of accumulation which this system forced in the years of socialisation on every member of the community.

These are only some of the psychological, economic and general sociological concomitants of the pattern described which are suggested in the essay, but which can not be pursued in such a very introductory context.

Notes

1. Hajnal, 1965. L'essai de Hajnal tente de démontrer en quelque sorte que les caractéristiques essentielles du mariage européen, c'est-à-dire l'âge généralement tardif auquel se marient les femmes et la proportion significative d'individus qui restent célibataires, remonte assez loin dans l'histoire de l'Europe, au moins jusqu'au Moyen Age. Les recherches entreprises depuis 1965 par le Cambridge Group for the History of Population and Social Structure ont pu vérifier le fait quant à l'âge; mais il n'a pas été possible de prouver l'existence du célibat pour un grand nombre de personnes vivant dans la société anglaise pré-industrielle, et certains faits viennent même à l'encontre de cette supposition. Les spécialistes des études sociales sont incapables de convaincre si, après avoir mis en relief certains traits particuliers à une culture, ils découvrent par la suite, comme le fit Margaret Mead à Samoa, que ces traits ont cessé d'apparaître dans la génération suivante.
2. Edité et introduit par Peter Laslett, avec l'aide de Richard Wall (1972), et donnant des exemples sur la taille et la structure (quelquefois aussi le développement dans le temps) de familles en Angleterre, France, Corse, Pays-Bas, Italie, Serbie, Japon, Etats Unis et autres pays, principalement à partir du 16ᵉ siècle.
3. *Cf.* Drake (1969), et les études de Wrigley (1966) sur l'âge des époux au moment du mariage et les différences d'âge entre eux à Colyton dans le Devonshire entre 1650 et 1750. On peut consulter d'autres ouvrages sur les résultats découlant des études de démographie historique tels que ceux de Louis Henry (en France), Livi Bacchi (pour l'Italie), Wells et Greven (pour les Etats Unis) et Hayami (pour le Japon), ainsi que de nombreux autres que l'on peut lire dans les *Annales de Démographie Historique* publiées chaque année à Paris.
4. Les chiffres venant d'Islande et de Hongrie doivent être employés avec prudence. Il faut bien se rappeler en jugeant les faits précités que l'âge du mariage en Occident, et sans aucun doute partout ailleurs, n'a cessé de varier de tout temps, et qu'il est

vraiment l'une des variables des structures sociologiques les plus interessantes. En fait, c'est l'âge relativement tardif auquel prend place le mariage et la différence d'âge relativement faible entre les époux que nous pensons générale.

5. Laslett, dans Laslett et Wall (1972: 154) tableau 4.15, montre que 84% des familles bourgeoises avaient des domestiques dans l'Angleterre traditionnelle. On a beaucoup écrit sur le rôle joué par les domestiques dans ces familles et cette tendance est encore vérifiée à notre époque. Il faut se rappeler cependant que seulement une minorité non encore déterminée de domestiques travaillaient non seulement dans des foyers, mais étaient aussi parfois ouvriers de ferme, ouvriers agricoles, apprentis etc., les hommes étant en nombre à peine supérieur aux femmes (*cf. ibid.*, tableau 4.13).
6. Note supplémentaire de juillet 1976: une version revue et étendue de ce court essai, présentant un plus grand nombre de données, constituera le chapitre premier de *Family life and illicit love in earlier generations*, Cambridge, 1977.

RÉFÉRENCES

Drake, M. (1969), *Population and Society in Norway.*

Hajnal, J. (1965), "European marriage patterns in perspective" in D.V. Glass and D.E.C. Eversley (eds.), *Population in History.*

Islande, Recensement de 1729, imprimé; copie xérographiée à Cambridge.

Kölked, (1973), Communication privée du Dr Rudolf Andorka.

Laslett, P., and Wall, R. (eds.) (1972), *Household and Family in Past Time*, Cambridge University Press.

Wrigley, E.A. (1966), "Family limitation in pre-industrial England", *Economic History Review*, 19: 82–109.

18. The family cycle in historical perspective: a proposal for a developmental approach*

TAMARA K. HAREVEN

The newly developing field of family history has contributed significantly to the revision of prevailing theories about the development of the family in Western society. The fact that pre-industrial households and families were nuclear in structure has now become generally accepted. Historical data has revised the myth that industrialization resulted in the transformation of the "traditional" extended family into the "modern" nuclear family. Certain historians of the family have gone so far as to argue that there has been little change in the family and household unit over the past two centuries.[1] A variety of historical studies have also shown the importance of disaggregating demographic trends and generalizing about household and family behavior in the past, and have demonstrated the structural and behavioral varieties of the family and the household under different historical conditions. While historians have thus had a profound impact on the sociology of the family, they have not yet sufficiently adopted the concepts and methods of developmental sociology to their own research.

This paper will address itself to the principles of the developmental sociology of the family cycle and to the possibility of their application to the historical study of the family. Secondly, it will attempt to show how

* An earlier short version of this paper was published in the *Journal of Social History*, Spring 1974.
I am indebted to Professors John Mogey and John Modell for their valuable insights and to Professors Maris Vinovskis and Michael Gordon for their constructive criticism. The research on nineteenth-century Boston mentioned in this paper was supported by a grant from Clark University's Graduate Research Fund. The Manchester, New Hampshire project is supported by a research grant from the National Endowment for the Humanities and the Merrimack Valley Textile Museum.

the historical study of the life cycle could make an important contribution to the sociology of the family.

The paper proposes a developmental approach to the historical study of the family. Underlying it is a conception of the family as a process, rather than as a static unit within certain time periods. The approach is based on the assumption that individuals go through a variety of family patterns and household structures over their individual life cycles, and that families and households evolve different types of structures, organizations, and relationships, which are generally obscured in the snapshot approach. While the family cycle approach encompasses all areas of familial and demographic behavior, namely, family structure, household organization, family size, kinship, family formation, dissolution, and economic behavior, this paper concentrates primarily on family and household structure in the nineteenth-century United States as a case in point. It discusses shared problems in current work, and proposes several possible approaches for future research.

The family cycle approach is of crucial importance to those interested in studying social change, since the variety of stages of individual and family development over the life cycle are intricately connected with historical change. One could argue that while the basic biological stages of individual development (childhood, adolescence, youth) may be universal, their social and cultural significance varies in different time periods, and is determined by historical conditions. Similarly, stages in the family cycle differed in different periods and among different socio-economic groups. Glick has shown that profound changes in the cycle of "the American family" since 1890 were caused not only by the changing age-structure of the population, but also by historical conditions. The stages of the family cycle conceptualized respectively by Hill, Duvall and Rodgers, may have occurred at different age levels and may have been recognized in different ways, not only within different historical periods, but even among various socio-economic and ethnic groups in the same period. Uhlenberg, for example, has shown in his study of the life cycles of cohorts of American women over the past centuries, that the uniform stages of the family cycle designated by Glick took different forms for women than for men.[2] Age at marriage, age at leaving home, child-spacing, periods of extension of the household unit or contraction, are not merely age-specific demographic phenomena. They are socially and culturally defined, and are, therefore, subject to historical change.

While sociologists have begun to unravel and conceptualize the contemporary family cycle as a unit of analysis, historians have not used the family cycle as the conceptual framework for the study of family patterns in the past. The only historians who have applied a developmental approach to the study of the family have concentrated on Colonial America. Under the influence of the French demographers and the Cambridge Group for the Study of Population and Social Structure, Colonial historians have employed family reconstitution techniques and have provided dynamic models of familial and demographic behavior in pre-industrial American communities. Demos, for example, specifically used the life cycle as the unit of analysis in his study of the family in Plymouth Colony. Greven followed a generational model in his analysis of family patterns in Colonial Andover, and Smith studied demographic change over an entire century in Hingham, Massachusetts.[3] Historians of nineteenth-century family patterns, on the other hand, have relied primarily on cross-sectional analysis, and have studied the family in limited time perspectives.[4]

A series of studies of family and household structure in various nineteenth-century communities, support their conclusions by data depicting conditions at one point in time, or during several points in time, rather than over the entire family cycle. These analyses are based primarily, and sometimes exclusively, on the manuscript schedules of the Federal Census, and are therefore limited by necessity to the period 1850–1880, during which the census data is organized by households and is open to research. The data is generally augmented by traces through city directories, which provide information on residential and occupational changes, but list no additional information on family structure. In most instances, the census data has not been linked to vital records.[5] Although the implicit questions which these studies are attempting to answer are of a developmental nature, the picture which emerges from the cross-sectional analysis is that of a snapshot view.

These studies of family patterns have presented a limited picture of the family in the nineteenth century: rural-urban differences in family structure appear to be minimal, and ethnicity, race, occupation and residential arrangements seem to have no dramatic impact on the varieties of family and household organization. (This lack of difference between rural-urban patterns does not apply to fertility, where demographers have already established clear patterns of rural-urban differences.) The distribution of household types generally falls within similar proportions: an average of 80% are nuclear, 12 to 15% are extended, and about 3 to 5% of all households consist of one member. This apparent constancy in the structure of nineteenth-century families and households has led some historians to the conclusion that household and family organization may not be the crucial variables in the study of nineteenth-century populations. It has been interpreted as a confirmation of the constancy of the nuclear family in the history of American communities, and seems to conform to Peter Laslett's conclusion that there has been little change in the family and the household in Western society over the past two centuries.[6]

Several scholars have gone so far as to argue that Talcott Parsons' ideal type of the modern American family as an isolated, nuclear, detachable, mobile unit was characteristic of the nineteenth-century family as well.[7] Students of nineteenth-century family structures who conclude that urban families were predominantly "intense", "isolated", and "nuclear", have frequently confused "household" with "family". Their almost exclusive reliance on the Federal Census Manuscript schedules listing of the household as the basic unit of analysis has led them to confuse the Bureau of the Census' enumeration unit with the actual organization of family life.[8] If, on the other hand, family is defined as a set of relationships which transcend the residential unit, we could conclude that while the majority of *households* studied were nuclear, indeed, at least one-half of the *families* within them were involved in elaborate kinship ties outside the household, and therefore conformed less to Parsons' ideal type of the American family.[9]

The major problem in this debate over family structure is its derivation from a static view of the family, and from the use of the standard classifications such as "nuclear", "extended", "augmented", for the characteristics of family and household types. While some sociologists have been questioning the validity of these categories for the interpretation of the family in periods of rapid social change, historians have continued to be bound by these classifications.[10]

The applicability of a developmental approach to the study of the family is supported by the data in my study of family structure in nineteenth-century Boston. This analysis of several thousand households sampled from select Boston neighborhoods, which were traced over time and linked longitudinally with vital records, reveals a constant flux in family and household organization. Men and women grew up in predominantly nuclear households, left their parental household in their twenties, and attached themselves as boarders and lodgers in strange households, until they married and set up their own nuclear households.

Middle-aged parents, whose children had left home, took in boarders. The same held true for men and women in their fifties and sixties, especially for unmarried women or widows, who generally took in strangers rather than attach themselves to an extended household. Once individuals became heads of households, they continued to remain in that position over their entire lifetime. The household types which they headed, however, changed over the life cycle. They headed a nuclear household first, became heads of an augmented, or occasionally an extended household in mid-cycle, and in old age, lived again in a nuclear or augmented household.[11]

In Boston, as well as in other nineteenth-century cities, lodging and boarding appeared consistently as a surrogate familial arrangement. While extended households constituted only between ten to twelve percent of the population, as many as one-fourth, and in certain areas one-third of all households took in strangers, especially after the children of the household had left home.[12] Boarding and lodging was more frequently correlated to age than to occupation. It was more commonly practiced by natives of Massachusetts and by migrants from rural New England than by foreign immigrants. Like marriage and widowhood, it was life cycle specific. A function of the individual as well as the family's stage of development, boarding and lodging was articulated to the life cycle of the boarders as to those who took them in. At least one-third to one-half of all individuals were likely to experience both – boarding in their early adulthood, and taking in boarders at a later stage of life. Between one-half to two-thirds of all urban residents were likely to have resorted to lodging and boarding as a transitional stage between their departure from their parents' households and their setting up households of their own.

While the largest proportion of boarders, regardless of age, lived with heads of households in the 40–50 age group, there was generally a "generation gap" between boarders and their heads. Most boarders under 35 tended to live in households headed by individuals who were their seniors by fifteen years or more. In Irene Taueber's phrase, boarding served as the "social equalization of the family". Comparisons of Boston with other urban communities support the hypothesis that most urban residents in nineteenth-century America lived through several types of family and household organizations over their lifetimes and that these forms varied significantly at different stages of their life cycles.

Another set of data, based on the cumulative individual career of laborers in an early twentieth-century textile community – Manchester, New Hampshire – suggests that individuals lived in different household types over different stages of life, and that their household arrangements were closely related to their work careers inside and outside the textile mills. Non-migrant young men and women continued to live in their parents' households while working in the mill. In the absence of parents they boarded or lodged with kin members or with strangers from their own ethnic group. After marriage, and until the birth of their first child, they shared households with other families. The migratory patterns of French Canadian laborers in this industrial population show a high correlation between the laborer's temporary sojourns and changes in household organization. The picture emerging from this study is one of a procession of individuals through different types of households, and one of continuous change in the structure of the households and families which encompassed them.[13]

A developmental approach to nineteenth-century family studies will require a new conceptual framework and a different methodology. The family cycle approach does not merely substitute a time unit of analysis for the currently used structural unit. Historians who will switch to longitudinal tracing or record linkage or cross-sectional analysis, without developing a conceptual scheme, will be moving from one mechanical category to another.

Family research in the next few years will have to determine what type of family cycles existed and what the significant stages of transition were. Historians of the individual life cycle (childhood, adolescence, youth) have already demonstrated the fact that stages of psychological development are socially defined, and that it would be impossible, therefore, to rely on universal stages. Similarly, stages in the family cycle are not governed simply by biological age grades.

Family sociologists have developed several schemes for the conceptualization and the classification of stages of the family cycle in contemporary societies. Historians will not only need to define such stages for past societies, but will need to interpret their relationship in the historical contexts. On the macro-scale, it will be the historian's task to delineate the major changes which had occurred in the family cycle over time, and to relate these changes to historical conditions. In addition to the changes in the life cycle of American families which Glick has outlined, it will be necessary to see the changes in the family cycle over time among specific racial and ethnic groups, on various occupational levels and in different settlement types.

The same holds true on the micro-scale. From the limited research accomplished to date, it is already evident that in nineteenth-century American society, different population groups experience different types of family cycles. Historical research is only beginning to analyze familial patterns in various periods. Over the next few years it will be necessary for historians to isolate the varieties of family cycles among different segments of the population under different historical conditions. The cycles of rural families were different from those of urban families, and the cycles of native American families differed from those of immigrants. The cycles of industrial families not only differed from these other groups, but actually represented a variety of patterns depending on what type of industry and what stages of industrialization these families were involved in. In the case of families of immigrants or migrants, for instance, it is necessary to analyze stages of the cycle in the pre-migration as well as post-migration period. These differences become critical particularly in studying patterns of seasonal migration where household composition is more fluid.

In exploring these different patterns historically, it will be essential to test the applicability to historical conditions of stages of the family cycle defined by sociologists. The demographic, functional and transactional stages of the family cycle which Hill, Duvall and Rodgers have conceptualized are all applicable to historical analysis.

The basic scheme developed by Hill defines the family cycle around three criteria: number of positions in the family, age composition of the family, change in the age-role content of the husband-father which occurs with his retirement from active employment. This framework renders the following stages: 1) Establishment (newly-married, childless); 2) New parents (infant to 3 years); 3) Preschool family (child 3 to 6 and possibly younger siblings); 4) School-age family (oldest child 6 to 12 years, possibly younger siblings); 5) Family with adolescent (oldest child 6 to 12, possibly younger siblings); 6) Family with young adult (oldest child 20 until first child leaves home); 7) Family as launching center for departure of first to last child; 8) Post-parental family, the middle years (after children have left home until father retires); 9) Aging family (after retirement of father).[14]

These stages were developed by Duvall and were further refined by Rodgers to allow a staggering of each stage in accordance with the progression of each child through the cycle, rather than just the first child. While they provide the first useful scheme for historians, they also clearly reveal the need for modification and adjustment in accordance with historical conditions. The Hill-Rodgers scheme is modelled on modern middle-class urban American families. In its application to historical circumstances, it will be necessary to adjust some of its criteria.

In certain societies in the past, the family cycle started with pre-marital pregnancies, rather than with marriage. The school-age stages were not as significant as the commencement of work of each child, and there was a distinct difference between families with male and families with female children. The "post-parental" family stage was also experienced differently in past societies, where due to demographic and economic reasons, long periods of retirement were not available to the majority of the population. Nor do the sociological schemes discussed above make allowance for the presence or absence of strangers in the household. The same holds true for kin interaction and the presence of kin inside the household. The current model is based on the assumption that the modern nuclear family functions in isolation. Although historical data has already confirmed the fact that only about ten to fifteen per cent of all urban families were extended, this percentage is still significant enough to justify the staging of the family cycle in accordance with the degree of interaction of the nuclear family with its kin members.

From a methodological point of view, the developmental approach will require increased reliance on two techniques in addition to cross-sectional analysis: 1) the tracing of families from one census to another and through city directories and vital records (namely, longitudinal record linkage); 2) the application of family reconstitution methods to nineteenth-century family studies. While longitudinal record linkages have been attempted by several historians of nineteenth-century family patterns, family reconstitution has been employed only by historians of the Colonial family. The presence of large mobile urban populations has intimidated historians from employing family reconstitution, since they feared it would be biased in favor of stable populations. This same bias applies, however, to studies of Colonial families, yet we have accepted family reconstitution for the Colonial period as adequately representative.

The methodological problems of both longitudinal record linkage and family reconstitution have been by no means resolved. In prevailing studies even cohort analysis and cross-sectional analysis have not been exploited to the full extent. Where the scarcity of data for complete record linkages seems forbidding, cross-sectional analysis could be used for infer patterns of the family cycle. This is true of Anderson's work on Lancashire, Berkner's work on Austrian villagers, Modell's work on migration, and Hareven's work on Boston.[15] The absence of a developmental approach to the historical study of the family is not merely the result of lack of methods and sources, but rather of lack of sensitivity to developmental questions.

Some exploration of the broader social significance of this approach follows the discussion of the conceptual and methodological problems involved in the historical study of the family cycle.

The life cycle approach could considerably broaden our understanding of the relationship of family process to other processes of social change. A study of the entire family cycle allows for the differentiation of two types of historical time: "family" time and "social" time. Family time designates such changes in the family cycle as marriage, childbirth, maturation, and leaving home. Although these processes and practices are not unaffected by external factors, they also follow internal rhythms which are governed and timed by family traditions, family economics and a variety of social and psychological conditions internal to the family. Social time, on the other hand, designates changing institutional conditions in the larger society, namely: occupational structure, migration, settlement patterns and changing policies and legislation governing family behavior.

Historians have generally assumed a standard correlation between family time and social time, and reductionist approaches have attempted to establish cause and effect relationships between the two. It is my contention, however, that family time is autonomous in certain areas. Historical changes in the family are slower than in other social institutions, and the accepted historical "stages" and "periods" in the study of Western society may or may not fit historical change in the family. The next assignment for social and cultural historians, particularly for family historians, should be the sorting of the relationship between family time and social time, family process and social process.

The need for such a reassessment is particularly evident in the study of the relationship between the family and social change, where historians have fallen into the trap of viewing familial or societal processes (e.g., urbanization, industrialization, migration) as dependent or as independent variables interchangeably. As a result, "the family" is treated either as an active agent or as a passive agent.[16] The family cycle approach, on the other hand, suggests a much more complex and dynamic set of relationships. The family (even the same individual family) can be an active agent at one stage of its cycle and a passive agent at another stage, just as it can switch from passive to active roles and vice versa in response to different societal conditions. Families with several children of working age at home would respond differently to the process of industrialization than families without children, or than the same family would five years later, after the children had left home.

Family "breakdown" has been subject to the demonology of the theories of "social disorganization", and has been generally interpreted as the result of pressures of urban life or migration. Several analyses of divorce cohorts in the nineteenth century show, however, that divorce, like marriage, was age-specific and was characteristic of certain stages of the life cycle. Individuals involved in family breakdown at one point in time, were found in stable family situations at another time.[17] In the study of migration and immigration, the family cycle approach will isolate those points in time when families are most open to migration, or those stages in the life cycle when individuals are most prone to abandon family ties or to postpone family formation and to migrate, or conversely, when individuals had to migrate in order to form family ties, or to maintain or complete their existing families.[18]

When exploring the relationship between societal change and family change, we cannot afford to keep one of these variables constant, while analyzing the other. We must assume instead that both family process and larger societal process are in constant motion. We must sort, therefore, the specific points of interaction between the two, before any broad generalizations about the "impact" of one or the other can be derived. The family cycle provides an adequate analytical category for this approach, because its stages are the points of interaction between individual time, family time and social time. It is precisely in this area that history and sociology of the family come together.

The family cycle offers a meaningful framework for the correlation of general demographic trends (mortality, nuptiality and fertility) to the patterns of individual family and household structure. At present, aggregate demographic analysis and the individual analysis of family and household are pursued independently of each other, while in the reality of family life, they are inseparable. "The changes that influence the demographic variable", Irene Taueber points out, "do so largely through the intermediation of the family. Marriage practices, family formation and family limitation practices are all essential determinants of fertility patterns and demographic transitions, and must be brought to bear on each other."[19]

On the other end of the spectrum of family history, the family cycle approach could provide a framework for the integration of demographic and quantitative data with the social, cultural and psychological information on family relations and on decisions affecting demographic behavior. It could rescue the entire area of the "qualitative" study of family from its current "limbo", because it provides the framework for the interpretation of "quantitative" analysis with "qualitative" statements of family roles and family behavior. Specifically, it could help delineate cognitive stages of the family cycle from normative and behavioral stages. Do the stages of the familial cycle defined by sociologists and historians merely serve as analytical tools designed to systematize seemingly disorderly data on human behavior, or do they reflect the behavioral reality of the families studied? And to what extent were these categories of family development perceived by the families that experienced them? What were the most important stages of transition in the family cycle and how were they experienced and articulated by the families going through them? How were they related to societal norms of familial behavior? It is precisely in the area of these questions that history, sociology, ethnography and psychology come together. Since the definition of family roles is specifically related to different stages in the individual or family life cycle, the approach suggested here could result in weaving together important aspects of the historical study of the family, which are now being studied in isolation.

Résumé

Le cycle de la vie familiale dans la perspective historique

Cet article étudie les principes de la sociologie du cycle de la vie familiale et leur possibilité d'application à une étude historique de la famille. Il cherche aussi à démontrer comment l'étude historique du cycle de la vie peut contribuer de façon importante à la sociologie de la famille.

On propose ici une conception de la famille étudiée en tant que processus, plutôt que comme unité statique à l'intérieur de certaines périodes de temps. Cette conception est basée d'une part sur l'affirmation que les individus traversent une variété de modèles familiaux et de structures de ménage au long de leur cycle de vie individuel et d'autre part que les familles et les ménages élaborent différents types de structures, d'organisations et de relations qui sont généralement obscurcis dans l'approche "instantanée". L'article corrobore ces affirmations théoriques avec des données historiques à partir de deux études de cas aux U.S.A.; l'un pour Boston (Massachussets) au 19e siècle et l'autre pour Manchester (New-Hampshire) au 20e siècle. Cette approche du cycle familial est d'une importance cruciale pour ceux qui sont intéressés par l'étude de changements sociaux, puisque la variété des étapes du développement individuel et familial du cycle de la vie sont intimement liés aux changements historiques.

Une approche développementaliste des études sur la famille au 19e siècle exige un cadre conceptuel nouveau et une méthodologie nouvelle. L'approche du cycle familial ne remplace pas seulement la dimension structurale généralement utilisée par une unité d'analyse temporelle. Les historiens qui s'orienteront vers le tracé longitudinal, l'enregistrement de liaisons ou une analyse en coupe, sans développer un schéma conceptuel, passeront d'une catégorie mécanique à l'autre.

Durant les prochaines années, il sera nécessaire pour les historiens d'isoler les variétés de cycles familiaux parmi les différents segments de population vivant dans des conditions historiques différentes.

D'un point de vue méthodologique, l'approche développementale exigera une confiance accrue dans deux techniques s'ajoutant aux analyses diachroniques: 1) le repérage des familles d'un recensement à un autre, à travers les recensements et les actes d'état civil (c'est-à-dire des techniques de couplage des données); 2) l'application de méthodes de reconstitution de la famille aux études sur la famille au 19e siècle.

Le cycle familial offre un cadre pertinent pour lier aux mouvements démographiques globaux (mortalité, nuptialité et fertilité) les modèles de structure de la famille individuelle et des ménages.

L'approche du cycle de la famille pourrait élargir considérablement notre compréhension des relations existant entre les processus du changement familial et ceux des changements sociaux. Une étude du cycle familial permettra de différencier deux types de temps historique: le temps "familial" et le temps "social".

NOTES

1. For a discussion of the development of the history of the family as a field, see Tamara K. Hareven (1971), "The history of the family as an interdisciplinary field", *Journal of Interdisciplinary History*, II/2, Autumn.
2. Paul C. Glick (1957), *American Families*, New York; (1947), "The family cycle", *American Sociological Review*, 12, April: 164–174; (1955), "The life cycle of the family", *Marriage and Family Living*, 18, February: 3–9; Reuben Hill (1970), *Family Development in Three Generations*, Cambridge, Mass.; E. M. Duvall (1957), *Family Development*, Chicago; Roy H. Rodgers (1962), *Improvements in the Construction and Analysis of Family and Life Cycle Categories*, Kalamazoo, Michigan; Peter R. Uhlenberg (1968), "A study of cohort life cycles: cohorts of native born Massachusetts women, 1830–1920", *Population Studies*, XXIII/3, November.
3. See John Demos (1970), *A Little Commonwealth: Family Life in Plymouth Colony*, Oxford,; Philip Greven, Jr. (1970), *Four Generations: Population, Land and Family in Colonial Andover, Massachusetts*, Ithaca, N.Y.; Daniel Scott Smith (1972), "The demographic history of Colonial New England", *Journal of Economic History*, 32, March: 180–183.
4. Richard Sennett (1969), *Families Against the City*, Cambridge, Mass., is the first example of this approach.
5. For examples of work in progress see studies by Stuart Blumin on Kingston, N.Y., Michael Katz for Hamilton, Ontario, Tamara Hareven for Boston, Lawrence Glasco for Buffalo, N.Y. Among these, Katz has compared age cohorts at several

census intervals, but has not traced families longitudinally. Glasco and Hareven have looked at varieties of urban family structures as life cycle specifics, but this approach should not be confused with the one advocated here, namely the analysis of the entire family cycle as a unit. Michael Katz (1972), "The Canadian Social History Project: Interim Report No. 4", The Ontario Institute for Studies in Education, Toronto University, mimeograph; Lawrence Glasco, "Family patterns of ethnic groups in Buffalo, N.Y., 1850–1870"; Stuart Blumin, "Rip Van Winkle's grandchildren: family structure in the Hudson Valley"; and Tamara K. Hareven, "Family structure and social change in nineteenth-century Boston". All these are manuscript essays prepared for the Clark University Conference on "The family: social structure and social change, April, 1972", to be published.

The difficulty of tracing individuals through vital records and directories is compounded by the high rate of population turnover and by social bias of directory listings. On this problem see Peter Knights (1971), *The Plain People of Boston*, New York. Another problem is in the absence of a reliable scheme of classification of individuals' relationships to the head of the household. The 1880 census is the only one that actually states this relationship.

6. Peter Laslett and Richard Wall (eds.) (1972), *Household and Family in Past Time*, Cambridge, England. See particularly Laslett's preface.
7. Talcott Parsons (1965), "The normal American family", in Bernard Farber, *et al.*, *Man and Civilization: The Family's Search for Survival*, New York.
8. Richard Sennett, for example, did not differentiate clearly between households and families and emphasized the intense loneliness of the nuclear family – thus ignoring the presence of kin members outside the household. See *Families Against the City*, where the debate over family adjustment to urban life rests on the difference between "nuclear" and "extended" households in a population group where extended families constituted only ten percent of the families studied.
9. Philip Greven and Lutz Berkner have emphasized these distinctions in their respective studies of Colonial Andover and rural Austria. Greven, *Four Generations*, and Berkner (1972), "The stem family and the developmental cycle of the peasant household: an 18th century Austrian example", *The American Historical Review*, April.
10. William Goode (1963), *Family Patterns and World Revolution*, New York. The sociological approaches and tools in longitudinal family research are eloquently discussed in Reuben Hill, "Methodological issues in family development research", in *Family Process*, 3/1: 186–205.
11. The Boston data is based on an analysis of family and residential patterns of approximately 6,000 individuals in nineteenth-century Boston, drawn by household from the 1880 census and traced back to 1850 through city directories, earlier censuses and vital records. For preliminary analyses of this data see Hareven (1972), "Family structure and social change in nineteenth-century Boston".
12. For a further elaboration on this theme, see John Modell and Tamara K. Hareven (1973), "Urbanization and the malleable household: an examination of boarding and lodging in American families", *Journal of Marriage and the Family*, August.
13. The Manchester data is based on preliminary findings from an analysis of reconstituted career and family patterns of 2,000 industrial laborers, representing different ethnic groups in Manchester, New Hampshire, 1910–1940. The unique feature of this study is the availability of a set of individual employee files which the Amoskeag Corporation's Employment Bureau had kept for each worker over his entire career. The combinations of these records with vital records, tenement rental contracts, and city directories allow the reconstruction of work careers, family cycles, as well as an exploration of kin relations outside the household.

14. Reuben Hill, "Methodological issues in family development"; Duvall, *Family Development*.
15. Michael Anderson (1971), *Family Structure in Nineteenth-Century Lancashire*, Cambridge, England; Berkner (1972), "The stem family...", *The American Historical Review*, April: 338–418; John Modell (1971), "Family and fertility on the Indiana frontier, 1820", *American Quarterly*, 23: 615–634; Hareven, "Family structure in nineteenth-century Boston".
16. The most persuasive statement in the role of the family in the process of industrialization is in Michael Anderson, *Family Structure in Nineteenth-Century Lancashire*. See also Goode, *World Revolutions*.
17. William H. Mulligan (1972), "Divorce in Worcester County, Mass.", unpublished seminar paper, Clark University.
18. The Manchester data cited above is most revealing on this subject. See also Anderson, *Lancashire*, and Sune Ackerman (1972), "Migration and family formation in a growing industrial district", research report from the Center for Migration Studies, University of Uppsala; Virginia McLaughlin (1971), "Working class immigrant families: first generation Italians in Buffalo, New York", Paper delivered at the Annual Meetings of the Organization of American Historians, New Orleans.
19. Irene Taueber (1969), "Continuity, change, and transition in population and family: interrelations and priorities in research", in *The Family in Transition*, National Institute of Health: 317.

19. Individual life cycles and family cycles. A comparison of perspectives*

JOËL M. HALPERN

This paper seeks to relate changing individual life cycles to changing cycles of family development. My data refer specifically to Yugoslavia (although it is hoped that some of the points made will have more general applicability). Within Yugoslavia primary reference is to a village in central Serbia which I have studied intermittently over the past twenty years, but comparative data will be presented from other regions as well.[1]

Over the past century in central Serbia, in common with many other regions of Europe, there has been a dramatic decrease both in mortality and in fertility (Table 1). The detailed implications of these commonplaces are only now beginning to get the attention they deserve. Also, it now seems clear that some earlier simplified assumptions associated with the processes of modernization and accompanying urbanization as these relate to the shift from the large extended family to the small nuclear one are now seriously being questioned and reevaluated.[2] We are beginning to come to terms with the implications that demographic changes have for social structure.

What seems clear is that for the fewer children born to individual mothers in this century, there are more options for kinship relationships and general life experiences. In the last century the larger number of deaths in infancy, early childhood and in childbirth, as well as the smaller chances of survival into the 60s and 70s were some of the restrictive parameters conditioning the development of family life and structuring the nature of family cycles.

* The research on which this paper is based was supported by grants from the National Science Foundation, the National Institute of Mental Health and the Research Committee of the University of Massachusetts. This paper is intended as an initial research report.

Table 1. *Fertility, mortality and rate of natural increase per 1000, 1880–1961: Central Serbia, Kragujevac district and Orasac village, compared*

	Fertility			Mortality			Rate of increase		
Years*	S	K	O	S	K	O	S	K	O
1880–1890		46.0			24.0			22.0	
1884–1895			39.5			22.2			17.3
1900–1910			37.5			20.5			17.2
1901–1910	38.3	38.1		23.1	21.1		15.2	17.0	
1921–1930	37.0	30.1		20.5	16.7		16.5	13.4	
1921–1931			36.4			15.6			20.8
1931–1940	28.8	24.2		13.7	15.1		10.9	13.3	
1948–1953			24.5			11.6			12.9
1951	24.5			13.1			11.4		
1961	17.2			8.4			8.8		

* According to years for which data from each of the 3 areas are available; S = Serbia, K = Kragujevac, O = Orasac

Sources *Prirodno kretanje stanovnistva Srbije od 1863–1954*, Zavod za Statistiku Narodna Republika Srbije, Beograd, 1957, prikaz 20: 21, 23, 25.
Vladimir Simeunovic, Stanovnistro Jugoslavije i Socijalistickih Republika 1921–1961, Zavod za Statistiku, Studije, Analize i Prikazi, 22, 1964: 43, 46.
Joel M. Halpern (1956), *Social and Cultural Change in a Serbian Village*, New Haven, Human Relations Area Files: 117.

Restrictive parameters on familial cycles

As an example of the consequences of restrictive parameters in terms of their effect on the nature of extended household composition, one can refer to the four-generation household which appears to have been a rarity a hundred years ago, in part because of the comparative infrequency of 60- to 80-year-olds, assuming twenty years to the generation (Tables 2, 3A and 3B).[3] In this respect the data from Orasac are suggestive of broader trends, for the increased frequency of the four-generation household must be taken together with the overall decline in household size leading to the emphasis on vertical as opposed to horizontal extension (Table 4). It seems, at least in the case of Orasac and the surrounding villages, that the households were large in great part because of the number of young children and particularly because of the frequency of the categories daughter and son, when households are analyzed with respect to their kin ties to the household head (see Table 5).[4]

Table 2. *Number and percentage of generations in households headed by males,* for selected census years, by selected villages*

	Number and percentage of generations										Total
Year and village	1	%	2	%	3	%	4	%	5	%	
1863 – Arandjelovac	114	54.0	91	43.1	4	1.9	2	.9	—	—	211
1863 – Banja	37	20.0	98	53.0	48	26.0	2	1.1	—	—	183
1863 – Bukovik	22	20.8	66	62.3	17	16.0	1	.9	—	—	106
1863 – Kopljare	6	6.7	64	71.1	19	21.1	1	1.1	—	—	90
1863 – Orasac	5	3.9	78	60.5	46	35.7	—	—	—	—	129
1863 – Stojnik	32	19.3	103	62.0	31	18.7	—	—	—	—	166
1863 – Topola	30	12.2	115	64.1	57	23.3	1	.4	—	—	245
1948 – Bobovac	34	14.3	90	37.8	92	38.7	22	9.2	—	—	238
1961 – Bobovac	58	21.8	66	24.8	105	39.5	36	13.5	1	.4	266
1948 – Lekenik	48	19.9	116	48.1	70	29.0	7	2.9	—	—	241
1961 – Lekenik	115	28.5	198	49.1	75	18.6	14	3.5	1	.2	403
1961 – Orasac	57	13.7	140	33.7	187	45.1	31	7.5	—	—	415
1931 – Slano	31	16.6	97	51.9	59	31.6	—	—	—	—	187
1948 – Slano	26	11.7	113	50.9	80	36.0	3	1.4	—	—	222
1961 – Slano	42	16.1	126	48.3	90	34.5	3	1.1	—	—	261
1961 – Veleste	23	6.0	206	53.4	151	39.1	6	1.6	—	—	386
1961 – Zupca	32	13.7	174	74.4	27	11.5	1	.4	—	—	234

* Households headed by males are used here, rather than all households, in order to render data from the 20th century more comparable to 19th century data, since there were virtually no female household heads recorded in 1863.

As the data from Orasac make clear, the husband-wife tie has tended to replace the father-child tie as the one of greatest frequency.[5] This is related to decreasing household size, for in more recent times fewer children are born and fewer remain at home. If we look at the category mother in age-specific terms, we see that this has significant implications for the duration or the potential duration of the husband-wife tie. Holding the factor of divorce constant for Orasac (in the case of this Serbian village it is still a minor factor) then, for example, the potential for a couple to experience 5 decades of life together seems progressively more likely as we approach our own time.

Thus, if we have fewer widows or widowers and more long-term married couples and comparatively fewer children produced by each mother, these parameters are already significant in influencing the kind of household cyclical development we might expect. But if we take as a model the kind of patrilineal, patrilocal and patriarchical culture that has existed in Serbia in the 19th century with the *zadruga* as the ideal prototype, we can already see the ways in which these demographic changes influence the

Table 3. *Percentage age structure of the population, 1863–1961**

A. Central Serbia and Orasac village, compared

	1921	1931	1948	1953	1961	
Age	Serbia	Serbia	Serbia	Serbia	Serbia	Orasac
0–19	46.2	43.7	41.4	37.8	34.7	30.8
20–39	28.8	32.3	29.2	31.1	34.9	31.0
40–59	16.5	16.7	20.9	22.2	20.0	21.5
60+	8.5	7.3	8.5	8.9	10.5	16.7

Source: Simeunovic, *op. cit.*, p. 102.

B. Kingdom of Serbia and Orasac village, compared

Age	1863 Orasac	1890 Orasac	1900 Serbia	1953 Orasac	1961 Orasac
0–10	42.3	31.8	29.6	19.7	17.7
11–20	20.5	23.6	24.1	17.6	14.9
21–30	17.4	15.0	15.8	18.9	13.2
31–40	10.2	12.0	11.9	9.1	17.0
41–50	5.0	8.0	8.5	13.8	8.6
51–60	3.6	6.0	5.6	10.6	13.1
61–70	1.0	3.0	2.9	6.7	9.4
71+	—	.6	1.5	3.6	5.2

Sources: *Statisticki Godisnjak, Kraljevina Srbije 1878–1899*, Beograd, Vol. 4, 1902: 55; and J. Halpern and David Anderson (1970), The Zadruga, a century of change", *Anthropologica*, N.S., XII, 1,: 86.

* National census data from the late 19th century uses different age categories from later surveys, hence the breakdown of this table to represent both systems.

extended family structure. Death and birth appear to have been major determinants in family cycle formation 100 years ago, while today demographic changes are reflected in the altering focus of dyadic relationships, especially that of husband and wife. One may grant that the coming into prominence of the husband-wife tie, in a society which formerly had a primary agnatic focus on the father-son and brother-brother tie, is as much a matter of changing ideology as of mere frequency; still, it is important to consider the effect that raising fewer children and living longer in a smaller extended family unit has had on husband-wife relationships.

Year and village			Size of household % in each category												
			1	2	3	4	5	6	7	8	9	10	Total	Mean*	Median
1863	Banja	pop.	2.07	1.90	4.92	3.80	7.33	10.35	13.29	10.35	9.32	36.67	1159	7.61	8
		hh.	12.97	5.95	10.27	5.95	9.19	10.81	11.89	8.11	6.49	18.38	185	5.81	6
	Bukovik	pop.	2.04	2.72	5.09	8.83	11.88	21.39	11.88	4.07	4.58	27.50	589	7.27	6
		hh.	10.28	7.48	9.35	12.15	13.08	19.63	9.35	2.80	2.80	13.08	107	5.29	5
	Kopljare	pop.	.44	.88	1.32	5.86	7.32	7.91	12.30	15.23	5.27	43.48	683	9.29	8
		hh.	3.33	3.33	3.33	11.11	11.11	10.00	13.33	14.44	4.44	25.56	90	6.84	7
	Orasac	pop.	.09	.37	1.39	3.70	5.55	8.32	11.65	12.57	7.49	48.89	1082	8.36	9
		hh.	.76	1.53	3.82	7.63	9.16	11.45	13.74	12.98	6.87	32.06	131	7.43	8
	Stojnik	pop.	1.48	2.17	3.55	8.29	12.34	16.58	10.37	9.48	7.11	28.63	1013	7.99	7
		hh.	8.38	6.59	6.59	11.98	14.97	16.77	8.98	7.19	4.79	13.77	167	5.66	6
	Topola	pop.	.68	2.61	2.42	6.96	9.01	12.00	12.62	13.92	10.07	29.71	1609	8.06	8
		hh.	4.40	8.40	5.20	11.20	11.60	12.80	11.60	11.20	7.20	16.40	250	6.16	6
1948	Bobovac	pop.	.96	6.76	13.90	18.24	20.59	11.47	7.21	7.65	5.29	7.94	1360	5.39	5
		hh.	4.19	14.84	20.32	20.0	18.06	8.39	4.52	4.19	2.58	2.90	310	4.33	4
1961	Bobovac	pop.	2.48	10.56	12.38	18.15	23.51	21.78	6.93	1.98	2.23	—	1212	4.66	5
		hh.	9.43	20.13	15.72	17.30	17.92	13.84	3.77	.94	.94	—	318	3.81	4
1948	Lekenik	pop.	2.33	11.99	15.99	22.65	19.57	14.99	4.66	4.66	2.25	.92	1201	4.52	4
		hh.	8.54	21.95	19.51	20.73	14.33	9.15	2.44	2.13	.91	.30	328	3.66	3.5
1961	Lekenik	pop.	3.98	13.59	19.66	22.54	19.29	13.59	4.72	.98	1.65	—	1633	4.14	4
		hh.	13.24	22.61	21.79	18.74	12.83	7.54	2.24	.41	.61	—	491	3.33	3
1961	Orasac	pop.	1.14	6.52	9.49	15.03	20.27	22.84	14.19	4.75	2.67	3.11	2023	5.34	5
		hh.	5.08	14.57	14.13	16.78	18.10	17.0	9.05	2.65	1.32	1.32	453	4.46	4
1931	Slano	pop.	.90	2.79	5.16	6.56	8.20	14.75	11.48	15.74	12.54	21.89	1220	7.16	8
		hh.	5.31	8.70	10.14	9.66	10.14	14.49	9.66	12.08	8.21	11.59	207	5.84	6
1948	Slano	pop.	2.71	4.03	8.75	10.83	16.67	15.0	13.61	10.0	4.37	14.07	1440	6.28	6
		hh.	12.71	9.36	13.71	12.71	15.72	12.04	9.36	6.02	2.34	6.02	299	4.69	5
1961	Slano	pop.	2.39	5.82	9.84	15.81	16.41	16.55	13.57	10.74	4.70	4.18	1341	5.60	5
		hh.	10.70	12.71	14.38	16.72	14.72	12.37	8.76	6.02	2.01	1.67	299	4.38	4
1961	Veleste	pop.	.48	1.03	3.85	4.25	10.08	11.65	14.88	12.90	7.26	33.64	2729	7.60	8
		hh.	3.31	3.56	8.91	7.38	13.99	13.49	14.76	11.20	5.60	17.81	393	6.39	6
1961	Zupca	pop.	1.29	3.62	9.83	18.28	19.40	16.55	10.26	8.28	4.66	7.84	1160	5.66	5
		hh.	6.05	8.47	15.32	21.37	18.15	12.90	6.85	4.84	2.42	3.63	248	4.67	4

* The mean is somewhat lower than that recorded in the author's "Town and countryside in Serbia in the nineteenth century: social and household structure as reflected in the 1863 census" (in *Household and Family in Past Time*, Peter Laslett and Richard Wall (eds.) (1972), Cambridge, Cambridge University Press: 409–417) because the 10 & + categories are collapsed in this table, e.g., household size relative to population is 8.3 for all 1863 villages, with 10.0 for Orasac and 9.3 for Kopljare, to cite the two highest.

Duration of father-son ties

It does not require great exercise of the imagination to visualize the greater potential for conflict if these ties were of long duration within a larger extended family. What is suggested is that two married brothers and their families, the basic units in the traditional ideal *zadruga* type, could co-exist for a longer period in the mid-19th century given the fact that the death of the father could be expected within one generation and not within two. Or, reciprocally, a father could exercise greater control over his married sons while they were in their 20s with young children, while when they reached their 40s and had marriageable children there would be a tendency toward fission. The data from the census of 1863 seem to suggest that there were simply not enough old men around to force decisions of fission, for that reason. That is, if a question of division came up, it did so after the father's death.

Less than a third of household heads were over age 50 in the 1863 census of Orasac, and the percentage is less for the other villages and towns of this period. The extended family ideal, the *zadruga* of married brothers and their families plus their parents, or a minimum of about eight people, was a setting participated in by half the population at a given point in time (49.46% of 6,650 persons in 1,149 households analyzed in the 1863 census data available lived in size 7 households or under).

Household size and composition

In 1863 only 10 out of 131 households in Orasac (7.63%) had 2 or more daughters-in-law[6] while 66% had no brothers, although 60% of the households in Orasac at that time contained relatives beyond the nuclear family.[7] But giving statistics in terms of households can be somewhat misleading, for what seems more important than frequency of households as such is the nature of particular kinds of family experiences to which the population as a whole was exposed; thus the mean and median household sizes are always larger when reference is made primarily to numbers of people rather than numbers of households. In Orasac in 1863 approximately 49% of the population lived in size 10 or larger households, and these households were only about a third of all households. Conversely, in Orasac in 1961 a little over 1% of the population lived alone, but this was more than 5% of the total households (see Table 4). These statistics, with their primary reference to households, do, however, provide a welcome corrective to the ideal type descriptions so often seen in discussing the extended family. One learns a great deal about the extended family from many studies, but one is rarely given sufficient information in order to correlate a selected case study with the life experiences of the population considered, to determine whether it was a common experience or an ideal pattern participated in by relatively few.[8]

In Orasac in 1863 almost 60% of the households contained relatives beyond the nuclear family. Only 252 people out of a population of 1,082 lived in a nuclear family setting. However, the majority of those in the extended family were actually the core nuclear family. Thus, out of 685 who lived in extended family households 419 were the head, his wife or children. It must also be borne in mind that doing analysis from a set of census data and projecting cyclical variations onto it through an analysis of different sets of relationships, while the focus of this paper does necessarily leave out the individual dynamics. A case where one proceeds to map out an individual's life experiences in terms of the number of different household types to which he belonged in his lifetime provides a perspective different from that of the family cycle view.[9]

It would seem reasonable to define a "different" household as one changed through the death or departure of an adult or the birth of a child, particularly a first child. But it would be necessary to restrict the definition of the role of births, particularly when dealing with large households in the 19th century, when a half dozen or more children were not unusual.[10]

Most ethnographic monographs focus on general typologies based on specific case histories or aggregate census data but neglect the complexities of a series of individual experiences within a family cycle or series of family cycles.

If birth and death are seen as biological forms of entry and exist and marriage as a volitional form of entry, with divorce as a volitional form of exit, the consanguine tie of out-marrying women can be seen as a relationship whose potential for reactivation is always present, even if cultural values or individual circumstances might make this unlikely at a given point in time. Finally, there are, of course, artificially extended kin ties such as adoption. These are basic considerations to be kept in mind in viewing the data presented here.

Table 5. *Age-specific kin ties, under 20 years, for selected census years, by selected villages**

Year and village	Ages	Head N	Head %	Son N	Son %	Daughter N	Daughter %	Brother N	Brother %	Sister N	Sister %	Grandson N	Grandson %	Grand-daughter N	Grand-daughter %	Daughter-in-law N	Daughter-in-law %	Bro's son N	Bro's son %	Bro's daughter N	Bro's daughter %	Wife N	Wife %
1863 Arandjelovac	Total[a]	219		104		92		13		8		3								1		101	
	0–9[b]	3	1.4	67	64.4	73	79.3	5	38.5	4	50.0	3	100.0							—		—	
	10–19	24	11.0	31	29.8	19	20.7	1	7.7	4	50.0	—								1	100.0	1	1.0
Banja	Total	185		227		195		92		50		41		38		40		41		34		130	
	0–9	—		114	50.2	113	57.9	11	12.0	13	26.0	35	85.4	32	84.2	—		28	68.3	22	64.7	—	
	10–19	15	8.1	69	30.4	74	37.9	38	41.3	32	64.0	6	14.6	6	15.8	1	2.5	11	26.8	12	35.3	1	0.8
Bukovik	Total	107		119		109		41		23		9		6		6		34		19		75	
	0–9	2	1.9	73	61.3	78	71.6	12	29.3	4	17.4	7	77.8	4	66.7	—		23	67.6	16	84.2	—	
	10–19	13	12.1	41	34.5	31	28.4	10	24.4	18	78.3	1	11.1	2	33.3	1	16.7	8	23.5	3	15.8	4	5.3
Kopljare	Total	90		153		131		50		36		15		9		14		25		25		76	
	0–9	1	1.1	79	51.6	85	64.9	12	24.0	10	27.8	10	66.7	9	100.0	—		16	64.0	19	76.0	—	
	10–19	8	8.9	56	36.6	44	33.6	16	32.0	23	63.9	3	20.0	—		1	7.1	5	20.0	6	24.0	2	2.6
Orasac	Total	131		257		203		68		25		56		39		50		43		46		—	
	0–9	—		119	46.3	127	62.6	6	8.8	4	16.0	48	85.7	36	92.3	—		36	83.7	35	76.1		
	10–19	5	3.8	79	30.7	73	36.0	18	26.5	20	80.0	8	14.3	3	7.7	2	4.0	3	7.0	11	23.9		
Stojnik	Total	167		193		169		82		38		22		14		25		49		31		135	
	0–9	—		103	53.4	105	62.1	11	13.4	10	26.3	20	90.0	13	92.9	—		21	42.9	22	71.0	—	
	10–19	14	8.4	62	32.1	63	37.3	31	37.8	23	60.5	2	9.1	1	7.1	3	12.0	21	42.9	8	25.8	6	4.4
Topola	Total	250		390		312		91		40		38		38		50		62		48		201	
	0–9	—		203	52.1	183	58.7	7	7.7	4	10.0	35	92.1	38	100.0	—		39	62.9	33	68.8	—	
	10–19	11	4.4	132	33.8	125	40.1	35	38.5	28	70.0	3	7.9	—		5	10.0	22	35.5	15	31.2	4	2.0
1948 Bobovac	Total	310		231		119		8		6		90		90		146		8		7		225	
	0–9	—		35	15.2	28	23.5	—		—		52	57.8	50	55.6	—		1	12.5	1	14.3	—	
	10–19	2	0.6	85	36.8	68	57.1	6	75.0	2	33.3	29	32.2	28	31.1	8	5.5	4	50.0	4	57.1	3	1.3
1961 Bobovac	Total	318		188		86		—	—	—		62		49		89		4		6		252	
	0–9	—		37	19.7	32	37.2					34	54.8	26	53.1	—		2	50.0	5	83.3	—	
	10–19	—		71	37.8	39	45.3					22	35.5	18	36.7	11	12.4	—		—		3	1.2
1948 Lekenik	Total	328		208		181		—		4		44		36		57		2		1		—	
	0–9	—		44	21.2	53	29.3			—		21	47.7	22	61.1	—		—		1	100.0		
	10–19	2	.6	84	40.4	84	46.4			1	25.0	16	36.4	13	36.1	5	8.8	2	100.0	—			

Year and village	Ages	Head N	Head %	Son N	Son %	Daughter N	Daughter %	Brother N	Brother %	Sister N	Sister %	Grandson N	Grandson %	Grand-daughter N	Grand-daughter %	Daughter-in-law N	Daughter-in-law %	Bro's son N	Bro's son %	Bro's daughter N	Bro's daughter %	Wife N	Wife %
1961 Lekenik	Total	491		286		218		3		5		53		41		50		—		—		358	
	0–9	—		100	35.0	89	40.8	—		—		35	66.0	29	70.7	—						—	
	10–19	2	.4	92	32.2	88	40.4	2	66.7	1	20.0	16	30.2	10	24.4	4	8.0					2	.6
1961 Orasac	Total	453		350		194		11		11		163		152		160		3		3		367	
	0–9	—		60	17.1	66	34.0	—		—		86	52.8	88	57.9	—		—		—		—	
	10–19	—		96	27.4	91	46.9	1	9.1	3	27.3	54	33.1	45	29.6	5	3.1	—		1	33.3	3	.8
1931 Slano	Total	203		277		222		87		58		36		30		—		1		11		—	
	0–9	—		67	24.2	65	29.3	—		—		31	86.1	28	93.3			—		6	54.5		
	10–19	1	.5	76	27.4	71	32.0	4	4.6	7	12.1	5	13.9	2	6.7			—		3	27.3		
1948 Slano	Total	299		301		271		21		52		48		42		—		10		6		—	
	0–9	—		69	22.9	79	29.2	—		—		25	52.1	26	61.9			6	60.0	2	33.3		
	10–19	2	.7	129	42.9	106	39.1	2	9.5	4	7.7	16	33.3	15	35.7			2	20.0	2	33.3		
1961 Slano	Total	299		269		189		20				56		60		—		4		1			
	0–9	—		52	19.3	44	23.3	—				34	60.7	40	66.7			1	25.0	—			
	10–19	1	.3	84	31.2	78	41.3	1	5.0			16	28.6	17	28.3			1	25.0	1	100.0		
1961 Veleste	Total	393		698		433		95		13		204		156		173		59		39		330	
	0–9	—		256	36.7	220	50.8	—		3	23.1	156	76.5	121	77.6	2	1.2	42	71.2	28	71.8	1	.3
	10–19	3	.8	188	26.9	195	45.0	11	11.6	7	53.8	42	20.6	34	21.8	13	7.5	8	13.6	10	25.6	2	.6
1961 Zupca	Total	248		336		284		4		2		14		14		31		—		—		206	
	0–9	—		137	40.8	125	44.0	—		—		13	92.9	13	92.9	—						3	1.5
	10–19	—		103	30.7	116	40.8	1	25.0	1	50.0	—		1	7.1	5	16.1					—	

* Great-grandchildren categories are not included here since great-grandchildren were essentially non-existent in the 1863 census and the situation was relatively infrequent in all villages. Most notable occurrences show up in 1948-Bobovac and 1961-Orasac. These data do not take into account the categories "mother" and "grandmother" and so understate the number of great-grandchildren relationships existing within a household.

a. Total number of individuals in this category for all age-groups.

b. This early age for household head presumably designates the heir and not actual authority.

Table 6. *Age specific kin ties, over 60 years, for selected census years, by selected villages*

Year and village		Ages	Head		Wife		Sister		Father		Mother		G-mother		Mo-in-law	
			N	%	N	%	N	%	N	%	N	%	N	%	N	%
1863	Arandjelovac	Total[a]	219		—		—		—		5		3		—	
		60–69	3	1.4							—		—			
		70–79	—								—		—			
		80 & +	—								—		—			
	Banja	Total	185		130		—		3		31		—		—	
		60–69	13	7.0	1	.8			—		—					
		70–79	3	1.6	—				1	33.3	1	3.2				
		80 & +	—		—				—		—					
	Bukovik	Total	107		75		—		—		13		—		—	
		60–69	3	2.8	1	1.3					4	30.8				
		70–79	—		—						2	15.4				
		80 & +	—		—						—					
	Kopljare	Total	90		—		—		—		18		3			
		60–69	4	4.4							3	16.7	2	66.7		
		70–79	—								2	11.1	—			
		80 & +	—								—		1	33.3		
	Orasac	Total	131		—		—		1		21		—		—	
		60–69	12	9.2					—		5	23.8				
		70–79	2	1.5					1	100.0	2	9.5				
		80 & +	—						—		—					
	Stojnik	Total	167		—		—		—		26		—		—	
		60–69	4	2.4							3	11.5				
		70–79	—								—					
		80 & +	—								—					
	Topola	Total	250		201						35		1		—	
		60–69	10	4.0	5	2.5					10	28.6	—			
		70–79	4	1.6	1	.5					3	8.6	—			
		80 & +	—		—						1	2.9	1	100.0		
1948	Bobovac	Total	310		225		6		8		67		8		3	
		60–69	36	11.6	24	10.7	1	16.7	2	25.0	19	28.4	4	50.0	1	33.3
		70–79	16	5.2	4	1.8	—		4	50.0	12	17.9	2	25.0	2	66.7
		80 & +	—		—		—		1	12.5	6	9.0	—			

Year and village		Ages	Head N	Head %	Wife N	Wife %	Sister N	Sister %	Father N	Father %	Mother N	Mother %	G-mother N	G-mother %	Mo-in-law N	Mo-in-law %
1961	Bobovac	Total	318		252		—		12		86		19		9	
		60–69	48	15.1	19	7.5			4	33.3	26	30.2	5	26.3	3	33.3
		70–79	9	2.8	2	.8			5	41.7	21	24.4	10	52.6	2	22.2
		80 & +	3	.9	1	.4			3	25.0	3	3.5	1	5.3	1	11.1
1948	Lekenik	Total	328		225		4		6		35		1		15	
		60–69	48	14.6	30	13.3	—		—		15	42.9	—		8	53.3
		70–79	18	5.5	2	.9	2	50.0	2	33.3	7	20.0	—		3	20.0
		80 & +	4	1.2	—		2	50.0	2	33.3	7	20.0	1	100.0	3	20.0
1961	Lekenik	Total	491		358		5		7		45		8		14	
		60–69	90	18.3	35	9.8	1	20.0	—		10	22.2	2	25.0	7	50.0
		70–79	21	4.3	8	2.2	—		5	71.4	18	40.0	6	75.0	4	28.6
		80 & +	6	1.2	—		—		1	14.3	7	15.6	—		2	14.3
1961	Orasac	Total	453		367		11		5		78		10		9	
		60–69	98	21.6	70	19.1	4	36.4	2	40.0	26	33.3	4	40.0	2	22.2
		70–79	44	9.7	21	5.7	—		2	40.0	24	30.8	5	50.0	2	22.2
		80 & +	11	2.4	—		—		—		7	9.0	1	10.0	2	22.2
1931	Slano	Total	203		165		58		3		34		—		2	
		60–69	49	24.1	27	16.4	4	6.9	1	33.3	11	32.4			—	
		70–79	30	14.8	10	6.1	—		2	66.7	11	32.4			1	50.0
		80 & +	1	.5	—		—		—		5	14.7			1	50.0
1948	Slano	Total	299		187		52		6		55		3		1	
		60–69	45	15.1	20	10.7	8	15.4	1	16.7	15	27.3	—		—	
		70–79	30	10.0	6	3.2	—		2	33.3	18	32.7	1	33.3	—	
		80 & +	12	4.4	1	.5	—		2	33.3	15	27.3	2	66.7	1	100.0
1961	Slano	Total	299		217		26		2		36		—		9	
		60–69	75	25.1	41	18.9	6	23.1	—		9	25.0			3	33.3
		70–79	23	7.7	9	4.1	2	7.7	1	50.0	13	36.1			2	22.2
		80 & +	14	4.7	2	.9	2	7.7	—		10	27.8			3	33.3
1961	Veleste	Total	393		330		—		2		71		3		1	
		60–69	61	15.5	26	7.9			—		27	38.0	1	33.3	1	100.0
		70–79	21	5.3	9	2.7			—		17	23.9	1	33.3	—	
		80 & +	10	2.6	1	.3			1	50.0	7	9.9	1	33.3	—	
1961	Zupca	Total	248		206		—		3		9		1		1	
		60–69	33	13.3	10	4.9			1	33.3	6	66.7			—	
		70–79	12	4.8	1	.5			1	33.3	1	11.1	1	100.0	1	100 .0
		80 & +	2	.8	—				—		—		—		—	

a. Total number of individuals in this category for all age groups.

Sons and household heads

A useful point of departure is the problem of longevity and its effect on the family cycle. Information can be gained by looking at age-specific kin ties at both ends of the life cycle (Tables 5 and 6), that is, the nature of kin relationships for those who are joining a household through birth and for those who are approaching the age of normal mortality and exit. Granting the imperfect nature of our comparative data, nevertheless certain contrasts between the mid-19th century and the mid-20th century from various cultural areas of Yugoslavia are readily apparent. In all the 1863 data the number of sons notably exceeds the number of household heads. In Zupca (1961), Slano (1931), and most notably in Veleste (1961), the number of sons continues to exceed the number of household heads. But even in Veleste, where the contemporary proportion is highest (about 1.8 proportion of sons as compared to household heads, opposed to 2.0 for Orasac in 1863), it still ranks below the 1863 figures.

The case of Slano is significant in that the data for 1948 marks something of a transitional point; here the number of sons barely exceeds the number of household heads (301 as opposed to 299), while by 1961 the situation had clearly been reversed. Age-specific kinship data for Orasac for 1928, 1948 and 1953 is not available, but a quantitative count of kinship designations is, and is comparable to the gross figures given in Table 5. By 1928 the number of household heads had already exceeded the number of sons but only by a ratio of 333 to 302; by 1948 the gap had widened proportionately from 495 to 391.

A number of factors are involved. First is the decline in the birth rate, so that fewer sons are born to each couple. Second, the migration of sons from the village in the post-war period, when opportunities were greater, has obviously played a role and is an unaccounted-for variable in our data. Third, multiple mature sons do not share the same household as formerly; contemporarily, only one mature son remaining with the father. Fourth, because of the increasing frequency of single person households or households of older married couples the position of household head does not imply a resident male heir with the same frequency as was formerly the case.

Related to these changes is the fact that in cases where diachronic data are available, the absolute numbers of sons have tended to rise in part related to overall population increases.[11] If the 0–9 and 10–19 age categories are compared within census periods, certain dynamics become apparent. In Orasac in 1961, for example, the greater number of sons in the latter age group is approximately offset by the decline in the number of grandsons (a gain of 36 versus a loss of 32). This implies (if one postulates that the birth rate has held approximately constant over the last ten years, and not considering migration) that in the contemporary context a proportion of those who are born as grandsons and to a lesser extent those who are born as great-grandsons (with respect to their relationship to the household head), become, in the course of a decade, sons. This can be seen as due to the death of a grandfather or great-grandfather, or the dividing off of a son from his father as that son's children mature. It is not the purpose, in an exploratory article such as this, to document each of these transitions conclusively but rather to suggest, on the basis of the summary data presented here, the kinds of transitions which may occur.

Impact of early mortality

In the 1863 villages in our sample and the structurally associated 20th century villages there is another process occurring, although it should not be assumed that it is entirely similar for both periods. In 1863 there was considerable attrition through earlier death. If one considers the population of Orasac, for example, there is an approximate difference of 2–3 percentage points in the proportion of the total population in the 0–10 as opposed to the 11–20 age groups in both 1953 and 1961 (as opposed to a difference of 8.2% in 1890 and approximately 22% in 1863).[12] (There remain significant regional differences in mortality; Macedonia overall is about 10% higher than Serbia proper – about 10 versus 9 per 1,000. Veleste is an Albanian village in southern Macedonia, and so the proportional difference may be even greater between Orasac and Veleste than between their two republics. The death rate is also about 10% higher in Bosnia, where Zupca is located.)[13]

With respect to the dynamics of the family in conservative 20th century communities such as Veleste, it is significant to look at the role of grandson versus that of brother's sons, e.g., the frequency of a *zadruga* of extended household of brothers and their nuclear families as opposed to one of a father and his married sons. In Veleste the category of grandson outnumbers that of brother's son by almost four to one, while for the 1863 data from Serbia, brother's sons tend to outnumber grandsons. If we add up the data from the 1863 villages, we find that there are a total of 172 grandsons of all ages while the figure for brothers' sons is 220, or about 22% higher. This is partly explained by the earlier death of the household head. If 1881–1882 and 1951–1952 are compared as sample years, fully 57% of all deaths in the latter period were of people over the age of 60, while the comparable percentage for the early 1880s was only 11%.[14] In 1881–1882, 28% of all deaths occurred in the 21–60 age group, the primary parental and grandparental years.[15]

Multi-generational households

A further view of the family cycle in the 1863 period is illustrated in the dramatic fall in the category of grandson and the rise in the category of brother as between the 0–9 and 10–19 age groups. Significantly the drop in the grandson category is not nearly as precipitous in Veleste, while there are no brothers in Veleste in the 0–9 age group since there is a higher rate of survival to old age for the household head than in the 1863 villages. (In Orasac in 1863 only 14% of the population was over the age of 40 as compared with over 20% in Veleste in 1961.) The situation of the categories of daughters, granddaughters and brothers' daughters for the most part parallels that of their male counterparts. The total number of sons, brothers' sons and grandsons is, of course, greater than daughters, brother's daughters and granddaughters, reflecting the fact that overwhelmingly it is women who marry out in this society. Unfortunately the number of great-grandchildren is too small for significant generalization as a category, but the growth in the proportion of four-generational households at the same time that overall household size is declining is important (see Table 2). This illustrates lineal extension and growth in structural complexity.

On the average the son or grandson is older today, reflecting in part the greater average life span and also the greater duration of these dyadic relationships within the context of the household. The occurrence of earlier succession to household head status: a household head under age 20 was not a rarity a century ago but did occur in about 8–12% of the cases. Today, in all villages, the proportion of such individuals is negligible, under 1%.

Looking at the over-60 group (see Table 6) we get a reciprocal picture. In only about 10% or less of the cases were household heads over age 60 in 1863. In a number of cases for 1863 more were under 20; approximately 20% seems to be a minimum figure for the proportion of household heads over 60 in the 20th century data, although in this respect there is much variation among cultural regions, i.e., Bobovac in 1948 with 16.8% and Slano in 1961, 37.5%. Veleste, which has the greatest proportion of extended households and most closely approaches the traditional *zadruga* organization, still has a greater proportion of household heads over 60, (23.4%) as many of the villages where complex extended families are less common. Notable is the virtual absence of the category wife and mother for the 1863 census in the over-60 category. The small proportion of wives in the over-60 category in the 20th century data is a reflection of the increasing number of female household heads in the older age categories.[16] The low proportion of wives is somewhat offset also by the other categories of elderly women such as mothers, grandmothers and sisters. The overall sex distribution in the later years tends to be increasingly female. Fathers tend to be a small category, not because men remain active so much longer in Yugoslavia than in other cultures but because they are formally regarded as head of the household in most of these culture areas as long as they can function to any perceptible degree. Most women seem to finish out their lives as mothers or grandmothers and men as household heads. In the over-70 category the mothers and grandmothers clearly outnumber the wives and female household heads.

The nature of role succession

What is the nature of role succession in the family cycle that we can postulate with respect to the 19th century and 20th century data? For the male in Serbia in the 19th century, it appears to have been son to household head. Alternately, the pathway was son to brother to household head, or in a clear minority of cases, brother's son to son to household head, and finally grandson to son to household head. Our focus has been on the changing roles of the individual and not on the household as such. A distinction needs to be made between the restructuring of a household, as on the death of the father, when one of the sons most likely succeeds to headship, if normal conditions prevail, and when subsequently two married brothers, each with his own family, decide to divide.

In the Serbian case, the most basic dynamic is the succession of son to household head. In Orasac in 1863 the percentage of sons is highest, at

46.4%, in the first age group, and progressively declines.[17] The age frequency pattern for household heads ranges from 3.8% to 12.1% in the 10–19 age group in 1863 (very young household heads are almost entirely absent in the 1961 census data (see Table 5); this category peaks at 28.2% in the 40–49 group and then declines progressively to 1.5% in the 70–79 group. There is some variation in the proportion of over age 60 household heads, ranging up to 5.6% for Topola and 8.6% for Banja; in the 20th century Bobovac, 1948, which has the lowest at about 17%, is still almost double the highest 1863 figure (see Table 6).

Since 19th century Serbian villages left few written records, there are no specific data on the particular timing of the succession of son to household head as might be reflected in formal written agreements found in some western and central European cultures. (An attempt has been made, for Orasac 1863, to examine a few selected households at various stages in the familial cycle. In these cases ages of household heads range from 18 to 40, heading households of 4 and 18 members respectively.)[18]

The proportionate number of household heads which grows until it reaches its peak in the 40–49 age group in Orasac, 1863, with a negligible number of women. Considering the male population, the proportions for the different age groups declines progressively after remaining relatively stable for the 10–19 and 20–29 age groups (20.7% and 18% respectively), reaching 10.2% for the 30–39 group and leveling off to 5.7% for the 40–49 and 50–59 groups. The major shift to the household head category seems to occur in the 20–29 group, and by 30–39 to be virtually complete (in 1863). By contrast, the brother category remains rather stable in absolute numbers from ages 10–19 through 30–39 (18 to 23 to 18 in terms of absolute numbers), but by the next age groups there is a drastic decline (to 2).

These figures are suggestive of the fact that the brother to household head transition occurs later relative to that of son to household head. There is a logic in this sequence of events in that the older son's succession to household head in the mid-19th century was most probably related to the death of the father, since only 1.5% of all households were composed of couples living alone. The internal evidence inclines toward the interpretation that younger married brothers would tend to stay together while their children were in the first ten years of life and would divide subsequently. Thus 83.7% of all brothers' sons and 76.1% of all brothers' daughters are in the 0–9 age category (see Table 5). Similarly, 85.7% and 92.3% of the grandsons and granddaughters are in the 0–9 age category.

It seems internally consistent to project that in the next decade most became sons and daughters in divided and reorganized households.

Role of women

The two increasing categories when the 0–9 and 10–19 age groups are compared sequentially are those of brother and sister. This is suggestive of the fact that while brothers' children as well as grand-children were becoming the children of the newly succeeded household head, others were becoming brothers and sisters to the new household head who replaced the deceased father – that is, the older brother, who in some cases might not even be married, replaces the deceased father, with the mother remaining in the household.[19] Genealogical evidence also suggests that occasionally a brother who became household head might also adopt the children of his deceased brother.

Considering the family cycle with respect to the exchange of women, by the 20–29 age group only 1.5% of the daughters and 4.0% of the sisters remain, and both of these categories disappear by the 30–39 age group. By contrast, the in-marrying daughter-in-law category peaks at age 20-29. The in-marrying women, of course, could become directly the wife of the household head, and this is undoubtedly the origin of the 25.9% of all wives by the 30–39 age group. This occurs at the same time that there is a relative 8% decline in the total proportion of women in these two age groups.

We would logically expect this increase to come out of the daughter-in-law category, which does, in fact, decline relatively, by 70% in this period. The sister-in-law category, like that of daughter-in-law, peaks in the 20–29 age group (75 and 80% respectively), and both these groups essentially phase out by age 40. They are not perfectly synchronized with their male counterparts of married sons since men did tend to be a few years older at age of marriage.[20] Marriage records from the 1880s and 1890s for Orasac, when statistics begin to be reliable for this area, give the age range as 16–24 years for brides and 16–27 for grooms. Almost none married under age 16 or over 30.[21]

By age 40 as of 1863, women had become wives relative to household heads, even if they had originally entered the household as daughters-in-law or sisters-in-law. This was also an age at which women begin to become widows, so that we have the appearance of the category mother, as might be expected, on a generational basis for the first time in the 40–44 age group and progressively increasing. Approximately only 2% of the population was over age 60 in 1863, so these categories are not pursued further.

The major kin transitions in the family cycle in Serbia, based on the 1863 Orasac example, then are son to household head, brother to household head, grandson to son, granddaughter to daughter, brother's son to son, and sons and daughters to brothers and sisters. Household heads do not become fathers (1 case in Orasac in 1863). In the other 1863 villages, this category is either absent or negligible, and even in the 1961 data, it is a non-significant category in all of the villages considered (see Table 6). Sisters and daughters marry out, while in-marrying women become wives, sisters-in-law or daughters-in-law and then subsequently wives of the household heads, paralleling the change of status of their husbands. Finally, wives become mothers on the decease of their husbands.

Looking at Orasac in 1961 we can, on the basis of the previous discussion, make some predictions based both on the changing demographic parameters and the changing kinship ideology.[22] First, given the disintegration of that specific part of the zadruga ideology in Orasac based on an alliance of married brothers we might assume that there are few married brothers and that the sister-in-law category, therefore, is virtually empty. In the 1961 Orasac data, there are actually no sisters-in-law and only 11 brothers (in a population of 2,023), with no brothers over 30. A brother is apparently only temporarily resident in his brother's house, probably because of the relatively recent death of their father. For 1961, it is logical to suppose that one will either shortly form his own household upon marriage or else will leave the village.

Fertility, longevity and lineal extension

More significant from the point of view of the total village social structure, we would expect, given the lower birth rate, that there are proportionately fewer sons and daughters with respect to the household head. In 1863 there were 3.5 sons and daughters per household head, while in 1961 the proportion was 1.2. The decline in fertility is well illustrated by birth records, which give birth order. When 1881 and 1951 are compared, we find that in the latter year the number of first and second births was about equal, about a fifth of the yearly total of infants born are third children and tenth are fourth children. There are no cases of a higher birth order. In 1881 half of the births were of a fifth child or higher.[23]

It is worth mentioning that although changes in kinship ideology and related factors of modernization are undoubtedly the principal reason for the decline in the fraternal *zadruga*, it is also true that there simply are not enough sons being born per father to form *zadrugas* in the traditional way. In 1863 there were 2 sons per household head but in 1961 only .8.

Increasing longevity has an immediate impact on the nature of an individual's participation in the family cycle. In 1863 approximately 25% of the children in the 0–9 age group were in the category of grandchildren with respect to the household head. In 1961, 58% were grandchildren. Given the much greater life span, with almost a fifth of the population over age 60 (see Table 3A) the various transitions would seem logically to take place at a later age; thus there should be older sons and daughters-in-law. The expected contrasts are dramatic: 29.4% of the sons are over 30 versus 5.5% in 1863, with 56.8% and 16% respectively for the over-30 age group of daughters-in-law in the two census periods. This relationship of a smaller number of children to longer living grandparents is clearly important in an individual's life experiences. But such differences do not readily appear in historically oriented qualitative descriptions of changes in family structures. Perhaps one reason might be because a century ago the existing observers were not sensitive to the sorts of things that interest us today and so there is a lack of comparative data.

The same transitions of son to household head and grandchild to child still occur, with the addition of the great-grandchild to grandchild transition. Overall there appears to be a twenty-year add-on, which reflects, of course, the coming into existence of the over-60 age group as a significant factor in the family cycle. Conceptually, like the large household, it was always there, but it was an ideal not often achieved in actuality. In 1961 most great-grandchildren are in the 0–9 age group, but about 20% are in the 10–19 age group. In 1863 no grandchildren were over age 19. In 1961 14% of the grandsons were in this category (see Table 2 for data on generations in household).

The twenty-year extended life span

It seems pertinent to state here that the statistics with which we are operating tend to understress the total nature of the transformation in social relationships related to the demographic transition. Thus our figures deal only with those grandchildren who remained in the village to be counted as part of their grandfathers' households. But there are sons and grandchildren who migrated to the market town or to Belgrade or other cities in Serbia and still visit the village regularly, or village grandparents who regularly interact with their urban kin. Such mobility was not an option in 1863, and we can reasonably assume that at that time almost all grandchildren remained within the household.

It is important to point out that about 55% of the grandchildren are still in the 0–9 age group. The transformation of grandchildren to children in terms of the family cycle helps to explain the approximate 50% increase in the son and daughter category of the 10–19 age group as compared to that of the 0–9 age group, even though the percentage of the total population in both age categories in 1961 is approximately the same (15% and 15.8% respectively).

Daughters continue to marry out, so there is a net quantitative decline in the number of daughters in 1961 Orasac data, from 91 to 16 from the 10–19 to the 20–29 age groups. By contrast, the numbers of sons drops by only 5, from 96 to 91.

There is, however, the appearance of a new category, that of son-in-law (12 in 1961 versus none in 1863). This helps to explain the presence of 21 over-30 daughters in 1961 (a few are widows of men killed in the second World War). The status of son-in-law is not the most desirable in a patriarchal society, but, given a shortage of sons, it would seem to be more common in contemporary times as well as more acceptable with the lessening of the patriarchal ideology. Here again the demographic parameters impact on the social structural possibilities. Certainly parents, when they decide to limit their number of children, do not thereby indicate an overt preference for a possible future son-in-law, but this is a possible consequence of such action.

Given the approximate 20-year extended lifespan in 1961 as opposed to a century earlier, the largest number of household heads is then predictably in the 50–69 age group in 1961 as opposed to 30–49 in 1863. However, a complicating factor in 1961 is the importance of emigration, an option which did not exist in 1863. There is thus a gap in the 40–49 generation in 1961. This group is only 8.8% of the overall population as opposed to 17.3% for the preceeding cohort and 12.7% for the older group. This gap does not exist in Moslem villages such as Zupca and Veleste, where there has been comparatively less permanent migration.

Those who were 40–49 in 1961 were 24–33 at the end of the war. Some men were killed, but there is also a deficit of women in the 40–49 age group, while in the 50–59 group, which participated in the war extensively, there is actually a greater number of men. Thus the 40–49 age group deficit seems to be due to emigration from the village and not to war losses.

This gap obviously affects the family cycle, so that fewer sons become household heads in the 40–49 age group: there are also fewer sons in the 20–29 age group, and presumably fewer grandchildren, which is why the younger groups have declined proportionately and the over-60 group has increased so dramatically, more than might be expected from the demographic transition as such.[24] This gap may also help explain why the proportion of household heads over 60 in Orasac is 33.7% as opposed to 23.4% for Veleste, although relative mortality rates do make some difference. The figures from Bobovac and Zupca (see Table 6) would also appear to confirm this view.

Despite emigration and the existing age gaps, family cycles continue to operate in the villages. Since the fathers now are not apt to die until they are in their 60s or 70s, sons don't become household heads by natural succession until they are in their 40s or 50s. There is, of course, the option of forming a separate household, but empirical observation in Orasac leads this observer to conclude that most cases where there are old couples living alone is due to the fact that their children have moved to town and not because of household fission.

Even with large-scale emigration there were still 19 sons and 19 daughters-in-law in the 40–49 age group in 1961. Given the still existing although considerably modified patriarchal ideology this does not necessarily imply the tension of waiting to inherit so prevalent in other cultures. In fact, most often a father turns over to his son much of the responsibility for the management of the household, even though he himself formally continues as household head. This is not to imply that conflict is absent but rather it appears manageable. The prolonged relationship of a single daughter-in-law to her mother-in-law would seem to be one worth examining in detail.

Limitations of census data and new categories

It needs to be stressed that the census data used here as a basis for calculation represent formal categories, and not necessarily power and decision-making roles. The fact that there are only 5 individuals in the category father among 453 households in 1961 does not imply that the over 60 and particularly over 70 household heads necessarily run matters. It is certainly significant that sons outnumber fathers in the over 50 age group in Orasac 1961, by 8 to 5.

In part because of the war but mainly because of the demographic transition, there is an almost four-fold increase in mothers, although the overall population has only approximately doubled in the past century. There also appears the new category of mother-in-law and some other affinals, the figures for which, although small, taken together with the growing role of the son-in-law, do suggest a minor but nevertheless perceptible shift away from the exclusive agnatic ideology prevalent a century earlier.

Not a simple transition

The changing affective nature of family relationships has been discussed in this paper only in passing, for its primary purpose has been to suggest ways in which demographic parameters condition family cycle. In contemporary Orasac this has meant smaller households than a century ago, but these are households in which there is a different diversity of relationships and relationships which last longer. While the roles of brothers, brothers' wives and brothers' children have almost entirely disappeared in terms of the role of laterally extended kin, and also in the pre-marriage years the multiple sibling relationships are now more restricted, there has been development of the important lineal extension with the coming into play of the greater role of grandchildren as well as great-grandchildren and some lateral extension to affinal kin such as son-in-law. Most important has been the greater duration of relationships, exemplified primarily by the over-60 kin and also by the greater proportion of individuals surviving over 40 combined with a lower birth rate.

Although divorce continues to be a minor factor in rural Serbia, there is no question but that a shared life for fifty years is not necessarily a golden option – but it is now an increasingly available option.

Previously there was superficial discussion among casual students of the family, expressing the attitude that where there were once extended families, there are now nuclear families, due to modernization. We know that smaller size does not necessarily mean exclusively nuclear families, and similarly the formerly larger size of family units did not necessarily imply an extended family unit. We now know that it is meaningless to talk in terms of a simple extended to nuclear family transition in European terms. It also seems necessary to abandon talk of a unilateral modernization of the family as such. In the 19th century, alternatives were lacking.[25] Relative longevity was not a 19th century possibility. Since the basic demographic parameters are so very different, the social forms could not possibly remain the same.

RÉSUMÉ

Cycles de vie individuels et cycles de vie familiaux
Comparaison des perspectives

L'objet du présent article est de rapprocher les cycles de vie individuels en évolution des cycles du développement familial en évolution en Yougoslavie. L'on se référera surtout à un village de la Serbie centrale et l'on comparera les recensements qui y ont été effectués en 1863 et en 1961. Des données comparées d'autres villages (1863) et régions (1961) ont été également présentées. Il y eut, en Serbie centrale au cours du siècle passé, comme d'ailleurs dans beaucoup d'autres régions d'Europe, une baisse spectaculaire du taux de mortalité et de natalité. Certaines des anciennes hypothèses portant sur des processus de modernisation – en ce qu'ils sont liés à la transformation de la grande famille étendue en une petite unité nucléaire – ont été révisées et le rapport existant entre la baisse du taux de natalité et l'allongement de la durée de la vie par rapport aux structures en évolution, a été étudié. Moins une mère a d'enfants et plus elle a de possibilités de nouer des relations de parenté qualitativement différentes. Les décès lors de la naissance, en bas-âge, et dans la première enfance, les chances réduites de survie à partir de 60–70 ans, ont constitué les paramètres restrictifs qui ont conditionné le développement de la vie de la famille, structurant ses cycles au cours du 19ᵉ siècle.

Les données du village d'Orasac en Serbie mettent en évidence que le lien mari-femme a tendance à remplacer celui de parent-enfant par sa plus grande fréquence. Ces changements sont étroitement liés à la réduction des dimensions de la famille. L'importance croissante de la dyade mari-femme, dans une société qui, auparavant, avait un foyer agnatique primaire fondé sur les liens père-fils et frère-frère, résulte d'une idéologie qui évolue, ainsi que d'un changement dans la démographie. Deux frères mariés et leurs familles, unités de base de la *zadruga* idéale traditionnelle, pouvaient co-exister pendant longtemps vers la moitié du 19ᵉ siècle du fait que le décès du père était prévisible au moment où ceux-ci atteignaient leur maturité. Les données du recensement de 1863 semblent indiquer qu'il n'y avait pas assez d'hommes âgés dans les familles pour déterminer la fission des familles élargies.

En ce qui concerne le type de succession des rôles masculins dans le cycle familial en Serbie au 19ᵉ siècle, nous sommes en droit de supposer – en nous fondant sur les données du 19ᵉ et du 20ᵉ siècle – que c'est le fils qui prend la place du chef de famille. Ou bien c'est le fils qui succède au frère, qui succède lui-même au chef de famille. Il semble, d'après les données, que la transition du frère au chef de famille advienne plus tard que celle du fils au chef de famille puisqu'au 19e siècle, ce dernier prenait probablement la tête de la famille à la mort du père. De même, tandis que les enfants du frère ainsi que les petits-enfants devenaient les enfants du nouveau chef du famille, d'autres devenaient des frères et soeurs du nouveau chef de famille, ce dernier remplaçant le père défunt.

Quant au mouvement des femmes, vers les années 40, la plupart d'entre elles étaient devenues la femme du chef de famille, même si initialement elles n'étaient entrées dans la maison qu'en tant que belles-filles ou belles-soeurs. Par ailleurs, à cet âge, beaucoup d'entre elles commençaient d'être veuves. Les principales transitions de parenté observées dans le cycle de la famille en Serbie, fondées sur l'exemple d'Orasac en 1863, sont du fils au chef de famille, du frère au chef de famille, du petit-fils au fils, de la petite-fille à la fille, du fils du frère au fils et des fils et filles aux frères et soeurs.

Malgré l'émigration et les vides existant dans les groupes d'âge, les cycles familiaux continuent de se dérouler aujourd'hui comme il y a 100 ans dans les villages de Yougoslavie. Puisqu'aujourd'hui les pères ne s'éteignent pas avant d'arriver à l'âge de 60 ou 70 ans, les fils ne deviennent pas chefs de famille par succession naturelle avant d'atteindre 40 ou 50 ans. Dans la pratique, le père donne très souvent à son fils la plus grande part des responsabilités pour gérer le ménage familial même s'il continue de rester officiellement le chef de famille.

N'oublions pas que les données de recensement utilisées comme base de calcul reflètent l'idéologie officielle et non pas nécessairement la réalité des choses. Le premier objectif du présent article est d'indiquer la manière dont les paramètres démographiques influencent les cycles familiaux. Ainsi, dans l'Orasac contemporain (1961), les familles sont plus petites qu'il y a un siècle mais les relations dyadiques sont de nature différente et durent plus longtemps. Le rôle des frères, femmes des frères et enfants des frères a presque entièrement disparu en ce qui concerne l'influence qu'il a sur la parenté étendue latérale; dans les années pré-nuptiales, les relations de parenté entre germains sont désormais plus réduites. La parenté linéaire s'est développée avec le nombre croissant d'arrières petits-enfants et l'apport de parents par alliance, comme dans le cas du gendre.

Nous savons maintenant que les familles de dimension plus réduite ne sont pas nécessairement des familles nucléaires et aussi que les anciennes grandes unités familiales n'étaient pas toujours des unités de familles étendues. On ne peut donc pas parler de changement de famille étendue à famille nucléaire.

NOTES

1. The following book-length studies by the author have been published on the Serbian village of Orasac in the region of Sumadija in central Serbia: *Social and Cultural Change in a Serbian Village*, New Haven, Human Relations Area Files, 1956; *A Serbian Village*, revised edition, New York, Harper and Row, 1967; *A Serbian Village in Historical Perspective* (with Barbara Kerewsky Halpern), New York, Holt, Rinehart & Winston, 1972.

   For 1863 data other villages to which reference will be made – Banja, Bukovik, Kopljare and Stojnik – are all located in the vicinity of Orasac. Arandjelovac and Topola are the nearby market towns. In 1863 the latter were essentially very small towns with many resident agriculturalists and some merchants and artisans. Other villages for which comparative data are given are: Veleste, an Albanian ethnic settlement near the towns of Struga and Ohrid in southern Macedonia; Zupca, a Moslem community in Bosnia, north of Sarajevo, in which a significant proportion of the men are peasant-workers employed as coal miners; Lekenik, a Catholic village near Zagreb; Bobovac, in the same region, but more isolated and with relatively few peasant-workers in comparison with Lekenik; Slano, on the Dalmatian Coast, north of Dubrovnik, a small trading center now developing tourism.

Census data for 1863 were obtained from the Serbian National Archives, and the use of material from 1931, 1948 and 1961 is based on availability. The 1931 census data was an accidental find, through the courtesy of a district clerk. Data from 1948 and 1961 were made available through the cooperation of the Federal Statistical Bureau and pertinent Republic statistical offices, whose assistance is here acknowledged with appreciation.

2. Examination of the data in Table 1 shows that there is fairly close correspondence in each of these statistical series for central Serbia, the district of Kragujevac and the village of Orasac. Fertility and mortality have declined by approximately half in the period considered, and the evidence seems to be that these trends are continuing, although clearly the major changes have already taken place and the amount of future decline in these rates would appear to be limited.

Peter Laslett remarks in his "Introduction" to *Household and Family in Past Time* (P. Laslett and R. Wall (eds.) (1972), Cambridge, Cambridge University Press: 8), "As the evidence is surveyed, it becomes difficult not to suppose that there has been an obstinately held wish to believe in what William Goode has trenchantly described as the 'classical family of Western nostalgia'. This belief, or misbelief, certainly seems to display a notable capacity to overlook contrary facts and to resist attempts at revision."

3. See Tables 2, 3A and 3B. The contrasts with respect to the existence of four-generation households are clearly illustrated in Table 2. The percentage figures are not the complete picture, in that for the 1863 census materials the overall sample size is smaller. The percentages range at approximately 1% or less for those villages in 1863 in which four-generation households occur, while in the 20th century the percentage is as high as 13.5% for the village of Bobovac in 1961. Not all villages have a significant percentage of four-generation households. However, in the latter part of the 20th century lower percentages may be due to the migration of younger generations, e.g., if the grandchildren and great-grandchildren have moved to town, so that the percentage of four-generation type relationships is perhaps understated by this data. Such mobility opportunities did not exist in central Serbia in the middle of the 19th century. (Only male household heads are considered in Table 2 since it was felt that in this way the overall data would be more comparable to the villages from 1863, where female headed households were a comparative rarity.)

Tables 3A and 3B document the great increase in the over 60 population, from some 3.5% for Serbia in 1900 to 10.5% for approximately the same area in 1961. The percentage of 16.7% for Orasac is relatively high but is roughly equivalent to that of the neighboring villages of Stojnik, Kopljare and Banja, although the overall Arandjelovac Commune is only 11%, reflecting migration to the local market town and general out-migration from the villages.

4. For example, comparing Orasac in 1863 and 1961, the total number of sons increased from 257 to 350 with an approximate doubling of the population, but the number of sons in the 0–9 years category actually decreased from 119 to 60. There are, of course, brothers' sons as a significant category in 1863, which added 43 to the total: this was more or less offset by approximately the same increase in the young grandson category in 1961.

5. See Halpern and Halpern, *op. cit.*, 1972, Table 1, p. 29. In 1863 the kin terms in order of frequency in terms of relationships to household head were son, daughter, household head and wife. In 1961, they were household head, wife, son, daughter.
6. See J.M. Halpern and D. Anderson (1970), "The zadruga, a century of change", in *Anthropologica*, N.S., XII/1: 91, Table 6.
7. *Ibid.*: 95, Table 9, and 90, Table 5.
8. This is the major point of the author's "Town and countryside in Serbia in the nineteenth century: social and household structure as reflected in the Census of 1863", in Laslett and Wall (eds.), *Household and Family in Past Time*, *op. cit.*
9. Such a case study is presented in Halpern and Halpern, *op. cit.*: 36–38.
10. *Ibid.*
11. The increase in sons has, however, been slower than population growth. Incomplete figures for Orasac in 1928 give a population of 1,585, and there was an approximately one-third increase (based on this admittedly incomplete 1928 estimate) to 2,023 in 1961. However, the number of sons increased by only about a sixth from 302 to 350, while the number of household heads grew by about a third (333 to 453) and the number of wives by more than a third (227 to 367).
12. This is shown in Table 3A and 3B; the differential listings of age groups for various census periods is due to the fact that the 19th and early 20th century statistics used the 0–10 years convention, while modern demographic publications use 0–9 years. An effort has been made to make the statistics comparable.
13. For example, see *Statisticki Godisnjak*, *FNRJ*, *1962*, Beograd, Savezni Zavod za Statistiku: 331, Table 302–309. In Veleste the proportionate drop in males is 14.1%, as opposed to 8.6% for females between the 0–9 and 10–19 age groups. In Zupca the overall decline is 4.9% and 7.7% for males between these two age groups. This contrasts with gains of 2.1 overall for Bobovac in 1961 and 3.6 for males in this latter community. By contrast, Lekenik in 1961 had decreases of 1.8% overall and 2.8% for males. At present no medical data is available which would help provide some specific data on mortality for these communities. Analysis of death registers in these communities would obviously be very useful.
14. The contrast between the 1860s and 1960s would be even more marked.
15. See Halpern, 1956, *op. cit.*: 121, Table 13.
16. The number of women over 60 who are household heads is, however, from a general point of view not very significant. This category did not seem to exist in 1863 and in the 20th century data ranges between 10 and 30 percent in a single case (Lekenik, 1961).
17. In Orasac in 1863 the progressive decline of the son category from the 0–9 age group over the four succeeding 10-year periods to the 40–49 age group is reflected in the following percentages: 46.3, 30.7, 17.5, 4.7, and .8.
18. Halpern and Halpern, *op. cit.*: 33–35.
19. See *ibid.*: 35, Figure 6, for an illustration of such a case.
20. Halpern, 1956, *op. cit.*: 370, Table 60.
21. *Ibid.*
22. The change in values concerning family structure has been extensively covered in Halpern, 1967, *op. cit.*, and Halpern and Halpern, 1972, *op. cit.* See the latter for an extensive bibliography of the literature.
23. Halpern, 1956, *op. cit.*: 139, Table 10.
24. A comparative perspective can be gained by looking at the data from Bobovac, Veleste and Zupca, villages which have all had comparatively little out-migration as contrasted with Orasac.
25. In the case of rural Serbia available field data indicate that there was considerable birth control in the 20th century, by means of abortion without the use of medical

techniques. It is also true, however, that in the 19th century a woman was much more likely to die from a badly performed abortion than in the 20th. It is difficult to separate out in any precise way the motivation for smaller families, related to 19th century ecological changes and the filling up of the central part of rural Serbia, and more generalized influences for modernization emanating from the growing towns. There was undoubtedly a perception that medical help was increasingly available, a development more pronounced in the post-war period.

20. Changes in the Bulgarian family cycle from the end of the 19th century to the present day

NIKOLINA ILIEVA and VERA OSHAVKOVA

1. *General*

Family in itself is a social system, but, at the same time, it is a primary unit in the system of society. Viewed from this second perspective, it mirrors in a specific way all those changes which are taking place in the socioeconomic and cultural relations of a country. That is why a comparative analysis of the changes in the family cycle, examined against the background of the socioeconomic transformations in Bulgaria from the end of the nineteenth century to the present day, would be quite indicative, since considerable progress has been achieved in this country in economic, social, and cultural respects.

We have chosen to study the period spanning the end of the nineteenth century to the beginning of the 1970s (almost one hundred years) because of the following considerations. During the eighteenth and the greater part of the nineteenth centuries Bulgaria was under Ottoman domination. This left its imprint on the entire life of the Bulgarian people and hence on the family, too. After liberation a rapid attempt at erasing this imprint began. Therefore, we have made it our task to follow in this article the changes which occurred in the family life cycle during the period of the sovereign development of our country.

2. *Characteristic features of the Bulgarian family life cycle after the liberation from Ottoman domination (1878) until the beginning of the 1940s*

In the post-liberation period (1878) petty-bourgeois relations were established in Bulgaria. The able-bodied members of the family were usually engaged in small private farming in the villages and petty artisanship in the towns. *Therefore, the village families and those of the small private craftsmen in the towns became the basic economic units of society*. The larger part of social labor was organized in these units. An exception was the capitalist economic enterprises which made their appearance at that time. The meagre economic relations of the small-scale farmer with the market, as well as the low degree of urbanization of the country, turned the family into a semi-closed economic unit. This kind of socioeconomic life determined to a great extent the stages of development and the character of the family life cycle in Bulgaria in this period.

Let us now examine the conditions then existing for selecting one's life partner and for creating a family. The poor economic conditions limited the possibilities for direct communication between the village lads and lasses. They could meet only for a short time and in such public places which were sanctioned by tradition: in the village square where the *horo* was danced on festive days; at the village *working-bee evenings*, which were held by one or another family, usually in winter, for doing some collective work; at the *village fountain* where the young girls went to fetch water. All those places were public spots attended also by adults. Moral norms did not permit young people to pair. Still further, in many villages for a long time there were two *horos* – one for the young women and the other for the young men.

It is certain that under such socioeconomic conditions and given the rigid moral norms the stage of so-called pre-marriage love-making did not exist; there was little more than mutual attraction evoked by outward appearances and physical beauty.

Marriage, however, was concluded not only and not mainly on the grounds of mutual affection. Very often the main incentive for picking one's marriage partner was of a material character, i.e., the fortune or lucrative trade of the young man or the rich dowry of the young girl. Most often well-off families (or those owning large plots of land) became allied by marriage. Poorer young people were forced to look for a husband or wife among their kin. Certainly there were cases of marrying beneath one's situation or, on the contrary, rising through marriage to a higher social position. But such matches were exceptions.

The consent (blessing) of the parents was a *sine qua non* for matrimonial alliance. This was a national tradition which was strictly observed; at its base lay the economic dependence of the young people on their parents. The sons and daughters of the property-owning strata of the population could inherit their share of the property after wedlock (and establishing their own family) only with the consent of their parents.

The predominating, extensive type of economy in Bulgaria and its mainly agrarian character during this period exerted their influence on the formation of a fixed family cycle. Thus, for instance, since the rural population was occupied with urgent work during the spring and summer seasons, weddings took place only in late autumn or in winter. The availability of more leisure time in those two seasons contributed to more festive wedding ceremonies and feasts which usually lasted for several days. Weddings were as a rule preceded by engagement. The period between those two events lasted anywhere from several months to a whole year. In the meantime the young girl could finish her trousseau.

The next stage of the family cycle is the birth of the children. The extensive type of production in private farming necessitated more working power. This was a major factor in peasant families at that time in Bulgaria, and they usually had a large number of children – rarely less than five, but not all remained alive. *This fact conditioned the longer duration of the child-bearing stage of the family cycle.* This stage most often continued throughout the fertility period of the wife. That is why it is not possible to separate this stage of the family life cycle from the next one – the rearing and upbringing of the children. *Those two stages were so closely interwoven that we must examine them as one.*

The considerable difference in the ages of the first-born and the last-born children made it possible for the older children, especially if they were girls, to look after the younger ones.

In the first decades after the liberation of Bulgaria (the end of the nineteenth and beginning of the twentieth centuries) compulsory school attendance covered only the first four grades. This was conditioned mainly by the simple character of the rural and handicrafts labor. It enabled the children to be included at an early age (according to their age and sex) into the labor activities of the private economy, thus easily solving also the problem of instilling in them working habits and behavioral norms. *Therefore, the time during which the children were entirely supported financially by their parents was a short one.* Although sons (in those cases in which they did not migrate to the cities to look for jobs) and daughters (until their marriage) continued to live with their parents, they participated in the money-making of the family.

The collective household system was predominant in the villages, i.e., several kindred families of relatives formed a collective household. For example, the family of the parents, together with those of the married sons, sometimes even with the families of the married grandchildren, formed a common household. This was necessitated by the low intensity of agriculture. The manufacturing character of farm production demanded pooling the labor of more people. A characteristic feature of the collective household was not only the collective tilling of the land but common revenue. It was kept by the head of household.

The artisan's family differed in many respects from the peasant family. It created its separate independent household, which consisted of the husband and wife, the unmarried children, and the parents of the husband if they lived in his house and not with one of his brothers. Irrespective of whether there were older people or not in it, the artisan's family had its own cash drawer, where, besides the revenues, the accounts of income and expenditure were kept.

The position of the wife both in the peasant and the artisan's family was that of a working partner. The wife not only did all the household chores, which at that time were numerous (bread making, spinning, weaving, etc.), but helped with the field work and in the workshop. All this made her equal with her husband: she had the right to make proposals and put forward initiatives, the right not only to consult but to take an active part in the solution of all important matters of the family. Mothers enjoyed particular respect. As to inheritance rights, compared with their brothers, daughters, by law, held an unprivileged position. The same was true of their education. As a rule daughters obtained less school training than sons.

The position of the wife in the family changed parallel with the development of the capitalist production relations. The use of women as workers in factory production or as hired laborers at the large landed estates brought about a devaluation of women's labor in Bulgaria, too. This was accompanied by the juridical, civic, and political inequality of women.

In the cities the family life cycle began to differ from that in the village. The first sign was the shortening of the childbirth stage which gradually blended with the next one – the raising of the young generation. However, since Bulgaria remained predominantly an agrarian country until the 1940s, the city-type family (town families also differed from one another depending on the social and class structure of the town) cannot be considered a typical representative of the Bulgarian family.

3. *Changes in the family life cycle under the influence of industrialization, urbanization, and social transformations in Bulgaria*

From the middle of the 1940s to the present day, the rapid process of industrialization and urbanization and the profound changes that have taken place in private ownership in villages and towns have brought about another significant socioeconomic phenomenon – the family has ceased to be *the economic organizational unit of society.* This, on its part, has brought about the disintegration of the collective household and other changes in the family cycle. On the other hand, the development of industrialization and communal services has taken over a number of those activities of family households which are not directly connected with the specific functions of the family, such as the biological and social reproduction of the population.

The socialization of the younger generation, achieved by means of lengthening compulsory education, boarding houses, participation in the labor brigade movement, youth organizations, and other similar activities, has enabled young men and women to select their marriage partners not only by physical attraction but by getting to know them better through friendly relations. *This has created the stage of pre-marriage love.*

A sociological enquiry which we carried out among the young people of three social groups gives their motivations in selecting their partners for life (Table 1).[1]

Table 1. *Basic motivations in selecting one's marriage partner (percentages)*

Motives	Young workers	University students	Labor Research Institute
1. Mutual love	18.8	31.5	4.5
2. Love and mutual respect	47.9	31.2	47.7
3. Material well-being	—	—	—
4. Love and good financial position	18.8	35.1	27.3
5. Kindred characters	14.5	2.2	20.3
Total	100.0	100.0	100.0

In essence this enquiry is sociological. It deals with three youth groups: young male and female workers of the Works for Telephone and Telegraph Technique, students of the Higher School for Dramatic Art, and young people of the Labor Research Institute, all of them living in Sofia. The data show some differences in the attitudes of the young people of the three different groups.

Although love is the predominant motivation (motivation 1 and 2) in all three social groups, there are differences in the opinions. Thus, whereas the students are almost unanimous for "Mutual love" and "Love and mutual respect", the remaining two groups lay stress mainly on "Love and mutual respect".

The motivation "Material well-being" as a basic one has not been indicated by either group. But the combination of "Love and good financial position" occupies the highest relative share with the students, while it is the lowest with the young workers. It is noteworthy that this motivation is designated most often by the girls of all three social groups. But here, too, there are differences of opinion. Thus, for instance, the majority of the girls from the Higher School of Dramatic Art show a preference for the "Love and mutual respect" motivation, while the young men of the same school prefer the "Kindred characters" motivation.

We dwell here only cursorily on the motivation for choosing a marriage partner, although we think that this is a very interesting question which deserves special attention.

Today young people wishing to get married alone decide this question. There is no legal structure which obliges them to have the consent of their parents. Traditions are observed in this respect, but no property considerations are involved. The abolition of private ownership freed not only the young people of any material consideration when marrying, but their parents, too.

The wedding ceremony has been kept as a positive tradition which today continues to be an important event in the life of the Bulgarian family, but it now reflects new content and new civic rites.

On the basis of the socioeconomic changes in society, a tendency has been noticed toward the formation of heterogeneous families. Data from a sociological enquiry[2] carried out on a nation-wide scale have shown that 68.8% of the workers' families are homogeneous, the rest being heterogeneous; for example, 25.7% are families where the wife is a worker and the husband an employee. Among employees (including the intelligentsia) 78.2% of the families are homogeneous, while in 17.3%

the wife is an employee and the husband a worker, etc. Among cooperative farmers 60.8% of the families are homogeneous, while in 26.5% the wife is a peasant woman and the husband a worker.

This process of forming socially heterogeneous families is a progressive one and will continue to develop parallel with the intensification of the economy and the build-up of social homogeneity in society.

The intensive manner of economic development in Bulgaria made necessary the raising of the standard of training and culture of all working people, including that of women. All this greatly affected the contemporary Bulgarian family – new stages appeared in the family life cycle, while others were transformed or their duration shortened. Here greater attention should be paid to the effect of female training and professional factors on the cycle of the family life.

The existing equal opportunities of men and women for education brought about the rapid growth of the relative share of women specialists in the country. Thus, 53% of the specialists with a secondary training are women, while in the more important professions where a university training is required the share of the women is as follows: 59.3% of teachers in the secondary and higher educational establishments, 58.0% of economists, 41.7% of physicians, 25.4% of engineers and 36.0% of agronomists. The introduction of the compulsory eighth-grade high-school training in 1957 and of the general tenth-grade high-school training in 1973 raised the culture of all strata of the female population. Parallel with this the professional activization of women rapidly developed. Today 81% of the married women in Bulgaria are engaged in public labor. We could safely say that *a new type of family cycle has established itself, where both husband and wife are engaged in public work*. This has transformed the traditional role of man as the bread-winner in the family. Today in more than 80% of the families this role is divided between the husband and wife. Thus the social prestige of women is increasing both in the family and in society. She has not only become economically independent and equal in the family community, but her social role in the family relations has been raised.

The transformation of the social status of women in Bulgaria leads immediately to changes in the cycle of the family life. First of all, *a shortening of the duration of the child-bearing stage in the contemporary Bulgarian family life cycle is noticeable*. Today in Bulgaria 55% to 60% of all childbirths fall annually to mothers not older than 25 years. This is evidence that today there is a conscious regulation of the number of the children in the family. While most families have two children, few have three. Whereas previously the child-bearing stage in the family lasted many years (almost the entire period of fertility of the woman), in the years after 1944 this period was considerably shorter. The reasons are two: the heightened education and general culture of the women and their professional activity. Women now lay more stress on improving their professional qualifications and on making a successful career.

The intensive factors of economic development sharply raised the requirements for the younger generations. This is reflected not only in the introduction of general high-school training but also in the demand that they demonstrate a wider range of cultural attainments such as knowledge of foreign languages, musical training, etc. Moreover, there is a marked attempt in the majority of high-school graduates to continue their training at the universities. That is why *the importance and prolongation of that stage of the family life cycle which embraces the education of the younger generation is considerably increasing*. Objectively, there is a marked prolongation of the period in which the children continue to be supported by their parents. The elongation of the training period of the younger generation necessarily leads to a delay of their economic independence.

The question now becomes in what way the family can respond to the increasing necessity for higher qualitative achievements by the younger generation and the simultaneously increasing demand for the labor activity of married woman? The answer lies in the assistance which society renders (in the socialist state) to the family for the fulfilment of one of its most important functions – the spiritual reproduction of the generation. In this respect we should point to the following social gains: working mothers are entitled to fully paid maternity leave (for pregnancy and delivery) beginning in the course of the fourth, fifth or sixth month depending on whether the child is the first, second, or third one. After the expiration of the fully paid leave mothers have the right to another leave of six, seven, or eight months (again depending on the number of children) paid at the rate of the minimum wage prescribed at the moment in the country. Highly qualified women workers and employees can, if they wish, start work immediately after the expiration of the fully paid maternity leave, while the state ensures them a subsidy amounting to half of the minimum wage to pay the expenses of a babysitter. After the expiration of the two paid leaves, working mothers can make the choice whether they themselves will continue to look after their child until he is three years old, while the post they occupy is kept for them until their return to work, and their length of service is not impaired by their absence, or whether they will send their child to the children's crêches and return to work. The fees charged by the crêches are very low and exist only formally. Despite this, many families prefer to look after their children themselves until the latter are two or three years old, particularly if they can ensure for themselves the help of the grandparents. There is a marked tendency when the child is three years old to send him to kindergarten. Today 75% of the children from three to seven years of age are taken care of in kindergartens. The fees are determined according to the monthly revenue of the family. The tendency is for the state to gradually take over full maintenance of the children in children's establishments. Special attention is paid to the introduction of full-board and semi-boarding systems, the provisions being at the beginning for these systems to include only children less than 11 years of age.

The help rendered by the crêches, the schools, the semi-boarding and full-board establishments *do not free the families from their obligations in the upbringing of their children*. There is, in fact, a peculiar distribution of obligations between them. Uniformity in education and mutually complementary work is bearing fruit – the younger generation receives the necessary training and upbringing.

We are of the opinion that the child-rearing stage of the family life cycle is the most complex, difficult, and responsible stage of the cycle. For the successful fulfilment of this function it is necessary for the parents to obtain preliminary preparation for raising and educating their children. There is no such organized and purposeful preparation for young families in Bulgaria. What we have now is based mainly on tradition. The lectures which the children's establishments and the schools deliver to parents and the publications on this topic are not enough. The lack of systematic preparatory work with the parents is the reason for the extant "variance" in the principles of education in the children's establishments and in some families.

Various kinds of services exist for alleviating mothers of household chores, leaving them more free time for raising their children. Some work, done previously in the household, is now taken care of by public services. These services represent a vast potential for economizing on time previously spent on household chores.

The active processes of urbanization and migration of the population, noticeable in the last 30 years in this country, exercise a considerable influence upon the transformation of the character of family relations. For one thing, urbanization has eliminated the basis which made possible and maintained the old type of family – the patriarchal family. It was a commune of three and more generations and had a collective household. This type of family and family relation has passed into history. Under the new socioeconomic conditions *the nuclear type of the family has established itself in both the towns and villages*. Even in cases when, because of housing shortages, the young family co-habitates with the parents, it becomes not only financially independent but has its own way of life and habits.

The establishment of the nuclear family is accompanied by a reduction in the number of children in the average family. This is true for families of all social groups. Most families have two children. The respective figures for the workers' families are 55.0%, for the employees 50.1%, and for the farmers – 55.3%. Peasant families with three children have a larger share – 12.3% – while in workers' families it is 6.0% and only 2% among employees.[3] The peasant group has the largest percentage of families of more than three children – 17.6%.

Owing to the introduction of a five-day working week, the leisure time of the population has increased, effecting some changes in the family life cycle. New habits are being acquired.

After the children reach the age when they do not need constant control, *there is a regular lengthening of the leisure time of the married couple*. This brings about *the formation of a new stage in the family life cycle – when the married couple can spare much more time for their spiritual needs:* cultural occupations, hiking, travelling, improving professional skills, creative occupations, etc. The formation of this stage is aided also by another fact we mentioned above – having the children in the first years of marriage. Thus, when the children are quite grown up, the parents still have before them a considerable amount of active working life. In the period under consideration (the end of the nineteenth century to the 1940s), this stage was not typical of the Bulgarian family. Its formation plays a positive role not only in the development of the personality but also in the creation of new common interests and relations between married people.

The increase in average longevity of the population in Bulgaria (from 45 years for 1921–1925 to 71 for 1965–1967)[4] created the necessary conditions after old-age pensioning – 55 years of age for women and 60 for men – for *a new stage in the family life cycle – the married couple is relieved both of the obligation for raising children and of participation in social labor*. This stage differs from the previous ones because of the transformation of the entire regimen of family life. A quite widespread practice in Bulgarian families in this stage is the voluntary obligation which aged married couples are taking to look after their grandchildren. It is a public responsibility, in the interest of the health of these people and in that of society, to fill their free time with useful occupations.

Bulgarian sociologists differ in their opinion as to whether the aged married couple should be engaged in looking after the second and sometimes third generation. We have in mind mainly those cases when the young mother returns to work after the expiration of the paid maternity leaves, but the parents prefer their children to be raised in family conditions at least until they are old enough for admittance to kindergarten. Part of the latter, of course, work half days only. The obligation for taking the child to the kindergarten, bringing him back, and looking after him at home is often left to the pensioned grandparents. Another problem is that about 25% of the children do not attend kindergartens.

We are of the opinion that this is a pleasant obligation which favorably stimulates aged married couples, since in most cases it is done with love and entirely voluntarily.

This survey is an endeavor to analyze, although in a synthesized manner, the changes which have taken place in the cycle of the family life in Bulgaria from the end of the nineteenth century to the present day. Some of the latest stages in the family cycle are studied for the first time in this country. That is why they might raise some discussions. Irrespective of this we hope that with the present publication an attempt has been made to not only trace these changes descriptively but to reveal the laws governing them.

Résumé

Changements dans le cycle de la vie familiale bulgare de la fin du 19e siècle à nos jours

Cet article tente de faire une analyse comparative des changements survenus dans le cycle familial, sous l'influence des transformations socio-économiques et culturelles en Bulgarie depuis la fin de 19e siècle jusqu'à maintenant.

La première des 2 parties principales examine les caractéristiques du cycle de la vie de la famille bulgare après la libération du joug ottoman (1878) et jusqu'au début des années 40. A cette époque, la famille de paysans et d'artisans constituait l'unité fondamentale de la société à l'intérieur de laquelle était organisée la plus grande partie des travaux publics.

Les conditions étaient telles que pour contracter un mariage, le consentement des parents était indispensable. Les jeunes étaient économiquement dépendants de leurs parents. En raison du caractère saisonnier de la production agricole, les mariages avaient lieu en général tard en automne et en hiver.

Le caractère extensif prédominant de l'économie bulgare en ce temps-là est l'un des principaux facteurs déterminant la demande accrue de main-d'œuvre. Ceci a influencé la longueur de la phase du cycle familial durant lequel les enfants apparaissent (naissent) dans la famille. C'est pourquoi il est impossible de distinguer cette phase du cycle de la vie familiale de la phase suivante: celle de l'élevage et de l'éducation des enfants.

Le ménage étendu, typique du village bulgare à cette époque, est caractéristique. Il comprenait 3 ou davantage de générations et était composé de plusieurs familles issues d'une lignée. Ce type de famille était fondé sur une production agricole privée demandant le travail coopératif de beaucoup de personnes.

On a comparé la vie familiale d'un ménage de paysans et celle d'un ménage d'artisans. La position de la femme est étudiée à l'intérieur de chacun de ces ménages.

C'est dans la deuxième période qu'interviennent des changements dans le cycle de la vie familiale sous l'influence de l'industrialisation, de l'urbanisation et des profondes modifications qui ont eu lieu depuis le début des années 40. Ces processus ont une conséquence socio-économique importante – la famille n'est plus désormais une unité économique dans la société bulgare, ce qui conduit à la désintégration de la famille collective. Le type conjugal de la famille a été imposé. Nombre de changements ont eu lieu dans le cycle de la famille.

L'abolition de la propriété privée des moyens de production a libéré le choix des époux des contraintes matérielles. Le consentement parental n'est plus une condition obligatoire pour contracter un mariage.

Un nouveau type de cycle familial se forme dans lequel les 2 époux sont actifs. Ceci bouleverse la conception selon laquelle l'homme est l'unique partenaire à devoir assumer l'existence de la famille. La phase durant laquelle naissent les enfants est raccourcie, ce qui a conduit à traiter comme phase indépendante l'éducation des enfants.

On a étudié la question du partage entre famille et société des obligations concernant la socialisation des enfants ce qui amène à créer quelques nouvelles phases dans le cycle de la famille. De plus, on étudie les différences dans le cycle de la vie familiale selon le groupe social – le mariage d'époux issus de classes sociales diverses étant considéré comme un processus progressif.

L'article s'est efforcé de déterminer à la fois les changements et les régularités observées dans le cycle.

Notes

1. A probing sociological enquiry carried out in Sofia by N. Ilieva (1971), *The Attitude of Youth towards the Family and Marriage.*
2. *Women in Production, Public Life and the Family*, 1969, Central Council of the Bulgarian Trade Unions, the Committee of Bulgarian Women, etc.
3. According to data from the sociological research in towns and villages, 1967, Sociology Institute at the Bulgarian Academy of Sciences.
4. *Statistical Yearbook of the People's Republic of Bulgaria*, 1972: 58–59.

21. Types de famille et cycle de vie dans la Yougoslavie rurale

CVETKO KOSTIĆ, RADA BORELI et
JEAN-FRANÇOIS GOSSIAUX

Continuité et ruptures, le cycle de la vie familiale se définit d'une manière opératoire comme une succession de phases aux bornes marquées par des événements. Le choix de ces événements, concernant généralement la vie des enfants: naissance, scolarisation, passage à l'âge adulte, etc., est habituellement fait, dans les divers travaux portant sur ce sujet, par référence aux changements qu'ils entraînent dans les différents rôles des membres de l'unité familiale. Les méthodes longitudinales, c'est-à-dire les enquêtes diachroniques portant sur une certaine population de foyers, unités statistiques, sont théoriquement les mieux adaptées aux études concernant le cycle de vie. L'observation suivie dans le temps d'un panel présente des difficultés matérielles évidentes qui rendent la méthode difficilement praticable. Un substitut possible en est l'enquête par entretiens rétrospectifs, mais celle-ci est affectée d'un certain nombre de défauts théoriques dont le moindre n'est pas le risque de déformation inhérent à l'appel à la mémoire. Un autre substitut est l'étude transversale, ("cross-sectional data") qui à partir d'une population observée à un instant donné, donc de données synchroniques et collectives, reconstitue un ensemble de faits diachroniques et individuels. L'inconvénient théorique de cette méthode est le caractère artificiel de cette reconstitution qui ne peut prendre en compte les transformations historiques de l'environnement. Le mérite majeur en est la commodité de réalisation, le coût (relativement) peu élevé et les possibilités d'application aisée de la technologie statistique.

Les données sur lesquelles s'appuie l'étude présentée ici sont issues d'une enquête sur la Yougoslavie des villages réalisée en 1965 conjointement par l'Institut de Sociologie de Belgrade, l'Institut Agraire de Zagreb et le Centre de Sociologie Européenne, sous la direction de Jean Cuisenier. L'axe en était un questionnaire soumis à 700 foyers issus de 14 villages, ces villages ayant été choisis de manière à être représentatifs des différentes sous-cultures identifiables dans la culture serbo-croate.[1] Cette enquête n'a pas été construite dans le but unique d'étudier le cycle de la vie familiale, mais porte sur un objet plus vaste, ayant trait notamment à l'économie rurale. Les méthodes transversales d'étude du cycle, qui sont les plus avantageuses en coût, présentent cet avantage supplémentaire, exploité ici, de pouvoir traiter un matériau non spécialisé, de pouvoir utiliser des données extraites d'une enquête à objet plus vaste et même de tirer parti de questions posées à d'autres fins. Ainsi nous utiliserons ici des variables démographiques qui peuvent être mises en œuvre dans d'autres études que celle de la vie familiale. L'enquête a été effectuée selon un sondage à deux niveaux, le premier niveau étant celui des villages, le second celui du choix des individus à l'intérieur de chacun de ces villages. Le taux de sondage au second niveau est assez élevé, allant d'un cinquième à un sur deux. Une variable de contrôle était la position sociale, à trois degrés, déterminée pour chacune des familles par des jurys locaux composés de notables. Le tirage aléatoire par village a été corrigé de manière à éviter une élimination de strates numériquement peu importantes. Toutefois, les échantillons sont au niveau du village statistiquement représentatifs de la population. Par contre, l'échantillon des villages n'est pas aléatoire et les 700 foyers de l'enquête ne constituent pas en ce sens un échantillon représentatif de l'ensemble des ruraux. Leur choix néanmoins permet de considérer les résultats de l'enquête comme une représentation pour la Yougoslavie rurale des phénomènes étudiés. Le questionnaire se composait d'un tronc commun au foyer, d'un sous-questionnaire propre à l'homme et d'un sous-questionnaire propre à la femme.

Persistance de formes d'organisation familiale différenciées, en liaison significative avec les sous-cultures coexistant en Yougoslavie, déroulement du cycle de vie de l'individu dans ces divers contextes, tels sont les points sur lesquels ce matériau est ici interrogé.

1. Famille élémentaire et famille étendue, *par Cvetko Kostić et Rada Boreli*

Les différentes classifications de types de famille rurale proposées par les sociologues yougoslaves sont établies sur la base du principe qui observe non seulement les relations réciproques entre membres d'une famille, mais aussi tient compte de leurs ressources, du milieu naturel où la famille est appelée à vivre, de l'influence de la tradition, de la position qu'occupe la femme, etc. On ne mentionnera que deux classifications: celle de Bogišić, et celle de Cv. Kostić. La plus ancienne a été proposée par Bogišić en 1882. D'après cette division, et suivant la localité, on distingue les familles *urbaines* et les familles *rurales*. Ces dernières se divisent ensuite en *familles isolées*, *corporations familiales* ("zadruga") et *familles musulmanes*. La famille rurale isolée se compose du mari, de la femme et de leurs enfants. "La corporation familiale comprend une famille multiple avec plusieurs frères, et même cousins ou parents éloignés avec, éventuellement, leurs femmes et enfants". Les familles musulmanes occupent une position particulière, d'après cette classification, à cause de la polygamie qui y règne et de l'influence de l'islamisme. Kostić propose une classification fondée sur la nature du milieu naturel dans lequel la famille est appelée à vivre. Il tient compte du relief du terrain et de la propriété foncière, des sources de revenu, de l'influence de la culture héritée, de la tradition et de la religion. D'après cette classification, on distingue cinq types de famille rurale: le type *alpin* (en Slovénie et en Istrie slovène), le type *maritime* (sur la côte adriatique croate et en Istrie et Dalmatie insulaire), le type *dinarique* (sur la côte dalmate et à l'intérieur du pays le long de la côte), le type *pannonien* (dans la plaine que parcourent la Save et le Danube) et le type "*Timok*" (riverain du fleuve du même nom).

Dans l'étude des données de l'enquête, nous avons utilisé une classification basée sur la composition de la famille. Ainsi les familles des 14 villages étudiés peuvent-elles être divisées en quatre types:

1. Famille élémentaire;
2. Famille élémentaire plus addition;
3. Famille incomplète;
4. Famille patrilinéaire étendue.

La famille élémentaire se compose du mari, de la femme et de leurs enfants. La famille élémentaire plus addition est une famille élémentaire à laquelle s'est joint un ou plusieurs parents. Elle est normalement composée du père, de la mère et de leurs enfants auxquels s'est jointe la veuve, mère de l'épouse; ou bien elle est composée des deux époux et du père de l'un d'eux, resté veuf; ou bien des deux époux et du frère ou de la sœur de l'un d'eux, non mariés, etc. A la famille incomplète manque un des deux parents, père ou mère, et elle se compose en général de la mère et du fils non marié; de la femme restée veuve ou de l'homme qui a perdu sa femme; du frère non marié et de sa sœur, etc. La famille patrilinéaire étendue se compose du père et de la mère, de leurs fils dont au moins un est marié, et de la famille de ce dernier.

L'examen des données montre que des changements importants se sont opérés au cours du dernier siècle. En effet l'enquête conduite par V. Bogišić en 1874, et exposée dans l'ouvrage intitulé *Recueil du droit coutumier contemporain des Slaves du Sud*, faisait ressortir que la famille patrilinéaire étendue représentait le type de famille le plus répandu dans la région alors enquêtée. En parlant du Sud de la Serbie et de la Macédoine, l'auteur dit: "Ils vivent en corporation familiale où sont rassemblées les familles des frères, fils et petits-fils". "Tant que le père, chef de famille, est en vie, ses fils mariés ne le quittent pas et vivent ensemble avec leurs familles."[2] Pour les villes en Vojvodina, il dit: "La famille y est élémentaire, mais dans les villages des environs la corporation familiale est le type de famille qui prédomine".[3] En Bosnie "on rencontre régulièrement des corporations familiales".[4] En Croatie, où le démembrement des corporations est fréquent, on trouve toujours des familles de ce type. En Dalmatie, "plusieurs familles élémentaires vivent ensemble".[3] En Bosnie, les familles rurales vivent en corporation, ce qui leur facilite l'organisation du travail quotidien et les aide à mieux s'adapter à l'économie locale. Dans les villages de l'Herzégovine "les familles vivent le plus souvent en corporation",[4] etc.

Or, dans notre enquête, menée en 1965, il apparaît que la famille élémentaire est nettement prédominante (66% des cas), suivie de la famille patrilinéaire étendue (17%), de la famille incomplète (9%), et de la famille élémentaire plus addition (6%). On peut donc conclure à une évolution de la famille rurale, parallèle à l'évolution économique.

Toutefois il existe des écarts notables entre villages. Ainsi dans le village serbe de Smedovac, 59% des familles vivent en famille patrilinéaire étendue. Ici c'est le type de famille de Timok qui est courant, le taux de natalité est bas, il existe une concentration de propriété foncière grâce aux alliances matrimoniales qui aident les familles à former des corporations familiales. Dans toute cette contrée les familles préfèrent n'avoir qu'un seul enfant et les familles entrent en corporation par l'intermédiaire des enfants qui se marient. Dans certains cas ce sont les parents qui continuent à vivre avec la famille du fils marié.

D'une manière générale, la famille étendue reste relativement fréquente dans les villages serbes (plus de 30% des cas). Par contre, dans l'ouest et le nord du pays elle apparaît comme un type en voie de désagrégation, jusqu'à n'être plus parfois qu'une forme exceptionnelle. Il en est ainsi notamment dans les villages croates de Busevac et Begovo-Razdolje (11%), à Gorenja Vas (Slovénie), Morović (Vojvodina) et Putović (Bosnie): 6%.

Bien que le mouvement de démembrement des corporations familiales commencé au 19e siècle se soit poursuivi, celles-ci se survivent sous la forme de la famille étendue, dont l'importance, réduite dans certaines régions, reste primordiale ailleurs.

2. Chronologie de la vie familiale
par Jean-François Gossiaux

Notre propos ici est de chercher une définition des phases du cycle de la vie familiale dans la Yougoslavie rurale, non pas en s'appuyant, ainsi qu'on le fait habituellement, sur l'évolution des rôles affectés aux membres de l'unité domestique, mais en n'utilisant que les évènements naturels touchant le foyer, c'est-à-dire sa croissance ou sa décroissance quantitative, sa composition du point de vue nombre et âge de ses membres, sans référence explicite aux variations de rôle qu'ils peuvent entraîner. Autrement dit, il s'agira de rechercher, parmi ces évènements, lesquels sont les plus pertinents pour servir de bornes entre les phases, en prenant en compte la dimension collective de la chronologie. En effet, même si au niveau individuel un événement a une signification vécue importante, sa survenance à des temps variables selon les individus lui enlève toute valeur de définition. Il s'agit de trouver une séquence d'évènements à peu près constante sur l'ensemble de la population. Les phases du cycle de vie ainsi dégagées, une étude systématique des relations entre rôles et position dans le cycle pourra être entreprise, sans qu'il y ait eu interférence dans les définitions des variables mises en rapport.

Comme pour toute méthode transversale, nous avons dû poser l'hypothèse de l'absence de changements historiques importants pour ce qui concerne la chronologie familiale dans les dernières décennies. Nous nous sommes par là-même interdit de rechercher une description trop fine du cycle, et le découpage du temps que nous avons obtenu est plus grossier que par exemple la description faite par Duvall et par Rodgers. Par contre, nous avons dû prendre en compte un trait propre à la société yougoslave, à savoir l'importance de la famille patrilinéaire étendue en tant que structure familiale, importance attestée par nos données mêmes, ainsi qu'il a été montré plus haut. J. Halpern,[5] s'attachant particulièrement au cas de la Serbie, a également démontré la pérennité de ce type de foyer, la *zadruga*, en dépit de certains changements survenus depuis le siècle dernier, ayant trait notamment au nombre de sous-unités familiales nucléaires (il y a eu réduction du nombre de ménages collatéraux, en général un seul enfant marié demeurant au foyer). Ainsi le système de phases que nous avons obtenu n'est pas une séquence parcourue par tout individu au long de sa vie familiale mais un ensemble de chemins distincts devant lequel il se trouve placé lorsqu'il fonde un foyer.

Nous avons adopté le parti d'étudier le cycle de vie familiale du point de vue individuel plutôt que du point de vue de l'unité domestique, ce qui signifie concrètement que nous avons introduit la variable "temps" par l'intermédiaire de l'âge du chef de famille et non par celui de l'ancienneté du mariage. Nous voulions ainsi examiner si les remariages occupaient une position relativement invariable dans la chronique individuelle. L'analyse a donné, comme nous le verrons plus loin, une indication négative sur ce point, et l'étude évoquée ici a en fait porté, pour des raisons précisées plus loin également, uniquement sur les individus mariés une seule fois. Donnée du point de vue individuel, la description du cycle obtenue peut toutefois être considérée comme valant aussi pour l'unité familiale, ayant été confirmée en utilisant l'âge de la femme comme indicateur de la variable "temps". Les phases ont donc été déterminées par la mise en rapport avec l'âge du chef de famille d'un certain nombre de variables descriptives de l'état de la famille, selon une technique statistique habituellement désignée sous le nom de segmentation[6] et dont le principe est le suivant:

Etant donné une variable numérique considérée comme "variable dépendante" et une série de variables "indépendantes" ou "explicatives" numériques ou qualitatives, l'analyse par segmentation a pour but de subdiviser l'échantillon en une série de sous-groupes homogènes du point de vue de la variable dépendante. Pour cela, la première étape consiste à diviser l'échantillon en deux sous-groupes aussi différents que possible du point de vue de la variable dépendante Y, à l'étape suivante l'opération est renouvelée sur chacun des sous-groupes ainsi définis, et la procédure est ainsi itérée jusqu'à ce que certains critères d'arrêt concernant notamment l'effectif et l'homogénéité des sous-groupes obtenus soient satisfaits. A chaque étape une variable explicative X_i devra être choisie, qui assure la différenciation la plus grande selon Y. Le partage d'un groupe G se fait en déterminant deux sous-groupes $G1$ et $G2$ dont les moyennes relatives à Y sont les plus différentes possibles. Plus précisément, le critère de choix de la dichotomie est le suivant: la variable explicative choisie est celle qui, prise isolément, explique la plus grande part de la dispersion de la variable dépendante, c'est-à-dire celle qui a la plus grande variance intergroupe. Autrement dit, on cherchera la dichotomie de G telle que si n_1 est l'effectif de $G1$, n_2 l'effectif de $G2$, $\bar{y}_1$ la moyenne de Y sur $G1$, $\bar{y}_2$ la moyenne de Y sur $G2$ et $\bar{y}$ la moyenne de Y sur G,

la quantité $BSS = n_1(\bar{y}_1 - \bar{y})^2 + n_2(\bar{y}_2 - \bar{y})^2$ soit maximum.

Concrètement, la démarche sera la suivante:

Une variable explicative X_i est en général polychotomique, c'est-à-dire présente plusieurs modalités. Ces modalités peuvent être regroupées en deux catégories disjointes X_i^+ et X_i^- de façon à former une partition de G: d'une part les individus ayant la caractéristique X_i^+ et d'autre part ceux ayant la caractéristique X_i^-. Plusieurs telles partitions sont possibles pour chaque X_i. On choisira parmi celles-ci la partition telle que les deux sous-groupes correspondants soient le plus différents possible au sens explicité plus haut, c'est-à-dire de manière à ce que la variance intergroupe BSS soit la plus forte possible. La partition ainsi déterminée est appellée "dichotomie de G associée à X_i". Pour chaque variable X_i la dichotomie associée étant ainsi définie, de même que la variance intergroupe correspondante BSS_i, on choisira la variable X_k qui possède la plus forte variance intergroupe, c'est-à-dire telle que

$$BSS_k = \operatorname*{Max}_i BSS_i$$

La variable X_k sera celle qui "segmentera" à cette étape.

Cependant le critère de "réductibilité" limite le choix. La variance de la variable choisie doit représenter une part suffisamment grande de la variance de l'échantillon (selon un coefficient choisi au départ). Si cela n'est pas, le groupe G n'est pas dichotomisé et est dit "non explicable".

A l'étape suivante, l'étude se porte sur celui qui parmi les sous-groupes déjà obtenus possède la variance interne la plus forte, c'est-à-dire celui sur lequel les valeurs de Y sont les plus dispersées. Cependant, ce groupe doit satisfaire à deux critères:

– posséder une taille suffisante, c'est-à-dire supérieure à un nombre choisi au départ;
– avoir une variance interne représentant une part suffisante de la variance totale de l'échantillon (toujours selon un certain coefficient); si cela n'est pas, il est dit "homogène".

La procédure s'arrête quand aucun sous-groupe ne peut plus être dichotomisé, c'est-à-dire quand tous les sous-groupes étant soit non explicables, soit homogènes, soit d'effectif trop faible, sont "terminaux". Le résultat final d'une étude se présente comme une arborescence dont les nœuds sont les sous-groupes. La segmentation est en fait une méthode de "classification descendante".

Nous avons indiqué plus haut que notre propos était de trouver une séquence d'événements à peu près constante sur l'ensemble de la population. Autrement dit, nous recherchons un certain nombre d'événements se produisant dans un ordre qui est sensiblement le même pour tous, dont la place dans la chronologie familiale est fixe. Supposons par exemple, qu'un événement *A* se produise régulièrement en milieu de cycle, alors qu'un autre événement *B* se situera selon les cas au début ou à la fin de la vie familiale. Notons P_A^- l'ensemble des individus pour qui *A* n'est pas encore survenu et P_A^+ l'ensemble complémentaire de ceux qui ont déjà vécu *A*, et considérons de même P_B^+ et P_B^-. L'hétérogénéité entre P_A^+ et P_A^-, pour ce qui est de l'âge, sera plus grande que celle existant entre P_B^- et P_B^+.[7] La technique de la segmentation permet de déterminer l'événement *E* le plus marquant au sens ainsi défini puis les événements les plus discriminants survenant respectivement avant et après *E*, et ainsi de suite. En fait, nous ferons ainsi apparaître non pas une, mais plusieurs séquences distinctes et superposées correspondant au maintien de la famille élémentaire ou à son évolution vers la famille étendue, ainsi qu'il a été indiqué précédemment.

Nous disposions par foyer des variables suivantes:
– nombre d'enfants nés
– nombre d'enfants vivants
– nombre d'adultes au foyer
– nombre de mineurs de 18 ans au foyer
– nombre d'enfants ayant quitté le foyer
– proportion d'enfants ayant quitté le foyer (0: aucun, 1: une partie, 2: tous)
– type de famille

Cette dernière variable était composée des modalités suivantes: 1) famille élémentaire, parents et enfants; 2) famille élémentaire parents seuls; 3) famille élémentaire + mère ou père veufs; 4) famille patrilinéaire étendue (chef de famille + fils marié) avec d'autres enfants que le fils marié demeurant au foyer; 5) famille patrilinéaire étendue sans autre enfant au foyer; 6) veufs ou veuves.

On remarquera que les variables utilisées ne sont pas indépendantes entre elles et que certaines présentent même une certaine redondance, par exemple le nombre et la proportion d'enfants ayant quitté le foyer, ou le nombre d'enfants nés et le nombre d'enfants vivants. Ceci permet d'utiliser pour une variable sous-jacente le meilleur indicateur sans préjudice pour la validité de l'analyse, puisque lorsqu'une variable "segmente" à une étape, la variable qui exprime le même phénomène disparait en quelque sorte derrière elle. La technique utilisée ici protège de ces "excès d'indicateurs" dont souffrent tant d'autres méthodes statistiques. Par ailleurs, la variable "nombre d'adultes" peut avoir des significations diverses et correspondre à des évènements différents selon le contexte de son apparition dans l'analyse.

Les segmentations successives, par la donnée à la fois des variables opérantes et du partage des modalités pour ces variables, déterminent des sous-populations caractérisées par un certain état de la famille et homogènes quant à l'âge. Si l'on passe du plan collectif et synchronique à un plan individuel et diachronique en vertu des hypothèses et approximations évoquées plus haut à propos des "méthodes transversales", aux sous-populations correspondent des phases décrites avec plus ou moins de précision suivant le nombre de segmentations prises en compte, et aux états définis par les modalités des variables segmentantes des événements qui bornent ces phases. La valeur de définition de ces événements est d'autant plus grande que la variable à laquelle ils correspondent apparaît plus tôt dans l'analyse.

Seuls les individus dont est né au moins un enfant ont été ici retenus. Une étude préalable a montré que le remariage n'intervenait pas comme variable segmentante. Evénement marquant le cycle de l'individu, il peut intervenir à des temps variables selon les cas et ne peut donc avoir de valeur définissante pour ce qui nous intéresse ici au niveau collectif: il n'y a pas d'âge pour les remariages.[8] Par contre, la présence dans l'analyse d'individus à qui correspondaient en fait deux cycles familiaux (ou tout au moins deux parties de cycle) successifs perturbait fortement la segmentation en troublant la signification des variables. C'est pourquoi

Figure 1. *A l'intérieur de chaque nœud figurent son numéro, les modalités de la variable segmentante le définissant, le nombre d'individus le composant, et leur moyenne d'âge*

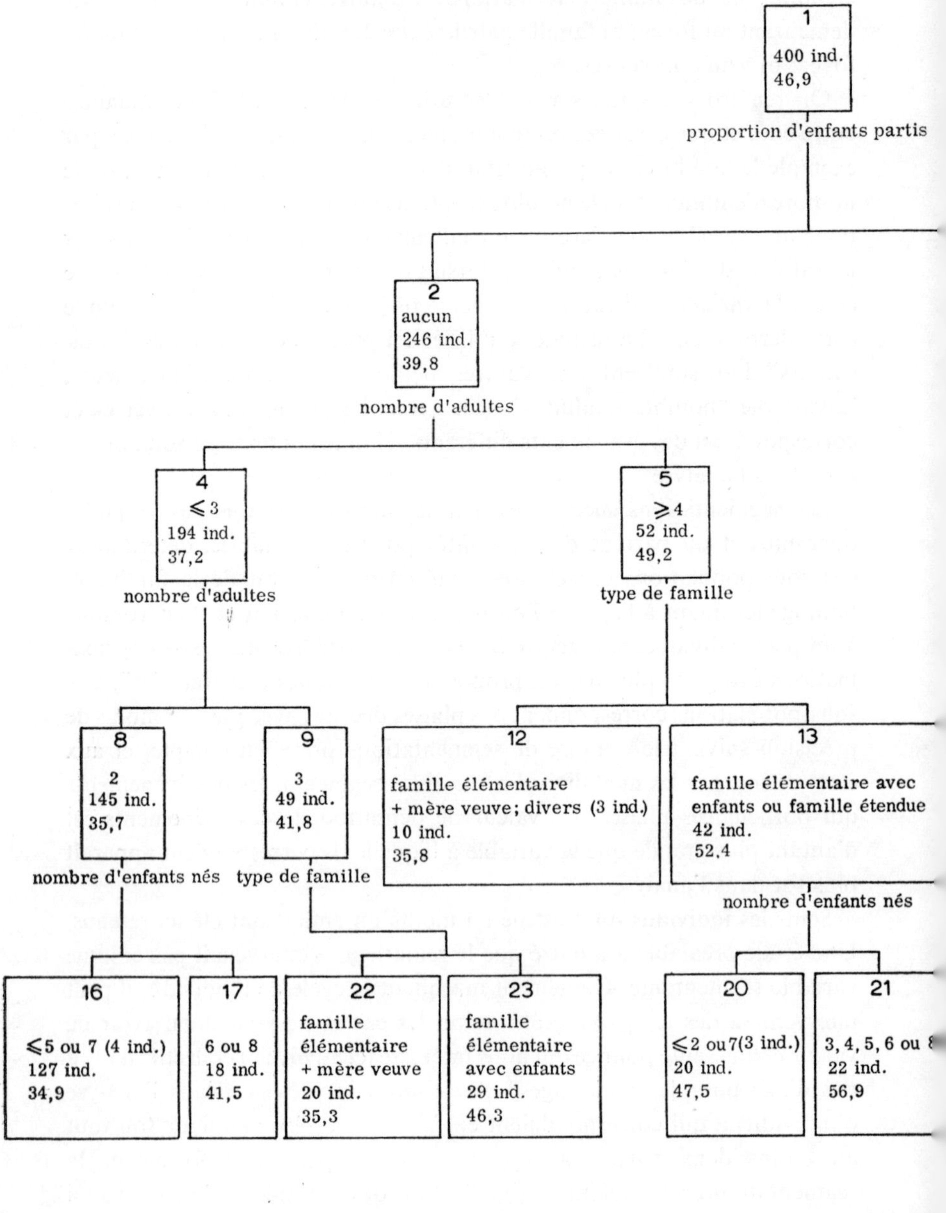

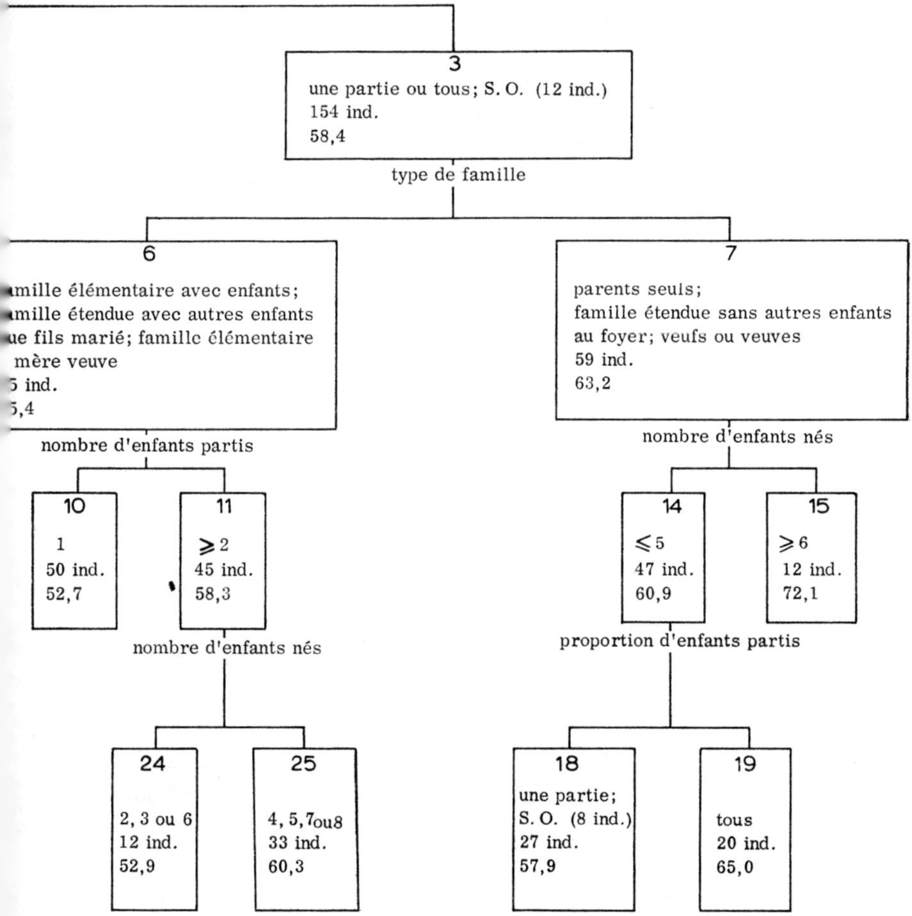
3
une partie ou tous; S. O. (12 ind.)
154 ind.
58,4
type de famille
6
amille élémentaire avec enfants;
amille étendue avec autres enfants
ue fils marié; famille élémentaire
mère veuve
5 ind.
5,4
7
parents seuls;
famille étendue sans autres enfants
au foyer; veufs ou veuves
59 ind.
63,2
nombre d'enfants partis
10
1
50 ind.
52,7
11
⩾2
45 ind.
58,3
nombre d'enfants nés
14
⩽5
47 ind.
60,9
15
⩾6
12 ind.
72,1
nombre d'enfants nés
24
2, 3 ou 6
12 ind.
52,9
25
4, 5, 7ou8
33 ind.
60,3
proportion d'enfants partis
18
une partie;
S. O. (8 ind.)
27 ind.
57,9
19
tous
20 ind.
65,0

nous n'avons fait entrer dans l'analyse que les individus qui n'avaient été mariés qu'une fois.

La figure 1 représente l'arborescence correspondant au résultat de la segmentation. La première variable segmentante est la proportion d'enfants partis. L'évènement le plus marquant, celui qui partage le cycle de la vie familiale en deux parties chronologiquement équivalentes est, quel que soit le type de famille vers lequel évolue l'unité domestique, le départ du premier enfant, c'est-à-dire la première rupture, la première amputation affectant la cellule familiale. La seconde segmentation, sur la partie droite de l'arbre, c'est-à-dire dans la seconde moitié du cycle, fait ressortir, par l'intermédiaire de la variable "type de famille", la phase finale qui commence après le dernier départ d'un enfant, l'unité domestique n'étant plus alors composée que des parents seuls ou, lorsqu'une famille patrilinéaire étendue a été constituée, des parents et du ménage du fils demeuré au foyer. Les branches issues du nœud 7 qui représente cette dernière phase, ne font plus apparaître d'événements marquants, étant donné que le seul qui pourrait survenir avant la dissolution naturelle de l'unité familiale est la mort d'un conjoint, plus précisément ici de l'épouse – puisqu'on travaille sur les chefs de famille et que la population des veufs dans l'enquête est trop faible pour intervenir seule dans une segmentation. La fission de 7 en 14 et 15 est simplement due au fait que les familles très nombreuses arrivent naturellement plus tard à la dernière phase du cycle, c'est-à-dire au départ du dernier enfant, que les autres. Par contre, la segmentation affectant le nœud 14 fait ressortir une particularité de la famille étendue par rapport à la famille élémentaire.[9] En effet, en raison des segmentations antérieures, la variable "proportion d'enfants partis" est ici équivalente au type de la famille. Si l'on écarte l'hypothèse selon laquelle les individus atteindraient un âge plus élevé dans une famille élémentaire qu'en étant à la tête d'une famille étendue, il apparaît que la dernière phase du cycle est atteinte plus rapidement dans les familles étendues que dans les familles élémentaires.[10] Certes, le départ concerne un enfant de moins dans les familles étendues mais d'autres analyses ont montré que le fils demeurant au foyer était plutôt un des aînés. Par ailleurs, le nombre d'enfants n'est pas sensiblement plus élevé dans les familles élémentaires. Il semble donc que le départ des enfants soit plus rapide dans les familles étendues.

Pour ce qui est de la partie du cycle qui va du départ du premier enfant (ou plus exactement du premier départ d'un enfant) à la phase finale, c'est-à-dire au dernier départ, et que représente le nœud 6 de la figure, il apparaît que l'évènement chronologiquement marquant à l'intérieur de cette période est le second départ. En effet, la segmentation du nœud 6 par la variable "nombre d'enfants partis" illustre la succession des scissions affectant l'unité familiale et fait ressortir la distance qui sépare la première de ces scissions des suivantes, lesquelles ne sont plus chronologiquement discernables au niveau de la population, comme le marque sur le nœud 11 la non-monotonicité du nombre d'enfants partis relativement aux moyennes d'âge correspondantes. La segmentation de ce nœud 11 par le nombre d'enfants nés n'est pas susceptible d'une interprétation claire. Certes, il est normal que les familles très nombreuses y soient affectées d'une moyenne plus élevée que les autres, étant naturellement plus lentes à acceder à la dernière phase. Mais la présence dans le nœud 24, d'ailleurs peu important numériquement, de la position "6 enfants" laisse supposer un effet d'échantillon.

La première moitié du cycle de vie, celle qui précède le départ du premier enfant et qui est représentée par la partie gauche de la figure 1, est essentiellement segmentée par les variables "nombre d'adultes au foyer" et "type de famille", celle-ci précisant et corrigeant celle-là. Ainsi apparaissent sur les familles élémentaires les événements marquants que constituent les passages successifs à l'âge adulte des enfants.[11] Par exemple, le nœud 8 représente la phase où aucun enfant n'a atteint l'âge adulte, le nœud 23 celle où un enfant a atteint cet âge et le nœud 13 a pour composante celle où au moins deux enfants sont adultes.[12] Le nœud 17, issu d'une segmentation du 8 par la variable "nombre d'enfants nés" correspond à la naissance de nombreux enfants, avec une périodicité élevée puisque toutes les naissances ont lieu avant le passage de l'aîné à l'âge adulte. Pour ce qui est de la segmentation de "13" en "20" et "21" par cette même variable "nombre d'enfants nés", la faiblesse des effectifs à ce niveau de la segmentation interdit d'écarter l'hypothèse d'un effet d'échantillon. Le décès d'enfants, dans les quelques familles à cycle achevé, peut également avoir joué un rôle.

En résumé, le cycle de vie dans la Yougoslavie des villages se divise du point de vue chronologique en deux moitiés dont la frontière est constituée par le premier départ d'un enfant. La première est marquée essentiellement par le passage à l'âge adulte des enfants, et notamment des deux premiers. L'événement principal de la seconde moitié est le départ du dernier enfant qui marque le début de la phase finale du cycle. Les analyses par segmentation effectuées sur les principales sous-cultures

Figure 2

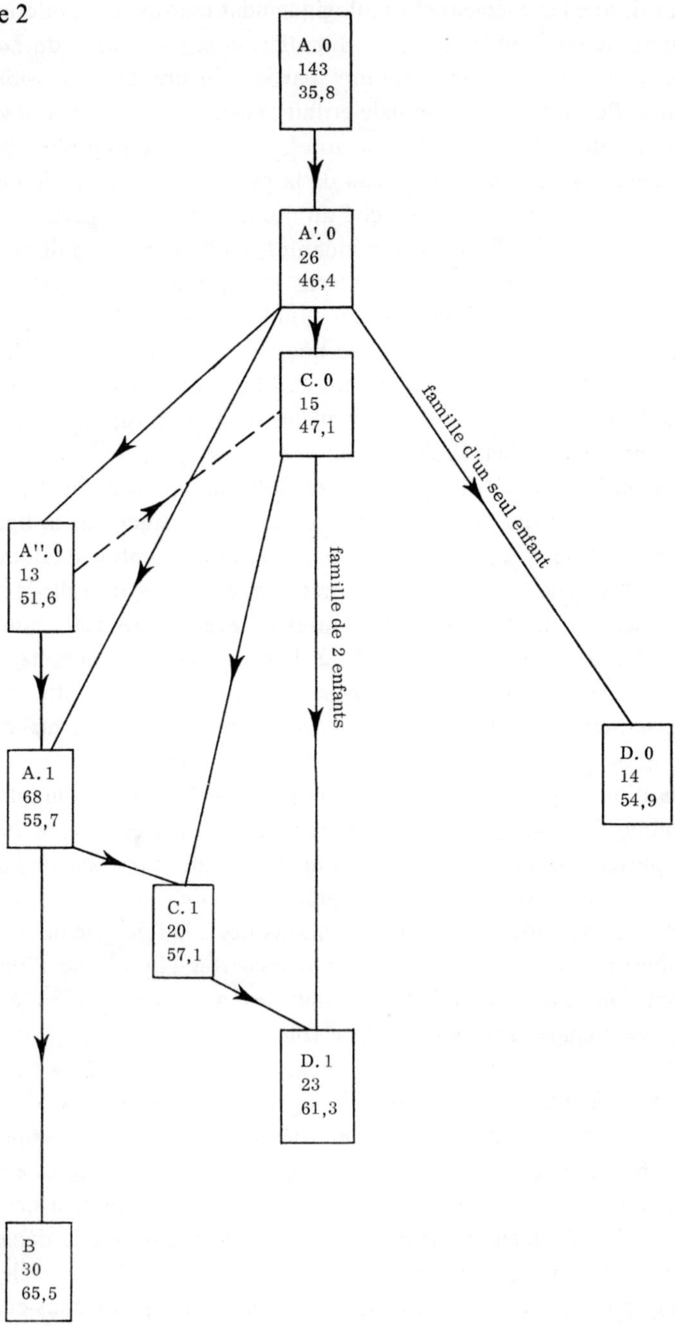
A. 0
143
35,8
A'. 0
26
46,4
C. 0
15
47,1
famille d'un seul enfant
A''. 0
13
51,6
famille de 2 enfants
D. 0
14
54,9
A. 1
68
55,7
C. 1
20
57,1
D. 1
23
61,3
B
30
65,5

(indiquées par les religions: orthodoxes, catholiques et musulmans), et sur les trois strates sociales distinguées par les notables villageois ont confirmé ce résultat qui apparaît donc avoir valeur générale pour la Yougoslavie rurale. En combinant les séquences ainsi définies et l'évolution de la cellule familiale en famille patrilinéaire étendue ou son maintien en famille élémentaire, nous avons obtenu les phases suivantes, opératoires pour l'étude des rapports entre cycle de vie et rôles sociaux:

- A.0 : famille élémentaire, aucun enfant adulte, aucun enfant parti
- A′.0 : famille élémentaire, 1 enfant adulte, aucun enfant parti
- A″.0 : famille élémentaire, au moins deux enfants adultes, aucun enfant parti
- A.1 : famille élémentaire, au moins 1 enfant parti, mais il reste des enfants au foyer
- B : phase finale de la famille élémentaire: tous les enfants sont partis, les parents restent seuls
- C.0 : famille patrilinéaire étendue, aucun enfant n'a quitté le foyer, et il y a au foyer d'autres enfants que celui qui est marié
- C.1 : famille patrilinéaire étendue, au moins un enfant parti, mais restent au foyer d'autres enfants que celui qui est marié
- D.1 : phase finale de la famille étendue, ne reste au foyer que l'enfant marié, après départ des autres enfants
- D.0 : phase finale de la famille étendue, seul vit avec les parents l'enfant marié, mais il n'y a eu aucun départ. En fait, cette phase ne concerne que les familles à enfant unique.

Le graphe orienté de la figure 2 représente les phases ci-dessus énoncées et les différents cycles possibles, chemins qui s'ouvrent à une famille après sa constitution, en A.0. Les sommets du graphe sont les phases, et les arêtes marquent la possibilité de passage d'une phase à l'autre. Sous le nom de chaque phase figurent l'effectif correspondant à cette phase dans l'enquête et l'âge moyen des individus. Les effectifs sont fonction de la fréquence du passage d'une phase à l'autre et de la durée des phases. La hauteur des sommets sur la figure est inversement proportionnelle à l'âge moyen de la phase qu'ils représentent. Ainsi une arête orientée "vers le haut" correspond-elle à un passage improbable, puisque l'âge moyen de l'extrêmité est inférieur à celui de l'origine. L'arête A″.0-C.0 par exemple, est dans ce cas. Les sommets B, D.1 et D.0 représentent les phases finales. Hormis l'hypothèse de mariage avant l'âge adulte, A′.0 est un point de passage pour tout cycle. Les chemins A.0–A′.0–A″.0–A.1–B ou A.0–A′0–A.1–B, – suivant que l'aîné quitte le foyer après ou avant le passage du second enfant à l'âge adulte – représentent le cycle d'une famille élémentaire. Pour atteindre D.1, la phase finale de la famille étendue (quand le fils aîné restant au foyer n'est pas l'unique enfant), plusieurs chemins sont possibles, se confondant plus ou moins longtemps avec celui d'une famille élémentaire. L'arête C.0–D.1 correspond à des familles de deux enfants. Mais quel que soit le chemin suivi, l'évolution vers une famille patrilinéaire étendue est, la comparaison des effectifs des phases D.1 et D.0 d'une part, B d'autre part, le montre, au moins aussi fréquente que celle vers une famille élémentaire, les parents restant seuls. La pérennité de la structure familiale traditionnelle apparaît donc ici, plus nettement que par la comparaison statistique brute entre famille patrilinéaire et famille élémentaire, effectuée sans référence à la phase finale.

La définition des cycles de la vie domestique que nous avons obtenue n'a, répétons-le, qu'une valeur chronologique, sans référence aux rôles sociaux, les rapports de ceux-ci avec la chronologie familiale étant l'objet d'études postérieures. Sur des données transversales, à l'aide d'une technique statistique, nous avons tenté de dégager une réalité collective et synchronique, plutôt qu'un vécu diachronique individuel. Notre matière est une société à un instant donné dont les membres sont à différents moments de leur vie, et non des vies domestiques dans une société sans date. Le but de l'analyse présentée ici était, préalablement à toute étude sociologique proprement dite, un découpage opératoire du cycle de vie, collectivement pertinent. Nous espérons avoir pu montrer le fonctionnement d'un outil statistique relativement simple adapté à cette problématique mettant en œuvre un ensemble de notions, cycle individuel et chronologie, objet collectif et vision synchronique, difficilement saisissables simultanément par d'autres techniques.

Summary

Types of family and life cycle in rural Yugoslavia

In the absence of diachronic data that would allow the application of longitudinal methods, one can attempt to approach the family life cycle by using a transversal study which, on the basis of a population observed at a given moment, i.e., on the basis of synchronic and collective data, establishes a set of diachronic and individual facts. This method is applied here to data gleaned from an investigation in rural Yugoslavia carried out in 1965, consisting essentially of a questionnaire submitted to 700 households from 14 villages chosen to be representatively characteristic of the different subcultures which can be identified in Serbo-Croate culture.

The family life cycle cannot be grasped without reference to an essential characteristic of rural Yugoslavian society: the importance in terms of family structure of the extended patrilineal family. This form of organization, a vestige of the traditional *zadruga* dominant in the last century, seems still to occur very frequently in certain regions, and particularly in Serbia, according to the results of the investigation.

The research reported in this paper is oriented toward determining the successive stages which constitute the life cycle, using as their limits only the natural events that affect the household, i.e., its composition in terms of number and age of its members. Its aim is, in effect, to define its position in the life cycle as a variable whose relations to the individual roles can be studied without interference in the definition of the variables brought together. The events that delimit the stages will be those which appear in an order which is demonstrably identical for all the individuals whose place in the family life cycle is fixed. The statistical method used to this end is a *segmentation* of which the dependent variable is the age of the head of the family. In this analysis, it is evident that the life cycle in the Yugoslavian villages is chronologically divided in two halves, the boundary of which is created by the first time a child leaves the household, a fundamentally determining event. The first half is essentially marked by the growth of the children to adult age, especially that of the two eldest; the second half is demarcated by the departure of the last child, the beginning of the final stage. Taking into account the type toward which the family evolves, parallel to the succession of these key events, we can construct an oriented graph representing the system of the stages of the different possible cycles, channels which are open to a household at the time of its beginning.

Notes

1. *Cf.* J. Cuisenier et A. Eliard, Séminaire sur la structure sociale dans la Yougoslavie des villages (Belgrade, 21–23 décembre 1966) organisé par le Centre de Sociologie Européenne (Ecole Pratique des Hautes Etudes, 6ᵉ section), l'Institut de Sociologie de Belgrade et l'Institut Agraire de Zagreb. Rapport général.
2. V. Bogišić (1882), *Recueil du droit coutumier contemporain*, Zagreb: 5.
3. *Ibid.*: 6.
4. *Ibid.*: 5.
5. Joël Halpern et D. Anderson (1970), "The zadruga, a century of change", *Anthropologica*, N.S., XII, 1.
6. "Programme A.I.D. Note méthodologique", Centre d'Etudes Sociologiques, publication interne.
7. Cette assertion serait fausse au cas où la population serait composée de deux sous-populations de tailles comparables telles que le début de cycle pour l'une correspondrait du point de vue âge à la fin du cycle pour l'autre. En fait, même si une certaine différence peut exister entre diverses sous-cultures relativement à l'âge où l'individu fonde un foyer, l'ampleur d'un tel décalage est minime par rapport à la durée totale du cycle.
8. Même dans une analyse particulière sur les musulmans, où les mariages multiples sont un fait culturel, la variable n'est apparue à aucun moment dans la segmentation.

9. La position S.O. (sans objet) qui apparaît dans le nœud 18 ainsi que dans le nœud 3, correspond au cas où tous les enfants sont décédés. Elle contribue certes à faire baisser la moyenne du nœud, mais la différence entre les modalités "une partie" et "tous" reste importante (5 ans).
10. Même si l'on admettait l'hypothèse selon laquelle les individus culturellement déterminés à devenir chef d'une famille étendue se marient plus tôt que les autres et donc présenteraient un certain décalage dans le déroulement de leur cycle, celle-ci ne suffirait pas à expliquer l'importante différence constatée.
11. L'hypothèse pourrait être faite selon laquelle la première segmentation par la variable "nombre d'adultes" est plus un artefact dû à l'existence de familles étendues et surtout des familles avec présence de la mère du chef de famille, que le révélateur de l'évènement qu'est le passage des enfants à l'âge adulte et notamment celui du deuxième enfant. En fait, si l'on élimine les familles avec présence de la mère veuve, l'âge moyen des chefs de famille de trois adultes est élevé de 4 ans et celui des chefs de familles élémentaires de quatre adultes, de 5 ans. Les nœuds 8, 23 et 13 ont d'ailleurs des âges moyens nettement différents, ce qui ne serait pas dans le cas d'un artefact.
12. Dans ce nœud figurent aussi les familles où un enfant est marié tout en demeurant au foyer. L'âge moyen des chefs de ces familles – si l'enfant n'est pas unique – est intermédiaire entre celui des chefs de familles élémentaires où un seul enfant est adulte et celui des chefs des familles élémentaires où deux enfants au moins sont adultes (mais restent encore au foyer). L'événement que constitue le mariage d'un enfant qui demeure au foyer est ainsi chronologiquement situé entre le passage à l'état adulte de l'aîné et celui du second enfant – ce qui situe cet enfant marié et restant au foyer comme l'aîné. Ceci ne concerne que les familles où aucun enfant n'est encore parti, mais d'après d'autres études, il semble, ainsi qu'il a été indiqué plus haut, qu'en général celui qui reste soit effectivement l'aîné et donc que les familles étendues se constituent avant le premier départ d'un enfant.

RÉFÉRENCES

Cuisenier, J., et Eliard, A. "Séminaire sur la structure sociale dans la Yougoslavie des villages (Belgrade 21–23 décembre 1966)", rapport général polycopié.

Halpern, Joël, et Anderson, David (1970), "The zadruga, a century of change", *Anthropologica*, XII/1.

Halpern Joël, et Kerewsky Halpern, Barbara (1972), *A Serbian Village in Historical Perspective*, New York, Holt, Rinehart & Winston.

"Note méthodologique (A.I.D.)", Centre d'Etudes Sociologiques, Paris, publication interne, 1970, ronéoté, 12p.

V. *Theoretical extensions of the concept*

Elargissement du champ théorique du concept

22. Content of relations with relatives

JOHN MOGEY

Introduction

All families go through a series of stages as their individual members pass through interaction patterns that are usually classed as pre-marital, marital, parental, and eventually by the loss of a role partner, simply residential. All families move through some such developmental sequence; some, through divorce, separation, or death, may enter the sequence of interactions more than once. Families also maintain contact with some relatives; they form units in a system of kinship interactions. This paper addresses itself to two separate problems: first, can any regular pattern be discovered between the frequency of interaction of kinsfolk and the content, or purposes, or functions served by this interaction?: second, do these patterns, or structures, if discovered, vary with the different stages of the developmental family cycle? When both of these questions have been answered, then the answers may be used to construct new theoretical propositions at a later period.

Research on the sociology of the family published in the last twenty years demonstrates that nuclear families as households maintain contact with their relatives; the notion that the nuclear family is isolated has been attacked from several fronts. Firstly, taking isolation to mean absence of interaction between persons, many authors have shown clearly that interactions with relatives are constant in most modern societies. These writers have also shown that relatives are more likely to be visited, or to be seen, when:

- they are closer kin, i.e., parents or grandparents (rather than second cousins);

- they are members of the same social class;
- they share an ethnic identity;
- they are similar in age, religion, or in their experience of social mobility.

(Aiken & Goldberg, 1969; Blau, 1956; Litwak, 1960, a & b; Litwak & Seleyni, 1969; Michel, 1960, 1972; Mogey, 1956; Munch, 1949; Reiss, 1962; Sharp & Axelrod, 1956; Sussman, 1959; Sussman & Burchinal, 1962; Sweetser, 1968; Willmott & Young, 1960; Young & Willmott, 1957).

Other papers show that patterns of contacts with relatives are independent of patterns of contact with neighbors, or with friends, or with participation in voluntary associations (Axelrod, 1956; Dotson, 1951; Greer, 1956; Litwak, 1960a). Interaction within a kinship system is therefore different from interaction in other small scale membership systems. In systems theory this probably means that kinship and other membership systems serve different functions for their members.

Some published material in the literature on family and kinship holds that patterns of contact in kinship systems have changed over the generations; that industrialism, urbanism, and modernization are related to the emergence of the isolated nuclear family from an extended family form (Goode, 1963; Parsons, 1954; Parsons & Bales, 1955).

This point about change requires that we distinguish interaction between individuals, which may be called social interaction, since its absence indicates the presence of social isolation, from contacts between social units like households and the families that inhabit them. In this second sense interaction may also lead to isolation, but this is structural isolation, the separate existence of social units. In its original formulation the concept of the isolation of the nuclear family referred to the tendency of families to set up households separate from those of other units in the kinship system, both spatially and financially (Farber, 1968, 1970, 1971; Parsons, 1954). It is this structural type of isolation that is held to have increased with modernization (Anderson, 1971; Furstenberg, 1966; Garigue, 1962; Greenfield, 1961; Shorter, 1971; Sweetser, 1966).

A recent monograph reviews the literature on social isolation (Klatsky, 1971) and tests propositions against data obtained from a 1965 national random quota sample of the U.S.A. (N = 1469 male adults). Using multivariate analysis, this paper confirms that kinship defines an independent system or network of contacts, since the boundary of the network depends on genealogical position. The minimal boundary includes three separate families, the family in which the male respondent is a spouse, the family in which he was a child, and the family in which his wife was a child.

Evidence shows that for this sample, frequency in son–father contacts correlates highly with frequency in all other types of contact. Within the system, frequency of contact depends most importantly on distance. Differences in frequency of contact with relatives which have been shown to occur between Catholic and Protestant families, between urban and rural dwellers, between dwellers in metropolitan cities and those in smaller cities, between working class and middle class households, can all be largely accounted for by distance.

Residential propinquity has earlier been shown to be a powerful predictor in the initiation of family life, that is to say in mate selection (Katz & Hill, 1958). More work will be needed to explore the possibility that on the one hand distance associated with frequency of contact with kin, and on the other hand residential propinquity as a variable in mate selection are equivalent. This is assuming that distance might be restated as residential propinquity.

Another confirmation of the point made above about the separation of kinship patterns from other systems is the finding in this monograph that social mobility had no measurable effects on frequency of contact with kinsfolk. This indicates that kinship is separate from stratification in this society. Two other variables added to the explanatory power of distance, ethnicity and age of husband, but their assistance was quantitatively minor.

Content of kinship contacts

Meeting relatives presumably serves some purposes other than pure sociability. Measures of frequency of contact provide only the minimum information about social interaction. Several studies describe the categories of purpose served by kinship contact (Hill, 1970; Sussman & Burchinal, 1962); many however report on the consequences of contacts in general for the family, rather than describe the specific content of contacts. These functions of the interaction range from the maintenance of the nuclear household itself, or the rate of the build-up of the inventory of household equipment, to the survival of the older individual through care and affection (Bott, 1971; Cummings & Schneider, 1961; Hill, 1970; Mogey, 1970; Shanas & Streib, 1965).

Data from a Boston study allow us to examine the relations between frequency of contact and the content of the interaction. The study population is the families of 2,000 male veterans enrolled in a longitudinal normative study of aging (Bell, Rose & Damon, 1966, 1972). The normative aging population are all in good health, since that is the condition for entry to the study, they cover all stages of the parental cycle, all ages between 25 and 75, have examples of most metropolitan occupations with a low labor turnover, are geographically stable and come from a varied ethnic background.

Since increased age and poor health, together with their associated chronic medical problems, are supposed to influence both the frequency and the content of contact between relatives, the fact that the original population of the sample was screened for good health is of great theoretical and analytical importance. In short, the effects of health and its relatively obligatory contribution both to frequency of contact and to type of aid, are controlled in these analyses.

A sub-sample was drawn from this population by selecting proportional numbers from each age group and occupation; this sub-sample rejected subjects who were unmarried, divorced, in their second marriage, or childless. The elimination of all households not inhabited by a nuclear family in its first marriage and with children, either at home or grown-up and in independent households, controls for a number of variables that normally complicate analyses of survey data about kinship systems.

By these means a relatively homogeneous set of 227 respondents was obtained. Their responses to questions about interactions with particular kinsfolk should contain patterns that support hypotheses about the operation of kinship systems. Unfortunately, since this is a secondary analysis of already collected data, the hypothesis that distance is the variable most closely associated with frequency of interaction with kinsmen cannot be tested, as information on distance was not obtained. However, it is possible to test the hypothesis that relations between father and son model the general pattern of frequency of contact between adult males and other relatives of the three families that constitute the minimal kinship system; these are, of course, the family of the respondent, the family of the father of the respondent, and the family of the parents of the respondent's spouse. Neither the normative aging sample, nor this sub-sample are random probability samples. Consequently, the distributions are not known to be representative of any larger universe. Interest centers on the patterns of interaction among the variables, not on the incidence of these patterns in a population, so a random probability sample is not essential.

The patterns of kinship interaction are, as a result of the sample design, free of contamination of age and poor health on interaction frequency. Correlations within the data show that the behavior of respondents is also free of significant correlations with: age; ethnicity; education; occupation, and other social class indicators. This means that any patterns discovered cannot be accounted for by these variables. This finding supports, by its negation of other possible relationships, the credibility of the earlier finding that distance accounts for most variations in frequency of contacts between relatives (Klatsky, 1971).

Since frequency of contact is simply the basic count of number of interactions it should relate equally to all measurements of the specific content of those interactions.

A search for patterns in a set of responses can best be completed through multivariate procedures and of these factor analysis is appropriate. Each subject was asked to respond to questions about:

frequency of contact – daily visits to once yearly visits
feelings of closeness – very close, moderately close, not at all close
financial aid
household help
child-rearing help
advice and moral support

These male veterans were asked specifically about:

subject's: mother and father, brothers and sisters
subject's spouse's: mother and father, brothers and sisters.

Two factor analyses were performed. First, all kinship interactions were subjected to a principal components factor program with orthogonal rotation (Rivero, 1970). After inspection of these results, data about brothers and sisters of respondent and of his spouse were omitted and the remaining intergenerational data subjected to an oblique principal components factor program. (Kamara, 1972) The orthogonal program searches for factors that are independent of each other, or in other words, assumes correlations between factors are zero. The oblique program allows for the possibility that factors may not be truly independent of each other.

The results of the orthogonal analysis are presented summarily in Table 1. Seventeen separate factors accounted for 71% of the variance. Only Factor 1 accounted for more than 10%; although all factors are statistically independent of each other, the repetition of the same combination of variables and the association of roles in the same factor should

Table 1. *Orthogonal factor analysis*

Factor	Roles	Type of content in relationship	% of variance accounted for
I	Father; Brother; Father-in-law; Brother-in-law; Mother-in-law; Sister	Household help	11
II	Father-in-law; Brother-in-law;	Advice and moral support; Childrearing help	7
III	Mother	Childrearing help; Advice and moral support	6
IV	Brother-in-law	Advice and moral support; Childrearing help; Household help	5
V	Father; Brother	Advice and moral support; Childrearing help; Frequency of contact; Feelings of closeness; Household help; Financial help	5
VI	Sister-in-law	Advice and moral support; Childrearing help	5
VII	Sister	Advice and moral support; Childrearing help; Household help	4
VIII	Mother-in-law; Sister	Frequency of contact	4
IX	Mother-in-law; Mother; Father-in-law	Advice and moral support; Childrearing help; Household help; Financial help	3
X	Father	Frequency of contact; Feelings of closeness; Financial help	3
XI	Brother	Advice and moral support Childrearing help	3
XII	Sister-in-law; Mother-in-law; Sister	Feelings of closeness; Household help; Childrearing help	3
XIII	Father-in-law; Brother-in-law	Frequency of contact; Feelings of closeness	3
XIV	Sister; Mother-in-law	Frequency of contact; Feelings of closeness; Financial help	3
XV	Mother	Frequency of contact; Feelings of closeness; Financial help	2
XVI	Brother-in-law; Sister-in-law	Financial security; Feelings of closeness	2
XVII	Brother-in-law; Sister-in-law	Financial security; Frequency of contact	1
Source: Rivero (1970): 97–102		Total variance	71%

be interpreted as meaning that kinship interaction forms a single complex system. Neither relations with in-laws nor relations with own family predominate. Frequency of contact is associated with many roles, including son–father on Factor V and Factor X; the discovery that frequency of contact is related to many other types of relation probably means that son–father relations are not a model for other relations in a kinship system. While the correlations reach the .05 level of significance, most are low.

The oblique solution in factor analysis allows a search for correlations between factors. In the analysis reported in Table 2 ten factors are used: preliminary trials with five, six and nine factors showed that a minimum of ten factors was needed to encompass the variation in the data. Under the oblique rotation program, the analysis accounts for 100% of the

Table 2. *Oblique factor analysis*

Factor	Intergenerational roles	Type of content in relationship	% of variance accounted for
I	Mother-in-law Father-in-law	Household help; Childrearing help	28
II	Mother Father	Frequency of contact	15
III	Mother, father Mother-in-law Father-in-law	Advice and moral support	13
IV	Mother Father	Household help	11
V	Father-in-law Mother-in-law	Financial help	9
VI	Mother Father	Feelings of closeness	8
VII	Father	Financial help	5
VIII	Mother Mother-in-law	Childrearing help; Household help	5
IX	Mother-in-law Father-in-law	Frequency of contact	4
X	Mother-in-law Father-in-law	Feelings of closeness	3

Source: Kamara, 1972

variance. In the oblique solution, four factors refer exclusively to relations with parents of respondent, four to relations with in-laws, and in two, both sets of relatives are linked together. As in the orthogonal factor matrix, no signs of greater emphasis on maternal relatives, nor on the more salient role of the female are apparent. Both matrilaterality and the importance of females in maintaining relations with relatives have been reported in other studies (Sweetser, 1968).

The importance of constructing oblique factors is that they can be intercorrelated. This is done in Table 3. The table shows the strength of

Table 3. *Factor correlations produced by the oblique solution*

Factor	Factor II	III	IV	V	VI	VII	VIII	IX	X
I	−.04	.21	.28*	.11	.02	−.08	.21	.33*	.25*
II		.01	.18	.02	.24*	.09	.04	.23*	.13
III			−.18	−.07	.09	−.02	−.09	−.08	−.16
IV				.03	.04	.29*	.14	.05	.03
V					.15	.11	−.07	.11	.26*
VI						−.03	−.02	−.02	−.20
VII							−.07	.04	.00
VIII								.00	.13
IX									.29*

Source: Kamara, 1972
$r = .232$, $df\ 72$, $p \leqq .05$*

association between factors; it does not unfortunately indicate directionality. For a matrix such as Table 3, those correlations that equal or exceed .23 are statistically significant. Omitting other correlations, the results can be arranged as in Figure 1. This is a diagram of the pattern of relations within a kinship system. Factors that combine parents and in-laws have low correlations and are omitted. The eight factors that remain divide equally between parents of both spouses. The diagram arranges them in an order that corresponds to a basic hypothesis of interaction theory. This holds that frequency of contact leads to feelings of closeness and this in turn leads to other consequences of interaction (Homans, 1961). If the theory was to be confirmed in this trial, the size of the correlations might be expected to vary with the level of the variable; our results give general support to this basic theoretical proposition, though the degree of fit is not completely isomorphic between the predictions and the findings. This analysis shows in addition that kinship systems are almost equally balanced between parent and in-law relatives.

Exchanges of activities in the form of household or child-rearing help relate most closely both to frequency of contact and to feelings of closeness. Advice and moral support, a more diffuse area of relations is also

Figure 1. *Diagram of kinship*

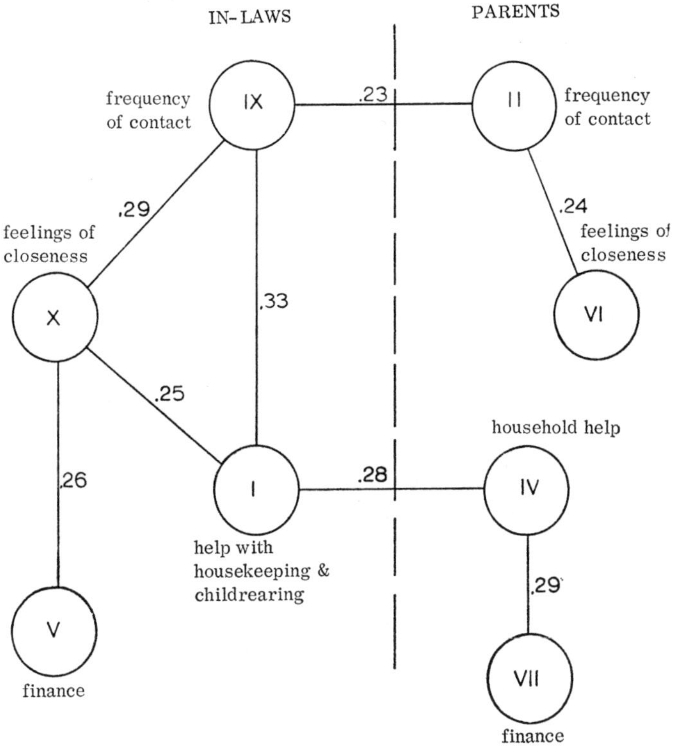

Sourc: Kamara, 1972

associated with household and child-rearing help. (Factors I and IV) As stated before, the kinship structure so described is free of significant correlations with age, ethnicity, education, occupation and other social class indicators. Kinship relations are therefore not significantly influenced by these measures of other social structures. This finding extends the reports in the literature that kinship, friendship and neighboring are independent social systems to the statement that kinship is also independent of major social structures.

Theory building

The data analyses summarized in earlier sections show that the amount of contact between relatives is largely a function of distance. Although these data refer to son–father contacts and, although the ability of son–father contacts to stand as an index of relations with other relatives is not proven, there can be no question that distance in the sense of residential propinquity explains most of the variance in frequency of contact with kin.

The Boston sample does two things:

1. it confirms earlier suppositions that relations between kin cohere in an independent social structure that has order as well as complexity (Rivero, 1970);
2. the content of these contacts intergenerationally falls into a neat pattern in which frequency of contact is associated with feelings of closeness and this, in turn, with the exchange of activities, on the one hand, and on the other hand, with the exchange of expressive behavior in the form of advice and moral support (Kamara, 1972).

Examples in the literature describe similar relationships in most societies, and across several generations. This presumed universality of kinship structures presupposes that they are independent of change in the rest of society. If kinship structures maintain continuity of patterns, while other social systems change, then they must be independent of these other systems. Such independence can never be absolute since individuals from kinship structures also participate in work, in political, in educational, in religious, in friendship and in many other types of organizational networks. The theoretical proposition may be stated as: family-kinship structures persist with few changes while larger structures of the society are rapidly changing.

Given that kinship structures persist with minor changes in the face of massive change in political and economic organizations, it is worth looking at the literature of sociology for other examples of continuity. All kinship systems described have been based on separate households for each family: the Boston samples were deliberately selected to include nuclear family households and no others.

Historians of the family, and students of census data, have in the past twenty years noticed that average household size is always about 4, plus or minus 1, persons. In advanced industrial societies the average fluctuates around 3 persons: in transitional societies, it fluctuates around 5 persons. For traditional or tribal societies, and for some transitional societies, the data either are not available, or are not reliable (Coale & others, 1965; Burch, 1967). This remarkable fact has been used to construct propositions about universal experiences in the home life of all humanity (Levy, 1970).

While average household size is bi-modal, the range is wide. In developed societies such as Sweden, over 60% of the population is clustered in households of 3 to 5 persons: in developing societies, such as U.A.R. or the Phillipines, about 30% of the population lives in households of 3 to 5 persons. In spite of variations in household size, the average is a good measure for comparing one society with another. Comparisons of household composition re-inforce this conclusion. In all 17 countries where census data allows the calculation of the proportion of all households that are nuclear families, 65% or more of all households are nuclear families in 16 of these countries, in 7 countries the ratio rises to 80% or more nuclear family households (Burch, 1967).

Wherever statistical data are adequate, households tend for the most part towards an average size of about four persons and the vast majority of these households are wholly composed of nuclear families. This is the social unit about which the frequency of contact, and the content of kin relations, has been presented.

Such a small unit composed of individuals differing in age, sex, and background, runs the risk of disintegration. Yet all the evidence is that families and households are remarkably stable over time. This stability persists in face of a regular cycle of developmental stresses: surveys of inner city ghettos in the U.S. find a remarkable stability of residence and of household structures there (Mogey, 1970). Theoretically household structures and family structures, although they inhabit the same space, need to be distinguished. The household may be tougher than the family, since it often survives divorce, desertion, separation, or death of a spouse or a child. This may be because households are simpler structures with fewer roles.

Families as sub-systems of all societies are organized around an axis of inequality. There is, by definition, difference in the sexes of spouses, and in ages of family members. More fundamentally, spouses reserve sexual rights to themselves, and treat children as unequals in the socialization process. In the household, on the other hand, a form of equality exists.

Households everywhere consist by definition of those individuals who share a common physical structure and eat at a common table. From this, it would seem that individuals in them develop and share a common life style: this may be termed equality, since each household member has equal rights to have his needs for shelter, food and esteem recognized: all members, in fact, are equal in status.

While not completely universal as the residential domestic unit of all societies, the household-family system shows a remarkable continuity both as to size and as to composition in those societies for which adequate data exist (Laslett, 1972). Over the past century, most modern societies had major transformations in their political systems, most underwent the economic shift from agriculture to factory production, most transport of goods changed from horse and wagon, first to canal boat, then to railway and now to trucks and highways. The household-family did change but the amount and direction of change seems to be much less than occurred in other parts of these societies: the change in household-family systems would seem to be in the rise in the ratio of nuclear family households from 75% (Anderson, 1971; Burch, 1967) to over 80% (C.P.R., 1973). In accounting for the small size of the average household, Coale (1965) developed a computer simulation based on age at death of 50 which predicted with good accuracy the range of actual sizes observed. Now that the average at death is over 70 in most industrial societies, the small size of the household should be predictable by the nuclearity of the family in the household, rather than by the death of a spouse.

The toughness and survival power of these small social systems can hardly be due to their internal structure. All social theorists recognize that households need so many different inputs to survive as a system, that it looks logical to postulate that major changes in societies should lead to major changes in household-family units. The evidence from the comparative history of the family and contemporary data from east European societies all demonstrate that the correlations between changes in macrostructures and changes in households will be low (Piotrowski, 1970).

Some indirect confirmation of this position can be drawn from studies that link together societal changes and family changes (Goode, 1963; Nimkoff & Middleton, 1960; Winch & Blumberg, 1968); Goode argues that a variety of family structures in pre-industrial societies has been transformed into a single conjugal family type with the coming of industrialization: Nimkoff and Middleton argue that hunting and gathering groups and advanced complex industrial societies share a predominance of the nuclear family as the domestic group: Winch and Blumberg find several different axes of societal complexity and several different sorts of family structures and make predictions that social class position in the society explained the household-family type. This is really to say that social classes have distinctive family patterns. This proposition finds no support either in Klatsky or in the Boston analyses. Indeed, a factor analysis of the data bank used by both Nimkoff and Winch found that of nine factors extracted: four referred to separate forms of economy such as hunting, agriculture, animal husbandry; four grouped together variables relating to the family system; and one was social stratification (Sawyer & LeVine, 1966). This additional factor structure supports the proposition made above in the present paper: that the household-family system is virtually independent of the major social organizations of society such as its polity, economy, and its stratification system.

This theoretical revision would see societies as consisting of two sets of sub-systems: one, a deviation-amplyfying sub-system set that undergoes social change through increases in organizational and institutional complexity; and two, a deviation-dampening set of sub-systems in which continuity is preserved and the impact of change on the individual reduced. This set of sub-systems includes neighborhoods and communities, kinship networks, households and families. Changes in localized community patterns from closed to open have been shown to be related to changes in marital role relations within families (Bott, 1971). One paper shows that interaction frequency amongst neighboring households is the crucial variable in this change in marital roles (Mogey and Morris, 1960).

No linear or direct relationship has yet been found between societal change and changes in the household family system. The proposition that there are in all societies a deviation-dampening set of sub-systems would explain some of the complex relations reported. Among these deviation-dampening systems are the neighborhood and the kinship networks. The data in this paper show that kinship interaction operates for all families irrespective of social class, the rate of social mobility, ethnicity or religion: but that kinship visitation is sensitive to distance, that is to neighboring as a social process. The content of kinship contacts is primarily the instrumental aids needed to preserve the independent functioning of the home: household help, child-rearing help and financial help; expressive aid in the form of advice and moral support is less central to the dynamics of kinship interaction.

These exchanges are shared between parents and children and also between the brothers and sisters of both generations and of both spouses, so the kinship system is a complex whole, even in the U.S.A., where bi-laterality and mobility work against the maintenance of regular patterns of interaction.

Kinship provides assistance:

1. to the household by financing the house and its equipment;
2. to parents as they engage in child-rearing;
3. to individuals through a sense of closeness which promotes self-awareness and feelings of security.

In these ways it promotes the functional survival and identity of the small nuclear family household.

The model of society as an amalgam of two separate systems fits the facts shown in the various analyses of kinship and other small scale social systems reviewed in this paper. If the model has merit, then the next step is to investigate the complex patterns by which neighborhoods and kinsfolk, households and families, interact to maintain their continuity in face of changes at work, in political attitudes, in statuses, and in other organizations. The unit for this type of study should be the interacting kinsfolk as a single system rather than their separate households.

RÉSUMÉ

Le contenu des relations de parenté

Les relations de parenté dans les sociétés modernes semblent être une expérience commune à la plupart des ménages. Les preuves, publiées ou non, de tels systèmes d'interaction parentale sont examinées pour découvrir si des modèles réguliers peuvent être établis.

Les données de cet article démontrent que les limites des systèmes de parenté dans les sociétés modernes sont claires; la fréquence d'interaction entre individus au sein de tels systèmes correspond principalement à la distance entre les lieux de résidence; des variables additionnelles telles que l'âge, le rôle social de père, mère, fils, fille ou de parents par alliance, la religion, la classe sociale, la mobilité sociale ont peu d'effets sur la fréquence des relations. Cette absence de corrélation entre la fréquence des relations et l'âge et le rôle social (qui a un lien avec l'âge) met en question les théories de développement du cycle de vie familiale comme sources de typologies pour l'analyse de la famille.

En outre, la fréquence des contacts correspond au contenu de ces relations: les corrélations les plus importantes relient la fréquence à des types spécifiques de contact tels que l'aide dans les tâches ménagères et dans l'éducation des enfants; certains contacts spécifiques entre générations correspondent à des formes plus diffuses d'aide telles que donner des conseils, des informations et un soutien moral; une aide financière correspond plus intimement à ces formes diffuses d'aide.

Les résultats de cette recherche servent partiellement de support à deux nouvelles affirmations théoriques. D'abord l'indépendance des systèmes de parenté par rapport à la classe sociale ou aux systèmes de stratification, et leur existence dans tous les groupes ethniques et résidentiels, est utilisée pour avancer la proposition que les systèmes de parenté fonctionnent indépendamment des structures sociales majeures dans toute société, c'est-à-dire qu'elles sont indépendantes des données politiques ou économiques et du système de stratification sociale.

Cette affirmation rend douteuse la position communément admise que des changements dans la société seront suivis par des changements dans la famille. Une ré-analyse des publications reflétant ce point de vue communément défendu offre quelque soutien aux propositions avancées dans cet article.

En second lieu, à l'intérieur de chaque système de parenté, les données suggèrent que la thèse de Homans selon laquelle la fréquence de l'interaction conduit à des sentiments d'intimité est soutenable même si les données de cet article ne peuvent appuyer des affirmations sur le sens des influences, ni sur leur causalité. La découverte que la fréquence des relations est expliquée principalement par la proximité résidentielle, ou la distance, transforme cette proposition de théorie de l'interaction en une théorie moderne de systèmes. Enfin, à partir de cette position nouvelle de théorie de systèmes, l'article suggère que les systèmes de parenté fonctionnent pour permettre aux unités familiales de tels groupes de résoudre leurs besoins d'identité, leur besoin d'aide supplémentaire pour l'éducation des enfants, et leurs besoins financiers pour l'entretien du ménage, et par cette immuabilité, rendre supportable les changements de la vie politique etc.

References

Aiken, Michael T., and Goldberg, David (1969), "Social mobility and kinship: a re-examination of the hypothesis", *American Anthropologist*, 71, April: 261–270.

Anderson, Michael (1971), *Family Structure in Nineteenth-Century Lancashire*, Cambridge, England, Cambridge University Press.

Axelrod, Morris (1956), "Urban structure and social participation", *American Sociological Review*, 21: 13–18.

Bell, B., Rose, C.L., and Damon, A. (1966), "The Veterans" Administration longitudinal study of healthy aging", *The Gerontologist*, 4: 179–184.

—— (1972), "Aging and human development. The normative aging study issue", *The Gerontologist*, 3: 1–200.

Blau, Peter M. (1956), "Social mobility and interpersonal relations", *American Sociological Review*, 21, June: 290–295.

Bott, Elizabeth (1971), *Family and Social Network*, New York, Free Press (Second edition).

Burch, T.K. (1967), "The size and structure of families: a comparative analysis of census data", *American Sociological Review*, 32: 347–363.

Coale, Ansley, J., Fallers, L.A., Levy, M.J., Scheider, D.M., and Tompkins, S.S. (1965), *Aspects of the Analysis of Family Structure*, Princeton, Princeton University Press.

Cummings, E., and Schneider, D.M. (1961), "Sibling solidarity: a property of American kinship", *American Anthropologist*, 63: 498–507.

Current Population Reports (1973), 251, June, Washington, D.C., Bureau of the Census: 20.

Dotson, Floyd (1951), "Patterns of voluntary associations among working-class people", *American Sociological Review*, 16: 687–693.

Farber, Bernard (1968), *Comparative Kinship Systems*, New York, John Wiley.
—— (1970), "Marriage law, kinship paradigms and family stability" in Presvelou and P. de Bie (eds.), *Images and Counterimages of Young Families*, Louvain, Belgium, Institute of Social Research: 79–120.
—— (1971), *Kinship and Class*, New York, Basic Books.
Furstenburg, Frank F. Jr. (1966), "Industrialization and the American family: a look backward", *American Sociological Review*, 31, June: 326–337.
Garigue, Philip (1962), *La Vie familiale des Canadiens français*, Montréal, Presses Univ. de Montréal.
Goode, W.J. (1963), *World Revolution and Family Patterns*, New York, Free Press.
Greenfield, Sidney M. (1961), "Industrialization and the family in sociological theory", *American Journal of Sociology*, 67: 312–322.
Greer, Scott (1956), "Urbanism reconsidered", *American Sociological Review*, 21: 20–25.
Hill, Reuben (1970), *Family Development in Three Generations*, Cambridge, Mass., Schenkman.
Homans, G.C. (1961), *Social Behavior; Its Elementary Forms*, New York, Harper.
Kamara, J. Lawrence (1972), "Family and kinship relationships: a study of intergenerational solidarity", Ph.D. dissertation, Boston University. Ann Arbor, Michigan: University Microfilms (This contains full reports on variables and the results of oblique factor analyses).
Katz, A.M., and Hill, Reuben (1958), "Residential propinquity and marital selection: a review of theory, method and fact", *Marriage and Family Living*, 20: 27–35.
Klatzky, Shiela R. (1971), *Patterns of Contact with Relatives*, Washington, D.C., American Sociological Association, Rose Monograph Series.
Laslett, T.P.R., and Wall, R. (1972), *Household and Family in Past Time*, Cambridge, England, Cambridge University Press.
Levy, Marion J., Jr. (1970), "Some hypotheses about the family", *Journal of Comparative Family Studies*, 1: 119–131.
Litwak, Eugene (1960a), "Occupational mobility and extended family cohesion", *American Sociological Review*, 25, February: 9–21.
—— (1960b), "Geographic mobility and extended family cohesion", *American Sociological Review*, 25, June: 385–394.
—— and Szelenyi, Ivan (1969), "Primary group structures and their functions: kin, neighbors, and friends", *American Sociological Review*, 34, August: 465–481.
Michel, Andrée Vielle (1960), "Kinship relations and relationships of proximity in French working-class households" in Norman W. Bell and Ezra F. Vogel (eds.), *A Modern Introduction to the Family*, Glencoe, The Free Press: 287–294.
—— (1972), *Sociologie de la famille et du mariage*, Paris, Presses Univ. de France.
Mogey, John M. (1956), *Family and Neighborhood*, Oxford, Oxford University Press.
—— (1970), "The Negro family system in the United States" in Reuben Hill and René Koenig (eds.), *Families in East and West. Socialization Process and Kinship Ties*, The Hague-Paris, Mouton: 442–453.
—— and Morris, R.N. (1960), "Causes of change in family role patterns", *Bulletin of Family Development*, 1: 1–10, Kansas City, Mo., Community Studies, Inc..
Munch, Peter A. (1949), "Social adjustment among Wisconsin Norwegians", *American Sociological Review*, 14, December: 780–787.
Nimkoff, M.F., and Middleton, R. (1960), "Types of family and types of economy", *American Journal of Sociology*, 66: 215–225.
Parsons, Talcott (1954), "The kinship system of the contemporary United States" in *Essays in Sociological Theory*, revised, New York, Free Press: 177–196.

—— (1964), "Evolutionary universals in society", *American Sociological Review*, 29: 339–357.

—— and Freed Bales, R. (1955), *Family, Socialization and Interaction Process*, New York, Free Press.

Piotrowski, Jerzy (1970), *Old People in Poland and Their Vital Capacity*, Warsaw, Institute of Social Economy.

Reiss, Paul J. (1962), "The extended kinship system: correlates of and attitudes on frequency of interaction", *Marriage and Family Living*, 24, November: 333–339.

Rivero, Eneida B. (1970), "Family structure and values: a methodological study for the prediction of health", Ph.D. dissertation, Boston University, Ann Arbor, Michigan: University Microfilms (This contains full reports on variables and the results of orthogonal factor analyses).

Sawyer, J., and LeVine, R. (1966), "Cultural dimensions: a factor analysis of the world ethnographic sample", *American Anthropologist*, 68: 708–731.

Shanas, Ethel, and Streib, G. (eds.) (1965), *Social Structure and the Family: Generational Relations*, Englewood Cliffs, New Jersey, Prentice-Hall.

Sharp, Harry, and Axelrod, Morris (1956), "Mutual aid among relatives in an urban population" in Ronald Freedman, *et al.* (eds.), *Principles of Sociology*, revised, New York, Holt, Rinehart and Winston: 433–439.

Shorter, E.A. (1971), "Illegitimacy, sexual revolution and social change in modern Europe", *Journal of Interdisciplinary History*, 2: 237–272.

Sussman, Marvin B. (1959), "The isolated family: fact or fiction", *Social Problems*, 6, Spring: 333–340.

Sussman, Marvin B., and Burchinal, Lee (1962), "Kin family network: unheralded structure in current conceptualizations of family functioning", *Marriage and Family Living*, 24, August: 231–240.

Sweetser, Dorrian (1966), "The effect of industrialization on intergenerational solidarity", *Rural Sociology*, 31: 156–170.

—— (1968), "Intergenerational ties in Finnish urban families", *American Sociological Review*, 33: 236–246.

Willmott, Peter, and Young, Michael (1960), *Family and Class in a London Suburb*, London, Routledge and Kegan Paul.

Winch, R.F., and Blumberg, R.L. (1968), "Societal complexity and familial organization" in R.F. Winch and L.W. Goodman (eds.), *Selected Studies in Marriage and the Family*, New York, Holt, Rinehart and Winston, 3rd edition.

Young, Michael, and Willmott, Peter (1957), *Family and kinship in East London*, London, Routledge and Kegan Paul.

23. Le processus de divorce

JACQUES COMMAILLE et ANNE BOIGEOL

De tous les travaux entrepris récemment en France sur le divorce,[1] aucun n'a adopté le cadre conceptuel découlant de l'approche développementale de la famille. Cela aurait-il été possible? En fait, le cycle de la vie familiale tel qu'il est systématisé pose un sérieux problème au chercheur travaillant sur le divorce. La classification en 8 phases de Duvall (1962) ou en 24 phases de Rodgers (1962), fait implicitement référence à un modèle dominant de l'institution familiale. Ce cycle ne débute qu'avec le mariage, se déroule avec la naissance et l'élevage des enfants, se poursuit par la période post-parentale et la retraite du père pour ne s'achever qu'à la mort. Mais le divorce, conçu semble-t-il comme un "événement perturbateur" pour reprendre la terminologie des démographes (Henry, 1959), est exclu de cette classification de même que tout autre comportement familial non conforme à ce modèle dominant. Cela est surprenant pour une approche élaborée et utilisée dans une société, la société américaine, où les dernières statistiques révèlent qu'un peu plus d'un mariage sur 3 se termine par un divorce (*Annuaire démographique de l'O.N.U.*, 1971). Sans atteindre ce niveau, la divortialité est également élevée dans la plupart des sociétés industrielles et bien souvent en constante augmentation. Pour la France, où l'on constate une sensible augmentation des divorces depuis 1964, les statistiques fournissent un nombre de divorces tel qu'actuellement un mariage sur huit se terminerait par un divorce.[2] Encore le divorce ne représente-t-il que l'aspect légal des dissolutions d'union, une récente analyse du recensement français de 1968 établirait que la proportion de séparés de fait parmi la population française serait presque aussi importante que la proportion de divorcés (Boigeol, Commaille, 1972). A tous ces comportements familiaux non prévus par les diverses classifications afférentes au cycle de la vie familiale, il faudrait ajouter le concubinage dont il est difficile de mesurer la fréquence mais qu'on peut supposer élevée dans certains pays comme la Suède où la nuptialité a baissé de 35% de 1966 à 1971 (Alexandersson, 1973).

En fait le problème posé est celui du fondement normatif de l'approche développementale. Toute pratique familiale s'écartant du modèle établi de l'institution familiale n'est pas traitée par le cycle de la vie familiale car implicitement définie comme déviante; ce qui rejoint *a contrario* cette constatation que le concept de désorganisation familiale est utilisé de manière normative et que "les essais de construction théorique se sont traditionnellement préoccupés des situations désirables par opposition aux situations indésirables" (Sprey, 1966). Or, en particulier, le divorce, son évolution, sa fréquence de plus en plus grande et les formes qu'il prend, suscite une réflexion moins sur la normalité ou la déviance du phénomène – bien que son intensité le consacre comme "normal" – que sur les transformations qu'il paraît révéler concernant la conception du mariage et de l'institution familiale en général, transformations qui ne semblent pas être prises en compte par l'approche développementale.

Le cycle familial est en partie prédéterminé par les normes sociales régissant les comportements familiaux

Une autre difficulté surgit quand on se propose de recourir à l'approche développementale pour analyser le divorce. La méthode la plus conforme serait, considérant la famille comme un système de "petit groupe" – "as a small group system" (Hill, 1964) – de se livrer à de véritables études de cas où, à travers une observation dans le temps du système d'intéraction que constituent le couple et les enfants, apparaîtraient les causes de la rupture. Or, ce que souligne l'observation de divorcés,[3] c'est le fait que le fonctionnement de ce "petit groupe" ne peut se comprendre que par référence à des règles se situant au niveau de la société globale; les comportements d'un couple ultérieurement dissous par le divorce sont déterminés par des facteurs préexistant à sa constitution ou déjà présents au moment de sa constitution mais venant peser à l'évidence sur le déroulement de son cycle. Il y a des normes régissant les comportements familiaux; ces normes sont issues du modèle établi de l'institution familiale, elles sont plus ou moins intériorisées par les individus et par les groupes sociaux auxquels ils appartiennent. Rejoignant les récentes orientations proposées par Rodgers qui insiste sur le fait que la famille n'est pas un système clos et qu'il y a nécessité de tenir compte de l'aspect "societal-institutional" dans l'approche développementale (Rodgers, 1973), on pourrait dire ainsi que le divorce est un processus déjà fortement prédéterminé par l'influence de variables institutionnelles.[4] Nous prendrons trois exemples pour illustrer cette constatation.

a) *Les rôles conjugaux* et leur répartition se révèlent être chez les divorcés moins le résultat d'ajustements et de désajustements successifs que le fruit de l'influence d'un certain modèle matrimonial qui s'imposait au couple dès sa constitution. L'échec du couple est souvent exprimé par référence à ce modèle de départ ["L'image que moi j'avais de la paternité... c'est essentiellement autour de cela que nous nous sommes séparés". Citation d'une divorcée – entretien XV].

Or, ce modèle apparaît traditionnel chez la plupart des divorcés, dans la mesure où le rôle de la femme est pour beaucoup d'entre eux surtout de rester au foyer et de se réserver à la vie de famille (tableau 1).
Cette conception rejoint d'ailleurs celle des Français dans la mesure où ceux-ci considèrent dans leur majorité (65%) que le travail de la femme (les enfants étant d'âge scolaire) présente surtout des inconvénients, essentiellement parce que "la femme qui travaille s'occupe moins de son foyer" (*Cahier de l'I.N.E.D.*, 1974). Par rapport à cette conception, il y a pourtant un décalage au niveau de la pratique effective des couples qui vont divorcer, lequel peut constituer une source de malaise, de conflits et de rupture: En effet, les femmes divorcées sont deux fois plus actives que les femmes mariées – 68% des femmes qui divorcent travaillent contre 34% des femmes mariées (Boigeol, Commaille, 1974) et l'enquête auprès des divorcés permet de penser que ce travail féminin est le plus souvent bien antérieur à la décision de divorcer. Cette activité de la femme implique une nouvelle répartition des rôles conjugaux s'accommodant éventuellement mal du modèle matrimonial dominant.

Toutefois, souligner l'influence essentielle de ce modèle préexistant au couple ou s'imposant à sa constitution n'est pas nier l'importance d'une analyse dynamique en terme de cycle de rôles. Il est certain que l'activité féminine selon le moment où elle intervient, la forme qu'elle prend au fur et à mesure du déroulement du cycle, peut favoriser à certains moments des équilibres ou, au contraire, précipiter les crises, la rupture éventuelle dont l'initiative sera prise plus ou moins rapidement selon le statut

Tableau 1

Question	Hommes %	Femmes %	Ensemble %
Quel est parmi les trois modèles suivants celui qui se rapproche le plus de l'image idéale que vous vous faites d'une famille?			
– Une famille où les deux conjoints ont un métier qui les absorbe autant l'un que l'autre et où les tâches ménagères et les soins donnés aux enfants sont partagés entre les deux	24	24	24
– Une famille où la femme a une profession moins absorbante que celle de l'homme et où elle assure une grande part des tâches ménagères et des soins des enfants	24	34	29
– Une famille où l'homme seul exerce une profession et où la femme reste au foyer	52	42	47
	100	100	100
Pensez-vous qu'un homme doive:			
– Réserver à la vie de famille presque tout son temps libre	35	33	33
– Avoir, en plus de la vie professionnelle certaines activités extérieures (syndicales, politiques, culturelles, philanthropiques)	65	67	67
	100	100	100
Pensez-vous qu'une femme doive:			
– Réserver à la vie de famille presque tout son temps libre	59	54	56
– Avoir, en plus de la vie professionnelle certaines activités extérieures (syndicales, politiques, culturelles, philanthropiques)	41	46	44
	100	100	100

de l'un ou l'autre époux: nous savons simplement pour l'instant que c'est aux âges jeunes que la proportion de demandes féminines en divorce est la plus forte et que ces âges sont aussi ceux où la femme est le plus fréquemment active (Boigeol, Commaille, 1974), (voir tableau 2), et où, comme nous le verrons plus loin, la probabilité de remariage est la plus grande.

De même, les modifications intervenant dans le statut de l'un des époux, la progression d'une carrière et son caractère unilatéral, peuvent venir renforcer les différences entre conjoints et avoir finalement une influence déterminante sur le processus de dissociation conjugale. Mais cette progression ne concerne bien souvent que les hommes, comme le laisseraient

Tableau 2

	Age de la femme								
	Moins de 20 ans	20–24 ans	25–29 ans	30–34 ans	35–39 ans	40–44 ans	45–49 ans	50–60 ans	60 ans et plus
Proportion de demandes féminines (en %)	56,8	63,1	66,2	66,4	64,2	62,0	58,9	53,7	41,5
Parmi les femmes en instance de divorce, proportion de celles qui sont actives (%)	57,9	71,6	71,3	69,0	64,8	63,2	61,6	55,3	36,7

penser certains entretiens auprès de divorcés ["J'ai commencé à travailler à 16 ans et j'ai été professionnel en atelier, pour être maintenant devenu ingénieur autodidacte ... Et je me rends compte maintenant qu'indépendamment de la maturité, de l'âge, on ne voit plus les choses de la même façon ... Quand vous avez une évolution, vous êtes amené à rencontrer des gens, ne serait-ce que sur le plan professionnel ou sur le plan des relations extra-professionnelles si vous avez une conjointe qui n'est pas à la hauteur, et bien ça vous empêche d'avoir des relations, ça vous nuit", citation d'un divorcé, entretien XXVII]. ["J'avais un mari très ambitieux ... Moi par contre, je ne l'étais pas trop (...) donc mon mari a fait des études (...) il s'est donc lui monopolisé sur des études ... Ce qui a fait qu'il y avait chez nous deux personnes qui ne se connaissaient plus de tout (...). On s'est éloigné mutuellement ... Lui avait une vie de son côté ... moi j'avais la mienne ... Une vie un petit peu de recluse", citation d'une divorcée, entretien XI].

b) *L'hétérogamie* sociale, l'hétérogamie d'âge et leur influence sur le divorce confirment *a contrario* qu'il y a des règles sociales concernant la constitution du couple et que la transgression de ces règles augmente la possibilité de rupture ultérieure dans le cours du cycle. De même qu'Alain Girard avait montré que le choix du conjoint était marqué en France par une forte homogamie sociale (Girard, 1964), de même les statistiques révèlent relativement plus de cas d'hétérogamie sociale chez les divorcés que chez les mariés (Boigeol, Commaille, 1974); ce qui rejoint d'ailleurs les constatations faites par Goode pour les Etats-Unis (1965). Dans le même ordre d'idées, on observe des écarts d'âge relativement plus grands chez les divorcés que chez les mariés, surtout dans les cas où la femme est plus jeune que son mari (Boigeol, Commaille, 1974).

c) *La conception prénuptiale* est un phénomène qui a la particularité, comme le divorce, d'être exclu du cycle de la vie familiale. Or, c'est un phénomène relativement fréquent en France et en constante augmentation: 20% des femmes françaises mariées avant 35 ans entre 1955 et 1960 ont eu une conception prénuptiale. Pour celles dont le mariage a eu lieu en 1970, la proportion est de 29%. En fait, la conception prénuptiale si elle est en dehors du cycle familial semble pourtant lourdement hypothéquer son déroulement ultérieur puisque les divorcés ont sensiblement plus de conceptions prénuptiales que les mariés (tableau 3).

Tableau 3

Age au mariage (par groupes d'âges)	Proportion de conceptions prénuptiales chez les époux en instance de divorce en 1971 (%)	Proportion de conceptions prénuptiales chez les mariés* (%)
15–19 ans	44,4	33,1
20–24 ans	29,7	18,4
25–29 ans	22,8	13,8
30–34 ans	21,3	11,7
Ensemble	33,6	20,0

* Les renseignements statistiques sur les Français mariés ont été obtenus à partir de l'enquête sur les familles réalisée en 1962 par l'I.N.S.E.E. Les proportions de conceptions prénuptiales ont été calculées sur les femmes de l'échantillon qui se sont mariées avant 35 ans entre 1955 et 1960.

Dans la mesure où, comme le démontre Christensen (1963), la conception hors mariage est socialement stigmatisée et où le contrôle social pousse à une régularisation de la conception prénuptiale par le mariage, la probabilité de rupture ultérieure est grande. ["On se marie jeune, on ne s'entend pas, on ne se connaît pas la plupart du temps. On se marie parce qu'on attend un enfant... Quelque temps après ça va déjà plus". Citation d'une divorcée, entretien VIII]. ["J'étais enceinte et je n'étais donc pas mariée ...; mon mari n'y tenait pas tellement... enfin... mon fiancé n'y tenant pas tellement mais vu mon état, mes beaux-parents ont essayé de forcer la chose... moi j'aimais mon mari. J'aimais mon fiancé, mais lui il était pas tellement d'accord... Enfin on s'est marié..." Citation d'une divorcée, entretien XXI]. Le poids du contrôle social ne se mesure d'ailleurs pas seulement à l'intensité du phénomène mais aussi aux répercussions qu'on peut observer sur le processus de rupture. Non seulement, l'existence d'une conception prénuptiale semble plus prédisposer au divorce mais aussi le divorce se fait plus vite: la durée moyenne de mariage lorsqu'il y a naissance ou conception prénuptiale est de 9 ans, elle est de 13 ans lorsque les conceptions ont eu lieu après le mariage. Le lien entre conception prénuptiale et précocité au divorce apparaît de façon spectaculaire si l'on considère les mariages ayant duré moins de 2 ans qui ont la proportion la plus forte de conceptions prénuptiales: 59 % (tableau 4).

Tableau 4

	Durée du mariage					
	0–1 an	2–4 ans	5–9 ans	10–14 ans	15–19 ans	20 ans et +
Conceptions prénuptiales (%)	59,4	46,0	34,4	27,9	28,5	21,2

Le processus de divorce et l'influence des variables institutionnelles

A partir d'une analyse du divorce, nous venons de mettre l'accent sur les aspects qui nous paraissent prédéterminer en partie l'histoire matrimoniale; mais cela ne revient pas à rejeter une approche dynamique des pratiques familiales, ce qui renvoie d'ailleurs à une préoccupation déjà ancienne des démographes: ceux-ci ont développé, dès la fin de la 2e guerre mondiale, l'utilisation de l'analyse longitudinale (Henry, 1966) dont la définition répond parfaitement à celle de l'approche développementale, bien que ne visant pas seulement la vie familiale, puisqu'il s'agit d'étudier le "déroulement des événements au sein d'une cohorte, génération ou promotion de mariage" (Henry, 1959). Sa finalité est, en outre, identique dans la mesure où l'analyse longitudinale affecte un événement démographique d'une probabilité donnée, de la même manière que l'approche développementale vise à "prédire les comportements par une connaissance des caractéristiques structurelles de la famille et de la phase dans laquelle elle se trouve" (Hill, 1964). Il reste, comme le note Louis Henry, que l'absence "d'enregistrement continu des événements" concernant une même promotion de mariages rend difficile une analyse longitudinale (Henry, 1959) et que de tous les travaux récemment entrepris en France sur le divorce, seules l'analyse de quatre cohortes de mariages d'après les registres d'état civil de la ville de Paris (Vallot, 1971) et l'analyse par promotion de mariages des divorces transcrits (Blayo, 1973) répondent aux critères de l'analyse longitudinale tels qu'ils sont définis par les démographes. Les enquêtes réalisées auprès des divorcés, soit par entretiens non directifs, soit par questionnaires, autorisent toutefois une analyse rétrospective de leur cycle familial mais de façon partielle; de même une étude de l'ensemble des divorces de l'année 1970, permet d'esquisser une analyse dans le temps. Mais la critique qui peut être adressée à toutes ces données est que "l'observation destinée à satisfaire les exigences de l'analyse longitudinale (...) doit beaucoup à des préoccupations dérivées de l'analyse transversale" (Henry, 1966). Pourtant, il semble bien que ce soit moins en terme d'événement qu'en terme de processus qu'il faille traiter du divorce, si l'on considère que la perception qu'ont les Français du divorce (*Cahier de l'I.N.E.D.*, 1974) corrobore l'opinion de la majorité des divorcés: 71 % d'entre eux estiment en effet que leur décision de divorcer, plutôt que de survenir à la suite d'une crise imprévue, a été précédée d'une lente dégradation des rapports avec leur conjoint ["Il y a une progression, l'impossibilité de supporter l'autre, tout s'accumulant ... ça devenait une rupture. C'est jamais comme ça un grief précis et puis c'est terminé", citation d'un divorcé, entretien III]. D'ailleurs il est significatif que pour un grand nombre de divorcés – 52 % des divorcés interrogés – l'éventualité du divorce avait déjà été envisagée auparavant ["Je crois que la première fois que j'ai dit à mon mari que je voulais quitter le domicile conjugal, ça doit bien remonter à 14 ou 15 ans ... les difficultés dataient de très longtemps", citation d'une divorcée, entretien VII].

Si le divorce doit bien s'analyser en terme de processus, il faut dire que ce processus ne concerne approximativement que les phases I à IV de la classification de Duvall (1962) puisque la répartition des durées de mariage[5] de l'année 1971 révèle qu'un peu plus de 70 % des divorces ont lieu moins de 15 ans après le mariage (tableau 5).

En fait, bien que nous n'ayons pas pris pour terme la date de jugement mais celle antérieure de la tentative de conciliation (la durée moyenne entre la tentative de conciliation et le jugement est de 13 mois), les durées de mariage obtenues restent des durées légales qui ne correspondent pas aux durées effectives de maintien du couple, qui sont sensiblement plus courtes, la cessation de cohabitation intervenant fréquemment beaucoup plus tôt que la décision judiciaire, ainsi que l'a déjà montré Chester (1971) et ainsi que le confirme l'enquête auprès des divorcés, puisque 78 % d'entre eux

Tableau 5

	Durée de mariage des couples en instance de divorce (année 1971)						
	0–1 an	2–4 ans	5–9 ans	10–14 ans	15–19 ans	20 ans et +	Ensemble
%	6,0	19,9	27,9	17,3	12,0	16,9	100,0
% cumulé	6,0	25,9	53,8	71,1	83,1	100,0	

Durée moyenne: 11 ans 8 mois; durée médiane: 9 ans 8 mois.

déclarent avoir cessé d'habiter avec leur ex-conjoint avant le début de la procédure.

Ce raccourcissement du cycle des divorcés par rapport à celui des mariés devrait à l'avenir s'accentuer si l'on tient compte des évolutions récentes observées parmi lesquelles:

– les proportions de divorces ont sensiblement augmenté chez les jeunes de 1935–1937 à 1967 (Roussel, 1970) et plus particulièrement de 1962 à 1968 (Jaulerry, 1971), ce qui s'explique par une plus grande précocité de l'ensemble des mariages en France.

– il y a une précocité au mariage légèrement plus forte chez les divorcés que chez les mariés (Boigeol, Commaille, 1974), mais la différence entre les deux s'atténue dans la mesure où la précocité de plus en plus grande de l'ensemble des mariages tend à rejoindre celle des mariages de divorcés (Jaulerry, 1971).

– il y a un lien entre précocité au mariage et précocité au divorce: plus le mariage est précoce, plus la durée de mariage est courte (tableau 6).

– de façon générale, la hausse des fréquences de divorce dans les récentes promotions de mariage laisse supposer une précocité au divorce de plus en plus forte, c'est-à-dire "une tendance à divorcer plus tôt dans le mariage" (Blayo, 1973).

Le raccourcissement en France du cycle des divorcés est un phénomène

Tableau 6

Age au mariage de l'époux	Durée moyenne du mariage (en années) Année 1971
Moins de 20 ans	9,9
20–22 ans	10,4
23–24 ans	11,8
25–29 ans	12,6
30–34 ans	12,2
35–39 ans	12,0

qui a pu être observé dans beaucoup d'autres pays où l'augmentation de la divortialité s'est accompagnée d'une réduction des durées de mariage; mais la France est encore en retrait par rapport à ce qu'on peut constater dans d'autres pays, en particulier aux Etats-Unis: si le mode de la distribution des divorces suivant la durée du mariage est placé à 5–6 ans en France, il est à 2 et même 1 an aux Etats-Unis (Blayo, 1973). Cette différence dans les comportements de divorce entre la société américaine et la société française – ou même à l'intérieur d'une même société: par exemple les Noirs et les Blancs aux Etats-Unis (Glick, Norton, 1971) – pose le problème de la possibilité d'une comparaison à partir de la classification de Duvall ou de Rodgers. Le fait que les ruptures conjugales ne se situent pas du tout dans les mêmes phases d'une société à l'autre signifie-t-il que le surgissement des moments critiques n'intervient pas du tout dans les mêmes périodes du cycle? Ou plutôt les différences sont-elles si fortes qu'elles ne peuvent s'expliquer que par des attitudes radicalement différentes à l'égard du mariage, ce qui renverrait à l'influence prépondérante des variables institutionnelles dans la détermination du processus de divorce.

Ces attitudes à l'égard du mariage peuvent varier selon les cultures et déterminer des types de processus; elles peuvent aussi varier selon les milieux sociaux de telle façon qu'il soit possible d'élaborer une typologie des cycles de divorcés, comme cela est esquissé dans le tableau 7 à partir d'une analyse de certaines caractéristiques des divorces en France.

Ce qui apparaît c'est, d'une part, que le déroulement du cycle des divorcés varie très sensiblement selon les milieux sociaux et, d'autre part, qu'il y a pour chaque catégorie socio-professionnelle une grande cohérence des comportements. Si l'on prend le type I, illustré par les agriculteurs exploitants, on observe qu'à un âge moyen au mariage relativement élevé, correspond un âge moyen au divorce également relativement élevé et une durée moyenne de mariage relativement plus longue, de même qu'on constate une proportion de conceptions prénuptiales relativement faible, une activité de l'épouse relativement moins fréquente et une divortialité faible. Inversement, dans le type III illustré par les cadres moyens et les employés, on observe qu'à une relative précocité au mariage correspond une relative précocité au divorce attestée par un âge moyen au divorce moins élevé et une durée moyenne de mariage plus courte, de même qu'on constate une proportion de conceptions prénuptiales relativement forte, une activité de l'épouse sensiblement plus fréquente et une forte divortialité.

S'il y a bien un processus de divorce, un cycle de divorcés, il se confirme qu'il est multiple et cela renvoie à une signification sociale du mariage, dont les divorcés sont porteurs et qui varie suivant les classes sociales. C'est bien une conception du mariage qui transparaît à travers l'âge au mariage, sa durée, la fécondité, le statut de la femme. Selon les milieux sociaux, le mariage est plus ou moins investi de fonctions sociales – parmi lesquelles la production et l'élevage des enfants, la gestion d'un éventuel patrimoine et sa transmission – qui contribuent à peser sur la décision de se marier, sur le déroulement du cycle et sur l'éventualité d'une dissolution du couple.

A ces modèles familiaux propres à chaque milieu social (et à chaque culture) sont associés des formes de contrôle social dont on peut essayer de mesurer globalement l'influence. En effet, à l'instar des analyses faites actuellement dans le domaine de la déviance (Robert, Kellens, 1973) ou bien antérieurement dans celui des maladies mentales (Bastide, 1965), le divorce se définit aussi par la réaction sociale qui s'exerce à son égard. Le contrôle social influe sur le processus à travers une plus ou moins grande résistance au divorce se manifestant selon les phases du cycle – comme on peut supposer qu'il détermine aussi en partie le cycle des mariés –. A cet égard, le décalage observé, entre la répartition des durées réelles de mariage et la répartition beaucoup plus précoce des durées fictives de mariage[6] ne s'explique-t-il pas partiellement par l'influence de ce contrôle social (*cf.* figure 1))

Ce contrôle social est d'abord incarné, en matière de divorce par les différents agents de l'institution judiciaire qui, au-delà de leur fonction formelle: appliquer le droit, ont des attitudes à l'égard de l'institution familiale qui influent certainement sur leur pratique (Commaille, Dezalay, 1971). Cette influence est toutefois difficile à appréhender par une approche extensive (Dezalay, 1974); ce que montrent les statistiques de l'activité judiciaire est assez restreint, dans la mesure où la saisie statistique se fait sur un aspect limité de l'action possible de l'institution et à un moment du processus de rupture pendant lequel la marge de manœuvre du juge est étroite. On observe pourtant qu'au niveau de la tentative de conciliation, plus le mariage est récent plus le magistrat ordonne un sursis à statuer, c'est-à-dire retarde la décision légale de rupture (tableau 8).

A ce contrôle social exercé par l'institution judiciaire fait écho celui des Français en général (*Cahiers de l'I.N.E.D.*, 1974), lequel varie également en intensité selon les phases du cycle. Ainsi, la résistance au divorce exprimée est la plus forte:

Tableau 7

	Age moyen au mariage (hommes)	Age moyen au divorce (hommes)	Durée moyenne de mariage	Conceptions prénuptiales (%)	Activité de l'épouse (%)	Divortialité* (‰)
Type I						
– agriculteurs exploitants	27,6 ans	42,9 ans	14 ans 11 mois	22,5	52,8	0,7
Type II						
– patrons de l'industrie et du commerce	26,3 ans	39,6 ans	13 ans	26,5	57,8	4,1
– professions lib. et cadres supérieurs	26,8 ans	39,9 ans	12 ans 11 mois	23,9	61,1	5,9
Types III						
– cadres moyens	24,9 ans	35,4 ans	10 ans 3 mois	31,9	72,5	7,1
– employés	24,7 ans	35,4 ans	10 ans 7 mois	34,6	70,5	9,1

* Ces taux de divortialité ont été calculés en rapportant le nombre de tentatives de conciliation de l'année 1970 pour chaque catégorie socio-professionnelle aux effectifs correspondants de couples mariés recensés en 1968.

Tableau 8

	Durée de mariage										
	Moins de 1 an	1 an	2 ans	3 ans	4 ans	5–9 ans	10–14 ans	15–19 ans	20–29 ans	30 ans et plus	Ensemble
% sursis à statuer	8,5	6,1	4,3	4,7	3,9	4,3	4,3	4,6	3,3	2,6	4,3

Figure 1. *Comparaison des durées de mariage réelles et fictives (en pourcentages cumulés)*

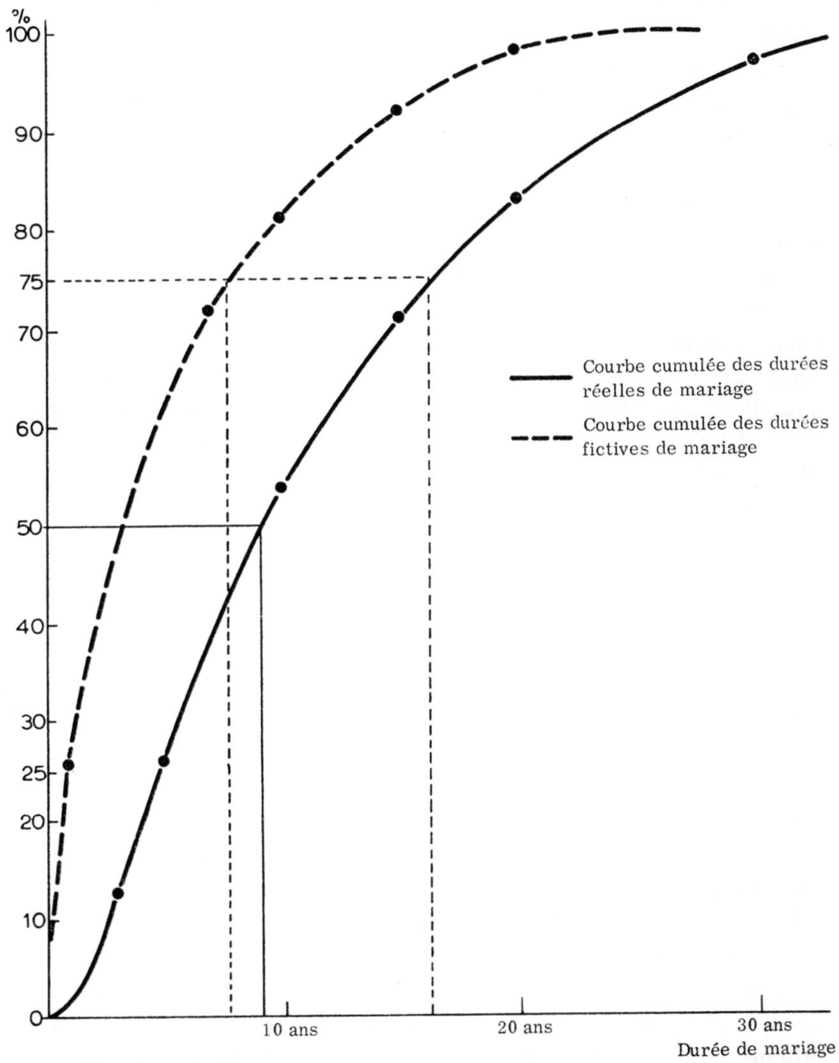

– d'abord dans les phases II à V du cycle Duvall quand tous les enfants ont moins de 16 ans,

– ensuite, au début du cycle quand le couple est marié depuis moins de 3 ans – ce qui peut apparaître comme la manifestation d'un souci de respect de l'institution du mariage.

Le divorce comme état transitoire

Dans la plupart des sociétés industrielles, le divorce a pris une nouvelle signification qui en fait un acte socialement mieux accepté (Ancel, 1973). De même, en France, on assiste à une évolution – non pas au niveau de la loi, pratiquement inchangée depuis 1884 – mais au niveau de la pratique judiciaire qui doit traiter de conflits conjugaux de moins en moins conformes au principe manichéen du divorce-sanction. Dans le cadre d'une approche dynamique de la famille, tous ces changements sont importants car ils confirment le divorce comme un état transitoire et non comme une fin en soi, au même titre que la mort. Pour la grande majorité des divorcés, le divorce n'est d'ailleurs pas perçu comme une faillite définitive mais comme une "épreuve pénible ne gâchant pas définitivement leur avenir" ou "comme une libération qui leur donne une nouvelle chance dans la vie" ["Je vis plus heureuse depuis que je suis divorcée (...) je vis beaucoup plus décontractée ... je parle beaucoup plus décontractée (...) j'avais un mari qui m'écrasait si vous voulez ... parce que lui il surnageait ... il surnageait non ... il gravissait les échelons ... moi au contraire je descendais le niveau (...) donc pour moi, le divorce c'est une libération ... c'est une reconversion à la vie si vous voulez", citation d'une divorcée, entretien XI] (voir tableau 9).

Bien sûr cette impression varie, en particulier pour la femme:

– selon son statut, quand elle est active, elle considère presque 2 fois moins souvent qu'il s'agit d'une faillite définitive.

– selon son âge, plus elle divorce jeune, moins elle considère qu'il s'agit d'une faillite définitive (ce qui est à comparer avec le fait que, d'une part, plus elle est jeune moins elle estime que le divorce a entraîné un changement dans son niveau de vie dans le sens d'une baisse et que, d'autre part, plus elle est jeune plus la durée est courte entre la décision de divorcer et la présentation de la requête au tribunal).

Si le divorce est une étape, la suite en sera dans bien des cas le remariage: 66,3% des hommes et 59,3% des femmes de la cohorte des divorcés de l'année 1950 étaient remariés en 1971 (*cf.* figure 2).[7] C'est une proportion légèrement inférieure à celle des Etats-Unis et de la Grande-Bretagne qui varie entre 70 et 80% (Dominian, 1968), mais déjà suffisamment remarquable pour renforcer cette interprétation du divorce comme simple prélude à un nouveau cycle.

Cette fréquence des remariages démontrerait que le divorce ne remet pas en cause l'institution matrimoniale mais participe en quelque sorte

Tableau 9

Question: En résumé, estimez-vous que votre divorce a été pour vous:	Hommes	Femmes	Femme		Age au divorce de la femme		Ensemble
			Active	Inac-tive	— de 30 ans	+ de 45 ans	
	(%)	(%)	(%)	(%)	(%)	(%)	(%)
– une faillite définitive de votre vie personnelle	7	12	11	21	8	18	10
– une épreuve pénible mais qui ne "gâche" pas définitivement votre avenir	49	39	39	36	26	35	43
– une libération qui vous donne une nouvelle chance dans la vie	40	43	44	39	60	40	42
– un événement dont vous connaissez encore mal les conséquences pour votre avenir	4	6	4	6	6	7	5
	100	100	100	100	100	100	100

Figure 2. *Remariages des époux divorcés en 1950 (en pourcentages cumulés)*

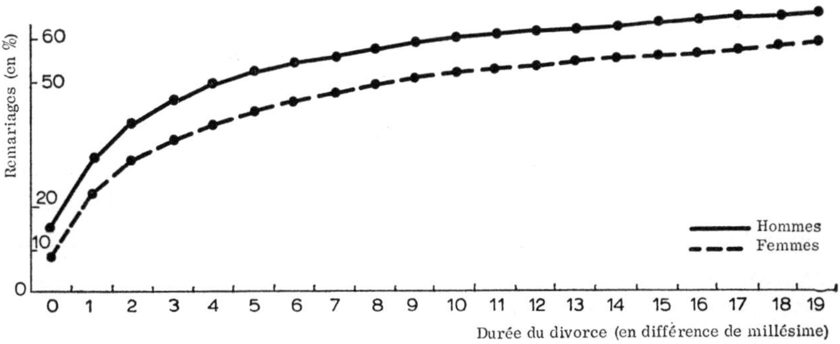

de son évolution. Si le mouvement devait s'accentuer et aboutir à cette situation extrême de la polygamie en chaîne ("sequential polygamy") dont parlent certains sociologues de la famille, cela n'inciterait-il pas à traiter autant de la succession des cycles que du cycle lui-même? La question peut être posée si l'on confronte deux observations allant, semble-t-il, dans le même sens:

– il y a un rajeunissement des âges au divorce

– la proportion de remariages est d'autant plus importante que l'âge au divorce est précoce (*cf.* figure 3).

(Encore faut-il nuancer selon le sexe: il y a globalement moins de remariages chez les femmes que chez les hommes mais plus la femme est jeune plus la différence s'atténue.)

Figure 3. *Remariages de la cohorte d'époux divorcés en 1962 (en pourcentages cumulés)*

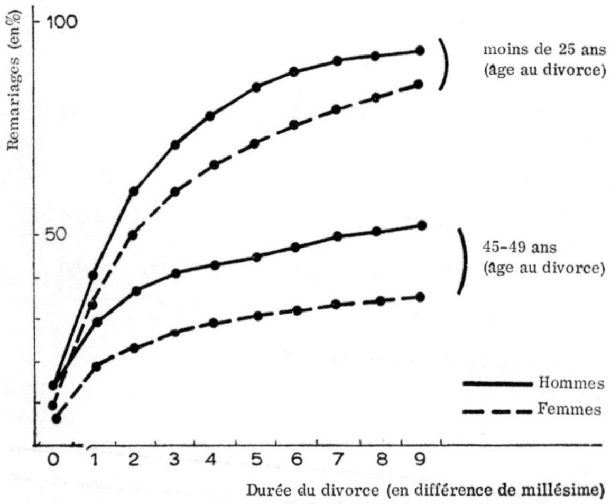

Les remariages qui se font rapidement après le divorce correspondent en fait aux situations où les divorcés avaient déjà le projet d'une nouvelle union avec une personne qu'ils connaissaient avant même que la rupture soit légalement consacrée. On peut supposer que c'est le cas pour beaucoup de divorcés puisque parmi les hommes divorcés et remariés en 1971, 48% avaient divorcé dans l'année ou l'année précédente, de même que 38% des femmes. L'enquête auprès des divorcés montre d'ailleurs que près de la moitié des divorcés remariés connaissaient leur nouveau conjoint au moment de la requête en divorce avec, pour les $\frac{2}{3}$ d'entre eux, la perspective de l'épouser dès que le divorce serait prononcé. Pourtant, il faut noter une évolution dans le calendrier des remariages: ceux-ci se font moins rapidement depuis quelques années et ce changement est particulièrement sensible lors des premières années suivant le jugement (*cf.* figure 4).

Figure 4. *Les remariages de 4 cohortes de divorcés (en pourcentages cumulés)*

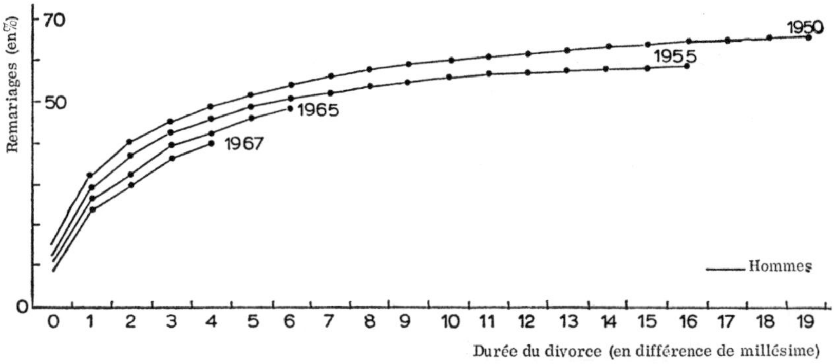

Une telle évolution, trop récente pour permettre d'annoncer une baisse de l'intensité du phénomène et pour être considérée comme irréversible, pourrait s'expliquer à la fois par le fait que le divorce serait relativement moins qu'auparavant associé à un remariage immédiat et par l'émergence de nouvelles attitudes à l'égard du mariage, lesquelles supposeraient des remariages précédés ou directement compensés par des concubinages post-divorce plus nombreux. On peut se demander si parmi les divorcés, ce n'est pas chez la femme qu'on trouverait le plus ces attitudes nouvelles; il est, en effet, intéressant d'observer que plus son appartenance sociale – mesurée par la catégorie socio-professionnelle du mari – est élevée, plus son niveau d'instruction est élevé, plus elle est active,[8] plus son lieu de résidence est urbanisé, moins elle se remarie (Deville, 1972).

Confirmant les récentes réflexions sur l'approche développementale (Rodgers, 1973) l'influence des variables institutionnelles sur l'ensemble des pratiques familiales apparaît fortement à travers une analyse du processus de divorce. C'est un modèle établi de l'institution familiale qui s'impose à la constitution du couple et contribue à déterminer son développement ultérieur. Mais le caractère normatif du concept de cycle de la vie familiale fait que celui-ci ne traite que des comportements conformes à ce modèle et néglige la pluralité des pratiques familiales, introduite par les variations selon les cultures et selon les milieux sociaux; cette pluralité concerne aussi bien les mariés que les divorcés (Goode, 1963) et pose moins le problème des cycles différents que celui de la différence des attitudes à l'égard de l'institution familiale. De même, le cycle de la vie

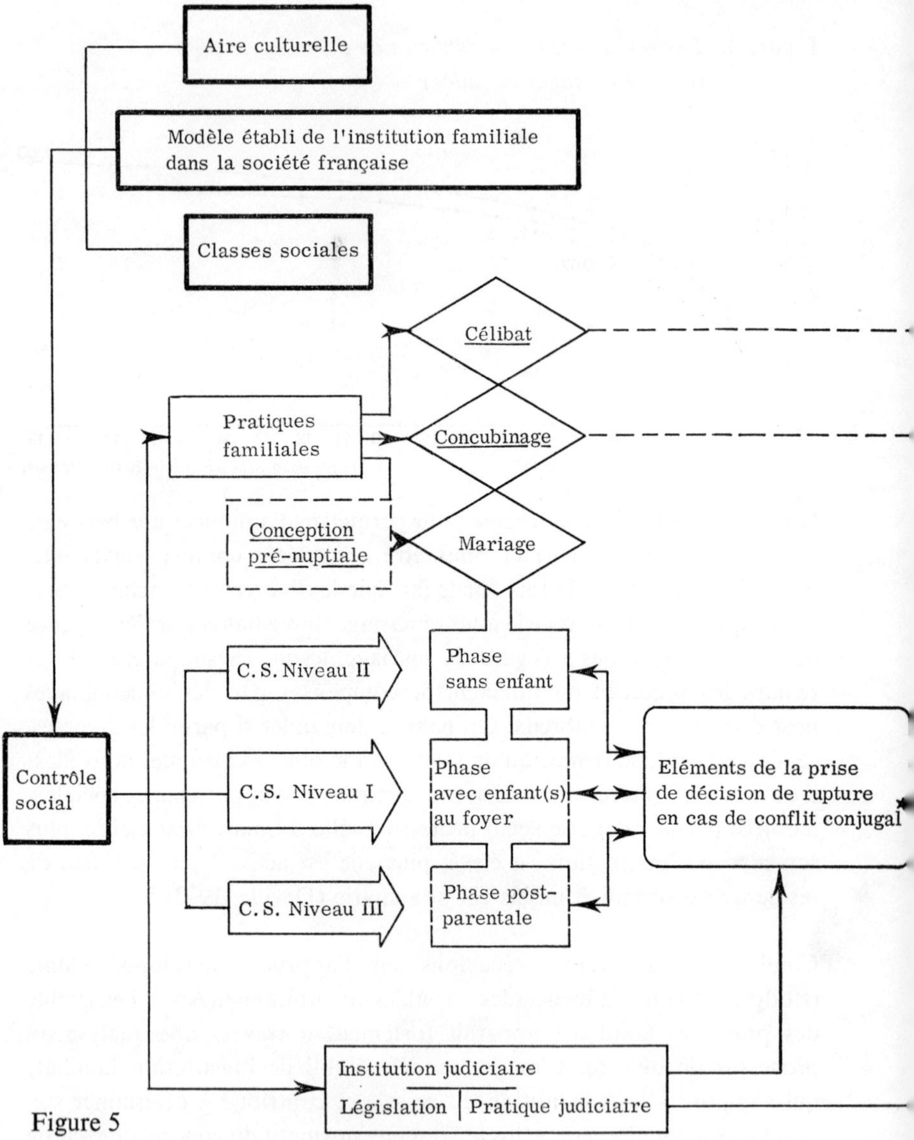

Figure 5

* Les élements de la prise de décision peuvent être:
- l'influence de l'environnement familial;
- l'influence de l'environnement non familial;
- les conditions objectives (âge de chacun des conjoints, présence d'enfants, statut socio-économique de chacun des conjoints, état des relations etc.);
- l'image du divorce;
- la perception de l'institution judiciaire;
- l'accès à l'institution judiciaire;
- le rôle de l'avocat;
- le rôle des experts (assistante sociale, psychologue, conseiller conjugal, etc.);
- le rôle du juge.

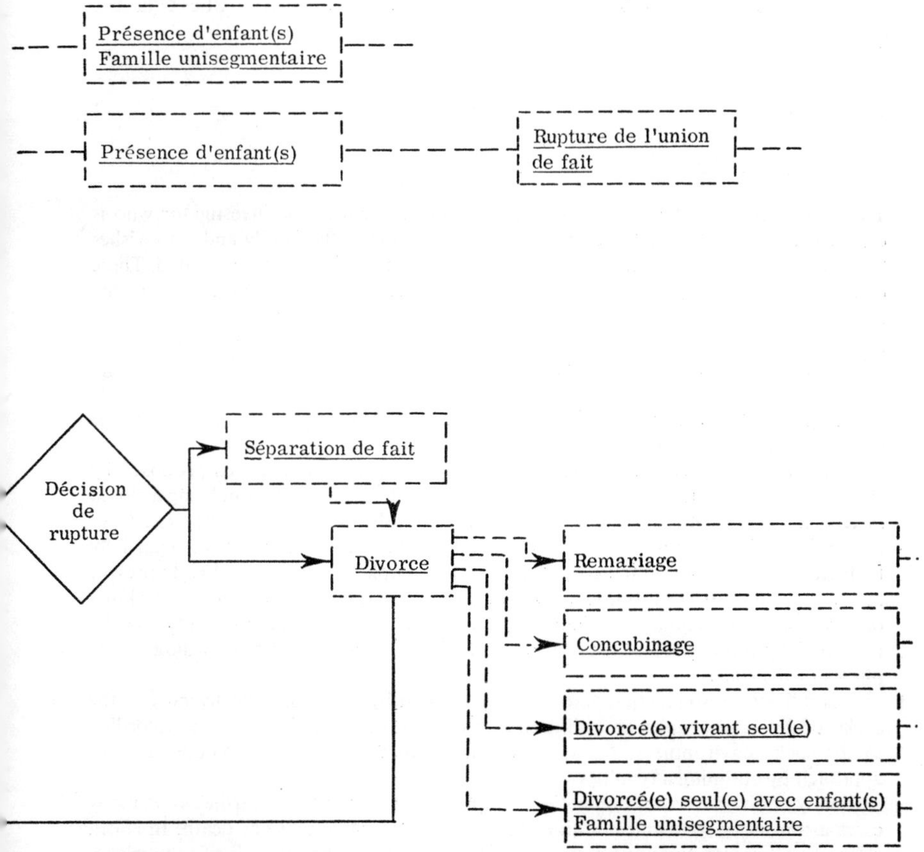

Contrôle social (C.S.) niveau I: la résistance au divorce est la plus forte, justifiée par la présence d'enfants mineurs.

Contrôle social (C.S.) niveau II: la résistance au divorce, bien que moins forte, reste à un niveau élevé, justifiée par le fait que le divorce précoce remet en cause l'institution du mariage.

Contrôle social (C.S.) niveau III: la résistance au divorce est beaucoup moins forte mais demeure, probablement à cause du risque de répudiation pour la femme.

Célibat: les pratiques familiales soulignées sont celles non prévues par le cycle de la vie familiale.

familiale n'intègre pas, outre le divorce, des pratiques familiales comme le concubinage ou le remariage dont il convient pourtant de consacrer l'existence avant même de savoir si elles marquent un changement fondamental de l'institution familiale. En plus du fait qu'il peut prendre des formes sensiblement variées, il faut aussi admettre que le mariage jusqu'à la mort de l'un des conjoints, pratique dominante, est néanmoins une possibilité parmi d'autres (*cf.* figure 5). Malgré sa tendance intrinsèque à l'homogénéïsation, la systématique du cycle de la vie familiale devrait être modifiée pour en tenir compte; il reste à démontrer que cela est possible.

SUMMARY

The process of divorce

The phenomenon of divorce poses an important problem to the investigator who is concerned with analysing it with regard to the life cycle of the family and who wishes to use the various classifications of that cycle that have already been formulated. These classifications, in fact, refer implicitly to a dominant model of the institution of the family which excludes all behavior which does not conform to its parameters. At the present time, marriage until the death of one of the partners is only one practice among others (see Figure 5 in this article). In particular, the evolution of divorce, its high frequency in most industrial societies, bears witness to the radical change taking place with regard to the conception of marriage and the institution of the family which the developmental approach fails to take into account.

Furthermore, in accordance with the recently developed orientations proposed by Rodgers, a study of divorce emphasizes the fact that the family, far from being a closed system, is permanently under the influence of societal – institutional variables. Consequently, the behavior of a couple ultimately divided by divorce is determined partially by factors which pre-exist the constitution of the couple or which are already present at the moment of its constitution but which come to the surface only with the unfolding of its cycle. The predominant influence of these societal – institutional variables may be measured by the impact of a social control whose intensity varies according to the phases of the cycle.

This influence also emerges and may be measured by examining the diversity of the cycles of divorced couples according to society, and, within a given society, according to the social environment. An attempt is made in this article to demonstrate this approach by outlining a typology.

Finally, if divorce is the culmination of a process, it represents, nevertheless, in many cases a transitory state and not an end in itself, in the same sense as death. In effect, a large majority of divorcees remarry (as demonstrated in an analysis of remarriages in France). The increasing frequency of divorces associated with an increasing frequency of remarriages leads one to wonder if it is not necessary to consider the succession of cycles as much as the cycle itself.

In spite of its intrinsic tendency to homogenize, the system of classification of the life cycle of the family should be modified in order to take into account these various factors generated by an investigation concerning divorce. It remains to demonstrate that these modifications are possible.

NOTES

1. Ces travaux qui comprennent essentiellement une rénovation des statistiques, une enquête auprès de divorcés, une enquête d'opinion auprès des Français, ont été réalisés à la demande du Ministère de la Justice, soit par un de ses services de recherche, soit par l'Institut National d'Etudes Démographiques sous la direction de A. Girard et L. Roussel que nous remercions très vivement pour avoir bien voulu nous communiquer l'ensemble des résultats à leur disposition.
2. A défaut d'analyse longitudinale, cette proportion est obtenue en rapportant les divorces d'une année aux mariages d'une année antérieure, déterminée par la durée moyenne de mariage des divorcés.
3. C'est-à-dire une enquête réalisée par l'Institut National d'Etudes Démographiques auprès de 900 divorcés.
4. Le terme "institutionnelle" est employé dans le même sens que le terme "societal-institutional" chez Rodgers.
5. Qui correspond à la différence entre date de mariage et date de la tentative de conciliation (1ère phase de la procédure de divorce en France).
6. Les durées fictives de mariage correspondent à la répartition dans le temps des projets de rupture avoués par les divorcés. La question était la suivante: avant de prendre la décision de divorcer, y a-t-il eu des moments au cours de votre vie conjugale où cette éventualité avait déjà été envisagée? Au bout de combien d'années après votre mariage, cette éventualité a-t-elle été envisagée?
7. Sauf mention d'une source particulière, les statistiques de remariage fournies ici sont inédites et ont été obligeamment mises à notre disposition par l'Institut National de la Statistique et des Etudes Economiques (I.N.S.E.E.).
8. Cette observation sur l'influence de l'activité est tirée de l'enquête auprès des divorcés.

RÉFÉRENCES

Alexandersson, B. (1973), "Réforme du droit de la famille de 1973", *Actualités suédoises*, 8, Institut Suédois, Paris.

Ancel, M. (1973), "Les modifications récentes apportées à la législation du divorce dans les pays de l'Europe occidentale", rapport ronéo, Centre Français de Droit Comparé, S.C.R. Ministère de la Justice.

Bastide, R. (1965), *Sociologie des maladies mentales*, Paris, Flammarion.

Blayo, C. (1973), "Evolution des désunions en France depuis 1950", *Population*, 3, mai-juin.

Boigeol, A., et Commaille, J. (1972), "La séparation de fait, analyse des résultats du recensement de 1968", *Population*, 2, mars-avril.

Boigeol, A., et Commaille, J. (1974), "Divorce, milieu social et situation de la femme", *Economie et Statistique*, 53, février.

Boigeol, A., Commaille, J., Lamy, M.L., Monnier, A., et Roussel, L. (1974), "Le divorce et les Français. I, Enquête d'opinion", *Cahier de l'I.N.E.D.*, 69, P.U.F.

Chester, R. (1971), "The duration of marriage to divorce", *British Journal of Sociology*, XXII/2, juin.

Christensen, H.T. (1963), "Timing of first pregnancy as a factor of divorce: a cross-cultural analysis", *Eugenics Quarterly*, III, septembre.

Commaille, J., et Dezalay, Y. (1971), "Les caractéristiques judiciaires du divorce en France", *Population*, numéro spécial, juin.

Deville, J.C. (1972), "Structure des familles, enquête de 1962", Collections de l'I.N.S.E.E., Série D, 13–14

Dezalay, Y. (1974), "A propos du divorce: les limites d'une analyse statistique", *Economie et Statistique*, 53, février.

Dominian, J. (1968), *Marital Breakdown*, Harmondsworth, Penguin Books.

Duvall, E.M. (1962), *Family Development*, Philadelphia, Lippincott Co.

Girard, A. (1964), "Le choix du conjoint", *Cahier de l'I.N.E.D.*, 44, P.U.F.

Glick, P.C., et Norton, A.J. (1971), "Frequency, duration and probability of marriage and divorce", *Journal of Marriage and the Family*, mai.

Goode, W.J. (1963), *World Revolution and Family Patterns*, New York, The Free Press.

—— (1965), *Women in Divorce*, New York, The Free Press.

Hemery, S., and Dinh, Q.C. (1972), "La situation démographique en 1970", Les Collections de l'I.N.S.E.E., Série D, *Démographie et emploi*, 17, décembre.

Henry, L. (1959), "D'un problème fondamental de l'analyse démographique", *Population*, 1, janvier-mars.

Henry, L. (1966), "Analyse et mesure des phénomènes démographiques par cohortes", *Population*, 3, mai-juin.

Hill, R. (1964), "Methodological issues in family development research", *Family Process*, III/1.

Jaulerry, E. (1971), "Les dissolutions d'unions en France, étudiées à partir des minutes de jugement", *Population*, numéro spécial, juin.

Monahan, T.P. (1962), "The changing nature and instability of remarriages", in *Selected Studies in Marriage and the Family*, New York, Holt, Rinehart and Winston.

O.N.U. (1971), *Annuaire démographique 1971*, O.N.U., New York.

Robert, Ph., et Kellens, G. (1973), "Nouvelles perspectives en sociologie de la déviance", *Revue française de sociologie*, XIV/3, juillet-septembre.

Rodgers, R.H. (1962), *Improvements in the Construction and Analysis of Family Life Cycle Categories*, Western Michigan University, Kalamazoo.

Rodgers, R.H. (1973), *Family Interaction and Transaction: The Developmental Approach*, Englewood Cliffs, New Jersey, Prentice-Hall, Inc.

Roussel, L. (1970), "Les divorces et les séparations de corps en France (1936–1967)", *Population*, 2, mars-avril.

Sprey, J. (1966), "Family disorganization: toward a conceptual clarification", *Journal of Marriage and the Family*, 4, novembre.

Vallot, F. (1971), "Mariages et divorces à Paris, analyse des actes de mariage de quatre cohortes", *Population*, numéro spécial, juin.

24. Modèles familiaux de la transmission patrimoniale et théorie du cycle

JACQUES LAUTMAN
avec le concours de Jean-François Gossiaux

Partant d'une réflexion sur la structure logique et les contraintes empiriques admises de la "théorie du cycle", cette contribution va tenter de montrer 1) qu'il est nécessaire d'élargir temporellement la perspective du cycle, 2) que certaines variables prises ordinairement pour indépendantes doivent au contraire être considérées comme dépendantes dans un schéma de représentation plus large de l'existence familiale qui reste à construire et dont l'universalité d'application, même aux seules sociétés développées, est loin d'aller de soi.

Remarques sur la structure logique des concepts de cycle et position dans le cycle

Les notions de cycle de la vie familiale et de positions dans le cycle sont une construction abstraite, supposée rendre des services pour l'analyse de la vie familiale. On ne peut parler que fort improprement de *théorie* du cycle. Cet abus de langage est fréquent, il n'en est pas moins condamnable. Il n'y a théorie que lorsqu'un ensemble de propositions logiquement reliées permettent de structurer les acquis descriptifs ou expérimentaux du champ défini par ces propositions. Ici, les propositions se réduisent grossièrement à deux, ce qui donne un pouvoir explicatif très limité.

1. La vie familiale dans les sociétés monogamiques et économiquement différenciées s'organise en un cycle qui s'ouvre avec le mariage et se clôt avec la mort des fondateurs.
2. La dynamique du cycle est constituée par la nature des relations, obligatoires ou non entre les fondateurs et leurs enfants éventuels avec les instances de socialisation autres que la famille.

Ces deux propositions ont permis essentiellement de construire des échelles de repérage indépendantes de l'âge des individus, et donc de comparer soit de culture à culture, soit de famille dite "normale" à famille dite "déviante", les vitesses de passage d'une phase du cycle à une autre, ou les possibilités d'accès à telle phase sous telles conditions. Par là, la position dans le cycle devient une variable qui synthétise davantage d'informations que la seule mention de l'âge. Elle permet également de contrôler l'influence de l'âge par rapport à un certain nombre de variables dépendantes.

Ces acquis et d'autres font du cycle un peu plus qu'un simple outil de repérage en ce sens que l'indexation est faite non de façon purement conventionnelle mais en référence à certaines coupures chargées de sens sociologique. Malgré ces avantages, force est de constater que la position dans le cycle n'a pas acquis droit de cité parmi les outils de la démographie et de la statistique sociale où l'on continue de s'en tenir à l'âge, l'âge au mariage, la différence d'âge entre les époux, le nombre de personnes au foyer, ou d'enfants à charge. Fait digne de remarque: la démographie sociale s'attache avec de bonnes raisons à tenir compte des conceptions prénuptiales en France, celles-ci sont liées de façon incontestable à la divorcialité ultérieure, or aucun découpage du cycle à ma connaissance n'a construit une case pour couples nouveaux avec enfants à naître moins de 9 mois après le mariage.

La première raison de ce faible succès, en dehors du cercle des sociologues de la famille, est probablement l'incapacité de fait où ceux-ci se sont trouvés de parvenir à un découpage relativement simple et généralement utilisé dans les enquêtes. Les raffinements, les subdivisions ou au contraire les regroupements auxquels nombre de collègues se sont livrés ont fait du cycle une plante délicate aux mutations nombreuses, propre au travail de serre surchauffée des enquêtes approfondies mais beaucoup moins à la pleine terre des sondages représentatifs ou des recensements.

Limitation de l'usage, mais non condamnation. Est-ce la seule? Dans son ambition d'être synthétiquement représentative du devenir familial, la division selon les phases du cycle souffre d'être à l'excès un découpage figé qui, jusqu'à présent, n'a été en mesure d'intégrer ni l'influence du passé sur le présent, ni celle que ses orientations au regard de l'avenir peuvent avoir sur l'état actuel. Deux couples situés à une même phase du cycle au bout du même nombre d'années de mariage et avec le même nombre d'enfants ne peuvent pas être considérés autrement que comme logiquement interchangeables. L'exemple déjà cité de l'influence des conceptions prénuptiales sur le devenir familial atteste l'excès de réductionnisme opéré par la position dans le cycle. De même, les modèles de fécondité élaborés en France ont-ils mis l'accent sur l'importance des attitudes au regard de l'avenir dans la détermination du nombre d'enfants souhaité ou admis.[1]

Dans un autre domaine de l'étude de la vie des ménages, celui des comportements d'épargne et de consommation, où l'usage de la position dans le cycle s'est révélé des plus utiles, on constate néanmoins que son pouvoir explicatif achoppe faute d'être en mesure de tenir compte des anticipations au regard du revenu comme du devenir éducatif des enfants. L'hypothèse de "revenu permanent", celles des anticipations au regard de l'inflation attestent là l'importance des représentations du futur sur les comportements actualisés.

Contrairement à ce qu'il semble en premier examen, la structure logique du "cycle de la vie familiale" n'autorise une représentation ordonnée que selon une seule dimension, celle du passage des enfants légitimes dans le foyer. Le cycle suppose implicitement que l'entrée dans la famille est un phénomène de pur développement – plus ou moins lent, plus ou moins fécond – et que leur sortie est une nécessité. Ce qui est extérieur aux trois faits: avoir des enfants, les socialiser, les émanciper, ne trouve pas place préparée dans la division selon les positions du cycle.

Or cela est cohérent avec la texture très fixiste des deux propositions rappelées plus haut qui sous-tendent les découpages. Si l'on regarde la première, on doit la considérer ou bien comme triviale, ou bien comme profondément inexacte. Elle correspond très exactement à la notion de famille conjugale normale selon la conception normative et valorisante de l'éthique chrétienne. L'extension du champ des enfants légitimes et des droits de l'enfant naturel atteste que le droit, pour normatif qu'il soit, admet déjà un clavier plus large. Abondance de faits montrent que la famille ne commence pas au mariage. Même si, à en croire les taux élevés de nuptialité, le mariage est moins en crise que d'aucuns ne le soutiennent; même si, comme l'a montré Alain Girard[2], les relations préconjugales et les conceptions prénuptiales conduisent au mariage, celui-ci n'est pas un commencement absolu. Les facteurs d'homogamie dont la présence est très généralement attestée montrent que le mariage de deux individus s'inscrit le plus souvent dans une histoire qui est celle de deux lignées. A l'autre bout apparent de l'existence du couple: la mort, la famille ne s'arrête pas. Certains choix fondamentaux qui prennent place dans le cycle et qui même servent à définir des changements de phase du cycle sont déterminés et par la représentation que le couple a de son futur, de celui de sa lignée, et par ses orientations au regard de l'avenir. Ainsi en va-t-il du nombre d'enfants, de leur éducation, de leur départ du foyer et aussi de l'aide qui leur est éventuellement accordée. Les dispositions prises, formellement ou non, au regard de la transmission des biens attestent que nombre de personnes entendent peser sur la vie des autres même après leur mort et font, de leur vivant, des choix inspirés par ce souci. Ces faits d'évidence bien connus des juristes spécialisés en droit de la famille sont-ils susceptibles d'une expression opératoire pour le sociologue de la famille? Telle est la question à laquelle nous allons tenter d'apporter quelques éléments concrets de réponse.

Nombre d'enfants et projet intergénérationnel. Peut-on considérer la naissance d'enfants dans la famille comme des évenements "absolus" ou ne convient-il pas plutôt d'interpréter ce fait brut pour en extraire un objet sociologiquement significatif? Les démographes ont approché le problème par la construction de modèles de fécondité, par des études de motivation, ces dernières permettant parfois de donner une interprétation concrète à un des termes du modèle, et également par des comparaisons diachroniques ou internationales. Dans le cas de la France, on admet souvent que la courbe en U selon la hiérarchie de prestige social reconnu (fécondité élevée chez les agriculteurs et dans les classes supérieures, natalité très faible dans les classes moyennes) exprime le malthusianisme des milieux d'employés motivés par le désir d'assurer la mobilité d'une descendance, à cette fin limitée.[3] La limitation prendrait sens par rapport à un projet dont la réalisation sortira de l'intervalle de durée de vie probable du ménage des parents.

En traitant par la méthode de l'analyse factorielle des correspondances[4] certaines données d'une enquête sur la transmission patrimoniale, nous avons établi des résultats fragiles puisque ne portant que sur 3 échantillons d'environ 500 personnes de profession non salariée (respectivement agriculteurs, commerçants et industriels, professions libérales) qui semblent confirmer la force d'une relation entre le nombre d'enfants et les attitudes au regard de l'avenir, mais jeter un doute sur l'univocité du sens à donner au choix de l'enfant unique.[5]

L'analyse a pris en compte à la fois des variables supposées descriptives telles que précisément le nombre d'enfants, et des variables supposées révélatrices d'orientations au regard de l'avenir telles que les dispositions prises pour la succession dans l'affaire.

Détaillons à titre d'exemple ce qu'on obtient chez les agriculteurs; le premier facteur avec une inertie de 0,57 oppose:

- un des enfants au moins travaille avec l'enquêté
- majorité des enfants dans la même profession
- scolarité limitée des enfants
- utilisation prévue de la donation-partage anticipé

- pas de successeur prévu
- enfants en partie dans groupe socio-professionnel plus élevé
- acceptation de la conversion des biens en valeur équivalente
- famille restreinte (0, 1 et rarement 2 enfants)
- non utilisation de la donation-partage[6]
- études longues des enfants

On peut interpréter le facteur comme opposant (colonne de gauche) ceux qui privilégient la stabilité en situation de la famille à ceux qui (colonne de droite) ont un projet de mobilité socio-professionnelle: orientation vers la permanence, orientation vers la mobilité.

Chez les premiers le nombre d'enfants n'apparaît pas peser d'un poids déterminant. En revanche, chez les seconds le modèle de l'enfant unique prédomine nettement.

Un deuxième facteur, avec une inertie sensiblement plus faible, oppose plus directement les familles nombreuses d'un côté, les familles restreintes de l'autre.

Avec la famille nombreuse, on trouve la succession souhaitée dans l'exploitation mais déclarée "tributaire de l'attitude des enfants", bref, une attitude peu volontariste au regard de l'avenir. Du côté de la famille restreinte, on trouve soit l'aîné ou l'enfant unique qui reprend l'exploitation, soit un départ organisé, c'est-à-dire des dispositions plus nettement prises à l'endroit de l'avenir. Le premier facteur a opposé stabilité à mobilité, le second sépare plutôt l'acceptation du destin à son organisation anticipée: l'opposition entre succession ou non succession dans l'entreprise cesse d'être pertinente, car la prévision peut, selon les cas, conduire à décider la continuation ou la cessation de l'exploitation.

Chez les agriculteurs donc, l'enfant unique est le résultat d'un choix qui exprime le volontarisme devant l'avenir associé éventuellement mais non nécessairement à un projet de mobilité. La famille nombreuse est davantage associée à une attitude plus passive ou plus optimiste sur les possibilités d'une stabilité locale et professionnelle de la famille.

Sur le groupe des commerçants et industriels, l'analyse conduit à des résultats plus différents et plus riches pour notre propos; le premier facteur oppose:

- enfant(s) travaille(nt) dans l'affaire avec ou sans succession déjà décidée
- intéresse financièrement les enfants
- leur a déjà fait des dons limités
- partage sera fait par référence aux enfants (et non en fonction de la retraite de l'intéressé)

- aucun enfant ne travaille dans l'affaire
- ne souhaite pas succession familiale dans l'affaire
- intention de ne pas faire de testament ni de donation anticipée
- pense que les enfants n'ont pas de droits sur les biens de famille

L'interprétation est assez aisée: d'un côté on trouve la vision familialiste dévouée aux enfants avec pour projet la continuité, de l'autre la vision courte, celle de l'individu qui borne son regard sur l'avenir à sa propre vie; de façon fort cohérente, il conclut que les enfants n'ont pas de droits sur les biens et qu'il n'a donc pas à agir en fonction d'eux. Le nombre d'enfants n'apparaît pas de façon déterminante dans les constellations caractéristiques de ce premier facteur. Il apparaît en revanche avec le deuxième facteur qui, comme il se trouve intégrer également plusieurs des variables lourdes du premier, permet d'affiner l'interprétation. Ce deuxième facteur oppose en effet:

- fera des parts égales
- songe à donation anticipée
- famille nombreuse
- intention de doter
- aide pour études

- un enfant
- ni don, ni testament
- pas d'aide pour études
- scolarité courte
- ne souhaite pas succession dans affaire

Certes, la division selon le deuxième facteur ne classe pas à gauche et à droite exactement les mêmes individus que celle selon le premier facteur (sinon il n'y aurait pas de deuxième facteur); néanmoins, l'importance des variables qui s'y retrouvent autorise à penser que ces partitions sont voisines. Selon le premier, la dominante en charge sur le facteur est le fait de travailler ou non dans l'entreprise paternelle. Selon le deuxième, toutes les variables associées à l'aide aux enfants sont, avec la famille nombreuse, opposées à la famille restreinte et au refus d'aide.[7]

Ainsi l'enfant unique irait avec le refus d'aide et la scolarité courte. L'interprétation n'est alors évidemment pas celle que suggère la descendance limitée des employés et sa promotion par l'école. Les commentaires et réponses aux questions ouvertes aident à préciser les contours du type humain auquel nous avons affaire ici. Hommes qui se sont faits eux-mêmes ces entrepreneurs du commerce ou de l'industrie sont de ceux qui ne sont pas assez devenus bourgeois pour penser en termes de lignée et qui en même temps ont rompu avec l'affectivité généreuse des familles populaires pour qui le souci des biens des enfants est primordial. Durs à eux-mêmes et aux autres, ils pensent que les enfants n'ont pas droit sur leurs biens, ce qui est tout à la fois l'expression d'un principe d'éducation par l'effort, d'un attachement à tous les attributs de la propriété et, éventuellement, d'un goût, ou d'un rêve de jouissance égoïste. Le très petit nombre d'enfants pourrait exprimer un refus de se créer des charges dans l'existence.

Ni chez les agriculteurs, ni chez les commerçants et industriels la ventilation en fonction du niveau de fortune ne modifie grandement les résultats. Il n'en va pas de même pour les professions libérales chez qui, au contraire, le montant global du patrimoine semble exercer deux influences, partiellement indépendantes mais susceptibles de converger. Sur le premier facteur dégagé par l'analyse l'un des pôles est constitué par le souci de transmission et exprimé de façon préférentielle par les propriétaires des patrimoines les plus élevés, dont la concentration autour de ce pôle est marquante. Or d'autre part les familles à patrimoine élevé ont, dans notre échantillon, la proportion d'enfants uniques la plus élevée. Cette dernière constatation serait de nature à ouvrir une interrogation sur l'interprétation usuelle et peut-être rapide de la fécondité élevée des classes supérieures. Si la sécurité matérielle et morale de certaines professions en même temps que l'ethos du milieu des classes dirigeantes, volontiers familialiste en France, vont souvent de pair avec un nombre d'enfants plutôt élevé, est-ce que le souci de la conservation du patrimoine quand celui-ci est important ne vient pas créer une motivation très contraire? On serait assez tenté d'accorder quelque crédit à l'hypothèse en comparant les familles de médecins et celles de membres des professions juridiques. Dans les premières il y a en moyenne peu de patrimoine hérité, la vie est confortable, l'épargne formée n'est pas considérable, les enfants sont nombreux. Dans les secondes au contraire, le patrimoine est considérable, même pour les avocats qui ne reprennent pas un office ou une charge et le nombre d'enfants est très réduit. Or comme l'accumulation vient de la génération antérieure, on peut, sous réserves, écarter l'hypothèse selon laquelle l'exiguïté des charges pour enfants serait la cause de l'enrichissement.[8]

Insérer le nombre d'enfants dans la chaîne des choix familiaux, et donner la place dans celle-ci aux options qui concernent la génération future, telle serait la première conclusion programmatique de cette analyse. La deuxième serait une invitation à prendre compte la diversité culturelle des familles selon des variables de milieu.

Milieu professionnel, milieu familial et reproduction des comportements. En poursuivant l'analyse précédente on peut se demander s'il y a une inertie qui conduirait l'enquêté à reproduire au profit de ses enfants ou héritiers les pratiques et modalités selon lesquelles il est devenu lui-même bénéficiaire ou héritier. Peut-on s'en tenir à des modèles selon le milieu professionnel ou conviendrait-il de chercher d'autres déterminants plus universels tels que des valeurs d'origine religieuse ou plus particularistes tels que des traits culturels locaux, voire des normes propres à un milieu très restreint ou à un groupe de familles? La pratique qui consiste à "faire un aîné" (qui peut ne pas être l'aîné par la naissance) est encore présente dans certaines familles et peut, malgré le code civil, trouver dans les dispositifs légaux en France certaines possibilités de réalisation. L'analyse à laquelle nous avons pu procéder sur nos données ne comportait pas de variables de localisation mais seulement les 7 variables suivantes:

- profession et groupe socio-professionnel
- rang de naissance de l'enquêté
- nombre d'enfants de l'enquêté
- religion
- modalités de la première réception (dot, héritage, etc. ...)
- souhaitez-vous qu'un de vos enfants vous succède professionnellement?
- avez-vous l'intention de faire un testament, une donation entre vifs?

La distribution des points les plus significatifs sur les différentes variables présente une configuration triangulaire indiquant la présence de deux axes d'opposition, le second opérant seulement une partition secondaire au sein de l'un des deux ensembles distingués par le premier.

La place des différentes professions est un premier fil conducteur. Une première constellation (droite du graphique) est en effet située tout autour des agriculteurs et c'est bien eux qu'elle décrit. Ils ont bénéficié de donations-partages anticipés et entendent bien agir de même à l'endroit

Figure 1. *Schéma simplifié de l'analyse factorielle des correspondances*

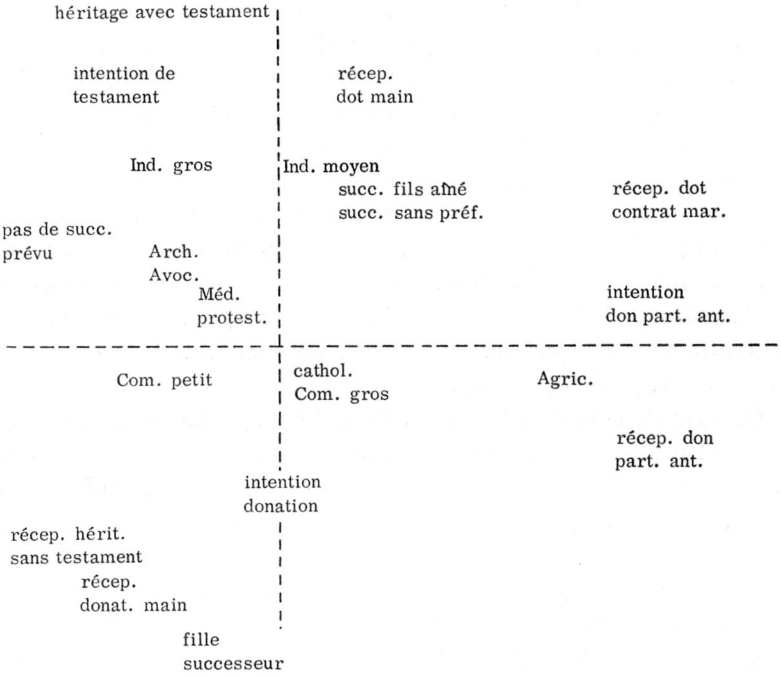

Agric. = agriculteur; Arch. = architecte; Avoc. = avocat;
Com. = commerçant; Ind. = industriel; Méd. = médecin.

de leurs enfants. Ils ont reçu des dots avec ou sans contrats de mariage. Ils souhaitent majoritairement que leurs fils leur succèdent.

En revanche, la gauche du tableau est traversée par un deuxième axe qui oppose nettement d'un côté:

- réception d'héritage avec testament
- intention d'héritage avec testament
- fils qui ne succèdera pas

et de l'autre:

- réception de donations
- intention de donations
- réception d'héritage sans testament
- possibilité ouverte à fille de succéder

Ici encore, la place des professions éclaire les choses. Dans le quadrant du haut à gauche on trouve les industriels gros et moyens (qui pratiquent le testament) et plus bas les professions libérales chez qui on ne s'étonnera pas que les enfants ne soient pas considérés comme des successeurs probables avec un haut degré de certitude. Le quadrant du bas est celui des commerçants, les gros ne se distinguent pas très fortement des petits.

Les autres variables ne se sont pas révélées très discriminantes par rapport à l'analyse factorielle étudiée. Le point central "catholique" est au point de croisement exact des deux axes,[9] le centre "protestant" en est très peu distant. Il n'y a donc pas quant aux modalités de l'héritage reçu ou à transmettre de différence imputable à une sous-culture religieuse. Seuls ceux qui ont été classés "autres" quant à la religion s'écartent un peu du centre pour se rapprocher de la région dans laquelle on rencontre les industriels et professions libérales.

De même le rang de naissance de l'enquêté n'apparaît lié à aucun des comportements étudiés. Il ne semble pas sur cette population que leurs parents se soient conduits différemment selon que l'enquêté fût ou non l'aîné. Tout au plus le point moyen "aîné" semble-t-il pencher du côté des agriculteurs, corroborant par là la sincérité de l'intention qui fait déclarer aux agriculteurs plus qu'aux autres souhaiter leur fils aîné comme successeur. De même la distribution des enquêtés selon le nombre de leurs enfants n'apporte-t-elle guère d'enseignements, sinon que les familles de 5 enfants, peu fréquentes, se rencontrent davantage chez les agriculteurs que dans les autres professions étudiées.

En revanche il est une catégorie de rapprochements frappants: pour chaque groupe professionnel les modalités de la réception par l'enquêté et ses intentions quant à la transmission apparaissent être les mêmes. En particulier "héritage avec testament" est très proche de "intention de tester", "réception sans testament" est assez proche de "intention de donation de la main à la main".

Les modalités de réception comme les intentions de transmettre, et avec moins de fermeté les souhaits quant à la continuité professionnelle par les enfants, sont liés d'assez près à la profession exercée et la probabilité est forte que les enquêtés se comportent à l'endroit de leurs enfants comme leurs parents se sont comportés vis-à-vis d'eux.

Que les agriculteurs se distinguent fortement des autres groupes ne sera pas pour nous étonner. Ils se caractérisent ici nettement par des réceptions de dot avec contrat de mariage, par leur pratique de la donation-partage anticipé tant en leur faveur qu'en faveur de leurs enfants, enfin par la conjonction moins illogique qu'il n'y paraît, de souhaits d'un fils comme successeur et d'incertitude quant au sort de leur exploitation.

Le contrat de mariage est, on le sait, plus fréquent chez les agriculteurs que dans d'autres milieux, la donation-partage anticipé est une formulation créée très explicitement à l'intention des chefs d'exploitations individuelles. L'intérêt est plutôt de voir que dans la population de l'ensemble étudié ces comportements suffisent à distinguer assez fortement les agriculteurs des autres, car enfin le contrat de mariage est tout de même loin d'être une exclusivité des agriculteurs.

Si l'on passe de l'autre côté du graphique, les faits mis en évidence sont plus nombreux. La catégorie des Patrons de l'Industrie et du Commerce éclate. Les gros commerçants sont proches des petits mais fort distants des industriels, cependant que ces derniers sont très proches des professions libérales. Vu la composition de l'échantillon, ce résultat peut surprendre, car rares étaient les très gros PDG. On y trouve surtout des patrons en nom et des gérants de S.A.R.L. dont on eût pu supposer qu'ils ne seraient pas socialement, financièrement et culturellement très distants des commerçants, au moins des gros. Il n'en est rien: il y a au regard des variables étudiées une certaine communauté entre industriels et professions libérales. Avec d'abord l'usage des testaments et la non-intention de continuité familiale dans le métier exercé. La position très excentrée du point "héritage reçu par testament" est digne de remarque: alors que le testament est un thème littéraire, un sujet de conversation, un objet de réflexion juridique important, la fréquence de la réception par testament apparaît des plus limitées dans des milieux qui pourtant ont quelque chose à transmettre. L'intention de testament est moins excentrée mais on peut se demander si une subtile distance entre intention et réalité ne viendra pas ramener la pratique au même niveau pour la génération actuelle.

Industriels et professions libérales ont également en commun de ne pas faire ce que font les agriculteurs et les commerçants. Or, si ces derniers ne pratiquent pas le testament c'est, on le voit très nettement, parce que chez eux la modalité dominante est la donation de la main à la main. Réception d'héritage avec testament et intention de tester: un milieu qui recourt à l'écrit et dans lequel la vieillesse est respectée: on ne se dépouille pas avant la mort. Voilà les industriels et les professions libérales. Donations entre vifs de la main à la main, voilà les commerçants: un monde où l'on cherche davantage à échapper à tout contrôle du fisc, où l'on craint moins également l'injustice de même que ses conséquences, où l'on admet davantage de se déssaisir partiellement avant la mort.

Or, l'étude des origines sociales avait montré que l'héritage professionnel au sens strict est relativement rare, ne dépassant jamais 20% dans aucun des sous-échantillons des professions libérales et 35% chez les commerçants. Il serait donc aventureux d'interpréter ces résultats et la constance intergénérationnelle qu'ils manifestent en s'en remettant à l'hypothèse de l'hérédité professionnelle. Pour notre part, nous préférons faire la supposition d'une *culture familiale* qui prédispose à l'entrée dans tel ou tel groupe professionnel.

Dans les professions libérales, l'origine sociale séparerait très nettement les membres des professions juridiques de ceux des professions médicales, les premiers ayant des origines beaucoup plus huppées que les seconds parmi lesquelles les pères salariés employés ou petits cadres sont assez fréquents. Cette différence ne se traduit guère dans les comportements ici analysés. Qu'est-ce à dire, sinon que la mobilité sociale a été préparée par un comportement global de la famille sur plusieurs générations – deux au moins? On songe aux textes de Schumpeter parlant de l'ascension et du déclin des familles:[10]

> L'ascension de certaines familles s'explique par une stratégie résolue dans le but d'améliorer les positions acquises ... La logique sociale ou la situation objective, si l'on n'y inclut pas les dispositions des individus ne détermine pas de façon univoque quelles proportions des bénéfices sera investie ni de quelle façon. Parler d'automatisme suppose qu'étant donné un statut initial des positions familiales il soit vrai que celles-ci tendent à se maintenir ...

Et plus loin[11] "Les familles franchissent les barrières et elles le font pour leur propre compte".

Conclusion

Les quelques exemples ici rassemblés entendent montrer l'importance pour la connaissance de la famille des déterminations du passé et des anticipations au regard de l'avenir. Plus encore que dans certains autres secteurs de la vie sociale la tranche qu'est le présent ne porte pas en soi sa signification. D'autre part les spécificités à l'intérieur d'une même culture globale ne peuvent pas être ignorées: William Goode écrivant que les pauvres ont tout moins que les autres, même la famille, a bien montré que l'usage du mot famille est trompeur, masquant une grande diversité, socialement réglée. Ce qui est vrai des relations familiales l'est tout autant des grandes phases du devenir, naissances, émancipation, choix professionnels, modalités de transmission.

Songeons à un dernier exemple de concrète actualité. En France, à l'heure actuelle, un mouvement puissant de l'opinion pèse pour que la diminution des heures travaillées dans la vie se fasse prioritairement par un abaissement de l'âge de la retraite plutôt que par une réduction de l'horaire hebdomadaire. L'extension de l'assurance-retraite obligatoire a conduit nombre de commerçants et artisans à envisager l'arrêt du travail avant d'avoir atteint l'épuisement physique. Est-ce nouveau? Oui, par rapport à la génération précédente dont les économies de prévoyance individuelle ont, avec l'inflation, fondu, quand elles n'étaient pas investies dans l'immobilier. Non, par rapport à la génération dite de la Belle Epoque. Lors, le modèle idéal des commerçants et industriels, dont la fréquence d'observation est certes mal connue, était de se retirer une fois un capital constitué.

Mais en plein à contre-courant de ce mouvement pour la limitation de la vie active, les cadres supérieurs dans leur majorité voient d'un mauvais œil des limitations dans le temps de leur travail, c'est-à-dire de leur pouvoir sur la société (bien davantage que de leur revenu). Le sens de la retraite varie lui aussi avec la position sociale et les projections auxquelles elle est associée.[12]

Summary

Family models of wealth transmission and cycle theory

In a first argument the author sets forth the limitations of the concept of the family life cycle. One can reproach it for not having taken into sufficient account that which lies outside the three basic functions of having legitimate children, socializing them and emancipating them. In a division according to the positions in the cycle, there is no place foreseen, for example, for new couples to whom a child will be born in less than eight months after marriage, while the number of such couples is significantly high among those which end in divorce.

In a second, more factual part the author presents for consideration a number of results from a longitudinal study on patrimonial behavior among active non-salaried workers in France (farmers, businessmen, industrialists and professionals), illustrating that one cannot consider death as the end of the line as far as the cycle is concerned or as far as the family is concerned. Certain fundamental choices, such as the number of children, their emancipation, the help that is given them, etc., are dependent upon the wish or the ability of the person concerned to influence his descendants even after his own death. For farmers, for example, the number of children and the length of their studies, i.e., of the cohabitation at home, is tied to the prospect of professional and social stability (single family, rarely two children). For businessmen and industrialists, on the contrary, the organization or projected future of the family is based on the large family. Families with one or two children most often do not want to help the children in their studies or to see them take over their enterprises (individualist model).

Far from being an explanatory element in the development of the family, the number of children would much sooner seem to be a complex result, dependent on, among other things, the attitudes and ideas with regard to the family in a long-term perspective.

Notes

1. P. Bourdieu et A. Darbel (1966) in Darras, *Le partage des bénéfices*, Paris, Ed. de Minuit.
2. Alain Girard (1962), *Le Choix du conjoint*, Paris, PUF, Cahier de l'INED, 59, 201 p.
3. M. Febvay (1959), "Niveau et évolution de la fécondité par catégorie socio-professionnelle", Communication au Congrès International de la Population, Vienne, 1959.
   G. Calot et J.C. Deville (1971), "Nuptialité et fécondité selon le milieu socio-professionnel", *Economie et Statistique*, 27, Paris, INSEE.
4. Sur la méthode on consultera J.P. Benzecri *et al.* (1973), *L'Analyse des données*, Paris, Dunod, 619 p.
5. Les enquêtés ayant tous dépassé 40 ans par construction de l'échantillon et souvent 50 en fait, on s'est permis de raisonner comme s'il était certain que les familles fussent "complètes".
6. Disposition juridique qui permet aux parents d'opérer de leur vivant la transmission de leurs biens et en particulier d'assurer la succession à la tête d'une entreprise.
7. La non-coïncidence des deux facteurs est essentiellement due au nombre "d'erreurs" sur les variables lourdes: il y a quelques familles nombreuses du côté droit du premier facteur et inversement.
8. La question est néanmoins sérieuse: les travaux sur la liaison âge/patrimoine montrent une épargne négative lors de l'établissement des enfants. Voir: A. Babeau (1974), *Un essai de modélisation rétrospective de l'accumulation patrimoniale*, Centre de Recherche sur l'Epargne, Université de Paris X, Offset.
9. Ce qu'on peut considérer comme une sorte de validation de la représentation obtenue.
10. Schumpeter (1971), "Les classes sociales en milieu ethnique homogène" in *Impérialisme et classes sociales* Paris, Ed. de Minuit: 171.
11. *Ibid.*: 187.
12. Anne-Marie Guillemard (1973), *La Retraite, une mort sociale*, Paris-La Haye, Mouton: 303.

25 The family life cycle. A problematic concept

JAN TROST

In this paper we will present some critical ideas on the family life cycles existing in the scientific literature. We compare one of the family life cycles with some Swedish data, and, finally, we present an alternative to the family life cycle – an alternative solving some of the problems involved in the family life-cycle approach. It should be stressed that the proposed system is no final solution but a suggested way of solving the problem of operationalizing some of the ideas in the developmental type of approach.

The family life cycle

The history of the concept of family life cycle is a fairly old one. It is probably as old as mankind, but as a research-oriented concept it can be found in the beginning of the twentieth century (*cf.* Aldous, 1972). Today, however, in circles of family researchers, the concept of family life cycle seems to be associated with a specific theoretical approach to the study of the family – this approach being the so-called developmental approach.

Irrespective of whether the concept of family life cycle is knitted to a theoretical approach or not, the most important part of the family life cycle is the idea or notion that time goes on. This leads us to a dynamic view when studying the family.

Another important part of the family life cycle is that significant changes occur at specific times or with certain events in the family, one being the birth of children, another the age variation or combination of the children in the family. Although never explicit, there is a suggestion of *rites-de-passage*-thinking in most of the family life cycles constructed and available to the author (*cf.* Aldous, 1972). When a child passes the age of three, one of the *rites de passage* seems to occur (slightly caricatured); another is when a child is six, a third at the launching of the children. However, it is a technical misunderstanding to believe that there really is a reference to *rites de passage* behind these constructions. (If one uses the term *rites de passage* in a transferred meaning, perhaps, but not in the proper sense.) However, as Björnsson (1971: 180) stresses, there are some parts of the idea of the life cycle that fit the concept of *rites de passage*. Björnsson claims that the individual passes "through certain significant stages, each of which confers upon him socially prescribed rights and obligations". Evidently, Björnsson means that this is true for the family group as well as for the individual.

Rodgers (1973: 13), using a developmental approach, states that the developmental approach seeks to explain family dynamics in terms of the common quality of the family's experience over its history and not in terms of unique elements. The same aim must be true for the family life cycles used by researchers other than developmentalists, too.

Some critical remarks

With the above mentioned paragraphs as a background, let us take a look at the concept of family life cycle from a more critical point of view. The concept of family life cycle is harmless *per se*. However, the use made of this concept is not always harmless. The concept might steer the research into wrong channels, or put blinds on the researcher, or, when used as an educational tool, act as a conserving agent.

Rodgers (1962: 23) claims that the stages in the family life cycle can be nothing but "analytical categories" because of the association between stage and something predetermined, indicating that all stages must be passed by all marriages. As Rodgers states, "a married couple may not have any children, which automatically precludes their ever passing through most of the stages" (1962: 22). Rodgers' solution is a modification of the family life scheme, including not only the importance of the first child but that of the last child as well. Thus, Rodgers' modified scheme consists of 24 categories. Rodgers also prefers to call his concept family career rather than family life cycle.

However, Rodgers' scheme does not solve the problem of the couple who never have children. According to Rodgers' pattern, that couple begins in the first category and then has to jump over to the next to last category. There are some curious aspects in this solution, one of them being that the couple will never be anything but young or old. Rodgers himself labels the third category "beginning families" – thus, a family might be a beginning family until their fiftieth year of marriage; after that they jump to the next to last category, i.e., the aging couple; or as Coughenour (1972) has it – we can let these couples stay in the first stage for ten years and after that move to an extra, final step, tailor-made for them. Whichever solution is applied, reality will be badly reflected. What is said is that the couple "began to cohabit at such and such an age, they cohabited for so many years, and they stopped cohabiting because of death" (Floyd Martinson, personal communication).

The concept of family, used in connection with the idea of the family life cycle, is defined as a marital group, perhaps with children, i.e., the old nuclear type of family. Through that definition some very important parts in the field of the family are excluded. Thus, for instance, the one-parent families are excluded, since they do not fit the existing family life cycles. All three types of one-parent families are non-fits: those resulting from divorce, those resulting from the death of one or the other spouse, and those that have never been knitted into a marriage group (the unmarried mother or father with children). The first two of these families have belonged to the family life cycle but have been removed from it at the time of dissolution. The exclusion might be reasonable when the remaining part is a single person – so wide a definition of family as to include one-parent households might seem extravagant to many; from some points of view, however, it is a reasonable definition.

Another type of non-fit family is the cohabiting unmarried couple (with or without children). They are not married, and marriage seems to be a prerequisite for entering the family life cycle. There are two ways of defending this statement when criticized: either, one could say that the cohabiting unmarried couple is so uncommon that it does not have to be counted, or one could claim that the cohabiting unmarried couple is not a family. Both arguments seem to be extraordinarily risky, since they limit the field and narrow the range of sight.

A few words might be added in relation to the cohabiting unmarried couple. The cohabitation system we now have in Sweden is very new and probably rapidly changing. It might stabilize in one way or another in a couple of years. Until about a decade ago unmarried cohabiting couples were uncommon – at least those cohabiting overtly.

We have always had a fairly high rate of children born out of wedlock and a high rate of pregnancy marriages but not long-lasting, everyday, unmarried cohabitation. The normal pattern was that the couple became formally engaged: they exchanged rings, and announced to their surroundings that from now on they were engaged. Once the announcement had been made it was natural for the couple to have sexual intercourse and to live together during vacations and weekends, and so on, but not to practice a real cohabitation. Cohabitation normally started at about the time of the wedding. During the last few years there has been an enormous increase in the number of cohabiting unmarried couples. The estimate now is that about ten percent of all couples living together are unmarried. An estimate of the situation ten years ago was less than one percent (*cf.* Trost, 1972a, 1972b).

Formal or informal engagements with social implications do not occur very much in Sweden nowadays. This has to do with the fact that engagement is not relevant in law any more, and the introduction of overt cohabitation seems to have minimized the reasons for being formally or informally engaged.

The marriage rate in Sweden is the lowest in the world. It has decreased during the last decade by about 50 percent. It does not seem unreasonable to suppose that we are moving toward a system where most people cohabit for a while and after some years marry. This system seems to be somewhat like the old system still existing (partly changing, however) in Iceland (*cf.* Björnsson, 1971). It should be noted that the unmarried cohabiting couples are not exclusively college and university students, as was believed some years ago and as the situation is supposed to be, for instance, in the United States, where the new type of unmarried cohabitation is supposed to be among college and university students and the old type among very poor people. It is not reasonable to assume this for Sweden (Näsholm, 1972).

The intention of this fairly long description of today's situation is to show that the traditional family life-cycle schemes do not fit, e.g., Swedish society. About ten percent of the syndyasmos (*cf.* Löcsei, 1970) cannot be classified in family life-cycle schemes. Something must be wrong, therefore, with the classification. One could claim that the cohabiting couples should be defined as married, but, if so, one underestimates some very important parts of reality, those having to do with the law as well as with informal traditions.

The fourth limitation of the family life-cycle scheme is that some couples start in category or stage I and then dissolve through death or divorce, which means that they are drop-outs. As mentioned above, they do not exist any more from the family life-cycle point of view. But, in relation to the main ideas of the developmental approach, it must be of utmost importance for the family to lose one of the spouses or the parents, at least as important as, for instance, the birth of a child in the family. (For a more extended critique of the family life cycle, see Trost, 1974).

Evidently, Burr (1970), in his random sample of 147 intact couples, selected to eliminate lower socioeconomic strata, has not found any childless couples in marriages older than seven years. Rollins and Feldman (1970), on the other hand, found that out of the 850 couples in their sample 6.2 percent were childless. The solution adopted by Rollins and Feldman was to omit or to eliminate these 6.2 percent from the analysis because "they were considered atypical in terms of stages of the family life cycle".

There can be at least three principal ways of looking upon the family life cycle:

(a) It should be an educational tool for the researcher, the student, and the practitioner, to be used as a rough description of society, without going into details and complications.
(b) It should be a simple classification, based upon an important and relevant theory (the developmental approach), making clinical application easier when working with case material.
(c) It should be an operationalization of theoretical ideas (the developmental approach), making aggregate research (sociology and social anthropology) easier.

This means that when using the family life cycle as indicated under (a) and (b) the critique here presented is not fully relevant; but it is very relevant when using the family life cycle as indicated under (c). If we want to describe and/or analyze the family in a region, most of the critique is applicable, and as soon as we want to use the family life cycle in comparative research (comparing one society at different times or two or more societies at the same time) the critique seems to be highly relevant.

Often the use is of type (a), as during the 13th International Seminar of the Committee on Family Research in Paris, 1973, when many papers dealt with the situations of families in one or two stages of the family life cycle. But that is no theoretical use – it is a way of labeling a specified sample, thus using the family life cycle as an abbreviation for a line of thought or as a part of the jargon of family researchers – which partly is *argot* language.

This seems to be one of the most important reasons (unconscious, probably) for using the family life cycle. An implication of this is that much of the use is of a non-theoretical character – our critique is mainly directed toward the intention of using the family life cycle as a scientific operationalization of the theoretical approach.

Swedish data and the family life cycle

With the aim of comparing a Swedish situation of today with the family life-cycle idea we have used, on the one hand, Hill's (1964: 192) scheme and, on the other hand, some data from Sweden. Hill's scheme of classification is as follows:

I Establishment (newly married, childless)
II New parents (infant–3 years)
III Preschool family (child 3–6 years and possibly younger siblings)
IV School age family (oldest child 6–12 years, possibly younger sibling)
V Family with adolescent (oldest 13–19, possibly younger sibling)
VI Family with young adult (oldest 20 until first child leaves home)
VII Family as launching center (from departure of first to that of last child)
VIII Postparental family, the middle years (after children have left home until father retires)
IX Aging family (after retirement of father)

This family life-cycle scheme can be used as an average illustration of the different types of schemes that exist. There are differences, but they are not of any great importance to us given the aim we have set.

The Swedish data are those used in the "Westtown project" (Trost, 1971), which is a panel study carried out in 1965 and 1970, interviewing couples in "Westtown" (a town of about 100,000 inhabitants in the middle of Sweden). The sample drawn consisted of all couples who had published their bans in any of the four parishes of Westtown from May 24, 1964, to March 7, 1965. Both spouses were interviewed separately both in 1965 and in 1970. This means that our data are average, normal Swedish families, started by marriage five to six years before the second data collection and immediately prior to the first data collection. Some checks have been made using the official files in the registers' offices. The only

Table 1. *Newly marrieds' career in the family life cycle during a five-year period*

	Number	%	
a. Fully according to the family life cycle			
1. Start stage I, still in stage I	17	5.8	
2. Start stage I, now in stage II	13	4.4	
3. Start stage I, through II, now in stage III	81	27.6	37.8
b. According to family life cycle but ending in divorce			
4. Start stage I, directly to divorce	7	2.4	
5. Start stage I, through II, now divorced	5	1.7	4.1
c. According to the family life cycle but starting with a pregnant bride			
6. Start stage I, through II, now in stage III	75	25.5	25.5
d. Start in stage II			
7. Start stage II, now in stage III	17	5.8	
8. Start stage II, through III, now in stage IV	23	7.8	
9. Start stage II, directly to divorce	4	1.4	
10. Start stage II, through III, now divorced	4	1.4	16.3
e. Start in stage III			
11. Start stage III, now in stage IV	8	2.7	
12. Start stage III, through stage IV, now in stage V	1	.3	
13. Start stage III, directly to divorce	2	.7	3.7
f. Start in stage IV			
14. Start stage IV, now in stage V	14	4.8	
15. Start stage IV, directly to divorce	3	1.0	5.8
g. Start in stage V			
16. Start stage V, now in stage VI	3	1.0	
17. Start stage V, through stage VI, now stage VII	3	1.0	
18. Start stage V, still stage V	1	.3	
19. Start stage V, directly to divorce	3	1.0	3.4
h. Start in stage VI	0	0	0
i. Start in stage VII			
20. Start stage VII, now stage VIII	2	.7	
21. Start stage VII, directly to divorce	1	.3	1.0
j. Start in stage VIII			
22. Start stage VIII, still stage VIII	1	.3	.3
k. Start in stage IX			
23. Start stage IX, still in stage IX	2	.7	
24. Start stage IX, ended in death of one of the spouses	1	.3	1.0
l. Jumpers			
25. Start stage I, directly to stage IX	2	.7	
26. Start stage I, directly to stage V	1	.3	1.0
Total	294		99.9

cases we present here are those which can be classified because sufficient information was obtained about the couple. All those cases where information was lacking are omitted. This normally is a serious limitation, but in this case it acts so that it reasonably underestimates the difficulties and the problems with the family life cycle. Initially the sample consisted of 409 couples, but owing to refusals and other reasons such as lack of information the total number of couples treated here is 294 (72 percent of the initial sample). For a comparison between our data and the family life cycle, see Table 1.

Of the cases, 76.3% started in stage I and thus at the time of marriage fitted the family life cycle (a, b, and c in Table 1). After five years, however, only 37.8% still remained in the family life cycle fully according to the concept (a in Table 1). However, some of these will in the future leave the family life cycle unnaturally: some of the 17 couples of type 1 will remain childless and thus not fit, and some will divorce or dissolve the marriage before reaching the final stages. The 4.1% (b in Table 1) starting in stage I and divorcing directly or after having reached stage II could be said to fit the family life cycle at least partly. The same could be said about those (c in Table 1) 25.5% starting in I, going through stage II and now, after five years, being in stage III but having started with a pregnant bride.

So, depending upon how orthodoxly or how critically one looks upon the family life-cycle idea, the result will be that between 37.8% and 63.2% of our couples still fit the idea of the family life cycle used here after five years.

As many as 16.3% start in stage II (i.e., with a child less than three years). These cases can be of different types. Some of them have a premarital child together, some of them are in the situation that one (or both) of the spouses has been married earlier and has children from earlier marriages, and some of them are in the situation that the bride had a premarital child of her own, the husband not being the father.

Almost 4% (e in Table 1) start in stage III, i.e., the oldest child is 3–6 years old. These cases are principally of the same kind as those starting in stage II.

Most of the types of cases in Table 1 are easy to imagine. One of them might not be so: number 26. The couple started in stage I and jumped directly to stage V. The reason for this is that the spouses adopted a fifteen-year-old child not related to either of them.

These data show, among other things, that when the first year of marriage is over, only about one-third of the couples belong to stage I.

This could be compared to the data that Hill (1970) presents. He finds that 88% of his couples belong to family life cycle category I after one year of marriage.

Five years after the formation of the marital dyad only 4.4% remain in stage II. In Hill's data 31% belong to this category. Almost 60% of the cases in our sample belong to stage III, compared to 65% in Hill's data. Hill has only 1% in category IV after five years, but in our data we have as many as 10.5% in family life cycle number IV. Hill has no cases in categories V and higher, but we have 10.1% in those categories. Of course, many of the last-mentioned figures are calculated based upon the idea that, although some of the couples do not start in stage I and thus do not fit the family life cycle, they are treated as if they were entered from the wrong side.

Hill (1970: 89ff.) shows that in his (and Rodgers, 1962) data 88% of the couples belong to family life cycle category I during the first year, after eight years only 1% remains, and by the ninth year none of them remains. This seems to be very curious. The fact that none of these couples remains childless might have to do with the type of sample that Hill uses.

A curious thing with many of the American studies is that there are no cases starting in stages later than stage I. It seems to have been very uncommon in the U.S.A. for unmarried mothers to keep their children. So for that reason few couples could be found starting in stage II, III, etc. But, on the other hand, there should be many: the divorce rate in the U.S.A. has for a long time been very high, as has the remarriage rate. So many of the remarriages must reasonably start at a later stage than stage I.

We fully agree with Hill's statement (Hill, 1970: 90) that "no simple classification can do justice to the variety of situations making up the careers of families over time". With the results presented here as a background it seems reasonable to complete the statement of Hill with the following statement: "No *simple* classification can do justice to the variety of situations making up the careers of families at any specific time".

Rodgers claims that the family life cycles "most frequently used in writings reflect statistically typical families moving through statistically typical careers" (Rodgers, 1973: 78). This seems to be intended as a precise description of over-simplification but, as our data have shown, the statement is an over-simplified description of over-simplifications. Rodgers goes on by saying that the researchers he refers to "have stated their problem implicitly as follows: 'let us take as our problem the explanation of some behaviour of families, which move through their careers as 'most' American families are expected to do'. Their family careers, then, are constructed to allow them to deal with their problem".

It should be noted that neither our data nor the data of Hill are representative of the population in Sweden and the United States, respectively. They might be representative of a sub-population but only geographically. Our own data, e.g., by definition exclude one-parent families, all unmarried cohabiting couples, etc. On the other hand, our cases can over time reach those family forms. Hill's data, on the other hand, have the same limitations by definition – excluding one-parent families, unmarried cohabiting couples, etc. – and, furthermore, they do not include families having moved over to "atypical" family forms.

An alternative to the cycle

With these examples we have, according to our own perception, shown that the family life-cycle schemes existing are risky to use in many respects. The modification made by Rodgers does not solve many of the problems we have pointed out. It seems fully reasonable that it is quite impossible to reach a stage in the nearest future, where we can find *one* (complicated or simple) operationalization of the ideas lying behind the family life cycle – this implies acquiring a multi-dimensional tool possible to use anywhere, at any time, and for whichever purpose it might be. This is quite in line with what Rodgers (1973: 79) says and what many othei colleagues have said for many hundreds of years, namely, that we might have one operationalization at one time and another at another time, and that the theoretical basis and not the operationalization is the impoı tant one. However, as mentioned above, the family life cycle is often used as if it belonged to the developmental approach itself and not only as a way of operationalizing some of the ideas in the theory.

In order to contribute something more than only negative criticism we will suggest here a system which might be usable when worked out in somewhat more detail, one which might be used in many types of studies and for many different analytical problems inside the family area. The system we propose does not solve all the problems of operationalization but it might not so easily be influenced by time and cultural situations. It is more research-oriented than the family life cycle, which, according to our perception (and as stated above), is more pedagogically than research oriented.

Our idea is to arrange a multidimensional table of a property-space type, consisting of a certain number of specific variables. The choice of variables to be included is made on the basis of the developmental approach. Each unit (family or household) could be classified in an *n*-digit code, where *n* equals the number of variables. The following list of variables is an example of what it could look like. The list is, however, not intended to be *the* list to be used. As mentioned above, it has to be worked out in further detail.

1. Marital status: if there is a marriage
   a) from a legal point of view or
   b) from a cultural point of view or
   c) not at all.
2. Cohabitation under marriage-like conditions, whether married or not.
3. Previous marital/cohabitational experience in household.
4. Duration of the syndyasmos.
5. Number of adults (e.g., 18 years and older) in the household.
6. Number of children (e.g., less than 18 years) in the household.
7. Age of oldest child in the household.
8. Age of youngest child in the household.
9. Sex composition of the children in the household.
10. Sex composition of adults in the household.
11. Type of habitation: one-parent or two-parent family.
12. Age of the adult(s) in the household: all are above or below, e.g., 65 years.
13. Departure of children from household.

If we combine these 13 variables we will reach several millions of cells, the majority of which, however, will be logically empty. All households will be classified in a 13-digit system.

With this system it is easy

(a) to reduce the number of variables to make the information easy to handle without a computer where no computer is available, or when use of computer is irrelevant, as when analyzing case-studies; or to reduce the number of variables when the interest being acute limits the information needed.

(b) to add a number of variables that for some theoretical or practical reasons may have to be added, thus changing the digit code without destroying the basic information given by the *n*-digit code.

(c) to label some of the code numbers in relation to some standard, e.g., the Duvall/Hill/Aldous family life-cycle scheme, making a total comparison possible with that scheme.

This might appear too complicated to handle, but it is not; in order to use an unshortened version one just has to have access to a computer, the most important qualification of which should be a large memory.

This system makes it possible to ensure that one's own data will be comparable to other researchers' data (if they use the same system). Difficulties in comparison is one of the worst communication problems in the scientific craft.

One of the most important advantages with the proposed *n*-digit system is that changes over time can fairly easily be shown and analyzed, independent of whether one uses longitudinal data, retrospective data, or register data.

This system, furthermore, is usable when the interest lies in predicting future composition of a population or a subpopulation when transition probabilities are known or can be estimated with high accuracy. Thus, for example, one can easily predict the composition in one year, two years, three years, etc., in a suburb where the situation at time t_0 is known. The transition probabilities for each value on the variables and each combination of values on combined variables can be estimated from the developmental approach, from life expectancy tables, from nuptiality trends, etc.

It is obvious that this proposal needs careful empirical as well as theoretical testing before one could reach the stage of an acceptable set of variables and cutting points for all researchers involved in this field.

There are some negative aspects in this system. Two of the more important are: first, the system is complicated. There is a need for a fairly good computer in order to use the entire system. Second, it is not easy to follow the concept of the stages, without using some kind of panel or retrospective data. However, that type of data is fairly commonly used and is needed for most of the analyses made under the heading of the developmental approach.

Conclusion

In this paper we have shortly summarized the idea lying behind the family life cycle and some thoughts relevant to the idea. We have mentioned some of the more important critical objections to the concept of the family life cycle:

The idea of stages is an unrealistic one because many families will never pass all stages but will jump from stage I to a much later stage.

Many important types of families are excluded (one-parent families, non-married cohabiting couples, etc.).

Families start in the family life cycle but are drop-outs through dissolution of the family group while the remaining parts of the family might be two-family groups, even without any substitution of new members.

Swedish panel data are applied to the family life cycle. These data show that depending upon how orthodoxly or how critically one looks upon the family life-cycle idea, between 35% and 60% of the families fit the idea of the family life cycle, after five years of marriage. The data consist of people who married at the time of the first data collection. The number of marriages fitting the cycle idea should be evaluated in relation to this. Finally, we propose a new system, an alternative to the family life cycle, for solving the operationalization of some ideas in the developmental approach. The solution proposed is a construction of an *n*-digit system, classifying each family or household by *n*-digits. When *n* is a high figure computers are normally necessary for handling data, while when *n* is a low figure data treatment can easily be made by hand. The system proposed is not *the* ideal operationalization, but it is one better than the family life cycle, at least from a research-oriented point of view.

Résumé

Le cycle de la vie familiale – un concept problématique

Le cycle de la vie familiale en tant que concept remonte aux origines de l'humanité mais le terme n'a fait son apparition dans les travaux scientifiques qu'à partir du début de ce siècle. Qu'il soit lié ou non à une théorie scientifique, le concept de cycle de la vie familiale se révèle d'une grande utilité mais comporte en même temps certains dangers.

Ce concept repose, entre autres, sur l'idée qu'avec le temps toute famille évolue et subit des modifications caractéristiques: des enfants naissent, grandissent, puis quittent le foyer familial, etc. – et que les étapes initiales de ce développement influencent ou expliquent les comportements ultérieurs, etc. Le cycle de la vie familiale présente un grand avantage: il est d'un emploi commode du point de vue pédagogique, ainsi que dans le jargon des specialistes. Mais il a l'inconvénient de fixer et de perpétuer les concepts traditionels. De plus, son cadre opératoire ne rend compte que d'un nombre limité de familles de notre société.

Le cycle de la vie familiale se fonde sur le groupe matrimonial et ignore de ce fait le cas de toute une série de constellations familiales, telles que la famille à un seul parent, ou le couple formé de deux partenaires qui cohabitent sans être mariés. Par ailleurs, ce concept repose sur la présence d'enfants nés du mariage et exclut *ipso facto* les unions sans enfants. Enfin, divisé tel qu'il l'est en stades successifs, le cycle de la vie familiale suppose que les enfants arrivent après le mariage des parents, alors que dans de nombreux cas les parents ont des enfants avant de se marier, débutant, pour ainsi dire, au "mauvais" stade. Nous nous sommes attachés à comparer la situation de la famille en Suède d'aujourd'hui au cycle de la vie familiale. Pour ce faire, nous avons eu recours à un échantillon empirique constitué par 300 jeunes couples environ que nous avons suivis de 1965 à 1971.

Nos résultats montrent que les deux tiers seulement des jeunes mariés ont commencé au stade I et que, 5 ou 6 ans après le mariage, un tiers d'entre eux seulement sont encore dans le cycle. Pas moins de 15% débutent au stade II (c'est-à-dire avec au moins un enfant de moins de 3 ans au moment du mariage). On notera au passage que l'échantillon examiné devait correspondre au cycle de la vie familiale puisqu'il était exclusivement constitué de couples mariés et qu'il ne comportait aucune famille à un parent ni aucun couple non marié. Il est donc vraisemblable que le cycle de la vie familiale rende moins bien compte encore de la réalité.

Nous avons mis au point une solution nouvelle au problème du cycle de la vie familiale. Partant des principes du "developmental approach" mais sous une forme sensiblement plus complexe que celle du cycle traditionnel, nous proposons de classer les familles à chaque moment significatif en fonction d'un certain nombre de variables qui peuvent être par exemple l'état civil, la durée du groupe, l'état civil antérieur, le nombre d'adultes, le nombre d'enfants, l'âge de l'aîné, l'âge du plus jeune, etc. Ainsi chaque famille sera caractérisée par une combinaison de n chiffres correspondant à sa situation à un moment donné. On aura recours à un ordinateur de grande capacité pour analyser les échantillons plus importants numériquement. La taille de n pourra varier mais une certaine standardisation de base est nécessaire afin de rendre possibles les comparaisons avec d'autres échantillons. Notre projet n'a cependant fait l'objet encore d'aucune expérimentation empirique.

REFERENCES

Aldous, J. (1972), "The developmental approach to family analysis", Vol. I, Minneapolis (mimeo).

Björnsson, B. (1971), *The Lutheran Doctrine of Marriage in Modern Icelandic Society*, Oslo, Universitetsförlaget.

Burr, W.R. (1970), "Satisfaction with various aspects of marriage over the life cycle: a random middle class sample" *Journal of Marriage and the Family*, 32/1, February: 29–37.

Coughenour, C.M. (1972), "Functional aspects of food consumption activity and family life cycle stages", *Journal of Marriage and the Family*, 34/4, November: 656–664.

Duvall, E.M. (1971), *Family Development*, New York.

Hill, R. (1964), "Methodological issues in family development research", *Family Process* III: 186–206.

—— *et al.* (1970), *Family Development in Three Generations*, Cambridge, Schenkman Publishing Company.

Löcsei, Pal (1970), "Syndyasmos in contemporary Budapest", Budapest (mimeo).

Näsholm, Astrid (1972), "Sammanboende gifta och sammanboende ogifta", SOU, 41, *Familj och äktenskap*, 1. Stockholm.

Rodgers, Roy H. (1962), "Improvements in the construction and analysis of family life cycle categories", unpublished doctoral thesis, University of Minnesota.

—— (1973), *Family Interaction and Transaction. The Developmental Approach*, Englewood Cliffs, N.J., Prentice-Hall, Inc.

Rollins, Boyd C., and Feldman, Harold (1970), "Marital satisfaction over the family life cycle", *Journal of Marriage and the Family*, February: 20–28.
Trost, J. (1971), *Methods and Distribution of Frequencies*, FF 16, Research Reports from the Department of Sociology, Uppsala, Uppsala University.
—— (1972a), "Various forms of cohabitation and their relation to psychical and social criteria of adaptation", Paper presented at the Third International Symposium on Society, Stress and Disease, Stockholm, May 29–June 3 (will be published in proceedings from the seminar, 1976, by Oxford University Press).
—— (1972b), "Marriage rates in Sweden" (will be published in Marie Corbin (ed.), *The Couple*).
—— (1974), "The family life cycle – an impossible concept?", *International Journal of Sociology of the Family*, 4: 37–47.

Conclusion
Type d'organisation familiale et cycle: changement ou mutation dans les sociétés européennes

JEAN CUISENIER

Le moment est venu d'esquisser un bilan et de dessiner des perspectives. Reuben Hill, Roy Rodgers et William J. Goode ont préparé les voies, en traçant l'histoire du concept et en ouvrant l'interrogation sur l'usage qu'on peut en faire pour la théorie. Jean Trost est allé aussi loin que possible dans la critique, remettant en question l'usage du concept non seulement pour l'analyse, mais aussi pour la description, allant même jusqu'à proposer un nouveau système pour rendre opératoires les idées sur le développement de la famille dans le temps. Entre ces premières interrogations et les propositions de Jan Trost, les contributions réunies dans ce livre invitent à suivre un chemin. Ruža First-Dilić, John Eriksen et Per Olav Tiller, Elina Haavio-Mannila, Veronica Stolte-Heiskanen, Takeji Kamiko, Wilfried A. Dumon et R. d'Hertefelt offrent une série d'analyses appliquant le concept de cycle à l'organisation familiale et à son développement dans le temps. Françoise Lautman, Robert Chester, Renate Künzel, Jean Kellerhals, Gérard Frinking, Andrjez Tymowski, Rhona et Robert Rapoport et Victor Thiessen étudient des faits particuliers de la vie familiale, comme le mariage, le divorce ou l'avortement à la place qui est la leur dans la durée propre des familles. Peter Laslett, Tamara Hareven, Joël Halpern, Nikolina Ilieva et Véra Oshavkova, Cvetko Kostić, Jean-François Gossiaux et Rada Boreli élargissent l'usage du concept de cycle à d'autres types de famille et à d'autres types de société que ceux pour qui il a été originairement élaboré. John Mogey, Jacques Commaille et Anne Boigeol, Jacques Lautman et Jean-François Gossiaux étudient le champ théorique du concept jusqu'au point où il faut bien se demander, comme Jan Trost, si de nouvelles propositions ne sont pas à faire. Que retenir du paysage qui vient ainsi de défiler, pour qui parcourt ce chemin? Vers quels itinéraires invite-t-il à s'engager pour des trajets futurs?

J'essaierai, en guise de conclusion, de dégager un certain nombre de soucis qui me paraissent s'être manifestés au long de ce livre, de préoccupations nouvelles dont toutes n'ont pas encore trouvé leur forme d'expression théorique, mais qui n'en fournissent pas moins des thèmes inspirateurs pour la recherche. Je risquerai ensuite quelques formulations théoriques d'un point de vue anthropologique, si l'on veut bien nommer *anthropologie* la discipline scientifique qui unifie, sur la base de mêmes fondements, les projets spécifiques de l'ethnologue, du sociologue, du démographe et de l'historien. Je tenterai enfin de repérer et baliser les voies sur lesquelles, d'un aveu commun, il faudra s'engager, si l'on veut réellement prendre en compte la dimension temporelle pour l'étude de l'organisation familiale dans toutes ses variétés.

1. *Soucis*

Les soucis nouveaux sont à peine nombrables, et il faudrait du recul pour les inscrire dans un champ théorique convenablement agencé. D'autres tenteront, ailleurs, de rationaliser l'ordre de leur apparition, et de trouver les rapports qui les lient entre eux. Je me bornerai ici à en nommer quelques-uns, considérés, par les contributions qu'on vient de lire, comme les plus vifs.

L'attention a été appelée à plusieurs reprises, et notamment par William Goode et Jan Trost, sur des formes d'organisation de la vie familiale que ne sanctionnent pas les législations existantes, mais qui n'en fonctionnent pas moins réellement. On vise ici non seulement les "communes" de hippies, dont la mode est déjà passée, mais aussi et surtout les ménages composites à plusieurs adultes sexuellement actifs: les couples sont relativement stables et gardent une certaine continuité, chacun exerce une profession, mais les tâches de la vie quotidienne, le soin et la garde des enfants se font en commun. On vise aussi les couples non mariés, liant des individus d'âge, de sexe et de carrière matrimoniale différents: un couple formé de deux divorcés commence, en principe, un cycle qui le rend formellement semblable à un couple de jeunes mariés, alors que les carrières matrimoniales antérieures donnent à chaque phase du nouveau cycle une signification différente, et au déroulement du cycle lui-même une orientation nouvelle. Et l'on aura garde d'oublier les faits de cohabitation prémaritale: tels les cas de jeunes qui vivent ensemble de façon intermittente pendant la période séparant les fiançailles et le mariage, lors des week-ends et des vacances notamment. L'important ici est moins le fait, que la tendance qui se manifeste en Suède par exemple depuis dix ans: la fréquence de ces cas augmente, la durée de la période de cohabitation prémaritale s'étale sur plusieurs années, au point qu'on peut se demander si un nouveau type de développement familial n'est pas en train d'apparaître, avec ses modèles, ses normes, ses valeurs. On ne peut éviter de se demander si ces formes d'organisation familiale non sanctionnées par le droit positif ont une valeur novatrice ou non. Annoncent-elles de nouvelles institutions, appelées à se généraliser dans les pays européens? Sont-elles seulement marginales et faut-il les traiter comme des déviances, des écarts à la norme tels qu'il y en a toujours dans les sociétés empiriquement observables? Sont-elles le signe d'une crise de l'institution familiale elle-même, qui serait menacée de disparition, ou le signe d'une évolution seulement, par transfert de fonctions remplies par l'agence familiale, dans sa forme d'organisation actuelle, à d'autres agences, dont les formes d'organisation évoluent simultanément? Quelle portée, quelles limites reconnaître à ces modes d'agencement de la vie entre adultes sexuellement actifs et enfants, dont les vieillards sont impitoyablement exclus?

Mais les types nouveaux d'organisation familiale sujets éventuellement de cycle ne sont pas les seuls à être visés. Le souci apparaît également de prendre en compte des événements importants pour la compréhension du cycle, que les séries statistiques officielles ne peuvent pas repérer. C'est ainsi que Robert Chester, Jacques Commaille et Anne Boigeol montrent sur données anglaises et françaises que le divorce est moins une coupure brutale dans le cycle qu'un événement dans un processus parfois très long, marqué par les étapes d'une séparation progressive.

Jean Kellerhals montre, pareillement, l'importance qu'a un événement singulier mal saisi par les statistiques officielles, l'avortement. Ces taux observés par enquête sont si élevés, que la notion courante d'après laquelle l'avortement serait un écart à la norme doit être révisée: l'interruption de grossesse est à comprendre plutôt comme un mode fondamental de régulation des équilibres familiaux. Ainsi voit-on se manifester une préoccupation constante: que signifient dans le cours d'une vie familiale, ces événements qui ne laissent que des traces muettes et souvent erratiques sur les registres officiels? De quels processus sont-ils le terme? A l'issue de quelles interactions surviennent-ils? Comment procéder pour les repérer et les interpréter? A quoi faut-il les référer?

Un troisième souci est celui qu'exprime, de façon populaire, le mouvement de libération des femmes. Qu'est-ce qui est ici en marche, vers quoi, jusqu'où? Certains parlent de révolution sexuelle. On a pu entendre soutenir que les agents les plus actifs des transformations dans l'organisation familiale sont les femmes. Est-ce que cela annonce une simple redistribution des tâches et une rediffusion partielle des rôles dans l'unité familiale, qui remplirait toujours les mêmes fonctions? Ou bien un changement plus fondamental, marqué par une nouvelle répartition de fonctions entre la famille et les autres agences sociales? Quels effets les modifications en cours dans l'organisation familiale ont-ils sur la division sexuelle du travail dans les professions? Sont-ils en rapport, ou non, avec l'augmentation des taux de féminisation de certaines professions, comme celles d'instituteur, de magistrat ou de médecin? De nouvelles divisions sexuelles du travail ne sont-elles pas en train de se reconstituer implicitement, mais sur quels critères? D'après quels usages?

Les préoccupations qui s'expriment à travers les débats sur la régulation des naissances ne sont pas séparables d'un quatrième souci, le dernier de ceux que je voudrais citer, celui du sens dans lequel évoluent les relations entre parents et enfants. Les modèles d'autorité, l'image du père, les fonctions de la mère ont profondément changé en moins de vingt ans, chacun le sait, et il est banal de le rappeler. Mais ce qu'on connaît moins, et qui demande étude, ce sont les rapports qui existent entre ces changements et les conditions dans lesquelles la famille fonctionne pour transmettre les savoir-faire, les manières de sentir, les goûts, les habitudes alimentaires, les évaluations esthétiques. La famille fonctionne toujours, dans beaucoup de sociétés européennes, comme une agence pour la procréation et la transmission des patrimoines, Jacques Lautman l'a montré ici même. Mais là-même où elle a cessé de remplir cette fonction de manière primordiale, n'intervient-elle pas toujours de façon majeure pour la transmission des savoirs, des chances et des pouvoirs? Les relations entre parents et enfants ont substantiellement changé pendant le cours de la vie commune au foyer familial. Mais ne sont-elles pas plus actives que jamais pour l'entrée dans la vie professionnelle et les débuts dans une carrière? Et les échanges entre générations ne retrouvent-ils pas un terrain privilégié d'exercice avec l'apparition d'une nouvelle période de l'existence liée à l'allongement de la durée moyenne de vie, celle qui va de l'âge de la retraite à l'âge de la vieillesse?

Tels sont, entre beaucoup d'autres, les soucis majeurs qui animent les praticiens des questions familiales. Ils ne sont encore qu'imparfaitement transcrits en hypothèses de recherche formulées en termes qui se prêtent à vérification. Et ils n'ont qu'un rapport plus ou moins direct avec la préoccupation majeure qui nous retient: saisir les faits familiaux dans leur développement temporel, caractériser le fonctionnement de l'organisation familiale dans le temps. Ils n'en conduisent pas moins à mettre en question la portée et les limites des idées relatives au cycle, ce pourquoi on a besoin de formulations théoriques précises. Quelles propositions peut-on donc avancer aujourd'hui pour préparer de nouvelles formulations?

2. *Vers de nouvelles formulations théoriques*

Toute formulation théorique consiste en la construction d'un problème, en la remise en cause de solutions acquises pour des problèmes voisins, en la critique d'apparentes évidences. Ici le problème est bien dégagé, et l'interrogation formulée en de nombreuses expressions. Je vais tenter de la ramasser sous sa forme la plus générale à la lumière des travaux rassemblés dans cet ouvrage.

Le concept de cycle de la vie familiale a été originairement construit dans une perspective psycho-sociologique pour décrire et analyser les ajustements successifs entre individus composant les familles nord-américaines au fur et à mesure que ces familles évoluent dans le temps. D'où le nom d'approche par le développement donné à cette perspective. En quinze ans de travaux, les schémas initialement proposés ont été élargis pour trois raisons:

1. Parce qu'on leur a donné des formulations théoriques plus strictes, ou même franchement nouvelles, comme Reuben Hill le montre dans sa contribution, comme Roy Rodgers en fait la preuve ici même et par son dernier livre *Family*.

2. Parce qu'on les a appliqués à des études transversales, comme disent les démographes, ou dans la synchronie, comme disent les linguistes, les ethnologues, et les sociologues, à des sociétés et des cultures contemporaines profondément étrangères, par leurs principes d'organisation et leurs systèmes de valeurs, à la société nord-américaine et aux sociétés qui lui sont apparentées: c'est le cas de travaux sur le cycle au Japon, dans les pays arabes ou dans les sociétés d'Europe orientale.

3. Parce qu'on les a appliqués longitudinalement en démographie

historique, diachroniquement en anthropologie et en sociologie historique, à des périodes variées des sociétés d'Europe occidentale et, depuis peu, de l'Amérique du Nord coloniale.

Le problème majeur est bien là: pouvons-nous, devons-nous employer ces schémas de description et d'analyse pour l'étude des sociétés européennes considérées dans leur variété culturelle et leur dimension historique, c'est-à-dire les transporter hors de leur champ d'application initial, la famille nord-américaine contemporaine, et les appliquer à un champ plus étendu, à des sociétés où le système social global est fondamentalement différent, comme les sociétés slaves anciennes et, par-delà les limites historiques de l'Europe, comme les sociétés asiatiques ou africaines? En ce cas, que devons-nous faire, si nous voulons vraiment considérer la famille comme un système social qui fonctionne dans la durée et qui a son devenir propre, distinct de celui des agents qui le composent et non moins distinct de celui des agences qui l'entourent?

Voilà le problème majeur. Comment l'a-t-on traité, et qu'a-t-on gagné à pareil traitement? J'avancerai volontiers les propositions suivantes:

1. Le schéma du cycle a un usage *descriptif* que personne, je crois, ne conteste vraiment. Toute unité familiale se prête en effet à une saisie par batterie de descripteurs, qui permet d'appréhender plus ou moins finement la succession des phases, telles qu'elles résultent de la combinaison des éléments constitutifs de l'unité, ainsi que des interactions et transactions entre agents. En revanche, l'usage *analytique* du schéma est sujet à critique, il n'y a pas de consensus sur les critères permettant de découper le *cycle* en *phases*.

2. L'absence de consensus sur les critères de découpage du cycle en phases n'est pas seulement accidentel ou conjoncturel. Il n'est pas dû, non plus, à de simples divergences dans les techniques ou dans les méthodes de recueil des données. Il est fondé en théorie, car il engage la conception de l'unité familiale elle-même. L'alternative ici est en effet ouverte:

– ou bien de construire l'unité familiale par combinaison de dyades apparentées: mari/femme, père/fils, etc. En ce cas, les divergences par la discrimination des phases du cycle ne sont pas graves: il s'agit de nuancer et de détailler, c'est-à-dire de compliquer, ou au contraire de simplifier, en considérant ou non l'âge des enfants, leur nombre, leur scolarité etc.;

– ou bien on construit l'unité familiale par analyse des fonctions qu'elle remplit dans la société globale: reproduction, socialisation, transmission, etc. Ce sont alors les événements marquants dans l'accomplissement de ces fonctions qui sont à prendre comme coupures entre les phases: une cérémonie marquant un rite de passage, l'affiliation d'un des membres du groupe à une organisation extérieure qui change la position du groupe dans la société locale ou la société globale, un héritage ou une donation qui transforme ses conditions de fonctionnement, etc. En ce cas, les divergences quant à la discrimination des phases sont graves, puisque l'institution familiale ne remplit pas les mêmes fonctions dans toutes les sociétés, et que, par conséquence, il ne peut y avoir de principe de découpage universellement applicable. Il y a lieu d'insister sur ce point: seule une logique du découpage des cycles en phases qui soit une combinatoire des dyades formant l'unité familiale peut fonder en théorie la construction d'un schéma d'analyse prétendant à l'universalité.

3. L'absence de consensus sur le découpage du cycle en phases a des conséquences méthodologiques graves. Il n'entraîne pas seulement, en effet, des difficultés factuelles pour la comparaison des résultats entre études qui se servent de découpages différents. Il entraîne surtout l'impossibilité pratique de faire admettre par les agences de l'Etat, qui sont les grands collecteurs de données statistiques, un cadre de rassemblement des données assez simple et assez puissant pour saisir le développement des familles dans le temps. On admettra que des progrès décisifs ont été faits dans la connaissance de la stratification sociale du jour où l'on a donné aux catégories socio-professionnelles statistiquement saisissables une définition rigoureusement uniforme. On admettra aussi que des progrès du même genre ont été accomplis dans la connaissance des mécanismes économiques dès l'instant où l'on a pu donner aux grandeurs macro-économiques, *production nationale*, *revenu national*, *formation brute de capital fixe*, une définition qui permette des enregistrements en comptabilité nationale. Et l'on a sous les yeux l'exemple de la démographie, dont les concepts majeurs d'analyse, *nuptialité*, *natalité*, *fécondité*, *mortalité*, etc. rendent possible l'exploitation de données primaires, et par conséquent l'application de modèles explicatifs à des sociétés globales tout entières. En l'absence de concepts d'analyse rendant possible des enregistrements statistiques à l'échelle des administrations d'Etat, une sociologie soucieuse d'étudier le développement de la famille dans le temps ne peut exploiter de données primaires. Elle se trouve enfermée, de ce fait, dans une alternative: pratiquer l'analyse secondaire sur données collectées selon d'autres principes, au prix de simplifications contraires à la puissance du modèle explicatif à proposer; mener des enquêtes fines sur échantillons limités, au prix de restrictions sur la portée

des conclusions qu'on peut légitimement en attendre. Si nous voulons que dans les années qui viennent l'approche par le développement fasse des progrès substantiels, il faut échapper à cette alternative, il faut mener l'action sur un double terrain: théorique, pour définir, société par société ou thème par thème, des phases du cycle telles qu'elles soient directement exploitables par les statistiques d'Etat; et administratif, pour convaincre, pays par pays, les administrations d'Etat à faire entrer certaines variables descriptives, sociologiquement pertinentes, dans leurs dispositifs d'enregistement des données.

4. Le choix du cycle comme perspective majeure pour l'analyse des faits familiaux ne fait pas le consensus, pour de nombreuses raisons. Je me bornerai, ici, à en indiquer les principales, qui procèdent toutes d'interrogations visant la structure et le fonctionnement de l'organisation familiale elle-même.

L'important en effet est-il le cycle, ou bien ce que Robert Rapoport a nommé le sous-cycle, c'est-à-dire les variations dans le temps observables au sujet de la manière dont fonctionnent les relations dyadiques telles que mari/femme, mère/fille, frère/sœur?

L'important est-il le cycle ou les variations dans le temps observable quant au fonctionnement des relations de filiation et d'alliance ou des relations de domesticité? Il faudrait évoquer ici les travaux de Joël Halpern, et rappeler qu'en de nombreuses sociétés étudiées par les ethnologues, la relation père/fils est socialement beaucoup plus importante que la relation mari/femme, et qu'en conséquence les variations temporelles les plus significatives à remarquer sont celles qui affectent cette relation. Il faudrait reprendre aussi les travaux de Peter Laslett, et insister sur le fait que l'unité familiale n'est pas bâtie seulement sur des dyades apparentées par des relations de filiation et d'alliance, mais aussi sur des dyades liées par des relations d'allégeance et de patronage, voire par des relations de service et de domesticité.

L'important enfin est-il l'unité familiale restreinte et son cycle, ou bien l'ensemble plus vaste auquel elle appartient, le réseau d'alliance et de filiation dans lequel l'individu prend place? John Mogey rappelle ici même que l'unité domestique n'est pas seule à avoir consistance et à justifier l'étude d'un développement dans le temps, et qu'en conséquence l'attention doit être portée non seulement sur les unités similaires auxquelles elle est apparentée, mais aussi sur les caractéristiques structurales et fonctionnelles de réseaux par quoi opèrent les agents formant de pareilles unités.

Il n'y a donc pas consensus sur le choix du cycle comme perspective majeure pour l'étude des faits familiaux dans le temps, et il ne peut y avoir consensus parce que les relations dyadiques rassemblées dans le système des relations familiales fonctionnent aussi dans d'autres systèmes, que ces systèmes sont parfois socialement et culturellement plus actifs que les unités familiales dans l'ordre même de la famille et de la parenté, et qu'en conséquence ils doivent être considérés en priorité pour le traitement d'un certain nombre de problèmes.

5. Il y a consensus pour reconnaître que le cycle est examinable selon trois perspectives différentes: au niveau de la société globale, pour rechercher comment elle détermine le ou les indices de cycle qu'elle institue; au niveau du groupe familial, pour analyser le système des rôles selon les modèles de cycle; au niveau de l'individu, pour analyser les manières dont les rôles sont tenus et les modèles auxquels l'on se refère pour la tenue de ces rôles. En revanche, le choix de l'unité d'observation privilégiée pour considérer le cycle ne fait pas le consensus. L'analyse des raisons profondes motivant ces divergences fait apparaître deux positions:

– L'une considère le cycle familial d'après les individus: on nomme alors cycle familial la partie de vie commune à 2, 3, 4, *n*, individus apparentés et vivant dans la même enceinte domestique, qui ont chacun au cours de la vie, un cycle individuel propre et différent. L'unité l'observation pertinente pour saisir la structure du système des relations dyadiques dans la famille et son isolation dans le temps est alors l'individu.

– L'autre considère le cycle familial d'après le groupe familial lui-même: on nomme alors cycle familial le développement de ce groupe dans le temps, l'évolution du système des relations dyadiques existant entre les membres qui le composent. Le groupe est saisi d'après son calendrier et sa chronologie propre, distincts du calendrier et de la chronologie des individus dont il est formé.

Je ne m'attarderai pas longuement sur cette dissension, qui me paraît inessentielle, puisque les deux points de vue sont complémentaires: on peut considérer les événements de la vie familiale et leur chronologie alternativement du point de vue des individus et du point de vue des groupes qu'ils forment quand ils composent une famille. Le choix de l'un ou l'autre point de vue est affaire de stratégie de recherche, non de théorie. Que l'on saisisse les faits de divorce et les faits d'avortement du point de vue de l'individu ou du point de vue de l'unité familiale ne change rien aux formulations théoriques que l'on se propose de vérifier.

6. L'articulation du cycle familial avec les autres phénomènes séquentiels de la société globale fait problème. Il y a évidemment consensus pour

reconnaître qu'il faut examiner cette articulation, c'est-à-dire pour ne pas considérer le cycle isolément, ou, pour reprendre la terminologie de Roy Rodgers, pour ajouter à un examen des interactions familiales un examen des transactions entre sous-système familial et autres sous-systèmes du système social. Là où le consensus est plus difficile à obtenir, c'est pour l'étude des schémas de transaction. William Goode a montré, depuis une quinzaine d'années déjà, que le système familial était relativement indépendant des autres systèmes, qu'on ne pouvait donc pas rendre compte des changements survenus dans les cycles comme s'ils étaient entièrement déterminés par des variables indépendantes telles que l'urbanisation ou l'industrialisation. Faut-il aller jusqu'à inverser la problématique courante, qui explique les changements dans l'organisation familiale par des changements dans la société globale ou de grands sous-systèmes du système social, et questionner: les changements dans le système politique, le système religieux, le système économique sont-ils déterminés, et dans quelle mesure, par le devenir propre de l'institution familiale? S'il y a variations simultanées, quelle part les variations propres du système familial ont-elles dans l'orientation de l'ensemble? Je crois pouvoir affirmer que le consensus est établi, désormais, sur l'inversion de la problématique courante, et sur l'attention à porter aux changements propres de l'organisation familiale. Mais si l'on hésite sur les modèles explicatifs à proposer, c'est parce qu'il y a une difficulté théorique majeure à considérer les phases du cycle alternativement comme des variables *déterminantes* et comme des variables *déterminées*.

7. Le consensus est établi pour considérer l'unité familiale comme un système, et pour privilégier les analyses qui procèdent par examen des dyades constitutives. Mais ne sait-on pas tout cela depuis Talcott Parsons, Max Weber et Emile Durkheim? Ainsi, pour éviter de répéter indéfiniment que les faits familiaux sont un caractère de système, vaut-il mieux, comme y engage Reuben Hill, tenter de tirer parti des acquisitions récentes de la théorie générale des systèmes. C'est ici que commencent les divergences: il n'y a consensus, en effet, ni sur la manière de concevoir les principes de fonctionnement du système familial, ni sur la fonction qu'y excerce l'équilibre. Caractérisé brièvement, un système familial consiste en une certaine allocation de rôles pour une certaine répartition de tâches. Quand les rôles ou les tâches changent, l'état du système change. C'est ainsi que lors des vingt dernières années, les tâches ont substantiellement changé, les rôles beaucoup moins. Les mouvements féministes tirent argument de ce fait, sociologiquement explicable lui-même, pour provoquer une

accélération dans le changement des rôles, et militent pour mettre en harmonie le nouvel état du système des tâches avec un nouvel état du système des rôles. Les mouvements pédagogiques, de leur côté, tirent argument du fait que les fonctions de socialisation majeure remplies par la famille sont désormais remplies par l'école, la télévision et les organisations de jeunesse, pour travailler à modifier en substance le rapport parents/enfants. Sur la constatation de ces changements, le consensus est aisé à établir. Il l'est moins sur leur interprétation: les modifications en cours dans le système des rôles sont-elles de simples passages d'un état de système à un autre; sont-elles, au contraire, une transformation du système lui-même? D'année en année, de petites modifications surviennent dans la répartition des rôles selon les sexes et dans les rapports entre parents et enfants: les états de système changent imperceptiblement. Mais la plupart des changements vont dans le même sens: la structure du système n'est-elle pas atteinte, l'équilibre traditionnel rompu, n'est-ce pas vers d'autres modes d'organisation familiale que l'on va, encore à peine expérimentés? Ou pour emprunter un instant le langage du linguiste, les changements enregistrables dans les systèmes familiaux européens sont-ils seulement lexicaux, la syntaxe du fonctionnement familial demeurant intacte? Affectent-ils, au contraire, les structures syntaxiques elles-mêmes?

3. *Orientations*

Des soucis viennent de s'esquisser, auxquels il faut répondre. Un langage vient d'être employé, dont on attend qu'il permette de décider entre la pluralité des interprétations possibles. C'est dire à quel point il est souhaitable que la recherche s'adonne lors des années prochaines, à quelques tâches majeures:

1. Ré-examiner la "pathologie" familiale, ces événements comme le divorce et l'avortement considérés au regard des normes légales et morales comme "anormaux", mais dont on sait depuis Emile Durkheim, qu'ils ont des lois, des causes, et un sens.

2. Ré-évaluer le travail féminin, non seulement dans la perspective "féminine", celle de la double carrière familiale et professionnelle des femmes; non seulement dans la perspective "masculine", celle des conséquences, sur les carrières professionnelles et familiales des hommes, des changements dans les carrières professionnelles et familiales des femmes; mais aussi et surtout pour les différentes agences sociales et pour la société globale elle-même.

3. Explorer et évaluer les formes marginales du couple et les formes nouvelles de l'organisation familiale, les comparer aux formes traditionnelles, apprécier la portée et la limite de ces véritables "expériences", estimer leur valeur de modèle ou leur fonction marginale.

4. Développer les études empiriques sur le découpage du cycle en phases d'après des déterminations non-démographiques.

5. Lancer des études sur l'articulation entre le cycle familial et les cycles auxquels il est lié, le cycle individuel, d'une part, le cycle lignagier, les réseaux l'endogamie et d'homogamie d'autre part.

Un type l'organisation familiale a pris forme, aux confins de l'Europe, il y a quelques millénaires, régissant, pour une bonne part, l'activité des agents sociaux. Des signes annoncent un changement, dont on peut se demander s'il n'est pas une mutation profonde. Puisse un nouvel examen, dans cinq ans, dans dix ans, nous permettre d'en décider.